European Archaeology Abroad

Global Settings, Comparative Perspectives

Sidestone Press

European Archaeology Abroad

Global Settings, Comparative Perspectives

edited by:
Sjoerd J. van der Linde, Monique H. van den Dries,
Nathan Schlanger & Corijanne G. Slappendel

Universiteit Leiden

Culture Programme

Published by Sidestone Press, Leiden
www.sidestone.com

ISBN 978-90-8890-106-5

Photographs cover: Archaeological work at Ancient Merv,
    Turkmenistan (Photograph: Justin Barton (flickr: Amen-Ra)).
Cover design: K. Wentink, Sidestone Press
Lay-out: P.C. van Woerdekom, Sidestone Press

This project has been funded with support from the
European Commission. This publication reflects
the views only of the authors, and the Commission
cannot be held responsible for any use which may
be made of the information contained therein. The
contributors to this publication have done so in their
personal capacity. The views and analyses they express
here remain their sole responsibility, and do not
necessarily reflect or represent those of the publishers,
the sponsoring organisations, their institutions or the
European Commission.

Contents

Notes on contributors

Rica Annaert is a PhD candidate at the Vrije Universteit Brussel (VUB) with research on early medieval communities in the Scheldt-valley region. She was the Belgian coordinator for the Archaeology in Contemporary Europe project as researcher archaeology at the Flanders Heritage Agency.
E-mail: henrica.annaert@rwo.vlaanderen.be

Xurxo M. Ayán Vila is archaeologist at the Institute on Heritages Sciences of the Spanish High Council for Scientific Research. His research interests include Iron Age Archaeology, Archaeology of Contemporary Past and Community Archaeology.
E-mail: xurxo.ayan@gmail.com

David Barreiro-Martínez works at the Institute of Heritage Sciences (Incipit) of the CSIC. He received his PhD in 2005 for the thesis 'Archaeology and Society: An Epistemological and Axiological Proposal for an Applied Archaeology'.
His research focuses on the theory and practice of Archaeological Heritage Management and Applied Archaeology. His specific interests are Landscape Archaeology, Cultural Landscape, the Philosophy of Science and Technology, Sustainable Development and Cooperation. He was also involved in the Archaeology in Contemporary Europe research network.
E-mail: david.barreiro@incipit.csic.es

Frank Braemer is senior researcher at the CNRS/University of Nice's lab 'Culture et environnement: Préhistoire Antiquité Moyen Age'. Specialist of Near Eastern protohistoric architecture and urbanism, he is co-director of the Syro-French archaeological mission in Southern Syria. During the years 2009-2010, he studied the current evolution of archaeological institutions and administration in the Mediteranean countries.
E-mail: frank.braemer@cepam.cnrs.fr

Els Cornelissen is a senior researcher and curator in charge of the Section of Prehistory and Archaeology at the Royal Museum for Central Africa in Belgium. Her current research interests are the technological changes at the end of the Stone Age in Central Africa as well as the impact of climate change there on prehistoric communities at the end of the Pleistocene. She has been actively engaged over the last decade in museum practice projects both in Tervuren and in Lubumbashi.
E-mail: els.cornelissen@africamuseum.be

Felipe Criado-Boado has been a full research professor at the Spanish National Research Council (CSIC) since 2001, and the director of the Institute of Heritage Sciences (Incipit) of the CSIC since May 2010. Incipit is a new institute created by the CSIC to promote advances and interdisciplinary studies on Cultural Heritage, as well as training and management. Amongst others, his areas of expertise are Landscape Archaeology, Interpretive theory, the Origins and developments of monumental architecture, Public Science and Community Science applied to cultural heritage management and Research. He has been the PI on several cooperation projects between the Incipit (CSIC) and the University of the Republic of Uruguay. He was also involved in the Archaeology in Contemporary Europe research network.

E-mail: felipe.criado-boado@incipit.csic.es

Ine Demerre is a maritime heritage researcher at the Flanders Heritage Agency (agentschap Onroerend Erfgoed) since 2005. She was responsible for the coordination and the research within the partnership of the international projects 'Managing Cultural Heritage Under Water' (Culture 2000) and 'Archaeological Atlas of the 2 Seas' (Interreg IVA).

E-mail: Ine.Demerre@rwo.vlaanderen.be

Camila Gianotti García has been an assistant professor at the Eastern Regional University Centre (CURE) of the University of the Republic of Uruguay since 2011. Between 1998 and 2010 she was a pre-doctoral research fellow at the Institute of Heritage Sciences of the Spanish National Research Council (CSIC). Her main areas of research are landscape archaeology, the origin and development of architecture in prehistoric hunter-gatherer societies and lowland archaeology. She is currently carrying out a range of projects and research on cultural heritage management, Public Archaeology and Community Archaeology, working in rural communities in Uruguay (Tacuarembó and Rocha). Since 2000 she has coordinated several cooperation projects between the University of the Republic of Uruguay and the Institute of Heritage Sciences (CSIC).

E-mail: camila.gianotti@lappu.edu.uy

Cristóbal Gnecco is professor in the Department of Anthropology at the University of Cauca (Colombia), where he works on the political economy of archaeology and discourses on the ethnic Other. He currently serves as Chair of the PhD Program in Anthropology at this university and as co-editor of the WAC journal *Archaeologies*. Gnecco holds a PhD degree from Washington University (USA). He has published 'Modernity and politics in Colombian archaeology' (In Handbook of South American Archaeology, edited by Helaine Silverman and William Isbell, Springer, New York, 2008), 'History and its discontents: stone statues, native histories, and archaeologist' (Current Anthropology 2008, 49), along with Carolina Hernández, and has co-edited with Carl Langebaek Contra la tiranía tipológica en arqueología. Una visión desde Sudamérica (Bogotá, 2006).

E-mail: cgnecco@unicauca.edu.co

Alfredo González-Ruibal is a staff scientist with the Institute of Heritage Sciences (Incipit) of the Spanish National Research Council (CSIC). His work focuses on the archaeology of the contemporary past and ethnoarchaeology. He has conducted research in Ethiopia and Equatorial Guinea, among other countries.

E-mail: alfredo.gonzalez-ruibal@incipit.csic.es

Maria Pia Guermandi, classical archaeologist, is responsible for GIS and ICT applications at the Institute for Cultural Heritage of Emilia Romagna Region. She is chief editor of the IBC website and national Counsellor of Italia Nostra, the oldest Italian Association for the safeguarding of cultural heritage. She was also involved in the Archaeology in Contemporary Europe research network.

E-mail: mpguermandi@regione.emilia-romagna.it

Randi Håland is a professor of African and Middle Eastern Archaeology at the Department of Archaeology University / Centre for Development Studies at the University of Bergen. She started to teach African Archaeology for two years at the newly established Archaeology Department in Khartoum in 1972. Since then she has continued research in Africa and taken on the supervision of doctorate students from Sudan, Palestine Botswana, Tanzania, Zimbabwe, Ghana, Palestine, and Nepal. Beside that, she has been directing archaeological research projects in Sudan, Tanzania, Nepal, Palestine and Zimbabwe for which the research interest has been on the transition to agriculture in the Nile Valley of the Sudan, the Iron Age in East Africa and the ethno-archaeology of Iron working. Her main research focus now is on Iron working seen in a cross-cultural cultural perspective.

E-mail: Randi.Haland@global.uib.no

Bill Jeffery, PhD is a consultant maritime archaeologist working as the Coordinator of the Maritime and Underwater Cultural Heritage Programme for CIE-Centre for International Heritage Activities. He is an active maritime archaeology field worker / part time academic in the African, Asian and Pacific regions and has conducted training programs in nine different countries. He is an Adjunct Assistant Professor and Research Associate with the University of Guam and a Research Associate with the Hong Kong Maritime Museum.

E-mail: billfjeffery@gmail.com

Arkadiusz Klimowicz is PhD student in the Institute of Prehistory (Poznań University), focusing on the socio-cultural aspects of changes in prehistory (particularly Near Eastern Neolithic) and development of methods and theory in archaeology. He is interested also in social and public issue of the current archaeology. Since 2001 he is a member of the Çatalhöyük Research Project, being involved simultaneously with several European scientific programs.

E-mail: areklim@amu.edu.pl

Patrycja Klimowicz is a field archaeologist participating in several excavations within Poland. She acquired an M.A. degree in archaeology in 2007 at the Institute of Prehistory in Poznań. She is interested in history of archaeology as well as development of methodology in the discipline.

E-mail: patklim@interia.pl

Kostas Kotsakis is professor of Prehistoric Archaeology at the Department of Archaeology of the Aristotle University of Thessaloniki. He has excavated extensively in Greece and Turkey. His main research topics are archaeological theory and method, history of Greek archaeology and Aegean material culture, in particular the Neolithic. He was the coordinator of the project named 'Digitization and Archiving of Archaeological Publications in the Daily and Periodical Press of the Period 1832-1932, and Construction of a Web Site' in the framework of Information Society Operational Programme and was a partner at the Archaeology in Contemporary Europe network.

E-mail: kotsakis@hist.auth.gr

Sonia Lévin, doctor in Greek archaeology from University Paris 1, worked on the coordination of the Archaeology in Contemporary Europe (ACE) project with Nathan Schlanger and Kai Salas Rossenbach, from Inrap, Paris during three years. She coordinated with Sjoerd van der Linde (Leiden University) and Nina Schücker (RGK) the ACE theme 'European archaeology abroad'.

E-mail: sonia.levin@ac-reunion.fr

José M. López Mazz is head professor of the Department of Archaeology at the Humanities Faculty of the University of the Republic of Uruguay. His specialized areas are lowland archaeology, the early population of South America, ethnoarchaeology of the Amazon, and the archaeology of the recent past. He is the director of the forensic anthropology group, and is the coordinator of an archaeological project based on locating and identifying persons who disappeared during the dictatorship in Uruguay. He has been the PI for a series of cooperation projects between the Incipit (CSIC) and the University of the Republic of Uruguay.

E-mail: lopezmazz@yahoo.com.ar

Sada Mire is a Somali born Swedish archaeologist, living and working in the UK and Somaliland. Sada is currently advisor to and former director of the Republic of Somaliland's Department of Tourism & Archaeology, which she founded in 2007. Next to being an executive director of the Horn Heritage Organization, Sada is a Research Associate at SOAS, and affiliated with also UEA and UCL. In addition, Sada has worked as a Technical Assistant for the United Nations Development Program in Somaliland on cultural resource management and capacity building, and is a member of the Council of the African Studies Association, UK.

E-mail: sada.mire@googlemail.com

Robert Parthesius is director of the Centre for International Heritage Activities (CIE). He is a maritime historian and works since the 1980s on the interface between history and archaeology of the maritime history. He holds a doctorate in the history of the European expansion from the University of Amsterdam. He is specialized in Dutch ships in tropical waters between 1595-1660, the development of the VOC network in Asia and the European-Asian cultural relations in the seventeenth and eighteenth centuries. Robert lectures Historical-Archaeology of the European expansion at the University of Leiden. In 2005 he initiated the establishment of the CIE.

E-mail: r.parthesius@heritage-activities.org

Gertjan Plets is a PhD student at Ghent University, focusing on community-based heritage management in the Altai Mountains, indigenous archaeology, indigenous perception of cultural landscapes and the perspectives of virtual three-dimensional preservation of heritage for developing countries.

E-mail: gertjan.plets@ugent.be

Ruth Plets is a post-doctoral research associate in the School of Environmental Sciences, University of Ulster. Her current research looks at Late Glacial sea-level minima in the Irish Sea. Her interests lie in marine geoarchaeology, high-resolution geophysics and sedimentology.

E-mail: r.plets@ulster.ac.uk

Nathan Schlanger's (*editor*) research interests include prehistoric technology and material culture studies, the history and politics of archaeology, and archaeological heritage management and policies. Among his recent publications are *Archaeology and the Global Economic Crisis: Multiple Impacts, Possible Solutions* (2010, ed. with K. Aitchison) and *La Préhistoire des Autres. Perspectives Archéologiques et Anthropologiques* (2012 ed. with A.-C. Taylor). He has been in charge of international research and development at the French national institute for preventive archaeological research (Inrap) since 2005, where he directed the Archaeology in Contemporary Europe

(ACE) project until 2010. He is also research associate at RARI, University of the Witwatersrand, Johannesburg, at the UCL Centre for Museums, Heritage and Material Culture Studies, and at UMR 8215 Trajectoires in Nanterre.

E-mail: schlanger1@gmail.com

Nina Schücker is a researcher at the Roman-Germanic Commission of the German Archaeological Institute in Frankfurt/Main. She was employed within the framework of the project 'Archaeology in Contemporary Europe' and specializes in the archaeology of the Roman Provinces.

E-mail: schuecker@rgk.dainst.de

Corijanne Slappendel *(editor)* is a Research Master student archaeology on the track Town and Country at Leiden University that deals with Classical, Mediterranean and Near-Eastern archaeology. She completed her thesis on the archaeology of Judaism in the Islamic world. During her studies she has worked also on the Archaeology in Contemporary Europe (ACE) book on European archaeology abroad, both as an editor and as a co-writer on the article on Dutch archaeology abroad. In the first instance this was through a position granted by the Royal Netherlands Academy of Arts and Sciences and later on as a student-assistent.

E-mail: c.g.slappendel@gmail.com

Maria Theresia Starzmann is an anthropologist focusing her work on post-/de-colonial theory and critical investigations of the history and practice of archaeology. She is currently Assistant Professor at the Institute of Middle Eastern Archaeology at Free University Berlin and is an Adjunct Research Associate at the Department of Anthropology at Binghamton University.

E-mail: mstarzmann@zedat.fu-berlin.de

Eleftheria Theodoroudi is a PhD candidate at the Aristotle University of Thessaloniki. Her thesis is on Identities and Material Culture in Late Bronze Age-Early Iron Age Macedonia Greece. She worked as a research assistant at the Archaeology in Contemporary Europe programme.

E-mail: eletheod@hist.auth.gr

Ibrahima Thiaw is a researcher and lecturer at Institut Fondamental d'Afrique Noire (IFAN), an institute within the University Cheikh Anta Diop of Dakar. His is also the director of the Museum Th. Monod d'Art African of Dakar. His research interests include historical archaeology, culture heritage management and public archaeology.

E-mail: ibrahima.thiaw@ucad.edu.sn

Monique van den Dries *(editor)* is assistant professor at the Faculty of Archaeology of Leiden University (The Netherlands), where she teaches on various aspects of heritage management. She holds a PhD (1998) in archaeology from Leiden University. Previously she was head of the archaeology division of the State Inspectorate for Cultural Heritage. She has recently experienced working with local communities abroad. Currently she is vice-president of the European Association of Archaeologists. She was also involved in the Archaeology in Contemporary Europe research network.

E-mail: m.h.van.den.Dries@arch.leidenuniv.nl

Sjoerd van der Linde *(editor)* is assistant professor in Archaeological Heritage Management at the Faculty of Archaeology, Leiden University. He was involved in the 'Archaeology in Contemporary Europe' Culture 2007 EU project as track-leader for the theme 'European Archaeology Abroad'. He has recently finished his PhD 'Digging Holes Abroad', which entails an ethnography of Dutch archaeological research projects. Sjoerd is also general director of the Foundation CommonSites.net.

E-mail: s.j.van.der.Linde@arch.leidenuniv.nl

FOREWORD

Some years ago, the European Association of Archaeologists (EAA) organized a debate on the issue of whether or not a European archaeology existed and what it was that made an archaeology 'European'. This book takes the next step, and seemingly not only departs from the premise there is such a thing as European archaeology but investigates the way in which its exerts and exerted its influence 'abroad', which presupposes a degree of geopolitical unity that may also not be entirely warranted.

Nevertheless, as the editors point out in their introduction to this important book and given all differences that exist between European countries, it is undeniably true that there has been a long period of "European" colonialism. Archaeology, and antiquarianism before it, have long regarded the lands beyond their European homelands as the contemporary past and in general they have served the colonial project well. There are many dimensions to this fascinating topic. Many of them are explored in this book, that is one of the outcomes of the ACE-project – "Archaeology in Contemporary Europe". This EU-financed project ran from 2007 – 2012 and constituted a collaboration of thirteen partners from ten countries from all parts of Europe.

The ACE network aimed to promote contemporary archaeology at a European level, by emphasizing its cultural, scientific, and economic dimensions, including its interest for the wider public and its impact beyond Europe. The latter was done in a special subtheme that focused on how values and motivations in the sociopolitical context of European states change and impact in relation to dealing with archaeological resources and the interaction with archaeologists, local communities and other stakeholders from the host country. The aim was to provide insights into an ethical and sustainable framework for undertaking archaeological heritage projects abroad, targeted at fostering benefits for archaeological resources and stakeholders alike.

This book offers a comparative analysis of projects originating from European countries elsewhere in the world, their motives and aims, and the context in which they were developed as well as their achievements or, perhaps better and more neutrally phrased, the effects they sorted.

Partners in the ACE network and many scholars from other countries in- and outside Europe have contributed to this book, that offers unique and highly interesting perspectives on the role of archaeology in a globalizing world. And also, to some degree, on the role of archaeology in globalizing the world.

Willem J.H. Willems
Leiden, December 2012

PREFACE

This publication was produced in the framework of the ACE project – "Archaeology in Contemporary Europe. Professional Practices and Public Outreach", with the support of the Culture 2007-2013 programme of the European Commission.

The ACE project, a multiannual cultural cooperation agreement lasting from 2007 to 2012, aims to promote contemporary archaeology at a European wide level, by emphasising its cultural, scientific, and economic dimensions, including its manifold interest for the wider public. With the acceleration of infrastructure and development works throughout the continent in the past decades, contemporary archaeology has become particularly important and challenging. While the process of development poses severe threats to archaeological heritage, it can also provide new opportunities for increasing our knowledge about the past and for enhancing sustainable archaeological heritage management for the benefit of all European citizens.

The ACE network is composed of thirteen partner institutions such as archaeological services, university departments, research institutes and cultural operators, originating from such countries as France, Germany, the United Kingdom, Italy, Spain, Poland, Belgium, Greece, the Netherlands and Hungary. The ACE partners have undertaken research, documentation and dissemination activities along four major thematic axes, each with its various strands and developments: I - 'Researching the significance of the past'; II - 'Comparative practices in archaeology'; III - 'The archaeological profession'; IV - 'Public outreach: invitations to archaeology' (see www.ace-archaeology.eu).

As part of the comparative axe (II), researchers from the University of Leiden, from the French National Institute for Preventive Archaeological Research (INRAP) and from the Römisch-Germanischen Kommission (RGK) spearheaded a specific strand dedicated to the question of 'European Archaeology Abroad', in both historical and contemporary perspectives. Activities under this strand included a questionnaire on the respective involvements of European countries and institutions in archaeology abroad, with an accompanying compilation of a wide-ranging bibliography. Several workshops were organised on the topic, and a full-day session held at the 16th annual meeting of the European Association of Archaeologists in Den Haag in September 2010.

The editors of this volume and many of its contributors are associated with the ACE project, and have undertaken in its framework the research they present here. Other contributors, notably in parts II and III have been invited to participate. The editors would like to thank all the contributors for their responsiveness and enthusiasm throughout the production of this volume.

European Archaeology Abroad: Global Settings, Comparative Perspectives

Nathan Schlanger*, Sjoerd van der Linde**, Monique van den Dries** and Corijanne Slappendel**

* UMR 8215 Trajectoires / French National Institute for Preventive Archaeological Research, France

** Faculty of Archaeology, Leiden University, The Netherlands

Encounters

A range of European scholars and their patrons have aspired, at least since the Renaissance, to 'travel back in time'. Unearthing the past has indeed served them well to ground the legitimacy of the prince, to flesh out narratives of common origins, to create material affinities through the reconstruction of remote ages, and also to contrive, demarcate and sometimes challenge territorial boundaries for the present and for the future. Granted all that, the question arises: why 'travel back' also in *space*? "Why roam far", this wanderlust of which speaks Goethe (see Schücker, this volume)? Indeed, why take the trouble to go and investigate ancient vestiges in far-remote lands, lands where one is a foreigner, at best a visitor? The prevalence of specifically nationalist motivations is already open to caveats within the European contexts: would it not be lacking or all the more limited in scope in the antipodes, where what is at stake after all is only (as it were) the past of the 'others'?[1]

Alongside conquest and commerce, the lure of adventure and romance has certainly played a part, exemplified by such voyages as Marco Polo's in the Far East, or later Lafitau's comparison of the customs of Native American 'savages' with those of ancient times. Emerging out of antiquarian practices and expectations, European archaeology abroad has long been fascinated with great and/or 'vanished' civilizations, civilizations towards which could be construed affinities of an

---

1 On the general development of archaeology in Europe see Trigger 1989; Malina and Vasicek 1990; Schnapp 1993, as well as Biehl, Gramsch and Marciniak 2002. Global views of archaeology are provided by Trigger 1984; Gran-Aymerich 1998; Diaz-Andreu 2007, and see also Moro-Abadia 2006.

analogical kind (as in the case of Spanish encounters in Mesoamerica, see for instance Gnecco (this volume), or in a different way, the British in India) or of an homological kind (as with the civilizations of the Mediterranean and the Near East). Nevertheless, the study of the past in 'extra-European' lands stood from the onset in close relationship with the colonial enterprise, if only in the purely pragmatic sense of being able to secure access to remote sites and to transport back the riches extracted. These connections are manifest already in the first bout of European colonialism, notably by Spain and by The Netherlands (see Ayán Vila and González-Ruibal (this volume), as well as Van den Dries, Slappendel and Van der Linde (this volume)). They became even more marked, and ideologically loaded, upon the second round of European imperial expansions – beginning with Napoleon's conquest of Egypt, following with the partition of Africa in the later years of the nineteenth century, and culminating with the intricate diplomatic-scientific manoeuvres surrounding the study of ancient Egypt, Mesopotamia and the lands of the Bible during the protracted collapse of the Ottoman empire.

One way to begin to understand what European archaeologists were doing abroad is to examine their activities and achievements through the lenses of established colonial categories. The distinction between 'exploitation' and 'settlement' colonies, although not as clear-cut as usually portrayed, is a good starting point. In the former case, probably best epitomized by the Belgian Congo since the late nineteenth century, the overall motivation of the colonizer is to exploit as quickly and efficiently as possible the available natural and human resources (as pointed out by Cornelissen (this volume), and see also the magnificent *Congo, een Geschiedenis*, by David van Reybrouck (2010)). In the latter case, of which both North Africa and Southern Africa are relevant examples, European settler populations saw themselves as 'here to stay', investing materially and ideologically in the creation of long term prospects, taking root in the land by, among other devices, seeking roots in its past. Not all Europeans have displayed any sustained interest in the local archaeological or historical past – far from it – but among those who did, a further distinction can be drawn between those who emphasized 'proximity' or on the contrary 'distance' with this past (these arguments are also fleshed out in Schlanger 2012; Schlanger and Taylor 2012).

Colonial categories

Those European scholars or antiquarians in search of proximity would notably identify elements propitious to their own historical positioning – the possibility, by appealing to ancient monuments and material vestiges, to contrive and proclaim some past affinities or commonalities upon which present realities can be legitimized, for the Europeans themselves and for their colonial subjects. Classic examples of this (in all senses of the word) are plenty around the Mediterranean basin, where Europeans have readily sought to portray themselves as heirs to the ideals of the Greek civilization (Theodoroudi and Kotsakis, this volume) and as the custodians, if not the imperial proprietors, of the *mare nostrum* heritage (Braemer, this volume; Guermandi, this volume; Lévin, this volume).

In other cases, however, European interests in the local past have rather served to establish or maintain 'distance' with colonized populations. Also here a single historical framework is postulated, but the aim is rather to demarcate with it, to rank and to schedule. Under the evolutionist paradigm prevailing in mid-nineteenth century archaeology, the challenge was to show the depth of time and of cultural achievements spanning between the African or the Polynesian, through savagery and barbarism, to the civilized – and civilizing – Englishman or Frenchman. With the advent of the diffusionist or culture-historical paradigm at the onset of the twentieth century, emphasis was rather put on heartlands, cultural circles, migration routes and distribution maps. This perspective could highlight civilizational entanglements, cast as common points of *departure* (as in the Mediterranean area, just discussed). It could also relate, towards the other end of the diffusionist process, to the conditions and destiny of *arrival*. Indeed, by conceiving of European expansion as the latest surge in a venerable series of dispersals and conquests, this historicization only confirmed the inevitable geopolitical and civilisational superiority of the latest comers. Particularly illuminating in this respect is the case of southern Africa, which scholarship since the end of the nineteenth century contrived to present as a '*cul de sac*' into which poured successive southbound waves of Hottentot, Bantu, Portuguese, Dutch and British immigrants, each re-enacting a pattern of expansion, occupation and replacement (see Etherington 2011; Fauvelle 2012).

It may be worth pointing out here that the practitioners of European archaeology abroad, in their overall majority, did not set to refute the historicity of the populations under their control. Alongside the denial of time and of coevalness as decried by anthropological critique, many references to the archaeological past have actually derived from a genuine interest in the historical emergence of human societies worldwide. In turn, this attested interest leads us to reiterate the obvious observation that the category of 'Europeans abroad' is and has always been a highly diversified one, in terms of national identities, social backgrounds, economic ambitions, and indeed ideological or moral stances. This plurality of actors and motivations make it difficult to consider European colonizers as a homogeneous group, identically disposed towards the native past and its archaeological heritage (Stoler 1989; Pels 1997; Van der Linde 2012). Within this recognized diversity, the distinction perhaps most salient for us to consider here is between those who may be called 'amateur' or 'antiquarian' archaeologists, and those deemed 'professional' or 'institutional'.

To the former group belong a whole range of individuals – administrators, military personnel, missionaries, settlers, traders etc. – whose presence in the colony is essentially unrelated to archaeology. When these individuals develop an interest in the local past (or rekindle a fascination with ancient vestiges already nurtured back home), this is usually manifest as a passionate but unmethodical or autodidact curiosity, typical of amateurs who find the time and the energy in between their ordinary occupations, albeit with limited means and sometimes ill-defined questions, to investigate the past (see examples in Thiaw (this volume) and

Cornelissen (this volume), as well as Plets, Plets and Annaert (this volume) and the interview with Mire (this volume)). When they interact with metropolitan science, they do so overwhelmingly (if at times resentfully) from a subordinate position, as providers of finds or data seeking instructions and recognition from the learned societies and the museums of the mother country (see examples in Robertshaw 1990; Griffiths 1996; Schlanger 2003 for Southern Africa).

Contrasting with this informal, local, almost 'antiquarian' archaeology (accepting for once the pejorative connotations of the term), there stands quite another form of European archaeology abroad – professional, institutional, emanating from, reproducing and occasionally anticipating established metropolitan structures, with qualified emissaries specifically commissioned to lead delegations and direct research expeditions to collect and analyse well documented archaeological evidence, and then to expedite its scientifically and aesthetically significant finds to would-be 'universal' museums and repositories in the west (see Braemer (this volume) and Lévin (this volume) and compare with the importance of private initiatives in Dutch archaeology, see Van den Dries, Slappendel and Van der Linde, (this volume)). If the 'amateur' archaeology outlined above can be said to be mired in a colonialist discourse, this 'professional' archaeology is rather dominated by considerations of imperial diplomacy and symbolic influence, including the pursuit of economic and political gain by the countries concerned (Schücker, this volume; Lévin, this volume). The metropolitan gaze, which orients actions and representations *in situ*, is in any case much more prevalent here, if not omnipresent. It was said for example of post-Napoleonic Egypt that while the present effectively belonged to the British, the French had as compensation control of the past. Extra-European territories have indeed become arenas in which nation-state rivalries were played out, while the excavation and restoration of monuments – again, preferably those of ostensibly 'great' civilizations – became projects of propaganda as much as of knowledge.

Contexts of practice

But whether bottom-up or top-down, European archaeology abroad has always thrived on its distinctive conditions of practice, closely determined by the 'colonial situation'. Beyond the romantic image of the orientalist excavation (typically involving swarms of picturesque natives unearthing imposing ruins), the political, legal and economic issues at stakes make of the archaeological knowledge produced both an expression and an instrument of the prevailing relations of domination. In comparison with the archaeology practised within Europe, things seem to be easier, or at least more manageable, in far distant lands. While the level of infrastructure and comfort admittedly leaves much to be desired, ready access to manpower remains one distinctive characteristic of archaeology abroad. Forced labour aside, various forms of salaried employment were experimented with, including payment by the time spend working onsite, or by the finds recovered and delivered intact. Indeed, the proper management of native human resources constitute a challenge for foreign expeditions in search of a workforce that would be efficient and reliable, albeit basically unqualified and interchangeable. The occasional recognition of selected individuals, generously singled out for their intuitive skills and savvy experience with ancient vestiges, only confirms the rule. Not only are these logistical questions likely to affect archaeological interpretations (what questions can be asked, what questions can be answered?) they also reflect on colonial capitalism of the kind long prevalent around the Mediterranean basin. Well attested in the times of W. Flinders Petrie and Max Mallowan (see for example Trümpler 2001; Quirke 2010; Schlanger 2010), many of these challenges still prevail today, as highlighted by Maria-Theresia Starzmann (this volume).

As importantly, also the efforts invested in the localization, exploitation and redistribution of archaeological resources fully benefit from the conditions of colonial jurisdiction. Very often, local administrations, development bureaus and suchlike offices of 'native affairs' had quite extensive powers of pre-emption and expropriation over private properties, whether customary or formalized, individual or collective. This ease of access includes the sites themselves, but also their contents, and notably the extracted small finds which then become object of commerce or negotiation between local deciders, diplomatic representations and recipient museums. Conversely, alongside the ensuing spoliations that have enriched the collections of Paris, London or Berlin, this juridical possession has also brought about an opportunity to exercise responsibility and custodianship, to conceive and to implement innovative measures for the protection and valorization of the archaeological heritage. Examples here might include the Archaeological Survey of India, able since the 1870s to develop measures that are increasingly unachievable in the mother-country; likewise the administrative system devised for North African antiquities in the interwar years, long before its implementation in France became conceivable, and likewise the archaeological state services and monument acts, introduced in colonial Indonesia long before the Netherlands, as indicated by Van den Dries, Slappendel and Van der Linde (this volume). The same potential is manifest in the organization of scientific institutions. The *Instituto di Correspondenzia* established in Rome in 1829 as a precociously international research centre soon gave birth to the German Archaeological institute (see Schücker, this volume), and also to the French system of 'schools' in Athens (1846) and in Rome (1873) (see Braemer, this volume; Lévin, this volume). The system was subsequently emulated by other European (and North-American) countries – including the creation of an original, language based, common Dutch – Flemish institute in Cairo (see Plets, Plets and Annaert, this volume; Van den Dries, Slappendel and Van der Linde, this volume). Whatever their forms and their sources of funding (ministries of foreign affairs, of culture or of higher education, universities, private foundations) these institutions represent dedicated, high-power research establishments of a kind still lacking within several European countries.

Last but not least, the unprecedented legal and operational opportunities offered to archaeology by its colonial settings are reflected also in the development of 'rescue', 'salvage' or rather, more accurately, 'preventive archaeology'. Indeed, the first large scale project worthy of that name was the one launched in 1907 prior to the construction of the first Aswan Dam, commissioned and funded by the British-directed and Ottoman regulated Egyptian administration of public works. Half a century later, the famous 1950s Nubia campaign prompted by the building of the second Aswan Dam – mentioned by Klimowicz and Klimowicz (this volume), as well as Ayán Vila and González-Ruibal (this volume), and Van den Dries, Slappendel and Van der Linde (this volume) – only confirms how important was the colonial or post-colonial context of these major investments and coordination efforts (Schlanger 2008). One immediate outcome of this has been the creation of the UNESCO World Heritage convention in 1972, initiating the globalization of the modern – albeit initially western – 'universal' heritage consciousness that we now witness worldwide.

Aftermath

The period following World War II has amply confirmed this heritage turn: its movements of decolonization and globalization gradually brought about several important changes in the practice of European archaeology abroad. The 'nationalist', 'colonialist' and 'imperialist' archaeologies of the previous period (as broadly defined by Trigger 1984) became increasingly challenged by the forces of post-colonialism and post-modernism, notably under the influence of Anglo-American social and interpretive archaeologies and under increasing critiques from local and 'indigenous' scholars (see Gnecco, this volume; Thiaw this volume). Together with a growth of global social movements that supported the rights of previously underrepresented and marginalized groups across states and societies, this ultimately saw the rise of a recognition of alternative voices and claims to archaeology.

These developments did not however occur everywhere in a similar pace or along the same lines. In some former European colonies, the new administrations in place were not always sufficiently prepared to adequately manage their archaeological resources. This is to some degree because very little had been done by foreign archaeologists in terms of transmitting knowledge, operational and managerial skills to local staff and scholars, mostly employed, as already noted, in unqualified roles. For some, like a few Italian scholars in North Africa, it has proved easy to recover the grounds lost and to keep working in isolation from the local context for several decades (see Guermandi, this volume). In other countries, like in Senegal (see Thiaw, this volume), historians or archaeologists were available to take over, but either they continued in the scientific traditions of the former colonizer in which they were trained (see also Gnecco (this volume), for a similar case in Colombia) or they found European expatriates still dominating local archaeological research. In those countries, it was not until the 1990s that things really started to change.

In any case, it is probably fair to say that over the last few decades, European archaeology has slowly come to terms with the notion that all archaeological interpretations are enmeshed within the socio-political, historical, cultural and economic frameworks in which they are generated, whether this concerns heritage on land or under water, in/or outside of Europe (see Demerre, this volume). This recognition has lead to the emergence of notions of community archaeology, multi-vocality, and more recently, collaborative practices within European practices and policies. Examples given in this volume – by Parthesius and Jeffery, Gianotti *et al.*, as well as by Randi Håland and Sada Mire in their respective interviews – all illustrate a trend towards a new form of collaborative, post-colonial heritage approach, not only with regards to the epistemological and theoretical foundations of archaeology and heritage notions, but also in terms of daily practices, academic interactions and funding policies. That granted, both Gnecco (this volume) and Thiaw (this volume) remind us that such new collaborative practices and policies also run the risk of reproducing a new form of neo-colonialism, abiding by a European or Western body of discourse.

At the same time, Håland (this volume) argues that also local powers and socio-economic contexts can seriously impede the implementation of even the most sincere collaborative practices. Similarly, the work by Starzmann (this volume) and Van der Linde (2012) warns us that collaborative practices often continue to rehearse the old power discrepancies between foreign researchers and local communities, so that the undertaking of transnational and intercultural projects should be integrated with value-based approaches and continuing self-reflexive ethnographies. The broadening of the concept of heritage to include intangible aspects, the notion of a heritage that cares not only for objects but also for the lives of people, as well as policies that better allow for the implementation and evaluation of the social aspects of archaeological science and cultural resource management, are clearly crucial elements for the future perspectives of European archaeology abroad. Perhaps, as Håland suggests in her interview (this volume), the situation will be better balanced when, for example, we will see African scholars leading archaeological collaborative projects on European soil.

Given the characteristics and history of international archaeological efforts, an important role is still being played by European archaeologists, heritage professionals and institutions in the research, management and development of archaeological heritage around the world. However, the undertaking of 'foreign' archaeology by European countries, especially in postcolonial contexts, is nowadays confronted with many ethical issues, such as indigenous claims to ownership and access to archaeology, the need for decolonizing epistemologies and practices, public accountability, western hegemony in heritage management discourses, its relation to post-colonial and neo-colonial political realities, the need to integrate its practice with wider heritage and development issues such as tourism and humanitarian aid, and finally the globalization of modern archaeological heritage management policies (following the Council of Europe's 1992 Malta convention, see Willems 2007; Naffé *et al.* 2008; Arazi 2011; Ashley and Bouakaze-Khan 2011, and see Cornelissen, this volume). As a result, the field of archaeology has made strides in decolonizing the discipline by recognizing the needs and interests of stakeholders in host countries, and by promoting equal partnerships and collaborations, through applying notions and methodologies such as 'public archaeology', 'community archaeology', 'indigenous archaeology', and, more recently, 'collaborative archaeology (Chirikure and Pwiti 2008, Hollowell and Nicholas 2009).

Such notions and methodologies do not come however without difficulties and challenges of their own. The power base in research, management, decision-making and benefits often continues to be skewed towards researchers from abroad, who are well endowed but usually do not stay long. Although it is widely acknowledged that concepts such as 'capacity building, 'community archaeology', 'partnerships', 'skills transfer' and 'multivocality' are all important factors in the conduct of archaeology abroad, such notions are often abstract and difficult to implement (Van der Linde 2012). In addition, little attention is given to the underlying notions of heritage, stewardship and materiality that underlie Western approaches to archaeological heritage and ethics. We need to question more seriously whether the values and concepts behind, for instance, European ethical codes and 'Malta' policies, are actually applicable to local circumstances in the host countries. Finally, more attention need to be paid in current debates on the ways motivations and activities of European archaeologists are influenced by the national socio-political and historical frameworks in which they operate. Although archaeology as an endeavor is increasingly multidisciplinary and international, it is often still carried out through institutional, financial and political frameworks on the national level of individual European nations states, each with their own specific historical legacies and international relationships.

Outline of the volume

Taken together, the above considerations constitute the context within which we composed this volume, *European Archaeology Abroad. Global Settings, Comparative Perspectives*. We explore the scope and impact of European archaeological policies and practices aimed at undertaking archaeological projects 'abroad', that is, in countries outside the respective contemporary national borders of the European space. Taking European archaeology abroad to be at once a historical process and as an ethical challenge, we focus on how values and motivations in socio-political and institutional European contexts change in relation to such issues as international collaboration with archaeologists, with local communities and with other stakeholders in the 'host country'.

The contributions in this volume are organized in three parts, dealing respectively with 'historical perspectives', with 'case studies' and with 'critical reflections'. Acknowledging that international and transcultural archaeological projects have a range of different stakeholders with specific and socio-politically situated motivations, the first part of this book aims, through comparative analysis, to historicize and identify the values and motivations behind different European archaeologies abroad. Dealing with a range of countries (namely Poland, Germany, the Netherlands, Belgium, France and Spain) the contributions here analyze the historical, institutional and socio-political frameworks in which 'foreign' archaeology has been developed and practiced. What values and motivations can one distinguish that have driven and presently drive foreign archaeology? How has the issue of 'international collaboration' in archaeology abroad been dealt with in the countries here studied? Finally, how has cooperation between local and foreign archaeologists unfolded, and how did engagements with local communities evolve over time?

The second part of this book presents case studies which explore how these values have been translated through contemporary socio-political, theoretical and administrative frameworks unto local or national circumstances in host countries, and how archaeological activities were and are nowadays received. This is illustrated through a range of examples, both from within and outside Europe. The range of issues considered includes international schools, capacity building, (post-)colonialism, globalization of 'Malta' archaeology, politics, language policies, community archaeology, etc. Overall, the main questions addressed are a) How do different European countries deal with the issue of 'international collaboration' with host countries, and how did this notion evolve and change over time?, as well as b) How is the notion of 'international collaboration' in contemporary archaeological practices received and valued by stakeholders in host countries? What lessons, in other words, can be learned from these contemporary case-studies regarding international and transcultural collaborations?

Indeed, we believe that the perceptions and values attached to European archaeological practices by stakeholders in host countries are actually fundamental for achieving equal partnerships and/or decolonized forms of archaeology. This question can be best answered by including perspectives and voices from the stakeholders themselves. This volume therefore includes as its third and final part several critical reflections on European values, motivations and collaboration projects, as perceived by archaeological heritage professionals based in and/or working in 'host-countries'. We do not pretend of course to be in anyway comprehensive or exhaustive here: understanding how international and transcultural projects are developed and negotiated over time, would entail far more detailed ethnographies of archaeological projects in postcolonial contexts than we can undertake (see for example Lydon and Rizvi 2010; Kleinitz and Näser 2011; Van der Linde 2012). Still, it is our hope that by providing throughout this volume some insights into the premises, policies and characteristics of European archaeology abroad, stakeholders the world over will be better placed to take informed decisions regarding what is feasible and desirable for the future prospects of archaeology.

References

Arazi, N. 2011. 'Safeguarding Archaeological Cultural Resources in Africa – Policies, Methods and Issues on (Non-)Compliance', *African Archaeological Review* 28: 27-38.

Ashley, C. and D. Bouakaze-Khan (eds). 2011. 'Conservation and Management of Archaeological Sites in Sub-Saharan Africa', *Conservation and Management of Archaeological Sites* 13(2-3): 95-102.

Biehl, P.F., A. Gramsch and A. Marciniak (eds). 2002. *Archaeologies of Europe. History, Methods and Theories.* Münster: Waxmann Verlag.

Chirikure, S. and G. Pwiti. 2008. 'Community Involvement in Archaeology and Cultural Heritage Management: An Assessment from Case-studies in Southern African and Elsewhere', *Current Anthropology* 49: 467–485.

Díaz-Andreu, M. 2007. *A World History of Nineteenth-Century Archaeology: Nationalism, Colonialism, and the Past.* Oxford: Oxford University Press.

Etherington, N. 2011. 'Barbarians Ancient and Modern', *The American Historical Review* 116: 31-57.

Fauvelle, F.-X. 2012. 'La Croix de Dias. Genèse d'une Frontière au Sud de l'Afrique', *Genèses* 86: 126-148.

Gran-Aymerich, E. 1998. *Naissance de l'Archéologie Moderne 1798–1945.* Paris: CNRS Editions.

Griffiths, T. 1996. *Hunters and Collectors: The Antiquarian Imagination in Australia.* Cambridge: Cambridge University Press.

Hollowell, J. and G. Nicholas. 2009. 'Using Ethnographic Methods to Articulate Community-Based Conceptions of Cultural Heritage Management', in Y. Hamilakis and A. Anagnostopoulos (eds), *Archaeological Ethnographies.* Public Archaeology 8(2-3). Leeds and Cambridge: Maney Publishing, 141-160.

Kleinitz, C. and C. Näser. 2011. 'The Loss of Innocence: Political and Ethical Dimensions of the Merowe Dam Archaeological Salvage Project at the Fourth Nile Cataract (Sudan)', *Conservation and Management of Archaeological Sites* 13(2-3): 253-280.

Lydon, J. and U. Rizvi (eds). 2010. *Handbook of Postcolonial Archaeology.* Walnut Creek: Left Coast Press.

Malina, J. and Z. Vasicek. 1990. *Archaeology Yesterday and Today. The Development of Archaeology in the Science and Humanities.* Cambridge: Cambridge University Press.

Moro-Abadia, O. 2006. 'The History of Archaeology as Colonial Discourse', *Bulletin of the History of Archaeology* 16: 4-17.

Naffé, B.O.M, R. Lanfranchi and N. Schlanger (eds). 2008. *L'Archéologie Préventive en Afrique: Enjeux et Perspectives: Actes du Colloque de Nouackchott, 1er-3 Fevrier 2007.* Saint-Maur-des-Fossés: Editions Sépia.

Pels, P. 1997. 'The Anthropology of Colonialism. Culture, History and the Emergence of Western Governmentality', *Annual Review of Anthropology* 28: 163-183.

Quirke, S. 2010. *Hidden Hands: Egyptian Workforces in Petrie Excavation Archives, 1880–1924*. London: Duckworth.

Robertshaw, P. (ed.). 1990. *A History of African Archaeology*. London: J. Currey.

Schlanger, N. 2003. 'The Burkitt Affair Revisited: Colonial Implications and Identity Politics in early South African Prehistoric Research', *Archaeological Dialogues* 10(1): 5-26, 42-55.

Schlanger, N. 2008. 'D'Assouan à Nouakchott, en Passent par Malte. Eléments pour une Histoire de l'Archéologie Préventive en Afrique', in B.O.M. Naffé, R. Lanfranchi and N. Schlanger (eds), *L'Archéologie Préventive en Afrique: Enjeux et Perspectives: Actes du Colloque de Nouackchott, 1er-3 Fevrier 2007*. Saint-Maur-des-Fossés: Editions Sépia, 31-38.

Schlanger, N. 2010. 'Manual and Intellectual Labour in Archaeology: Past and Present in Human Resource Management', in S. Koerner and I. Russell (eds), *Unquiet Pasts. Risk Society, Lived Cultural Heritage, Re-designing Reflexivity*. London: Ashgate Publishing Ltd., 161-171.

Schlanger, N. 2012. 'Situations Archéologiques, Expériences Coloniales', *Les Nouvelles de l'Archéologie* 128: 41-46.

Schlanger, N. and A-C. Taylor. 2012. 'Archéologie et Anthropologie: Chemins Parcourus et Engagements Partagés', in N. Schlanger and A.-C. Taylor (eds), *La Préhistoire des Autres. Perspectives Archéologiques et Anthropologiques*. Paris: La Découverte, 11-27.

Schnapp, A. 1993. *La Conquête du Passé: aux Origines de l'Archéologie*. Paris: Editions Carré [English translation from 1996: *The Discovery of the Past*. London: British Museum Press].

Stoler, A.L. 1989. 'Rethinking Colonial Categories: European Communities and the Boundaries of Rule', *Comparative Studies in Society and History* 31: 134-161.

Trigger, B. 1984. 'Alternative Archaeologies: Nationalist, Colonialist, Imperialist', *Man (new series)* 19(3): 355-370.

Trigger, B. 1989. *A History of Archaeological Thought*. New York: Cambridge University Press.

Trümpler, C. 2001. *Agatha Christie and Archaeology*. London: British Museum Press.

Van der Linde, S. 2012. *Digging Holes Abroad. An Ethnography of Dutch Archaeological Research Projects Abroad*. Archaeological Studies Leiden University 27. Leiden: Leiden University Press.

Van Reybrouck, D. 2010. *Congo. Een Geschiedenis*. Amsterdam: De Bezige Bij.

Willems, W. 2007. 'The Work of Making Malta: The Council of Europe's Archaeology and Planning Committee, 1988 – 1996', *European Journal of Archaeology* 10: 57-71.

Part One

Historical Overviews

1.1 Foreign schools and institutes around the Mediterranean Sea: relics of the past or renewed tools for scientific partnership?

Frank Braemer

National Centre for Scientific Research,
French School of Rome, France

Abstract

Foreign schools and institutes form a central system in the organization of archaeological research around the Mediterranean Sea. Stemming from a long tradition, these schools and institutes currently have to adapt to new conditions of archaeological research in specific host countries, as well as to the broader evolution of scientific research organization on a European, national and community level.

A comparative analysis of the medium-term programme proposals of European foreign schools and institutes allows for defining the current evolution of this system of research, its pivotal strategic aims and the future role that it can play around the Mediterranean Sea.

Résumé

Écoles et instituts étrangers autour de la mer Méditerranée : vestiges du passé ou instruments renouvelés pour un partenariat scientifique?

Les écoles et les instituts étrangers constituent un système central dans l'organisation de la recherche archéologique autour de la mer Méditerranée. Ces écoles et instituts, issus d'une longue tradition, doivent maintenant s'adapter à de nouvelles conditions de recherches archéologiques dans certains pays d'accueil, ainsi qu'à l'évolution de l'organisation de la recherche scientifique aux niveaux européen, national et communautaire.

Une analyse comparative des programmes à moyen terme proposés par les écoles et instituts européens, permet de définir l'évolution actuelle de ce système de recherche, ses objectifs stratégiques déterminants et le rôle qu'il pourra jouer à l'avenir sur la mer Méditerranée.

Extracto

Las Escuelas y las Instituciones Extranjeras alrededor del mar Mediterráneo: ¿Reliquias del Pasado o Herramientas Renovadas para una Asociación Científica?

Las escuelas y las instituciones extranjeras forman un sistema central en la organización de los estudios arqueológicos alrededor del mar Mediterráneo. Estas escuelas e instituciones, que proceden de una larga tradición, actualmente tienen que adaptarse a nuevas condiciones de investigación arqueológica en los específicos países huésped, tanto como a la evolución más amplia de la organización de investigaciones científicas a nivel europeo, nacional y local.

Un análisis comparativo de las propuestas de programa a medio plaza de escuelas e instituciones europeas permite definir la evolución actual de este sistema investigadora, los fines estratégicos cruciales y el futuro papel que puede tener alrededor del mar Mediterráneo.

ملخص

المعاهد والمدارس الأجنبية حول البحر المتوسط: قطع أثرية من الماضي أم تجديد للشراكة العلمية

فرانك برامر

المركز القومي للبحث العلمي

تشكل المدارس والمعاهد مراكزيا في تنظيم البحوث الأثرية في جميع أنحاء ضوء الأبيض المتوسط. وانطلاقا من تقاليد عريقة، يجب على هذه المدارس والمعاهد أن تتكيف، في الوقت الحالي، مع الظروف الجديدة للبحوث الأثرية في بلدان مضيفة محددة، وكذلك مع التطور الأوسع لتنظيم البحوث على المستوى المجتمعي المحلي، والوطني، والأوربي، على المستوى العلمية.

ويسمح التحليل المقارن لاقتراحات البرامج متوسطة المدى الخاصة بالمدارس والمعاهد الأجنبية والأوربية بتحديد التطور الحالي لهذا النظام من البحث، وأهدافه الاستراتيجية المحورية، والدور المستقبلي الذي يمكن أن تلعبه في كل أنحاء دول البحر الأبيض المتوسط.

Keywords

Foreign schools, archaeological research, Mediterranean sea

Introduction

A new system of historical and archaeological research institutions around the Mediterranean Sea developed during the last third of the nineteenth century when Germany, Great Britain, France, and the United States established study and training centres in Athens, Rome, Cairo and Madrid. The creation of these national establishments started with the French school at Athens in 1846, after an original phase of international collaboration in a kind of 'scholars' republic' which was promoted by German scholars and the *Institut de Correspondance Archéologique* at Rome from 1829 until 1870.

This article will not go deeply into the academic and diplomatic contexts of the creation and competition between these 'big nations' to assert their cultural influence on the Mediterranean world. Numerous papers offer good studies of such issues (Gran Aymerich and Grand Aymerich 1998; Delaunay 2000; Gran Aymerich 2000; Chevalier 2002; Jansen 2008; Petricioli 2009). Rather, taking this historical background into account, this article will provide an overall picture of the system today in order to better understand its evolutions and its inertia, and to discuss its near future.

In this article, the system of institutes, schools and research centres around the Mediterranean is analysed by examining their structure, their scientific strategy, their staff policies and by trying to describe the operational place they hold in the field of archaeology today. Subsequently, some major strategic issues will be defined which these institutions will have to face in the future.

When looking at the mission statements, reports and pamphlets of the foreign schools and institutes during their beginning in the nineteenth century, we can distill a common strategy to develop stable and institutionalized organizations undertaking historical research in the regions in which western civilization was thought to have originated. With the period of independent 'traveller-scholars' in the mid-nineteenth century coming to an end, a new working environment was therefore needed. In effect, four major aims can herein be distilled, which were 1) to organize excavations on important archaeological sites, develop facilities for scientific work such as libraries and sites' archives, and publish scientific journals, bulletins and monographs; 2) to train the 'elite' of archaeological and historical research, having the vocation to teach and develop scientific research in universities and academic bodies; 3) to open the system primarily to the scientific community of the country of origin, as well as 4) to establish a continuous connection with other academic institutions by sharing scientific results within the framework of learned societies, universities and national and local archaeological authorities.

By the end of the nineteenth century, the example of France, Germany and Great Britain was followed by several others countries, leading to the appearance of more foreign schools and institutes in Rome, Athens and Cairo. The archaeological presence extended to Jerusalem at the turn of the century with the peculiarity of convent schools developing archaeological programmes (mainly from the Dominican, Franciscan and the German Lutheran Church). A second wave of

Countries	Spain	Italy	Greece	Turkey	Cyprus	Syria	Lebanon	Israël	Pal. Aut.	Jordan	Egypt	Morocco
Germany	1943	1871	1872	1929		1982	1961		1900	1976	1907	
Australia			1980									
Austria		1881	1898									
Belgium		1939	1985									
Canada			1980									
Denmark		1956	1992			1995						
Spain		1910										
Finland		1954	1984			2010						
France	1920	1873	1846	1930		1929/1985	1946	1952	1890	1975	1880	(x)
Georgia			1997									
United Kingdom		1901	1886	1947		2010			1919	1975	1882	
Hungary		1894										
Eire			1995									
Italy			1909						1901		2008	
Norway		X	1989									
Netherlands		1904	1976	1958		2006					1971	2006
Poland		1927									1960	
Romania		1931										
Sweden		1925	1948									
Switzerland		1947	1975									
USA		1894	1881		1978			1900		1968	1948	

1st wave   2nd wave   3rd wave   last creations

Table 1. Establishment dates of foreign institutes and schools around the Mediterranean Sea (Table: F. Braemer).

archaeological institutes in the 1930s and 1940s can be directly associated with the decline of the Ottoman Empire when, after the creation of the modern Turkish state, institutes at Istanbul and later at Ankara appeared. Likewise, in Middle Eastern countries under western mandate, the creation of institutes in Jerusalem, Damascus and Beirut for example was directly connected to the establishment of departments of antiquities in these new states (table 1).

In Greece, the national law of antiquities required the creation of an institute in Athens for any country that wanted to obtain an excavation licence. This requirement was at the basis of a second wave of institutions appearing in Greece from the 1960s onwards. Later, the establishment of institutes and centres at Amman, Damascus, and Nicosia followed primarily the movement of conflicts in the Middle East after 1967.

The development of foreign institutes is not in a phase of extinction. The Netherlands for example, only recently reorganized and widened their network of offices for university cooperation in eight Mediterranean countries. Most of these integrate projects of archaeological and historical research (Van den Dries, Slappendel and Van der Linde, this volume). Next to this, private foundations supporting academic institutions have promoted the development of new institutes, such as for instance Denmark and Finland at Damascus. In addition, existing institutes have been increasing their network in the Middle East: the Centre for British Research in the Levant (CBRL) for instance created an office at Damascus, the *Institut Français du Proche-Orient* (IFPO) created offices at Erbil (Iraq) and Jerusalem, and the *Deutsches Archäologisches Institut* (DAI) in Cairo undertakes research in Libya, whilst the Spanish academic community is pressing for the creation of institutes at Athens and Amman (Ayán Vila and González Ruibal, this volume).

In 2010, the foreign archaeological research network was distributed over more than 67 centres, permanent schools and institutes around the Mediterranean Sea. France maintains 14 institutes, Germany 9, the USA, the United Kingdom, and the Netherlands 6, Denmark, Belgium, Switzerland, Austria and Italy 3, Finland and Sweden 2, whilst Poland, Spain, Australia and Canada each have one institute (figure 1).

This very brief history shows that the development of the foreign archaeological research network is still alive and dynamic. Scientific communities have always been the main supporters of the foreign research institutes, as they often regarded such a system as providing an effective solution to their international research needs. It is also striking to note the global similarities in structure and functioning from one institute to another. Matters of fieldwork, research tools and scientific communication are all based upon the same model to support national teams in their international scientific competitive endeavours. Permanent structures abroad are as such logistical 'hubs' for any archaeological project. Furthermore, one can see some striking similarities between the career paths and training schemes of academic archaeologists in Europe, which often include a significant period of stay in foreign countries where research centres are located. Taken together, this is why

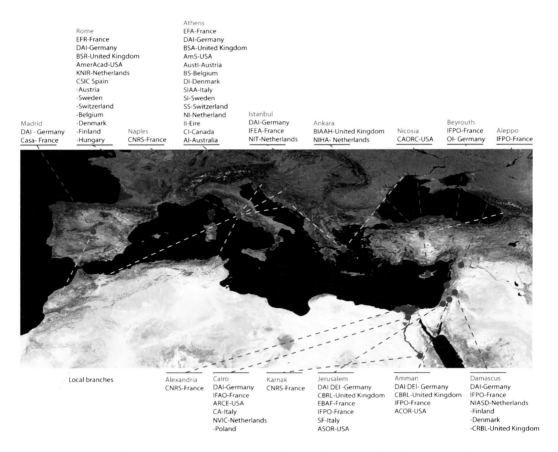

Rome
EFR-France
DAI-Germany
BSR-United Kingdom
AmerAcad-USA
KNIR-Netherlands
CSIC Spain
-Austria
-Sweden
-Switzerland
-Belgium
-Denmark
-Finland
-Hungary

Athens
EFA-France
DAI-Germany
BSA-United Kingdom
AmS-USA
Austl-Austria
BS-Belgium
DI-Denmark
SIAA-Italy
SI-Sweden
SS-Switzerland
NI-Netherland
Il-Eire
CI-Canada
AI-Australia

Istanbul
DAI-Germany
IFEA-France
NIT-Netherlands

Ankara
BIAAH-United Kingdom
NIHA- Netherlands

Nicosia
CAORC-USA

Beyrouth
IFPO-France
OI- Germany

Aleppo
IFPO-France

Madrid
DAI - Germany
Casa- France

Naples
CNRS-France

Local branches

Alexandria
CNRS-France

Cairo
DAI-Germany
IFAO-France
ARCE-USA
CA-Italy
NVIC-Netherlands
-Poland

Karnak
CNRS-France

Jerusalem
DAI DEI -Germany
CBRL-United Kingdom
EBAF-France
IFPO-France
SF-Italy
ASOR-USA

Amman
DAI DEI- Germany
CBRL-United Kingdom
IFPO-France
ACOR-USA

Damascus
DAI-Germany
IFPO-France
NIASD-Netherlands
-Finland
-Denmark
-CRBL-United Kingdom

Figure 1. Map of foreign institutes and schools around the Mediterranean Sea (Illustration: K. Wentink, based on work by F. Braemer).

we can consider these centres, schools and institutes abroad as a fundamental part of the occidental training and research system in Mediterranean archaeology and history.

Archaeology occupies a pre-eminent position in these institutions. Besides being of scientific value, archaeology also provides a major interface between research and politics – a result of what Etienne (2000: 4-5) called the "plasticity of presentation" of archaeology. Indeed, "archaeology owes its strong historical links with politics to the opportunities it offers as being sometimes science, sometimes a cultural vector", as well as in its capacity to become intrinsically linked to politics of memory, international relationships and development strategies (Etienne 2000: 4-5). As a result, archaeology often provides one of the states' most useful vectors of cultural initiatives, which means that institutes abroad are often not only scientific organizations, but also symbols of cultural influence and tools of 'soft diplomacy'. The creation of archaeological institutes and schools has as such always been based upon political choices (see for example Theodoroudi and Kotsakis, this volume), which explains the involvement of ministries of foreign affairs in most of them.

Organization

Foreign research centres are very autonomous in their functioning. A general director, often surrounded by scientific directors, administrators, and a scientific board organizes the centre's daily functioning and negotiates funding matters with government bodies. Only the research centres of the German archaeological institute are strongly integrated into a network mirroring the federative structure of Germany itself, although the Netherlands recently restructured their system of foreign institutes to promote internal integration as well. In France, the Ministry of Foreign Affairs and the Ministry of Higher Education have tried from time to time to group the various institutes and schools into a more homogeneous structure – without much success, except for a common web portal (Levin, this volume) and more recently, some common rules provided by a unique government decree. Within French and UK institutes and schools, the dominant attitude is that their scientific interests are not convergent: in general, they seem to value their own identity and autonomy more than their collective scientific and institutional strengths.

The financial support for foreign schools and institutes depends on the specific administrative organization of each country. Traditionally, this is provided by the ministries of higher education and research in France and the Netherlands, by the British Academy in the UK, by ministries of foreign affairs in Germany and France, by the ministry of culture in Italy, whilst national research centres in Spain and France also support wider infrastructure facilities and salaries. Recent developments in the research organization of Europe have led to the creation of foundations in the Netherlands, Denmark and Finland that are financing foreign institutes. Finally, scientific projects are increasingly funded by national and European research agencies: in 2010, around half of the total DAI budget (approximately fifteen M€) was for example funded in this way.

Research

Most of the schools and institutes define their scientific interest as belonging to the historical sciences, frequently with an additional emphasis on the social sciences in a diachronic perspective. Only the DAI and the Italian School in Athens explicitly limit their field of investigation to the archaeology before 'modern' times. Around the Mediterranean Sea, it is generally Classical Archaeology and Egyptology that takes up the central place.

At present, the strategic research plans by the British schools and institutes in Athens, Ankara and Amman/Jerusalem offer one of the clearest research objectives of all the foreign research schools and institutes. To summarize, these are, firstly, to develop excellent research projects involving British researchers and members of the centres themselves. Secondly, their objective is to facilitate the training of British academic talents at pre-doctoral, doctoral and post-doctoral levels through providing scholarships and grants. Thirdly, they aim to offer services to the entire international scientific community, such as libraries, archives, reference collections and publications. Fourthly, their objective is to be the main broker and general point of advice for British researchers in the specific host countries, and finally, their aim is to promote collaboration between British researchers, local academic communities and other European researchers through shared projects, seminars and conferences.

This summary shows that the objectives and aims initiated at the end of the nineteenth century are still relevant. There is however a certain variety from one institute to another. This is not only the result of practical constraints such as availability of financial resources and personal capacity, but also of the impact of strategic choices such as what research disciplines are considered as relevant, the relative weight (funding and scientific) that is placed upon the different objectives, and the organization of scientific programmes. In general, scientific programmes are based upon very broad topics: this is the direct consequence of the institutionalized modes of scientific and financial evaluation that have been standardized in Europe during the last two decades.

Many of the schools and institutes abroad have a leading role in the direction of archaeological operations. The DAI network manages circa 80 archaeological research projects around the Mediterranean Sea per year, which represent more than half of all the German activities in this area (29 in Turkey, ten each in Italy, Greece and Egypt, nine in Spain, and two each in Tunisia and Morocco). French schools abroad manage approximately 50 operations per year, which account for more than a third of French archaeological activity abroad (nineteen projects by the French school in Cairo in Egypt and Sudan, fourteen by the school in Athens in Greece, Cyprus and Albania, twelve by the school in Rome in Italy, Albania, Croatia, Serbia, Morocco and Tunisia, and four projects by the school in Madrid in Spain and Morocco). Schools, institutes and societies related to the British Academy and the Egypt Exploration Society coordinated at least 50 British archaeological projects, mostly financed by external resources (thirteen in Egypt, twelve in Turkey, nine in Greece, five in Libya, four in Italy, three in Syria and two in Cyprus).

As such, a large part of the archaeological projects abroad around the Mediterranean are managed by this system every year. Beyond these projects, many of the schools have the capacity to manage 'great' archaeological sites for a very sustained period, such as for example Olympia since 1875, Delphia since 1893 and Karnak since 1895. These sites were, and still are, major sources for the construction and interpretation of historical narratives by means of fieldwork and documentation research. The sustained presence of foreign institutions in for example Greece and Egypt, also allowed for the organization of long-term data and information collection systems by means of archaeological journals, chronicles and regional or thematic archaeological maps.

The academic life at the schools and institutes in general crystallizes around the library, which often forms a fundamental part of the centres' identity. Apart from being an academic working tool, the libraries often fulfil a role in welcoming colleagues and students of host countries, as well as in housing collections that are important for researchers of both home and host countries. The continuation of annual funding for maintaining and updating these collections is thus a priority for all.

Academic editing is another basic activity of all the schools and institutes, many of which also have a role as publishers and booksellers. As such, every foreign institution maintains a journal and book series, which is important not only for its continuation of a long tradition in publishing archaeological field data, but also for it capacity to increase visibility, promote identity and expand the library collections through book exchanges.

Finally, it is noteworthy that the American and British schools in Athens, the British Institute in Ankara, and the French school in Cairo all maintain important archaeological scientific laboratories, providing opportunities to both local and foreign researchers.

Who works there?

Comparing the institutions' archaeological staffs is not an easy task due to differences in employment status and scientific areas of interest. However, when looking at the German, French and British systems, it can be noted that senior researchers generally form the directorate of each institute, who are always recruited on their academic merit, and who normally live locally for around 3 to 8 years as a result of specific research programmes. These management teams account for a total of circa 100 people around the Mediterranean (consisting of circa 35 from the DAI, 45 from the French network, and around 20 from the British network). Roughly 55 to 60 people can be considered as fellows, members, and 'pensionnaires' of the institutions; they normally live abroad for a three to four year stay. These people are always recruited on the basis of post-doctoral positions, except for the French schools in Rome and Athens and the Italian school in Athens which recruit at doctoral level. At the doctoral level, the general rule is a short stay of 3 months up to two years, with different accompanying systems of grants and awards. Finally, a large set of grants is provided for undergraduate and graduate students and junior researchers for short-term stays (one to twelve months) abroad.

In a rather exclusive way, these positions are often available only for citizens of the countries funding the institutes, in evident contradiction with European legislative rules. Only Spain opens up its positions at a European level. The United Kingdom widens the eligibility of candidacy to students having studied in the UK and still being resident. Different formulas of association allow the integration of several colleagues and students from host countries to research projects. Finally, local contracts – either for foreigners or local people – are devoted to the support of research, such as in the areas of documentation, topography, restoration, laboratory work, fieldworks, archival studies, and library tasks. These account for just over a hundred persons.

Around 250 to 300 people are working in archaeology at the foreign schools and institutes around the Mediterranean Sea, with an expatriate stay of more than six months; circa 130 to 140 people for the French schools, 90 to 95 for the German centres, and 40 to 45 for Great Britain. At least 100 months of grants per year for short-term scholarships complement this system.

Research training

All the institutions have a similar teaching and training mission, in several complementary ways. The first approach towards teaching is by offering courses, seminars, fieldwork and technical workshops – all open to the centres' members but often also to students of the country of origin and the host countries. Secondly, the scientific activities of the institutions (archaeological projects, seminars, conferences, colloquiums) are opened to, or managed by PhD students, which is an effective way of vocational training for a professional integration in the social research environment. Furthermore, training is often realized through a direct, yet informal and personal relationship between students and supervisors. Only the Italian School at Athens advocates a formal teaching structure.

As a result, this educational and training system produces researchers who are launched on the European scientific professional market, mainly at post-doc level but also at a more general research level. The director of the French School in Rome for example, emphasized in his last annual report the 'return on investment' that the constitution of this researcher's pool represents for France, out of which it recruits its university professors and its researchers. Indeed, this holds true for 90% of French schools members, but also for circa 65-75% of DAI members. In other words, a curriculum vitae including a research period at a foreign school or institute often provides an additional advantage for an application for university positions. The nineteenth century idea of the 'grand tour' as an element of academic identity building seems as such very much alive. Obtaining a recruitment abroad thereby presents a good career move for young researchers, as they are becoming part of a perceived 'research elite', benefiting from high-level facilities in prestigious institutions.

Some strategic issues

The system of historical and archaeological research organizations around the Mediterranean Sea is changing very slowly due to the weight of tradition and the academic community's inertia. Research funding programmes at a European level, the increasing data production by preventive and 'Malta' archaeology and the local development of universities and research centres all around the Mediterranean necessitate the adaptation of the system. As such, there is a need for renewed partnerships with host countries in a less unilateral way.

Europe

"Europe is the only effective framework for scientific research at an international level. It is thus necessary to make this an immediate and short-term objective" according to the director of the *Institut Français du Proche-Orient* (IFPO) in an on-line message.[1] This European dimension was not, until recent times, a major concern for schools and institutes. The staff recruitment, as well as the financing of archaeological projects, remains often exclusively national, which means that European international collaboration abroad is generally reduced to some minimal organization of colloquiums and workshops. There are however some opportunities for change.

The massive reduction of funding in particular related to the Middle East could urge schools and institutes to build scientific associations but also to share premises with institutes of other European countries. In Syria for example, such an initiative has led to an association between the IFPO and the Spanish *Casa Araba* at Aleppo. This might lead to a new form of European multinational institutional centre in the area – such as exists for example at Nairobi between British and French institutes.

A new collaboration between national funding agencies – such as the *Deutsches Forschung Gemeinschaft* (DFG), the *Agence Nationale de la Recherche* (ANR) and the Art and Humanities Research Council (AHRC) – offers a less 'Kafkaesque' organization than those of European programmes and is probably going to become a great incentive for scientific collaboration. An agreement between the ANR and the DFG for example already foresees the development of new projects in Rome. A recent common declaration by directors of European schools and institutes directors in Rome signals similar developments.

These opportunities for collaborations and the partnerships they facilitate, and the European move towards opening up recruitment in higher education, gradually leads to the abandonment of a tradition of purely national recruitment. It is likely that young researchers will increasingly go to schools and institutes that offer them the most suitable programmes and research according to their research needs. As they will also choose the best linguistic and cultural environment for their research objectives, they might have to jump national barriers, as they are already doing within European 'Erasmus' and post-doc research schemes abroad. This is a consequence and a benefit of the Bologna process that facilitates a harmonization of academic courses.

On the European level, scientific cooperation schemes are developing new opportunities for multi-national projects and mobility exchange programs for European citizens. Simultaneously, this means that the former dominant bilateral system of cooperation is weakening: European researchers can no longer apply for common programs in Europe whilst at the same time operating only under their national flags abroad. On the other hand, the cultural and scientific cooperation schemes funded by each individual European nation-state is often more important

---

1   Retrieved 15 January 2009 from http://www.ifporient.org/node/1.

than those of the European Community. This creates a rather contradictory situation, which leads to the fact that researchers and foreign schools prefer to maintain more or less all the diverse forms of funding for scientific cooperation.

Research framework

It is important to point out that the system of schools and institutes is far from taking care of the total number of archaeological projects in the Mediterranean. Whilst Classical archaeology and Egyptology remain pre-eminent topics within the current and future projects by the schools and institutes, and whilst Late Antiquity and Medieval periods occupy a significant place, there is an explicit deficit in research programmes dealing with pre- and protohistoric periods (although less in the Middle East and Turkey), with archaeological sciences and with heritage management studies, although these latter should not be separated from archaeological fieldwork projects.

The British School in Athens is the only institution that prioritizes a scientific objective "to break the barrier that exists between the study of prehistory and that of the historic periods in the Greek world, and to promote comparative studies" (British School at Athens 2006). The development of archaeological laboratories and reference collections began rather recently in the British schools at Athens and Ankara, and at the IFAO in Cairo. In the latter case, this initiative was stimulated by Egyptian legislation that prohibits the export of samples. However, true interdisciplinary research that does not see archaeological techniques and sciences as auxiliary but as an important move towards developing new areas of research and data production, is not undertaken. By and large, the archaeological research interests and methods of the institutions stay within the traditional core of those disciplines that motivated their original creation. As a result, most of the schools and institutes only manage with difficulty to create meaningful and innovative interrelationships with other disciplinary communities. As such, the move towards developing a new archaeological discipline will not likely be initiated here.

Another strategic issue in terms of archaeological research within these institutions is their exclusive implication with so-called research-led archaeology. Nevertheless, a major part of new field data nowadays comes from preventive or developer-led archaeology. The increasing gap between these two practices and modes of production of archaeological data constitutes a major risk for the discipline. If information about the totality of produced data does not circulate in a fluid way between these two worlds, and is not accessible to international research, archaeological researchers will work and think whilst remaining partially blind. We therefore need a collective reflection on this issue, which will doubtless involve a redistribution of the roles and functions of research practices. Such a reflection has begun for example with the joint on-line publishing of databases in Italy (the 'Fasti on-line'[2] of the AIAC) and in Greece (the 'Excavation chronicle' by the French and British schools).[3] Such initiatives, although useful, are still far from

---

2   See www.fastionline.org/.
3   See http://chronique.efa.gr/.

all that is needed. Academic institutions both at home and abroad have to redefine their role amongst commercial archaeology as resulted from the implementation of the Malta Convention, amongst increasing initiatives in cultural tourism and within broader governmental heritage management structures.

Nevertheless, initiatives in the field of data management, processing and storage are certainly promising, and it is necessary to strengthen collaborations in building new databases, archaeological maps and heritage inventories. Such a role of institutes and schools was already clearly suggested about ten years ago, during an Egyptology conference in Cairo. Here, a demand was discussed to return databases and knowledge about archaeological sites obtained by foreigners in their fieldworks to Egypt, and to participate in the enrichment of these databases with the aim of archaeological heritage management and protection. Simultaneously, there is a need to integrate heritage management studies more strongly within the research domain of schools, institutes and academic institutions if researchers want to truly take part in discussions about heritage valuation.

Uncertain futures

Continuing efforts for ensuring funding and political support for the schools and institutes is essential because such support can never be automatically assumed. National political support for institutions that are far away from the metropolis are not as strong and constant as they have been in the past. The current economic crisis, the budgetary programmes of austerity and the increasing Europeanization increasingly lead to questions about the right of existence for foreign, distant institutions.

The Dutch Institute in Istanbul for example, was 'expelled' from the consular buildings, and could only return to its activities thanks to a Turkish private foundation that presently accommodates it. Protest movements and interventions at the highest political level were necessary so that the DAI in Rome was not closed during safety works on its premises, and to make sure that the Italian School in Athens was removed from the list of 'useless' structures that was established during the summer of 2010 by the Italian Ministry of Finance. In addition, the Austrian Institute in Rome was at the time of research threatened with closure. In general, an increasingly political voice appears that regards these structures as having less strategic value than in the past. This is due to several factors, such as a decreasing value of the humanities and classical studies in international academic competitions and as a form of 'cultural power', the fact that archaeology is increasingly becoming an element of economic development within a market approach, and because of an uncertainty about sharing academic institutions at the national or European levels. Reversing this political view requires a coherent effort by the academic community at a political level. But there is hope, as can be seen by the efforts made by the DAI, which has nowadays become an official supporter of the German Ministry of Foreign Affairs' cooperation network, and a renewed actor on the national and international scientific scene.

Conclusion

The system of a research network of foreign schools and institutes is supported by a major part of the national and international academic communities. But now that the academic and political motivations behind the original system's creation are becoming obsolete, what are the necessary adjustments? The system has always been devoted to the reproduction of academic research and teaching in the European home countries, but recent developments in academic research and teaching within the host countries impose a necessary *aggiornamento* of the ancient partnerships. Foreign schools and institutes located in European countries have to rearrange their scientific strategies not only in a bilateral way with local universities and research bodies, but also in terms of developing programmes and research tools with other foreign schools. The recent trend in cooperation between national funding agencies and the increased mobility of researchers form a strong stimulus to adjust to. This is also the case for schools and institutes located in non-European countries, where partnerships with local universities and research bodies have to adjust to changes occurring in academic organizations such as the increasing influence of international standards in teaching.

Classical and Medieval archaeology can no longer remain the central scientific horizon of the system. Opening up to prehistory and modern times and a stronger integration with archaeological sciences are fundamental if the system wants to remain a major element in the conduct of archaeology abroad. Integration with the field of heritage management studies is also an important new domain to be explored.

But the major challenge is likely to be the degree to which 'academic', research-led archaeological programmes can integrate new data coming out of preventive and developer-led archaeology. Foreign schools and institutes should therefore create links with local counterparts and actors from the field of preventive and development-led archaeology, and elaborate a clear positive role of the institutions for the future.

Acknowledgements

This paper was prepared within the framework of an analytical mission about the international situation of archaeology around the Mediterranean, sponsored by the directors of the French *Centre National de la Recherche Scientifique* (CNRS), *Institut des Sciences Humaines et Sociales* and the *Ecole Française de Rome*.[4]

---

4   The full report is available at the worldwide web at http://halshs.archives-ouvertes.fr/docs/00/60/24/63/PDF/Rapport_Mission_Archeo.pdf.

References

British School at Athens. 2006. *Strategic Plan for Research 2006-2009*. Athens: British School at Athens.

Chevalier, N. 2002. *La Recherche Archéologique Française au Moyen-Orient 1842-1947*. Paris: Editions Recherches sur les Civilisations.

Delaunay, J.-M. 2000. 'La Recherche Archéologique, une Manifestation de Puissance? L'Archéologie et les Archéologues au Coeur des Relations Internationales Contemporaines. L'Ecole Française d'Athènes, un haut-Lieu du Nationalisme Français?', in R. Etienne (ed.), *Les Politiques de l'Archéologie du Milieu du XIXè Siècle à l'Orée du XXIè*. Paris: Ecole Française d'Athènes, 125-154.

Etienne, R. 2000. 'Introduction', in R. Etienne (ed.), *Les Politiques de l'Archéologie du Milieu du XIXè Siècle à l'Orée du XXIè*. Paris: Ecole Française d'Athènes, 3-6.

Gran-Aymerich, E. 2000. 'L'Archéologie Française en Grèce: Politique Archéologique et Politique Méditerranéenne 1798-1945', in R. Etienne (ed.), *Les Politiques de l'Archéologie du Milieu du XIXè Siècle à l'Orée du XXIè*. Paris: Ecole Française d'Athènes, 79-112.

Gran-Aymerich, E. and J. Gran-Aymerich. 1998. *Naissance de l'Archéologie Moderne, 1798-1945*. Paris: CNRS Editions.

Jansen, C. 2008. 'The German Archaeological Institute Between Transnational Scholarship and Foreign Cultural Policy', *Fragmenta* 2: 151-181.

Petricioli, M. 2009. 'Le Missioni Archeologiche Italiane nel Mediterraneo tra Politica e Cultura', in F. Salvatori (ed.), *Il Mediterraneo delle Città: Scambi, Confronti, Culture, Rappresentazioni*. I Libri di Viella 86. Roma: Viella, 199-206.

1.2 FRENCH ARCHAEOLOGY ABROAD: A SHORT HISTORY OF ITS INSTITUTIONAL AND POLITICAL FRAMEWORK

Sonia Lévin

French National Institute for Preventive
Archaeological Research, France

Abstract

Since its antiquarian origins, French archaeology has had affinities with the ancient remains of distant lands. Successive colonizations were not the only justification of such foreign academic interests, even though archaeological projects abroad were always influenced by politics. From the ambassadors of the *Ancien Régime* to the actual involvement of French diplomacy in the funding and the mediation of archaeology, the French state has promoted the development of archaeology in foreign – or colonized – territories. Before the creation of a dedicated advisory commission for overseas excavations within the Ministry of Foreign Affairs in 1947, the Ministry of Public Instruction was the main supervisor of such projects, mainly through the promotion of individual missions and the creation of permanent archaeological schools. Nowadays, the Ministry of Foreign Affairs and the National Centre for Scientific Research (CNRS) are forming common objectives. Together with archaeological professionals from universities, higher education, museums and Inrap, they aim to conduct archaeology on the five major continents – with a growing concern for sustainable development and enhanced collaboration with 'guest' countries.

Résumé

L'archéologie française à l'étranger : un bref historique de son cadre institutionnel et politique

Dès ses origines du temps des antiquaires, l'archéologie française a toujours eu des affinités avec les vestiges archéologiques des pays lointains. Les colonisations successives ne sont pas la seule raison de cet intérêt académique pour l'étranger, bien que les projets archéologiques à l'étranger ont toujours été influencés par la politique. L'État français a de tout temps promu le développement de l'archéologie dans les territoires étrangers ou colonisés, depuis les premiers ambassadeurs de l'Ancien Régime jusqu'à une véritable implication diplomatique française dans le financement et la médiation de l'archéologie. Avant la création d'un comité consultatif des fouilles à l'étranger par le Ministère des Affaires Étrangères en 1947, le Ministère de l'Éducation Nationale supervisait de tels projets, principalement par la promotion de missions isolées et la création d'écoles d'archéologie permanentes. Aujourd'hui, le Ministère des Affaires Étrangères et le Centre National de la Recherche Scientifique (CNRS) ont des objectifs communs : avec des professionnels de l'archéologie de formation universitaire ou issus d'écoles supérieures, de musées ou de l'Inrap, leur but est de mettre en place une pratique archéologique sur les cinq continents principaux - avec une préoccupation croissante pour le développement durable et en favorisant la collaboration avec les pays concernés.

Extracto

La arqueología francesa en el extranjero: una breve historia de su estructura institucional y política

Desde sus orígenes antiguos la arqueología francesa siempre ha tenido afinidades con los vestigios antiguos de países lejanos. Las colonizaciones sucesivas no fueron el único motivo de aquellos intereses académicos extranjeros, aunque la política siempre ha afectado los proyectos arqueológicos extranjeros. Desde los embajadores del *Ancien Régime* hasta la participación actual de la diplomacia francesa en el establecimiento y la mediación de la arqueología, el Estado francés ha fomentado el desarrollo de la arqueología en territorios extranjeros o colonizados. Antes de la fundación de una dedicada comisión asesora para excavaciones de ultramar dentro del Ministerio de Asuntos Extranjeros en 1947, el Ministerio de Enseñanza Pública era el supervisor principal de tales proyectos, principalmente a través del fomento de misiones individuales y de la fundación de escuelas permanentes de arqueología. Hoy en día el Ministerio de Asuntos Extranjeros y el Centro Nacional para Investigaciones Científicas (CNRS) están formando objetivos comunes. Tienen, junto con los profesionales de las universidades, de la enseñanza superior, de los museos y de Inrap, el objetivo de ejecutar la arqueología en los cinco continentes principales con una creciente preocupación por el desarrollo sostenible y la colaboración reforzada con los países huésped.

ملخص

علم الآثار الفرنسي في الخارج: تاريخ مختصر لإطاره السياسي والمؤسسي

سونيا ليفين

المعهد القومي للبحوث الأثرية الوقائية، فرنسا

منذ أصوله القديمة، كان علم الآثار الفرنسي على صلات مع الأطلال القديمة في بلدان بعيدة. ولم يكن الاستعمار المتعاقب هو المبرر الوحيد لهذه المصالح الأكاديمية، على الرغم من تأثير المشاريع الأثرية في الخارج الأجنبية بالسياسة دائماً. ومن سفراء النظام القديم إلى الإشراك الفعلي للدبلوماسية

الفرنسية الدولة قامت الآثار، علم في والوساطة التمويل في الفرنسية
وقبل المستعمرات. أراضي أو الأجنبية الأراضي في الآثار علم تطوير بتطوير
لوزارة تابعة الخارج في التنقيب أعمال لأعمال متخصصة إشرافية لجنة إنشاء
هذه مثل على رئيسي الفرنسي هي العام التعليم وزارة كانت ،1947 عام الخارجية
بشكل الأثرية المدارس إنشاء والفردية البعثات تشجيع خلال من يعرف، المشاريع
مع علماء الأجنب، إلى جنب الحاضر، الوقت وفي .المركز مع بالتعاون الخارجية
من الأثرية اللقائية للبحوث القومي والمعهد والفتاح والعهد القومي لتشكيل بالعلم يتشكيل المشتركة.
من المتزايد القلق مع الكبرى القارات في أثرية بحوث إجراء إلى فهدف تهدف
.المضيفة البلدان مع التعاون وتعزيز المستدامة التنمية أجل

Keywords

French archaeology abroad, CNRS, Ministry of Public Instruction, Ministry of Foreign Affairs, diplomacy, national archives

Introduction

One could say, provocatively perhaps, that French archaeology was 'born' abroad. The first sustained and formal French interests in the material culture of the past occurred outside French territory proper. This French territory was historically more extended than today, but there seems to be no systematic link between the archaeological interests and the political status of the countries where material remains were discovered. The first French colonial empire, which included territories in North America, the Antilles and islands in the Indian Ocean, as well as Eastern Indian and African lands, effectively came to an end by the last decades of the eighteenth century. The second colonial empire, mostly comprised of territories in North and Sub-Saharan Africa but also in Indochina and Oceania's islands which were mainly obtained after 1830 and by and large relinquished with the era of independence. This phenomenon of colonization does however not explain the politics of archaeological explorations fully. Since the Renaissance, French amateurs and researchers have been interested in ancient civilizations located overseas but not necessarily, not only, in annexed or colonized lands.

Archaeology, as a body of knowledge, practices and practitioners, has always been connected with travel; this is not a specifically French characteristic (Kaeser *et al.* 2008: 26-29). Either in the field or in their general scientific interaction with colleagues, archaeologists do not work in isolation: international conferences and missions involve physical travels, whereas correspondences and publications testify to the circulation of words, images and ideas. On the whole, French archaeology has engaged with those more or less informal networks and international institutions, which reach beyond political boundaries and linguistic traditions.

However, alongside individual initiatives and projects, also the French state has been consistently involved with organizing and ensuring the continued existence of scientific missions and institutions abroad, and this involvement is still ongoing at the onset of the twenty-first century. As a first approximation, three successive phases can be distinguished in the history of French archaeology abroad: 1) antiquarian origins, from the Renaissance onwards, 2) nineteenth century institutionalization beginning with Bonaparte's expedition to Egypt, and 3) contemporary frameworks from the mid-twentieth century until today. This tripartite division will serve us as a framework with which to present the main institutional and organizational developments of French archaeology abroad, including its lasting and its changing features.

Diplomacy and war at the service of archaeology

In the world of antiquarians, as thoroughly studied by Alain Schnapp in '*The Conquest of the Past*' (Schnapp 1993), going abroad appears to be something of a French speciality. Indeed, in contrast to the more local observations by their British or Scandinavian colleagues, French antiquarians overall preferred long-distance destinations; being more attracted by antiquities from far away lands than by the ones coming out of their own soil. A good example is the magistrate Nicolas Fabri de Peiresc (1580–1637). After a classical 'tour' in Italy in 1559, he extended his scientific curiosity to the rest of the world, collecting and archiving ancient remains from Egypt, from the northern fringes of Europe, from Persia, and other remote places (Schnapp 2004).

Since the sixteenth century, French scholars had systematically joined ambassadors in eastern countries: 'a good ambassador can only be a good collector at the service of his king' (Schnapp 2004: 16). Of course collecting is still a long way from 'proper' archaeological scientific exploration, but the social position and the curiosity of those collectors enhanced the value of the material testimonies inherited from the past. The framework of royal institutions also constituted a basis for missions abroad. Since its creation in 1663, the *Académie des Inscriptions et Belles-Lettres* has stimulated epigraphic and antiquities studies. The *Académie des Sciences* (created in 1666) and the *Académie d'Architecture* (created in 1671) also resulted in centralized policies for observation and scientific missions. These prestigious institutions still exist, gathered within the *Institut de France* in Paris, where they hold precious archaeological archives (Lamarque, Piernas and Queyroux 2007). They still provide support for scientific research, and have long-standing links with French archaeological schools abroad, such as the *École Française d'Athènes* (EFA) or the *École Française de Rome* (EFR) (Braemer, this volume). This support from the French centres of power and knowledge, mainly through royal diplomacy and the early scientific institutions, has been invaluable to many early scholars interested in antiquities abroad.

The scale of scientific explorations changed upon their association with military expeditions – of which Napoleon Bonaparte's expedition to Egypt (1798–1801) is the first and most emblematic. A group of some 160 scholars, from the *Museum d'Histoire Naturelle* and the *Institut de France* and its academies, linked up with the military corps of the French empire. Initially, Bonaparte wanted these scholars to serve his political and territorial ambitions, but the research they undertook was of such scope and quality that it gave a lasting impetus to Egyptology.

According to Eve Gran-Aymerich, this expedition remained the most important model throughout the nineteenth century for all other military expeditions in the Mediterranean (Gran-Aymerich 1998, 2000: 10), in Greece with the Morea expedition (1829–1831), in Persia, in Lebanon, as well as in Algeria. Indeed, the Algerian colonial conquest, from 1830 onwards, was soon after followed by a commission for scientific exploration (Dondin-Payre 2003).

In the nineteenth century archaeology abroad cannot be dissociated from the European fascination with the Orient. Attracted by the picturesque mores and customs prevalent in Egypt, Babylonia and the 'Lands of the Bible', metropolitan bourgeoisie, artists and aristocrats became fascinated by the monumental ruins there. Archaeological excavations in Egypt, Persia and Mesopotamia, still under Ottoman rule, therefore required an undeniable diplomatic tact, sporting rivalries between western powers. The study of oriental civilizations in certain geographical locations thereby became intrinsically linked to the oriental policies of France and Britain (Fenet, Filliozat and Gran Aymerich 2007: 52). It was in this context that the '*diplomat-archaeologists*' could conduct their excavations. Iraq was for instance a chosen field for competition between Britain and France. While the British Sir Henry Rawlinson (1810–1895) was excavating Nimrud and Assur, Paul-Émile Botta (1802–1870), French consul in Mossoul, had been working in Khorsabad since 1843 (Chevalier 2002). Another pioneer, Ernest de Sarzec (1837–1901), vice-consul in Bassorah, excavated Tello from 1877 onwards. In parallel with the fascination with the Orient, the collection of artefacts also remained a major drive behind foreign explorations: archaeological remains were sent back to the supporting museums, specifically to the Louvre Museum which had opened its doors in 1793, after the French Revolution.

The institutionalization of archaeology and its integration into cultural diplomacy

On 7 and 8 April 2010, a conference on the 'International Cooperation for the Protection and the Repatriation of Cultural Heritage' was held in Cairo. Co-ordinated by the then vice-minister of culture, Zahi Hawass, the conference focused on the restitution of 'looted' antiquities disseminated over the world. France, Great Britain and Germany – as western 'culprits' – were not invited. Zahi Hawass officially called the 22 countries present into action to co-operate in getting back the cultural objects from their respective countries. For Egypt, he pointed out the Nefertiti bust exhibited in Berlin, the Rosetta stone presented by the British Museum, as well as the Denderah zodiac owned by the Louvre. Taken together, these claims form an introduction to the evolution of international archaeological cooperation: they point to the increased calls of ownership by those countries where 'French archaeology abroad' was historically conducted.

In France, as in other European countries, the nineteenth century saw the formation and the institutionalization of archaeology as a scientific discipline. Institutions were created to support archaeological developments at home, but also – perhaps particularly – in Mediterranean countries where rivalries occurred between several European nation-states. Since the beginnings, both in the mother country and in foreign territories, this emerging archaeology had to deal with a complicated relationship between science and politics. As stated by Díaz-Andreu (2007), the archaeological discourse in the nineteenth century was built by and for the nation (although Díaz-Andreu does not deny the personal aspirations and 'passions', she argues that these occurred at the service of the nation). In the context of war and growing nationalism, motivations for establishing foreign schools went clearly beyond the realm of 'pure' scientific requirements. While the value of these schools for the recognition and the long-time achievements of archaeology is evident, it is also undeniable that they were implicated in the competition between nation-states. For example, in the programmes and aims of the *École Française d'Athènes* (EFA) between 1870 and 1950,[1] we can identify a direct consequence of the 1870 Franco-Prussian war. The defeat against Germany was a shock for French intelligentsia, and the resulting need to consolidate scientific research became a national concern, with direct implications for the development of the EFA. German archaeological science was not only active early in all the domains of the discipline (such as epigraphy, pottery studies and sculpture), but it could be regarded as a competitor for archaeological investigations in Greece. This led for instance to the creation of a German Institute in Athens in 1873 (see Schücker, this volume), the excavation of Olympia from 1875 onwards (see also Kotsakis and Theodoroudi, this volume), and the appearance of a German scientific journal dedicated to Greece in 1876. France had not only lost its archaeological monopoly – the EFA was no longer the only foreign establishment in Greece – but it was also challenged on a scientific level: in a sense, the war back at home had 'woken up' French archaeology abroad.

During the whole of the nineteenth century, the Ministry of Public Instruction (which was created in 1828, and later became the 'Ministry of National Education') was the main public actor for the conduct of French archaeology abroad. This happened through the creation of foreign archaeological schools (Braemer, this volume), through the supervision of large-scale scientific missions – with dedicated committees like the *Commission de l'Exploration Scientifique du Mexique* in 1862–1893 (Prevost Urkidi and Le Goff 2009) – but also through the supervision of individual scientific missions. Before the official creation of the *Service des missions* within the 'science and letters division', the Ministry of Public Instruction occasionally attributed grants to travellers. The ministry considered these as 'enhancements and support towards scholars and lettered men'. This new institution was created in 1842 to encourage and finance all travels aimed at physical and geographical research as well as linguistic or historical studies and, in general, at all sciences that could interest civilization. This date of 1842 signifies the reinforced implication of the ministry for those field researchers who had the will to collect scientific data *in situ*, be it in unexplored countries or in libraries and archival repositories. The success of those missions gave rise to the creation some

---

1   See the website of the École Française d'Athènes, 'Histoire de l'École 1870–1950'. Retrieved 20 July 2011 from http://www.efa.gr/Ecole/Histoire/acc_ecole_hist.htm.

thirty years later (1874) of a more controlled, permanent *Commission des Missions*. Scientific scholars from different specialities – archaeology among them – gathered in this commission to evaluate the applications, and to advise the minister on the best projects in terms of their scientific quality. The destinations of these travels were sometimes linked to the colonial expansion and to political and commercial interests (Lévin, this volume), but this is not a systematic rule.

Both the *Service des Missions* and the *Commission des Missions* were incorporated in 1935 into the *Caisse des Recherches Scientifiques*, which four years later became the *Centre National de la Recherche Scientifique* (CNRS). A substantial part of the scientific missions undertaken during the nineteenth and early twentieth century by scholars sponsored by the Ministry of Public Instruction has been recently studied by Le Goff and Coutsinas (2007) in the framework of the European research network AREA (ARchives of European Archaeology) (Schnapp *et al.* 2007). Years are still needed to investigate and classify all those archaeological missions, but some areas have already been covered and inventories of those archives can be found on the website[2] of the French National Archives; specifically on Greece, Asia Minor and the Near East (Coutsinas and Le Goff 2009a, 2009b), which seem to constitute the main archaeological destinations for French scholars. Sub-Saharan Africa has been published too (Lévin and Le Goff 2009; see also Lévin, this volume) to try to understand the rather more limited and late French interest for African archaeology (see Lévin and Schlanger 2009).

These state archives paint a picture of the various historical contexts and positions taken at the highest level of the state regarding the development and institutionalization of French archaeology around the world. Indeed, beyond its support to individual missions, the Ministry of Public Instruction has also been involved during the nineteenth century with the creation of four permanent archaeological institutions: the *École Française d'Athènes* (EFA), the *École Française de Rome* (EFR), the *Institut Français d'Archéologie Orientale* in Cairo (IFAO, for an inventory of its archives see Sbeih and Le Goff 2009) and the *École Française d'Extrême Orient* (EFEO) in Phnom-Penh, Hanoï and other locations. Together with the *Casa Velázquez* created in Madrid in 1928, these schools are still active today under the supervision of the Ministry of Public Instruction/National Education. Several other schools and research institutes were created at the end of the nineteenth century or in the course of the twentieth century, but they have been placed under the supervision of the Ministry of Foreign Affairs (as will be seen in the third part of this paper; see also Braemer, this volume).

The already mentioned *École Française d'Athènes* (EFA) was created thanks to "two revolutions, one political, the other literary; the Greek revolution and the romantic revolution", as put by one of its directors, Théophile Homolle (1848–1925). Indeed, France had actively participated in the advent of the Greek state, during and following its independence wars, between 1821 and 1830. First of the foreign archaeological schools established in Athens (and first of the French schools abroad), and in competition with other European powers (especially with

---

2   See http://www.archivesnationales.culture.gouv.fr/arn/.

Germany as we have seen before), the EFA is still a high level research institution for Greek archaeology. From 1989 onwards, the EFA has increased its support for operations outside Greece, such as in Albania.

Conceived first as a 'Roman' division of the French School of Athens (in 1873), then as a full-time school of archaeology (in 1874), the French School of Rome was established in 1875. It occupies the *Palazzo Farnese*, shared ever since with the French embassy in Italy. As a central place for French research in Italy and the central Mediterranean Sea in the fields of history, archaeology and the social sciences, the EFR nowadays mainly works in partnerships with French and Italian scholars, but it also has cooperation projects in the Maghreb, in countries along the Adriatic Sea (Albania, Croatia, Serbia and Slovenia) and in countries of the European Union. Apart from broadening its scope geographically, the EFR also broadened its scope scientifically, by advancing multidisciplinary projects and by focusing on new archaeological periods of interest.

The position of French scholarship in Egyptology and in Egypt is ancient. It was upon Bonaparte's expedition and the discovery of the Rosetta Stone that Champollion deciphered the hieroglyphs in 1822. Another Frenchman, the curator Auguste Mariette (1821–1881), created the Egyptian Antiquities Service, which was directed by a succession of French scholars until the Egyptian Revolution of 1952. In December 1880, a decree inspired by Gaston Maspero (1846–1916) and signed by the minister of Public Instruction Jules Ferry (1832–1893), created a permanent mission in Cairo. It was institutionalized as the *Institut français d'Archéologie Orientale* (IfAO) in 1898, attesting to its prerogatives beyond Egypt. Nowadays, the relations with the Egyptian Antiquities Service are of a different nature (Andreu-Lanoë 2011). In addition to issues such as research, heritage management and publications, also questions of looting and restitution have arisen, as we have seen in the introduction.

The *École Française d'Extrême-Orient* (EFEO), the French School of Asian Studies, was created in Paris in 1900, and situated at several locations in what was then French Indochina (1887–1954), on the joint initiative of the Oriental Studies section of the *Académie des Inscriptions et Belles-Lettres* and the colonial government. The former envisaged scholars working on sites in Asia – along the pattern already established in Athens, Rome, and Cairo – whereas the latter wanted to establish an institution that would be responsible for the inventory and preservation of the cultural heritage of Indochina. After 1945 a new period began for the EFEO. Despite the Indochina war (1946–1954), and thanks to a real desire for scholarly cooperation with the newly independent states in the area, its members continued their work in continental south-east Asia. This work entailed ethnology, Buddhist studies, linguistics and literature, but above all archaeology. This also gave rise to reconstruction projects at monumental sites such as Angkor Wat, mainly using the newly developed reconstruction method of *anastylosis*. In 1957, the French School was obliged to leave its offices in Hanoi, and finally, in 1975, also those in Phnom Penh. But after a troubled period, its geographic and scientific coverage has been extended again. Together with the Asian network for French archaeology abroad, the EFEO now has many offices again: in Kuala Lumpur, Hong Kong, Taipei, Tokyo, Seoul, and, from the late 1990s onwards, also in Beijing, Bangkok and Yangon.

In summary, this century saw the institutionalization and worldwide coverage of French archaeology, either through individual missions, or through the establishment of permanent schools – both with the support of the Ministry of Public Instruction. Archaeology in this period became a diplomatic tool, as for instance in its support for Greek independence. We also witnessed unilateral diplomatic efforts to assert the supremacy of French science, either in competition with other European powers (such as in Athens and Rome) or more hegemonic in countries like Egypt and Indochina. As to the latter countries, it is difficult to speak of scientific cooperation, as no local, equivalent scientific systems were developed or allowed to grow. Moreover, countries where France had played an important archaeological role in the past have since become independent, with increasing claims to the ownership and control of their own cultural and archaeological heritage.

Paving the way for today's global network

Since the end of World War II, the Ministry of Education is no longer the main ministry in charge of French archaeology abroad. French archaeology abroad has become a specific concern of the Ministry of Foreign Affairs. Emerging out of the *Ancien Régime*'s network of ambassadors and diplomats, the Ministry of Foreign Affairs is an ancient and long-lasting administration, but it is only since the second half of the twentieth century that it has turned to deal again with archaeology.

Since 1945, the CNRS has focused its research on 'metropolitan' archaeology at home, confiding the administrative responsibility of archaeology abroad to the Ministry of Foreign Affairs.[3] A dedicated 'Committee of excavations and archaeological missions' was established there in 1947: this institutional framework, still operating today, will be presented in more details below.

At present however, a new definition of what 'French archaeology abroad' entails seems to be in order. While the Mediterranean and Middle East still represent an important part of its geographical range, French researchers now have other destinations as well. French archaeology is practised literally everywhere, and not just in former colonies or francophone countries. With the support of the Ministry of Foreign Affairs' archaeological commission, five main geographical-cultural areas are covered: the Americas (mainly South and Central America), Europe-Maghreb, the Ancient East (including for example Iraq, Iran and Syria), Africa-Arabia (see Lévin, this volume) and Asia-Oceania.

In addition, 'archaeology' is no longer restricted to large-scale excavations revealing the monumental temples or 'lost' cities of ancient civilizations: archaeology, as we understand it now, is a multidisciplinary, scientific practice

---

3   After the creation of the CNRS in 1939, archaeology was split into two sections: the 'fifteenth section' for excavations on metropolitan territory and the 'sixteenth section' for excavations abroad.

within which various specialists – from the humanities and the natural sciences – co-operate for a better knowledge of past societies and environments, through the study of material remains. Just as the number of scientists participating in excavations has increased, in the field, in laboratories, in libraries or even archival repositories, so have archaeological operations as a whole broadened considerably beyond a strictly speaking 'French' origin or perspective. Moreover, international cooperation (first and foremost with the hosting country, but also with other scholars and institutions from different countries) has become increasingly frequent. As a consequence of growing globalization, of student exchanges, of professional mobility and of professional frameworks, as well as new outlooks and enhanced possibilities for funding archaeological projects through international cooperation, archaeology is increasingly becoming a genuinely trans-national scientific and cultural undertaking.

As the leading public research scientific institution in France, the CNRS nowadays has some 26,000 permanent employees and more than 1,200 laboratories or research units around the world. The main administrative units of French archaeology are referred to as Unité Mixte de Recherche (UMR). These 'mixed research units' bring together CNRS scholars and laboratories with one or several University(ies), with School(s) of Higher Education, with the Ministry of Foreign Affairs and occasionally with the Ministry of Culture (which is usually more involved with metropolitan archaeology). Nowadays, all these UMRs facilitate co-operative programmes with their international counterparts, even if the research units themselves are based in France. All in all, nearly forty UMRs have an archaeological activity abroad (see the list table annexed: Table 1).

Also National Museums conduct archaeological activities abroad. The *Musée du Louvre* develops scientific policies in its specialized departments (Egyptian antiquities, Eastern antiquities, Greek, Roman and Etruscan antiquities) and its curators are involved in research and field operations, most specifically in Egypt. Also undertaking archaeology abroad within UMRs are the *Museum National d'Histoire Naturelle (MNHN)*, with its prehistoric and Palaeolithic projects, and the *Musée National des Arts Asiatiques* (Musée Guimet) for Asian studies. But there are other long-term archaeological operations with ancient historical roots and legacies. One case in point is the *Délégation Archéologique Française en Afghanistan* (DAFA), which was created in 1922, closed in 1982, and reopened in 2002 with the support of the Afghan authorities, to undertake research, cooperation and training.[4]

In cooperation with the CNRS and the UMR units, the funding and supervising of archaeological excavations and surveys abroad is centralized by the '*Commission Consultative des Recherches Archéologiques à l'Étranger*' of the Ministry of Foreign Affairs. Drawing on scientific criteria with expert panels, and including other considerations, the commission contributes every year to the funding and supervision of some 160 missions undertaken by French institutions. In 2010 (Lévin, this volume), the commission developed new missions in Oman, Saudi

---

4   See the website of the Délégation Archéologique Française en Afghanistan, http://www.dafa.org.af.

Arabia, Laos, Guatemala, Peru, Romania, Croatia, Tunisia, Syria and Kurdistan. It also gave its agreement to the renewal of 150 missions, distributed in about sixty countries all over the world. The dedicated budget was, as in 2009, 2.8 m€, averaging € 17,500 per project.[5] Most of the operations selected for funding are conducted in collaboration with local teams and also integrate training and capacity-building programmes – more than one hundred local archaeologists have been trained in ten years, according to the commission. The Ministry of Foreign Affairs is also involved in global archaeological heritage management, as for example in Angkor Wat, a UNESCO World Heritage Site since 1992.

The Ministry of Foreign Affairs also supervises the network of 27 permanent French Research Institutes Abroad (*Instituts Français à l'Étranger*).[6] Spread over some 37 locations all over the world, these institutes specialize in social and human sciences.[7] Twelve of them have specific archaeological goals, and they are managed as UMIFRE units (*Unité Mixte des Instituts Français de Recherche à l'Étranger*).

Finally, it may be noted that the institutional division between the Ministry of Foreign Affairs and CNRS is to a large extent redundant – French institutes or archaeological projects abroad are almost never funded exclusively by one or the other. The same can be said in relation to universities, to the *Académie des Inscriptions et Belles-Lettres*, the French schools abroad or Inrap (see below). As a rule, permanent institutes or missions always try to combine and balance their budgets with these different sources. Thus, just as in France itself, UMR or UMIFRE units are under the double tutelage of the CNRS and the Ministry of Foreign Affairs. Traditionally, the CNRS guarantees the scientific programmes and standards, while the Ministry oversees relevant diplomatic issues. As suggested in the *Institut Français du Proche-Orient*'s report for 2008 and 2009,[8] the scientific objectives of the CNRS may well be congruent with the diplomatic aims of the Ministry of Foreign Affairs: this is the case with local partnerships, cultural cooperation, international influence and expertise, etc. International scientific collaboration as such is handled by CNRS researchers and local scientists in the field, whilst the Ministry of Foreign Affairs tries to ensure good interactions with the policies and actors of the hosting country (*e.g.* excavation licenses, heritage legislation and protection measures, the preservation of remains in local museums, etc.).

---

5   See the website of France Diplomatie, 'Archaeologie, Sciences Humaines et Sociales'. Retrieved 3 May 2012 from http://www.diplomatie.gouv.fr/fr/enjeux-internationaux/echanges-scientifiques-recherche/archeologie-sciences-humaines-et/.

6   See the website of *Instituts Français à l'Étranger,* http://www.ifre.fr/index.php/recherche/petite-histoire-des-ifre

7   More generally, 145 institutes and cultural centres supported by the Ministry of Foreign Affairs – of the same order as the British Council or the Goethe Institute centres – are established in 92 countries, in addition to 1075 *Alliances Françaises* (French language schools) in 134 countries. The whole network received € 138 million in 2006, and consists of 783 expats and international volunteers, plus 10,000 locally recruited staff.

8   The Institut français du Proche-Orient (IFPO) since 2003 results from the Institut français d'études arabes de Damas (IFEAD, created in 1922), the Institut français d'archéologie du Proche-Orient (IFAPO, 1946, Syria and Lebanon), and the Centre d'études et de recherches sur le Moyen-Orient contemporain (Cermoc, 1977, Lebanon and 1988, Jordan).

Policies for development

For countries where archaeology is a quite recent concern, development issues are increasingly taken into account. Indeed, for the French Ministry of Foreign Affairs 'archaeology is a source of pride and self-esteem, for both the states and the peoples concerned, and should thus be at the core of any sincere cooperation' (Saint-Geours 2004). Archaeology, an activity partially linked to colonization, is anchored today in modern relations between states. France increasingly advocates a holistic vision of international cooperation: scientific work, the necessary restitution of data, transfer of knowledge and know-how, all became gradually joined concerns in sustainable development. Such a view also incorporates environmental protection, preservation of sites in relation to mass tourism, economic development, and an appropriation by citizens to deal with their own heritage. Angkor Wat is perhaps the most symbolic, though particularly complicated, example of this approach. From 1991 onwards, all these issues arose here at the same time; most notably that of balancing site management at both local and Cambodian state levels, as well as at a global, universal level. The responsibility of cooperation is nowadays seen to include the training of students and professionals, the sharing of expertise, and local participation in the preparation of development plans and relevant legal frameworks. The consolidation of national archaeological services is clearly a major aim.

In this respect, the Ministry of Foreign Affairs has developed or encouraged three specific diplomatic paths that are concerned with cooperation and development issues, and which provide opportunities for funding and undertaking archaeological projects abroad. The first of these diplomatic paths is the *Service de Coopération et d'Action Culturelle* (SCAC, Cooperation and Cultural Action Service), which is an embassy-level service in charge of developing and implementing co-operative actions in the field of culture and development. As such, the SCAC has some means of cooperation (technical support, scholarships etc.) which can be dedicated to archaeological actions. Some recent SCAC actions include assistance in setting up a new visitor signalling system on the archaeological site of Apollonia (SCAC Tirana, Albania) or cooperation with the DAFA to set up an archaeological computer room at Kabul University (SCAC Kabul, Afghanistan). The SCAC is the interlocutor of funding bodies and works in close collaboration with the AFD, the *Agence Française pour le Développement*.[9]

The second diplomatic path is the Ministry *Fonds de Solidarité Prioritaires* (FSP, Priority Solidarity Funds): longer-term funding lines available for research, institutional and socio-cultural development in certain 'priority' countries. Some archaeological programmes have already benefited from these funds, particularly in sub-Saharan Africa (see Lévin, this volume) and the Far East. As indicated by a

---

9   As a bilateral development bank and the central operator of France's foreign aid policy, AFD's activities on five continents are aimed at reducing poverty and inequalities, financial sustainable economic growth and protecting 'Global Public Goods' of benefit to all humanity. AFD activities fall within the framework of the United Nations' Millennium Development Goals. See also the website of the Agence Française pour le Développement, http://www.afd.fr/jahia/Jahia/lang/en/home/GouvernanceAFD.

representative of the FSP during a colloquium on archaeology in West Africa and Maghreb (Bazzana and Bocoum 2004: 13).

> *"We think, indeed, that archaeological research, protection and the development of heritage are an integral part of development aid strategies; it is one of the specificities of the French conception of public aid to integrate this dimension into the strategies of cooperation which also concerns infrastructure, the construction of roads, highways, ports or hospitals. (…) International cooperation in archaeology will continue to remain, in the years to come, fundamental for the Ministry of Foreign Affairs."*

Thirdly, and also diplomatically related, is the *Institut de Recherche pour le Développement* (IRD). This scientific and technological public institution is placed under the double tutelage of the Ministry of Research and the Ministry of Cooperation, which was integrated within Foreign Affairs in 1999. For more than 60 years, the IRD has overseen research, valuation and training activities in Africa, in the Mediterranean Sea, in Latin America, in Asia and in overseas French contexts.

To complete this extensive picture of French archaeology abroad, it will be worth mentioning the recently created (2002) *Institut National de Recherches Archéologiques Préventives* (Inrap). This public service institution is in charge of preventive (rescue) archaeological operations ahead of development work in metropolitan France and its overseas territories. Since the creation of the institute, its missions have included the sharing of research skills and heritage management values, at both a national and international level. Besides facilitating the participation of its own experts and archaeologists in research projects abroad, Inrap has forged institutional links aiming at the exchange of expertise, training and policy development with a range of organizations, including the Institute of Archaeology at the Russian Academy of Science, the Max Planck Institute for Evolutionary Anthropology, the Israel Antiquities Authority, the APSARA authority in Angkor Wat, and the Albanian Agency for Archaeological Services. It has undertaken joint seminars with local partners and heritage managers in Moscow, Tirana, Aksum and Nouakchott (see Naffé, Lanfranchi and Schlanger 2008), and hosted a range of trainees on its excavations. One of Inrap overarching objectives has been to promote, at a more global level, the heritage protection measures enshrined in the European Malta Convention (1992).[10] In this context, it has a partnership agreement with the UNESCO World Heritage Centre, and it also actively participates in European-funded projects, such as the ACE project. Most Inrap operations abroad, in addition to their scientific aims, are geared towards development and cooperation issues. The recent Inrap publication 'Archéologie sans Frontières' (Schlanger 2011) illustrates some of these aims and achievements.

---

10 Http://conventions.coe.int/Treaty/en/Treaties/Html/143.htm.

Conclusions

The beginnings of French archaeology abroad consisted of a 'proto-archaeological' science. Characterized as the time of antiquarians, it generally lasted from the sixteenth to the eighteenth century, until Bonaparte's expedition to Egypt (1798–1801). During this period, archaeology was conducted, sporadically, through diplomatic operations or in contexts of conflict. As such, diplomacy and war served several individual scholars as their pretext to experiment and develop research on archaeological heritage. With the institutionalization of archaeology in the nineteenth century, on the contrary, French archaeology abroad became a fully-fledged diplomatic tool; with the implementation of state-funded archaeological schools in Mediterranean countries and with the implication of the Ministry of Foreign Affairs in the management of archaeology outside its national borders. Finally, from the second half of the twentieth century onward, the contemporary institutional and scientific framework of French archaeology was established, which increasingly focused on international collaboration.

Today, French archaeology is active at a global level – its emphasis increasingly placed at the diplomatic level, upon its funding and to an extent supervision by the Ministry of Foreign Affairs. This diplomatic emphasis concerns not only collaborations with countries having their own archaeological, scientific and cultural policies, but also with countries that still have to develop these policies. The challenge today for French archaeology abroad is thus to encourage and help formalize the integration of scientific research and understanding of the past with various development, economic and social frameworks – especially in the framework of preventive archaeology, which is becoming a worldwide necessity. As can be gathered from the above-mentioned diplomatic and scientific networks, the archaeological community, at least, feels very clearly the relationship between the practice of archaeology abroad and various development aid funding and policies. The challenge for the coming years will surely be to ensure that diplomacy, with its networks and funding, remains as much as possible at the service of archaeology, which itself, wherever practised, recovers and promotes its social values.

Acknowledgements

I wish to thank all my colleagues of the Archaeology in Contemporary Europe project for their contribution to the exploration of our archaeological practices abroad. In particular, I would like to thank Nathan Schlanger without whom the ACE-project would not have existed.

References

Andreu-Lanoë, G. 2011. 'Perspectives pour la Coopération Archéologique Franco-Égyptienne', in N. Schlanger (ed.), *Archéologie sans Frontières*. Archéopages hors série. Paris: Institut national de recherches archéologiques préventives, 107-109.

Bazzana, A. and H. Bocoum (eds). 2004. *Du Nord au Sud du Sahara, Cinquante Ans d'Archéologie Française en Afrique de l'Ouest et au Maghreb. Bilan et Perspectives*. Paris: Éditions Sépia.

Chevalier, N. 2002. *La Recherche Archéologique Française au Moyen-Orient 1842-1947*. Paris: Éditions Recherches sur les Civilisations.

Coutsinas, N. and A. Le Goff. 2009a. *Missions Scientifiques et Littéraires en Grèce et en Asie Mineure, Dossiers individuels (1846-1937)*. Retrieved 20 July 2011 from http://www.archivesnationales.culture.gouv.fr/chan/chan/fonds/edi/sm/F/F17Missionsgrece.pdf.

Coutsinas, N. and A. Le Goff 2009b. *Missions Archéologiques au Proche-Orient, Dossiers Individuels (1849-1938)*. Retrieved 20 July 2011 from http://www.archivesnationales.culture.gouv.fr/chan/chan/fonds/edi/sm/F/F17_Proche%20Orient_2933-3014_17265-17294.pdf.

Díaz-Andreu, M. 2007. *A World History of Nineteenth-Century Archaeology, Nationalism, Colonialism, and the Past*. Oxford: Oxford University Press.

Dondin-Payre, M. 2003. 'L'Archéologie en Algérie à Partir de 1830: une Politique Patrimoniale?', in P. Poirrier and L. Vadelorge (eds), *Pour une Histoire des Politiques du Patrimoine*. Paris: Comité d'Histoire du Ministère de la Culture, 145-170.

Fenet A., P.-S. Filliozat and E. Gran –Aymerich 2007. 'La Société Asiatique, une Société Savante au Coeur de l'Orientalisme Français', *Nouvelles de l'Archéologie* 110, 51-56.

Gran-Aymerich, E. 1998. *Naissance de l'Archéologie Moderne*, 1798-1945. Paris: CNRS.

Gran-Aymerich, E. 2000. 'Introduction', in P. Jacquet and P. Périchon (eds), *Aspects de l'Archéologie Française au XIXème Siècle, Actes du Colloque International tenu à La Diana à Montbrison les 14 et 15 Octobre 1995*. Recueil de Mémoires et Documents sur Le Forez 28. Montbrison: Société de La Diana, 7-17.

Kaeser M.-A., S. Lévin, S. Rieckhoff and N. Schlanger (eds). 2008. 'The Making of European Archaeology / Poczatki archeologii Europejskiej', in *Catalogue of the AREA Network Exhibition*. Bruxelles: Culture Lab.

Lamarque M., G. Piernas and F. Queyroux. 2007. 'L'Archéologie devant le Parlement des Savants. Les Archives de l'Institut de France Explorées par le Programme AREA', *Nouvelles de l'Archéologie* 110, 30-38.

Le Goff A. and N. Coutsinas. 2007. 'Les Dossiers Individuels de Mission Conservés aux Archives Nationales et leur Apport à l'Histoire de l'Archéologie. L'Exemple de la Fouille d'Aphrodisias en 1905', *Nouvelles de l'Archéologie* 110, 40-47.

Lévin, S. and A. Le Goff. 2009. *Missions Scientifiques et Littéraires dans l'Afrique Subsaharienne Dossiers Individuels (1828-1937)*. Retrieved 20 July 2011 from http://www.archivesnationales.culture.gouv.fr/chan/chan/fonds/edi/sm/F/F17Afrique.pdf

Lévin S. and N .Schlanger. 2009. 'Logiques Individuelles, Logiques d'État: Archéologie et Sciences Coloniales en Afrique Subsaharienne d'après les Archives du Ministère de l'Instruction Publique', *Nouvelles de l'Archéologie* 116, 41-44.

Naffé, B., R. Lanfranchi and N. Schlanger (eds). 2008. *L'Archéologie Préventive en Afrique, Enjeux et Perspectives, Actes du Colloque de Nouakchott 1er-3 Février 2007.* Saint-Maur-des Fossés: Editions Sépia.

Prevost Urkidi N. and A. Le Goff. 2009. *Commission de l'Exploration Scientifique du Mexique (1862-1893).* Retrieved 20 July 2011 from http://www.archivesnationales. culture.gouv.fr/chan/chan/fonds/edi/sm/F/F17%202909-2914.pdf.

Saint-Geours, Y. 2004. 'La Place de l'Archéologie dans la Politique de Coopération Scientifique et Culturelle du Ministère des Affaires Étrangères', in Ministère des Affaires Étrangères (ed.) and P. Mongne (dir.), *Archéologies, Vingt ans de Recherches Françaises dans le Monde.* Paris: Maisonneuve and Larose, Editions Recherche sur les Civilisations (ERC), Association pour la Diffusion de la Pensée Française (ADPF), 68-69.

Sbeih L. and A. Le Goff. 2009. *Institut Français d'Archéologie Orientale du Caire (1880-1946).* Retrieved 20 July 2011 from http://www.archivesnationales.culture.gouv.fr/chan/chan/fonds/edi/sm/F/F%2017_institut_du_Caire.pdf.

Schlanger, N. (ed.). 2011. *Archéologie sans Frontières.* Archéopages Hors Série. Paris: Institut national de recherches archéologiques préventives.

Schnapp, A. 1993. *La Conquête du Passé.* Paris: Éditions Carré (see English translation 1996, *The Discovery of the Past.* London: British Museum Press).

Schnapp, A. 2004. 'La Naissance du Regard Archéologique: des Antiquaires aux Archéologues', in Ministère des Affaires Étrangères (ed.) and P. Mongne (dir.), *Archéologies, Vingt Ans de Recherches Françaises dans le Monde.* Paris: Maisonneuve and Larose, Editions Recherche sur les Civilisations (ERC), Association pour la Diffusion de la Pensée Française (ADPF), 12-20.

Schnapp, A., N. Schlanger, S. Lévin S. and N. Coye. (eds) 2007. *Archives de l'Archéologie Européenne (AREA). Pour une Histoire de l'Archéologie Française. Les Nouvelles de l'Archéologie* 110. Paris: Éditions de la Maison des Sciences de l'Homme, Éditions Errance.

1.3 BELGIAN ARCHAEOLOGISTS ABROAD: FROM ANTIQUARIANS TO INTERDISCIPLINARY RESEARCH

Gertjan Plets*, Ruth Plets** and Rica Annaert***

* Ghent University, Belgium

** School of Environmental Sciences,
University of Ulster, Northern Ireland

*** Flanders Heritage Agency, Belgium

Abstract

Belgian archaeological research abroad dates back to the late nineteenth century. However, until the 1930s, research projects outside Belgium were undertaken only very sporadically. This changed when the Royal Museums for Art and History (RMAH) started large excavation programmes in Syria and Egypt. The period after World War II witnessed a growth in investigations abroad largely due to the increasing research by universities.

Furthermore, Belgian research itself followed the global trend of increasing scientific interdisciplinary cooperation in archaeological research. At present, Belgian institutes also integrate the broader socio-cultural context of archaeological heritage research through an extensive collaboration with local stakeholders, which can assist in a number of areas such as the development of local educational programmes or sustainable heritage management practices.

Résumé

Archéologues Belges à l'Étranger : d'Antiquaires à une recherche Interdisciplinaire

Les premières recherches archéologiques belges à l'étranger datent de la fin du XI-Xème siècle. Pourtant, jusque dans les années 1930, des projets de recherches en dehors de la Belgique, étaient entrepris mais de façon sporadique. Ceci a changé lorsque le Musée Royal d'Art et d'Histoire (Royal Museum for Art and History, RMAH) a entamé de vastes programmes de fouilles en Syrie et en Égypte. La période qui a suivi la deuxième guerre mondiale a connu une croissance des recherches à l'étranger, principalement en raison d'une augmentation des recherches universitaires.

De plus, les recherches belges ont suivi la tendance mondiale d'une croissance de la coopération interdisciplinaire dans la recherche archéologique. Aujourd'hui, les instituts belges intègrent un contexte socio-culturel plus large dans leurs recherches archéologiques et historiques, par une collaboration intensive avec des parties prenantes au niveau local, ce qui peut aider dans différents domaines, comme le développement de programmes locaux d'enseignement ou d'une gestion durable du patrimoine culturel.

Extracto

Los Arqueólogos belgas en el Extranjero: de Anticuarios a Investigación Interdisciplinaria

La investigación arqueológica belga en el extranjero data de fines del siglo diecinueve. Sin embargo, hasta los años treinta del siglo pasado muy raramente se emprendían proyectos de investigación fuera de Bélgica. Esto cambió cuando El Museo Real de Arte e Historia (RMAH) emprendió amplios programas de excavaciones en Siria y Egipto. El periodo después de la Segunda Guerra Mundial muestra un crecimiento de investigaciones en el extranjero, predominantemente debido al aumento de las investigaciones en las universidades.

Por lo demás, las investigaciones belgas mismas han seguido la tendencia global de la creciente colaboración interdisciplinaria científica en la investigación arqueológica. Actualmente las instituciones belgas también integran el amplio marco socio-cultural de la investigación del patrimonio arqueológico a través de una colaboración extensiva con los interesados locales. Estos pueden asistir en cierto número de campos, como el desarrollo de programas educativos locales o de las prácticas sostenibles de la gestión del patrimonio.

ملخص

علماء الآثار البلجيكيين في الخارج: من الآثار إلى البحوث متعددة التخصصات

خيرتريان بليستس*، روت بليستس** وأوريكا آنارت ***

* جامعة غينت، بلجيكا

** مدرسة علوم البيئة، جامعة أولستركي، إيرلندا الشمالية

*** وكالة التراث الفلمنكية، بلجيكا

يعود تاريخ الأبحاث الأثرية البلجيكية في الخارج إلى أواخر القرن التاسع عشر. ومع ذلك، كانت مشاريع الأبحاث خارج بلجيكا، حتى ثلاثينيات القرن العشرين، تتم بشكل متقطع. وقد تغير ذلك عندما بدأ المتحف الملكي

القرتفلا تتدهش دقو .رصمو ايروس يف ةعساو قيبقنت جمارب خيراتلا نونفللاو نونفلا
ريبك دح ىلإ ،عجري ،يملعلا تاثعبلا يف اومن ةيناثلا ةيملاعلا برحلا دعب ام
.تاعماجلا يف ثاحبألا ةدايز ىلإ

يملاعلا هاجتالا ةعباتم و نحن ايكيجلب يف ثاحبألا بلب تهجتا دقف ،كلذ ىلع ةوالعو
موقت ،نآلاو .ةيرثألا ثاحبألا يف تاصصختلا ددعتم يملعلا نواعتلا ةدايزل
ثارتلا ثاحبأل ةعساو ألا يفاقثلا يعامتجالا قايسلا ديدج ةيكيجلبلا ةداعإ
نأ نكمي امم ،نييلحملا ةحلصملا باحصأ عم قطانملا نواعت لالخ نم ةيرثألا
تاسارمم ةيلحملا ةيميلعتلا جماربلا ريوطت لثم تالاجملا نم ددع يف يف دعاسي
.ثارتلل ةمادتسملا ةرادإلا

Keywords

Belgium, Belgian Archaeology, antiquarianism, interdisciplinary collaboration

Introduction

The history of domestic and foreign Belgian[1] archaeology is relatively unknown and has never been studied in a thorough and concise manner. Although some studies focus on the history of research for a certain archaeological period, topic, or region (*e.g.* Mekhitarian 1985; Maret 1990; De Mulder 2011), none provides a complete and integrated overview of the evolution of Belgian archaeology as a discipline. Such a study is imperative for Belgian archaeology but will not be a straightforward task, as it will involve a vast period of archival work to unravel the financial, cultural and academic trends underlying this evolution.

When focusing on the Belgian archaeological undertakings abroad, most information is scattered and only available through 'grey literature'. As such, this paper starts by providing an introductory insight into the history of archaeological research abroad and the different 'players' that participated in this research. Subsequently, it will explore the changing research mentality and agenda of projects based on some illustrative research initiatives, dealing for instance with the motives of research and the engagement with other stakeholders.

Because the term 'archaeological research' has a broad meaning, the definition of 'Belgian archaeological research abroad' in this paper will be limited to all archaeological activities that involve a direct contact with archaeological monuments and sites (*e.g.* excavation, survey, petrography, geo-archaeology and site management). Furthermore, research is considered to be 'Belgian' when a Belgian institution (*i.e.* a university, museum, private or governmental institution)

---

1   The kingdom of Belgium became independent after a revolt against the Netherlands in 1830. Since its existence, Belgium has undergone a series of culturally and economically driven governmental changes. The unitary Belgian state of 1830 has since evolved into a federal state with three regions (Flanders, Wallonia and Brussels) and three communities (Flemish, French and German), each with their own jurisdictions and governments. The communities govern matters such as language and culture (*i.e.* education, sports, media and welfare), while the regions have power over more territorial affairs (*e.g.* spatial planning).

has a significant role in the research. Research conducted by a Belgian citizen employed by or working for a non-Belgian institution is therefore not included.

The first Belgian 'archaeologists' were rich, highly educated people (such as doctors, noblemen, clergymen and teachers) acting out of personal interest, and their research had a limited academic or professional motive. The first real step towards the professionalization of archaeology was made in the late nineteenth century when archaeologist Baron A. de Loë was employed by the Royal Museum for Armour, Antiquities and Ethnology (RMAAE), the current Royal Museums for Art and History (RMAH). De Loë introduced new techniques to his research, which resulted in an increased attention for recording and a noticeable progress in research quality. In 1903 he also founded the National Service for Excavations, which was funded by the Belgian government (Cahen-Delhaye 1999: 106; De Mulder 2011: 56-57). After World War II the Government Service for Excavations, the successor of the National Service for Excavations, became integrated into the Royal Institute for Cultural Heritage (*Koninklijk Instituut voor het Kunstpatrimonium / Institut Royal du Patrimoine Artistique*, KIK/IRPA). From 1963 onwards, this service became an independent excavation service, and in 1989 this service split into a Flemish and Walloon excavation service.

From the beginning of the twentieth century, the attention for archaeology at the universities also evolved out of a growing interest in history, geology (*such as the excavation of the famous Neandertal caves of Wallonia*) and art history. It was not until after World War II that archaeology became taught as an independent discipline.

As for Flanders, all archaeological research takes place within a Malta-related context since 2005–2006. Archaeological contractors are nowadays the main executors of archaeological research; universities have become increasingly less active in the field (De Clercq *et al.* 2011) and recent reforms have steered those government agencies responsible for archaeology towards a policy-supporting role.

Actors involved in archaeology abroad

In Belgium, there has never been a central governmental organization in charge of the supervision, execution or funding of archaeological research abroad. In general, there are two main categories of actors involved in archaeological research abroad, which we will briefly discuss in this section. The first category consists of scientific organizations, such as universities, museums and scientific academies (also called schools) that undertake or support archaeological research abroad. The second category comprises agencies and foundations that subsidize this research.

Universities

There are five Flemish universities and three Walloon academies.[2] Three of the five Flemish universities and all three Walloon academies have an archaeology department and have been active abroad since the late 1940s.

The Catholic University of Leuven, founded in 1425, is the oldest Belgian university. Their first excavation abroad took place in the late 1940s in Alba Fucens, Italy (Mertens 1981), by F. De Visscher (professor and then head of the *Academia Belgica*). Subsequently, the university was involved in a long list of excavation programmes, mainly focusing on the Classical world and the Near East. In 1968 the university split up into a Flemish university based in Leuven (*Katholieke Universiteit Leuven*, KUL, and a Walloon university (*Université Catholique de Louvain*, UCL), which moved to a new campus in Louvain-La-Neuve.[3] After this separation, each university went its own way but remained specialized in the same archaeological research areas (see figure 1). Nowadays, the KUL is active in Egypt, Sudan, Syria, Greece and Turkey (Vermeersch 2002; Bretschneider and Van Lerberghe 2008; Waelkens 2009), and the UCL is active in Greece, Egypt and Italy (MacGillivray *et al.* 1984; Belova and Krol 2004; Cavalieri *et al.* 2007). The UCL also has a branch in Namur, as part of the *Académie Universitaire de Louvain*, which has been active in Ostia, Italy since 1992 (De Ruyt 1995).

Ghent University was founded in 1817. The first 'scientific' international archaeological project took place in 1951 in Fars, Iran, under the direction of L. Vanden Berghe (Overlaet 2007). Subsequently, there have been annual expeditions to Greece, Iraq, Turkey, Jordan, Spain and Iran.[4] At present, the university has major projects in Italy (Vermeulen 2009), Portugal (Taelman *et al.* 2008) and Siberia (Gheyle 2009).

The University of Liège (ULG - part of *Académie Universitaire Wallonie-Europe*), was established in 1817 and is one of the first Belgian universities that specialized in archaeology, owing its long archaeological tradition to the early Palaeolithic excavations in the caves of the Meuse basin. Nowadays, archaeologists at ULG are still primarily active in Belgium. During the last 25 years however, several important excavations of Palaeolithic sites have also been undertaken by ULG scholars in Iran, Turkey, Romania, Moldavia, Morocco, Lebanon, China, and Egypt (Otte, pers. comm.).[5]

---

2   Since the reforms of 2007, the Walloon universities have been grouped into three academies (Académies), as a consequence of the revised subsidy policy of the Walloon government. See also 'Programmes de recherches à l'étranger'. Retrieved 21 January 2010 from http://dev.ulb.ac.be/crea/ AccueilFrancais.php?page=Etranger.

3   For more information about the parting of the Catholic University of Leuven see Jonckheere and Todts (1979).

4   See 'Vakgroep Archeologie - Onderzoeksprojecten' on the website of the University of Ghent. Retrieved 21 December 2011 from http://www.archaeology.ugent.be/ onderzoeksprojecten.

5   See 'Fouilles' on the website of the University of Liège. Retrieved 19 December 2011 from http:// www2.ulg.ac.be/prehist/fouilles/fouilles.html.

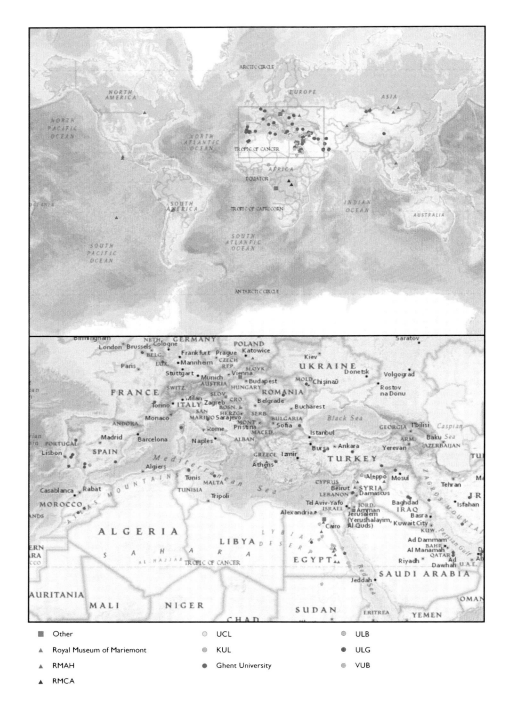

Figure 1. *Overview of the projects of the different Belgian institutions mentioned in this chapter, illustrating the focus on the Mediterranean and the Near East (Illustration: Flanders Heritage Agency).*

The Free University of Brussels was founded in 1834 and underwent the same reform as the University of Leuven. In 1969 the university split into the Walloon ULB (*Université Libre de Bruxelles* – part of *Académie Universitaire Wallonie-Bruxelles*) and the Flemish VUB (*Vrije Universiteit Brussel*).[6] Both universities have an archaeology department. Whilst the Walloon ULB has an extensive archaeology programme and has been very active abroad in the Classical world, the Near East, Africa and recently also in Latin-America (ULB 2010), the Flemish VUB archaeology department is considerably smaller with less research abroad. The foreign activities of the VUB are grouped in the Mediterranean Archaeological Research Institute (MARI), focusing in particular on the Bronze and Iron Age of Cyprus and the Near East.[7]

Museums

Five museums have a history of carrying out archaeological research abroad: the RMAH, KIK/IRPA, the Royal Museum of Mariemont, the Royal Museum for Central Africa and the Royal Belgian Institute of Natural Sciences. The archaeological research programmes of the Royal Museum of Mariemont, and KIK/IRPA and the Royal Belgian Institute of Natural Sciences are however small-scale (Van Loo and Bruwier 2010; Royal Belgian Institute of Natural Sciences, pers. comm.), and will not be discussed in this paper.

Out of all these museums, the Royal Museum for Art and History (RMAH) is the most actively engaged in archaeological projects abroad. It was founded in 1835 and, since 1905, has partaken in many projects in Egypt, Syria, Easter Island, Italy, Greece, Vietnam, Mexico, Russia, Jordan, Poland, Portugal, Mongolia, Ukraine, Uzbekistan, Bolivia and Peru (Koninklijke Musea voor Kunst en Geschiedenis 1991, 1992, 1993, 1999, 2000, 2001, 2004). An important aspect of the museum's policy is public outreach and as a consequence, many of the scientific publications are aimed at a wide audience.

The Museum of Belgian Congo[8] (MBC) was established following the Brussels International Exhibition of 1897 and was initially aimed at obtaining the Belgian people's support for King Leopold II's practices in his 'private' colony of the Congo Free State. Leopold II later turned over this personal property to Belgium, mainly due to international outrage over the brutality of his reign, and annexation by the government of Belgium was accomplished in 1908. After the independence of Congo, the MBC was redefined as the Royal Museum for Central Africa (RMCA), widening the geographic scope in which its activities were to take place. Through time, the archaeology department evolved into an important scientific entity within the museum, specifically dedicated to the prehistory of central Africa (Maret 1990:

---

6   See 'Historiek en basis filosofie' on the website of Vrije Universiteit Brussel. Retrieved 19 January 2010 from http://www.vub.ac.be/home/historiek.html.

7   See also the website of the Mediterranean Archaeological Research Institute (MARI) at http://www.vub.ac.be/mari/.

8   For further reading about the activities and current strategies of the RMCA, see Cornelissen, this volume.

134). It is presently still active in Africa (Cornelissen, this volume), with as its main scientific goal the reconstruction of Africa's Sub-Saharan history through the study of material culture and the environment.[9]

Belgian scientific schools abroad

In total there are three Belgian schools with an archaeology department abroad (see also Braemer, this volume): the *Academica Belgica in Rome*, the Belgian School at Athens and the Netherlands-Flemish Institute in Cairo. All have a supporting role for research that takes place in that specific country.

The *Academia Belgica* was inaugurated in 1939 in Rome. Since its existence it has supported Belgian historians, linguists, artists and archaeologists who study the Italian culture. It has been an important agent in supporting excavations in Italy in Castro, Alba Fucens, Artena and Herdonia (Academia Belgica 1989).

The Belgian School in Athens was founded by Belgian members of the French School at Athens in 1962. Its original aim was to supervise excavations in Greece that were conducted by Belgian universities. Currently, it supports research in Sissi, Ténos and Torikos.[10]

The Netherlands-Flemish Institute in Cairo (NVIC) is an academic centre which helps scholars and students from the supporting Dutch and Flemish research centres (museums and universities) with their activities in the field of Arabic and Islamic studies, Egyptology, archaeology and papyrology. Most recently, it has supported Belgian research in Egypt in Elkab, Qurta, El Hosh and Deir El-Basha.[11]

Funding institutions

The majority of the above mentioned scientific organizations have their own research budget, which is granted by the communities. However, this is often insufficient for the full scope of activities, and additional financial support is needed. There are many private and governmental institutions in Belgium which subsidise or support research and a full list is beyond the remit of this paper. However, the most important providers of additional funds are the Walloon and Flemish communities through the National Fund for Scientific Research (*Le Fonds National de la Recherche Scientifique*, FNRS or *Nationaal Fonds Wetenschappelijk Onderzoek*, N-FWO).

The FNRS/N-FWO was founded in 1928 after a speech by King Albert I in 1927 in which he pleaded for more attention to science and innovation.[12] Since its beginnings, the FNRS/N-FWO has had one main goal, which is to (financially) support and stimulate scientific research. Initially it was privately funded, but since 1948 the Belgian state has become the main investor. In 1992 the FNRS/N-FWO split into the Flemish FWO (*Fonds voor Wetenschappelijk Onderzoek Vlaanderen*)

---

9   See the website of the RMCA or *Koninklijk Museum voor Midden Afrika* in Tervuren at http://www. africamuseum.be/home.

10   See the website of the Belgian School at Athens at http://www.ebsa.info/.

11   See the website of the Netherlands-Flemish Institute in Cairo at http://www.institutes.leiden. edu/nvic/.

12   See also the website of the FWO, *Fonds Wetenschappelijk Onderzoek* at http://www.fwo.be/.

and the Walloon FRS (*Fonds de la Recherche Scientifique*) allowing each linguistic group to define its own science policy. Nowadays, the communities are the most important funders, but a small part is still funded by private investors.[13]

One of the first major projects funded by the FNRS/N-FWO was an archaeological excavation in 1930 in Apamea, Syria (Balty 1985: 217) and a scientific mission to Easter Island (Halleux and Xhayet 2007). To date, the FNRS/N-FWO has been the most important institution in subsidizing foreign research by Belgian universities and museums through funds for research projects.

Project proposals are nowadays evaluated on the following topics: collaboration between different research units, innovativeness of the project, innovativeness of the used methodology, international scientific level of the research unit and significance of the project (both on a national and international scale).[14] As for archaeology, both domestic and foreign projects get funding, however projects outside Belgium usually tend to get a more privileged review, due to the more international scope and scientific output (*i.e.* international publications).

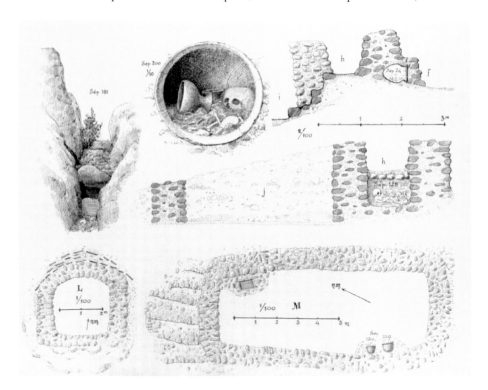

Figure 2. Drawings of some El Argar (third millenium BCE) funerary contexts, excavated by the brothers Siret in Spain. Given their background in geology, they paid considerable attention to accurate recording. (Illustration: Koninklijke Musea voor Kunst en Geschiedenis/ Musées Royaux d'Art et d'Histoire).

---

13   See http://www.fwo.be/.
14   See http://www.fwo.be/.

An overview of Belgian archaeology abroad

1830–1940: Towards the first major excavation projects

The first Belgian archaeological activity outside Belgium was undertaken by amateurs (such as clergymen, engineers and geologists) who excavated, registered and/or collected archaeological finds during their work or travels abroad (in for example Mexico, Congo and Spain). However, due to their limited training and the scarcity of sources they left behind, it is almost impossible to trace back the scope and agenda of these first archaeological undertakings. They varied from proper archaeological work with great attention for registration and context (see figure 2; Siret and Siret 1888) to undertakings solely focusing on the acquisition of finds.

In 1905, J. Capart (archaeologist and deputy conservator of the Egyptology department of the RMAH) was granted the concession to excavate a tomb in Sakkara, Egypt. The work by Capart can be regarded as the first professional excavation abroad. In subsequent years, this pioneer excavated several other sites in Egypt (Mekhitarian 1985: 225). A general interest in the classical world (figure 3), which was also in line with the personal interest of members of the Royal Family, can be distilled in the first major excavations funded by the FNRS/N-FWO. These missions were undertaken by the RMAH and included excavation programmes in Apamea, Syria (1930) (Balty 1985: 217) and Elkab, Egypt (1937) (Mekhitarian 1985: 225) – which are both still running until today. These first professional archaeological projects, orchestrated by the national museum, mainly focused on excavating archaeologically-rich contexts such as temples or graves, and on the acquisition of antiquities. Such an interest in prestigious art pieces is also illustrated by the expedition to Easter Island (figure 4) from 1934 to 1935. Funded by the FNRS/N-FWO, a Belgian team sailed to Easter Island to acquire a *moia* statue for display in the RMAH (Forment 1985). Sadly this statue was removed without real archaeological fieldwork, which is illustrative of the object-oriented archaeology of the time.[15]

Next to research in the classical world, the prehistoric archaeological work in the Congo continued. Although this research was mainly performed by Belgians who were not originally trained as archaeologists, the merit of the research projects by J. Collete, F. Cabu and M. Bequaert are widely acknowledged for specifying central Africa's place in prehistory (Maret 1990).

1945–1990: Universities digging abroad

In the late 1940s a group of Belgian archaeologists started excavations in Alba Fucens, Italy, under the direction of the Academia Belgica and the University of Leuven (Mertens 1981). Ghent University, on the other hand, began a survey and excavation programme in Fars, Iran, in 1951 (Vanden Berghe 1954). These universities, where archaeology was increasingly taught as an independent

---

15 See 'Het mysterie van POU'. Retrieved 15 December 2011 from www.fedramagazine. be/UserFiles/Pdf/pdf165_nl.pdf.

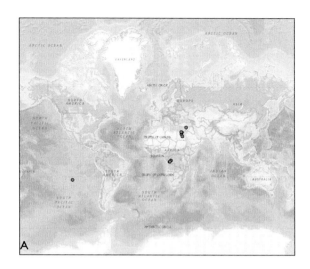

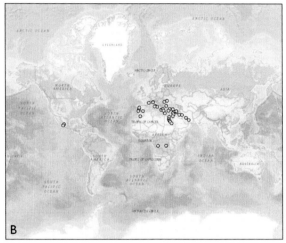

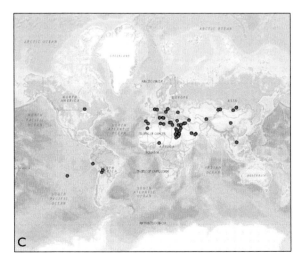

*Figure 3. Distribution of research
activities across different periods.
A: 1830-1940; B: 1945-1990; C.
1990-2009 (Illustrations: Flanders
Heritage Agency).*

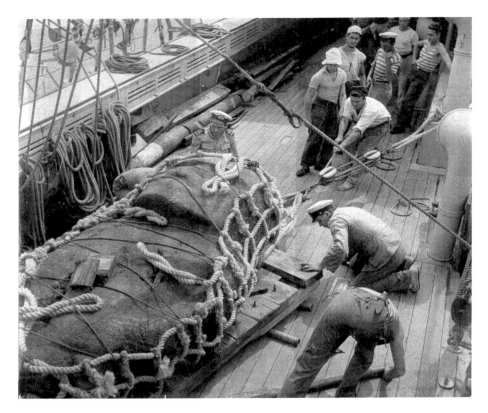

Figure 4. An Easter Island statue is loaded on board the Mercator. (Photo: Nederlands Fotomuseum).

discipline, were new actors who increasingly started up excavation projects which resulted in a growing number of research projects abroad and a changing research attitude. In addition, the major projects of the RMAH were restarted after World War II, and investigations in Congo continued (Maret 1990).

Since the 1950s, the more prominent role of universities in the undertaking of research abroad led to a growing multi-disciplinary approach,[16] clearly breaking with the antiquarian tradition. Excavation programmes such as at Alba Fucens in Italy (Mertens 1981), Apamea in Syria (Balty 1985: 222), Pessinus in Turkey (Pessinus Excavations Project 2008), and Elkab in Egypt (Limme 1985) became for example characterized by an increasing integration of biologists, topographers, geographers and geologists into archaeological research.

16 Multi-disciplinary research involves different academic disciplines that relate to a shared goal, but with multiple disciplinary objectives. Participants exchange knowledge, but they do not aim to cross subject boundaries in order to create new integrative knowledge and theory (Tress, Tress and Fry 2004: 488).

This growing multi-disciplinary aspect subsequently evolved into inter-disciplinary research[17] in the 1980s. A prime example of this is the archaeometry research by the universities of Ghent and Leuven. This project was one of the earliest that determined the provenance of classical marble from the Mediterranean based on an intense collaborative study between archaeologists, chemists and geologists (Moens, De Paepe and Waelkens 1992).

The research programmes during this period were often subject to international tension caused by changing post-war political relationships. The independence of Congo in 1960 was a particularly important event which meant that archaeological research in the region was hampered by political instability. Other international conflicts affecting research by Belgians included the Yom Kippur War between Israel and Egypt (1973) which turned the area around El Kab into a militarized zone, which meant that RMAH archaeologists started to excavate elsewhere in Egypt (Limme 1985); the Iranian Revolution of 1979 made it impossible for Ghent University archaeologists to continue their research in Luristan, West-Iran; and the first Gulf War in 1990 halted research led by L. Demeyer (Ghent University) in Iraq.

1990–Present: Community archaeology and the post-Soviet era – two new worlds for Belgian archaeology

For both new and existing research programmes, the main scope was still the Classical world. But the political developments in the Soviet Union opened up a new world for some Belgian institutes, and the number of Belgian activities in Russia and other former Soviet areas saw a remarkable increase (Koninklijke Musea voor Kunst en Geschiedenis 1991, 1992, 1993, 1999, 2000, 2001, 2004; Gheyle 2009; Otte, pers. comm.).[18]

It is interesting to note that the excavation or survey programmes during this period, both in and outside Europe, have mainly been research-led projects and less frequently related to rescue and preventive work. Moreover, a significant rise in non-invasive surveys and prospective work is noticeable during this period, which can be attributed to the growing field of landscape-archaeology and new techniques like geophysics and Geographical Information Systems.

Another interesting development is the ever intensifying cross-cultural cooperation between Belgian institutions, local archaeological institutes and local stakeholders.[19] Such collaborations increasingly transcend the purely functional (for example the use of infrastructure and facilities for fieldwork) and academic (such as joint research and publishing with host institutes); nowadays, research collaborations abroad increasingly take on board the educational opportunities of

---

17 Interdisciplinary involves several unrelated academic disciplines in a way that forces them to cross subject boundaries. The concerned disciplines integrate disciplinary knowledge in order to create new knowledge and theory and achieve a common research goal (Tress, Tress and Fry 2004: 488).

18 See also 'Fouilles' on the website of the University of Liège. Retrieved 19 December 2011 from http://www2.ulg.ac.be/prehist/fouilles/fouilles.html.

19 See Cornelissen, this volume, about collaborative projects in Congo.

heritage sites, community archaeology, the development of a local framework for heritage tourism, capacity building at governmental and university levels, as well as the intangible values of archaeology. Examples of such collaborative, indigenous and community projects are commonly found in non-Western contexts and vary from collaborations where a local museum is constructed,[20] to projects where local children of Easter Island are taught the history of their island (Vlaams Instituut voor het Onroerend Erfgoed 2009) and to initiatives where local communities are assisted with the development of a framework for sustainable heritage tourism (Sagalassos 2011).[21]

The results of excavations or surveys can also be implemented into local heritage management structures. This is one of the objectives of the Altai project (in Siberia) by Ghent University. Specifically, the aim of the research is to develop and maintain sustainable heritage management solutions for some of the ethno-natural parks in the Altai Mountains. Such heritage management approaches are community-based, starting from a careful assessment of the perception of cultural heritage by local indigenous populations. The Altaians for example perceive the numerous burials sites as spiritual charged places; disrespect for these monuments is not tolerated which has already led to culturally charged disputes with archaeologists. This means that an integration of socio-cultural and economic needs of the indigenous population within archaeological conduct is imperative. In addition, the possibilities and restrictions of sustainable heritage tourism are implemented into the management plan, which again are mainly based on indigenous values and the vulnerability of the archaeological heritage (Plets *et al.* 2011).

Conclusion

In this brief history of Belgian archaeological research abroad, several types of players have been distilled that are active abroad, and each has had its own influence on the 'way' in which archaeology was performed. The museums, which initiated the professionalization of archaeology in Belgium, were also the first Belgian non-amateurs that started up professional excavation projects abroad, which had much to do with prestige and the acquisition of antiquities. The universities subsequently moved the more object-oriented approach towards a more multi-disciplinary and eventually inter-disciplinary archaeology, with still a focus on the classical world. This traditional scope of Belgian archaeology abroad was however remarkably widened with the disappearance of the Iron Curtain. A final, less-pronounced trend is the recent attention to and active involvement of the indigenous population.

As mentioned in the introduction, Belgian archaeology – both outside and inside Belgium – lacks a thorough reflection of its own history. This paper should as such be considered as a starting point for future research on Belgian archaeology

---

20   See also the 2005 speech in English in the section on the Pessinus Excavations Project on the website of *Universiteit Gent* at http://www.archaeology.ugent.be/pessinus/ 2005speechenglish.

21   See also 'Planning for Sustainable Tourism in Sagalassos and Ağlasun' on the website of the Sagalassos Archaeological Research Project. Retrieved 16 December 2011 from http://www.sagalassos. be/en/community_archaeology/sustainable_tourism.

abroad. As a small country with a limited budget for scientific research, comparison with its neighbouring countries is thereby imperative.

Acknowledgements

The authors would like to acknowledge the *agentschap Onroerend Erfgoed* (OE),[22] Ghent University, the Royal Museum for Central Africa and the Royal Museum for Art and History. Special thanks go to Jean Bourgeois (Ghent University), Dirk Huyge (RMAH) and Marc De Bie (Free University of Brussels and OE) for their assistance.

References

Academia Belgica 1989. *Le Cinquantenaire de l'Academia Belgica 1939-1989*. Rome: Academia Belgica.

Balty, J. 1985. 'Les Fouilles d'Apamée de Syrie Du Premier Comité des Fouilles au Centre Belge de Recherches Archéologiques à Apamée de Syrie, in H. De Meulenaere, J.C. Dalty, G. Delmarcel and G. Derveaux (eds), *Liber Memorialis 1935-1985*, Brussels: Koninklijke Musea voor Kunst en Geschiedenis/Musées Royaux d'Art et d'Histoire, 217-224.

Belova, G. and A. Krol. 2004. *Preliminary Report on the Third Season of Archaeological and Geophysical Survey at Kom Tuman, Tell Aziziya and Kom Dafbab*. Retrieved 27 January 2010 from http://www.cesras.ru/eng/arch/memph/r_2004.htm.

Bretschneider J. and K. van Lerberghe (eds). 2008. *In Search of Gibala, An archaeological and historical study based on eight seasons of excavations at Tell Tweini (Syria) in the A and C fields (1999-2007)*. Aula Orientalis-Supplementa 24. Sabadell, Barcelona: Editorial AUSA.

Cavalieri, M., M. Bottacchi, F. Mantovani and G. Ricciardi. 2007. 'Misure di Resistivit à Mediante Finalizzate allo Studio del Sito di Torraccia di Chiusi', *Archeologia e Calcolatori* 18, 159-185.

Cahen-Delhaye, A. 1999. 'De Loë (Alfred), baron', in *Nouvellle Biographie Nationale* 5. Brussels: Académie Royale des Science, des Lettres et de Beaux-Arts de Belgique, 106-108.

De Clercq, W., M. Bats, J. Bourgeois, P. Crombé, G. De Mulder, J. De Reu, D. Herremans, P. Laloo, L. Lombaert, G. Plets, J. Sergant and B. Stichelbaut. 2011. 'Developer-led Archaeology in Flanders. An Overview of Practices and Results in the Period 1990-2010', in R. Bradley, C. Haselgrove, M. Vander Linden, and L. Webley (eds), *Development-led Archaeology in Northwest Europe*. Oxford: Oxbow Books.

De Mulder G. 2011. *Funeraire Rituelen in het Scheldebekken tijdens de Late Bronstijd en de Vroege IJzertijd. De Grafvelden in hun Maatschappelijke en Sociale Context*. Gent: Universiteit Gent, 27-47.

---

22 Up until January 2012 OE was known as the Vlaams Instituut voor het Onroerend Erfgoed (VIOE).

De Ruyt, C. 1995. 'Fouilles Récentes dans la Ville Romaine d'Ostie (Italie)', *Revue Belge d'Archéologie et d'Histoire de l'Art* 64, 166.

Forment, F. 1985. 'Enkele Resultaten van de Frans-Belgische Zending naar het Paaseiland (29 juli 1934 – 3 januari 1935) in een Nieuw Daglicht Geplaatst', in H. De Meulenaere, J.C. Dalty, G. Delmarcel and G. Derveaux (eds), *Liber Memorialis 1935-1985*. Brussels, Koninklijke Musea voor Kunst en Geschiedenis/Musées Royaux d'Art et d'Histoire, 257-262.

Gheyle, W. 2009. *Highlands and Steppes. An Analysis of the Changing Archaeological Landscape of the Altay Mountains From the Eneolithic to the Ethnographic Period*. Ghent: University Ghent, 380.

Halleux R. and G. Xhayet. 2007. *La Liberté de Chercher Histoire du Fonds National Belge De la Recherche Scientifique*. Liège: Editions de l'Université de Liège.

Jonckheere, W. and H. Todts. 1979. *Leuven Vlaams: Splitsingsgeschiedenis van de Katholieke Universiteit Leuven*. Leuven: Davidsfonds.

Koninklijke Musea voor Kunst en Geschiedenis. 1991. 'Jaarverslag KMKG - Rapport Annuel MRAH', unpublished report. Brussels: Koninklijke Musea voor Kunst en Geschiedenis/Musées Royaux d'Art et d'Histoire.

Koninklijke Musea voor Kunst en Geschiedenis. 1992. 'Jaarverslag KMKG - Rapport Annuel MRAH', unpublished report. Brussels: Koninklijke Musea voor Kunst en Geschiedenis/Musées Royaux d'Art et d'Histoire.

Koninklijke Musea voor Kunst en Geschiedenis. 1993. 'Jaarverslag KMKG - Rapport Annuel MRAH', unpublished report. Brussels: Koninklijke Musea voor Kunst en Geschiedenis/Musées Royaux d'Art et d'Histoire.

Koninklijke Musea voor Kunst en Geschiedenis. 1999. 'Jaarverslag KMKG - Rapport Annuel MRAH', unpublished report. Brussels: Koninklijke Musea voor Kunst en Geschiedenis/Musées Royaux d'Art et d'Histoire.

Koninklijke Musea voor Kunst en Geschiedenis. 2000. 'Jaarverslag KMKG - Rapport Annuel MRAH', unpublished report. Brussels: Koninklijke Musea voor Kunst en Geschiedenis/Musées Royaux d'Art et d'Histoire.

Koninklijke Musea voor Kunst en Geschiedenis. 2001. 'Jaarverslag KMKG - Rapport Annuel MRAH', unpublished report. Brussels: Koninklijke Musea voor Kunst en Geschiedenis/Musées Royaux d'Art et d'Histoire.

Koninklijke Musea voor Kunst en Geschiedenis. 2004. 'Jaarverslag KMKG - Rapport Annuel MRAH', unpublished report. Brussels: Koninklijke Musea voor Kunst en Geschiedenis/Musées Royaux d'Art et d'Histoire.

Limme, L. 1985. 'Het Comité voor Belgische Opgravingen in Egypte', in H. De Meulenaere, J.C. Dalty, G. Delmarcel and G. Derveaux (eds), *Liber Memorialis 1935-1985*. Brussels: Koninklijke Musea voor Kunst en Geschiedenis/Musées Royaux d'Art et d'Histoire, 231-237.

MacGillivray, J.A., L.H. Sackett, D. Smyth, J. Driessen, D.G. Lyness, B.A. Hobbs and A.D.D. Peatfield. 1984. 'An Archaeological Survey of the Roussolakkos Area at Palaikastro', *The Annual of the British School at Athens* 79, 129-159.

Maret, P. 1990. 'Phases and Facies in the Archaeology of Central Africa', in O. Robertshaw (ed.), *A History of African Archaeology*. London: James Currey, 109-134.

Mekhitarian, A. 1985. 'Les Fouilles Belges en Egypte de 1905 à 1955', in H. De Meulenaere, J.C. Dalty, G. Delmarcel and G. Derveaux (eds), *Liber Memorialis 1935-1985*. Brussels: Koninklijke Musea voor Kunst en Geschiedenis/Musées Royaux d'Art et d'Histoire, 225-229.

Mertens, J. 1981. *'Alba Fucens', Centre Belge de Recherches Archéologique en Italie Centrale et Méridionale*. Rome: Academia Belgica.

Moens, L., P. De Paepe and M. Waelkens. 1992. 'Multidisciplinary Research and Cooperation: Keys to a Succesful Provenance Determination of White Marble', in M. Waelkens, N. Herz and L. Moens (eds), *Ancient Stones: Quarrying, Trade and Provenance - Interdisciplinary Studies on Stones and Stone Technology in Europe and Near East from the Prehistoric to the Early Christian Period*. Leuven: Leuven University Press, 247-255.

Overlaet, B. 2007. 'Soundings at Tall-i Kamin (Kur River basin), Fars, Iran', *Iranica Antiqua* 42: 61-103.

Plets, G., W. Gheyle, R. Plets, E.P. Dvornikov and J. Bourgeois. 2011. 'A Line through the Sacred Lands of the Altai Mountains: Perspectives on the Altai Pipeline Project', *Mountain Research and Development* 31(4): 372-379.

Siret, H. and L. Siret. 1888. *Les Premiers Âges du Métal Dans le Sud-Est de l' Espagne*. Antwerp: Impremerie Polleums, Ceuterick et Lefébure.

Taelman, D., S. Deprez, F. Vermeulen and M. De Dapper. 2008. 'Lapicidinae Ammaiensis: een Geoarcheologische Case-Study voor de Civitas Ammaiensis (Noordelijke Alentejo, Portugal)', *Tijdschrift voor Mediterrane Archeologie*: 28-36.

Tress, G., B. Tress and G. Fry. 2004. 'Clarifying Integrative Research Concepts in Landscape Ecology', *Landscape Ecology* 30: 479-493.

Vanden Berghe, L. 1954. 'Archeologische Navorsingen in de Omstreken van Persepolis', *Jaarbericht Ex Oriente Lux* 13: 394-408.

Van Loo, A. and M.C. Bruwier (eds). 2010. *Héliopolis*. Bruxelles: Fonds Mercator.

Vermeersch, P. 2002. *Paleolithic Quarrying Sites in Upper and Middle Egypt*. Leuven: Leuven University Press, 365.

Vermeulen, F. 2009. 'Prospections Géo-Archéologique dans la Vallée de la Potenza (Les Marches, Italie): Évolution d'un Paysage Adriatique dans l'Antiquité', in F. Dumasy and F. Queyrel (eds), *Archéologie et Environnement dans la Méditerranée Antique*. Genève: Droz, 81-93.

Vlaams Instituut voor het Onroerend Erfgoed. 2009. 'European Archaeology Abroad', unpublished VIOE-report. Brussels: Vlaams Instituut voor het Onroerend Erfgoed.

Waelkens, M. 2009. *Sagalassos-Jaarboek 2008: Het Kristallen Jubileum van Twintig Jaar Opgravingen*. Academic Collection. Leuven: Peeters.

1.4 Spanish archaeology abroad

Xurxo Ayán Vila and Alfredo González-Ruibal

Institute of Heritage Sciences, National Research Council, Spain

Abstract

This article provides an assessment of the evolution of Spanish foreign archaeology from the period of formation of the Empire in the sixteenth century to the present. Within the European context, the Spanish case is anomalous because in the nineteenth century Spain became a 'colony of archaeology' for German and French archaeologists. In the twentieth century, the fascist regime of Francisco Franco (1939-1975) contributed to a rise of Spanish archaeology in Africa. The advent of democracy (1978) consolidated the undertaking of annual archaeological missions, mainly at sites of the 'great civilizations' (in the Maya, Inca and Aztec areas as well as in Italy, Greece and the Near East). The last decade has witnessed a diversification in the type of projects and destinations, as part of the development of the Spanish international cooperation policy, strongly supported by the last socialist government (2004-2011).

Résumé

L'Archéologie Espagnole à l'Étranger

Cet article présente l'évolution de l'archéologie espagnole à l'étranger, depuis la formation de l'empire au cours du XVIème siècle jusqu'à nos jours. Dans le contexte européen, le cas de l'Espagne est atypique étant donné que l'Espagne est devenue, au cours du XIXème siècle, une 'Colonie d'archéologie' pour des archéologues allemands et français. Pendant le XXème siècle, le régime fasciste de Francisco Franco (1939-1975) a contribué au développement de l'archéologie espagnole en Afrique. L'arrivée de la démocratie (1978) a conforté les missions archéologiques annuelles, qui étaient principalement effectuées sur des sites de 'grandes civilisations' (dans les régions des civilisations Maya, Inca et Aztèque, ainsi qu'en Italie, en Grèce et au Proche Orient). La dernière décennie a connu une diversification des types de projets et de destinations, ce qui résulte du développement, de la part de l'Espagne, d'une politique de coopération internationale, fortement soutenue notamment par le dernier gouvernement socialiste (2004-2011).

Extracto

La Arqueología Española en el Extranjero

Este artículo presenta una evaluación de la arqueología española desde el periodo de la fundación del imperio hasta la fecha. El caso español es divergente dentro del marco europeo porque en el siglo diecinueve España llegó a ser una 'colonia arqueológica' de arqueólogos alemanes y franceses. El régimen fascista de Francisco Franco (1939-1975) del siglo veinte contribuyó a una expansión de la arqueología española en África. La llegada de la democracia (1978) fortaleció el emprendimiento de misiones arqueológicas anuales, sobre todo a sitios de las 'grandes civilizaciones' (en las regiones de los maya, inca y azteca tanto como en Italia, Grecia y el Oriente Próximo). La última década ha mostrado una diversificación en el tipo de proyectos y destinos, siendo parte del desarrollo de la política española de colaboración internacional, que fue apoyada fuertemente por el último gobierno socialista (2004-2011).

ملخص

علم الآثار الإسباني في الخارج

خوروخ وآیان فيلا وأودیريفلا جونزاليس روبیال

معهد علوم التراث، المجلس القومي للبحث، إسبانيا

يقدم هذا المقال لتطور علم الآثار الإسباني الأجنبي منذ فترة تشكيل الإمبراطورية في السياق وحتى الوقت الحاضر. وفي الإمبراطورية الأوربي، وللمفارقة أصبحت إسبانيا في القرن التاسع عشر "للأثرين الألمان والفرنسيين. وفي القرن العشرين، ساهم النظام الفاشي بقيادة فرانكو (1939-1975) في صعود علم الآثار الإسباني في أفريقيا. وقد عزز مجيء الديمقراطية (1978) من إرسال البعثات الأثرية السنوية "إلى مواقع الحضارات العظيمة" (في منطقة المايا، والإنكا والأزتك، بالإضافة إلى إيطاليا واليونان والشرق الأدنى). وقد شهد العقد الأخير تنوعاً في أنواع المشروعات والأماكن المستهدفة، كجزء من تطور السياسة الإسباني في التعاون الدولي، بدعم من قوى من الحكومة الاشتراكية السابقة (2004-2011).

Keywords

Spanish Empire, colonial archaeology, francoist dictatorship, Spanish international cooperation

Introduction

Spain constitutes a significant example in the history of West-European archaeology. Indeed, it would be very hard to understand the very origins of the archaeological discipline without considering the historical circumstances in which the Spanish Empire reached its peak and began to decline. Whilst pioneering Spanish efforts were made between the sixteenth and eighteenth centuries to explore and study renowned sites of the great ancient civilizations of America and Classical Antiquity, both the Spanish Empire and its archaeology started to lose importance from 1812 onwards. The Peninsular War against Napoleon (known in Spain as the 'War of Independence') and Spain's ensuing loss of the American colonies marked a turning point towards a peripheral position within the European context. This happened at the same time as colonial capitalism was beginning to develop in the rest of Europe. From this moment on, Spain's role in European archaeology was to change drastically. Its new position became that of an area in which to conduct fieldwork, like in the countries of South America or the Middle East. Spanish archaeology also became absolutely dependent on foreign scientific paradigms, especially German cultural historicism (Díaz-Andreu and Mora 1995).

During the first third of the twentieth century, archaeology became institutionalized as an academic discipline at universities, under the inevitable influence of the Spanish Civil War (1936–1939). The triumph of fascism, with Francisco Franco's seizure of power and long dictatorship (1939–1975), was to foster a new, international Spanish archaeology focusing on minute North African colonies and Nasser's Egypt. The return of democracy in 1978 laid the foundations for international cooperation policies, consolidating the presence of Spanish archaeological teams in Central and South America as well as in Africa. On the other hand, the past would still weigh heavily on Spanish archaeology, in that classical archaeology continued to regard Italy, Greece, Egypt and the Middle East as the main destinations of its archaeological missions, to compete on a par with other European archaeologies. This is, in short, the history of Spanish archaeology abroad, which we shall now proceed to examine further in this article.

From the Renaissance to the Enlightenment

During the Late Middle Ages the Catalan-Aragonese Crown had expanded towards the west Mediterranean region. The resulting integration of southern Italy, Sicily, Sardinia and Corsica allowed the new political entity's rulers and intellectual elites to take part in the artistic and ideological renovation of the Renaissance period. At the same time, the unifying process begun by Queen Isabella I of Castile and Ferdinand of Aragon had laid the foundations for a Spanish Empire that was to develop under Emperor Charles I. The Italian territories were to play a major role in this geopolitical context into the eighteenth century (figure 1). Early modern Spanish viceroys of Italy and their patronage contributed to a growing interest in the antiquities found in central and southern Italy.

In the 1730s, the military engineer Roque Joaquín de Alcubierre began the first excavations of the city of Herculanus. In 1748 he rediscovered Pompeii and over the following three years he conducted archaeological works in Cumas, Sorrento, Mercato di Sabato, and Bosco de Tre Caste (Fernández Murga 1989). These pioneering attempts to develop a Spanish classical archaeology were enthusiastically supported by the King of the Two Sicilies, Charles de Bourbon (the future Charles III of Spain), who not only funded the excavations and sponsored the study and preservation of the materials, but also encouraged the publishing of several treaties

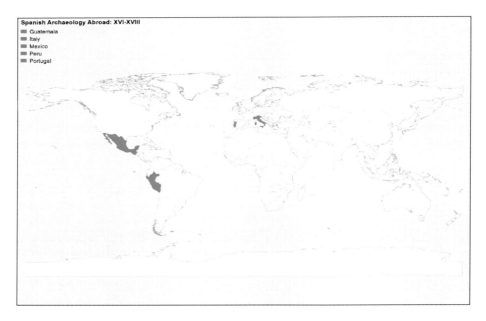

Figure 1. Spanish Archaeology Abroad: sixteenth to eighteenth century AD (Illustration: César Parcero).

and the opening of the museum *Museo Ercolanense de Portici* to house all the findings. In 1755 the Royal Herculanum Academy (*Regale Academia Ercolanense de Napoles*) was created. The impact of these works was such that scholars, intellectuals and travellers were drawn from all over Europe, including the art and history specialists Charles de Brosses, Walpole, Caylus and also Winckelmann, the father of Art History and a harsh critic of Alcubierre's use of tunnels for his excavations (Schnapp 1996: 242-245). Following Alcubierre's death in 1780, these works were continued by Francisco de la Vega, who was responsible for the first architectural consolidation of the ruins and for detailed recordings of the process of excavation. The sculptures discovered during the Crown-sponsored excavations in Italy, along with others purchased by antiquarians, were incorporated into the royal collection, and in the early nineteenth century were transferred to the Prado Museum in Madrid.

Charles III of Bourbon would become a great advocate of the Enlightenment ideas within the Spanish Empire and played a fundamental role in the development of an antiquarian archaeology stretching from Italy to the Spanish American territories. Curiosity for American artefacts and cultures in the sixteenth century focused on Maya, Aztec and Inca riches. Some examples of this interest are the chronicles of Fray Toribio de Benavente, Sahagún, Olmos Mendieta in Mexico, Landa in Yucatán and Cieza de León in Peru. At this time, however, the cultural legacy was not valued on artistic or scientific grounds, so pieces made of precious metals were often melted down and many monumental sites were re-used as construction materials (Alonso-Sagaseta de Ilúrdoz 2000: 15-18). In the eighteenth century, on the other hand, the Enlightenment was to bring about the first archaeological works in the New World, at the Mochica-Chimú city of Chan-Chan in Peru and the Maya city of Palenque (Chiapas), where architect Antonio Benasconi and colonel Antonio del Rio drew the first topographic map of the site and copies of bas-reliefs. Subsequently, the study of the site was commissioned to the French officer Guillaume Dupaix who published the results of his work in 1844. Such interest on the part of the Bourbon Monarchy served the dynasty's legitimizing political strategy to boost their prestige by collecting artistic riches and spoils of ancient civilizations in their dominions (Mora 1998).

For this same purpose they created the Cabinet of Antiquities of the Royal Academy of History (1738). In charge of collecting antiques or – to use the eighteenth century term – 'relics' (*antiguallas*), the institution gathered coins, epigraphs and other curious objects, mostly from Spain. Among them were findings as celebrated as the Corinthian Helmet from the Huelva estuary, the missorium of Theodosius I (a large silver platter with a representation of the emperor and his retinue), the veil of Hisham II and the Ivory Ark of Don Martín de Aragon. These collections grew quickly and were gathered in a Cabinet of Antiquities (*Gabinete de Antigüedades*) which, alongside its priceless collection of documents constitutes an invaluable tool in understanding both this institution and the history of Spanish archaeology (Almagro Gorbea 1999; Almagro Gorbea and Maier 2003). Housing documents collected during its more than 250-year-long history, the original aim of the Cabinet was to preserve artefacts from all over Spain and its colonies. Initially the responsibility of an academy secretary, the artefacts' importance and number grew to the point that a position of antiquarian was created to look after the growing collections and to inform about any issues connected to the antiquities. Since then, this position of antiquarian in the Spanish academic system has been held by some of the most prominent figures in Spanish archaeology and provides an essential key to understanding its developments.

The Cabinet's vigorous start during the Enlightenment was accompanied by the creation of an Antiquities Commission in 1792 which was to be abruptly interrupted by the French invasion of Spain in 1808. The Napoleonic invasion, which in the long run would bring about the emancipation of the Spanish American colonies, ironically contributed in Spain to the advancement of enlightened ideas in relation to protecting antiquities. The first legal norm for the protection of the looted archaeological site of the Roman city of Italica (Seville) was issued in 1810, when Napoleonic authorities decided to restore the old Roman name of Italica. They drew up financial plans for annual excavations which were in fact not realized until 1839–1840.

The installation of the liberal regime: the era of Queen Elisabeth II (1833–1868)

Through the complex and long-term dynamics of these developments, archaeological data had, by the 1830s, become part of an ideological discourse. The historiographical discourse which archaeology contributed to construct had become an instrument in the emergence of an intellectual elite. The sum of their individual studies had built a body of knowledge that was more curious than scientifically rigorous (Hernández Hernández and de Frutos González 1997: 141; see also below). The Enlightenment idea of 'historical knowledge' as an antiquarian's work of recapitulation, collection and erudite wisdom had gained prominence and within this framework archaeology was seen as an auxiliary tool of history, like numismatics and epigraphy. and not as a discipline in its own right. In the absence of a professional body of archaeologists, all archaeological works were carried out by antiquarians and amateur scholars. Their efforts were channelled and regulated by a centralized system which would in 1844 lead to the setting up of Provincial Commissions of Historical and Artistic Monuments (*Comisiones Provinciales de Monumentos Históricos y Artísticos*). These institutions' founding documents stated such aims as collecting archaeological objects with a view to creating antiquities museums, the protection of heritage, spreading regional culture and the excavation of archaeological sites (Adán Álvarez 1997: 259).

In order for these field activities to materialize, an authorization was required which was at first granted by the government and then by the Royal Academy of History (*Real Academia de la Historia*) (Hernández Hernández and de Frutos González 1997: 145). The process was characterized by a gradual transition from the practice of private collecting to more institutionalized forms, which also meant that scientifically-based approaches were eventually swept aside by the antiquarian approach. The institutionalizing process at this time ran parallel to cementing a Spanish national identity through the idea of 'national heritage'. The traces of that pre-conceived identity were sought in the monumental and documentary legacy from the past. In this light, archaeological remains and antiques acquired a new symbolic value as the building blocks of a national culture, which was allegedly common to all Spaniards and as the silent witnesses of the nation's glorious past. Archaeological data changed from objects of art to instruments of ideological transmission.

The shaping of the knowledge and power system underlying the nineteenth century Spanish state took place alongside the creation of state institutions to train professionals in the task of managing the state's cultural heritage (Mederos Martín 2010). In 1856 an official school, the *Escuela Superior de Diplomática* was set up in Madrid which offered training in a number of fields, from archaeology to numismatics to those wishing to become state librarians, antiquarians and registrars. In 1858 access to these very positions was regulated by the *Cuerpo Facultativo de Archiveros y Bibliotecarios del Estado*. A Royal decree did institute the National Archaeological Museum (*Museo Arqueológico Nacional*) on 12 March 1867. This institutional framework and the Royal Academy of History, which encouraged archaeological excavations and the search for antiquities, espoused an erudite and antiquarian method in which archaeological artefacts and sites were seen as sacrosanct documents of a glorious past. Celebrated sites such as Numancia (Jimeno Martínez and de la Torre Echavarri 2005), Sagunto, Tarraco, Merida and Emporion (Buscató and Pons 2001) were excavated.

Spanish historians at the time were far more interested in the adventures and heroic quests of Spanish sea explorers. Indigenous material culture from the Americas was literally shelved in antique cabinets, as were dissected animals and plants and the documents of scientific missions. Throughout the nineteenth century Spanish archaeologists showed no interest whatsoever in local Amerindian communities. Although the 1840s saw a new colonial phase develop with interest focusing on the North of Morocco and the Gulf of Guinea (Equatorial Guinea), and although Spanish domination would continue in the Philippines until the war with the USA in 1898, it is important to note that the Spanish situation in the European context during the nineteenth century was quite peculiar. While other nations were expanding their empires or creating new ones, Spanish imperial possessions were shrinking and by 1898 had virtually vanished. This explains in part that, whilst other European countries developed imperial archaeologies and global museums, Spain's efforts were invested in creating a national network of antiquarians and museums (Mederos Martín 2010). Furthermore, Spain became a colonized nation in archaeological terms, with German and French archaeologists excavating Spanish sites and enriching their museums with Spanish antiquities. In fact, this new imperialist phase coincided with the Romantic movement and with a growth in Orientalist interest stimulated by Washington Irving's *Tales of the Alhambra*. This nineteenth century cultural fashion would bring to Spain scholars and specialists like Edouard de Vemoil or Emil Hübner. Their interest in the country's cultural heritage in a sense made them the predecessors of French and German archaeologists and prehistory scholars visiting Spain in the late nineteenth and early twentieth century (Blech 2002). The only recorded case of a Spanish foreign archaeological mission during this phase is the one conducted by ambassador Eduard Toda i Güell, who published his findings in a collection entitled 'Egyptological Studies' (*Estudios Egiptológicos*).

The second wave of the institutionalization of archaeology. The Spanish restoration and the Second Republic (1874–1939)

From 1881 onwards, state control increased through a new reform of the Monuments Commissions (*Comisiones de Monumentos*). All their curation and excavation activities were placed under the supervision of the Central Academies of Fine Arts and History. A 'Higher Board of Excavations' (*Junta Superior de excavaciones*) was created in 1907, which set the guidelines for archaeological policies through published works which were then circulated to the Provincial Commissions. The foundations were laid for a complete professionalization of archaeology (Peiró Martín and Passamar Alzuria 1990). The discipline would be taught at universities and a set of laws were passed for the protection of heritage alongside institutions which contributed to the development of archaeology. These included the Centre for Historical Studies (1910) whose archaeology section was directed by Manuel Gómez Moreno and the Palaeontogical and Prehistoric Research Commission (1912–1939) under the Marquis of Cerralbo (Díaz-Andreu

1997: 403-405). The process culminated in the regulation of archaeological works with the Law of Archaeological Excavations and a Royal Decree which developed its contents (1912) (Adán Álvarez 1997: 261).

At the same time, the need for a modernization of Spanish science was addressed between 1907 and 1936 through the creation of a Board for the Continuation of Studies (*Junta para la ampliación de Estudios*). This institution's grants meant an opportunity for Spanish archaeologists to receive training in Europe (Sánchez Ron 1988). The intellectual influence of German universities in particular became so strong that cultural historicism was to become the prevailing paradigm in Spanish archaeology for decades. Such renowned figures as Adolph Schulten (1870–1960) and Hugo Obermaier conducted excavations at Tartessos and Numancia (1877–1947). Father Obermaier had studied under Cartailhac and the Abbé Breuil and, as professor of Primitive History at the Central University of Madrid (*Universidad central of Madrid*) he made a lasting impression on a generation of disciples who were to become prominent figures themselves after the war, such as Carlos Alonso del Real, Antonio Tovar, Julio Caro Baroja, Martín Almagro Basch and Martínez Santa-Olalla (Moure Romanillo 1996). This international phase in the history of Spanish archaeology also saw the foundation of the Spanish School *Escuela Española de Historia y Arqueología en Roma;* the first (and to date only) official Spanish foreign archaeological delegation, styled after German archeological institutes and British and French schools of archaeology (see Braemer, this volume).

Still largely an area for archaeological fieldwork for other European powers at this point, Spain was not in a position to develop an overseas colonial archaeology. But defeat in the Cuban war against the USA in 1898 and the loss of the last imperial possessions were triggering a nationalist movement of regeneration which aspired to resume nineteenth-century colonial endeavours in Africa (Fernández Martínez 1997). These ambitions are clear in the proceedings of the Third Congress of the Spanish *Africanista* Society held in Valencia in 1909 (Congreso Africanista 1909); voicing the interests of tycoons trying to open up new markets in the wake of the 1898 losses, the text reveals that the ambitions focused on the minute possessions left to Spain by the Berlin Conference in present-day Equatorial Guinea, as well as on the traditional Spanish interests in Morocco and Western Sahara. The concluding sections include the advice given to future patriot investors by the president of the Official Chamber of Agriculture (*Cámara Agrícola Oficial*) of Fernando Poo (present-day isle of Bioko) in a paragraph entitled 'The Colonisation of Fernando Poo' (López Canto 1909). An interesting ethnographic note states that "the natives of the territories of Muni, named after the nearby river is, as all Guineans, very similar to the *bubi*; that is, indolent but very warlike, his best friend being the shotgun, which he looks after dearly" (López Canto 1909, LIII). Violence and coercion as adequate means of colonization were typical of the *africanista* discourse which the book captures in another chapter eloquently entitled, in translation, 'Why a Spanish military intervention in Africa is necessary' (Maestre 1909). This point of view was quickly endorsed by *africanista* army officials engaged in the Moroccan wars (Gozalbes Cravioto 2008). It would also become commonplace in the propaganda of the philo-fascist dictatorship of Primo de Rivera (1923–1936) as a way of defending their technocratic renovation. The colonial and patriotic ideology of the Spanish Moroccan military reached its peak in the 1936 military coup and their victory under the leadership of the (also *africanista*) general Francisco Franco in the ensuing Civil War. The consequences of their victory last to this very day.

Unlike in other countries, the imperialist undertaking did not coincide with an imperial science (Fernández Martínez 2001). No institutions were created to study the colonies, nor was expert training given to the staff commissioned in Morocco or Guinea. Most colonial knowledge was obtained from neighbouring empires: sometimes it was literally copied. It was an old-fashioned empire of soldiers, priests and planters, rather than civil servants, traders and scientists. The lack of interest in acquiring knowledge is obvious in archaeology. In Equatorial Guinea, a colony officially acquired in 1778, there was not a single archaeological expedition until the 1940s.

Archaeology during the francoist dictatorship (1939–1975)

On 24 November 1939 a decree ordered the creation of the National Research Council (*Consejo Superior de Investigaciones Científicas*, CSIC), an autonomous body within the Spanish Ministry of Education. At the inauguration ceremony held on 30 October 1940, Ibáñez Martín clearly advocated the purpose of this new institution under the auspices of the new Francoist power, by stating that "we want a Catholic science" (Mora 2003: 96-99). Its centralized character meant the dismantling of all regional institutions and legislation bodies operating below the category of the state (Díaz-Andreu 1997: 548). This new institutional landscape mirrored Francoist repression of nationalist movements and its direct consequences included the disappearance of their cultural and scientific institutions (Gracia Alonso 2009; figure 2). A long silence awaited the *Seminario de Estudios Gallegos* in Galicia, the *Institut de Estudis Catalans* and the Catalan school of Archaeology created by Bosch Gimpera (in charge of the department of Justice of the Catalan government before the war) and the Society for Basque studies Eusko-Ikaskuntza in Euzkadi.

The centrepiece of the new post-war system was the General Commission of Archaeological Excavations (*Comisaría General de Excavaciones Arqueológicas)*, placed under a National Fine Arts Head Office (Díaz-Andreu and Ramírez Sánchez 2004). The new administrative structure's commissioners were responsible for any archaeological finding recorded in their province. A strong populist inclination can be seen in the fact that the system generally favoured individuals without any academic training in archaeology but who could match their knowledge of local antiquities with credentials in the political apparatus of *Falange*, the new single party (Díaz-Andreu 2003: 46). During the most philo-fascist period of the regime's life, researchers with close links to the party wielded considerable power which forced the discipline of archaeology into serving the regime's ends (Díaz-

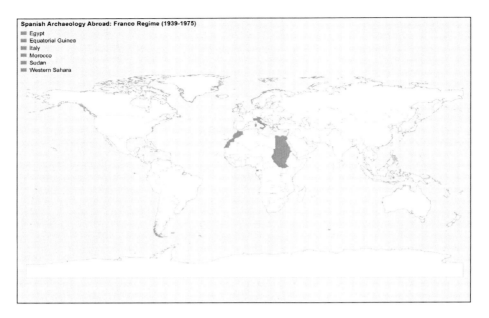

Figure 2. Spanish Archaeology Abroad: Franco Regime 1939–1975 (Illustration: César Parcero).

Andreu 1993; Cortadella 1997; Wulff Alonso and Álvarez Martí-Aguilar 2003; Gracia Alonso 2008).

Once the political system presented as Spain's 'catholic version of fascism' (*nacionalcatolicismo*) was installed in 1939, the *africanista* idea of empire and the aspirations for the fatherland which went with it were enshrined as the political project for the 1940s. In the early post-war years, fascist-styled archaeology proceeded to legitimize general Francos's aspirations. The new regime fostered a generation of Franco-supporting archaeologists like Alonso del Real, Almagro Basch, Tarradell, Pericot, García Bellido and Martínez Santa-Olalla, whose Palaeolithic and rock-art studies in Morocco or the Sahara (figure 3) proposed a very dubious cultural and historic unity over both sides of the Strait of Gibraltar. Their articles, headed by dedications to the *Caudillo* ('leader', or General Franco) as the 'friend of Africa' were published in the journal *Africa* (a successor to the *Journal of Colonial Troops* created in 1929) or in the Annals of the Institute of African Studies (1947–1966). The best example is perhaps provided by Martínez Santa-Olalla, prominent in the fascist knowledge-power system until the mid-1950s, who in 1943 wrote a truly surrealistic scientific article entitled 'Andalusians in Neolithic Morocco' (Martínez Santa-Olalla 1943). The sky was the limit for an archaeology which tried to legitimate the very same claims Franco had put forth to Hitler at their meeting in Hendaye to discuss Spanish participation in the Second World War. Although enthusiasm cooled off eventually, 1945 still saw archaeological research being conducted at the river Muni and Fernando Poo (Equatorial Guinea) to where regular fieldtrips were organized. Whip in hand and

Figure 3. Spanish archaeological expedition to Western Sahara (1943) (Photo: Museu d'Arqueologia de Catalunya, in Gracia Alonso 2009).

wearing a pith helmet, Martínez Santa-Olalla himself would conduct the works of the first archaeological expedition into territories where missionary expeditions had once been fashionable. The atmosphere is well captured by Martín Almagro Basch's 1946 book *Prehistory of North Africa and the Spanish Sahara* dedicated to the 'Spanish army of Africa, preserver of Spain's heroic, civilising and missionary spirit'.

The dictatorship's international recognition upon Spain's entering the UN in 1955 opened up new vistas for a regime whose foreign policy still made repeated references to Africa. Propaganda insisted on presenting Franco as a friend of the Arab world, especially after the independence of Morocco in 1956. It is important to bear in mind that Moroccan troops played an important role in Franco's army during the Civil War and there was always a paternalistic relationship between the Franco regime and the Maghreb nations. Excellent relations with Middle Eastern monarchies and authoritarian leaders like Nasser (as much as the need to project a positive international picture of the Dictatorship) explain the first archaeological foreign missions, naturally headed by the regime's favourite archaeologists (Almagro Basch 1968). The best example of this new context is provided by the Spanish salvage expedition to Nubia which, led by Martín Almagro Basch, was the first of a series of Spanish campaigns in Egypt and Sudan during the next decades. They were presented as yet another sign of the *Caudillo's* modernization of Spain, a country which could now boast an international archaeology to match the traditional European powers' campaigns with its own specialists on successful missions abroad. The Ptolemaic temple of Debod, donated by Nasser

Figure 4. Reconstruction of the Ptolemaic temple of Debod in Madrid (1968-1972). The entire building was donated to Spain by the Egyptian government when the Great Dam of Aswan was build, thanks to the excellent relationships between Nasser and Franco (Photo: Archive of TVE).

and re-erected in Madrid (figure 4) is the best metaphor of the late technocratic phase of the Francoist dictatorship. The context also laid the foundations for Spanish archaeology abroad in the upcoming democratic period with its interest in classical archaeology and interventions focusing mainly on monumental and emblematic complexes in highly symbolic areas like the Middle East, the 'cradle of civilization'.

From foreign archaeological missions abroad to international cooperation

Franco's death in 1975 coincided with the *Green March* which signalled the Moroccan occupation of Western Sahara, a traumatic end to an archaic colonial situation bringing tragic consequences to this day. Spanish archaeological research, still at its peak in the early 1970s, was brought to an abrupt end. The Spanish transition to democracy culminated in a Constitution being approved (1978) and a decentralized system of largely self-governing regions being established. Despite this truly federal structure, the Spanish central government retained its powers to make decisions concerning international relations. As a result, since 1985, the Department of Fine Arts and Cultural Property (*Dirección General de Bellas Artes y Bienes Culturales del Ministerio de Cultura*) has devised an annual

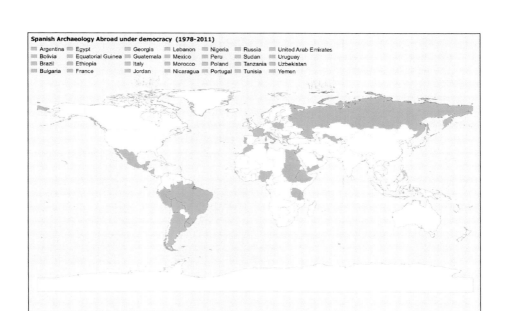

Figure 5. Spanish Archaeology Abroad under democracy 1978-2011 (Illustration: César Parcero).

financial programme for archaeological projects overseas.[1] Its beneficiaries are generally research groups continuing to work according to the same guidelines which were set up during the late Francoist phase. Disciples of the old masters continue to lead new archaeological missions to Egypt, Sudan, Syria or Morocco. Political context also plays a major part in the development of new projects (figure 5). Factors include bilateral agreements with certain governments and a renewed interest under Juan Carlos I in relations with Latin America (addressed by the 1992 celebrations of the Spanish 'discovery' of America); also important is Spain's mediating role in Central American civil conflicts or the privileged relations with Arab countries like Jordan or Morocco and the continuation of old colonial links as is the case with Equatorial Guinea.

A bird's eye view of projects approved in 1999 suggests four permanent trends over 20 years of democracy. The first trend consists of projects in the Middle East and Egypt; including excavations at Tell Halula, Tell Qara Quzaq and Tell Jamis (Syria), at Tiro-Albass (Lebanon), at the Omeya Palace of Amman and Jebel al-Mutawwaq (Jordan); as well as at Oxirrinco and Heraklepolis Magna and prospection works in Yemen. A second trend includes projects in Italy, such as at Pompeii, Plinius' villa in Perugia and Sardinia. The third trend covers projects in Latin America, such as pre-Columbian archaeological projects in Guatemala and projects focused at coastal settling in Nicaragua. The fourth and final trend consists

---

1   http://www.academia.edu/1156109/INFORMES_Y_TRABAJOS_N_5._EXCAVACIONES_ ARQUEOLOGICAS_EN_EL_EXTERIOR.

of projects in Africa, including excavations at Mogador and Lixus (Morocco) and surveys in the Blue Nile area (Sudan-Ethiopìa).

Nine years later, in 2008, these overseas archaeological interventions continued to be developed mainly by universities (especially in Madrid and Catalonia), by the National Research Council and the Spanish School of History and Archaeology in Rome (under CSIC). Of the 30 approved projects, ten were excavations at Roman sites in Italy, nine were excavations in the Maghreb and the Middle East, whilst four research projects were developed in South America (Argentina, Uruguay, Peru and Guatemala) and five in sub-Saharan Africa (Ethiopia and Tanzania) (figure 6). As such, the last decade saw an increase in the number of projects, financial support and geographic range, which is the result of resources being more easily available during a period of economic growth with a socialist government's backing since 2004. Although the archaeology of great civilizations continues to exert a clear influence, the scope of research has been broadened with extensive projects in prehistoric archaeology and ethnoarchaeology developed in the framework of new university agendas. We can also see that long-term projects, like those developed in Egypt, Jordan and Syria, continue to receive solid institutional back-up, irrespective of their scientific results, which are sometimes perceived as rather marginal (especially in Egypt and Jordan).

At the same time the past two decades have seen the emergence of private organizations and funds developing remarkable archaeological work in Egyptology (which is, meaningfully, the only area that has managed to attract private

Figure 6. Spanish archaeological excavation at Meroitic site of Amir Abdallah, Sudan, 1978-1980 (Photo: Víctor Fernández).

funding). The Barcelona-based Clos Foundation *(Fundaciò Arqueòlogica Clos,* 1993) has excavated and rehabilitated sites and monuments in Egypt, while the Institute of Ancient Egyptian Studies *(Instituto de Estudios del Antiguo Egipto,* 1997) has developed the Sen-en-Mut project, funded by Telefonica (Spain's main telecommunications company). In addition, the Caja Madrid Foundation has been financing the Djehuty tomb project, which has captured remarkable media attention since 2004.

Between 2004 and 2011, Spanish archaeology abroad developed into several new directions under policies implemented by Rodríguez Zapatero's socialist government, such as the ambition to create a network of archaeological research schools in the East Mediterranean and the Middle East, alongside the institutes at Cairo, Athens and Amman. The official aims behind this creation include supporting bilateral cooperations in the field of history and cultural heritage, promoting archaeological and historical research as well as the preservation, curation and support of heritage, providing Spanish researchers with the technical assistance and administration needed to carry out their work, and the publication of research. Unfortunately, the economic crisis and resulting budget cuts of 2010 and 2011 have prevented this initiative from materializing for the time being.

Another remarkable aspect was the increased support for Spanish international cooperation initiatives by the Spanish Agency for International Cooperation (since 1998), which presently consists of 44 technical cooperation offices (OTCs), fifteen cultural centres and six training centres which are spread around all participating countries and linked to the corresponding embassies. The guidelines in a general plan for Spanish internatioal cooperation between 2009–2012 included the idea of financing collaborative projects in the field of heritage management that incorporate the theoretical concepts of social and public archaeology such as to monitor archaeological teams in the Uruguayan lowlands, to conduct a training project for Ethiopian archaeologists, and to facilitate cultural resources management in Equatorial Guinea. This new agenda of Spanish inernational cooperation, which was more focused on providing assistance to the poorest countries and less on buttressing political strategies with traditional allies, is slowly influencing the purely scientific projects financed by the Ministry of Culture. In recent years, there has been a growing presence of Spanish archaeologists in countries such as Ethiopia, Tanzania and Ghana which are far from the traditional geostrategic sphere of influence by Spain. However, an orientalist trend, also existing in other countries such as France and the US, persists in manifold, often unconscious, ways. The cover of a recent publication by the Department of Fine Arts and Cultural Property (figure 7; Ministerio de Cultura 2011), which includes reports on archaeological projects abroad, for example displays a photograph that could have been taken in the nineteenth century: a group of Egyptians workers in turbans and jalabiyas dig up a monumental wall with the majestic Nile in the background. The image speaks volumes on what is still being conceived as 'archaeology abroad' by the general public, political institutions, and even by parts of academia.

Figure 7. Official collection of reports published by the Spanish Ministry of Culture. (Illustration: Instituto del Patrimonio Cultural de España).

Finally, an important challenge that faces current Spanish archaeology is its paradoxical lack of internationalization; Spanish archaeology outside Spain is still very much science abroad, not international science. As all Spanish cultural activities in foreign countries depend on support by the Ministry of Foreign Affairs, the emphasis has been mainly on political prestige (putting flags in the correct places), rather than academic excellence; with some important exceptions (most significantly palaeo-anthropological research), the publication record of Spanish archaeological teams abroad remains rather poor.

Conclusion

When placed within the context of international archaeology, Spain represents an interesting and exceptional case. Having built its empire prior to the development of archaeology as a scientific discipline, Spain had already lost nearly all of its territories by the time European archaeological science was first used in the interest of colonialism in Asia, Africa and Oceania. The way in which Spanish academic archaeology developed in the nineteenth century is another contributing factor to the idea of a 'failed' nation-state. While world powers established archaeological schools and institutes and carried out excavations in the four corners of the world, Spain became a probing area for a colonial archaeology which was mainly led by France, Germany, Great Britain and the USA. The richness of the Spanish archaeological heritage, the historical emergence of urban culture in the Iberian South and the Islamic past drew researchers to Spain as much as they continue to do so to this day. The anaemic state of nineteenth century Spanish science suffered from a remarkable dependence on foreign influence, the development of prehistoric archaeology in Spain being largely influenced by foreign researchers. The loss of Cuba, Puerto Rico and the Philippines in 1898 brought about an unprecedented identity crisis which exposed the need for a modernization of Spanish science. A process of institutionalization followed where grants provided by the Board for the Continuation of Studies (*Junta por la Ampliación de Estudios*, 1907) enabled young Spanish researchers to benefit from training in Western Europe. This process of institutionalization consolidated archaeology as a power-legitimizing knowledge, as would become very clear during the Francoist period.

Political circumstances have obviously played an important factor in driving Spanish archaeology beyond its national borders. Archaeology was once an instrument of fascist colonialism in the 1940s and 50s, then a means of polishing the dictatorship's international image in the 1960s and 1970s; today it is a tool for international cooperation with democratic governments.

Recent projects, like setting up a network of archaeological schools in the Mediterranean and the Middle East, clearly portray the peculiarity of Spanish geopolitics and the pre-eminence of a research tradition which espouses classical archaeology and intervention in monumental architecture as investments in symbolic and scientific capital in the international arena. It also constitutes a good example of the Spanish government's late emulation of archaeological policies traditionally implemented by European powers.

The long-term scope adopted in this article allows us to appreciate the change from a colonized and self-conscious archaeology to a discipline with an international position. The Spanish state continues to maximize the modernizing aspects of its image in attempts to make its name as a commercial brand by supporting successful national sports or world-famous archaeological projects in and outside Spain. Atapuerca, Nadal, Jorge Lorenzo, Barça and the national football team all play in the same league; a context involving memory, identity, prestige, geopolitics, diplomacy and, of course, power.

References

Adán Álvarez, G.E. 1997. 'La Comisión de Monumentos de Oviedo (1844-1978): Génesis y Desarrollo', in G. Mora and M. Díaz-Andreu (eds), *La Cristalización del Pasado: Génesis y Desarrollo del Marco Institucional de la Arqueología en España*. Málaga: Universidad de Málaga, 259-264.

Almagro Basch, M. 1946. *Prehistory of North Africa and the Spanish Sahara*. Barcelona: National Council for Scientific Research.

Almagro Basch, M. 1968. *El Estado Actual de la Investigación de la Prehistoria del Norte de África y del Sáhara*. Madrid: Instituto de Estudios Africanos.

Almagro Gorbea, M. 1999. 'Historiografía Sobre la Arqueología Española en la Real Academia de la Historia', in J. Blánquez Pérez and L. Roldán Gómez (eds), *La Cultura Ibérica a Través de la Fotografía de Principios de Siglo*. Madrid: Universidad Autónoma de Madrid, 179-198.

Almagro Gorbea, M. and J. Maier (eds). 2003. *250 Años de Arqueología y Patrimonio. Documentación Sobre Arqueología y Patrimonio Histórico de la Real Academia de la Historia. Estudio General*. Madrid: Real Academia de la Historia.

Alonso-Sagaseta de Ilúrdoz, A. 2000. *Colecciones de Arqueología y Etnología de América de la Universidad Complutense de Madrid*. Madrid: Consejo Social de la Universidad Complutense.

Blech, M. 2002. 'Las Aportaciones de los Arqueólogos Alemanas a la Arqueología Española', in S. Quero Castro and A. Pérez Navarro (eds), *Historiografía de la Arqueología Española: las Instituciones*. Madrid: Museo de San Isidro, 83-117.

Buscató, L. and L. Pons. 2001. 'La Real Academia de la Historia y los Yacimientos de Rhode y Emporion en el siglo XIX', *Boletín de la Real Academia de la Historia* 198(1): 155-174.

Congreso Africanista. 1909. *Tercer Congreso Africanista Celebrado en el Salón de Actos de la Exposición Regional de Valencia, en los Días 9, 10, 11, 13 y 15 de Diciembre de 1909, por Iniciativa de los Centros Comerciales Hispano-Marroquíes*. Barcelona: Imprenta de España en África.

Cortadella, J. 1997. 'El Professor Nino Lamboglia (1912-1977) y la Arqueología Clásica en España', in G. Mora and M. Díaz-Andreu (eds), *La Cristalización del Pasado: Génesis y Desarrollo del Marco Institucional de la Arqueología en España*. Madrid-Málaga: CSIC, 573-580.

Díaz-Andreu, M. 1993. 'Theory and Ideology in Archaeology: Spanish Archaeology under the Franco Régime', *Antiquity* 67: 74-82.

Díaz-Andreu, M. 1997. 'Nación e Internacionalización. La Arqueología en España en las Tres Primeras Décadas del Siglo XX', in G. Mora and M. Díaz-Andreu (eds), *La Cristalización del Pasado: Génesis y Desarrollo del Marco Institucional de la Arqueología en España*. Málaga: Universidad de Málaga, 403-416.

Díaz-Andreu, M. 2003. 'Arqueología y Dictaduras: Italia, Alemania y España', in F. Wulff Alonso and M. Álvarez Martí-Aguilar (eds), *Antigüedad y Franquismo (1936-1975)*. Málaga: Diputación Provincial de Málaga, 33-74.

Díaz-Andreu, M. and G. Mora. 1995. 'Arqueología y Política: el Desarrollo de la Arqueología Española en su Contexto Histórico', *Trabajos de Prehistoria* 52(1): 25-38.

Díaz-Andreu, M. and M. Ramírez Sánchez. 2004. 'Archaeological Resource Management under Francos's Spain: the Comisaría General de Excavaciones Arqueológicas', in M.L. Galaty and Ch. Watkinson (eds), *Archaeology Under Dictatorship*. Hingham: Kluver-Plenum, 109-130.

Fernández Martínez, V. 1997. 'La Arqueología Española en África', in G. Mora and M. Díaz-Andreu (eds), *La Cristalización del Pasado: Génesis y Desarrollo del Marco Institucional de la Arqueología en España*. Málaga: Universidad de Málaga, 705-720.

Fernández Martínez, V. 2001. 'La Idea de África en el Origen de la Prehistoria Española: una Perspectiva Postcolonial', *Complutum* 12: 167-184.

Fernández Murga, F. 1989. *Carlos III y el Descubrimiento de Herculano, Pompeya y Estabia*. Salamanca: Universidad de Salamanca.

Gozalbes Cravioto, E. 2008. 'La Arqueología Española en Marruecos (1921-1936): Memorias y Desmemorias', in G. Mora, C. Papí and M. Ayarzagüena (eds), *Documentos Inéditos para la Historia de la Arqueología*. Madrid: Sociedad Española de Historia de la Arqueología, 183-196.

Gracia Alonso, F. 2008. 'Relations between Spanish Archaeologists and Nazi Germany (1939-1945). A Preliminary Examination of the Influence of Das Ahnenerbe in Spain', *Bulletin of the History of Archaeology* 18(1): 4-27.

Gracia Alonso, F. 2009. *La Arqueología Durante el Primer Franquismo (1939-1956)*. Barcelona: Bellaterra.

Hernández Hernández, F. and E. de Frutos González. 1997. 'Arqueología y Museología: la Génesis de los Museos Arqueológicos', in G. Mora and M. Díaz-Andreu (eds), *La Cristalización del Pasado: Génesis y Desarrollo del Marco Institucional de la Arqueología en España*. Málaga: Universidad de Málaga Española de Historia de la Arqueología, 141-147.

Jimeno Martínez, A. and J.I. de la Torre Echavarri. 2005. *Numancia. Símbolo e Historia*. Madrid: Akal.

López Canto, F. 1909. 'La Colonización de Fernando Poo', in Congreso Africanista, *Tercer Congreso Africanista Celebrado en el Salón de Actos de la Exposición Regional de Valencia, en los Días 9, 10, 11, 13 y 15 de Diciembre de 1909, por Iniciativa de los Centros Comerciales Hispano-Marroquíes*. Barcelona: Imprenta de España en África.

Maestre, T. 1909. 'Por qué puede ir España a la acción militar en el Noroeste de África', in. Congreso Africanista, *Tercer Congreso Africanista Celebrado en el Salón de Actos de la Exposición Regional de Valencia, en los Días 9, 10, 11, 13 y 15 de Diciembre de 1909, por Iniciativa de los Centros Comerciales Hispano-Marroquíes*. Barcelona: Imprenta de España en África, 106-138.

Martínez Santa-Olalla, J. 1943. 'Los Andaluces en Marruecos durante el Neolítico. Las Primeras Pinturas Rupestres del Marruecos Español', *África* 18: 9-11.

Mederos Martín, A. 2010. 'Análisis de una Decadencia. La Arqueología Española del Siglo XIX. i. El Impulso Isabelino (1830-1867)', *Cuadernos de Prehistoria y Arqueología de la Universidad Autónoma de Madrid* 36: 159-216.

Ministerio de Cultura. 2011. *Informes y Trabajos 5. Excavaciones en el Exterior 2009*. Madrid: Ministerio de Cultura. Retrieved 19 November 2012 from http://www. academia.edu/1156109 /INFORMES_Y_TRABAJOS_N_5._EXCAVACIONES_ ARQUEOLOGICAS_EN_EL_EXTERIOR.

Mora, G. 1998. *Historias de Mármol. La Arqueología Clásica Española en el Siglo XVIII*. Málaga: Ediciones Polifemo.

Mora, G. 2003. 'El Consejo Superior de Investigaciones Científicas y la Antigüedad', in F. Wulff Alonso and M. Álvarez Martí-Aguilar (eds), *Antigüedad y Franquismo (1936-1975)*. Málaga: CEDMA, 95-109.

Moure Romanillo, A. 1996. 'Hugo Obermaier. La Institucionalización de las Investigaciones y la Integración de los Estudios de Prehistoria en la Universidad Española', in A. Moure Romanillo (ed.), *'El Hombre Fósil' 80 Años Después*. Santander: University of Cantabria, Marcelino Botín Foundantion, 17-50.

Peiró Martín, I. and G. Passamar Alzuria. 1990. 'El Nacimiento en España de la Arqueología y la Prehistoria (Academicismo y Profesionalización, 1856-1936)', *Kalathos* 9-10: 9-30.

Sánchez Ron, J.M. 1988. 'La Junta para la Ampliación de Estudios e Investigaciones Científicas Ochenta Años Después, 1907-1987', in *La Junta para la Ampliación de Estudios e Investigacioens Científicas Ochenta Años Después*. Madrid: CSIC, 1-61.

Schnapp, A. 1996. *The Discovery of the Past*, New York: Harry Abrams.

Wulff Alonso, F. and M. Álvarez Martí-Aguilar (eds). 2003. *Antigüedad y Franquismo (1936-1975)*. Málaga: Diputación Provincial de Málaga.

1.5 Polish archaeology in Egypt and Sudan: an historical overview

Patrycja Klimowicz and Arkadiusz Klimowicz

Institute of Prehistory, Adam Mickiewicz University, Poznań, Poland

Abstract

This paper analyses the phenomenon of Polish archaeological excavations in Egypt and Sudan within their changing socio-historical contexts. In particular, it will focus on the motives and objectives that lay behind the emergence of the Polish School of Mediterranean Archaeology as well as the complex circumstances accompanying its development.

The paper will illustrate both the relationships between successive stages of Polish archaeology abroad and the general context in which the scientific research was carried out. The confrontation of archaeological projects conducted out of Poland with the contemporaneous domestic and international situation will form a major topic of discussion. The last section of the paper will be devoted to changing patterns in relationships and cooperation between archaeologists and local communities, arguing that it constitutes a crucial element in Polish archaeological research in Egypt and Sudan.

Résumé

L'archéologie Polonaise en Égypte en au Soudan. Un Aperçu Historique

Cet article présente une analyse du phénomène de recherches archéologiques polonaises en Égypte et au Soudan, compte tenu de leurs contextes socio-historiques changeants. L'article porte en particulier sur les motivations et les objectifs qui sont à l'origine de la création de l'École Polonaise d'Archéologie Méditerranéenne, et sur les circonstances complexes de son évolution.

L'article vise à illustrer l'enchaînement des étapes successives du développement de l'archéologie polonaise à l'étranger, ainsi que le cadre général des ces recherches scientifiques. La confrontation entre des projets archéologiques réalisés à l'étranger et la situation nationale et internationale forment le thème de la discussion. La dernière partie de l'article se concentre sur l'évolution des relations et de la coopération entre les archéologues et les communautés locales, en affirmant que cela est un élément crucial pour la recherche archéologique polonaise en Egypte et au Soudan.

Extracto

La Arqueología polaca en Egipto y Sudan. Un resumen histórico.

Este informe analiza el fenómeno de las excavaciones polacas en Egipto y Sudan dentro de sus marcos socio-históricos variables. Se enfocan en particular los motivos y objetivos que se encuentran detrás del surgimiento de la Escuela Polaca de Arqueología Mediterránea tanto como las circunstancias que acompañan su desarrollo.

El artículo demostrará ambas relaciones entre las fases sucesivas de la arqueología polaca en el extranjero y el marco general en el que se realizó la investigación científica. La confrontación de proyectos que se realizan fuera de Polonia en la actual situación nacional e internacional será un tema esencial de debate. La última sección del artículo se dedicará a las estructuras variables en las relaciones y la colaboración entre arqueólogos y las comunidades locales, en que argumenta que constituye un elemento crucial en la investigación arqueológica polaca en Egipto y Sudan.

ملخص

علم الآثار البولندي في مصر والسودان: لمحة تاريخية

باتريشيا كليموويتش أو أركاديوش كليموويتش

معهد ما قبل التاريخ، جامعة آدم ميكيفيج، بوزنان، بولندا

تحلل هذه الورقة ظاهرة الحفريات الأثرية البولندية في مصر والسودان ضمن سياقاتها الاجتماعية والتاريخية المتغيرة. وسيتم التركيز، على وجه الخصوص، على الدوافع والأهداف والموضوعات التي تكمن وراء ظهور المدرسة البولندية لعلم آثار البحر المتوسط فضلا عن الظروف المعقدة التي طورها.

وتوضح هذه الورقة كلا من العلاقات بين المراحل المتعاقبة من علم الآثار البولندي في الخارج، والسياق العام الذي تم تنفيذ البحث العلمي فيه. وسوف تشكل مواجهة المشاريع الأثرية التي تجري خارج بولندا مع الوضع المعاصر، دوليا، موضوعا رئيسيا للمناقشة. وسوف يخصص القسم الأخير من هذه الورقة إلى أنماط التغيير في العلاقات والتعاون بين علماء الآثار والمجتمعات المحلية، بحجة أنها تمثل عنصرا حاسما في البحوث الأثرية البولندية في مصر والسودان.

Keywords

Polish School of Mediterranean Archaeology, Polish Centre of Mediterranean Archaeology, excavations in Egypt and Sudan

Introduction

Our aim in this paper is to presents a broad historical overview of the long-term activities of Polish archaeologists in the Middle East. This brief account will address some of the major aspects leading to the establishment of a Polish School of Mediterranean Archaeology (see discussions in English in Jakobielski and Karkowski 1992; Laskowska-Kusztal 2007). As part of our overview, we propose to regroup Polish archaeological activities in the Middle East into four successive stages. This will enable us to take into consideration the changing socio-political contexts and cooperation policies that have significantly influenced archaeological research over the last 100 years.

In doing so, however, we will not be able to discuss all areas or subjects. For instance, no mention will be made of the presence of Polish research in Egypt and Sudan prior to the twentieth century. Very few Polish individuals had actually participated in archaeological explorations in the Middle and the Near East during the nineteenth century (Tyszkiewicz 1994). Most of these were actually men of noble birth, with good social and financial positions, whose motivations were focused on increasing their private collections and galleries of ancient art. As such, their activities in the region cannot really represent reliable scientific research.

Polish archaeologists in scientific missions organized by the Partitioning Powers in the years 1907–1914

Polish archaeological research undertaken in Egypt and Sudan have had relatively fewer spectacular results than similar endeavours carried out by other European countries, such as France, Great Britain, Germany and the Netherlands. Already before official Polish missions in North Africa began in 1937 (see next section), several qualified archaeologists of Polish origin were carrying out research on the banks of the river Nile since the beginning of the twentieth century, at a time, it is worth recalling, when Poland did not exist on the map of Europe as a sovereign state.

These activities were however of a marginal character, with little impact on scientific research and public interest. As just noted, the territory of Poland was in those years still partitioned between Russia, Prussia and Austria. Being subordinated to the alien interests and economic systems of these three partitioning powers was not conducive to the development of any idea of archaeological excavations abroad. Only the residents of the region located in southern Poland (Galicia) had opportunities to conceive research concepts, in the more liberal context and autonomy achieved within the federation of the Austro-Hungarian Empire (Knopek 2005: 328). Most Polish researchers therefore concentrated around Galician universities (Cracow, Lvov) as well as the Cracov branch of the Polish Academy of Arts and Science. These institutions had only limited resources at their disposal, which made it impossible to organize their own research expeditions outside Europe. Moreover, only few archaeologists and historians of art were interested in this type of research, as most academics and intelligentsia believed that it was of utmost importance and priority to preserve the Polish national heritage and to

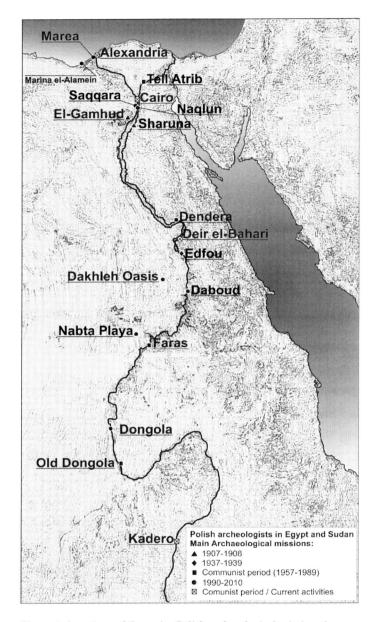

Figure 1. Locations of the major Polish archaeological missions in Egypt and Sudan taking into account their chronological division (Illustration: A. Klimowicz).

protect the historical monuments of the former Kingdom of Poland, instead of exploring the history of other countries.

In that difficult period, only a few Polish archaeologists participated in archaeological excavations along the banks of the Nile. The first was Tadeusz Smoleński (1984-1909), who arrived in Cairo on his doctor's recommendation due to a poor state of health. Once in Africa, he immediately took an interest in the culture of ancient Egypt and started his Egyptological studies. When in 1907 the Hungarian merchant Fülöp Back applied to the Egyptian Antiquities Service for financing excavation work, Smoleński was chosen to head the Austro-Hungarian research (Smoleński 1907; Pilecki 1969; Śliwa 2002, 2007, 2008; Vörös 2008: 20-29). As a result, two campaigns were carried out between 1907 and 1908, on the sites of Sharuna (Kom El-Ahmar Sawaris) and El-Gamhud (figure 1). However, Smoleński died soon after the completion of the project, at the age of twenty-five.

A few years later, an agreement was reached between the Cracov Branch of the Polish Academy of Arts and Science and the Academy of Sciences in Vienna: in return for subsidizing the Viennese expedition, researchers of Polish origin, such as Piotr Bieńkowski, Karol Hadaczek and Tadeusz Wałek-Czernecki, were allowed to participate in the work headed by Herman Junker (Śliwa 1998; Knopek 2005: 329-330). Nevertheless, the results of the research expedition were rather poor in terms of the quantity and scientific value of the uncovered monuments, and the project did not fulfil the organizers' expectations. Apart from the participation of several Polish representatives in archaeological missions, who were then able to collect some artefacts, study and exhibit them in Polish museums, these archaeological activities abroad did not generate much interest among the general public. However, the individuals and institutions who gained professional experience in this way could have formed a solid basis for the further development of Polish Egyptology. These developments were however hindered by the outbreak of the First World War and by subsequent changes in the international arena, which resulted in suspending Polish excavation activities on the Nile for almost a quarter of a century.

First Polish archaeological excavations in Egypt and the Nile in the Interwar Period (1937–1939)

While Poland regained its independence after the First World War, the situation remained very unstable and the country's borders were eventually defined only in 1922 (Dębicki 1962; Biskupski 2000). The difficult economic and social situation resulting from the unification of three different regions, previously ruled by the partitioning powers, had a huge influence on the situation of science in general (Jaczewski 1982; Nałęcz 1991). A lack of specialists posed major difficulties, and most archaeologists got their education in different districts of partitioned Poland as well as in other European countries already before the War. This notably had effects on the whole higher education system, which needed to be totally reorganized and modernized. Not surprisingly given these priorities, the first steps towards excavation work in North Africa were taken only as late as in the mid-1930s.

Archaeological excavations in that particular region were mainly conceived in the circle of classical archaeologists and following their interest in Greek and Roman culture, rather than an interest in Egyptology itself (Michałowski 1974a, 1983: 59). Moreover, the focus on Egypt resulted mostly from material considerations. Compared to other Mediterranean and Near Eastern states, Egypt had in place a relatively liberal law which allowed foreign archaeological missions to keep a part of their archaeological finds (Michałowski 1974b, 1986: 104). It must be recalled that researchers at that time were guided by such considerations, and that the possibility of expanding the limited collections of ancient artefacts then owned by Polish museums was a central motivation, as it was in other countries. Indeed, another important incentive was the possibility of participating in the ongoing international archaeological 'competition', so as to raise the profile of the Polish state. This conviction expressed the popular opinion of those days, whereby the level of culture in any country as well as its degree of civilization could be measured by the undertaking of its own excavations in Egypt (Michałowski 1974a: 8-11; Szafrański 2007a: 44).

Research in Egyptian archaeology was initiated at Józef Piłsudski University in Warsaw (Warsaw University): in accordance with the Ministry of Religious Denominations and Public Education, two of its professors were sent to Egypt in the mid-1930s. One was the originator of the idea, Kazimierz Michałowski (1901-1981) (figure 2), who represented classical archaeology, and the other was the ancient historian Tadeusz Wałek-Czernecki. During their stay in Egypt they began talks with the French Institute of Eastern Archaeology in Cairo (IFAO) in order to initiate cooperation (Michałowski 1990: 259). This partnership was necessary to ensure assistance and obtain permission to excavate in Egypt, given that there was no Polish institution in the region at that time.

Figure 2. Kazimierz Michałowski at the beginning of his career, in 1937 (Photo: the National Archive of Digital Sources; English version of the sentence quoted after Szafrański 2007).

Field prospections and in-depth research made it possible for the Polish-French team to localize a site in Upper Egypt called Edfu for their excavation (see figure 1). This site was chosen in view of the possibility of securing interesting archaeological finds as early as in the first season. The presence of some remains of an ancient agglomeration dating to the Ptolemaic period ensured spectacular results in a very short time. They proved to be of vast importance for strengthening the idea of research in the eyes of the public in Poland (Michałowski 1957: 193).

The organization of excavations at Edfu called for the support of several state institutions, as none of them was able to cover the expenses of such a mission on its own. The following institutions participated in funding the project, in accordance with their financial capacities: the Ministry of National Denominations and Education (responsible for education), the Ministry of Foreign Affairs, the Municipality of Warsaw and the Chancellor of Józef Piłsudski University (Michałowski 1986: 154). This question of financing excavations in Egypt soon became the subject of discussions by the press. In 1937 it was suggested that Poland could not afford these expensive archaeological missions in North Africa, and that the funds should have been used to subsidize local archaeological research, such as in the newly discovered well-preserved site of Biskupin in western Poland (Michałowski 1986: 154-155). These reactions in the press reflected the

Figure 3. Opening ceremony of the Ancient Art Gallery in the National Museum in Warsaw (September 1937). Present persons: Vice-Minister of the National Denominations and Education J. Błeszyński, President of Warsaw; S. Starzyński, Ambassador of France to Poland; Leon Noel, co-leader of the excavation at Edfu; K. Michałowski (Photo: the National Archive of Digital Sources).

involvement of local archaeologists in state propaganda, whose priority was to identify the ethnogenesis of the Slavs and to prove the Slavic origins of the territory of Poland since Late Bronze Age (Michałowski 1974a: 21).

The three years of cooperation at Edfu, between 1937 and 1939, proved however to be extremely fruitful. The uncovered monuments and artefacts, transported to Poland in over 90 boxes, became the basis of the Ancient Art Gallery opened, as early as in 1937, in the newly established National Museum in Warsaw (figure 3). The exhibition served as a reply to the alleged waste of public money. Its success strengthened the position of the mission at Edfu, gained public support and developed a general interest in the cultures of Ancient Egypt (Michałowski 1937, 1938, 1957, 1990: 642-643; Aksamit 2007: 31-40).

The Second World War interrupted this research, which had become the starting point for the development of the Polish School of Mediterranean Archaeology under the leadership of Warsaw University. At this point, the role of Professor Kazimierz Michałowski must be emphasized. Thanks to him, the small-scale mission at Edfu became not just a short episode in Polish science: on the contrary, the work in Upper Egypt formed the foundation of the development of Mediterranean archaeology, and brought substantial contribution to that science in post-war reality in Poland (Bernhard 1986a).

Polish excavations in Egypt and Sudan during communist times. The origins of the Polish School of Mediterranean Archaeology (1957-1989)

After the Second World War, Poland found itself under the influence of the Soviet Union (figure 4). The communist government and ruling party (the Polish United Workers' Party) commenced the reconstruction of the country destroyed by the war. All state structures were reorganized according to the Soviet model. This pertained also to academic institutions, which were to follow the principles of Marxism (Lech 1998: 57-95; Biskupski 2000; see also Klimowicz and Klimowicz, this volume).

These new conditions affected Polish Egyptology as well. Despite the enormous wartime destruction of Warsaw by the Germans, Poland's capital city remained the focal point of developments also in this branch of archaeology. In 1946 the National Museum in Warsaw became the centre where all ancient artefacts were gathered from all over the country. Three years later, the Ancient Art Gallery was reopened. It exhibited all the monuments from the Edfu mission which survived the war. While Michałowski continued to direct the Department of Mediterranean Archaeology, his efforts to take up research in Egypt remained fruitless, as Polish researchers were unable to carry out any work outside the Soviet-bloc countries (Michałowski 1964: 315-318; Lech 1998: 83-84; see also Klimowicz and Klimowicz, this volume). The years between 1949 and 1955 have been termed 'the Stalinist period', a time when it proved especially difficult to develop any field of science in the People's Republic of Poland. The Communist system applied strong pressure for the vulgar implementation of the Marxist doctrine in all aspects of life

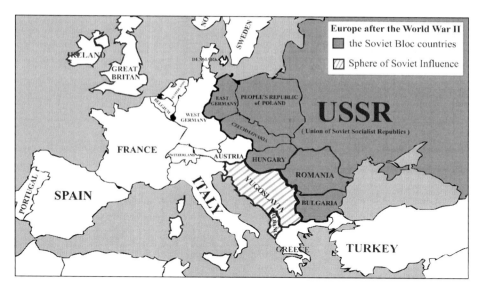

Figure 4. Europe's geopolitical situation in the second half of the twentieth century, highlighting 'the Eastern Bloc' countries and the Soviet sphere of influence within the Continent (ca. 1955–1989) (Illustration: A. Klimowicz).

(Lech 1998: 85), and the main task of the government at that time was to steer the country towards nationalization of the industry and the development of a centrally planned economic system.

This situation altered very slowly, beginning with the death of J.V. Stalin in 1953, and gradual transitions in the international arena, especially within 'the Eastern Bloc'. As a result, Polish archaeologists could by the mid-1950s increasingly enjoy contacts with the outside world. At the same time, Northeastern Africa also evidenced significant shifts, including the full independence gained by Egypt and Sudan, and their implementations of post-colonial diplomatic relations. In the second half of the 1950s, when 'the Cold War' was flourishing, the Egyptian policy led by G.A. Nasser launched closer economic, military and cultural cooperation with the Soviet Union and with the countries of 'the Warsaw Pact'.[1]

This changing orientation, away from the traditional colonial powers, created favourable conditions for Polish excavations to be renewed in the Nile Valley (Michałowski 1986: 218-228; Lech 1998: 83-84). In 1956, a new permit was obtained for carrying out research at Tell Atrib (figure 1). The excavations there were however delayed due to 'the Suez Crisis', so that the Polish expedition reached the ancient *Athribis* only as late as in February 1957. Along with a Dutch mission, it was the only group of foreign archaeologists allowed in Egypt at that time of political conflicts (Michałowski 1974a: 47-51; see also Van den Dries, Slappendel

---

1   The period between 1955 and 1973 is considered to be the peak of Soviet-Middle Eastern involvement. Alongside arms sales and an ever expanding external trade, this involvement is also manifest in the opportunity given to thousands of Arab exchange students to complete their cost-free university education in Eastern European countries (Beck 1963; Kreutz 1999).

and Van der Linde, this volume). Already in 1958, Michałowski undertook archaeological explorations in Nubia and subsequently in the Nile Delta: the report of that survey was presented to the Director of the Egyptian Antiquities Service as well as to the Egyptian Minister of Culture (Michałowski 1959, 1974a: 69; Szafrański 2007a). When, in 1960, the government of the United Arab Republic of Egypt began the construction of the Aswan High Dam, the Polish archaeological missions immediately joined the international cooperation efforts to save the ancient monuments of Nubia (both in Egypt and the Sudan) destined to be submerged by the rising waters of the Nile (Hassan 2007: 81).

These rapid developments in Polish research in Egypt and Sudan, especially the involvement of the International Nubian Programme carried out under the auspices of UNESCO, made it necessary to create a permanent archaeological base in Egypt. The Polish Centre for Mediterranean Archaeology of Warsaw University (PCMA) was created in Cairo in 1959, and rapidly became an essential anchor for Polish archaeological missions in the region (Michałowski 1974a; Daszewski 1986; Bernhard 1995). The Centre (figure 5) was responsible for the organization and implementation of all Polish archaeological expeditions in the Middle and Near East, including excavations and monuments restoration. Unlike most other Eastern European institutions of the type (*i.e.* Czechoslovakia, Hungary), PCMA as a unit of Warsaw University was in fact placed under the Ministry of Education, and did not report to the Ministry of Foreign Affairs (Jakobielski 2001).

Figure 5. Premises of the Polish Centre of Mediterranean Archaeology of Warsaw University in Cairo - abbreviated PCMA (Photo: M. Drzewiecki).

Kazimierz Michałowski became the first and enduring director of the Centre. His authoritative position was also manifested in him having responsibility for the three institutions concerned with excavation work in Egypt: Warsaw University (with its Cairo outpost), the National Museum in Warsaw, and The Department of Mediterranean Archaeology of the Polish Academy of Sciences (Bernhard 1986b: 17-23, 1995: 7-18). It should be emphasized that, as one of the most influential representatives of the scientific community in Poland, Michałowski had a key role in gaining funding from the state – the state providing then the only support for science and research in the absence of any private sector. The financial aspect of these Near Eastern activities was often raised by journalists, who wondered whether Poland could afford to conduct archaeological excavations abroad. Michałowski's firm reply was that "Poland cannot afford to be absent in this research!" (Jakobielski, pers. comm.).

This response emphasized the cultural significance of excavations abroad, and the opportunity they provided to introduce Polish achievements to the world arena. In this way Michałowski reconciled questions of costs, cultural objectives and symbolic influence. This firm position made it possible to secure funding for the three mentioned institutions and to undertake research abroad without serious economic difficulties. This created favourable circumstances for the development of the discipline, which had no parallel in the human sciences at that time. Moreover, the secured financial contributions were carefully divided in accordance with the activities undertaken: funds for Warsaw University were dedicated to cover the excavation costs, those for the National Museum provided the expeditions with equipment, and those for the Polish Academy of Science were used for producing reports and monographs, as well as for specialist analyses (Jakobielski, pers. comm.).

These activities were related to the aim of establishing scientific institutions which would be autonomous from political and ideological involvements (see also Klimowicz and Klimowicz, this volume). Michałowski's ostensibly neutral attitude implied that engaging in political matters might have a deleterious influence on the discipline. In his opinion, benefit from direct financial assistance from the Ministry of Education could reduce to a minimum the relations with the Communist government itself. As a consequence, the activities of Polish archaeologists abroad have been considered to be "non-aligned" (Szafrański 2007a: 55-56).

The Polish archaeological mission in Nubia specifically addressed the needs of the Sudanese government, and it was as such that excavations at Faras began in February 1961 (see also Klimowicz and Klimowicz, this volume). The sensational discovery of well-preserved mural paintings in the ruins of the Coptic cathedral was a great scientific and cultural success of the Polish team (Emery 1965: 98; Burstein 2008: 56-57). Faras has become the most famous site explored by Polish researchers, but it is worth recalling that at the beginning of the 1960s they carried out numerous other projects, such as in Aleksandria, Deir-el-Bahari or Old Dongola (see figure 1). The number of archaeological expeditions grew systematically, and with them greater independence for Professor Michałowski's students. Most research in Egypt and Sudan at that time was carried out under the auspices of the PCMA of Warsaw University, the only exception being the joint American-Polish-Egyptian Combined Prehistoric Expedition headed by Fred Wendorf and Romuald Schild (Wendorf, Said and Schild 1970; Schild and Wendorf 1980, 2002; Wendorf and Schild 1998).

The research work in Egypt and Sudan became very popular in Poland and it was constantly presented by the media. Michałowski was frequently interviewed by the press, radio and television, as were later his assistants. Consequently, the achievements of Polish archaeology were acclaimed and recognized by the general public at home (Lech 1998: 84-85; see also Klimowicz and Klimowicz, this volume). This period of enormous interest in excavations abroad coincided with a period of prosperity in Poland. The 1970s saw economic reforms and industrial modernization, which also resulted in more public subsidies for the Polish School of Mediterranean Archaeology.

In 1981, after Kazimierz Michałowski passed away, his students were faced with the necessity of organizational changes as none of them was capable of replacing the *Master* and heading the three institutions simultaneously. The changes coincided with the introduction of Martial Law (in 1981) and the escalation of constraints in Poland. Nevertheless, the decade brought many significant successes with regard to excavation as well as conservation. Considering the extensive efforts of the 1980s, special attention must be drawn to the implication of Polish archaeologists at Saqqara (in 1987) and to the prehistoric prospection of the Western Desert (1986), including the documentation of rock art and the Stone Age sites survey (Krzyżaniak 1988; Myśliwiec 2007).

Polish excavations in the Nile Valley after 1989

The collapse of the Communist system in the Eastern Europe in 1989 created a new geopolitical reality that also affected science significantly. Following a transitional period, Polish archaeologists gained more freedom and more opportunities to engage in collaborative projects with other countries. Research cooperation with western institutions soon increased significantly, and the PCMA began to publish reports and monographs more frequently in English. However, the shift from a *centrally planned economy* to a free *market economy* generated a chronic under-funding of the scientific domain, due to hyper-inflation and an unstable monetary sector. Warsaw University still remained the major centre of education for young archaeologists, but it no longer had a research monopoly position in the Nile Valley. Also the tripartite scheme of costs and activities mentioned in the previous section collapsed. The new conditions made it necessary to turn for support to scholarly institutions and to private sponsors.

Such cases of inadequate funding soon made it necessary for various museums and universities from across the country (Cracow, Poznań and Gdańsk) to co-operate in order to be able to undertake field research abroad. A greater number of archaeologists from all over Poland were thus to participate in North African expeditions. Their work led to setting up permanent exhibitions of Egyptian and

Sudanese ancient artefacts in several cities. This in turn increased considerably public interest in archaeological research in Northern Africa, and also opened new opportunities for acquiring donations from private sponsors. The number of projects co-ordinated by the Warsaw university PCMA centre grew dramatically, and it soon became apparent that its organization and Cairo premises were too limited. With the assistance of the Foundation for Polish Science, a new building much more suited to the needs of Polish archaeologists and international teams was purchased in 1994.

Character and patterns of the cooperation
International circumstances accompanying the presence of Polish archaeologists abroad

On the question of international cooperations (Polish-Egyptian; Polish-Sudanese), it must be acknowledged that they had many opportunities to develop favourably over the century of Polish archaeology abroad. As noted above, archaeological research activities were often in tune with the broader constructive patterns of worldwide relations. For instance, the presidency of G.A. Nasser (1954–1970) coincided with a resurgence and intensification of Polish archaeological activities in the Nile Valley (see also Klimowicz and Klimowicz, this volume), and this was partly due to the amicable relationships developed by Nasser with the Soviet Union in the mid-1950s. This Egyptian inclination towards the Eastern Block gave Polish researchers the opportunity to resurrect their work in the Middle East. These circumstances changed notably during the era of President Anwar al-Sadat (1970–1981), who improved US-Egyptian diplomatic relations and expulsed much of the Soviet personnel (Saliba 1975: 55). Coincidently Poland itself became at that juncture more open to capitalist influences, notably as a result of receiving aid and loans from Western European countries in the 1970s.

From the perspective of international relations, it is worth recalling the official agreements signed by People's Republic of Poland with the Republic of Egypt (in 1957) and with the Republic of Sudan (in 1967). These agreements were the first of their kind, and opened cultural, scientific and technical cooperation between these nations. The contracting parties assured each other of further strengthening the bonds of friendship and of promoting cooperation in the field of science and culture, in particular of fostering mutual assistance between their Academies of Sciences and research institutes. Most important with regards to archaeology, both parties agreed to develop facilities for admission to libraries, archives, and museum collections, and also to create an extended exchange programme of free transfer of information and expertise.

Remarkable gestures of appreciation for these inter-state cooperations were expressed by national decorations: thus, several Polish archaeologists (*e.g.* S. Jakobielski, L. Krzyżaniak) received the Order of the Two Niles (2nd Class) conferred by the Sudanese President. Bestowing the country's highest national decoration on foreign archaeologists recognized their involvement in saving and protecting the archaeological heritage of Sudan. Similarly, one of the most significant Polish Orders of Merit for enhancing Polish research activities in Egypt was granted in 1989 by the Polish President to Dr Abou al-Youn Barakat (Sohag and Alexandria Universities).

Without doubt, the Polish archaeological research carried out in the Middle Eastern republics served to reinforce links between the nations. However, these relationships extended over time beyond the frame of archaeology and political affairs (Szafrański 2007a: 55). This seems to be confirmed by the activities of the Polish-Arab Friendship Association. Many of its prominent members were actually archaeologists, and some of them performed even presidential functions there (*e.g.* K. Michałowski, T. Dzierżykay-Rogalski, Z. Szafrański). With its aims to improve relations between Polish and Arab people, the association encourages a broadly-defined Polish-Arab dialogue and organizes conferences and cultural and artistic events.

Cooperation with Local Communities

Polish researchers abroad could always count on Egyptian assistance. This was the case not only at the level of official contacts with authorities, but also on the ground, in terms of ongoing cooperation with local communities and workers, with whom Polish archaeologists interacted on a daily basis. The latter type of relationships, which include some often anonymous inhabitants of remote parts of the countries, at this point call for special attention. In this respect too, the figure of Professor K. Michałowski, the unquestioned founder of the Polish School of Mediterranean Archaeology, deserves further recognition. His abilities in organizing missions abroad were accompanied by an unusual talent for winning the favour of local communities and indigenous authorities. This provided a model for archaeologists to follow. His rules were formulated explicitly at the beginning of every season, as a type of agenda for conduct. The protocol was obligatory for all members of the Polish missions, and effectively shaped their behaviour pattern.

With hindsight, it appears that some of these rules of behaviour differed from those of other archaeological missions at that time. For instance, the custom of shaking hands with the Egyptian supervisor (*Rais*) and workers (*Fellaheen*) assumed harmonious relations between the staff members and the local communities (Michałowski 1974a: 30). The request that archaeologists refrain from being seated during working hours within the excavation area followed from a similar logic, as an expression of respect for the *fellaheen's* labour. Another very important issue in this context was the necessary adaptation to the socio-cultural environment, including the wearing of appropriate cloths (*e.g.* avoiding shorts) and the respect of indigenous rules associated especially with the religious conviction of local communities. For instance during the fast of the *Ramadan* the staff refrained from eating, drinking and smoking during daylight hours in the work area (Jakobielski, pers. comm.).

In addition, the archaeologists always ensured that their expeditions would be well equipped with medicines, and to provide also for the workers and their families. These circumstances undoubtedly created an atmosphere of trust, loyalty and sometimes led to honest long-lasting friendships (Jakobielski, pers. comm.). An unusual approach to the *fellaheen* included the possibility of individual promotion upon general approval. Consequently, a worker may be appointed by the director of the excavation on the nomination of the *Rais* (supervisor) after in-depth recognition of his skills and abilities, acquiring as a result considerable position and responsibilities in the expedition. One of the enduring *Rais* received on his retirement a pension from the PCMA in recognition of his loyalty and dedication to his work. In some cases, relationships between Polish archaeologists and Egyptian workers and their families have extended over three generations (Szafrański 2007a: 50).

Another example of the attitude towards the local communities propagated by Michałowski was the custom of a courtesy visit to the Elders' homes, in order to introduce the director of excavation to the prominent people living in the immediate vicinity of the site. During these meetings the elders were informed about the archaeological objectives, actual events and contingent discoveries. Of course, these successful relationships with local communities were also strengthened by the fact that the United Arab Republic and the Republic of Sudan, as newly independent states in decolonized Africa, preferred hosting researchers from countries which had never had any colonial involvement in the area (Michałowski, 1974a: 30, 47-48; Hassan 1998: 207-209). With this behaviour, Michałowski gave intellectual authority and leadership to his students and collaborators, instilling principles that may be seen as his worthy legacy.

Scholarly Cooperations

Following the idea that whatever is discovered needs to be returned as closely as possible to its original form, conservation efforts have always been a crucial part of Polish archaeological activities abroad. The presence of highly-specialized teams of restorers, engineers and architects was an integral part of the missions since the late 1950s. These contributions to the renovation of famous monuments world-wide led to the recognition of the 'Polish School of Conservation' (Szafrański 2007a: 53). Building on their experience in the reconstruction of devastated Poland after the Second World War, Polish conservation experts have repeatedly shared their specialized knowledge and experience in several cooperation projects with the Egyptian and Sudanese Antiquities Services.

The list of joint conservation efforts is a long one. First among those is the Temple of Hatshepsut, the Polish-Egyptian preservation mission in Deir el-Bahari (1960s) which soon led to other similar projects all over Egypt (Lipińska 2007; Szafrański 2007b). For instance the preservation mission on the Mosque of Qurqumas (1972-2001) and the Sultan al-Ashraf Inal complex (1989) occurred in the Cairo's City of Dead, Marina el-Alamein on the Mediterranean coast (1988) and Tuna el-Gebel in the Middle Egypt (2004) (Daszewski 2007; Witkowski 2007). These jointly restored monuments, did also, as importantly, cement the bonds of international friendship. Excellent cooperation between Polish researchers and the Egyptian Antiquities Service has been emphasized with regard to the successfully dismantled

Nubian temples at Tafa and Dabod (1960-61). In this context the Abu Simbel Temples represented the most challenging attempt of transferring this example of Nubian art and subsequently returning them to their former magnificence.

Mutual cooperation involving Polish conservation expertise was particularly reinforced during the Nasser presidency. At that time, thousands of Arab students took the opportunity to complete their cost-free university education in Eastern European countries, including Poland (Kreutz 1999; see also Klimowicz and Klimowicz, this volume). Such an opportunity was possible due to already discussed Soviet influence in the Middle East (Daigle 2004). At the beginning, Egyptian and Sudanese archaeology students were enrolled in Warsaw University at Polish expense. Over time, the scholarship system evolved to meeting the changing needs and fields of expertise in the discipline. In this respect, the remarkable achievements of Polish conservation projects in saving the heritage of ancient civilizations led to the organization of restoration courses for foreign students. Nowadays, most of these former students are prominent inspectors employed in the Egyptian and Sudanese Antiquities Services (Szafrański 2007a: 53).

Although international contacts in higher education have changed considerably in recent times, it is still noteworthy that Middle Eastern students have a preference for attending PhD courses in Poland, be it in Warsaw, in Poznań or in Cracow.

Conclusions

The phenomenon of Polish archaeological research in Egypt and Sudan is composed of numerous elements. The stormy history of Poland as well as the changes occurring in the international arena during the twentieth century, discussed above in detail in four historical contexts, have all undoubtedly influenced the unique development of the Polish School of Mediterranean Archaeology. In retrospect, it is clear that the School owes its conception to one man, Kazimierz Michałowski, whose vision and ambition to create from scratch an internationally recognized school of Polish archaeological research in the Near East eventually came to fruition.

Although this School initially built on the experience of other European researchers (mainly French), it gradually came to acquire its own, distinctive character. One of the essential traits of Polish archaeological activity in the southern Mediterranean (*e.g.* Syria, Cyprus, Libya, Lebanon, Palestine) has been its willingness to develop advanced specialization in research areas of lesser interest to international counterparts, such as research on the Predynastic period in Egypt, as well as on the Greek, Roman and Coptic periods. Although we did not set out here these international developments in relation to the patterns and areas of interest of Polish archaeology in Poland itself, it may nonetheless be noted that within Poland there had always been strong emphasis on the prehistoric periods, especially the Stone Age (including the Neolithic), as well as the Middle Ages.

In any case, the interdisciplinary cooperation of Polish archaeologists and experts in a wide range of studies, as well as the open-minded attitude displayed in interactions with local populations, have received international recognition and even appreciation. An additional feature characteristic of Polish archaeological missions abroad has been an attempt to maintain a balance between scientific concerns and political involvement (see also Klimowicz and Klimowicz, this volume). The latter condition guaranteed that Polish researchers working abroad have not been associated with diplomatic activities and have never been put in an uncomfortable position in the context of the changing socio-political configurations prevailing over the last century.

Acknowledgements

We would like to thank Stefan Jakobielski and Arkadiusz Marciniak for their help and for the opportunities to exchange valuable matters. We want to express our gratitude to Mariusz Drzewiecki and the National Archive of Digital Sources (Narodowe Archiwum Cyfrowe) who agreed to make their photos accessible for the paper. We also would like to thank for assistance and help in preparing the text for print: Sjoerd van der Linde, Corijanne Slappendel and Nina Schücker, as well as all scholars who co-participated in the European Archaeology Abroad Project.

References

Aksamit, J. 2007. 'Tell Edfu', in E. Laskowska-Kusztal (ed.), *Seventy Years of Polish Archaeology in Egypt*. Warsaw: Wydawnictwa Uniwersytetu Warszawskiego, 31-40.

Beck, C.F. 1963. 'Czechosovakia's Penetration of Africa 1955-62', *World Politics Quarterly Journal of International Relations* 15(3): 403-416.

Bernhard, M.L. 1986a. 'Edfu', in Z. Kiss (ed.), *50 Lat Polskich Wykopalisk w Egipcie i na Bliskim Wschodzie*. Warszawa: Dom Słowa Polskiego, 23-28.

Bernhard, M.L. 1986b. 'Kazimierz Michałowski', in Z. Kiss (ed.), *50 Lat Polskich Wykopalisk w Egipcie i na Bliskim Wschodzie*. Warszawa: Dom Słowa Polskiego, 17-22.

Bernhard, M.L. 1995. 'Korzenie', in M.L. Bernhard (ed.), *Od Nilu do Eufratu. Polska Archeologia Śródziemnomorska 1981-1994*. Warszawa: Uniwersytet Warszawski, 7-18.

Biskupski, M.B. 2000. *The History of Poland*. London: Greenwood Press.

Burstein, S.M. 2008. 'When Greek was an African Language: The Role of Greek Culture in Ancient and Medieval Nubia', *Journal of World History* 19(1): 41-61.

Daigle, C.A. 2004. 'The Russian Are Going: Sadat, Nixon and the Soviet Presence in Egypt', *Middle East Review of International Affairs* 8(1): 1-15.

Daszewski, W.A. 1986. '50 Lat Polskich Wykopalisk w Egipcie i na Bliskim Wschodzie. 25 Lat istnienia Stacji Archeologii Śródziemnomorskiej Uniwersytetu Warszawskiego', in Z. Kiss (ed.), *50 Lat Polskich Wykopalisk w Egipcie i na Bliskim Wschodzie*. Warszawa: Dom Słowa Polskiego, 7-16.

Daszewski, W.,A. 2007. 'Marina el-Alamein', in E. Laskowska-Kusztal (ed.), *Seventy Years of Polish Archaeology in Egypt*. Warsaw: Wydawnictwa Uniwersytetu Warszawskiego, 191-204.

Dębicki, R. 1962. *Foreign Policy of Poland 1919-1939. From the Rebirth of the Polish Republic to World War II*. New York: Praeger Publisher.

Emery, W.B. 1965. *Egypt in Nubia*. London: Hutchinson of London.

Hassan, F.A. 2007. 'The Aswan High Dam and the International Rescue Nubia Campaign', *African Archaeological Review* 24: 73-94.

Hassan, D.T. 1998. 'Memorabilia: Archaeological Materiality and National Identity in Egypt', in L. Meskel (ed.), *Archaeology Under Fire. Nationalism, Politics and Heritage in the Eastern Mediterranean and Middle East*. London: Routledge, 200-216.

Jaczewski, B. 1982. 'Nauka', in J. Tomicki (ed.), *Polska Odrodzona 1918-1939. Państwo, Społeczeństwo, Kultura*. Warszawa: Wiedza Powszechna, 507-554.

Jakobielski S. and J. Karkowski (eds). 1992. *50 Years of Polish Excavations in Egypt and the Near East: acts of the Symposium at the Warsaw University*. Warsaw: Cieszyńska Drukarnia Wydawnicza.

Jakobielski, S. 2001. 'Taki Był Profesor'. *Podkowiński magazyn kulturalny* 4-1(31/32). Retrieved 10 January 2011 from http://free.art.pl/podkowa.magazyn/nr3132/michalowski.htm.

Knopek, J. 2005. 'Aktywność Polskich Badaczy w życiu Afryki Północnej do Początku XX wieku', *Cywilizacja i polityka* 3, 316-332.

Kreutz, A. 1999. 'Post-Communist Eastern Europe and the Middle East: the Burden of History and New Political Realities', *Arab Studies Quarterly* 21(2). Retrieved 10 January 2011 from http://www.findarticles.com/p/articles/mi_M2501/IS_2_21/AI_55683884/PG_4.

Krzyżaniak, L. 1988. 'Dakhleh Oasis Project: Interim Report on the First Season of the Recording of Petroglyphs, January/February 1988', *The Journal of the Society for the Study of Egyptian Antiquities* 17(4): 182-191.

Laskowska-Kusztal, E. (ed.). 2007. *Seventy Years of Polish Archaeology in Egypt*. Warsaw: Wydawnictwa Uniwersytetu Warszawskiego.

Lech, J. 1998. 'Between Captivity and Freedom, Polish Archaeology in the 20th century', *Archeologia Polona* 35-36: 25-222.

Lipińska, J. 2007. 'Deir el-Bahari. Temple of Tothmus III', in E. Laskowska-Kusztal (ed.), *Seventy Years of Polish Archaeology in Egypt*. Warsaw: Wydawnictwa Uniwersytetu Warszawskiego, 105-114.

Michałowski, K. 1937. 'Wykopaliska w Edfu. Kampania R. 1937', *Biuletyn Historii Sztuki i Kultury* 5: 271-278.

Michałowski, K. 1938. 'Wykopaliska w Edfu. Kampania R. 1938', *Biuletyn Historii Sztuki i Kultury* 6: 201-207.

Michałowski, K. 1957. 'Polskie Wykopaliska w Edfu', in S. Strelcyn (ed.), *Szkice z Dziejów Polskiej Orientalistyki 1*. Warszawa: Państwowe Wydawnictwo Naukowe, 31-41.

Michałowski, K. 1959. 'The Polish Archaeological Reconnaissance Trip to Nubia'. *Review of the Polish Academy of Sciences* 6(3): 47-85.

Michałowski, K. 1964. 'Archeologia Śródziemnomorska w Ostatnim Dwudziestoleciu w Polsce Ludowej', *Meander* 19: 315-328.

Michałowski, K. 1974*a*. *Od Edfu do Faras. Polskie Odkrycia Archeologii Śródziemnomorskiej*. Warszawa: Wydawnictwa Artystyczne i Filmowe.

Michałowski, K. 1974*b*. 'Polska Archeologia w Pogoni za Straconym Czasem', in W.H. Boulton, *Wieczność Piramid i Tragedia Pompei*. Warszawa: Wiedza Powszechna, 231-256.

Michałowski, K. 1983. 'Polish Mediterranean Archaeology', in W. Tyloch (ed.), *Oriental Studies in the Sixty Years of Independent Poland*. Warsaw: Polish Scientific Publishers, 59-64.

Michałowski, K. 1986. Wspomnienia. Warszawa: Państwowy Instytut Wydawniczy.

Michałowski, K. 1990. *Opera Minora 1*. Warszawa: Państwowe Wydawnictwo Naukowe.

Myśliwiec, K. 2007. 'Saqqara", in E. Laskowska-Kusztal (ed.), *Seventy Years of Polish Archaeology in Egypt*. Warsaw: Wydawnictwa Uniwersytetu Warszawskiego, 79-90.

Nałęcz, D. 1991. *Kultura Drugiej Rzeczypospolitej*. Dzieje Narodu i Państwa Polskiego 3. Warszawa: Krajowa Agencja Wydawnicza.

Pilecki, J. 1969. 'Pionierska działalność Tadeusza Samuela Smoleńskiego w Dziedzinie Egiptologii Polskiej', in J. Reychman (ed.), *Szkice z Dziejów Polskiej Orientalistyki* 3. Warszawa: Państwowe Wydawnictwo Naukowe, 227-233.

Saliba, N.E. 1975. 'The Decline of Nasirism in Sadat's Egypt', *World Affairs* 138(1): 51-59.

Schild, R. and F. Wendorf. 1980. *Prehistory of the Eastern Sahara*. New York: Academic Press.

Schild, R. and F. Wendorf. 2002. 'Forty Years of the Combined Prehistoric Expedition', *Archaeologia Polona* 40: 5-22.

Smoleński, T. 1907. 'Austo - węgierskie wykopaliska w Górnym Egipcie 1907 roku', in B. Ulanowski (ed.), *Sprawozdania z czynności i posiedzeń Akademii Umiejętności w Krakowie*. Kraków: Drukarnia Uniwersytetu Jagiellońskiego, 19-20.

Szafrański, Z.E. 2007a. 'Our Milestones', in E. Laskowska-Kusztal (ed.), *Seventy Years of Polish Archaeology in Egypt*. Warsaw: Wydawnictwa Uniwersytetu Warszawskiego, 41-64.

Szafrański, Z.E. 2007b. 'Deir el-Bahari. Temple of Hatshepsut ', in E. Laskowska-Kusztal (ed.), *Seventy Years of Polish Archaeology in Egypt*. Warsaw: Wydawnictwa Uniwersytetu Warszawskiego, 91-104.

Śliwa, J. 1998. 'Profesor Piotr Bieńkowski (1865-1925). W stulecie utworzenia Katedry Archeologii Klasycznej w Uniwersytecie Jagiellońskim', *Alma Mater* 7. Retrieved 10 January 2011 from http://www3.uj.edu.pl/alma/07/29.html.

Śliwa, J. 2002. 'Tadeusz Smoleński (1884 - 1909) i Początki Polskiej Egiptologii', *Alma Mater* 44: 27-29.

Śliwa, J. 2007. 'Amon-Re kocha Tego, Kto go Umiłował. Skarabeusz Egipski Odkryty w Szarunie w Roku 1907', *Meander* 1-2: 82-85.

Śliwa, J. 2008. 'Tadeusz Smoleński (1884 - 1909). W Stulecie Krakowskich Wykopalisk w Egipcie', *Alma Mater* 99: 196-200.

Tyszkiewicz, M. 1994. *Egipt Zapomniany Czyli Michała hr. Tyszkiewicza Dziennik Podróży do Egiptu i Nubii (1861–1862)*. Warszawa: PRO-EGIPT.

Vörös, G. 2008. *Egyptian Temple Architecture: 100 Years of Hungarian Excavations in Egypt, 1907-2007*. Budapeszt: The American University in Cairo Press.

Wendorf, F., R. Said and R. Schild 1970. 'Egyptian Prehistory: Some New Concepts', *Science, New Series* 169(3951): 1161-1171.

Wendorf, F. and R. Schild. 1998. 'Nabta Playa and Its Role in Northeastern African Prehistory', *Journal of Anthropological Archaeology* 17: 97-123.

Witkowski, M.,G. 2007.'Amir Qurqumas Complex in Cairo', in E. Laskowska-Kusztal (ed.), *Seventy Years of Polish Archaeology in Egypt*. Warsaw: Wydawnictwa Uniwersytetu Warszawskiego, 191-204.

1.6 Dutch archaeology abroad: from treasure hunting to local community engagement

Monique van den Dries, Corijanne Slappendel and Sjoerd van der Linde

Faculty of Archaeology, Leiden University, The Netherlands

Abstract

Dutch archaeology abroad can be divided into four phases. The first phase (seventeenth to nineteenth century) is characterized by a major role for private investors in terms of collecting antiquities and the funding of expeditions, and subsequently in the development of archaeology as a scientific activity as well as in heritage preservation. During the second phase (1900-World War II), scientific interest grew further and an ethnological interest came to dominate the activities abroad. This interest was focused on the Dutch colonies. The third phase (World War II-1990) showed a growing interest in relationships with countries with which no colonial bond existed. New institutions were established, mainly in Mediterranean countries, to support archaeological research abroad. Long-term projects prevailed and the western scientific objectives and views on heritage management dominated. The involvement of the Dutch government with culture was quite strong, both at the national and international level. Culture became part of the welfare state and was heavily stimulated and funded. The last phase, up until the present day, is characterized by the opposite, a decrease in state interference (especially when it comes to funding) and a subsequent return of private initiatives. Interestingly, there is a renewed (politically instigated) interest in the former colonies, *i.e.* in preserving Dutch colonial heritage. This all coincides with changing circumstances and rising demands in guest countries, forcing archaeologists to find new ways of funding and organizing projects abroad. Consequently, awareness of local people's values is rising and knowledge sharing, capacity building and development aid are emerging in Dutch archaeology abroad.

Résumé

L'Archéologie Néerlandaise à l'Étranger : D'une Chasse aux Trésors à un Engagement de la Communauté Locale

L'histoire de l'archéologie néerlandaise à l'étranger se décompose en quatre phases. La première phase (XVIIème-XIXème siècle) se caractérise par le rôle majeur des investisseurs privés, grâce à leur collection d'antiquités, au financement d'expéditions et, par la suite, au développement de l'archéologie en tant qu'activité scientifique et préservation du patrimoine. Au cours de la seconde phase (1900-seconde guerre mondiale) l'intérêt scientifique a augmenté et l'éthnologie est apparue pour dominer les activités à l'étranger. Cet intérêt s'est concentré sur les colonies néerlandaises. La troisième phase (seconde guerre mondiale-1990) a connu un intérêt croissant pour les relations avec des pays non colonialisés. De nouvelles institutions ont été fondées, principalement dans les pays méditerranéens, pour conforter la recherche archéologique à l'étranger. Des projets à long terme ont prévalu et les valeurs et visions scientifiques occidentales sur l'héritage patrimoniale, ont dominé. L'État néerlandais s'est fortement impliqué dans le domaine culturel, tant au niveau national qu'au niveau international. La culture a alors fait partie intégrante de l'état-providence, et a été fortement confortée et financée. La dernière phase, jusqu'à nos jours, est caractérisée, à l'inverse, par une diminution de l'intervention de l'État (en particulier lorsqu'il s'agit de financement) et par conséquent par le retour d'initiatives privées. Fait intéressant, il y a un regain d'intérêt (de motivation politique) pour les anciennes colonies, dicté par le souhait de préserver l'héritage colonial des Pays-Bas. Tout ceci coïncide avec des circonstances changeantes et des exigences croissantes dans les pays concernés, ce qui oblige les archéologues à trouver de nouveaux moyens de financement et d'organisation des projets de recherche à l'étranger. Par conséquent, il y a une meilleure prise de conscience des valeurs des peuples locaux et donc un meilleur partage des connaissances, un renforcement des capacités et une meilleure aide au développement dans l'archéologie étrangère néerlandaise.

Extracto

La Arqueología Neerlandesa en el Extranjero: De la Busca de Tesoros al Compromiso a la Comunidad Local

Se puede dividir la arqueología neerlandesa en el extranjero en cuatro fases. La primera fase (el siglo diecisiete hasta el siglo diecinueve) se caracteriza por un papel importante para inversores privados en el sentido de coleccionar antigüedades y de financiar expediciones y, consecuentemente, por el desarrollo de la arqueología como una actividad científica, tanto como por la preservación patrimonial. Durante la segunda fase (1900 – Segunda Guerra Mundial) el interés científico aumentó más y un interés etnológico llegó a dominar las actividades en el extranjero. Los intereses se concentraron en las colonias neerlandesas. La tercera fase (Segunda Guerra Mundial – 1990) mostró un interés creciente en relaciones con países con los que no había habido una relación colonial. Se fundaron nuevas instituciones principalmente en los países mediterráneos para sostener la investigación arqueológica en el extranjero. Los proyectos a largo plazo prevalecieron y dominaron los objetivos occidentales científicos y las opiniones sobre la gestión. La implicación del gobierno neerlandés en la cultura fue considerable, tanto a nivel nacional como internacional. La cultura llegó a ser parte del estado del bienestar y se la estimulo y subsidió en gran medida. La última fase, hasta el presente, se caracteriza por el contrario, una disminución en la intervención estatal (en particular en el sentido de fondos) y una reducción de iniciativas privadas. Es interesante que haya un nuevo interés (estimulado por la política) en las antiguas colonias, pe. en la preservación del patrimonio colonial neerlandés. Todo esto coincide con las circunstancias variables y las exigencias crecientes en los países huésped, lo cual obliga a los arqueólogos encontrar nuevas maneras de financiar y organizar los proyectos en el extranjero.

Consecuentemente crece la conciencia de los valores de la población local, y el compartir de conocimientos, la creación de capacidades y la ayuda al desarrollo están surgiendo en la arqueología neerlandesa en el extranjero.

ملخص

علم الآثار الهولندي في الخارج: من صيد الكنوز إلى تعاون المجتمع المحلي

مونيك فان دن دريس، كورينا بالسبيندال وشرود فان دن در ليند

كلية علم الآثار، جامعة ليدن، هولندا

المرحلة الأولى: إلى أربعة مراحل يمكن تقسيم علم الآثار الهولندي في الخارج إلى أربعة مراحل. يتميز هذا الدور بالدور (من القرن السابع عشر إلى القرن التاسع عشر) وتتميز هذه المرحلة بالكبير الذي عبه مستثمرو القطاع الخاص فيما يخص جمع الآثار وتمويل البحافظة على نشاط علمي في علم الآثار كنشاط ريور في ذلك. وبعد ذلك (من المرحلة الثانية من 1900 وحتى الحرب العالمية الثانية). كذلك كثلاث التراث وقد الأنشطة الخارجية. وقد ظهرت المرحلة الثالثة (من نما الاهتمام العلمي وسيطر الاهتمام الانثولوجي على الأنشطة الخارجية. وقد ظهرت المرحلة الثالثة (من تركز هذا الاهتمام على المستعمرات الهولندية. وقد ظهر اهتمام متزايد في العلاقات مع البلدان البحر العالمية الثانية وحتى 1990) الحرب العالمية الثانية في ضوء بلدان حوض البحر وقد تم إنشاء المعاهد في بلدان حوض الأثرية في الخارج. وقد سادت المتوسط بشكل رئيسي من أجل تعزيز البحوث الأثرية في الخارج. وقد سادت قرار إدارة حول نظريات الغربية وجهة نظر في سيطرت الأهداف كما الأمد، طويلة المشروعات كذلك للتراث. وكان إشراك الحكومة الهولندية على قوى الثقافة على المستويين لقد أصبحت الثقافة جزء من دولة الرفاه وقد تم تحفيزها والداخلي. والمحلي. الحاضر، حتى تمتد تلت والتي الأخيرة، المرحلة وتتميز (خاصة بالنسبة للتمويل) وبعد ذلك عودة وتموليها بكثرة. حيث انخفض تدخل الدولة (خاصة بالنسبة للتمويل) وبعد ذلك عودة بالعكس، حيث انخفض تدخل الدولة (دوافع سياسية) كانه أن المثير للاهتمام هناك لتجدد الاهتمام في الدراسات الخاصة. وتزامن المستعمرات السابقة، أي الحفاظ على التراث الاستعماري الهولندي. ويتزامن كل هذا مع الظروف المتغيرة، وارتفاع الطلب في البلدان المضيفة، مما يدفع علماء الآثار إلى لبس طرق جديدة لتمويل وتنظيم المشاريع في الخارج. وبالتالي، زيادة الوعي بالقيم الشعبية المحلية؛ أدبار تبادل المعرفة، وبناء القدرات، والمساعدة التنمية في الظهور في علم الآثار الهولندي في الخارج.

Keywords

antiquities, archaeology abroad, Netherlands, heritage policy, mutual heritage, development aid, community engagement

Introduction

The appointment in 1818 of the first professor of archaeology, *i.e.* the classicist Caspar Reuvens (1793–1835), is usually taken as the starting point of Dutch professional, academic archaeology. His primary task was to build a collection of antiquities that could provide a basis for teaching and research. This collection, that would later become the asset of the National Museum of Antiquities in Leiden, consisted mainly of material that he bought from collectors who were buying antiquities abroad, mainly in the Mediterranean region, and of material collected in the Dutch colonies (South Africa, Indonesia, Surinam and the Dutch Antilles).[1] As such, the roots of archaeology in the Netherlands – like in many other European countries – lie in antiquarianism, in collecting and studying antiquities from abroad.[2]

This focus on collecting continued to exist throughout the nineteenth century and the first decades of the twentieth century, although the collection strategy of the Dutch was elaborated by participating in excavations of other European countries abroad and eventually by conducting excavations themselves. After World War II, the academic interest was broadened to countries with which no 'colonial relation' existed. In addition, it can be noted that the classical world remained of interest – its study now developed into 'Mediterranean archaeology'. In the last couple of decades archaeological activity abroad has shown some new developments again – in terms of aims, motives, funding and geographic distribution – with a remarkable return of interest in former Dutch colonies and trading posts.

In this paper we will provide a general historic overview of the archaeological activities that have been carried out abroad by Dutch 'archaeologists', specifically exploring their changing aims and motivations. These changes reflect general trends in the development of western archaeology (see *e.g.* Trigger 1984, 2006), but some aspects are typically Dutch. As activities abroad often related to what was happening 'internally', some national developments and policies are discussed as well.

---

1   Contacts with Indonesia date back to before 1600, related to the trading activities of the East India Company (VOC). Indonesia (Netherlands East Indies) became part of the Kingdom of the Netherlands in 1815 (National Archives of the Netherlands, Netherlands Institute for Cultural Heritage, Netherlands Cultural Heritage Agency 2010). Relations with Surinam go back to 1667 when Abraham Crijnsen made it a colony of the Dutch Province of Zealand. In 1682 it was handed over to the West Indian Company (National Archives of the Netherlands, Netherlands Institute for Cultural Heritage, Netherlands Cultural Heritage Agency 2010: 114).

2   Reuvens only enhanced this collection with excavated material from the Dutch soil as of 1827 (Forum Hadriani).

Seventeenth to nineteenth century: private initiatives and enterprises

The seventeenth century is generally considered to be the 'golden age' for the then Republic of the Seven United Netherlands. Already in this period the foundation was laid for much of the archaeological activity that the Dutch would conduct abroad in the following centuries. As a result of explorations in other parts of the world[3] and the subsequently founded chartered companies *Vereenigde Oost-Indische Compagnie* (VOC, 1602), *Noordsche Compagnie* (1614) and *West-Indische Compagnie* (WIC, 1621) setting up trading posts and colonies in Asia, Africa and America and whaling posts in the arctic region, the Republic dominated European trade and became a 'state of global trade'. This brought along economic prosperity, the emergence of rich merchants and flourishing science and arts. The ships and merchants, but also the missionaries who worked in overseas areas brought back all kinds of exotic material and stories about the local 'natives' and more and more people became interested in exotic objects and antiquities. This gave a tremendous boost to antiquarianism. In contrast with neighbouring European countries, in the Netherlands these collections were mainly in private hands, mostly of merchants

Figure 1. The oldest, still functional museum in the Netherlands, Teylers Museum in Haarlem. It was opened to the public in 1784, showing both art and scientific objects from the private collection of Pieter Teyler van der Hulst (1702–1778), and has kept its original display till today (Photo: Teylers museum).[4]

---

3   Well-known explorers are Willem Barentsz (1550–1597), who sailed to the arctic to find a northern passage to the east and ran into Nova Zembla, and Abel Tasman (1603–1659), who sailed for the VOC from Indonesia south and found New Zealand and Tasmania.

4   See www.teylersmuseum.eu.

and other rich citizens (Halbertsma 2003: 6). These collections were displayed in '*rariteitenkabinetten*' (cabinets of curiosities), which remained popular throughout the seventeenth and eighteenth centuries until the first public displays in museums opened at the end of the eighteenth century (figure 1).

But not just the antiquities and curiosities that were encountered in the Dutch colonies (South-Africa, Indonesia, Surinam and the Caribbean) drew attention. The Renaissance – with Europeans regarding themselves as heirs and descendants of the Ancient Roman and Greek civilizations (*e.g.* Hingley 2005; see also Theodoroudi and Kotsakis, this volume) – did have a huge influence on Dutch cultural life in the sixteenth century too. So from the start of this 'modern' antiquarianism, the Mediterranean had also been of interest to scholars and collectors. An additional interest in the remains of the Near East, and in particular Mesopotamia, Palestine and Egypt, arose from Christianity and the biblical stories. These areas were regarded as the background scenery to biblical and classical stories, relating to the roots of western civilization (*e.g.* Nieuwenhuyse 2006).

The University of Leiden (founded in 1575) played a substantial role in furthering this interest. It was the main institutional collector of books, *naturalia*, *artificialia* and antiquities in the seventeenth and eighteenth century. It acquired its first Egyptian antiquities in 1620 from merchants travelling to the Mediterranean (Rijksmuseum van Oudheden 1981; Raven 2007), such as mummified bodies, and showed them to the public in the anatomic theatre (*Theatrum Anatomicum*). Moreover, throughout the eighteenth century the education in classical philology was very important at Leiden University (Otterspeer 2008: 105).

Under the influence of the Enlightenment, scientific interest in anthropology and ethnology developed too, to fill the gaps in the knowledge of the planet and its inhabitants, and expeditions gained a scientific rather than a purely economic goal. Since the second half of the eighteenth century for example, Indian objects from Surinam were collected and transferred to the Netherlands, where they were exhibited in the Royal Cabinet of Curiosities in The Hague (Versteeg 1998).

For a long time arts, antiquities and science had been dominated by powerful individuals and the nobility, but things started to change towards the end of the eighteenth century. The maritime expansion policy was first replaced by consolidation and as of the second part of the seventeenth century the Republic was losing trading power and subsequently colonies to other European countries (England, France, Spain). Numerous wars, disasters, plagues and revolts contributed to the Republic's downfall that ended in the founding of the Batavian Republic (1795), by which it became a vassal of France. Consequently, absolutism grew, giving the monarchs power over nobility and cultural affairs. In 1798, the Republic's government followed the French example and established a national gallery in The Hague.[5] Subsequently Louis Bonaparte, who was appointed King of the Netherlands (from 1806 until 1810) by his brother, emperor Napoleon,

---

5   See www.rijksmuseum.nl.

founded a new national museum (*Rijksmuseum*) and a Royal Institute for Sciences (in 1808),[6] both in Amsterdam.

Also under French influence Dutch antiquarianism developed towards archaeology, as national antiquities were more and more considered important for defining a national identity (compare Levin, chapter 1.2 this volume). At the same time this promoted academic research as identity claims needed legitimization through scientific evidence (Willems 2008: 284). This period of cultural flourishing temporarily ceased when Napoleon took over after the forced abdication of Louis Bonaparte in 1810, and at his order many works of art were confiscated and taken to Paris (Halbertsma 2003: 1). After the defeat of Napoleon in 1813, when the kingdom of the Netherlands was founded and King Willem I took office, an ambitious cultural policy emerged. The Netherlands wanted to become a player in the international arena again. Moreover, antiquities were 'hot' and the trade in them commercially interesting. So, in 1818 a national museum for antiquities (later *Rijksmuseum van Oudheden,* RMO) was initiated. Caspar Reuvens, who by royal decree had been appointed professor of archaeology at Leiden University, was asked to establish an archaeological museum after the example of other European museums. Almost immediately, Reuvens became very successful in purchasing Mediterranean antiquities from merchants (especially Greek antiquities) and from special agents that were commissioned by the Dutch state to keep an eye on the market of Classical and Egyptian antiquities (Rijksmuseum van Oudheden 1981: 44).

One of those agents was Jean-Émile Humbert (1771–1839), a Dutch military officer who worked for the Tunisian ruler as chief engineer at the harbour project of La Goulette (Halbertsma 2003: 72), when he discovered in 1817 the ancient Punic city of Carthage. He sold his material to the RMO, which subsequently had the ministry finance a new three-year expedition to Tunisia (1822–1824) to excavate new objects at Carthage and to buy other antiquities (Halbertsma 2003: 79).[7] After that, Reuvens managed to have the state pay for Humbert being posted in Livorno, at that time one of the main centres for the trade in antiquities (Rijksmuseum van Oudheden 1981: 44). There Humbert and Reuvens bought large parts of the museum's Italian and North-African collections.

The museum was funded by the Ministry of Education, National Industry and the Colonies (by royal decree through the intervention of minister Falck), especially between 1818 and 1830 (Rijksmuseum van Oudheden 1981: 48). This 'governmental urge' depended for a large part on the interests of people like minister Falck and King Willem I, with whom Reuvens seems to have had a close relationship (Halbertsma 2003: 2).[8] After 1830, state funding diminished considerably and the

---

6   See www.knaw.nl.

7   One of Humbert's first achievements after he arrived in Tunesia was the purchase of nine Roman statues, amongst which a statue of the Roman emperor Traianus in full armour (Halbertsma 2003: 81) which can still be found in the museum today.

8   The money was not only spent on collecting antiquities from abroad, Reuvens also conducted the first excavation in the Netherlands, in 1826 in Arentsburg, to collect Provincial Roman material for the RMO.

enhancement of the collection became more and more dependent on endowments, such as from the King and Dutch consuls.

Whereas at the beginning of the nineteenth century the European archaeological museums tried to get the best collections on the Roman and Greek civilizations, followed by those of Egypt and Mesopotamia, in the second part of the century interest grew in prehistoric civilizations. That happened when the RMO also started to acquire material from the colonies, according to Reuvens' principle to collect antiquities of any extinct culture (Rijksmuseum van Oudheden 1981: 34). From Surinam, the RMO received archaeological objects since 1860 (stone axes and pottery) from C.J. Hering, a collector of botanical and zoological material and a 'self-taught' archaeologist who lived in Paramaribo (Versteeg 1998). At request of Dr Leemans, then director of the RMO, he even did some research on non-moveable objects, like the well-known petroglyphs along the Marowijne River (Versteeg 1998).[9] Hering (1899) also wrote the first paper on the antiquities of Surinam, entitled *'De Oudheden van Suriname'*.

King Willem I not only wanted classical antiquities, he also dispatched scholars to collect materials from overseas (colonial) regions. Throughout Europe such objects were increasingly exhibited in dedicated museums, so also in the Netherlands a National Ethnography Museum was founded in Leiden in 1837 (now National Museum of Ethnology, NME), when the state bought the Japanese collection of Ph.F. von Siebold. At first the museum's collection was composed of various Japanese collections, but from the second half of the nineteenth century, the collection was gradually expanded with material from Indonesia, the South Pacific, Africa, America, Tibet and Siberia.[10] In 1903, also the Indonesian and American material of the RMO was handed over to the NME, and from then on the two museums focused on different geographical regions (Rijksmuseum van Oudheden 1981: 34).

Despite the active purchasing of objects and the founding of museums, there was, however, no formal state policy on culture (Ministerie van Onderwijs, Cultuur en Wetenschap 2007; Pots 2009; Von der Dunk 2010). Unlike countries such as France, the Dutch Republic still had no strong influence on cultural life. There was even resistance to the state interference as reflected in the foundation of national museums and institutes (Pots 2009); cultural life was mostly considered as a responsibility of (rich) civilians. One of the strongest advocates of this *laissez faire* policy was the liberalist politician J.R. Thorbecke (1798–1872). In his opinion, the state was only responsible for order, compliance control and to facilitate and stimulate private initiatives.

---

9   In a report from 1883 it was mentioned that the Dutch government had assigned Hering the task of investigating the carvings on the rocks of the Maroni and Coppename Rivers and to investigate any other remains of early inhabitants of Dutch Guiana (Geijskes 1960: 70).

10   See www.rmv.nl.

It was only in 1870 that an official government policy on Art and Science was established. The driving force behind this was Victor de Stuers (1843–1916), who was the principal of the Department of Arts and Sciences of the Ministry of the Interior. In contrast to Thorbecke, De Stuers strongly believed that the government should have an interest in art and culture and has a responsibility in safeguarding museum objects and monuments (Tillema 1982). He instigated a policy on culture and cultural heritage as the lack of government steering had caused a serious neglect of the Dutch cultural heritage (Ministerie van Onderwijs, Cultuur en Wetenschap 2007). For that reason, he is considered to be the founding father of the government care for monuments in the Netherlands.

This growing awareness and government interference also seems to have had an influence on the archaeological activities abroad, although this was not the same everywhere. In the colonies in the west, the interest was mainly directed towards the ethnography of the indigenous populations.[11] In Indonesia the interest was – like in Africa (see several chapters in this volume) – first of all directed towards evolutionary archaeology, especially after Darwin published his 'On the origins of species' in 1859. This interest led in 1891 to the discovery on Java of *Pithecanthropus erectus* (now known as *Homo erectus*) by the Dutch physician Eugene Dubois (Van de Velde 2001: 932; Toebosch 2003: 86).

However, it was also here that a first concern emerged about the loss and destruction of remains of ancient civilizations. Compared to the relatively scarce remains of the Indian culture in Surinam (Versteeg 1998), there were many more monumental remains in Indonesia, like the temple complex of Borobodur. People who were sent to the colonies as deputies made attempts to record these remains. However, the time was not ripe yet for establishing a specific government organization concerned with archaeological research, for attempts to do so were not successful. Private attempts, like the founding of the Archaeological Society in Jakarta in 1885, were more successful (Soejono 2001). These organizations were mostly acting at their own responsibility and their archaeological activities were mostly not officially organized (*e.g.* Geijskes 1960: 70). Nevertheless, according to Soejono, the foundation for the development of archaeology as a discipline in Indonesia was laid by the Dutch in this period (Soejono 2001: 648), as attention was paid to documentation, restoration, excavation and interpretation.[12]

11　This is also reflected in the rapidly growing interest in photos of other cultures towards the end of the nineteenth century (Roodenburg 2002).

12　The main interest of archaeologists in Indonesia in this period concerned the classical Hindu period, with the Borobodur complex and the temple complexes at Prambanan, both on Java as the most important examples (Van de Velde 2001: 932). Interest in the Islamic past of Indonesia was minimal in this period. Already in 1778 the Batavian Society of Arts and Sciences was established, having a great impact on historical, ethnographic and archaeological research (Soejono 2001: 648). Documentation of temple complexes and archeological remains at Borobodur and Prambanan on Java in the form of drawings, photographs, inventories, restorations, observations, surveys and excavations took place.

1900-World War II: institutionalization

At first, not much changed at the start of the twentieth century. The government kept its grip on the safeguarding of the cultural heritage, while simultaneously there was still a lot of space for private initiatives. Private initiatives blossomed (Pots 2009), especially in the Dutch cities, and they had a very important role in the safeguarding of monuments.[13]

On the international level there were no real cultural relations during the first three decades of the twentieth century (Van Wijngaarden 1992: 10). Several European countries already had research institutes abroad since the late nineteenth century (see Braemer, this volume), but not the Netherlands. The first Dutch institute abroad was founded only in 1904, in Rome (Mols 1998).[14] The initial aim of this Royal Dutch Institute in Rome (*Koninklijk Nederlands Instituut*, KNIR) was to study the archives of the Vatican, which had been unlocked by the Pope in 1880, although Roman antiquity and art history were research subjects as well.

The RMO remained the main player in the Dutch archaeological arena. As of 1940 the state had housed its new *Rijksbureau voor Oudheidkundig Bodemonderzoek* at the RMO and until 1947, when the succeeding State Service for Archaeology was founded in Amersfoort, it was the central excavation and documentation centre for the Netherlands (Van Es 1972). It established a well-documented collection of antiquities that was representative of Dutch archaeology (Rijksmuseum van Oudheden 1981: 37). Also abroad, the RMO staff remained active in collecting and studying antiquities. Pieter Boeser (1858–1935) was appointed conservator for the department of Egyptology in 1892 and he was the first Egyptologist from the RMO to visit Egypt, in 1904 (Rijksmuseum van Oudheden 1981: 37). He also became the first teacher of Egyptology (in 1902) at Leiden University.

Apart from the RMO staff, Dutch archaeologists and academics that were specialized in for example classical studies, philology and theology were involved in archaeological excavations and surveys in the Mediterranean region (including Italy, Greece, Egypt, the Near East and Mesopotamia) that were carried out by other countries. One of these was Henri Frankfort (1897–1954), who had become a student of William Flinders Petrie in London and was asked by the Egypt Exploration Society to lead the excavations in Abydos (in 1925), Amarna (in 1926) and Armant (1928–1929) (Rijksmuseum van Oudheden 1998; Raven 2007).

Although these academics were not conducting excavations on behalf of the Netherlands, they sometimes did bring material to the Netherlands. For instance, Franz M.Th. de Liagre Böhl (1882–1976), who had studied theology in Groningen (and who would become professor at Leiden University and director of the

---

13 Private associations, like the Nederlandse Oudheidkundige Bond (1899), Bond Heemschut (1911), Vereniging Hendrick de Keyser (1918), Menno van Coehoorn (1932) were started by civilians who were worried about the loss of historic buildings and other monuments due to building activities and infrastructural works. To prevent their destruction, the latter two associations bought numerous old buildings, the former focused on a lobby to stimulate the development of heritage legislation. See: www.knob.nl; www.heemschut.nl; www.coehoorn.nl; www.hendrickdekeyser.nl.

14 This was an initiative of Bakhuizen of the University of Utrecht (Mols 1998).

Institute for the Near East), was involved in the German excavations of E. Sellin at Tell Balata/Sichem in Palestine in 1925–1927 (Böhl 1926; Wright 1957: 21-22; Nieuwenhuyse 2006: 20) and brought material to the RMO (Vriezen 1976). Also from Amarna lots of material was brought to the Netherlands. It was given to the banker C.W. Lunsingh Scheurleer (1881–1941), in return for his financial support of the excavations by the Egypt Exploration Society (Brijder and Jurriaans-Helle 2002).

Again in contrast to many other European countries, it took a long time before the Dutch started their own excavations abroad. The first one was carried out by university scholars. Carl Wilhelm Vollgraff (1876–1967), a philologist at the University of Utrecht and as of 1908 professor of philology at Groningen University (Kamerbeek 1968), undertook the first Dutch excavation in 1904, in Argos (Feye 1988).[15] One reason for this late development probably was that in this early period most academics active in this region were philologically trained and hardly interested in field archaeology (Van de Velde 2001: 932). Another factor might be that in our country it simply was not possible yet to be trained as field archaeologist. Archaeology was only taught as part of classical philology or classical arts. It was only in 1921 that by royal decree a university degree in (Classical) archaeology was established and could be obtained at Leiden University (Feye 1988: 4; Van de Velde 2001).[16] Likewise, it was not until 1939 that it became possible to obtain a degree in Egyptology in the Netherlands when Adriaan de Buck became professor of Egyptology at Leiden University.

Another major issue was the financing of excavations. Travelling to and working in Greece for example was expensive as there were no facilities. Vollgraff for example had no school abroad to facilitate his work, no excavation tradition, no students and no money. At first he carried out his work in Argos through his membership of the French School and his financial sources were provided by wealthy individuals (like A.E.H. Goekoop). Others however could only join foreign campaigns of other countries: professor De Waele of the University of Nijmegen directed American excavations in Greece (*e.g.* Korinthe and Olynthus), and professor Haspels from the University of Amsterdam directed (in 1934) the French excavations in Delos. Moreover, the economic crisis in the 1930s made it financially impossible to conduct excavations abroad (Feye 1988: 11).

The crisis had yet another, unexpected, effect; it led to the foundation of a second Dutch archaeological museum. When the banker Lunsingh Scheurleer suffered badly in the crisis and had to sell his antiquities collection in 1929, it was bought by the Allard Pierson Foundation in Amsterdam.[17] Together with

---

15 Vollgraff was philologist at the University of Utrecht from 1903, and from 1908 professor of philology at Groningen University.

16 Prof. dr A.W. Byvanck held the chair in Classical Archaeology and Ancient History from 1922 till 1954.

17 This foundation was named after Prof. dr Allard Pierson (1831–1896), who in 1877 became the first professor in classical art in Amsterdam. It was founded in 1926 by the University of Amsterdam to take care of the collection of antiquities and books from the legacy of Prof. dr Jan Six, the successor of Prof. dr Allard Pierson.

the antiquities collection of professor Jan Six (1857–1926), the first professor of aesthetics and art history at Amsterdam University (1896), and the collection of Egyptologist professor F.W. Freiherr von Bissing (1873–1956), it formed in 1934 the basis of the Allard Pierson Museum (Brijder and Jurriaans-Helle 2002). Since then the majority of its collection has been enriched with gifts and donations of private collections, but also with material from excavations that the University of Amsterdam conducted in the Mediterranean.

Throughout this period, the Dutch remained archaeologically active in the Caribbean region as well, where they were involved in several archaeological expeditions. In Surinam, the interior was still hardly known when in 1901 the first scientific expeditions were carried out, among others by the *Koninklijk Nederlands Aardrijkskundig Genootschap* (Royal Dutch Geographic Society, KNAG), a private organization founded in 1873 to stimulate the interest for geographical studies.[18] Such expeditions were often financed by the organization themselves, although companies sometimes supported them financially if they expected economic gain from the discoveries (like mining opportunities). Claudius Henricus de Goeje (1879–1955), who worked for the *Hydrografische Dienst* (Hydrographic Service) and who was an expert on mapping, was 'borrowed' by the KNAG to join these expeditions. Besides the known rock carvings, several archaeological features like whet grooves and ceramic remains of earlier inhabitants were discovered (Geijskes 1960: 71). In 1927 an expedition encountered the 'wild', 'Stone Age' bush Indians, who still used stone implements. De Goeje wrote ethnographic reports, translated Indian words and collected objects for the National Ethnology Museum in Leiden.[19]

Such expeditions were also conducted in the Dutch Antilles, for instance by the anthropologist and curator of the Dutch National Museum of Ethnology, J.P.B. de Josselin de Jong (Kuiper 1965: 399; Hofman 2008: 6). These too led to publications on the indigenous populations of Aruba, Curaçao en Bonaire (1918 en 1923), but also on the meaning of the archaeological research on the islands (Kuiper 1965: 399).

In Indonesia, apart from an interest in objects, there was a remarkable attention for the preservation of archaeological remains. Already in 1901, the government of the Dutch East Indies created a Colonial Archaeological Commission and between 1907 and 1911 had put much effort in the restoration of the ninth century Hindu temple at Prambanan and the eighth century Buddhist temple at Borobodur (Bloembergen and Eickhoff 2011: 411) (figure 2). The Commission was succeeded by the Colonial Archaeological Service in 1913, the official task of which was to take an inventory of the antiquities in the whole archipelago, to investigate and hold watch over them and to prevent any decay. This task was even supported by a monument act, as of 1931 (Bloembergen and Eickhoff 2011: 412),

18 The expeditions are described at http://www.knag-expedities.nl/pages/expedities.php.
19 In 1943 he described nine tribes in his 'the Neolithic Indians in Surinam'. He was appointed as professor at Leiden University in 1946 and started to teach on the language and ethnology of Surinam and Curaçao.

which is remarkable as both the service and the act are much earlier dated than the establishment of the Archaeological State Service (1947) and the first Monument Act (1961) in the Netherlands itself.[20] With the establishment of the Colonial Archaeological Service, archaeological activities became more centrally organized than before and for the first time archaeological research was being published (Soejono 2001: 649).

Despite this government interest, private initiatives remained equally important in Indonesia. Prominent individuals, like civil servants and experts from other government institutions, still provided additional funding and private institutes, like the Kern Institute (1924) in Leiden, were established.[21] This institute's goal was to collect study material such as photographs, documents (books, manuscripts, maps, letters) and casts, as the objects of archaeological investigations were lacking in the Netherlands. It collected material through donations and legacies rather than purchases, as it had limited financial means, especially during the crisis of the

Figure 2. The Borobodur on Java, photographed in 1872 before the restorations began (Photo: Tropenmuseum).

---

20 A first provisional monument act was drawn up in 1946 in the Netherlands (Van de Velde 2001: 922).

21 The Kern Institute was founded by sanskritist and archaeologist Prof. dr J.Ph. Vogel and called after Hendrik Kern, the first Professor in Sanskrit in the Netherlands as of 1865. Its aim was to study the Indian art history and archaeology at Leiden University. It has now developed into a centre of expertise for Indological studies with a unique and famous collection of over 57,000 books, photos, manuscripts and other documents. See http://www.instituutkern.nl.

1930s and World War II. Through its collections it has had a major influence on the promotion of the study of Indian archaeology.

Although archaeology had become more institutionalized and the Indonesian interest in archaeological knowledge was stimulated by the staff of the Archaeological Service, the Indonesians themselves were only trained as field technicians and assistants and they were given the least paid jobs at the Archaeological Service (Bloembergen and Eijckhoff 2011: 420-421; Soejono 1987: 213). It was only after the war of independence that Indonesians were trained as archaeologists, in an attempt to revive the Archaeological Service (Bloembergen and Eickhoff 2011: 411).

Post World War II - 1990: broadening horizons and long-term relationships

After World War II things clearly evolved in a different direction, literally. This had to do with three developments. Firstly, the relationships with the largest colonies, *i.e.* Indonesia and Surinam, changed.[22] With Indonesia the relationship had deteriorated since the war of independence and the subsequent founding of the sovereign Republic of Indonesia (1949). At first, the archaeological activities stagnated, but the technical staff at Prambanan – which consisted of Indonesians – successfully continued the work of the Archaeological Service (Soejono 1987: 213). Thus, when the Dutch returned after the war, actually two Archaeological Services existed, the Djwatan Purbakala (set up in 1946 and owned by the Indonesian Republic), and the original Dutch colonial service in Batavia (that still had a Dutch director, the archaeologist Bernet Kempers). This situation lasted until 1957, when all Dutch archaeologists were repatriated (Soejono 1987: 213; Bloembergen and Eickhoff 2011: 424).

In Surinam things developed slightly different. It first of all took much longer before the colonial ties were cut; Surinam became a sovereign state in 1975, and thereafter the scientific ties continued for quite a while. These ties had however not been as tight as with Indonesia. As of 1947, when the *Stichting Surinaams Museum* (SSM) had been founded in Paramaribo, Surinam had conducted archaeological research mostly independently – although it did not have a 'professional' archaeologist – and it continued doing so after 1975 (Bruijning, Voorhoeve and Gordijn 1977: 31). There were nonetheless contacts between the director, D.C. Geijskes, and archaeologists and other scientists in Holland. After 1975, the archaeologist of the SSM was a Dutch archaeologist, paid by Dutch development funds (Versteeg 1998). In fact the three main professional archaeologists that have been active in Surinam until today (A. Boomert, A. Versteeg and B.S. Mitrasingh) were all Dutch archaeologists. After 1981, Dutch payments from the development

---

22   South Africa was already lost to the British in 1806. The relationship with the Dutch Antilles lasted, as the islands remained part of the Dutch Kingdom until today. From the 1980s on, archaeological research in this region became firmly established as a collaboration between the Anthropological and Archaeological Institute Dutch Antilles (AAINA), the Archaeological Museum Aruba (AMA) and Leiden University (Hofman 2008: 6).

funds came to an end due to the political instability and, consequently, attention from the Netherlands for Surinamese archaeology diminished too.

Next to the changing relation with the colonies, the second development was that the attitude of the Dutch State concerning culture and cultural policy changed. Whereas in the academic world the occupation led to a post-war aversive attitude towards German scientific work (Van de Velde 2001), in the political arena almost the opposite occurred. The German example of a national cultural policy had raised sympathy for a strong government role (Pots 2009: 6). In combination with the loss of cultural identity that the nation was suffering from, all aspects of culture, art and cultural heritage gained a lot of attention (Ministerie van Onderwijs, Cultuur en Wetenschap 2007). Culture was seen as related to social welfare and in 1965 culture was moved from the Ministry of Education and Science and was combined with recreation and social welfare in a new ministry (*Ministerie van Cultuur, Recreatie en Maatschappelijk werk*, CRM) (Ministerie van Onderwijs, Cultuur en Wetenschap 2007: 35). This attention was primarily visible in the budget that was made available (Ministerie van Onderwijs, Cultuur en Wetenschap 2007: 32). As the economy was growing, more funding could be provided. Another effect was that spending was increasingly regulated by comprehensive policies. Culture had clearly become an integrated part of the welfare state.

The third development was the emergence of a strong Dutch international cultural policy. After the war there was a general European need to improve international relations. This is illustrated by the emergence of bilateral cultural agreements between countries, followed by various European cultural treaties. Also the Netherlands wanted to promote itself abroad, to improve its image and to subsequently stimulate the export of products and tourism. Culture was considered an important instrument in this (Van Wijngaarden 1992: 10). By means of cultural agreements, cultural exchange was stimulated, including international academic relations. This policy focused on establishing liaisons within Europe, at first with the countries from the west, and from the 1960s also with the nations at the eastern side of the 'iron curtain'. International cultural relations became increasingly important, also in politics, and led to more financial facilities.

These three developments are also reflected in the archaeological activities that the Dutch conducted abroad. Archaeological activities in the colonial regions diminished and the Mediterranean (Italy, Greece, Turkey, Egypt, Syria) became the principal region for archaeological research, where predominantly surveys and architectural studies were carried out, and to a lesser extent excavations (Feye 1988; Van Wijngaarden 1992; Nieuwenhuyse 2006; Moorman 2008).[23] Moreover, the academic interest was broadened to countries in Eastern Europe and Africa. One example is the excavation of the settlement of Djadovo in Bulgaria, where

---

23 For instance Prof. dr S.C. Bakhuizen of the University of Utrecht did fieldwork in the 1970s in Greece (Goritsa), where they surveyed and mapped rural Greek settlements of the Classical and the Hellenistic periods (Feye 1988); Prof. dr de Waele of Nijmegen University and Prof. dr Maaskant-Kleibrink of Groningen University were active in Satricum, Italy (Van Dijk, Hijmans and Seiverling 1988). Overviews of archaeological projects running in the Mediterranean until the 1990s are given by Feye 1988, Van Dijk, Hijmans and Seiverling 1988, and Van Wijngaarden 1992.

from 1962 tot 1991 the University of Amsterdam worked with the Bulgarians (Fol *et al.* 1989). The projects that the University of Utrecht started in the late 1960s in Mali and Cameroon constitute another example. Originally they were carried out in the context of a long-term biological research on human adaption to the environment of the Sahel, but they soon included archaeological research as well (Bedaux *et al.* 1978; Bedaux 1981).

As a result of the increased academic activity in the Mediterranean and the Near East, and the increasing influence of the Dutch state on cultural affairs, scientific institutions abroad were founded to facilitate scientific projects in the countries. Institutions that specifically were involved in archaeology are the institutes in Rome, Cairo, Istanbul and Athens (Holleman 1996: 144; Mols 1998; Van Haarlem 1999).[24] These institutions, which were managed by the universities, acted as foreign embassies for these universities and they had a logistic and supportive task for archaeological research, such as in helping archaeologists to apply for permits (except in Greece).[25] Additional tasks for example concerned teaching and supplying accommodation for students and researchers.

Compared with other European countries, the Netherlands were very late in establishing institutes abroad (see the other chapters in this volume). Apart from the institute in Rome (KNIR) that dates to 1904, the institute in Istanbul (NHAI) was established only in 1953, those in Cairo (NVIC), Athens (NIA)[26] and Damascus (NIASD) in 1971, 1982 and 1997 respectively. The institutes were directed by the universities directly, not by the ministry. Some received financial support by the umbrella organization of the institutes, the Dutch Academic Institutes Abroad (*Nederlandse Wetenschappelijke Instituten in het Buitenland*, NWIB). The NWIB was (and still is) directed by a council of deans of those Dutch universities that

---

24 There are several Dutch institutions abroad with a focus on culture and science. Five of them support archaeological activities abroad. These are the Royal Netherlands Institute in Rome (KNIR, http://www.nir-roma.it/nl/het-instituut-mainmenu-8.html), The Netherlands Institute in Athens (NIA, http://www.nia.gr/basicpagenederlands.htm), the Netherlands Historical Archaeological Institute in Istanbul (NHAI, http://www.nit-istanbul.org/index.htm), The Dutch Flemish Institute in Cairo (NIVC, http://www.institutes.leiden.edu/nvic/about/general-nvic.html) and the Netherlands Institute for Academic Studies in Damascus (NIASD, http://www.niasd.org/). Of these, the institutes in Rome, Athens and Cairo come under the umbrella of the Nederlandse Wetenschappelijke Instituten in het Buitenland (NWIB, http://www.nwib.nl/index.html).

With regard to the Caribbean the National Anthropological Memory Management (NAAM) should be mentioned, though this actually is not a Dutch institution. Since 1998 it is the successor to the Archaeological Anthropological Institute for the Dutch Caribbean (AAINA; Archaeologisch Antropologisch Instituut Nederlandse Antillen which had been established by the government in the late 1970s (Witteveen and Francisco 2009, 13).

25 In Greece there were only permits for surveys, not for excavations. Greek law restricted excavation-rights to those foreign countries that have a fully-fledged archaeological institute in Greece (see Theodoroudi and Kotzakis, this volume).

26 Already in the 1960s, the University of Utrecht (Prof. dr J.H. Jongkees and others) wanted to start a Dutch archaeological and historical institute in the Peloponnese, but could not proceed with it due to the Greek political situation. Instead, the Archaeological Survey School of Holland was founded, in 1976. It was succeeded by the Archaeological School of the Netherlands at Athens in 1982, which was recognized by the Greek government in 1984. From then on the institute could take the responsibility for archaeological fieldwork (Feye 1988).

were involved in projects abroad.[27] This was the case for the institutes in Rome, Athens, Cairo, Damascus, Florence, Tokyo and St. Petersburg. In the case of the NIA, The Dutch Ministry of Education and Science was willing to provide temporary financial assistance, but the long-term funding had to come from the Dutch universities themselves.

Usually, the institutions financed their own expeditions, but in many cases this was not sufficient and additional external funds were needed. Often these funds were provided by the Dutch Organization for Scientific Research (NWO), the organization in charge of granting subsidies for academic research.[28] Sponsoring by private organizations/or individuals was not common, not for archaeological projects abroad nor within the Netherlands. Funding from European sources was not yet common either, an exception being the support for student exchanges through the ERASMUS programme (Van Wijngaarden 1992).[29]

Next to the universities and the institutes abroad, the National Museum of Antiquities kept an important position in the international archaeological arena, although it conducted its first own excavation only in 1957, at the cemetery of Abu Roash (figure 3) in Egypt (Raven 2007). Adolf Klasens, then curator and later director (1959–1979) of the RMO, unearthed 380 graves there from the period of the earliest pharaohs (ca. 3000–2700 BC) to study the burial ritual and grave architecture. The largest part of the artefacts (almost 1200 objects) was given to the RMO, perhaps because the investigation had been financed by NWO.

The RMO also joined the Nubian salvage campaign (Klasens 1962; Raven 2007) – the international campaign initiated by UNESCO in the 1960s to save some of the sites that would be drowned by the building of the Aswan dam (see also A. Klimowicz and P. Klimowicz, this volume). Klasens directed rescue excavations near the temples of Abu Simbel and to thank the Dutch, the Egyptian government donated the Isis-temple from Taffeh. This temple was rebuilt in 1979 in the main hall of the RMO and has become one of the museum's top attractions.

In 1975 the archaeological activities of the RMO moved to Saqqara, to the necropolis of the ancient Egyptian capital of Memphis, where excavations would be undertaken for the next three and a half decades.[30] Also the Allard Pierson Museum became active in Egypt in this period. From 1986 onwards it conducted excavations of the early dynastic and Middle Kingdom site at Tell Ibrahim Awad (Nieuwenhuyse 2006).[31]

Most of the projects abroad lasted very long, some even decades, like those at Saqqara (Egypt), Tell Sabi Abyad (Syria), Tell Deir Alla (Jordan), Satricum (Italy) and Halos (Greece) (e.g. Feye 1988; Van der Kooij and Ibrahim 1989; Nieuwenhuyse

27 The University of Amsterdam, University Utrecht, Leiden University, Groningen State University, the Free University of Amsterdam and the Radboud University Nijmegen, see http://www.ru.nl/nwib.
28 See www.nwo.nl.
29 In the inventory of projects by Van Wijngaarden (1992) only two out of the 41 projects seem to have received funding from European programmes (e.g. the ERASMUS programme for student exchange).
30 See www.saqqara.nl.
31 See also http://www.institutes.leiden.edu/nvic/research/researcharcheo-nvic.tml#tell-ibrahim-awad.

Figure 3. The first excavation of the RMO in 1957 at Abu Roash, a small village just north of the pyramids of Gizeh (Photo: RMO).

2006; Raven 2007; Moorman 2008; Sa'd Abujaber 2009).[32] This tradition of long running projects had already started with Vollgraff, who excavated in Argos between 1903 and 1930 (Feye 1988: 7). These projects were mostly drawing upon the personal relations between foreign and local archaeologists, illustrated by the fact that many projects moved along with their directors to other institutions.[33]

---

32 Some long-running projects were started in this period, like the Deir Alla excavation by Leiden University since 1959, led by H.J. Franken and taken over by G. van der Kooij. In 1964 a field survey in the Assad Region in Syria was carried out by M. van Loon, leading, amongst others, to the excavations at Tell Bouqras, Tell Hammam et-Turkman and Tell Sabi Abyad (Nieuwenhuyse 2006). This also accounts for the excavation at Satricum in Italy, which was set up by the Netherlands Institute in Rome (NIR) in 1977, and taken over by the National Museum of Antiquities in 1985 and continued by the University of Amsterdam in 1991.

33 The excavation at Tell Sabi Abyad in Syria is good example, which was initially set up by The University of Amsterdam in 1986 but was taken over by the National Museum of Antiquities in 1991 as professor Van Loon moved to the RMO at that time.

This 'loyalty' to a region has always been highly valued and considered of major importance for research (Koninklijke Nederlandse Akademie van Wetenschappen 2007: 34). The interaction with traditions from the host countries resulted in innovations in theoretical approaches and excavation techniques and the projects abroad were even referred to as 'scientific laboratories'.[34]

Another characteristic of the work abroad was a general lack of collaboration, both between Dutch parties on projects abroad – despite the fact that excavation locations were often in the same areas – and with other institutions in the host countries (Van Wijngaarden 1992: 24). Although the host countries increasingly had archaeological services at their disposal themselves and awareness was growing that local relations and collaboration were important, the focus of the relationship was often simply to obtain permission to do research. Moreover, the Dutch institutes worked primarily with and for Dutch scientists and not with local communities. Nor did many archaeologists themselves have much contact with the local population. Illustrative of the relation with the local communities is a remark by professor Marianne Maaskant-Kleibrink of Groningen University, who noted at the end of the 1980s in a critical analysis of the academic archaeological world: "Who wants to affront snakes and scorpions or worse, the local population, that preferably see you leave. In their view we only want to take their ancestors' gold." (Maaskant-Kleibrink 1988: 14, translation by the authors). She also immediately acknowledged that the poor relationship with local people was due to the archaeologists themselves, as they failed to reach out to the public, the media and the press.

Towards the end of this period, during the late 1980s especially, in the Netherlands the government role began to change again. Due to an economic decline, expenses were seriously cut[35] and the firm role of the state, the welfare state with its strong tradition of subsidizing culture was increasingly questioned again. Funding opportunities diminished and – also in relation to culture – the alternative of decentralization and privatization of archaeological work was slowly gaining ground (Ministerie van Onderwijs, Cultuur en Wetenschap 2007: 13). The government had the intention to diminish the influence of the state on cultural affairs. As of 1987, cultural policy was no longer directed on an annual basis but defined for four years through a culture policy (*Cultuurnota*) and on the basis of advice by experts joined in advisory boards (Ministerie van Onderwijs, Cultuur en Wetenschap 2007: 45).

Moreover, the main aim of the internal cultural policy was to enlarge public support for culture and participation by young people, woman and minority groups (Ministerie van Welzijn, Volksgezondheid en Cultuur 1993). The then responsible Ministry of Wellbeing, Health and Culture (which was created in 1982) was mostly involved with national cultural policy and Dutch archaeological

---

34 For developments in the content of the work see among others Van de Velde 2001; Nieuwenhuyse 2006; Moorman 2008; Versluys 2008, 2011.

35 The goverment share in the total budget for culture diminished from 42 percent to 29 percent between 1981 and 1991 (Ministerie van Welzijn, Volksgezondheid en Cultuur 1993).

heritage, not with archaeology abroad (Van Wijngaarden 1992); the universities were rather autonomous in that area. Since the 1940s, international cultural policy was predominantly part of the ministry of foreign affairs and until late in the 1990s there was hardly any cooperation on this domain between the ministries (SICA 1999).

1990–Today: globalization and the return of private initiatives

An inventory by Van Wijngaarden in 1992 showed that at the start of the 1990s around 40 archaeological projects were being carried out in the Mediterranean region: in Italy (17 projects), Greece (7 projects), Jordan, Syria, Turkey (together 12 projects) and Egypt (3 projects) (Van Wijngaarden (1992: 22). In other parts of the world, like Asia, Africa and the Caribbean some projects were set up as well, but they were not abundant and they have not been systematically recorded.

In terms of research focus, things were changing quite drastically. Whereas from the nineteenth century onwards, Dutch archaeologists working abroad mainly had a classical background and were trained in classical philology (Van de Velde 2001: 923), a shift had occurred during the last fifty years from a rather cordial relationship between art history and classical archaeology to an almost ideological dichotomy (Versluys 2011: 688). Art history was almost suspect, presumably as a result of post-colonial thinking (Versluys 2011: 691). Consequently, from around 1995 it was preferred to call the research domain 'Mediterranean archaeology' instead of 'classical archaeology', to avoid an association with art history (Moorman 2008: 52; Versluys 2011: 690). The new term also expressed the focus that Mediterranean archaeologists have on landscape or rural archaeology (Moorman 2008: 49; Versluys 2008).

With regard to the research institutes abroad, the effects of the financial cutback of the 1980s became clearly visible. The archaeological departments of the universities were expected to finance the institutes themselves, but this was difficult to organize due to severe cost-cutting exercises at the universities too. Especially the archaeological school in Athens had a difficult time when the minister stopped funding it in 1991. Having an expensive institute just for archaeological work could no longer be afforded, so the archaeological school was changed into The Netherlands Institute at Athens (NIA) and it broadened its focus to all Greece-oriented studies. Consequently, six universities participate at present. Also the NVIC in Cairo had difficulties and as of 1988 it was jointly financed by Dutch and Flemish governments (Van Haarlem 1999).

In general, it was increasingly necessary to find additional funding for research from other sources. Due to the dispersive character of Dutch international cultural policy, it could sometimes be obtained from other departments than the Ministry of Education, Culture and Science. The Ministry of Foreign affairs for instance subsidized projects in Mali from 1996 until 2005 that aimed to preserve the cultural heritage of the Dogon (Bedaux 2007), and the Ministry of Development Cooperation funded projects like the excavation of Tell el-Ibrahim Awad in the

Nile Delta in Egypt (Van Wijngaarden 1992: 22). Sometimes it was possible to generate new sources through creative and innovative initiatives. An interesting example in this regard is the research (from 1991 until 2003) by archaeologists of the University of Amsterdam (*Instituut voor Prae- en Protohistorie*) on the Russian island of *Nova Zembla* (Novaya Zemlya), where they wanted to find remains of the ship of Willem Barentsz with which he got stuck in the ice in 1596 and of the Barentsz house which his crew built with the remains of that ship in an attempt to survive the arctic winter (Zeeberg, Floore and Gerritsen 1996). The Dutch archaeologists not only collaborated with Russian researchers who paid their own share, but they also got financial support from various commercial companies, such as a newspaper publishing house. In return for this support, a journalist of the publishing house joined the expeditions and was allowed to report on the expedition (Blankesteijn and Hacquebord 1992).

Other examples are the excavations at Berenike (Egypt) and tell Sabi Abyad (Syria). The main sources of funding of the first were NWO and the Dutch Ministry of Foreign Affairs, but substantial additional funding was provided for many years (1994–2000) by the National Geographic Society and some other private foundations.[36] For Sabi Abyad funding was even obtained from a large multinational oil company.[37]

Apart from the changes in funding, some other fundamental changes took place in Dutch cultural policy. Firstly, the influence of the collective European policy on culture was clearly emerging, through the work of primarily UNESCO, ICOMOS and the Council of Europe, with the signing of the Council of Europe's European Convention on the Protection of the Archaeological Heritage in Valletta in 1992 as one of the most prominent and influential events. Secondly, in national politics the final signal was given that culture was no longer considered to be part of the welfare policy by removing cultural affairs from the Ministry for Welfare, Health and Culture in 1994 and joining it with education and science in the Ministry of Education, Culture and Science (Ministerie van Onderwijs, Cultuur en Wetenschap 2007). Most of the government attention of this new ministry was drawn to internal cultural issues, such as developing a more planned and effective heritage management, which – after the signing of the Valletta Convention – became increasingly important.

With the signing and subsequent ratification (1998) of this convention, the state dominance of internal cultural policy shrank even further. In the Netherlands developer-funded archaeology became leading and the authority was handed over to the municipalities (see *e.g.* Van den Dries and Willems 2007). Moreover, it was decided in 2007 that instead of deciding on financing small organizations and small proposals, the ministry would only decide on the scope of the general, basic infrastructure; the allocation of financial means to cultural projects was handed over to 'funds' such as the one for cultural participation (Ministerie van Onderwijs, Cultuur en Wetenschap 2007: 47).

---

36   See http://www.archbase.com/berenike/neder1.html.
37   See http://www.sabi-abyad.nl.

According to the Royal Dutch Academy of Arts and Sciences (*Koninklijke Nederlandse Akademie van Wetenschappen*, KNAW) the implementation of the Malta Convention in the national policy has had the effect that the attention of government funding programmes, of talented researchers and students for 'Malta-archaeology' has grown, and that archaeologists working in non-European regions sometimes have felt neglected (Koninklijke Nederlandse Akademie van Wetenschappen 2007: 53). It was feared that this would marginalize the other fields of research, *i.e.* the archaeology conducted abroad. The long-lasting projects that were started after World War II – the so-called 'scientific laboratories' – were confronted with increasing research costs and demands in the host countries while development-led funding was lacking, and in some cases archaeologists were expected to pay for research themselves (Koninklijke Nederlandse Akademie van Wetenschappen 2007: 68).

Interestingly, however, the introduction of commercial archaeology also brought along a new phenomenon in the archaeology conducted abroad – although on a limited scale, *i.e.* that of archaeological contracting. An illustration of this are the projects carried out during the 1990s by RAAP. This Dutch foundation was invited by other countries to carry out surveys, geophysical research and excavations on a commercial basis. It was active in Germany (Andrikopoulou-Strack and Bloemers 2005), France, Portugal and Cambodia (Orbons 2005).

Despite the tendency to withdraw, OCW did continue to have a strong influence on the archaeological activities abroad. In the first *Cultuurnota* (1997–2000) of the Secretary of State Aad Nuis, the policy focused on priority countries, such as to bordering countries (Flanders and North Rhine-Westphalia), young democracies (Middle and Eastern Europe), countries from where minorities migrated (Morocco, Turkey) and – interestingly – countries the Netherlands had historical ties with (*e.g.* Surinam, Dutch Antilles, Indonesia, South Africa).[38] This policy was further strengthened when as of 1997 the Ministry of Foreign Affairs tuned its foreign cultural policy in with that of the Ministry of Culture. The Homogenous Group for International Cooperation (HGIS) was launched and an annual sum of 16 million guilders (1997–2003) was reserved for international cultural policy, the so-called HGIS-cultural resources. These financial resources were used for projects that suited the priorities as defined by the cultural policy of the Ministry of Education, Culture and Science, so for priority countries and on 'shared cultural heritage'.

Since then the concept of 'mutual heritage' has been a focal point of Dutch international cultural policy. Even the Royal Dutch Academy of Arts and Sciences stated in its foresight study of 2007 that the archaeology of the Dutch expansion was an essential element of all Dutch archaeological research groups (Koninklijke Nederlandse Akademie van Wetenschappen 2007: 80). The common cultural

---

38 The concept of 'mutual heritage' seems already to have been used in relation to the colonial heritage in Indonesia since 1988 (Van Roosmalen 2003, note 1).

heritage policy[39] was extended and even further elaborated by the 2009–2012 policy guideline 'Arts without Borders' (Ministerie van Onderwijs, Cultuur en Wetenschap 2009), which enlarged the number of countries designated to have common cultural heritage to eight: Brazil, Ghana, India, Indonesia, Sri Lanka, Russia, Surinam and South Africa (figure 4). It furthermore aimed to connect the international culture policy with the culture and development cooperation policy. From the 1980s there had been a growing interest in the cultural dimension of development aid and it was now considered important to structurally support cultural life in developing countries and to pay attention to the cultural roots of their citizens through the cultural policy as well (Ministerie van Onderwijs, Cultuur en Wetenschap 2009: 7).

Especially the common cultural heritage policy has had a marked effect. There has been a considerable increase in research and heritage management interest in the remains of former activities abroad, such as trading posts, whaling stations, forts, lost VOC vessels, etc. and various projects searching relics of Dutch presence in the former VOC and WIC activity areas were undertaken.[40] For instance in 1997 archaeologists of the University of Amsterdam explored the peninsula of Araya and in 1999 La Tortuga (both Venezuela) for seventeenth century relics of the Dutch WIC exploitation of the region for salt production (Van Beek 2002). Another example is the research just outside of the Galle harbour, Sri Lanka, where Dutch archaeologists (of the University of Amsterdam and the State Agency for Cultural Heritage) have been working on an inventory of the ship wreck sites and then on the excavation of the *Avondster* (see Parthesius and Jeffery, this volume). It was financially supported through the HGIS culture fund (Parthesius 2002). The latter example illustrates another recent development, *i.e.* that it has renewed the opportunity for private initiatives and foundations to have a role again in heritage management activities abroad; increasingly, all kinds of NGOs are becoming involved in these activities.[41]

---

39   The definition that the policy framework uses is: ".. relics of a past that the Netherlands has shared with others: buildings and engineering constructions, archives, underwater wrecks and museum exhibits, and intangible heritage. They include heritage in other countries dating from the era of the Dutch East and West India Companies and from Dutch colonialism in Asia, Africa, and South America, as well as heritage deriving from a period of intensive cultural relations such as between the Netherlands and Russia. The term may also include artefacts (including archives) commissioned in other countries and built or supplied by Dutch people. Finally, it includes heritage in the Netherlands of other countries which have had a particularly strong (reciprocal) influence on Dutch culture." (http://en.nationaalarchief.nl/sites/default/files/docs/common_ cultural_heritage_policy_framework.pdf).

40   Illustrative of all this interest is the production of the Atlas of Mutual heritage (in 2001), a digital catalogue of original seventeenth and eighteenth century pictures and data of the VOC- and WIC-places abroad (Gosselink 2002: 110), and a digital guide of published and unpublished Dutch sources for studying the history of the interaction with the Atlantic world. For the atlas see www.atlasmutualheritage.nl; for the guide see http://awad.kitlv.nl/Introduction.

41   Apart from the Centre for International Heritage Activities (CIE), various private initiatives have emerged, like the New Holland foundation for mutual heritage (www.newhollandfoundation.nl), the *Commissie Overzeese Vestingwerken* (COV) of the Menno van Coehoorn foundation, the research on the VOC ship De Gouden Buys (www.degoudenbuys.nl), etc.

Figure 4. Fort Orange, Itamaracá Island, Brazil, a mutually accepted example of common heritage (Photo: LeRoc via Wikimedia Commons).

The decentralized approach to culture also affected the RMO: in 1995 it had to be privatized. Nevertheless, the museum continued excavating abroad; until 1998 it worked in Sakkara together with the Egypt Exploration Society of London, and from 1999 the project became a joint venture with Leiden University. It is now financed by the two partners and by additional funding from various parties, such as NWO, the Dutch Embassy in Cairo, cultural foundations and private persons. The project is still running today and if the political situation allows it excavations are continued, although unlike in the old days the finds rightly stay in Egypt now.

Next to the decentralization and the renewed interest in the former colonies, there is yet another intriguing development in cultural policy in the Netherlands. We witness an increased interest of politicians in national identity and national heritage, both on the liberal and the socialist wings, and there is a growing political influence on culture, despite the fact that funding is diminishing and private responsibilities are further emphasized. This interest and influence is reflected in political involvement in plans to build a museum of national history, in the development of a historical canon of the Netherlands,[42] the foundation of a fund for folk culture, and so forth.[43]

---

42   Http://entoen.nu.

43   The contemporary relation between politics and heritage is nicely discussed in Erfgoed Nederland 2010.

At present: culture and development

Despite the fear of the KNAW for the neglect of foreign archaeology, annually around 30 research projects are still being carried out abroad – mainly by universities and private organizations, and to a lesser extent by the State Agency and the two national archaeological museums. These archaeological activities are still conducted in the Mediterranean region (Italy, Greece, Turkey, Jordan, Palestine, Egypt, Syria),[44] but the share of projects in this region seems to be decreasing: in 2009, 20 projects were counted, while Van Wijngaarden documented 40 projects in 1992. The share of other regions is however increasing: in 2009 we counted 32 projects in other parts of the world,[45] whereas there were only a few in 1992. There is also a remarkable change in the funding. In 1992, Van Wijngaarden noticed that half of the projects in the Mediterranean region were financed by the universities, that 17 were (co-)funded by NWO, but that hardly any EU-money was involved. In 2009, 17 out of a total of 52 projects were exclusively (or primarily) funded by NWO and only 2 by the universities. Another 9 were privately funded, 8 were supported by a Dutch government department, and 14 by the EU. Also many projects are nowadays co-funded by local universities or other local government and non-government organizations.

It seems that Dutch archaeologists are pragmatic. They tend to adapt to the changing circumstances and try to find other funds to carry out their research. Bluntly put, they follow the money. They also seem to be pragmatic in realizing their goals; they adjust their project policies, discourses and aims to the new conditions and demands of the funding organizations (cf. Van der Linde 2012). Especially funds for development seem to emerge as a new financing source.

Moreover, we believe that the fears expressed in the KNAW report are rather self-centred, focusing on the Dutch perspective, on the possible loss of its 'scientific laboratory'. The need of having to find financial funds elsewhere may however have positive effects for the countries in which the research is carried out. Especially the funding through the HGIS culture fund and special development programs stimulate for instance that local capacity building and community involvement increases, as examples from Sri Lanka, Tanzania (Parthesius and Jeffery, this volume), Mali (Bedaux 2007)[46] and Palestine (Van den Dries and Van der Linde 2012)[47] show.

---

44 This is based on an inventory that was taken at the start of 2009, before the 'Arab spring' changed the situation drastically.

45 Including the Caribbean, Latin America, the Baltic States, Eastern Europe, the Polar region, Asia, etc.

46 Mali: the Ministry of Foreign affairs provided funding for restoration works of houses in Djenné, the excavation of the threatened site of Dia; help building knowledge and expertise on museum curation and display; to raise awareness of the community on cultural values and to prevent illegal disappearance of Dogon artefacts to foreign countries (Bedaux 2007). Context is UNESCO world heritage-list. Cultural preservation was considered development aid. Safeguard remains that play a role in building identities. In cooperation with the National Museum for Ethnography.

47 This is also an example of a project that is funded by the Dutch Ministry of Foreign Affairs, through the Dutch representative in Ramallah. See also www.tellbalata.com.

Figure 5. A Dutch and a Jordanese student working together on Tell Hammeh in Jordan, 2009 (Photo: Xander Veldhuijzen).

This change in funding coincides with the rise of postmodernism and post-processualism in Dutch social sciences and archaeology. A gradual, though often still theoretical, shift can be seen from research carried out of purely scientific interest, to a sharing of knowledge and collaboration on a more equal basis with local archaeologists, to projects that advocate purely ethnographic and indigenous archaeologies. The approach to local communities is as such simultaneously changing as well, as the values of local stakeholders towards research, heritage and collaboration are increasingly being recognized as rightful perspectives too. This is also reflected by the emerging attention for the local population by the institutes abroad.[48]

Although there is an increasing awareness that a good relationship with local people and stakeholders is important, this still deserves much more attention. Apart from being based on good intentions, collaborative approaches are sometimes also simply a reaction to a dependency on local authorities for being able to realize research goals, for instance to acquire an excavation permit. Moreover, there is still a lot of self-interest involved; the aims are far from altruistic, as the government policy to stimulate the preservation of especially the remains of the colonial era

---

48   Gert-Jan Burgers of the KNIR for instance showed in a presentation at Leiden University that there is attention for local communities in Rome. He experienced however a struggle to balance these activities with the scientific work (Mulder, De Campenhout and Sesmilo 2011).

illustrates.[49] Consequently, the activities are not always appreciated by stakeholders in the other countries involved.[50] Considering the past, this is understandable and it illustrates the different values that the various stakeholders may hold and how easily these differences can be overlooked. Archaeological research projects abroad could therefore benefit from an integration with value-based heritage approaches as well with continuous ethnographic reflection (Van der Linde 2012).

It must also be noted that where relations are good, these are often of a personal character and not very sustainable. When the involved researcher stops the work or changes jobs and moves to another institution, the research also ends or – at best – moves along to another institution. Another difficulty is the fact that contemporary funding generally lasts a few years at most, while it is essential for heritage management solutions and capacity building programmes to have long-lasting relationships in order to be effective and sustainable. These matters illustrate that the current funding and institutional frameworks of Dutch archaeology should better allow for the implementation, resourcing and evaluation of long-term research collaborations in which heritage and collaboration issues are seen as a fundamental part of archaeological conduct, and not as a well-intended afterthought (Van der Linde 2012).

We can nevertheless conclude that in Dutch archaeological projects abroad, local involvement is growing. Site management, the concern for archaeological remains and the acknowledgement of subaltern values towards heritage is generally growing, and project policies and archaeologists are increasingly aiming at a more equal and ethical collaboration between foreign scientists and local people (figure 5). The countries involved are swiftly developing their own heritage methods, values, approaches and capacity as well. It is our belief that these developments together may ultimately contribute to archaeological research practices that add value to all parties involved.

Acknowledgements

We want to thank Lizzy Polman en Alexandra van Dijk for their assistance with the ACE questionnaire and the compilation of the bibliography in the early stages of our research. We also want to thank our colleagues at Leiden University and the other Dutch universities, as well as all other people who took the time to

---

49 Intriguing in this respect is that the cultural policy framework for 2013-2016 cuts heavily in cultural funding (200 m€), but keeps the common heritage policy as a priority (Ministerie van Onderwijs, Cultuur en Wetenschap 2012). Recently, the three main heritage institutes involved in carrying out this policy proudly presented the highlights of our shared past "to inform as many people as possible" (National Archives of the Netherlands, Netherlands Institute for Cultural Heritage and Netherlands Cultural Heritage Agency 2010: 4), without a critical reflection on the pros and cons of this approach.

50 This was the case with the celebration of the 400th birthday of the VOC in Indonesia. Indonesia considered this a fact to be commemorated instead of being celebrated (Fienieg *et al.* 2008: 23). A project in which the mutual heritage approach did work is Fort Orange in Brazil. Here both countries considered this shared heritage. See MOWIC foundation. 2000. 'Fort Orange Project'. Retrieved 11 November 2010 from http://mowic.nl/Afgraving.htm. See also Hefting 2005.

answer our questions and who provided us with useful information and comments. Furthermore, we thank the Rijksmuseum van Oudheden, Teylersmuseum, the Tropenmuseum and Xander Veldhuijzen for letting us use their photos. We are grateful to Laurens Jansen and Salam-al-Waked for their permission to use the photo of the latter. Finally, we thank the Koninklijke Nederlandse Akademie van Wetenschappen (KNAW) for making it possible to have an academy research assistant (Corijanne Slappendel) on this project.

References

Andrikopoulou-Strack, J.-N. and J.H.F. Bloemers. 2005. 'LAND & RAAP: met Malta voor de muziek uit in Duitsland', in M.H. van den Dries and W.J.H. Willems (eds.), *Innovatie in de Nederlandse Archeologie. Liber Amicorum voor Roel W. Brandt*. Gouda: SIKB, 23-35.

Bedaux, R.M.A. 1981. 'La Contribution Hollandaise a la Recherche Archéologique en Afrique sub-Saharienne', in Agence de Coopération Culturelle et Technique, *Etudes Africaines en Europe Bilan et Inventaire* 1. Paris: Agence de Coopération Culturelle et Technique and Éditions Karthala.

Bedaux, R.M.A. 2007. 'Cultureel Erfgoed' in Mali, in H. Pennock, J. Leistra, T. de Boer and M. van Heese (eds), *Erfgoedverhalen voor Charlotte van Rappard-Boon*. The Hague: Erfgoedinspectie.

Bedaux, R.M.A., T.S. Constandse-Westermann, L. Hacquebord, A.G. Lange and J.D. van der Waals. 1978. 'Recherches Archéologiques dans le Delta Intérieur du Niger', *Palaeohistoria* 20: 92-220.

Blankesteijn, H. and L. Hacquebord. 1992. *Op Zoek naar het Behouden Huys. Een Expeditie naar Nova Zembla in het Kielzog van Willem Barentsz*. The Hague: Uitgeverij BZZTOH.

Bloembergen, M. and M. Eickhoff. 2011. 'Conserving the Past, Mobilizing the Indonesian Future: Archaeological Sites, Regime Change and Heritage Politics in Indonesia in the 1950s', *Bijdragen tot de Taal-, Land-en Volkenkunde* 167: 405-436.

Böhl, F.M.T. 1926. 'De Geschiedenis der Stad Sichem en de Opgravingen Aldaar', *Mededeelingen der Koninklijke Akademie van Wetenschappen, Afdeeling Letterkunde: Geschiedenis, Volkenkunde, Rechtswetenschap* 62: 24.

Bruijning, C.F.A., J. Voorhoeve and W. Gordijn. 1977. *Encyclopedie van Suriname*. Amsterdam: Elsevier.

Brijder, H. and G. Jurriaans-Helle (eds). 2002. *A Guide to the Collections of the Allard Pierson Museum*. Amsterdam: Allard Pierson Museum.

Council of Europe. 1992. *European Convention on the Protection of the Archaeological Heritage (Revised), Valetta, 16 January 1992*. Council of Europe Treaties 143. Retrieved 27 April 2011 from http://conventions.coe.int/Treaty/en/Treaties/Html/143.htm.

Erfgoed Nederland. 2010. *Neerlands Hoop, Erfgoed en Politiek*. Erfgoed NU series. Amsterdam: Erfgoed Nederland.

Fienieg, A., R. Parthesius, B. Groot, R. Jaffe, S. van der Linde and P. Roosmalen. 2008. 'Heritage Trails: International Cultural Heritage Policies in a European Perspective', in G. Oostindië (ed.), *Dutch Colonialism, Migration and Cultural Heritage*. Leiden: KITLV Press, Koninklijk Instituut voor Taal-, Land- en Volkenkunde, 23-69.

Feye, K. 1988. 'Nederlands Archeologisch Onderzoek in Griekenland', *Tijdschrift voor Mediterrane Archeologie* 1(1), 4-12.

Fol, A., R. Kantincarov, J. Best, N. de Vries, K. Shoju and H. Suzuki (eds). 1989. *Djadovo: Bulgarian, Dutch, Japanese Expedition, Vol. 1, Mediaeval Settlement and Necropolis (11th-12th Century)*. Tokai: Tokai University Press.

Geijskes, D.C. 1960. 'History of Archaeological Investigations in Surinam', *Berichten van de Rijksdienst voor het Oudheidkundig Bodemonderzoek* 10: 70-77.

Gosselink, M. 2002. 'De Atlas of Mutual Heritage. Overzees Erfgoed Digitaal', in M.H. Bartels, E.H.P. Cordfunke and H. Sarfatij, *Hollanders Uit en Thuis*. Hilversum: Uitgeverij Verloren, 105-110.

Halbertsma, R. 2003. *Scholars, Travellers, and Trade: the Pioneer Years of the National Museum of Antiquities in Leiden, 1818-1840*. London and New York: Routledge.

Hefting, O.F. 2005. 'Towards restoration of Fort Orange. Research of Fort Orange in Brasil', in L.G.W. Verhoef and R. van Oers (eds), *Dutch Involvement in the Conservation of Cultural Heritage Overseas*. Delft: IOS Press/Delft University Press, 157-170. Retrieved 19 November 2012 from http://www.newhollandfoundation.nl/teksten/Fort_Orange-Hefting.pdf.

Hering, C.J. 1899. *De Oudheden van Suriname - Catalogus Nederlandsche West-Indische Tentoonstelling*. Haarlem: Koloniaal Museum, 54-58.

Hingley, R. 2005. *Globalizing Roman Culture: Unity, Diversity and Empire*. Oxon: Routledge.

Hofman, C. 2008. *'Indianenverhalen', Het kwetsbare Verleden van de Antillen*. Leiden: Leiden University. Retrieved 8 December 2011 from www.leidenuniv.nl/tekstboekjes/content_docs/ oratie_hofman.pdf.

Holleman, T. 1996. *In de Schaduw van het Parthenon. Archeologisch Nederland. Jaarboek 1995*. Den Haag: SDU Uitgevers.

Kamerbeek, J.C. 1968. 'Levensbericht C.W. Vollgraff', in *KNAW Jaarboek 1967-1968*. Amsterdam: Koninklijke Nederlandse Akademie van Wetenschappen, 346-354.

Klasens, A. 1962. *The Excavations of the Leiden Museum of Antiquities at Abu-Roash*. Leiden: Rijksmuseum van Oudheden.

Koninklijke Nederlandse Akademie van Wetenschappen. 2007. *De Toren van Pisa Rechtgezet. Over de Toekomst van de Nederlandse Archeologie*. Verkenningen KNAW. Amsterdam: Koninklijke Nederlandse Akademie van Wetenschappen. Retrieved 12 October 2012 from http://www.knaw.nl/smartsite.dws?id=26103&pub=20061111.

Kuiper, F.B.J. 1966. 'Levensbericht J.P.B. de Josselin de Jong', in Huygens Institute - Royal Netherlands Academy of Arts and Sciences (KNAW), *Jaarboek 1965-1966*. Amsterdam: Koninklijke Nederlandse Akademie van Wetenschappen, 397-403. Retrieved 12 October 2012 from http://www.dwc.knaw.nl/DL/levensberichten/PE00001156.pdf.

Maaskant-Kleibrink, M. 1988. 'Opgraven of Niet', *Tijdschrift voor Mediterrane Archeologie* 1(1): 13-17.

Ministerie van Onderwijs, Cultuur en Wetenschap. 2007. *Cultuurbeleid in Nederland*. The Hague: Ministerie van Onderwijs, Cultuur en Wetenschap.

Ministerie van Onderwijs, Cultuur en Wetenschap. 2009. *Grenzeloze Kunst*. The Hague: Ministerie van Onderwijs, Cultuur en Wetenschap. Retrieved 12 October 2012 from http://www.sica.nl/sites/default/files/pdf/Grenzeloze_Kunst.pdf.

Ministerie van Onderwijs, Cultuur en Wetenschap. 2012. *Meer dan Kwaliteit: een Nieuwe Visie op Cultuurbeleid*. The Hague: Ministerie van Onderwijs, Cultuur en Wetenschap.

Ministerie van Welzijn, Volksgezondheid en Cultuur. 1993. *Cultuurbeleid in Nederland*. The Hague: Ministerie van Welzijn, Volksgezondheid en Cultuur, Directoraat-Generaal voor Culturele Zaken.

Mols, S. 1998. 'Nederlandse Instituten in het Buitenland. Aflevering 1: Italië', *Archeobrief* 9: 12-13.

Moormann, E.M. 2008. 'Op Vakantie? Nederlands Archeologisch Onderzoek in de Mediterrane Wereld', *Tijdschrift voor Mediterrane Archeologie* 40(20): 48-56.

Mulder, E., E. de Campenhout and M.-E. Sesmilo. 2011. 'Gert-jan Burgers - Handling the Ancient City: The Multifold Cultural Layers of Rome', in T.W. Breukel, V. Neiteler and E.F. Rogmans (eds), *The City: Past, Present and the Future. Honours Class Archaeology 2010-2011*. Graduate School of Archaeology Occasional Papers 9. Leiden: Faculty of Archaeology, 59-60.

Nieuwenhuyse, O. 2006. 'Nederlandse Archeologen in het Midden Oosten', *Archeobrief* 20(3): 20-24.

National Archives of the Netherlands, Netherlands Institute for Cultural Heritage, Netherlands Cultural Heritage Agency. 2010. *Footsteps and Fingerprints. The Legacy of a Shared History*. Zwolle: Uitgeverij Waanders.

Orbons, J. 2005. 'Van Ideeën, via Improvisaties naar Innovaties in Prospectiemethoden', in M.H. van den Dries and W.J.H. Willems (eds), *Innovatie in de Nederlandse Archeologie. Liber Amicorum voor Roel W. Brandt*. Gouda: SIKB, 55-64.

Otterspeer, W. 2008. *The Bastion of Liberty. Leiden University Today and Yesterday*. Leiden: Leiden University Press.

Parthesius, R. 2002. 'Handel, Productie en Consumptie. Het Wrak van het VOC-schip *Avondster* in de Haven van Galle (Sri Lanka). Een Potentiële Bron van Kennis over de Europese Expansie in Azië', in M.H. Bartels, E.H.P. Cordfunke and H. Sarfatij, *Hollanders Uit en Thuis*. Hilversum: Uitgeverij Verloren, 61-70.

Pots, R. 2009. 'De Tijdloze Thorbecke, Over Niet-oordelen en Voorwaarden scheppen in het Nederlandse Cultuurbeleid', *Boekman, Tijdschrift voor Kunst, Cultuur en Beleid* 81, 2-14. Originally published in Boekmancahier 50. Retrieved 12 October 2012 from http://www.boekman.nl/documenten/BM81-Pots.pdf.

Raven, M.J. 2007. *Hakken in het Zand - Nederlandse Opgravingen in Egypte*. Leiden: Rijksmuseum van Oudheden.

Rijksmuseum van Oudheden. 1981. *Rijksmuseum van Oudheden/National Museum of Antiquities*. Nederlandse Musea 6. Haarlem: Joh. Enschedé en Zonen Grafische Inrichting B.V.

Roodenburg, L. 2002. *De Bril van Anceaux. Volkenkundige Fotografie vanaf 1860*. Leiden: Rijksmuseum voor Volkenkunde. Retrieved 12 October 2012 from http://volkenkunde. nl/sites/default/files/attachements/bril_van_anceaux.pdf.

Sa'd Abujaber, R. 2009. 'Dutch Cultural and Archaeological Activities in Jordan during the Last Fifty Years', in E. Kaptijn and L.P. Petit (eds), *A Timeless Vale. Archaeological and Related Essays on the Jordan Valley in Honour of Gerrit van der Kooij on the Occasion of his Sixty-fifth Birthday*. Archaeological Studies Leiden University 19. Leiden: Leiden University Press, 9-17.

SICA. 1999. *SICAmag 3*. Retrieved 12 October 2012 from http://www.sica. nl/content/nl-internationaal-cultuurbeleid-nederland.

Soejono, R.P. 1987. 'Archaeological Research in Indonesia', *Journal of Southeast Asian Studies* 18(2): 212-216.

Soejono, R.P. 2001. 'Indonesia', in T. Murray (ed.), *Encyclopedia of Archaeology. History and Discoveries* 2(E-M). Santa Barbara, California: ABC-Clio, 647-654.

Tillema, J.A.C. 1982. *Victor de Stuers: Ideeën van een Individualist*. Assen: Van Gorcum.

Toebosch, T. 2003. 'Hertenrits: de Insectendeskundige, Iwan de Verschrikkelijke en Oom Bob, over Opgravingen in de Oost en de West', in T. Toebosch (ed.), *Grondwerk 200 Jaar Archeologie in Nederland*. Amsterdam: Sun, 78-94.

Trigger, B.G. 1984. 'Alternative Archaeologies: Nationalist, Colonialist, Imperialist', *Man* 19: 355-370.

Trigger, B.G. 2006. *A History of Archaeological Thought*. Cambridge: Cambridge University Press.

Van Beek, B.L. 2002. 'Zout uit het Caribisch Gebied. Archeologische Verkenningen nabij het Fort Araya en op het Eiland La Tortuga, Venezuela', in M.H. Bartels, E.H.P. Cordfunke and H. Sarfatij, *Hollanders Uit en Thuis*. Hilversum: Uitgeverij Verloren, 71-84.

Van den Dries, M.H. and W.J.H. Willems. 2007. 'Quality Management - The Dutch Perspective', in W.J.H. Willems and M.H. van den Dries (eds), *Quality Management in Archaeology*. Oxford: Oxbow Books, 50-65.

Van den Dries, M.H. and S.J. van der Linde. 2012. 'Collecting Oral Histories for the Purpose of Stimulating Community Involvement at Tell Balata, Palestine', in N. Schücker (ed.), *Integrating Archaeology*. Frankfurt: RGK.

Van der Kooij, G. and M.M. Ibrahim (eds). 1989. *Een Verhaal voor het Opgraven. Opgravingen te Deir Alla in de Jordaanvallei*. Leiden: Rijksmuseum van Oudheden.

Van der Linde, S.J. 2012. *Digging Holes Abroad. An Ethnography of Dutch Archaeological Research Projects Abroad*. Archaeological Studies Leiden University 27. Leiden: Leiden University Press.

Van de Velde, P. 2001. 'Netherlands', in T. Murray (ed.), *Encyclopedia of Archaeology History and Discoveries* 3(N-Z). Oxford: ABC Clio, 919-934.

Van Dijk, W., S. Hijmans and E. Seiverling. 1988. 'Archeologisch Veldwerk in het Mediterrane Gebied. Een Inventarisatie van Nederlandse en Vlaamse Activiteiten', *Tijdschrift voor Mediterrane Archeologie* 1, 24-38.

Van Es, W.A. 1972. 'The Origins and Development of the ROB for Archaeological Excavations in the Netherlands', *Berichten ROB* 22, 17-71.

Van Haarlem, W. 1999. 'Nederlandse Instituten in het Buitenland. Aflevering 3: Egypte', *Archeobrief* 12, 14-16.

Van Roosmalen, P. 2003. 'Changing Views on Colonial Heritage', in R. van Oers and S. Haraguchi (eds), *Identification and Documentation of Modern Heritage*. UNESCO World Heritage Papers 5. Paris: UNESCO, 121-129. Retrieved 12 October 2012 from http://whc.unesco.org/documents/publi_wh_papers_05_en.pdf.

Van Wijngaarden, G.J. 1992. *Nederlandse Archeologie in het Buitenland: Cultuurbeleid en Praktijk*. Archeologisch Informatie Cahier 3. Leiden: Archeologisch Informatie Centrum.

Von der Dunk, T. 2010. 'Le Roi Louis et l'Architecture: une Politique Nationale', in A. Jourdan (ed.), *Louis Bonaparte: Roi de Hollande (1806-1810)*. Paris: Nouveau Monde, 275-317.

Versluys, M.-J. 2008. 'Romeinse Archeologie: Theoretische Ontwikkelingen in de Laatste Decennia. Een Nederlands Perspectief'. *Tijdschrift voor Mediterrane Archeologie* 20(40), 29-35.

Versluys, M.-J. 2011. 'Archéologie Classique et Histoire de l'Art aux Pays-Bas: des Liaisons Dangereuses', *Perspective, La Revue de l'INHA* 4: 687-701.

Versteeg, A.H. 1998. 'The History of Prehistoric Archaeological Research in Suriname', in Th.E. Wong, D.R. de Vletter, L. Krook, J.I.S. Zonneveld and A.J. van Loon (eds), *The History of Earth Sciences in Suriname*. Amsterdam: Netherlands Institute of Applied Geoscience TNO/Royal Netherlands Academy of Arts and Sciences, 203-234.

Vriezen, Th. C. 1976. 'Levensbericht F.M.Th. de Liagre Böhl', in Huygens Institute - Royal Netherlands Academy of Arts and Sciences (KNAW), *Jaarboek 1976*. Amsterdam: Koninklijke Nederlandse Akademie van Wetenschappen, 218-223.

Willems, W.J.H. 2008. 'Archaeological Resource Management and Preservation', *Geoarchaeological and Bioarchaeological Studies* 10: 283-289.

Witteveen, I. and E. Francisco. 2009. *Final Report. NAAM expert meeting 2009. Safeguarding the Netherlands after the Constitutional Changes*. Curacao: Cultural Heritage Expertise Center.

Wright, G.E. 1957. 'The Archaeology of the City', *The Biblical Archaeologist* 20, 19-32.

Zeeberg, J.J., P. Floore and R. Gerritsen. 1996. *Nova Zembla, Recente Expedities in het Noordpoolgebied*. Rijswijk: Uitgeverij Elmar.

1.7 Warum in die Ferne schweifen?[1] An overview of German archaeology abroad

Nina Schücker

Roman-Germanic Commission of the German
Archaeological Institute, Germany

Abstract

This paper presents a historical overview of German archaeology abroad, reflecting upon various aims and motivations for conducting research on foreign history and culture besides the driving academic questions. German archaeology developed in the nineteenth century when Germany did not yet exist as a single state. After the foundation of the German Empire in 1871, excavations abroad were promoted to a high extent as a factor in the competition with other European nation states. In the period of National Socialism, archaeology abroad became a discipline misused for the purposes of propaganda and looting. In the following decades, archaeology developed differently in the two German states. Whilst foreign fieldwork projects by the German Democratic Republic were limited to a small number in Bulgaria, Russia and some Arab states, the German Archaeological Institute (*Deutsches Archäologisches Institut*) in the west even expanded overseas. The end of the Cold War offered new opportunities for collaboration and opened new fields of research in East and West Germany respectively as well as worldwide. Today, co-operative international projects are seen as instruments in foreign cultural policy and intercultural dialogue.

Résumé

Pourquoi chercher si loin? Un Aperçu de l'Archéologie Allemande à l'Étranger

Cet article présente un aperçu historique de l'archéologie allemande à l'étranger, montrant les différents objectifs et motivations pour étudier l'histoire et les cultures étrangères, outre les questions académiques couramment posées. L'archéologie allemande s'est développée au cours du XIXème siècle, avant que l'Allemagne ne soit

---

1 'Why roam far?' following Johann Wolfgang von Goethe, Erinnerung: "Willst du immer weiter schweifen?" (see Goethe 1981: 133).

réunifiée. Après la fondation de l'Empire allemand en 1871, des fouilles à l'étranger se sont développées principalement pour leur rôle dans la compétition avec d'autres nations européennes. Durant la période du National-Socialisme, l'archéologie à l'étranger a été utilisée à mauvais escient, à des fins de propagande et de pillage. Au cours des décennies suivantes, l'archéologie s'est développée de manière distincte dans les deux États allemands. Alors que les fouilles étaient réduites à un nombre limité par la République démocratique allemande en Bulgarie, en Russie et dans les États Arabes, en Allemagne de l'Ouest, l'Institut Archéologique Allemand (Deutsches Archäologisches Institut), s'étendait même outre mer. La fin de la guerre froide a ouvert de nouvelles possibilités de collaboration et de nouveaux domaines de recherche, respectivement pour l'Allemagne de l'Est et l'Allemagne de l'Ouest, ainsi qu'au niveau mondial. Aujourd'hui des projets coopératifs internationaux sont vus comme des instruments de la politique culturelle à l'étranger et du dialogue interculturel.

Extracto

¿por qué buscarlo más allá? Un Resumen de la Arqueología Alemana en el Extranjero

Este artículo muestra un resumen histórico que refleja los fines y las motivaciones para realizar investigaciones históricas y culturales extranjeras, además de las cuestiones académicas que subyacen. La arqueología alemana se desarrolló en el siglo diecinueve cuando Alemania todavía no existía en forma de un solo estado. Después de la fundación del Imperio alemán en 1871 se fomentaron las excavaciones extranjeras a un grado alto, siendo un factor en la competición con otros estados nación europeos. Durante el periodo del Socialismo Nacional la arqueología llegó a ser una disciplina mal usada para los propósitos de propaganda y saqueo. En las décadas siguientes la arqueología se desarrolló de manera diferente en los dos estados alemanes. Mientras los proyectos de trabajo de campo en el extranjero se limitaban a un reducido número en Bulgaria, Rusia y en algunos estados árabes, el Instituto Arqueológico Alemán (Deutsches Archäologisches Institut) en el occidente incluso se extendió al extranjero. El fin de la Guerra Fría ofreció nuevas oportunidades para colaboración y dio paso a nuevos campos de investigación tanto en Alemania del Oeste y del Este respectivamente, como en todo el mundo. Hoy en día los proyectos de cooperación internacional son vistos como instrumentos de la política cultural extranjera y del diálogo intercultural.

ملخص

لماذا نسافر بعيداً؟ نظرة عامة لعلم الآثار الألماني في الخارج

نينا شوكر

اللجنة الرومانية الجرمانية للمعهد الجرماني الأثري الألماني، ألمانيا

تقدم هذه اللورقة نظرة تاريخية على علم الآثار في الخارج، وهي تلقي الضوء على
مختلف الأهداف والدوافع للقيام بالبحث في التاريخ والثقافة الأنجنبيتين
إلى جانب الأساس الأكاديمية التي تقود البحث. لقد نشأ علم الآثار الألماني
في القرن التاسع عشر عندما لم تكن الألمانيا دولة موحدة. وبعد تأسيس
الإمبراطورية الألمانية في 1871، تم ترويج البعثات الأثرية في الخارج إلى
حد كبير عامل في المنافسة مع الدول القومية الأوربية الأخرى. وفي مرحلة
الاشتراكية القومية، أصبح علم الآثار ميدان بحث يساء استغلاله من أجل
الدعاية القومية، وفي العقود التالية، تطور علم الآثار بطريقة مختلفة في كلا
الدولتين الألمانيتين. وبينما اقتصرت مشروعات العمل الميداني الأجنبية
التي قامت بها جمهورية ألمانيا الديمقراطية على عدد صغير في بلغاريا،
وروسيا وبعض الدول العربية، إذ بالمعهد الأثري الألماني في الغرب يقوم
بتوسيع مشروعاته إلى الخارج. وقد تقدمت نهاية الحرب الباردة فرصة جديدة
للتعاون، كما تفتحت ميادين بحث جديدة في شرق وغرب ألمانيا على التوالي
وفي العالم أجمع. أما اليوم، فتعتبر المشروعات التعاونية الدولية وسائل في
السياسة الثقافية الأنجنبية والحوار بين الثقافات.

Keywords

Germany, history of research, archaeology

Introduction

Public perception of archaeology seems to be that of exciting adventures in fascinating landscapes in far-away countries. A considerable percentage of the German population regards the archaeological profession as closely connected with fieldwork abroad, especially around the Mediterranean (Bohne and Heinrich 2000; Jansen 2008a: 151; cf. Ceram 1949).[2] Even if it is shaped by television documentaries and films, this stereotype is true to a certain extent. For various reasons, investigations abroad have always played an important role, already since the early days of German archaeology. A huge number of projects in foreign countries – among them long-term activities – have been run by or involved Germans. In 1829, the later German Archaeological Institute (*Deutsches Archäologisches Institut*) was founded in Rome. In the first decades of its existence, the field of activity was related to this location (Jansen 2008a: 152, 157-159). Today, as a scholarly organization under the auspices of the Foreign Office, again most of its projects are embedded in international cooperations and deal with ancient cultures outside Germany.

---

2   The famous publication 'Gods, Graves and Scholars' is a German fact book on the history of archaeology in Italy, Greece, Egypt and the Near East, South and Central America by Kurt Wilhelm Marek (1915–1972), published in 1949 under the pseudonym C.W. Ceram. It has been translated into 28 languages and sold over 12 million copies. It made (foreign) archaeology popular in Germany in the 1950s and 1960s. Retrieved 19 July 2011 from http://de.wikipedia.org/wiki/G%C3%B6tter,_Gr%C3%A4ber_und_Gelehrte; see Grunewald 2006.

In the following a historical overview is given of the development of German archaeology abroad over the last three centuries, referring to some projects, research institutes and funding institutions. It deals with the changing framework for international research, including motivations and reasons that go beyond academic issues. Since this text represents a general summary, it has not been possible to include here the accounts and achievements of specific individuals.[3] This might have helped us avoid undue generalizations. Since individuals as well as institutions are always affected by the political and social situation in Germany and abroad, taking these into account would have illustrated and illuminated the recorded historical facts.[4] Despite the impact of political and social circumstances on all archaeological agents and on the development of research strategies and policies, the individual interests and research objectives of scholars – accompanied by the spirit of adventure and the yearning for far-away places – have always been the fundamental motivation for conducting fieldwork abroad (cf. Trümpler 2008a: 16).

Early years

Germany had not yet been unified when archaeology developed from humanistic interest in classical culture and art in the eighteenth century. In these very early days of the discipline, work in the field of antiquities needed private assets and a diverse range of support. Financial sponsorship was obtained from German sovereigns whose interest in the spirit of humanism was mainly focused on the impressive remains of ancient civilizations in Italy and Greece. The antiquary Johann Joachim Winckelmann (1717–1768), who probably is the best-known German scholar of these years and is considered to be one of the founders of archaeology, conducted most of his scientific work in Rome. His writings, in which he expressed his admiration for Greek culture, had a significant impact on German archaeology and on German cultural and intellectual history in general (Wünsche 1986; Maier 1994: 35-37; Gramsch 2006: 2; Schnapp 2009; Holtz 2010: 196-202).[5]

In the nineteenth century, a high regard for classical as well as oriental cultures became common also among the middle classes (Gramsch 2006: 3-4; Berlin-Brandenburgische Akademie der Wissenschaften 2007; Pawlitzki 2009). Ancient

---

3   Cf. the publication 'Archäologenbildnisse' (en. 'Effigies of archaeologists' by Lullies and Schiering 1988) which portrays German-speaking classical archaeologists. In the text in hand only eight of them are mentioned by name.

4   Neither contemporary publications and unpublished historical documents nor all research literature could be included here. At present, a great interest in the history of archaeological research is remarkable (especially in the period of National Socialism which has been extensively studied since the 1990s). Cf. several exhibitions (e.g. 'Das große Spiel. Archäologie und Politik zur Zeit des Kolonialismus (1860–1940)' in Essen 12 February-13 June 2010, 'Die geretteten Götter aus dem Palast vom Tell Halaf' in Berlin 28 January–14 August 2011; 'Lawrence von Arabien. Genese eines Mythos' in Oldenburg 21 November 2010–27 March 2011 and Cologne 30 April–11 September 2011.

5   For Winckelmann see: Leppmann 1986; Lullies and Schiering 1988: 5-7; Bruer 1994; Gröschel 1994; Maier 1994: 37-40; Rahms 1994; Marchand 1996: 7-16; Schneider 1997; Sünderhauf 2004; Wangenheim 2005; Pawlitzki 2009: 10, 24-25; Schnapp 2009: 280-288.

art was highly valued for aesthetic reasons; and academic interest in these relics grew alongside a desire to form art collections. As more and more explorers travelled around southern Europe and visited the original sites, networks for conducting and funding geographical, epigraphic and archaeological work came into existence (Minner 2005: 25).[6]

The *Instituto di corrispondenza archeologica*, which later became the German Archaeological Institute, was founded in Rome in 1829 by a group of international scholars, artists and diplomats under the patronage of the Prussian Crown Prince and later king Friedrich Wilhelm IV (1795–1861).[7] When its initiator Eduard Gerhard (1795–1867) was appointed to the Royal Museum (*Königliches Museum*) in Berlin, national interests became integrated within the institute. In 1859, in the interests of security of planning, the Prussian Foreign Office took on the responsibility for most of its financing (Lullies and Schiering 1988: 20-22; Marchand 1996: 40-62; Ridley 1996; Unte 2003: 163-169; Meyer 2004: 158-160, 169-170; Ellinger 2006: 194; Fröhlich 2007: 141, 164; Parzinger 2007: 158-159; Jansen 2008a: 151-152; Schnapp 2009: 327-334; Stürmer 2009).

In 1842, Prussia funded the first German investigations in Egypt and Sudan, a four year expedition led by Karl Richard Lepsius (1810–1884). The engagement was not only motivated by the interest in art and science, but also by the desire of acquiring precious objects for the Berlin Museum (Marchand 1996: 62-65; Berlin-Brandenburgische Akademie der Wissenschaften 2007; Müller-Römer 2009; Hafemann 2010; Holtz 2010). As a result of diplomatic efforts, the mission was licensed to take antiquities of 'all kind, size and number to Berlin as a present of viceroy Mohamed Ali to his brother, the king of Prussia Friedrich Wilhelm IV'.[8]

In these years, Greece was ruled by Otto of Wittelsbach (1815–1867), Prince of Bavaria, and German officials ran most of the administration. Ludwig Ross (1806–1859) was appointed *ephoros* (royal representative) for the supervision of ancient monuments, and later became the first professor of archaeology at the University of Athens, until the Greeks protested against foreign civil servants in 1843 (Goette and Palagia 2005; Minner 2005; Niemeier 2005).[9]

The last quarter of the nineteenth century saw the foundation of the German Empire in 1871 and the building of a German national consciousness. Rivalries between the European states determined the political behaviour as well as the self-conception of the population. The relatively small number of high-ranking ancient art objects in the Berlin museums was perceived as unacceptable by the Germans. As an opportunity for compensation, archaeology was considered as a subject of national interest, and excavations became a tool in the competition with France and

---

6   Cf. for travels in Italy: Hamdorf 1986a: 123-133, and Greece: Hamdorf 1986b: 247-263.
7   Blanck 2008; Dennert 2009: 103-104; Holtz 2010.
8   English translation by the author, German quotation from Müller-Römer 2009: 6. "… jeder Art, jeder Größe und in jeder in seinem freien Belieben stehenden Zahl mit nach Berlin zu nehmen, als persönliches Geschenk des Vizekönigs Mohamed Ali an seinen Bruder, den König von Preußen Friedrich Wilhelm IV".
9   Cf. Lullies and Schiering 1988: 29-30; Hamilakis 2008: 273-275. For investigations in regions other than the Mediterranean see *e.g.* Skripkin 1997.

Great Britain. Thus, nationalism, imperialism and acquisition of antiquities were the key factors for the high status of foreign archaeology in the German Empire during these early years.[10] This was expressed in 1886 by the Egyptologist Adolf Erman (1854–1937): "Prussia needs to excavate, so that we do not find ourselves once again at a disadvantage".[11] Another driving factor was religion – in relation to investigations in the Biblical Lands (Maier 1994; Marchand 1996: 65-74, 220-227; Schneider 1997: 190-191; Crüsemann *et al.* 2000: 3-12; Bruch 2002: 9-10; Löhlein 2003, 2009; Schipper 2006; Crüsemann 2008a; Jansen 2008a: 152-156; Lang 2008; Matthes 2008; Trümpler 2008a: 16-17, 2008b; Dittmar 2010).[12]

The imperial age

As a result, research in foreign countries undertaken by private scholars, on behalf of public institutes as well as societies, was promoted to a high degree. In 1871 the Institute for Archaeological Correspondence (*Institut für archäologische Korrespondenz*) became a research body directly under the aegis of the imperial government. The Imperial German Archaeological Institute (*Kaiserlich Deutsches Archäologisches Institut*) was in fact the first scientific institution of the newly-founded German Reich (Wickert 1979; Schneider 1997: 191; Bruch 2002: 9-10; Löhlein 2003; Meyer 2004: 160-164, 170-185; Ellinger 2006: 194; Fröhlich 2007: 141; Jansen 2008a: 154-155). Other important bodies undertaking fieldwork abroad were the Prussian Academy of Sciences (*Preußische Akademie der Wissenschaften*), and the German Oriental Society (*Deutsche Orient-Gesellschaft*) as well as the Royal Prussian Museums (Marchand 1996: 192-220; Wilhelm 1998a; Ellinger 2006: 96-100; Parzinger 2007: 159; Crüsemann 2008a).[13] Permanent branches were opened abroad, which again has to be understood as part of the desire to draw level with other European countries. In 1874, a department of the Imperial German Archaeological Institute was established at Athens, where France had already been running its *École* for more than 25 years (Wickert 1979: 83-120; Jantzen 1986: 1-16; Maier 1994: 52; Fittschen 1996; Niemeier 2007; Jansen 2008a: 154-156). In 1886, a first step in the institutionalization of German archaeology in Turkey was taken, when Carl Humann (1839–1896), excavator in Pergamon, was designated as Foreign Director (*Auswärtiger Direktor*) of the Berlin Museum in Izmir; later the office moved to Istanbul (Dörner and Dörner 1989: 86-87; Parzinger 2007: 159-160; Cobet 2008: 347). In 1900, the German Protestant Institute of Archaeology of the Holy Land (*Deutsches Evangelisches Institut für Altertumswissenschaft des Heiligen Landes*) was founded, following the

---

10   Not to be underestimated is the political weight of archaeologists in time of war due to their cultural competence and language skills, which is true for the Germans Leo Frobenius (1873–1938) and Max von Oppenheim (Kröger 2008; Trümpler 2008a: 18, 2008c).

11   English translation by the author, German quotation from Kloft 2006: 298, 321; Löhlein 2009: 64 and Matthes 2008: 227, 229: "Preußen muss graben, damit wir nicht wieder einmal das Nachsehen haben".

12   See Hübner 2002 for the German Society for the Exploration of Palestine (*Deutscher Verein zur Erforschung Palästinas*).

13   For the Orient Committee (*Orient-Comité*) see Crüsemann 1998.

visit of the German Emperor Wilhelm II (1859–1941) to Jerusalem two years earlier (Bienert *et al.* 2000; Freischlader 2000; Fritz 2000; Petersen 2008).[14] And in 1907 the Imperial German Institute for Egyptian Archaeology (*Kaiserlich Deutsches Institut für Ägyptische Altertumskunde*) began its work in Cairo. The first German excavations in Egypt had already started in Abu Ghurob in 1898, followed by work in Abusir by the German Oriental Society in 1902 (Bittel *et al.* 1979: 98-100; Krauss 1998a; Thissen 2006; Rummel 2007: 1; Jansen 2008a: 156).

A strong interest was also displayed by the German public in ancient cultures, especially those of Greece, Asia Minor and the Near East, in relation to close political contacts and economic interests in the region.[15] Although archaeology abroad and the collection of foreign cultural heritage was a political and social objective (also within the professional archaeological community), the respective research tasks of individual excavations gradually became more important. Large-scale projects that started in these years included investigations in for instance Pergamon (1878), Miletus (1899), Assur (1903), Babylon (1898) and Tell el-Amarna (1911) (Maier 1994: 53-55; Marchand 1996: 92-103, 188-227; Schneider 1997; Krauss 1998b; Maul 1998; Wilhelm 1998b; Radt 1999; Dürring 2000: 425-426; Löhlein 2003, 2008: 391-394, 2009; Marzahn and Salje 2003; Cobet 2008: 348-352; Crüsemann 2008a, 2008b; Heimsoth 2008; Marzahn 2008a; Matthes 2008; Petersen 2008; Teichmann 2008; Voß and Pilgrim 2008: 297-305; Wawrzinek 2010: 89-90).

Upon the division of the finds, significant discoveries like the Pergamon Altar, the Miletus Market Gate, the Ishtar Gate and the Nefertiti Bust were brought to Berlin. At the same time excavations started in Olympia, but because of the existing contract, finds had to remain in Greece, a state of affair that was criticized by German politicians (Maier 1994: 48; Marchand 1996: 77-91, 209; Crüsemann *et al.* 2000: 23-26; Bruch 2002; Kalpaxis 2002; Klinkhammer 2002; Sösemann 2002; Niemeier 2007; Cobet 2008: 348-352; Crüsemann 2008a; Marzahn 2008b; Trümpler 2008a: 17-8; Löhlein 2009: 65; Wrede 2009).

In these early days of the discipline, fieldwork was undertaken by archaeologists but also by autodidactic academics from different disciplines, for example architects, engineers and jurists. Well-known Germans working abroad in those years were *e.g.* Eduard Robert Koldewey (1855–1925), Ludwig Borchardt (1863–1938), Carl Humann, Walter Andrae (1875–1956), Max von Oppenheim (1860–1946) and Wilhelm Dörpfeld (1853–1940).[16] Support was given by the German emperors Friedrich III (1831–1888), who had been a student of the archaeologist Ernst Curtius (1814–1896), and Wilhelm II, who was personally interested in archaeology.

---

14 Excavations carried out by the institute started late in Madaba and in Som near Irbid (both Jordan) in 1966 (Fritz 2000: 45-46).

15 For work outside the area mentioned see *e.g.* Yaldiz 2008 on the expeditions to Turfan (1902–1904).

16 For E.R. Koldewey see Lullies and Schiering 1988: 116-117; Crüsemann 2008b; Marzahn 2008a. For L. Borchardt see Dürring 2000; Voß and Pilgrim 2008. For C. Humann see Lullies and Schiering 1988: 69-70; Dörner and Dörner 1989; Radt 1999: 309-314; Kästner 2008. For W. Andrae see Marzahn and Salje 2003. For M. von Oppenheim see Teichmann 2008; Wawrzinek 2010: 87-92, 107-108. For W. Dörpfeld see Lullies and Schiering 1988: 112-113; Radt 1999: 319-323; Dierichs 2003.

But other people also spent their private money on field research. Examples of this are Heinrich Schliemann (1822–1890), excavator of Troy, Mycenae and Tiryns, and Simon James (1851–1932), who in 1898 was the initiator of the German Oriental Society (Lullies and Schiering 1988: 39-40; Matthes 1996, 2008: 231-232; Wilhelm 1998a; Löhlein 2003, 2008, 2009; Gramsch 2006: 9; Crüsemann 2008a; Petersen 2008; Trümpler 2008a: 16; Wrede 2009).[17]

From the First to the Second World War

The First World War made a deep cut into German society. Archaeological activities in wartime were of subordinate importance and – when carried out – of a very different motivation and nature compared to those in peacetime (Wickert 1979: 160; Maier 1994: 55; Marchand 1996: 242-262; Müller-Scheeßel *et al.* 2001: 342, 529; Schnurbein 2001: 150-151, 156, 162; Ungern-Sternberg 2006: 242-244; Cobet 2008: 349; Heber 2008: 312; Kröger 2008; Trümpler 2008c, 2008d; Kitova 2010; Parzinger 2010; cf. Wawrzinek 2010: 91).

The parliamentary Weimar Republic which was established in 1919 was faced with numerous political and social problems that affected each individual in society, and the archaeological discipline as a whole. Moreover, the end of the Ottoman Empire changed the framework of research in the Near East (Altekamp 2008a). The economic crisis had an effect on research funding. Funds which had been made available by the Emergency Society for German Sciences (*Notgemeinschaft der Deutschen Wissenschaft*) were essential to conduct fieldwork projects abroad, *e.g.* in Uruk-Warka (Iraq) (Deutsche Orient-Gesellschaft n.d.: 2; Marchand 1996: 263-301; Ess 1998; Junker 1998: 283; Schnurbein 2001: 216; Unte 2003: 331-365; Kirchhoff 2007). In those years, the country's inner turmoil was reflected in the behaviour of the archaeological community; efforts undertaken to re-establish good contacts abroad ran counter to the emerging nationalistic tendencies in German society (Schnurbein 2001: 158-161, 166-167; Ungern-Sternberg 2006: 252-254; Kirchhoff 2007: 102, 164; Jansen 2008a: 164, 2010: 85). In 1929, at the end of a period of relative stability for the Weimar Republic, the Archaeological Institute of the German Empire (*Archäologisches Institut des Deutschen Reiches*) – as it was named in 1921 – celebrated its 100th anniversary.[18] On this occasion the offices in Istanbul (until then a department of the Berlin Museum) and in Cairo (until then an independent body) became part of the institute (Bittel *et al.* 1979: 65-85, 93-105; Junker 1998: 283; Ellinger 2006: 194; Jansen 2008a: 161-162;

---

17   For H. Schliemann see Lullies and Schiering 1988: 45-46; Cobet 1992; Marchand 1996: 118-124; Aslan and Thumm 2001; Jähne 2001; Mühlenbruch 2008. For S. James see Matthes 1998, 2008: 232-234. For the Deutsche Orient-Gesellschaft see its website at www.orient-gesellschaft.de and a publication of unknown date entitled 'Deutsche Orient-Gesellschaft. Seit 1898 im Dienste der Forschung' (Deutsche Orient-Gesellschaft n.d.).

18   For fieldwork of the Archaeological Institute of the German Empire during the Weimar Republic in Greece, Turkey and the Palestinian Territories see Wickert 1979: 160 and Müller-Scheeßel *et al.* 2001.

Parzinger 2007: 159-160; Rummel 2007: 1-2; Dennert 2009: 125; cf. Schnurbein 1993).

Between 1933 and 1945 archaeology was integrated in the National Socialist ideology, and most archaeologists adapted themselves to the political system for various reasons ranging from opportunism, career ambitions, envy and fear of reprisal to loyalty and personal conviction. One focus was on pre- and early history and the Germanic past, but also classical archaeological investigations were promoted as a result of Adolf Hitler's particular interest in this area. New institutions were set up: the *Amt Rosenberg* and the *SS-Ahnenerbe*. Already existing institutes continued their work, for example the Archaeological Institute of the German Empire. At the beginning of the National Socialist dictatorship, German foreign cultural policy was designed to present Germany in a positive way – as was attempted at the 1936 Summer Olympics in Berlin. On the occasion of this propaganda event, German excavations were resumed in Olympia. In 1938, after the annexation ('*Anschluss*') of Austria to the German Reich, the Austrian Archaeological Institute lost its independence and became a branch of the Berlin Institute. A new department was established in Madrid in 1943 as Spain was an allied state. Even though such deliberations had existed before, this must be seen in a political context as a declaration of friendship with the Spanish dictatorship. During the war, German archaeologists were culpably entangled in many immoral activities. A combination of foreign assignments, acts of war and looting of foreign cultural artefacts characterized the involvement of German archaeology in the regime. In the occupied territories, Germans took over control not only of local research institutes but also their prestigious projects. Fieldwork was carried out in Austria, Belarus, Croatia, Czechia, Estonia, France, Greece, Italy, Latvia, Luxemburg, Poland, Russia, Serbia, Slovakia and the Ukraine. German archaeologists were also working in Belgium, Denmark, the Netherlands, Norway and Sweden (Bollmus 1970, 2002; Kater 1974: esp. 145-190, 292; Bittel *et al.* 1979: 117-139; Jantzen 1986: 49-50; Arnold 1990; Faber 1995; Hiller von Gaertringen 1995: 466-468, 481-489; Marchand 1996: 343-354; Junker 1997, 1998, 2001: 512-513; Schneider 1997: 193; Kandler 1998: 49-53; Leube 1998, 1999; Heuss 2000: 144-159, 2002a, 2002b; Müller 2000; Schnurbein 2001: 216, 219-227; Halle 2002, 2009; Haßmann 2002: 108-110; Maischberger 2002; Meyer 2004: 164, 186-189; Ellinger 2006: 108-113, 194-200; Fröhlich 2007: 139-156, 2008; Legendre, Olivier and Schnitzler 2007a, 2007b; Altekamp 2008b; Jansen 2008a: 160-161, 164-173, 2008b, 2010; Legendre 2008; Jagust 2009; Schöbel

2009; Manderscheid 2010; Müller 2010: 118-120; Stern 2010; Vigener 2010; Mahsarski 2011: 201-284).[19]

The Cold War

The situation in the aftermath of the Second World War was characterized firstly by the former involvement in the National Socialist system. In the first years, efforts were undertaken to re-establish a working environment and to restore confidence which was completely destroyed owing to the crimes of National Socialism (Schnurbein 2001: 239-248; Fröhlich 2007). As in many other sectors of German society, working through the involvement in the former system was not promptly addressed in the archaeological community (Schneider 1997: 194; Haßmann 2002: 120-122; Kunow 2002: 162-163; Steuer 2005; Gramsch 2006: 13-14; Jagust 2009: 285-288; Strobel and Widera 2009: 9-14; Manderscheid 2010; Müller 2010: 119, 121; Saalmann 2010: 98-101; cf. Barbanera 2010: 33). In the subsequent period of the Cold War, the existence of two German states led to a diverging development of archaeological research. One of the urgent tasks of German archaeology in the second half of the twentieth century was to maintain contacts between East and West Germany as well as East and West European colleagues (Schnurbein 2001: 276-284; Neumayer 2007; Heber 2008: 331).

The German Archaeological Institute became a West German authority (Bittel *et al.* 1979; Jantzen 1986: 57-68; Meyer 2004: 189-191). Offices abroad were reopened, and departments in the Near East newly established (Baghdad in 1955, Teheran in 1961). This rapid expansion was supported by academic interest and enabled by the economic success of the Federal Republic. In addition, it was politically desired due to the fact that culture and research seemed to be suitable means by which to enhance the international image of Germany. Furthermore,

---

19 For Austria see Trnka 1994; Rudolf 1995; Kandler 1998: 53-59, 2000; Jernej 2007: 281-283. For Belarus see Heuss 2000: 149-150. For Croatia see Kater 1974: 292-293; Leube 1998: 405. For Czechia see Kater 1974: 292; Leube 1998: 407; Haßmann 2002: 108; Motyková 2002; Mahsarski 2011: 220-222. For Estonia see Heuss 2000: 149. For France see Schnitzler 1991, 2002, 2007; Pétry 1993; Leube 1998: 397, 1999: 564, 2007: 103-111; Legendre 1999, 2002, 2007, 2008; Heuss 2000: 144-147; Becker and Schnurbein 2001: 474-506; Müller-Scheeßel *et al.* 2001: 524; Schnurbein 2001: 221-227; Maischberger 2002: 216; Olivier 2002, 2007; Schnitzler and Legendre 2002; Fehr 2007; Mahsarski 2011: 214-220. For Greece see Jantzen 1986: 47-56; Hiller von Gaertringen 1995; Leube 1998: 396-397, 406, 1999: 564; Stürmer 2002; Arnold 2006: 20; Altekamp 2008b. For Italy see Junker 1998: 289-299; Maischberger 2002: 214; Fröhlich 2007: 146-147, Altekamp 2008b; Dennert 2009: 124. For Latvia see Heuss 2000: 149. For Luxemburg see Bollmus 1970: 334; Gatzen 2007; Jagust 2009: 293. For Poland see Bollmus 1970: 333-334; Kater 1974: 80, 292; Arnold 1990: 469, 2006: 19; Leube 1998: 405, 407, 2004; Piotrowska 1998: 266-270; Heuss 2000: 149; Gediga 2002; Haßmann 2002: 106; Mączyńska 2002; Makiewicz 2002; Heber 2008; Kaczmarek 2009. For Russia see Heske 1999: 4-5; Müller 2000: 29, 32-33, 35-40. For Serbia see Kater 1974: 292-294; Leube 1998: 405, 407; Heber 2008: 329; Saalmann 2010: 97-98. For Slovakia see Bollmus 1970: 334; Kater 1974: 292; Leube 1998: 405, 407, 2001: 8-16; Kolník 2002. For Ukraine see Kater 1974: 295-296; Heuss 2000: 152-153, 2002a: 413-414, 2002b; Huismann 2009; Schöbel 2009: 275-280; Mahsarski 2011: 271-272. For Belgium, Denmark, the Netherlands, Norway and Sweden see Becker and Schnurbein 2001: 474-489; Eickhoff 2002, 2007; Haßmann 2002: 103-106; Johansen 2002; Martens 2002; Fehr 2007; Gob 2007; Halle 2007; Leube 2007: 112-117; Schreiber Pedersen 2007; Mahsarski 2011: 205-213.

German foreign policy was integrated in the western alliance and its strategy towards the eastern bloc, a system in which Iraq and Iran were regarded as important regional powers (Marchand 1996: 363; Jansen 2008a: 161-162, 173-177). In this political context, the activities of leading individuals remained important. The renewed confidence in German colleagues was often due to charismatic characters, such as Gerhard Bersu (1889–1964), the director of the Roman-Germanic Commission of the German Archaeological Institute (*Römisch-Germanische Kommission des Deutschen Archäologischen Instituts*). Forced out of his post and into exile by the National Socialists, he returned to Germany after the war and took up his former position (Krämer 2001; Schnurbein 2001: 200-204, 249-252, 267; Becker 2002: 61-62; Maischberger 2002: 211-212).

Owing to its responsibility for the genocide of European Jews, Germany's relationship with the state of Israel was deeply problematic. Diplomatic relations between the Federal Republic and Israel were established in 1965. Already in 1964, the Evangelical Church in Germany (*Evangelische Kirche in Deutschland*) reopened its German Protestant Institute of Archaeology in Jerusalem, which had been closed in 1939. As a result of the war in 1967, a branch was set up in Amman to continue excavations in Jordan. In 1972, Volkmar Fritz (1938–2007) was the first German after World War II to direct an excavation in Israel (Bienert *et al.* 2000; Fritz 2000, 2007; Zwickel 2007; Hübner and Kamlah 2008: 85).[20]

It was at a relatively late stage that the German Archaeological Institute expanded further overseas to other continents, again as a result of foreign policy interests. In 1979, the Commission for General and Comparative Archaeology (*Kommission für Allgemeine und Vergleichende Archäologie*) was founded, later renamed as Commision for non-European and Comperative Archaeology (*Kommission für Außereuopäische und Vergleichende Archäologie*), which outlines the working area of the department centred in Bonn. This late development may be due to the fact that German archaeology had been under a strong humanistic influence and focused on studies in classical antiquity, but also to the fact that German colonialism had been relatively small scale (Wurster 1994; Parzinger 2007: 160-161; Jansen 2008a: 162-163).[21]

In the German Democratic Republic, the German Academy of Sciences at Berlin (*Deutsche Akademie der Wissenschaften zu Berlin*), later renamed Academy of Sciences of the German Democratic Republic (*Akademie der Wissenschaften der Deutschen Demokratischen Republik*) was the most important research institution. While in the beginning several archaeological departments existed, in 1969 the Central Institute for Ancient History and Archaeology (*Zentralinstitut für Alte Geschichte und Archäologie*) was founded. It comprised nearly all archaeological and ancient historical subject areas. The Central Institute conducted many large-scale projects, but, largely due to restrictions on travel and foreign exchange, East German archaeologists were involved only in a limited number of fieldwork projects abroad in allied states such as Bulgaria and Russia as well as Egypt, Iraq,

---

20   1972–1975: Israeli-German excavation in Hirbet el-Mešāš (Tel Masos).
21   For German archaeology in Namibia see Kinahan 1995, 2002.

Sudan and Syria (Behrens 1984: 31; Willing 1991: 108-116, 171-181, 233-241; Gringmuth-Dallmer 1993a; Coblenz 1998: 543-545, 560, 2002: 309-310, 314-318, 323, 336, 338; Schnurbein 2001: 276-284; Gramsch 2006: 13-14; Wendel 2007).[22]

Recent developments

The end of the Cold War offered new opportunities for collaboration and archaeological research abroad. The unification of the two German states changed the archaeology sector. In 1990, the Academy of Science was dissolved. A substantial number of staff of the Central Institute was taken over by the German Archaeological Institute. As a result of access to new research areas that had been behind the iron curtain and of new employees with specialist knowledge, a branch for the Archaeology of Eurasia (*Eurasien-Abteilung*) was created (Gringmuth-Dallmer 1993a: 280; Willing 1996; Parzinger 1998; Schnurbein 2001: 261, 263, 284-289; Jacobs 2002; Mante 2007: 84-86; Neumayer 2007).

Today, German archaeologists are working in many countries throughout the world, still with a focus on the Mediterranean, the Near East, the Balkans and Eurasia. German research in these areas is determined by operators such as public institutions, universities and to a lesser extent NGOs. The private archaeology sector is relatively small in Germany, and companies play no part in (preventive) archaeology abroad. The only exceptions are survey companies who normally do not act autonomously, but as part of bigger research projects. The most significant institutions in the field of international research are the German Archaeological Institute with its various branches abroad and the Romano-Germanic Central Museum (*Römisch-Germanisches Zentralmuseum*).

The Romano-Germanic Central Museum, a foundation and member of the Gottfried Wilhelm Leibniz Association (*Wissenschaftsgemeinschaft Gottfried Wilhelm Leibniz*), is financed by both the federal government and the individual German states with substantial involvement of the state of Rhineland-Palatinate and a contribution by the city of Mainz, where its head office is located. Its workshops are among the largest facilities in the field of restoration worldwide; in addition it runs temporary departments abroad. In 1990 (projected until 2013), a branch in Xi'an (China) was established as a collaboration of several German and Chinese institutions and as an initiative of the former Federal Ministry of Research and Technology (*Bundesministerium für Forschung und Technologie*), today Federal Ministry of Education and Research (*Bundesministerium für Bildung*

---

22   Bulgaria: *Mitteilungen zur Alten Geschichte und Archäologie in der Deutschen Demokratischen Republik* volume 1(1973)-17(1989); Egypt: volume 9(1981)-14(1986), 16(1988), 17(1989); Iraq: volume 10(1982), 11(1983); Russia: volume 9(1981), 11(1983), 12(1984); Syria: volume 12(1984)-17(1989); Sudan: volume 2(1974), 4(1976), 11(1983), 17(1989). Behrens 1984, 31; Herrmann 1988, 265-267; Herrmann and Klengel 1989; Lehmann 2000; Siefer 2000; Müller-Scheeßel *et al.* 2001, 358-359, 518(118); Schnurbein 2001, 288; Becker 2002, 62. Until now only a few historical studies have addressed archaeology in the GDR, therefore additional literature is listed here even if that does not deal specifically with archaeological investigations abroad; Gringmuth-Dallmer 1993b, 2001; Härke 2002; Kunow 2002, 166-172; Mante 2007.

und Forschung), in cooperation with the Archaeological Institute of the Shaanxi province (Greiff, Shenping and Zorn 2006; Pluntke, Lehnert and Frey 2009).[23]

The German Archaeological Institute is a federal agency under the German Foreign Office. It maintains permanent branches in 14 countries abroad: Italy (Rome), Greece (Athens), Egypt (Cairo), Turkey (Istanbul), Spain and Portugal (Madrid, Lisbon), Israel and Jordan (Jerusalem and Amman, as the German Protestant Institute of Archaeology), Mongolia (Ulaanbaatar, branch of the Commission for Archaeology of Non-European Cultures), in Iraq, Syria and Yemen (Baghdad, Damascus, Sana'a, all branches of the Orient department) as well as Iran and China (Teheran, Beijing, branches of the Eurasia department). All of these as well as the domestic branches (*e.g.* Roman-Germanic Commission) are conducting projects abroad and are working closely with archaeological heritage management organizations, research institutes and universities of the host countries. From a political point of view, this work does not only serve scholarly interests but aims to contribute to the foreign cultural and educational policy of Germany. On the Foreign office's website this dimension is stated: "As a tool for defining and communicating cultural identity, exploring the nation's past is deemed an important political priority. In this context the ... work [of the German Archaeological Institute] is a reflection of Germany's interest in, respect for and knowledge of the world's major cultures and makes a valuable contribution to intercultural dialogue"[24] (Deutches Archäologisches Institut 1969, 1983, 1999a, 1999b, 2000, 2004a, 2004b, 2004c, 2008; Bittel *et al.* 1979; Jantzen 1986; Rheidt 1999; Becker 2002; Gerlach 2003).

As one project of great political interest, the work of the Roman-Germanic Commission in Kosovo is worth noting. The RGK was initially limited to archaeology in Germany, but has gradually expanded its geographical focus; recently one of its main research areas is the Balkans (Schnurbein 1993, 2001; Müller-Scheeßel *et al.* 2001). In this framework the first bilateral cooperation agreement between Germany and the newly-founded Kosovo was on the archaeology of Ulpiana, a Roman town next to Priština. The joint work by the Archaeological Institute and Museum of Kosovo and German archaeologists was aimed at the scholarly development of the area and is intended to serve as an example for the introduction of modern methods and cultural management.[25]

German universities are public corporations within the responsibility of the states. Their work consists of both teaching and research. Archaeological training in Germany is structured to a wide range of individual subjects; some of them, *e.g.*

---

23 For current research see the annual journal *Jahrbuch des Römisch-Germanischen Zentralmuseums* and the website www.rgzm.de.

24 Quotation retrieved 4 August 2011 from http://www.auswaertiges-amt.de/EN/Aussenpolitik/ KulturDialog/Wissenschaft/DAI_node.html. Cf. information http://www.dainst.org/en/content/ foreign-cultural-activities?ft=all – http://www.dainst.org/en/objectives?ft=all. For current research see the annual journal *Archäologischer Anzeiger* and the website www.dainst.org.

25 Retrieved 4 August 2011 from http://www.dainst.org/en/pressrelease/kooperationsvertrag_ ulpiana?ft=all;
http://www.dainst.org/en/pressrelease/bundeswehr-st%C3%A4rkt-deutsch-kosovarische-kooperation?ft=all – http://www.dainst.org/de/project/ulpiana?ft=all.

Egyptology, are focused on foreign history and culture. Therefore, their fieldwork projects can only take place abroad. The content of teaching is left to the professors and lecturers in charge. Thus, the implementation of excavations in Germany and abroad depends on individual research interests of professors. An online study in 2008 showed that 34 of 38 German universities that teach archaeology run at least one fieldwork project abroad in cooperation with the local heritage management.[26] Investigations are almost exclusively financed through third-party funds. Larger activities are usually co-operative projects involving several partners from other German institutions as well as in the hosting countries. The majority of German university projects take place in Turkey, followed by Syria, Italy, Egypt, Greece, Austria and Spain. The great interest in the archaeology of Turkey can be explained in part by scholarly traditions and the fact that the area is the focus of several archaeological disciplines, such as Near Eastern, Classical and Christian Archaeology as well as pre- and early history. The German Archaeological Institute has traditionally been active in the region, which paves the way for future cooperations.

External research funding is provided by a number of foundations, societies and organizations that promote scholarly research, such as the Gerda Henkel and the Fritz Thyssen Foundations (*Stiftung*) or smaller bodies which address themselves to a specific investigation, for example Friends of Troy (*Freunde von Troia*). The most important body in the field of science and humanities is the German Research Foundation (*Deutsche Forschungsgemeinschaft*). It funds research projects in all fields of science and the humanities.[27]

This overview was focused on fieldwork projects, but some more aspects of cooperation and exchange should at least be mentioned. The one-year travel scholarship awarded since 1859 to postgraduates by the German Archaeological Institute still provides an excellent opportunity for young scholars to gain good knowledge of foreign countries, their culture and archaeological heritage as well as to get in contact with colleagues abroad. Other aspects are exchange programmes, conferences, multi-lateral exhibitions, publishing work and book exchange.[28]

---

26 For the projects see the websites of the universities.
27 www.gerda-henkel-stiftung.de; www.fritz-thyssen-stiftung.de; http://www.uni-tuebingen.de/troia/eng/freunde.html; www.dfg.de (cf. Schnurbein 2001: 273-276).
28 Cf. Kalb, Rasbach and Sasse-Kunst 2001: 410-413; Rassmann, Rittershofer and Schnurbein 2001; Schnurbein 2001: 168, 173-174, 184-187, 190-199, 203, 205, 267-271; Becker 2002; Greiff, Shenping and Zorn 2006; Dennert 2009: 105-107, 137-140; Pluntke, Lehnert and Frey 2009. In former times other issues were also associated with the travel scholarship, see Jansen 2008a: 164.

Turkey	28	17 %		
Egypt	19	11 %	87	52 %
Near East (others)	40	24 %		
Italy	13	8 %		
Greece	7	4 %	21	13 %
Southern Europe (others)	1	1 %		
Central Europe	4	2 %	4	2 %
Northern Europe	3	2 %	3	2 %
Western Europe	2	1 %	2	1 %
Balkan	12	7 %	21	13 %
Eurasia	9	5 %		
Africa	12	7 %		
Far East	1	1 %	18	11 %
America	5	3 %		
Unspecified	11	7 %	18	11 %

Table 1. Archaeological projects abroad (167), funded by the German Research Foundation in 2009.[29]

Conclusion

Using the example of German archaeology abroad, it has been shown that since its very beginning the discipline and its individual agents are affected by the respective political and social conditions. Funding and administrative procedures have always been the most obvious interfaces in this context. Even though the circumstances have constantly been changing this still holds true today.[30]

Due to its impact on cultural identity, archaeology is of long-term importance, which in turn serves as a ground for the discipline itself. With their international activities, archaeologists are able to make a valuable contribution to knowledge of the world's history, but also to the international images of sending and receiving states. With this in mind, sustainably planned and responsibly realized fieldwork projects based on partnership represent good opportunities for collaborations, exchanging knowledge, building confidence and individual friendship to be extended beyond the archaeological sector. This very positive assessment of opportunities and possibilities attributed to modern international research again reflects contemporary attitudes and political aims.

---

29   Cf. Deutsche Forschungsgemeinschaft, DFG annual report 2009, Projects in Egyptology and Ancient Near Eastern Studies, Prehistory, Classical Archaeology in Individual Grants Programme (Deutsche Forschungsgemeinschaft 2010).

30   This could partly have been because of 300 years of history of archaeological work. For the current example of the 'sphinx of Hattuša' which in 2011 was reclaimed by the Turkish government see various articles in German and Turkish newspapers (cf. press review archive of the German Archaeological Institute, 2011).

Acknowledgements

I would like to thank H. Baitinger, U. Rothe and H.-U. Voß for their help.

References

Altekamp, S. 2008a. 'Germanità. Archäologische Kolonialfantasien', in C. Trümpler (ed.), *Das große Spiel. Archäologie und Politik zur Zeit des Kolonialismus (1860–1940)*. Essen, Köln: Ruhr Museum, DuMont Buchverlag, 580-585.

Altekamp, S. 2008b. 'Klassische Archäologie und Nationalsozialismus', in J. Elvert and J. Nielsen-Sikora (eds), *Kulturwissenschaften und Archäologie*. Historische Mitteilungen Beihefte 72. Stuttgart: Steiner, 167–209. Retrieved 26 July 2011 from http://edoc.hu-berlin.de/oa/ bookchapters/ reD5IMz1lbPVM/PDF/291OSMHgfjGYo.pdf.

Arnold, B. 1990. 'The Past as Propaganda: Totalitarian Archaeology in Nazi Germany', *Antiquity* 64(244): 464-478.

Arnold, B. 2006. ''Arierdämmerung': Race and Archaeology in Nazi Germany', *World Archaeology* 38(1): 8-31.

Aslan, R. and D. Thumm. 2001. 'Ein Traum und seine Auswirkungen. Troia und die Anfänge der Archäologie', in Archäologisches Landesmuseum Baden-Württemberg, (ed.) *Troia. Traum und Wirklichkeit*. Begleitband zur Ausstellung 'Troia - Traum und Wirklichkeit'. Darmstadt: Wissenschaftliche Buchgesellschaft, 323-329.

Barbanera, M. 2010. 'R. Bianchi Bandinelli und die Klassische Archäologie in Italien in den Zwanziger bis Fünfziger Jahren', *Hephaistos* 27: 33-40.

Becker, K. 2002. '100 Jahre Römisch-Germanische Kommission', *Archäologie in Deutschland* 2002(2): 60-63.

Becker, K. and S. von Schnurbein. 2001. 'Dokumente zur Geschichte der Römisch-Germanischen Kommission', *Bericht der Römisch-Germanischen Kommission* 82: 447-506.

Behrens, H. 1984. *Die Ur- und Frühgeschichtswissenschaft in der DDR von 1945–1980. Miterlebte und Mitverantwortete Forschungsgeschichte*. Arbeiten zur Urgeschichte des Menschen 9. Frankfurt am Main, Bern, New York, Nancy: Verlag Peter Lang.

Berlin-Brandenburgische Akademie der Wissenschaften. 2007. *Preußen in Ägypten - Ägypten in Preußen. Die Königlich Preußische Expedition nach Ägypten (1842-1845). Sonderausstellung im Museum für Islamische Kunst, 30. November 2007–3. Februar 2008*. Retrieved 22 Juni 2011 from http://aaew.bbaw.de/dateien/weitere%20archive/ Lepsius-Ausstellung/ FuehrungPreuss Aeg.pdf.

Bienert, H.-D., J. Eichner, B. Müller-Neuhof and D. Vieweger. 2000. 'Beyond the Jordan: From Jerusalem to Amann. Das Deutsche Evangelische Institut für Altertumswissenschaft des Heiligen Landes in Aman. Past - Present - Future', in H.-D. Bienert and B. Müller-Neuhof (eds), *At the Crossroads. Essays on the Archaeology, History and Current Affairs of the Middle East*. Amman: German Protestant Institute, 239-271.

Bittel, K., F.W. Deichmann, W. Grünhagen, W. Kaiser, T. Kraus and H. Kyrieleis. 1979. *Beiträge zur Geschichte des Deutschen Archäologischen Instituts 1929 bis 1979. Teil I. Das Deutsche Archäologische Institut*. Geschichte und Dokumente 3. Mainz: Verlag Philipp von Zabern.

Blanck, H. 2008. 'The Instituto di Corrispondenza Archeologica', *Fragmenta* 2: 63-78.

Bohne, A. and M.U. Heinrich. 2000. 'Das Bild der Archäologie in der Öffentlichkeit. Eine Befragung in Bonn und Köln'. Retrieved 5 November 2010 from http://www. danguillier.de/ darv1.html

Bollmus, R. 1970. *Das Amt Rosenberg und seine Gegner. Studien zum Machtkampf im Nationalsozialistischen Herrschaftssystem*. Studien zur Zeitgeschichte. Stuttgart: Deutsche Verlags-Anstalt.

Bollmus, R. 2002. 'Das «Amt Rosenberg», das «Ahnenerbe» und die Prähistoriker. Bemerkungen eines Historikers', in A. Leube (ed.), *Prähistorie und Nationalsozialismus. Die mittel- und osteuropäische Ur- und Frühgeschichtsforschung in den Jahren 1933–1945*. Studien zur Wissenschafts- und Universitätsgeschichte 2. Heidelberg: Synchron Wissenschaftsverlag der Autoren, 21-48.

Bruch, R. vom. 2002. 'Internationale Forschung, Staatsinteresse und Parteipolitik. Die Olympia-Ausgrabung als frühe Phase deutscher auswärtiger Kulturpolitik', in H. Kyrieleis (ed.), *Olympia 1875-2000. 125 Jahre Deutsche Ausgrabungen. Internationales Symposion, Berlin 9.-11. November 2000*. Mainz am Rhein: Verlag Philipp von Zabern, 9-17.

Bruer, S.-G. 1994. *Die Wirkung Winckelmanns in der Deutschen Klassischen Archäologie des 19. Jahrhunderts*. Akademie der Wissenschaften und der Literatur. Abhandlungen der Geistes- und Sozialwissenschaftlichen Klasse 1994(3). Stuttgart: Franz Steiner Verlag.

Ceram, C.W. 1949. *Götter, Gräber und Gelehrte. Roman der Archäologie*. Hamburg: Rowohlt Verlag.

Cobet, J. 1992. 'Zwischen Realismus und Romantik. Gedenken an Heinrich Schliemann', in J. Cobet and B. Patzek (eds), *Archäologie und Historische Erinnerung. Nach 100 Jahren Heinrich Schliemann*. Essen: Klartext Verlag.

Cobet, J. 2008. 'Theodor Wiegand - das Osmanische Reich und die Berliner Museen', in C. Trümpler (ed.), *Das große Spiel. Archäologie und Politik zur Zeit des Kolonialismus (1860–1940)*. Essen, Köln: Ruhr Museum, DuMont Buchverlag, 346-353.

Coblenz, W. 1998. 'Bemerkungen zur Ostdeutschen Archäologie zwischen 1945 und 1990', *Ethnographisch-Archäologische Zeitschrift* 39: 529-561.

Coblenz, W. 2002. 'Archaeology under Communist control: the German Democratic Republic, 1945-1990', in H. Härke (ed.), *Archaeology, Ideology and Society. The German Experience*. Gesellschaften und Staaten im Epochenwandel 7. Frankfurt am Main, Berlin, Bern, Bruxelles, New York, Oxford, Wien: Peter Lang (second revised edition), 308-341.

Crüsemann, N. 1998. 'Ein Vorläufer der DOG: Das Orient-Comité', in G. Wilhelm (ed.), *Zwischen Tigris und Nil. 100 Jahre Ausgrabungen der Deutschen Orient-Gesellschaft in Vorderasien und Ägypten.* Zaberns Bildbände zur Archäologie. Sonderhefte der Antiken Welt. Mainz am Rhein: Verlag Philipp von Zabern, 13.

Crüsemann, N. 2008a. '„Ja! Wir werden das Licht des Deutschen Genius auch dorthin tragen". Der Beginn der Ausgrabungen in Assur im Spiegel Preußisch-Deutscher Orientpolitik unter Wilhelm II.', in J. Marzahn, G. Schauerte, B. Müller-Neuhof and K. Sternitzke (eds), *Babylon. Wahrheit. Eine Ausstellung des Vorderasiatischen Museums Staatliche Museen zu Berlin mit Unterstützung der Staatsbibliothek zu Berlin.* München: Hirmer, 35-44.

Crüsemann, N. 2008b. 'Das große Puzzle. Von Ziegelbruchstücken aus Babylon zum Berliner Ischtar-Tor', in C. Trümpler (ed.), *Das große Spiel. Archäologie und Politik zur Zeit des Kolonialismus (1860–1940).* Essen, Köln: Ruhr Museum, DuMont Buchverlag, 336-345.

Crüsemann, N., U. von Eickstedt, E. Klengel-Brandt, L. Martin, J. Marzahn and R.-B. Wartke. 2000. *Vorderasiatisches Museum Berlin. Geschichte und Geschichten zum Hundertjährigen Bestehen.* Berlin: Staatliche Museen zu Berlin Preußischer Kulturbesitz.

Dennert, M. 2009. 'Die Christliche Archäologie und das Deutsche Archäologische Institut', *Römische Quartalschrift für Christliche Altertumskunde und Kirchengeschichte* 104(1/2): 103-140.

Deutsches Archäologisches Institut. 1969. *Ausgrabungen. Forschungen. Seit 1950.* Berlin: Brüder Hartmann.

Deutsches Archäologisches Institut. 1983. *Ausgrabungen, Funde, Forschungen.* Kulturgeschichte der Antiken Welt Sonderband. Mainz am Rhein: Verlag Philipp von Zabern.

Deutsches Archäologisches Institut. 1999a. *Kayip Zamanlarin Peşinde. Alman Arkeoloji Enstitüsü Anadolu Kazıları. Auf der Suche nach verschwundenen Zeiten. Die Ausgrabungen des Deutschen Archäologischen Instituts in der Türkei.* Istanbul: Yapı Kredi Kültür Sanat Yayıncılık.

Deutsches Archäologisches Institut. 1999b. *Zehn Jahre Ausgrabungen und Forschungen in Syrien. 1989-1998.* Damaskus: Deutsches Archäologisches Institut Damaskus.

Deutsches Archäologisches Institut. 2000. *Archäologische Entdeckungen. Die Forschungen des Deutschen Archäologischen Instituts im 20. Jahrhundert.* Zaberns Bildbände zur Archäologie. Sonderbände der Antiken Welt. Mainz am Rhein: Verlag Philipp von Zabern.

Deutsches Archäologisches Institut. 2004a. '175 Jahre Deutsches Archäologisches Institut 1829-2004. Bericht über die Festveranstaltungen in Berlin', *Archäologischer Anzeiger* 2004(2): 1-154.

Deutsches Archäologisches Institut. 2004b. *Zwischen Kulturen und Kontinenten. 175 Jahre Forschung am Deutschen Archäologischen Institut.* Berlin: Deutsches Archäologisches Institut.

Deutsches Archäologisches Institut. 2004c. *Deutsches Archäologisches Institut Rom. Aufgaben und Unternehmungen. Herausgegeben aus Anlaß der Hundertfünfundsiebzigjahrfeier am Palilientag 2004*. Rom: Inmediaprint.

Deutsches Archäologisches Institut. 2008. *Aktuelle Forschungsprojekte. Deutsches Archäologisches Institut, Orient-Abteilung*. Berlin: Deutsches Archäologisches Institut.

Deutsche Forschungsgemeinschaft. 2010. *Deutsche Forschungsgemeinschaft. Jahresbericht 2009. Aufgaben und Ergebnisse*. Retrieved 8 July 2011 from http://www.dfg.de/download/pdf/dfg_im_profil/geschaeftsstelle/publikationen/dfg_jb2009.pdf.

Deutsche Orient-Gesellschaft. n.d. *Deutsche Orient-Gesellschaft. Seit 1898 im Dienste der Forschung*. Berlin: Deutsche Orient-Gesellschaft.

Dierichs, A. 2003. 'Erinnerung an Wilhelm Dörpfeld, dem Schichten mehr als Schätze galten', *Antike Welt* 34(6): 665-666.

Dittmar, P. 2010. 'Kaiser Wilhelm zahlte 8000 Taler für Fälschungen', *Die Welt online 16.02.2010*. Retrieved 8 July 2011 from http://www.welt.de/die-welt/kultur/article6415177/Kaiser-Wilhelm-zahlte-8000-Taler-fuer-Faelschungen.html.

Dörner, F.K. and E. Dörner. 1989. *Von Pergamon zum Nemrud Dağ. Die Archäologischen Entdeckungen Carl Humanns*. Kulturgeschichte der antiken Welt 40. Schriften der Hermann-Bröckelschen-Stiftung 8. Mainz am Rhein: Verlag Philipp von Zabern.

Dürring, N. 2000. 'Nofretete und andere Kleinigkeiten. Ludwig Borchardt und die frühe Ägyptologie', *Antike Welt* 31(4): 424-426.

Eickhoff, M. 2002. 'Die Politisch-Gesellschaftliche Bedeutung der Archäologie während der deutschen Besetzung der Niederlande. Reflexionen am Beispiel von F. C. Bursch und A. E. van Giffen', in A. Leube (ed.), *Prähistorie und Nationalsozialismus. Die mittel- und osteuropäische Ur- und Frühgeschichtsforschung in den Jahren 1933–1945*. Studien zur Wissenschafts- und Universitätsgeschichte 2. Heidelberg: Synchron Wissenschaftsverlag der Autoren, 555-573.

Eickhoff, M. 2007. '„Der Unterschied zwischen den Russen und uns". Die Vor- und Frühgeschichtsforschung in den besetzten Niederlanden 1940-1945', in J.-P. Legendre, L. Olivier and B. Schnitzler (eds). *L'Archéologie Nationale-Socialiste dans les Pays Occupes à l'Ouest du Reich. Actes de la Table Ronde Internationale «Blut und Boden» tenue à Lyon (Rhône) dans le cadre du Xe congrès de la European Association of Archaeologists (EAA), les 8 et 9 septembre 2004*. Gollion: Infolio éditions, 351-364.

Ellinger, E. 2006. *Deutsche Orientalistik zur Zeit des Nationalsozialismus, 1933–1945*. Thèses 4. Edingen-Neckarshausen: Deux Mondes.

Ess, M. van. 1998. '1912/13: Uruk (Warka). Die Stadt des Gilgamesch und der Ischtar', in G. Wilhelm (ed.), *Zwischen Tigris und Nil. 100 Jahre Ausgrabungen der Deutschen Orient-Gesellschaft in Vorderasien und Ägypten*. Zaberns Bildbände zur Archäologie. Sonderhefte der Antiken Welt. Mainz am Rhein: Verlag Philipp von Zabern, 32-41.

Faber, R. 1995. 'Humanistische und Faschistische Welt. Über Ludwig Curtius (1874-1954)', *Hephaistos* 13: 173-186.

Fehr, H. 2007. 'The «Germanic Heritage» of Northern Gaul: Early Medieval Archaeology in Occupied France and Belgium', in J.-P. Legendre, L. Olivier and B. Schnitzler (eds), *L'Archéologie Nationale-Socialiste dans les Pays Occupes à l'Ouest du Reich. Actes de la Table ronde Internationale «Blut und Boden» tenue à Lyon (Rhône) dans le Cadre du Xe Congrès de la European Association of Archaeologists (EAA), les 8 et 9 septembre 2004.* Gollion: Infolio éditions, 325-335.

Fittschen, K. 1996. 'Die Gründung des Deutschen Archäologischen Instituts in Athen, Ernst Curtius (1814-1896) zum Gedächtnis'. *Mitteilungen des Deutschen Archäologischen Instituts Athenische Abteilung* 111: 1-44.

Freischlader, L. 2000. 'Die Orientreise Kaiser Wilhelms II. im Jahre 1898. Vorgeschichte, Verlauf und Ergebnisse', in H.-D. Bienert and B. Müller-Neuhof. *At the Crossroads. Essays on the Archaeology, History and Current Affairs of the Middle East.* Amman: German Protestant Institute, 181-223.

Fritz, V. 2000. 'Für die Biblische und Kirchliche Vorzeit. Hundert Jahre Deutsches Evangelisches Institut für Altertumswissenschaft des Heiligen Landes', *Antike Welt* 31: 43-47.

Fritz, V. 2007. 'Volkmar Fritz (1938-2007)', Biblical Archaeological Review August 29. Retrieved July 2011 from http://www.bib-arch.org/news/fritz-obit.asp.

Fröhlich, T. 2007. 'Das Deutsche Archäologische Institut in Rom in der Kriegs- und Nachkriegszeit bis zur Wiedereröffnung 1953', in M. Matheus, *Deutsche Forschungs- und Kulturinstitute in Rom in der Nachkriegszeit.* Bibliothek des Deutschen Historischen Instituts Rom 112. Tübingen: Max Niemeyer Verlag, 139-179.

Fröhlich, T. 2008. 'The study of the Lombards and the Ostrogoths at the German Archaeological Institute of Rome, 1937-1943', *Fragmenta* 2: 183-213.

Gatzen, A. 2007. 'Die Ausgrabungen auf der Aleburg bei Befort im Jahre 1941', in J.-P. Legendre, L. Olivier and B. Schnitzler (eds), *L'Archéologie Nationale-Socialiste dans les Pays Occupes à l'Ouest du Reich. Actes de la Table ronde Internationale «Blut und Boden» tenue à Lyon (Rhône) dans le Cadre du Xe Congrès de la European Association of Archaeologists (EAA), les 8 et 9 septembre 2004.* Gollion: Infolio éditions, 257-270.

Gediga, B. 2002. 'Die Ur- und Frühgeschichte in Breslau in den Jahren 1933-1945', in A. Leube (ed.), *Prähistorie und Nationalsozialismus. Die mittel- und osteuropäische Ur- und Frühgeschichtsforschung in den Jahren 1933–1945.* Studien zur Wissenschafts- und Universitätsgeschichte 2. Heidelberg: Synchron Wissenschaftsverlag der Autoren, 503-509.

Gerlach, I. (ed.). 2003. *25 Jahre Ausgrabungen und Forschungen im Jemen 1978-2003. 25 Years Excavations and Research in Yemen 1978-2003.* Hefte zur Kulturgeschichte des Jemen 1. Berlin: Deutsches Archäologisches Institut, Orient-Abteilung, Außenstelle Sanaa.

Gob, A. 2007. 'Deutsche Grösse. Une exposition á la Gloire de l'Empire Allemande en 1942 à Bruxelles', in J.-P. Legendre, L. Olivier and B. Schnitzler (eds), *L'Archéologie Nationale-Socialiste dans les Pays Occupes à l'Ouest du Reich. Actes de la Table ronde*

Internationale «Blut und Boden» tenue à Lyon (Rhône) dans le Cadre du Xe Congrès de la European Association of Archaeologists (EAA), les 8 et 9 septembre 2004. Gollion: Infolio éditions, 337-349.

Goethe, J.W. von. 1981. *Goethe. Johann Wolfgang von Goethe. Werke. Kommentare und Register.* Hamburger Ausgabe in 14 Bänden 1(1). München: C.H. Beck'sche Verlagsbuchhandlung.

Goette, H.R. and O. Palagia (eds). 2005. *Ludwig Ross und Griechenland. Akten des internationalen Kolloquiums, Athen, 2.–3. Oktober 2002.* Internationale Archäologie. Studia Honoraria 24. Rhaden/Westfalen: Verlag Marie Leidorf GmbH.

Gramsch, A. 2006. 'Eine kurze Geschichte des archäologischen Denkens in Deutschland'. *Leipziger online-Beiträge zur Ur- und Frühgeschichtlichen Archäologie* 19. Leipzig: Professur für Ur- und Frühgeschichte der Universität Leipzig. Retrieved 11 July 2011 from http://www.uni-leipzig.de/histsem/uploads/media/Nr.19-Gramsch.pdf.

Greiff, S., Y. Shenping and B. Zorn. 2006. '15 Jahre Entwicklung von Methoden zur Erhaltung von Kulturgütern durch das Römisch-Germanische Zentralmuseum Mainz und das Archäologische Institut der Provinz Shaanxi', in *Der Vergangenheit eine Zukunft geben. 15 Jahre Deutsch-Chinesische Entwicklung und Erprobung von Verfahren zur Erhaltung von Kulturgut.* Bonn, Berlin: Bundesministerium für Bildung und Forschung (BMBF) Referat Öffentlichkeitsarbeit, 188-193.

Gringmuth-Dallmer, E. 1993a. 'Die Ur- und Frühgeschichtsforschung an der Berliner Akademie der Wissenschaften nach Wilhelm Unverzagt. Versuch einer Bilanz', *Ausgrabungen und Funde* 38: 275-280.

Gringmuth-Dallmer, E. 1993b. 'Archaeology in the former German Democratic Republic since 1989', *Antiquity* 67(254): 135-142.

Gringmuth-Dallmer, E. 2001. 'Die Berliner Akademie der Wissenschaften und die Mittelalterarchäologie in der DDR', *Mitteilungen der Arbeitsgemeinschaft für Archäologie des Mittelalters und der Neuzeit* 12: 25-31.

Gröschel, S.-G. 1994. 'Heros Winckelmann', *Antike Welt Jubiläumsausgabe*: 11-25.

Grunewald, E. (ed.). 2006. *Götter, Gräber und Gelehrte: Archäologie des Romans der Archäologie. Begleitbuch zur Ausstellung der Landesbibliothek Oldenburg. Schriften der Landesbibliothek Oldenburg* 42. Oldenburg: Isensee Verlag.

Hafemann, I. (ed.). 2010. Preußen in Ägypten, Ägypten in Preußen, *Kaleidogramme* 59. Berlin: Kulturverlag Kadmos.

Halle, U. 2002. *„Die Externsteine sind bis auf weiteres Germanisch!". Prähistorische Archäologie im Dritten Reich.* Sonderveröffentlichungen des Naturwissenschaftlichen und Historischen Vereins für das Land Lippe 68. Bielefeld: Verlag für Regionalgeschichte.

Halle, U. 2007. 'Go West. German Archaeology during the Third Reich (Netherlands and Belgium)', in J.-P. Legendre, L. Olivier and B. Schnitzler (eds), *L'Archéologie Nationale-Socialiste dans les Pays Occupes à l'Ouest du Reich. Actes de la Table ronde Internationale «Blut und Boden» tenue à Lyon (Rhône) dans le Cadre du Xe Congrès de la European Association of Archaeologists (EAA), les 8 et 9 septembre 2004.* Gollion: Infolio éditions, 303-311.

Halle, U. 2009. 'Deutsche Ost-, deutsche Westforschung: Ein Vergleich', in J. Schachtmann, M. Strobel and T. Widera (eds), *Politik und Wissenschaft in der prähistorischen Archäologie. Perspektiven aus Sachsen, Böhmen und Schlesien*. Berichte und Studien 56. Göttingen: V&R Unipress GmbH, 53-68.

Hamdorf, F.W. 1986a. 'Klenzes archäologischen Studien und Reisen, seine Mission in Griechenland', in Glyptothek München (ed.), *Ein Griechischer Traum. Leo von Klenze. Der Archäologe. Ausstellung vom 6. Dezember 1985–9. Februar 1986, Glyptothek München*. München: Staatliche Antikensammlung und Glyptothek, 117–212.

Hamdorf, F.W. 1986b. 'Reisen in Griechenland – eine Chronik der Wiederentdeckung', in Glyptothek München (ed.), *Ein griechischer Traum. Leo von Klenze. Der Archäologe. Ausstellung vom 6. Dezember 1985–9. Februar 1986, Glyptothek München*. München: Staatliche Antikensammlung und Glyptothek, 247–263.

Hamilakis, Y. 2008. 'Decolonizing Greek Archaeology: Indigenous Archaeologies, Modernist Archaeology and the Post-Colonial Critique', in D. Damaskos and D. Plantzos (eds), *A Singular Antiquity. Archaeology and Hellenic Identity in Twentieth-century Greece*. Athens: The Benaki Museum, 273-284.

Härke, H. 2002. 'The German experience', in H. Härke (ed.), *Archaeology, Ideology and Society. The German Experience*. second, revised edition. Gesellschaften und Staaten im Epochenwandel 7. Frankfurt am Main, Berlin, Bern, Bruxelles, New York, Oxford, Wien: Peter Lang (second, revised edition), 13-40.

Haßmann, H. 2002. 'Archaeology in the 'Third Reich', in H. Härke (ed.), *Archaeology, Ideology and Society. The German Experience*. Gesellschaften und Staaten im Epochenwandel 7. Frankfurt am Main, Berlin, Bern, Bruxelles, New York, Oxford, Wien: Peter Lang (second, revised edition), 67-141.

Heber, S. 2008. 'Wilhelm Unverzagt und die archäologischen Untersuchungen in Zantoch (1932-1934)', *Ethnographisch-Archäologische Zeitschrift* 49(3): 309-333.

Heimsoth, A. 2008. 'Die Bagdadbahn und die Archäologie. Wirtschaftliche und wissenschaftliche Planungen im Osmanischen Reich', in C. Trümpler (ed.), *Das große Spiel. Archäologie und Politik zur Zeit des Kolonialismus (1860–1940)*. Essen, Köln: Ruhr Museum, DuMont Buchverlag, 354-367.

Herrmann, J. 1988. 'Archäologische Feldforschungen und Ausgrabungen des Zentralinstituts für Alte Geschichte und Archäologie in der Mitte und zweiten Hälfte der 80er Jahre. Ausgrabungen und Funde', *Archäologische Berichte und Informationen* 33(6): 265-276.

Herrmann, J. and H. Klengel 1989. 'Worte des Gedenkens', *Mitteilungen zur Alten Geschichte und Archäologie in der Deutschen Demokratischen Republik* 17: 7-14.

Heske, I. 1999. 'Von Haithabu nach Kiew und in den Kaukasus - Aspekte des NS-Kunstraubes durch Ur- und Frühgeschichtler', *Nachrichten und Informationen zur Kultur* 1: 2-6.

Heuss, A. 2000. *Kunst- und Kulturgutraub. Eine vergleichende Studie zur Besatzungspolitik der Nationalsozialisten in Frankreich und der Sowjetunion*. Heidelberg: Universitätsverlag C. Winter Heidelberg GmbH.

Heuss, A. 2002a. 'Der Kulturgutraub der Prähistoriker in der ehemaligen Sowjetunion', *Jahresschrift für mitteldeutsche Vorgeschichte* 85: 407-418.

Heuss, A. 2002b. 'Prähistorische «Raubgrabungen» in der Ukraine', in A. Leube (ed.), *Prähistorie und Nationalsozialismus. Die mittel- und osteuropäische Ur- und Frühgeschichtsforschung in den Jahren 1933–1945*. Studien zur Wissenschafts- und Universitätsgeschichte 2. Heidelberg: Synchron Wissenschaftsverlag der Autoren, 545-553.

Hiller von Gaertringen, J. 1995. 'Deutsche archäologische Unternehmungen im besetzten Griechenland 1941–1944', *Mitteilungen des Deutschen Archäologischen Instituts Athenische Abteilung* 110: 461-490.

Holtz, B. 2010. 'Weltoffenheit oder Machtkalkül? Friedrich Wilhelm IV. und sein Interesse am Orient', in I. Hafemann, *Preußen in Ägypten, Ägypten in Preußen*. Kaleidogramme 59. Berlin: Kulturverlag Kadmos, 181-202.

Hübner, U. 2002. '125 Jahre Deutscher Verein zur Erforschung Palästinas', *Antike Welt* 33: 653-658.

Hübner, U. and J. Kamlah 2008. 'Volkmar Fritz (1938-2007)', *Zeitschrift des Deutschen Palästina-Vereins* 124(1): 84-88.

Huismann, F. 2008. 'Wilhelm Jordan. Als Wissenschaftler im besetzten Osten', in J.E. Schulte (ed.), *Die SS, Himmler und die Wewelsburg*. Paderborn, München, Wien, Zürich: Ferdinand Schöningh, 209-226.

Jacobs, J. 2002. 'German Unification and East German Archaeology', in H. Härke (ed.), *Archaeology, Ideology and Society. The German Experience*. Gesellschaften und Staaten im Epochenwandel 7. Frankfurt am Main, Berlin, Bern, Bruxelles, New York, Oxford, Wien: Peter Lang (second revised edition), 343-355.

Jagust, F. 2009. 'Follow the Money. Bemerkungen zum Verhältnis von Geld, Prähistorie und Nationalsozialismus', in J. Schachtmann, M. Strobel and T. Widera (eds) *Politik und Wissenschaft in der prähistorischen Archäologie. Perspektiven aus Sachsen, Böhmen und Schlesien*. Berichte und Studien 56. Göttingen: V&R unipress GmbH, 285-299.

Jähne, A. 2001. 'Heinrich Schliemann. Troiaausgräber wider Willen', in Archäologisches Landesmuseum Baden-Württemberg (ed.), *Troia. Traum und Wirklichkeit*. Begleitband zur Ausstellung 'Troia - Traum und Wirklichkeit'. Darmstadt: Wissenschaftliche Buchgesellschaft, 330-337.

Jansen, C. 2008a. 'The German Archaeological Institute Between Transnational Scholarship and Foreign Cultural Policy', *Fragmenta* 2: 151-181.

Jansen, C. 2008b. 'Völkische und rassistische Tendenzen in den deutschen Wissenschaften 1900-1940', in J.E. Schulte (ed.), *Die SS, Himmler und die Wewelsburg*. Paderborn, München, Wien, Zürich: Ferdinand Schöningh, 141-160.

Jansen, C. 2010. 'Archäologie im Dritten Reich. Eine Einführung', *Das Altertum* 55: 83-88.

Jantzen, U. 1986. *Einhundert Jahre Athener Institut 1874-1974*. Das Deutsche Archäologische Institut. Geschichte und Dokumente 10. Mainz: Verlag Philipp von Zabern.

Jernej, R. 2007. 'Archäologie in Kärnten 1938-1945', in J.-P. Legendre, L. Olivier and B. Schnitzler (eds), *L'Archéologie Nationale-Socialiste dans les Pays Occupes à l'Ouest du Reich. Actes de la Table ronde Internationale «Blut und Boden» tenue à Lyon (Rhône) dans le Cadre du Xe Congrès de la European Association of Archaeologists (EAA), les 8 et 9 septembre 2004*. Gollion: Infolio éditions, 271-286.

Johansen, O.S. 2002. 'Anmerkungen zur archäologischen Tätigkeit in Norwegen in den Jahren 1940-1945', in A. Leube (ed.), *Prähistorie und Nationalsozialismus. Die mittel- und osteuropäische Ur- und Frühgeschichtsforschung in den Jahren 1933–1945*. Studien zur Wissenschafts- und Universitätsgeschichte 2. Heidelberg: Synchron Wissenschaftsverlag der Autoren, 619-622.

Junker, K. 1997. *Das Archäologische Institut des Deutschen Reiches zwischen Forschung und Politik. Die Jahre 1929 bis 1945*. Das Deutsche Archäologische Institut, Geschichte und Dokumente 11. Mainz: Verlag Philipp von Zabern.

Junker, K. 1998. 'Research under Dictatorship: the German Archaeological Institute 1929–1945', *Antiquity* 72(276): 282-292.

Junker, K. 2001. 'Zur Geschichte des Deutschen Archäologischen Instituts in den Jahren von 1933 bis 1945', in B. Näf (ed.), *Antike und Altertumswissenschaft in der Zeit von Faschismus und Nationalsozialismus. Kolloquium Universität Zürich 14.-17. Oktober 1998*. Mandelbachtal, Cambridge: Edition Cicero, 503-517.

Kaczmarek, J. 2009. 'Archäologie in Westpolen und im Warthegau zwischen 1918 und 1945', in J. Schachtmann, M. Strobel and T. Widera (eds), *Politik und Wissenschaft in der prähistorischen Archäologie. Perspektiven aus Sachsen, Böhmen und Schlesien*. Berichte und Studien 56. Göttingen: V&R unipress GmbH, 251-265.

Kalb, P., G. Rasbach and B. Sasse-Kunst. 2001. 'Die Bibliothek der Römisch-Germanischen Kommission', *Bericht der Römisch-Germanischen Kommission* 82: 395-345.

Kalpaxis, T. 2002. 'Die Vorgeschichte und die Nachwirkungen des Olympia-Vertrages aus griechischer Sicht', in H. Kyrieleis (ed.), *Olympia 1875-2000. 125 Jahre Deutsche Ausgrabungen. Internationales Symposion, Berlin 9.-11. November 2000*. Mainz am Rhein: Verlag Philipp von Zabern, 19-30.

Kandler, M. 1998. 'Unter fremden Namen. Die Jahre 1938–1945', in M. Kandler (ed.), *100 Jahre Österreichisches Archäologisches Institut. 1898-1998*. Sonderschriften des Österreichischen Archäologischen Instituts 31. Wien: Österreichisches Archäologisches Institut, 49-60.

Kandler, M. 2000. 'Guido List, Adolf Hitler und Carnuntum', in *Altmodische Archäologie. Festschrift für Friedrich Brein*. Forum Archaeologiae 14(3). Retrieved 12 July 2011 from http://farch.net.

Kästner, U. 2008. 'Carl Human und die Entdeckung des Pergamonaltars. Vom Privatunternehmen zum Staatsauftrag', in C. Trümpler (ed.), *Das große Spiel. Archäologie und Politik zur Zeit des Kolonialismus (1860–1940)*. Essen, Köln: Ruhr Museum, DuMont Buchverlag, 324-335.

Kater, M.H. 1974. *Das „Ahnenerbe" der SS 1935-1945. Ein Beitrag zur Kulturpolitik des Dritten Reiches*. Studien zur Zeitgeschichte 6. Stuttgart: Deutsche Verlags-Anstalt.

Kinahan, J. 1995. 'Weißer Riese-Schwarze Zwerge? Empirismus und ethnische Deutung in der Archäologie Namibias', *Archäologische Informationen* 18(1): 7-18.

Kinahan, J. 2002. 'Traumland Südwest: two Moments in the History of German archaeological Inquiry in Namibia', in H. Härke (ed.), *Archaeology, Ideology and Society. The German Experience.* Gesellschaften und Staaten im Epochenwandel 7. Frankfurt am Main, Berlin, Bern, Bruxelles, New York, Oxford, Wien: Peter Lang (second revised edition), 356-377.

Kirchhoff, J. 2007. *Wissenschaftsförderung und forschungspolitische Prioritäten der Notgemeinschaft der Deutschen Wissenschaft 1920-1932.* Retrieved 12 April 2011 from http://edoc.ub.uni-muenchen.de/7870/.

Kitova, L. 2010. 'Das Wirken Gero von Merharts in Krasnojarsk', in A. Müller-Karpe, C. Dobiat, S. Hansen and H. Parzinger (eds), *Gero von Merhart. Ein deutscher Archäologe in Sibirien. 1914–1921. Deutsch-Russisches-Symposium. 4.–7. Juni 2009. Marburg.* Kleine Schriften aus dem Vorgeschichtlichen Seminar Marburg 59. Marburg: Vorgeschichtliches Seminar der Philipps-Universität Marburg, 67-71.

Klinkhammer, L. 2002. 'Großgrabung und große Politik. Der Olympia-Vertrag als Epochenwende', in H. Kyrieleis (ed.), *Olympia 1875-2000. 125 Jahre Deutsche Ausgrabungen. Internationales Symposion, Berlin 9.-11. November 2000.* Mainz am Rhein: Verlag Philipp von Zabern, 31-47.

Kloft, H. 2006. 'Adolf Erman und die Alte Geschichte. Der Briefwechsel mit Eduard Meyer und Ulrich Wilcken', in B.U. Schipper (ed.), *Ägyptologie als Wissenschaft: Adolf Erman (1854-1937) in seiner Zeit.* Berlin: Walter de Gruyter GmbH, 294-329.

Kolník, T. 2002. 'Prähistorische Forschung in der Slowakei 1933–1945. Zur Rolle der österreichischen und deutschen Ur- und Frühgeschichte bei der Entwicklung der slowakischen Forschung', in A. Leube (ed.), *Prähistorie und Nationalsozialismus. Die mittel- und osteuropäische Ur- und Frühgeschichtsforschung in den Jahren 1933–1945.* Studien zur Wissenschafts- und Universitätsgeschichte 2. Heidelberg: Synchron Wissenschaftsverlag der Autoren, 481-501.

Krämer, W. 2001. 'Gerhard Bersu ein deutscher Prähistoriker 1889–1964', *Bericht der Römisch-Germanischen Kommission* 82(2001): 5-101.

Krauss, R. 1998a. '1902–1908: Grabungen im Pyramidenfeld von Abusir', in G. Wilhelm (ed.), *Zwischen Tigris und Nil. 100 Jahre Ausgrabungen der Deutschen Orient-Gesellschaft in Vorderasien und Ägypten.* Zaberns Bildbände zur Archäologie. Sonderhefte der Antiken Welt. Mainz am Rhein: Verlag Philipp von Zabern, 76-79.

Krauss, R. 1998b. '1911–1914: Vier Grabungswinter in Amarna', in G. Wilhelm (ed.), *Zwischen Tigris und Nil. 100 Jahre Ausgrabungen der Deutschen Orient-Gesellschaft in Vorderasien und Ägypten.* Zaberns Bildbände zur Archäologie. Sonderhefte der Antiken Welt. Mainz am Rhein: Verlag Philipp von Zabern, 82-89.

Kröger, M. 2008. 'Archäologen im Krieg: Bell, Lawrence, Musil, Oppenheim, Frobenius', in C. Trümpler (ed.), *Das große Spiel. Archäologie und Politik zur Zeit des Kolonialismus (1860–1940).* Essen, Köln: Ruhr Museum, DuMont Buchverlag, 448-461.

Kunow, J. 2002. 'Die Entwicklung von archäologischen Organisationen und Institutionen in Deutschland im 19. und 20. Jahrhundert und das „öffentliche Interesse". Bedeutungsgewinne und Bedeutungsverluste und deren Folgen', in P.F. Biehl, A. Gramsch and A. Marciniak (eds), *Archäologien Europas / Archaeologies of Europe. Geschichte, Methoden und Theorien / History, Methods and Theories.* Tübinger Archäologische Taschenbücher 3. Münster, New York, München, Berlin: Waxmann, 147-183.

Lang, M. 2008. 'Der Babel-Bibel-Streit', in C. Trümpler (ed.), *Das große Spiel. Archäologie und Politik zur Zeit des Kolonialismus (1860–1940).* Essen, Köln: Ruhr Museum, DuMont Buchverlag, 114-123.

Legendre, J.-P. 1999. 'Archaeology and Ideological Propaganda in annexed Alsace (1940-1944)', *Antiquity* 73(279): 184-190.

Legendre, J.-P. 2002. 'Grabungsstätten und Forschungsthemen im Département Moselle. Die Grabungsarbeiten von Ennery (1941) und Saint-Pierre-aux-Nonnains (1942)', in H.-P. Kuhnen (ed.), *Propaganda. Macht. Geschichte. Archäologie an Rhein und Mosel im Dienst des Nationalsozialismus.* Schriftenreihe des Rheinischen Landesmuseums Trier 24. Trier: Rheinisches Landesmuseum, 71-80.

Legendre, J.-P. 2007. 'Les Fouilles de la Nécropole Mérovingienne d'Ennery (1941): Dichtung und Wahrheit (fiction et réalité)', in J.-P. Legendre, L. Olivier and B. Schnitzler (eds), *L'Archéologie Nationale-Socialiste dans les Pays Occupes à l'Ouest du Reich. Actes de la Table ronde Internationale «Blut und Boden» tenue à Lyon (Rhône) dans le Cadre du Xe Congrès de la European Association of Archaeologists (EAA), les 8 et 9 septembre 2004.* Gollion: Infolio éditions, 217-230.

Legendre, J.-P. 2008. 'Archäologie und NS-Propaganda im annektierten Lothringen: das Landesdenkmalamt Metz und seine Abteilung Vor- und Frühgeschichte (1940-1944)', *Ethnographisch-Archäologische Zeitschrift* 49(3): 335-352.

Legendre, J.-P, L. Olivier and B. Schnitzler 2007a. 'Introduction. L'Archéologie Nazie en Europe de l'Ouest', in J.-P. Legendre, L. Olivier and B. Schnitzler (eds), *L'Archéologie Nationale-Socialiste dans les Pays Occupes à l'Ouest du Reich. Actes de la Table ronde Internationale «Blut und Boden» tenue à Lyon (Rhône) dans le Cadre du Xe Congrès de la European Association of Archaeologists (EAA), les 8 et 9 septembre 2004.* Gollion: Infolio éditions, 21-42.

Legendre, J.-P, L. Olivier and B. Schnitzler 2007b. 'L'Archaeologie Nationale-Socialiste et la Germanisation de l'Europe de l'Ouest: Esquisse d'un Bilan', in J.-P. Legendre, L. Olivier and B. Schnitzler (eds), *L'Archéologie Nationale-Socialiste dans les Pays Occupes à l'Ouest du Reich. Actes de la Table ronde Internationale «Blut und Boden» tenue à Lyon (Rhône) dans le Cadre du Xe Congrès de la European Association of Archaeologists (EAA), les 8 et 9 septembre 2004.* Gollion: Infolio éditions, 405-426.

Lehmann, W. 2000. 'Forschung in Museen: Verflucht sei der Staudamm', *Der Tagesspiegel,* 24 August 2000. Retrieved 8 July 2010 from http://www.tagesspiegel.de/weltspiegel/ gesundheit/ forschung-in-museen-verflucht-sei-der-staudamm/161524.html.

Leppmann, W. 1986. *Winckelmann. Ein Leben für Apoll.* Frankfurt am Main: Fischer Taschenbuch Verlag GmbH.

Leube, A. 1998. 'Zur Ur- und Frühgeschichtsforschung in Berlin nach dem Tode Gustaf Kossinnas bis 1945', *Ethnographisch-Archäologische Zeitschrift* 39: 373-427.

Leube, A. 1999. 'Zur Vor- und Frühgeschichte an der Friedrich-Wilhelms-Universität in den Jahren 1933-1945', in E. Cziesla, T. Kersting and S. Pratsch (eds), *Den Bogen spannen … Festschrift für Bernhard Gramsch*. Beiträge zur Ur- und Frühgeschichte Mitteleuropas 20. Weissbach: Beier und Beran.

Leube, A. 2001. 'Anmerkungen zur Deutschen Prähistorie 1938-1945. Brandenburg und die Slowakei', *Slovenská Archeológia* 49(1): 1-18.

Leube, A. 2004. 'Deutsche Prähistoriker im besetzten Polen 1939-1945', in B. Hänsel (ed.), *Parerga Praehistorica. Jubilämumschrift zur Prähistorischen Archäologie. 15 Jahre UPA*. Universitätsforschungen zur Prähistorischen Archäologie 100. Bonn: Verlag Dr. Rudolf Habelt GmbH, 287-347.

Leube, A. 2007. 'Deutsche Prähistoriker im besetzten Westeuropa 1940-1945. Das „Ahnenerbe" der SS in Westeuropa', in J.-P. Legendre, L. Olivier and B. Schnitzler (eds), *L'Archéologie Nationale-Socialiste dans les Pays Occupes à l'Ouest du Reich. Actes de la Table ronde Internationale «Blut und Boden» tenue à Lyon (Rhône) dans le Cadre du Xe Congrès de la European Association of Archaeologists (EAA), les 8 et 9 septembre 2004*. Gollion: Infolio éditions, 93-119.

Löhlein, W. 2003. 'Majestät brauchen Scherben. Wenn Wilhelm II. statt seines Szepters den Spaten schwang', *Antike Welt* 34(6): 659-664.

Löhlein, W. 2008. 'Mit Zepter und Spaten. Kaiser Wilhelm II. und die Archäologie', in C. Trümpler (ed.), *Das große Spiel. Archäologie und Politik zur Zeit des Kolonialismus (1860–1940)*. Essen, Köln: Ruhr Museum, DuMont Buchverlag, 390-397.

Löhlein, W. 2009. 'Wilhelm II. und die Archäologie', *Archäologie in Deutschland* 2009(3): 64-66.

Lullies, R. and W. Schiering (eds). 1988. *Archäologenbildnisse. Porträts und Kurzbiographien von Klassischen Archäologen deutscher Sprache*. Mainz am Rhein: Verlag Philipp von Zabern.

Mączyńska, M. 2002. 'Ur- und Frühgeschichte in Kraków in den Jahren 1933-1945', in A. Leube (ed.), *Prähistorie und Nationalsozialismus. Die mittel- und osteuropäische Ur- und Frühgeschichtsforschung in den Jahren 1933–1945*. Studien zur Wissenschafts- und Universitätsgeschichte 2. Heidelberg: Synchron Wissenschaftsverlag der Autoren, 511-516.

Mahsarski, D. 2011. *Herbert Jankuhn (1905 – 1990). Ein deutscher Prähistoriker zwischen nationalsozialistischer Ideologie und wissenschaftlicher Objektivität*. Internationale Archäologie 114. Rahden/Westfalen: Verlag Marie Leidorf GmbH.

Maier, F.G. 1994. 'Von Winckelmann zu Schliemann. Archäologie als Eroberungs-wissenschaft des 19. Jahrhunderts', *Antike Welt Jubiläumsausgabe*: 35-59.

Maischberger, M. 2002. 'German Archaeology during the Third Reich, 1933-45: a Case Study Based on Archival Evidence', *Antiquity* 76(291): 209-218.

Makiewicz, T. 2002. 'Archäologische Forschung in Poznań während des Zweiten Weltkrieges', in A. Leube (ed.), *Prähistorie und Nationalsozialismus. Die mittel- und osteuropäische Ur- und Frühgeschichtsforschung in den Jahren 1933–1945*. Studien zur Wissenschafts- und Universitätsgeschichte 2. Heidelberg: Synchron Wissenschaftsverlag der Autoren, 517-533.

Manderscheid, H. 2010. 'Opfer - Täter - schweigende Mehrheit. Anmerkung zur deutschen Klassischen Archäologie während des Nationalsozialismus', *Hephaistos* 27: 41-69.

Mante, G. 2007. *Die deutschsprachige prähistorische Archäologie. Eine Ideengeschichte im Zeichen von Wissenschaft, Politik und europäischen Werten*. Internationale Hochschulschriften 467. Münster, New York, München, Berlin: Waxmann.

Marchand, S.L. 1996. *Down from Olympus. Archaeology and Philhellenism in Germany, 1750-1970*. Princeton, New Jersey: Princeton University Press.

Martens, J. 2002. 'Die Nordische Archäologie und das «Dritte Reich»', in A. Leube (ed.), *Prähistorie und Nationalsozialismus. Die mittel- und osteuropäische Ur- und Frühgeschichtsforschung in den Jahren 1933–1945*. Studien zur Wissenschafts- und Universitätsgeschichte 2. Heidelberg: Synchron Wissenschaftsverlag der Autoren, 603-617.

Marzahn, J. 2008a. 'Die deutschen Ausgrabungen in Babylon', in J. Marzahn, G. Schauerte, B. Müller-Neuhof and K. Sternitzke (eds), *Babylon. Wahrheit. Eine Ausstellung des Vorderasiatischen Museums Staatliche Museen zu Berlin mit Unterstützung der Staatsbibliothek zu Berlin*. München: Hirmer, 67-78.

Marzahn, J. 2008b. 'Von der Grabung zum Museum. Babylon wird sichtbar', in J. Marzahn, G. Schauerte, B. Müller-Neuhof and K. Sternitzke (eds), *Babylon. Wahrheit. Eine Ausstellung des Vorderasiatischen Museums Staatliche Museen zu Berlin mit Unterstützung der Staatsbibliothek zu Berlin*. München: Hirmer, 91-98.

Marzahn, J. and B. Salje (eds). 2003. *Wiedererstehendes Assur: 100 Jahre deutsche Ausgrabungen in Assyrien*. Mainz am Rhein: Verlag Philipp von Zabern.

Matthes, O. 1996. 'Eduard Meyer und die Deutsche Orient-Gesellschaft', *Mitteilungen der Deutschen Orient-Gesellschaft zu Berlin* 128: 173-218.

Matthes, O. 1998. 'James Simon - Gründer und Mäzen der DOG', in G. Wilhelm (ed.), *Zwischen Tigris und Nil. 100 Jahre Ausgrabungen der Deutschen Orient-Gesellschaft in Vorderasien und Ägypten*. Zaberns Bildbände zur Archäologie. Sonderhefte der Antiken Welt. Mainz am Rhein: Verlag Philipp von Zabern, 4.

Matthes, O. 2008. 'Deutsche Ausgräber im Vorderen Orient', in C. Trümpler (ed.), *Das große Spiel. Archäologie und Politik zur Zeit des Kolonialismus (1860–1940)*. Essen, Köln: Ruhr Museum, DuMont Buchverlag, 226-235.

Maul, S.M. 1998. '1903–1914: Assur. Das Herz eines Weltreiches', in G. Wilhelm (ed.), *Zwischen Tigris und Nil. 100 Jahre Ausgrabungen der Deutschen Orient-Gesellschaft in Vorderasien und Ägypten*. Zaberns Bildbände zur Archäologie. Sonderhefte der Antiken Welt. Mainz am Rhein: Verlag Philipp von Zabern, 47-65.

Meyer, H. 2004. 'Der Rechtsstatus des Deutschen Archäologischen Instituts. Rechtsgutachten', *Archäologischer Anzeiger* 2004(2): 155-220.

Minner, I.E. 2005. '„… so gilt mir Griechenland als mein zweites […] Vaterland". Die Griechenland-Erfahrung von Ludwig Ross im Spannungsfeld privater und beruflicher Heimatsuche', in H.R. Goette and O. Palagia (ed.), *Ludwig Ross und Griechenland. Akten des internationalen Kolloquiums, Athen, 2.–3. Oktober 2002.* Internationale Archäologie. Studia Honoraria 24. Rhaden/Westfalen: Verlag Marie Leidorf GmbH, 25-39.

Motyková, K. 2002. 'Die Ur- und Frühgeschichtsforschung in Böhmen 1918–1945 und die tschechisch-deutschen Beziehungen', in A. Leube (ed.), *Prähistorie und Nationalsozialismus. Die mittel- und osteuropäische Ur- und Frühgeschichtsforschung in den Jahren 1933–1945.* Studien zur Wissenschafts- und Universitätsgeschichte 2. Heidelberg: Synchron Wissenschaftsverlag der Autoren, 471-479.

Mühlenbruch, T. 2008. *Heinrich Schliemann. Ein Itinerar.* Kleine Schriften aus dem Vorgeschichtlichen Seminar Marburg 58. Marburg: Philipps-Universität.

Müller, T.T. 2000. '„Wir werden uns dieser Aufgabe mit derselben Zähigkeit widmen, mit der sich die Schutzstaffel allen anderen Aufgaben gewidmet hat"'. „Ahnenerbe", Urgeschichtsforschung und SS', *Nachrichten und Informationen zur Kultur* 4: 19-44.

Müller, U. 2010. 'Die "Kieler Schule" - Ur- und frühgeschichtliche Forschung zwischen 1927 und 1945', *Das Altertum* 55: 105-126.

Müller-Römer, F. 2009. 'Richard Lepsius – Begründer der modernen Ägyptologie. Vortrag beim Collegium Aegyptium des Instituts für Ägyptologie an der LMU München am 29.10.2009'. Retrieved 5 July 2011 from http://archiv.ub.uni-heidelberg.de/propylaeumdok/volltexte/2009/ 460/pdf/Mueller_Roemer_Lepsius.pdf.

Müller-Scheeßel, N., K. Rassmann, S. von Schnurbein and S. Sievers. 2001. 'Die Ausgrabungen und Geländeforschungen der Römisch-Germanischen Kommission', *Bericht der Römisch-Germanischen Kommission* 82: 291-361.

Neumayer, H. 2007. 'Frankfurt am Main, 31.10.2006, 16.00 Uhr', *Archäologisches Nachrichtenblatt* 12(2): 107-112.

Niemeier, W.-D. 2005. 'Ludwig Ross – Wegbereiter der Altertumswissenschaft im neuen Griechenland', in H.R. Goette and O. Palagia, *Ludwig Ross und Griechenland. Akten des internationalen Kolloquiums, Athen, 2.–3. Oktober 2002.* Internationale Archäologie. Studia Honoraria 24. Rhaden/Westfalen: Verlag Marie Leidorf GmbH, 1-11.

Niemeier, W.-D. 2007. 'German Archaeological Institute at Athens', in E. Korka (ed.), *Foreign Archaeological Schools in Greece – from the 19th to the 21st Century.* Athena: Melissa, 89-101.

Olivier, L. 2002. 'L'Archéologie du «3ème Reich» et la France. Notes pour Servir à l'Étude de la «Banalité du Mal» en Archéologie', in A. Leube (ed.), *Prähistorie und Nationalsozialismus. Die mittel- und osteuropäische Ur- und Frühgeschichtsforschung in den Jahren 1933–1945.* Studien zur Wissenschafts- und Universitätsgeschichte 2. Heidelberg: Synchron Wissenschaftsverlag der Autoren, 575-601.

Olivier, L. 2007. 'Une «Ambassade de l'Archéologie Allemande en France»: le Bureau «Préhistoire et Archéologie» du Kunstschutz (1940-1944)', in J.-P. Legendre, L. Olivier and B. Schnitzler (eds), *L'Archéologie Nationale-Socialiste dans les Pays Occupes à l'Ouest* du Reich. *Actes de la Table ronde Internationale «Blut und Boden» tenue à Lyon (Rhône) dans le Cadre du Xe Congrès de la European Association of Archaeologists (EAA), les 8 et 9 septembre 2004*. Gollion: Infolio éditions, 145-162.

Parzinger, H. 1998. 'Archäologie am Rande der Steppe. Die Eurasien-Abteilung des Deutschen Archäologischen Instituts', *Antike Welt* 29: 97-108.

Parzinger, H. 2007. 'Zwischen Kultur und Wissenschaft: eine Rückkehr in die Zukunft?', in K.-D. Lehmann (ed.), *Vogel Phönix. Die Stiftung Preußischer Kulturbesitz*. Berlin: University Press, 158–162.

Parzinger, H. 2010. 'Archäologisches in Daljóko', in A. Müller-Karpe, C. Dobiat, S. Hansen and H. Parzinger (eds), *Gero von Merhart. Ein deutscher Archäologe in Sibirien. 1914– 1921. Deutsch-Russisches-Symposium. 4.–7. Juni 2009. Marburg*. Kleine Schriften aus dem Vorgeschichtlichen Seminar Marburg 59. Marburg: Vorgeschichtliches Seminar der Philipps-Universität Marburg, 49-61.

Pawlitzki, B. 2009. *Antik wird Mode. Antike im bürgerlichen Alltag des 18. und 19. Jahrhunderts. Katalog einer Ausstellung im Winckelmann-Museum vom 28. Juni bis 6. September 2009*. Ruhpolding, Mainz: Verlag Franz Philipp Rutzen.

Petersen, L. 2008. 'Die Orientreise des deutschen Kaisers 1898 und die Ausgrabungen in Baalbek', in C. Trümpler (ed.), *Das große Spiel. Archäologie und Politik zur Zeit des Kolonialismus (1860–1940)*. Essen, Köln: Ruhr Museum, DuMont Buchverlag, 398-409.

Pétry, F. 1993. 'L'Archéologie en Alsace au Temps de l'Annexion: le Cas exemplaire des Fouilles du Mont Sainte Odile', *Cahiers Alsaciens d'Archéologie, d'Art et d'Histoire* 36: 77-88.

Piotrowska, D. 1998. 'Biskupin 1933–1996: Archaeology, Politics and Nationalism', *Archaeologica Polona* 35-36: 255-285.

Pluntke, L., U. Lehnert and A. Frey 2009. 'Ludwig Lindenschmit: Begründer der Werkstätten des RGZM', in A. Frey (ed.), *Ludwig Lindenschmit d. Ä. Begleitbuch zur Ausstellung aus Anlass seines 200. Geburtstages. Römisch-Germanisches Zentralmuseum, 10. September 2009 bis 10. Januar 2010*. Mosaiksteine, Forschungen am Römisch-Germanischen Zentralmuseum 5. Mainz: Verlag des Römisch-Germanischen Zentralmuseums.

Radt, W. 1999. *Pergamon. Geschichte und Bauten einer antiken Metropole*. Darmstadt: Primus-Verlag.

Rahms, H. 1994. 'Aufklärung und Überschwang. Winckelmanns Werk in neuer Sicht', *Antike Welt Jubiläumsausgabe*: 31-34.

Rassmann, K., K.-F. Rittershofer and S. von Schnurbein 2001. 'Die Veröffentlichungen der Römisch-Germanischen Kommission', *Bericht der Römisch-Germanischen Kommission* 82: 363-394.

Rheidt, K. 1999. 'Archäology heute: weltweit und interdisziplinär. Neue Forschungen des Deutschen Archäologischen Instituts', *Antike Welt* 30: 455-462.

Ridley, R.T. 1996. 'The founding of the German Archaeological Institute: unpublished documents', *Mitteilungen des Deutschen Archäologischen Instituts Roemische Abteilung* 103, 275-294.

Rudolf, E. 1995. 'Pompeji vor den Toren Wiens. Die 'Führergrabung' von Carnuntum 1938/40', *Hephaistos* 13: 187-220.

Rummel, U. (ed.) 2007. *Meeting the Past. 100 years in Egypt. German Archaeological Institute Cairo 1907-2007. Catalogue of the special Exhibition in the Egyptian Museum Cairo, 19th November 2007 to 15th January 2008*. Cairo: Deutsches Archäologisches Institut.

Saalmann, T. 2010. 'Wilhelm Unverzagt und das Staatliche Museum für Vor- und Frühgeschichte in Berlin in der NS-Zeit', *Das Altertum* 55: 89-104.

Schnapp, A. 2009. *Die Entdeckung der Vergangenheit. Ursprung und Abenteuer der Archäologie*. Stuttgart: J.G. Cotta'sche Buchhandlung Nachfolger.

Schneider, L. 1997. 'Abschied vom Deutschen Griechentum: 200 Jahre Klassische Archäologie', *Hephaistos* 15: 187-95.

Schnitzler, B. 1991. 'Le Casque de Baldenheim. Un Exemple de Détournement Idéologique Appliqué à l'Archéologie', *Cahiers Alsaciens d'Archéologie, d'Art et d'Histoire* 34: 83-7.

Schnitzler, B. 2002. 'Archäologische Ausgrabungen und Forschungsthemen im Elsaß', in H.-P. Kuhnen (ed.), *Propaganda. Macht. Geschichte. Archäologie an Rhein und Mosel im Dienst des Nationalsozialismus*. Schriftenreihe des Rheinischen Landesmuseums Trier 24. Trier: Rheinisches Landesmuseum, 57-70.

Schnitzler, B. 2007. 'Les Fouilles du Reichsbund für Deutsche Vorgeschichte au Mont Sainte-Odile en Alsace (1942-1944) et leur «Réinterprétation» a la Fin de la Guerre', in J.-P. Legendre, L. Olivier and B. Schnitzler (eds), *L'Archéologie Nationale-Socialiste dans les Pays Occupes à l'Ouest du Reich. Actes de la Table Ronde Internationale «Blut und Boden» tenue à Lyon (Rhône) dans le Cadre du Xe Congrès de la European Association of Archaeologists (EAA), les 8 et 9 septembre 2004*. Gollion: Infolio éditions, 231-240.

Schnitzler, B. and J.-P. Legendre 2002. 'Die Archäologie im Elsass und im Département Moselle zwischen 1940 und 1944', H.-P. Kuhnen (ed.), *Propaganda. Macht. Geschichte. Archäologie an Rhein und Mosel im Dienst des Nationalsozialismus*. Schriftenreihe des Rheinischen Landesmuseums Trier 24. Trier: Rheinisches Landesmuseum, 47-56.

Schnurbein, S. von. 1993. 'Die Auswahl der Grabungsplätze durch die Römisch-Germanische Kommission des Deutschen Archäologischen Instituts in den Jahren seit 1956', in S. Dušek (ed.), *Archäologische Denkmalpflege und Forschung. Kolloquium anlässlich der Jahrestagung 1992, Weimar, 18.5.-21.5.1992*. Weimar: Thüringisches Landesamt für Archäologische Denkmalpflege, 41-45.

Schnurbein, S. von. 2001. 'Abriß der Entwicklung der Römisch-Germanischen Kommission unter den einzelnen Direktoren von 1911 bis 2002', *Bericht der Römisch-Germanischen Kommission* 82: 137-289.

Schöbel, G. 2009. 'Die Ostinitiativen Hans Reinerths', in J. Schachtmann, M. Strobel and T. Widera (eds), *Politik und Wissenschaft in der prähistorischen Archäologie. Perspektiven aus Sachsen, Böhmen und Schlesien*. Berichte und Studien 56. Göttingen: V&R unipress GmbH, 267-283.

Schreiber Pedersen, L. 2007. 'Deutsche Archäologie im okkupierten Dänemark 1940-1945', in J.-P. Legendre, L. Olivier and B. Schnitzler (eds), *L'Archéologie Nationale-Socialiste dans les Pays Occupes à l'Ouest du Reich. Actes de la Table ronde Internationale «Blut und Boden» tenue à Lyon (Rhône) dans le Cadre du Xe Congrès de la European Association of Archaeologists (EAA), les 8 et 9 septembre 2004.* Gollion: Infolio éditions, 379-390.

Siefer, W. 2000. 'Schliemanns Erben im Reich der Schwarzen Pharaonen', *Focus Magazin* 1. Retrieved 8 July 2011 from http://www.focus.de/wissen/wissenschaft/schliemanns-erben-im-reich-der-schwarzen-pharaonen_aid_181583.html.

Skripkin, A.S. 1997. 'Archäologische Untersuchungen deutscher Gelehrter im unteren Wolgagebiet', *Kölner Jahrbuch* 30: 321-27.

Sösemann, B. 2002. 'Olympia als publizitisches National-Denkmal. Ein Beitrag zur Praxis und Methode der Wissenschaftspopularisierung im Deutschen Kaiserreich', in H. Kyrieleis (ed.), *Olympia 1875-2000. 125 Jahre Deutsche Ausgrabungen. Internationales Symposion, Berlin 9.-11. November 2000.* Mainz am Rhein: Verlag Philipp von Zabern, 49-84.

Stern, T. 2010. 'Von der Denkmalpflege zum Propagandastachel – Archäologiefilme im Nationalsozialismus', *Das Altertum* 55: 143-160.

Steuer, H. 2005. 'Archäologische Forschung in der Nachkriegszeit', *Archäologisches Nachrichtenblatt* 10(4): 397-408.

Strobel, M. and T. Widera. 2009. 'Einleitung', in J. Schachtmann, M. Strobel and T. Widera (eds), *Politik und Wissenschaft in der prähistorischen Archäologie. Perspektiven aus Sachsen, Böhmen und Schlesien.* Berichte und Studien 56. Göttingen: V&R unipress GmbH, 9-29.

Stürmer, V. 2002. 'Hans Schleif. Eine Karriere zwischen Archäologischem Institut und Ahnenerbe e.V.' , in A. Leube (ed.), *Prähistorie und Nationalsozialismus. Die mittel- und osteuropäische Ur- und Frühgeschichtsforschung in den Jahren 1933–1945.* Studien zur Wissenschafts- und Universitätsgeschichte 2. Heidelberg: Synchron Wissenschaftsverlag der Autoren, 429-449.

Stürmer, V. 2009. 'Eduard Gerhard – Begründer der institutionellen Archäologie in Berlin', in A.M. Baertschi and C.G. King (eds), *Die modernen Väter der Antike. Die Entwicklung der Altertumswissenschaften an Akademie und Universität im Berlin des 19. Jahrhunderts.* Transformationen der Antike 3. Berlin, New York: Walter de Gruyter, 145-164.

Sünderhauf, E.S. 2004. *Griechensehnsucht und Kulturkritik. Die deutsche Rezeption von Winckelmanns Antikenideal 1840-1945.* Berlin: Akademie Verlag.

Teichmann, G. 2008. 'Max Freiherr von Oppenheim – Archäologe, Diplomat, Freund des Orients', in C. Trümpler (ed.), *Das große Spiel. Archäologie und Politik zur Zeit des Kolonialismus (1860–1940).* Essen, Köln: Ruhr Museum, DuMont Buchverlag, 238-249.

Thissen, H.J. 2006. 'Adolf Erman und die Gründung des Deutschen Archäologischen Instituts in Kairo. Prolegomena', in B.U. Schipper (ed.), *Ägyptologie als Wissenschaft: Adolf Erman (1854-1937) in seiner Zeit.* Berlin: Walter de Gruyter GmbH, 193-201.

Trnka, G. 1994. 'Das Gräberfeld von Gusen. Zu den Ergebnissen der "SS-Grabung" 1941-1943', *Arche* 4: 20-24.

Trümpler, C. 2008a. 'Das große Spiel. Archäologie und Politik zur Zeit des Kolonialismus', in C. Trümpler (ed.), *Das große Spiel. Archäologie und Politik zur Zeit des Kolonialismus (1860–1940)*. Essen, Köln: Ruhr Museum, DuMont Buchverlag, 14-19.

Trümpler, C. 2008b. 'Die moabitischen Fälschungen', in C. Trümpler (ed.), *Das große Spiel. Archäologie und Politik zur Zeit des Kolonialismus (1860–1940)*. Essen, Köln: Ruhr Museum, DuMont Buchverlag, 104-113.

Trümpler, C. 2008c. 'Das Deutsch-Türkische Denkmalschutz-Kommando und die Luftbildarchäologie', in C. Trümpler (ed.), *Das große Spiel. Archäologie und Politik zur Zeit des Kolonialismus (1860–1940)*. Essen, Köln: Ruhr Museum, DuMont Buchverlag, 474-483.

Trümpler, C. 2008d. 'Die Thronende Göttin und die Tell Halaf-Reliefs', in C. Trümpler (ed.), *Das große Spiel. Archäologie und Politik zur Zeit des Kolonialismus (1860–1940)*. Essen, Köln: Ruhr Museum, DuMont Buchverlag, 484-493.

Ungern-Sternberg, J. von. 2006. 'Deutsche Altertumswissenschaftler im Ersten Weltkrieg', in T. Maurer (ed.), *Kollegen, Kommilitonen, Kämpfer. Europäische Universitäten im Ersten Weltkrieg*. Pallas Athene. Beiträge zur Universitäts- und Wissenschaftsgeschichte 18. Stuttgart: Franz Steiner Verlag, 239-254.

Unte, W. 2003. *Heroen und Epigonen. Gelehrtenbiographien der klassischen Altertumswissenschaft im 19. und 20. Jahrhundert*. Itinera Classica 2. St. Katharinen: Scripta Mercaturae Verlag.

Vigener, M. 2010. 'Der „gegebene Ortsgruppenleiter"? – ein Archäologie in der Auslandsorganisation der NSDAP in Rom', *Das Altertum* 55: 127-142.

Voß, S. and C. von Pilgrim. 2008. 'Ludwig Borchardt und die deutschen Interessen am Nil', in C. Trümpler (ed.), *Das große Spiel. Archäologie und Politik zur Zeit des Kolonialismus (1860–1940)*. Essen, Köln: Ruhr Museum, DuMont Buchverlag, 294-305.

Wangenheim, W. von. 2005. *Der verworfene Stein. Winckelmanns Leben*. Berlin: Verlag Matthes und Seitz.

Wawrzinek, C. 2010. 'Helden ohne Mythos. Orient-Reisende während des 1. Weltkrieges', in F. Both, J. Black, M. Fansa and D. Hoffmann (eds.), *Lawrence von Arabien. Genese eines Mythos. Begleitband zur Sonderausstellung „Lawrence von Arabien"*. Schriftenreihe des Landesmuseums für Natur und Mensch 78. Mainz am Rhein: Philipp von Zabern, 87-108.

Wendel, M. 2007. 'Die Ausgrabungen in Iatrus und Karasura: Zu einigen Aspekten der Frühmittelalterforschung in Bulgarien', in J. Henning (ed.), *Post-Roman Towns, Trade and Settlement in Europe and Byzantium 2. Byzantium, Pliska, and the Balkans*. Berlin: Walter de Gruyter, 509-526.

Wickert, L. 1979. *Beiträge zur Geschichte des Deutschen Archäologischen Instituts von 1879 bis 1929*. Das Deutsche Archäologische Institut. Geschichte und Dokumente 2. Mainz: Verlag Philipp von Zabern.

Wilhelm, G. 1998a. '100 Jahre Ausgrabungen der Deutschen Orient-Gesellschaft', in G. Wilhelm (ed.), *Zwischen Tigris und Nil. 100 Jahre Ausgrabungen der Deutschen Orient-Gesellschaft in Vorderasien und Ägypten*. Zaberns Bildbände zur Archäologie. Sonderhefte der Antiken Welt. Mainz am Rhein: Verlag Philipp von Zabern, 5-13.

Wilhelm, G. 1998b. '1898–1917: Babylon. Stadt des Marduk und Zentrum des Kosmus', in G. Wilhelm (ed.), *Zwischen Tigris und Nil. 100 Jahre Ausgrabungen der Deutschen Orient-Gesellschaft in Vorderasien und Ägypten*. Zaberns Bildbände zur Archäologie. Sonderhefte der Antiken Welt. Mainz am Rhein: Verlag Philipp von Zabern, 15-28.

Willing, M. 1991. *Althistorische Forschung in der DDR. Eine wissenschaftsgeschichtliche Studie zur Entwicklung der Disziplin Alte Geschichte vom Ende des Zweiten Weltkrieges bis zur Gegenwart (1945-1989)*. Historische Forschungen 45. Berlin: Duncker und Humblot.

Willing, M. 1996. 'Das Ost-Berliner „Zentralinstitut für Alte Geschichte und Archäologie" im deutschen Vereinigungsprozeß (1989-1992)', *Geschichte in Wissenschaft und Unterricht* 47(7/8): 466-482.

Wrede, H. 2009. 'Olympia, Ernst Curtius und die kulturgeschichtliche Leistung des Philhellenismus', in A.M. Baertschi and C.G. King (eds). *Die modernen Väter der Antike. Die Entwicklung der Altertumswissenschaften an Akademie und Universität im Berlin des 19. Jahrhunderts*. Transformationen der Antike 3. Berlin, New York: Walter de Gruyter, 165-208.

Wünsche, R. 1986. '„Göttliche, paßliche, wünschenswerthe und erforderliche Antiken". L.v.Klenze und die Antikenerwerbungen Ludwigs I.', in Glyptothek München (ed.), *Ein griechischer Traum. Leo von Klenze. Der Archäologe. Ausstellung vom 6. Dezember 1985–9. Februar 1986, Glyptothek München*. München: Staatliche Antikensammlung und Glyptothek.

Wurster, W.W. 1994. 'Was macht die KAVA in Bonn? Eine exotische Forschungsinstitution des Deutschen Archäologischen Instituts stellt sich vor', *Antike Welt* 25: 226-236.

Yaldiz, M. 2008. 'Die deutschen Turfan-Expeditionen nach Xinjiang (1902–1914): Im Wettstreit auf der Suche nach einer verlorenen Kultur', in C. Trümpler (ed.), *Das große Spiel. Archäologie und Politik zur Zeit des Kolonialismus (1860–1940)*. Essen, Köln: Ruhr Museum, DuMont Buchverlag, 188-201.

Zwickel, W. 2007. 'Und die Bibel hat doch nicht immer Recht. Der konstruktiven Phantasie des Ausgräbers half der kritische Sinn des Exegeten: Zum Tode von Volkmar Fritz', *Frankfurter Allgemeine Zeitung* 197: 31.

Part Two

Case Studies

2.1 FRENCH ARCHAEOLOGY IN AFRICA: HISTORICAL, INSTITUTIONAL AND POLITICAL FRAMEWORKS

Sonia Lévin

French National Institute for Preventive
Archaeological Research, France

Abstract

In this globalized age, approaching archaeological activities following national perspectives may seem outdated. However, such an approach proves actually useful to evaluate and comprehend the archaeological activities undertaken in foreign countries, especially in former colonies. This paper focuses on the archaeological research undertaken by French scholars and institutions in the countries that the French republic appropriated in Africa, more than a century ago. It tries to discover what the aims and frameworks were for the initial French archaeological research in Africa, in particular in the Sub-Saharan region. Following the evolution from individual pioneers' explorations to genuine international collaborations, this paper then assesses the present-day French foreign policies and the archaeological operations in the former African colonies.

Résumé

L'Archéologie Française en Afrique : Les Cadres Historiques, Institutionnels et Politiques

Dans cette ère de mondialisation, aborder les activités archéologiques suivant des perspectives nationales peut paraître dépassé. Pourtant, une telle approche s'avère utile pour évaluer et comprendre les activités archéologiques entreprises à l'étranger, particulièrement dans les anciennes colonies. Cet article se concentre sur la recherche archéologique effectuée par des chercheurs et des institutions françaises, dans des pays africains appropriés par la République française il y a plus d'un siècle. L'article vise à découvrir quels étaient les objectifs et le cadre, des premières recherches archéologiques françaises en Afrique, notamment dans la région subsaharienne. En suivant l'évolution des recherches effectuées par des pionniers à titre individuel, jusqu'à de véritables collaborations internationales, l'article analyse la politique étrangère française et les recherches archéologiques menées dans les anciennes colonies africaines.

Extracto

La Arqueología Francesa en África: Marcos Históricos, Institucionales y Políticos

En estos tiempos globalizados el planteamiento de actividades arqueológicas siguiendo las perspectivas nacionales puede resultar anticuado. Sin embargo, tal planteamiento resulta realmente útil para evaluar y comprender las actividades arqueológicas que se emprenden en países extranjeros, en particular en las ex colonias. Este artículo enfoca la investigación arqueológica emprendida por científicos franceses e instituciones en los países de los cuales la Republica francesa se apropió en África hace más de un siglo. El artículo trata de descubrir cuáles fueron los fines y marcos de la investigación inicial arqueológica francesa en África, en particular en la región Sub-Sahara. Este artículo, siguiendo la evolución de exploraciones individuales pioneras a verdaderas colaboraciones internacionales, determina las actuales políticas extranjeras francesas y las operaciones arqueológicas en las antiguas colonias africanas.

ملخص

علم الآثار الفرنسي في أفريقيا: أطر تاريخية، مؤسسية وسياسية

سونيا ليفين

المعهد القومي للبحوث الأثرية الوقائية، باريس، فرنسا

في عصر العولمة هذا، قد يبدو وتناول الأنشطة الأثرية التي تتبع المنظورات الوطنية قديما. ولكن، مثل هذا المنهج يثبت فائدته في تقييم وفهم الأنشطة الأثرية التي تم القيام بها في بلدان أجنبية، خاصة في المستعمرات القديمة. وتركز هذه الورقة على البحث الأثري الذي قام به علماء فرنسيين ومؤسسات فرنسية في أفريقيا، في الدول التي استولت عليها الجمهورية الفرنسية في أفريقيا. حاول الورقة اكتشاف ما هي أهداف وأطر البحث الأثري الفرنسي. كما تحاول هذه الورقة في افريقيا، خاصة في منطقة جنوب الصحراء. ومن قبل ما يزيد عن القرن. الفرنسي البدائي في أفريقيا، الرواد المنفردين إلى التعاونات الدولية خلال متابعة من تطور من اكتشافات استكشافات، تقيم هذه الورقة تقييم سياسات فرنسا الأجنبية الحالية والعمليات الأثرية في المستعمرات الأفريقية السابقة.

Keywords

French Archaeology, Sub-Saharan Africa, Centre National de la Recherche Scientifique, Ministry of Public Education, Ministry of Foreign Affairs, diplomacy, national archives

Introduction

Studies of ancient civilizations around the Mediterranean have a long history, with Napoleon's emblematic expedition to Egypt (1798–1801) as one of its main catalysts. In fact, the archaeological past of the Maghreb and of Egypt, in particular in Classical, Muslim and Pharaonic times, is still better known than that of Sub-Saharan Africa. For a long time there has been a lack of interest in the cultures and history of this region. Partly this can be explained by geographical and historical factors, since Sub-Saharan Africa and the Mediterranean basin did not seem to have established much contact during Classical antiquity and the Punic and Roman periods from the eleventh century BC until the seventh century AD (Ennabli 2004). But there must have been more to it. There was for instance as of 1881 a French Institute of Oriental Archaeology (IFAO) in Cairo (see Lévin, this volume), but none in Sub-Saharan countries. In this paper I will therefore first explore the archaeological activities and organizational structures established during the French colonial past in Africa, and look into the scientific interests French researchers had in those countries. I will then consider the subsequent emergence of Africanists and French archaeologists specializing in the region, and examine how archaeology has come to gain a role in economic and social development.

The French structures in Africa during the colonial past

In 2010, France celebrated the fiftieth anniversary of the independence of fourteen African countries: Mauritania, Senegal, Mali, Guinea, Ivory Coast, Niger, Burkina Faso, Togo, Gabon, Benin, Republic of Congo, Central African Republic, Cameroon and Chad. Those countries - organized in two federations, French West Africa (*Afrique Occidentale Française*, AOF) and French Equatorial Africa (*Afrique Équatoriale Française*, AEF) - were part of the colonial realm which France had assembled in the course of the nineteenth century.

From the start of the colonial period, there was some scientific interest for Africa, French researchers led scientific expeditions to these countries. From 1842 until the creation of the *Centre National de la Recherche Scientifique* (CNRS, National Centre for Scientific Research) in 1939, these were mostly expeditions conducted by a small selection of researchers that had the support of the Ministry of Public Education. The records of those individual missions are kept in the French National Archives: for the nineteenth century and the beginning of the twentieth century they attest to a relatively limited influence of the French state on the scientific and literary exploration of what used to be called black Africa (*e.g.* the former European colonies south of the Sahara).

Two thirds of a total of 150 of those African explorers' missions were run in the two decades between 1880 and the turn of the century. These were the years of the largest colonial expansion into Sub-Saharan Africa (Lévin and Le Goff 2009). This assembling of French colonial possessions happened during the French Third Republic (1870–1940). It was notably at the instigation of Jules Ferry (1832–1893),

Minister of Public Instruction (and later of Foreign Affairs), that colonization was considered to be a constituent of French greatness. Following the decisions of the Berlin conference (1884–1885), the Third Republic established many colonies in Africa, as well as in French Indochina, Madagascar and French Polynesia.

Various documents from that period make it clear that the missions often had simultaneous political, commercial and scientific aims (Lévin and Schlanger 2009). There was however no global, centralized or solid programme for the scientific exploration of Africa. According to Emmanuelle Sibeud, this could have reflected a political choice:

> *"[...] while the explorations relied on the diffuse practices of collection popularized by learned societies which rapidly expanded at the end of the nineteenth century in France, they do not emerge from a coherent project of scientific exploration of French Africa. The absence of such a project is all the more surprising given that the symbolic appropriation of the continent is a powerful motive, and has a readily available model at the end of 1870s with the scientific exploration of Algeria. It is however in the logic of a management voluntarily scattered of the explorations which allows in fact the political logic of the conquest to constantly extend beyond all other logics"* (Sibeud 2007: 30-31, translation by the author).

It was in any case through such missions that most of the objects were collected of the first ethnological museum in Paris, the *Museum Ethnographique des Missions Scientifiques* (since then called *Musée d'ethnographie du Trocadéro*), created in 1878 by anthropologist Ernest-Theodore Hamy (1842–1908). Hamy had collected prehistoric artefacts in Egypt and gained interest in the material manifestations of human activity; as an employee of the *Muséum National d'Histoire Naturelle* he proposed to start a new museum, specifically dedicated to ethnography. He wrote various archaeological publications on the Stone Age of Guinea, Gabon and Ivory Coast,[1] but otherwise archaeology was rarely pursued in Sub-Saharan Africa. Only three missions (out of a total of 150) make any mention of some archaeological aim[2]. The ancient relics of this region were clearly overshadowed by the monumental remains of North Africa and Egypt, despite the fact that they were dating from the same period.

Until World War I there was no relevant framework, orientation and structure of the archaeological research in the whole of French Africa (Coulibaly 1997). This is particularly surprising given the fact that the conquest of Algeria in 1830 was from the onset accompanied by a commission for scientific exploration, and also that since the end of the nineteenth century the French School in Rome had undertaken sustained archaeological investigations in the Maghreb. As well, it is worth pointing out that North Africa had an archaeological service (connected with universities, museums and antiquities services) already in the 1930s, before metropolitan France (Gran-Aymerich 2001).

---

1   L'Âge de la pierre au Gabon (1897), L'Âge de la pierre dans la Dubreka (1897), L'Âge de la pierre dans la Côte d'Ivoire (1905), all in *Bulletin du Muséum d'histoire naturelle* (Paris).
2   These were made by Georges Revoil in 1880, by Franz De Zeltner in 1907 and by G. Waterlot in 1935–1937.

Despite this metropolitan neglect of archaeology in Subsaharan Africa, the activities of officials and intellectual pioneers on the ground led, in 1915, to the creation of the French West Africa Committee on Historical and Scientific Studies, which provided an institutional framework for research. Archaeology had quite a significant position within this Committee: almost 70 articles were published in the reports and bulletins of the Committee between 1915 and 1936. While these works were burdened by racial prejudices, they usefully considered the entire AOF-region as a geographical entity, without being confined to the political and artificial subdivision of its contemporary borders (see Bocoum 2004 and particularly Thiaw, this volume, for the development of archaeology in Senegal and western Africa).

In 1936 an important step was taken with the creation of the *Institut Français d'Afrique Noire* (IFAN, French Institute for Black Africa) in Dakar, Senegal. IFAN constituted "the most active agent of the emergence of a credible archaeological pole in western Africa" (Bocoum 2004). Its task was to study the societies and their natural environments in western Africa. It was primarily an institute for research and training, but its results were also disseminated to the wider public, via for example broadcasts on Radio Senegal.

From 1936 until 1958, the 'federal' IFAN had branches in Mali, Senegal, Mauritania, Niger, Upper Volta, Togo, Dahomey, Guinea and Sudan, co-ordinating the archaeological research that was conducted in these regions. In 1960, IFAN was integrated with the University of Dakar, while its local and associated branches became autonomous. After independence, the wide geographical scope of IFAN was reduced to Senegal, and in 1966 it was renamed the *Institut Fondamental d'Afrique Noire* (Fundamental Institute of Black Africa). In 1986, after the death of professor Cheikh Anta Diop (1923–1986), one of its most eminent researchers, it took its current name of IFAN Cheikh Anta Diop.

It is noteworthy that, unlike Cairo and Indochina during the colonial period, there has never been a dedicated French archaeological school in Sub-Saharan Africa on the model of those of Athens and Rome (see Lévin, this volume).[3] It is actually only recently that the Ministry of Foreign Affairs has begun to fund some French research institutes in this region, albeit those active in the broad field of human and social sciences and not just archaeology. Among these institutes, several are conducting archaeological activities, in Ethiopia, Sudan, South Africa,

---

3   The *École Française d'Extrême-Orient* (EFEO) was founded in 1900 in Hanoi as a joint initiative of the Oriental Studies section in the French Academy of Inscriptions and Belles-Lettres and the colonial government of French Indochina (http://www.efeo.fr/).

Nigeria and Kenya.[4] Interestingly, there are such institutions also in South Africa and Kenya (IFAS and the two IFRA branches) – that is, in what was Anglophone Africa in colonial times.

Growing interests and the emergence of an institutional network

Between the two World Wars interest grew in African studies in France. The first large-scale ethnographic expeditions to Africa took place during that period, including one to Ethiopia (1928) and the famous Dakar-Djibouti mission (1931–1933) that crossed Africa from west to east with the purpose of collecting ethnographic material and information in the colonized areas (Sibeud 2008: 108). Anthropologist Marcel Griaule (1898–1956) played an important role in this rising interest in Africa through his missions and studies of the Dogon in Mali. In this period the *Société des Africanistes* was created (in 1930), based at the National Museum of Natural History in Paris (*Muséum National d'Histoire Naturelle*). The aim of this association was to study Africa and its people from the most remote times to the present: its major activity also today consists of publishing its pluri-disciplinary *Journal des Africanistes*.[5]

At the end of World War II, the interest in African archaeology and French archaeology abroad became the concern of the State, in particular of the Ministry of Foreign Affairs (see Lévin, this volume). As of 1945 the CNRS concentrated its research on metropolitan archaeology and entrusted its administrative responsibility for archaeology conducted abroad to the dedicated 'Commission of excavations and archaeological missions' of the Ministry of Foreign Affairs. In 1947, this commission defined Prehistory, Egypt, Ethiopia and North Africa as specific research topics, but Sub-Saharan Africa was not mentioned. In fact, it was

---

4   In 1991 the *Maison Française des Études Éthiopiennes* was created, succeeding the *Mission Archéologique en Éthiopie* established in 1955. It was founded for co-ordinating the French excavations in the ancient city of Aksum. In turn it was succeeded in 1997 by the *Centre Français des Études Éthiopiennes* (CFEE) (*Unité de Service et de Recherche* 3137; *Unité Mixte des Instituts Français de Recherche à l'Étranger* 23), in Addis Abeba that was formally recognized by the Ethiopian Ministry of Culture. It assists and hosts historical or contemporary researches on Ethiopia and the Horn of Africa (see Derat *et al.* 2011).
    In Khartum the *Section Française de la Direction des Antiquités et des Musées Nationaux du Soudan* (SFDAS) (USR 3336; UMIFRE 4) has been established. Following a cooperation protocol for archaeological activities included in the *Accord de Coopération Culturelle et Technique* signed in 1969 by France and Sudan, the SFDAS is integrated into the Sudanese service for antiquities, and its director is answerable to the national Antiquities' director.
    The *Institut Français d'Afrique du Sud* (IFAS) (USR 3336; UMIFRE 25) was established in 1995 in Johannesburg. It was meant to take part in the construction of the new South Africa, in the field of human and social sciences. It includes in its studies programmes 'the history of the demographic processes on the long term: history, rock art, archaeology, oral sources, ethnomusicology on the populations of hunters-gatherers and semi-nomadic breeders San and Khoekhoe'.
    The Institut Français de Recherche en Afrique (IFRA) (USR 3336; UMIFRE 24) has two branches, one in Nigeria (IFRA Ibadan) and one in Kenya (IFRA Nairobi). The latter is mainly focused on contemporary, social and political themes of research, but the first conducts archaeological research.
5   Http://www.africanistes.org/.

following the African missions and interests of Abbé Henri Breuil (1877–1961), in charge of the subcommittee on prehistoric research since 1960, that French prehistoric research developed in Sub-Saharan Africa (Coye 2006).

Since that time, the African continent has witnessed an ever increasing interest in its ancient history, by French and more generally European scholarship. It is worth recalling in this respect the major international project UNESCO launched in 1964. Following decolonization, this project aimed to solve the general ignorance on Africa's history by rewriting it, this time from an African perspective free from racial prejudices. Archaeology is well-represented in these eight volumes General History of Africa (GHA), at least in its first two volumes concerning Methodology and Prehistory, and Ancient Africa.[6]

At present six major laboratories, combining researchers from the universities and the CNRS (so-called joint labs or *unités mixtes de recherche*, UMR), are specialized in African studies. Of these, only two are exclusively dedicated to archaeology.[7] The main specialized team dealing specifically with African archaeology in France is the unit 'Africa, societies and environments' within UMR 7041. It is a joint team with researchers from CNRS, Paris I University and Paris X University, based on the campus at Nanterre (in the *Maison de l'Archéologie et de l'Ethnologie - René Ginouvès*). Researchers, students and teachers dedicate themselves to archaeological research on the African continent. In collaboration with local students and researchers, the unit is working in the Sahara (notably in Chad), in East Africa and in Angola.[8]

The other laboratory is the UMR 5608, called TRACES (*Travaux et Recherches Archéologiques sur les Cultures, les Espaces et les Sociétés*). It consists of a joint team from CNRS, University Toulouse II Le Mirail, the Ministry of Culture and

---

6   Overseen by an international scientific committee of which two-thirds was African, this monumental piece of work mobilized more than 230 historians and other specialists during more than 35 years and it constitutes a model of scientific cooperation. The publications were translated into thirteen languages, including Arabic, English, French and three African languages. The dissemination of this History of Africa to local communities was of high concern to UNESCO, so in March 2009 the second phase of the project was launched, 'the Pedagogical Use of the General History of Africa'. Through this four-year project it is aimed to incorporate the contents of the GHA into the primary and secondary school curriculum in order to enhance the knowledge of African students of their continent's history. Something that was strongly pleaded for by the African countries. Http://www.unesco. org/new/en/culture/themes/dialogue/general-and-regional-histories/general-history-of-africa/.

7   The other four are: *Centre d'Étude d'Afrique Noire* (CEAN, Institut d'Études Politiques Bordeaux) mostly devoted to the analysis of political change in Africa (http://www.cean.u-bordeaux.fr/anglais/); the *Centre d'Études des Mondes Africains* (CEMAF) (UMR Paris I, EPHE, University of Provence) providing masters programmes in African history, political science, law and anthropology (see http://www.cemaf.cnrs.fr/); the Laboratory of University Paris 1 and CNRS called MALD (*Mutations Africaines dans la Longue Durée*) (see http://www.cemaf.cnrs.fr/). It publishes the journal *Afrique & Histoire*; and the *Institut d'Études Africaines* (UMR 6124 CNRS; *Maison Méditerranéenne des Sciences de l'Homme*, University of Provence), publishing *Clio en Afrique: Bulletin d'Anthropologie et d'Histoire Africaines en langue française* (see http://www.mmsh.univ-aix.fr/iea/).

8   Mega-Chad is an international network of multidisciplinary researches on the history and the evolution of societies in the pond of the Lake Chad. Established gradually, following a first multidisciplinary meeting in 1984 in Paris, it consists of approximately 500 correspondents distributed over twenty countries in nearly all continents (see http://www.afrikanistik.uni-bayreuth.de/de/publications/Mega-Tchad/index.html).

Communication and the *Institut National de Recherches Archéologiques Préventives* (INRAP). It conducts an ambitious transversal research on 'Saharan and Sub Saharan history and archaeology'.[9] One of its projects, concerning the Bantu expansion from Equatorial to Southern Africa, is centred on the rhythms and the modalities of this expansion drawing on a range of field operations and museum studies.

In 2010, the total amount of subsidies granted by the Ministry of Foreign and European Affairs for archaeological operations was 2.8 million euro, distributed among some 160 missions, concerning 200 French researchers in 65 countries (see Lévin, this volume). Of these projects, 40 were carried out in Africa and Arabia, mostly in Egypt (the Nile Valley), Yemen and Sudan. Projects were also undertaken in various other countries, such as South Africa, Cameroon, Madagascar, Mali, Kenya, Uganda, Tanzania, and Chad.

Current development tools and archaeology

Today, all French archaeological activity in Africa is undertaken within the framework of various development-related policies and structures. This implies support from the Service of Cooperation and Cultural Action (SCAC), an office present in many French embassies for implementing collaboration activities in the domains of culture and development, occasionally including archaeology (see Lévin, this volume). For example, SCAC-Luanda (Angola) financed several missions of the TRACES laboratory of Toulouse on the Bantu expansion research.

Given France's engagement in development practices in Africa, archaeology has increasingly found a place in these programmes.[10] One of the main actors is the *Institut de Recherche pour le Développement* (IRD, previously the *Office de la Recherche Scientifique et Technique Outre-Mer*). This scientific public institution under the supervision of both the Ministry of Research and the Ministry of Foreign Affairs was founded in 1948 to support the implementation of the national structures of research abroad. For more than 60 years, it has undertaken research, valuation and training activities in Africa, the Mediterranean Sea, Latin America, and Asia and in overseas tropical French territories. Its researches are concerned with the study of environments, the sustainable management of living resources, and social and health development and they are conducted in close collaboration with local stakeholders.

Archaeology had from the onset a place within the activities of the IRD, of which the main objective was making heritage inventories. As a result, the IRD supports activities such as the development of the BANI-database (Base of physical Anthropology of Niger) which was conceived to present the collection of skeletal remains of the Research Institute in Human Sciences of the University of Niamey (Niger). In close collaboration with the embassy in Yaoundé (Cameroon), and with

---

9   Http://traces.univ-tlse2.fr/19776613/0/fichepagelibre/&RH=themes_traces&RF=Afrique.

10   Several initiatives across sub-Saharan Africa are reported in a special issue of the journal *Les Nouvelles de l'Archéologie* (Paris 2010).

support of the European Commission, the IRD also conducts a valuation of the respective weight of natural pressures and cultural choices in the evolutions of the tropical societies in the long term.

Another French public institution which has recently become involved in heritage and development in Africa is the *Institut National de Recherches Archéologiques Preventives* (INRAP, the French National Institute for Preventive Archaeological Research). Among other activities INRAP organized in 2007, together with the SCAC in Mauritania and the Mauritanian Institute of Scientific Research, a colloquium in Nouakchott on preventive archaeology in Africa (see Naffé, Lanfranchi and Schlanger 2008). At this meeting African and European archaeologists from France, Belgium and Spain addressed together new perspectives for reconciling the continent's economic and social development with the preservation of its archaeological heritage. Since 2004, INRAP has also been involved in archaeological collaboration projects in Algeria, Morocco and Ethiopia, and it supported archaeological missions in Egypt, Libya, Tunisia, Somalia, Djibouti, and beyond the North and the Horn of Africa, in Mali and South-Africa (see Schlanger 2011).

France is also active within international organizations. It participated for example in the Africa 2009 project of the International Centre for the Study of the Preservation and Restoration of Cultural Property (ICCROM),[11] a twelve year long capacity building programme launched in Abidjan, Ivory Coast, in 1998.[12] It is based on the principle that the problems related to the preservation in Africa should not only be handled through technical solutions but also through a consideration of the relationship between the cultural heritage and its social, environmental and economic aspects. A major actor in this programme was CRAterre, the Center for the Research and Application of Earth Architecture in Grenoble.[13]

Another major vehicle for international collaboration is the France-UNESCO Convention for architectural, urban and landscape heritage that was signed in 1997 (and came into force in 1999).[14] Through this agreement technical and financial cooperation is organized between UNESCO, the French State and international cultural actors. It recently facilitated three cultural/archaeological projects in western Africa: the inscription of megalithic sites between Senegal and Gambia to the World Heritage list; the inventory of cultural heritage in Senegal; and the

---

11 ICCROM is an intergovernmental organization dedicated to the conservation of cultural heritage, projected at the ninth UNESCO General Conference in New Delhi in 1956 and established in Rome in 1959.

12 Http://www.africa2009.net/english/programme/index.shtm.

13 This research and training laboratory on earth structures and buildings was created in 1979 by the National Superior School of Architecture in Grenoble. It now consists of around 30 persons of diverse nationalities and disciplinary backgrounds (architecture, anthropology, sociology, engineering, archaeology). (see http://craterre.org/).

14 To celebrate the tenth anniversary of this agreement, in 2009, UNESCO produced a booklet with the results of the work in the fields of conservation and cultural development (see http://whc.unesco.org/uploads/activities/documents/activity-589-1.pdf).

Niger-Loire project on governance and culture.[15] It also supports a training centre on cultural heritage and local development, the School of the African Heritage, in Porto Novo (Benin).[16]

Most of the French institutional actors described above (*e.g.* the Ministry of Foreign Affairs, the IRD, the embassies, the *Institut Français de Recherche en Afrique*, INRAP, etc.) were present during a meeting on African cultural heritage in Mombasa, in June 2010. In this meeting it was acknowledged that over the past two decades a practice and discourse of heritage resource management was being established in Africa, and that there are lively debates going on concerning the perceptions of cultural heritage, the management of archaeological resources and the development of indigenous management models. Subsequently, the participants debated on the incompatibility of western heritage approaches with local African views, the importance of intangible heritage, the exclusion of local communities, and the need for capacity building and socio-economic benefits. African and European heritage specialists exchanged strategic reflections on the link between heritage and sustainable development, between heritage and identical constructions, and on the role of the local communities in the processes of conservation and valuation of the heritages.

Such debates are crucial, but they have only recently started. Developments in heritage management are only recent, as are archaeology training programmes in Africa: in 2005 Lassina Simporé (University of Ouagadougou) was the first doctor in archaeology who was completely trained in a French-speaking African university (Abandé 2007). Such developments show however that we can be confident that African scholarships will soon find their own answers to the challenges of archaeology and heritage management – with, it is hoped and expected, the support of France.

Conclusion

Leaving aside various individual initiatives and contributions (which had to remain beyond the scope of this paper), I have attempted here to provide an overview of the development of archaeological interest in the French colonies in Africa. I have also tried to show how this interest has evolved into the diverse archaeological collaborations that are nowadays being conducted throughout the African continent. At the same time, this presentation has been based on a French perspective – the complementary perspective provided by Thiaw, this volume, is as indispensible

---

15 See http://loirevalley-worldheritage.org/Actions/Main-projects/Projets-termines/River-to-river-cooperation/Niger-Loire-governance-and-culture; http://whc.unesco.org/en/activities/23/.

16 Created by the ICCROM in 1998, this *École du Patrimoine Africain* (EPA) is a non-governmental international organization for higher education that is specialized in the preservation and the mediation of the tangible and intangible cultural heritage. It trains professionals in preservation and heritage management in 26 countries of francophone Sub-Saharan Africa. Its sister organization, the Centre for Heritage Development in Africa (previously called the Programme for Museum Development in Africa) that is based in Mombasa (Kenya), covers English-speaking countries of Sub-Saharan Africa. Together they cover the Portuguese-speaking countries (see http://www.epa-prema.net/en.html).

for understanding the broader picture. Moreover, I have here considered these developments from a theoretical or 'armchair' position: in the field, the situation is much more complex, and far from ideal. Funding remains a major issue. Neither in Africa nor in France or the rest of Europe, are culture and heritage priorities of national funding. For example, of the 250 cultural manifestations that were organized to celebrate 50 years of independence from France (in 2010), not a single one was dedicated to archaeology.

Nevertheless, I have tried to show that nowadays French archaeologists no longer intend to impose their scientific paradigms and approaches of the African past, but rather seek to encourage local scholars and communities to appropriate their own pasts. This is done, as appropriate, by providing or developing specific tools and skills. No foreign archaeological operation in Africa – involving scholars from France, Europe or North America – should be conducted without the active collaboration and training of local archaeologists with their own research and management structures. In the colonial area, 'French archaeology in Africa' could probably be defined as 'archaeology financed by French funds, carried out by researchers from French universities and scientific institutions, according to their methods and theories'. Hopefully 'French archaeology in Africa' has nowadays a completely different meaning, implying international collaboration with respect for local values, stakeholders and ideas.

Yet, in both national and international contexts, the networks and collaborations clearly have to be reinforced in the years to come. It must be ensured that the potential of development is realized, and that good and fair use is being made by all the actors concerned of the resources available for archaeological research and heritage management in Africa.

Acknowledgements

I thank Sjoerd van der Linde, perfect chair of our session on European archaeology abroad during the conference of the European Association of Archaeologists in The Hague, in 2010 and Nathan Schlanger for his readings and comments.

References

Abandé, A. 2007. 'L'A.O.A.A. et la Question de la Prévention en Archéologie: une Perspective Régionale', unpublished paper.

Bocoum, H. 2004. 'L'Archéologie Française en Afrique de l'Ouest: Rétrospectives et Enjeux', in A. Bazzana and H. Bocoum (eds), *Du Nord au Sud du Sahara, Cinquante Ans d'Archéologie Française en Afrique de l'Ouest et au Maghreb. Bilan et Perspectives.* Paris: Sépia, 29-36.

Coulibaly, É. 1997. 'L'Archéologie, Science Oubliée des Études Africanistes Françaises' in A. Piriou and E. Sibeud (eds), *L'Africanisme en Questions.* Paris: Centre d'Études Africaines des Hautes Études en Sciences Sociales, 89-111.

Coye, N. (ed.). 2006. *Sur les Chemins de la Préhistoire. L'Abbé Breuil du Périgord à l'Afrique du Sud.* Paris: Somogy.

Derat M-L., F.-X. Fauvelle-Aymar, A.-M. Jouquand and B. Poisonnier. 2011. 'Archéologie du Christianisme Éthiopien: Quinze Ans de Collaboration Scientifique entre le Centre Française et l'Inrap', in N. Schlanger (ed.), *Archéologie sans Frontières*. Archéopages hors série. Paris: Institut national de recherches archéologiques préventives, 37-46.

Ennabli, A. 2004. 'Entre Afrique Antique et Afrique Sub-Saharienne: un Obstacle Infranchissable?', in A. Bazzana and H. Bocoum (eds), *Du Nord au Sud du Sahara, Cinquante Ans d'Archéologie Française en Afrique de l'Ouest et au Maghreb. Bilan et Perspectives*. Paris: Sépia, 23-24.

Gran-Aymerich, E. 2001. 'L'Archéologie Française à l'Étranger, Méditerranée, Afrique et Proche-Orient (1945-1970)', *Revue pour l'Histoire du CNRS* [online] 5. Retrieved 20 July 2011 from http://histoire-cnrs.revues.org/3402.

Lévin, S. and A. Le Goff. 2009. *Missions Scientifiques et Littéraires dans l'Afrique Subsaharienne Dossiers Individuels (1828-1937)*. Retrieved 20 July 2011 from http://www.archivesnationales.culture.gouv.fr/chan/chan/fonds/edi/sm/F/F17Afrique.pdf.

Lévin, S. and N. Schlanger. 2009. 'Logiques Individuelles, Logiques d'État, Archéologie et Sciences Coloniales en Afrique Subsaharienne d'après les Archives du Ministère de l'Instruction Publique', *Les Nouvelles de l'Archéologie* 116, 41-45.

Naffé, B., R. Lanfranchi and N. Schlanger (eds). 2008. *L'Archéologie Préventive en Afrique, Enjeux et Perspectives, Actes du Colloque de Nouakchott 1er-3 Février 2007*. Saint-Maur-des-Fossés: Éditions Sépia.

Paris, F. (ed.) 2010. *La Coopération Française en Afrique 1. Préhistoire et Protohistoire*. Les Nouvelles de l'Archéologie 120/121. Paris: Éditions de la Maison des Sciences de l'Homme, Éditions Errance.

Schlanger, N. (ed.). 2011. *Archéologie sans Frontières*. Archéopages Hors Série. Paris: Institut national de recherches archéologiques préventives.

Sibeud, E. 2007. *Une Science Impériale pour l'Afrique? La Construction des Savoirs Africanistes en France 1878-1930*. Paris: Éditions des Hautes Études en Sciences Sociales.

Sibeud, E. 2008. 'The Metamorphosis of Ethnology in France, 1839-1930', in H. Kuklick (ed.), *A New History of Anthropology*. Oxford: Blackwell Publishing, 96-110.

2.2 Archaeology in the Democratic Republic of Congo: old and current strategies for ancient issues

Els Cornelissen

Section of Prehistory and Archaeology,
Royal Museum for Central Africa, Belgium

Abstract

The origin of the Prehistory and Archaeology unit of the Royal Museum for Central Africa in Belgium lies in the colonial past, in what is now called the Democratic Republic of the Congo. This legacy, clearly represented in collections, archives and expertise, explains the continuous efforts of the museum to stimulate both archaeological research and collaboration with museums in the DR Congo. Despite these efforts, explicit government policies in the DR Congo and the Belgian indirect international aid programmes, the university and museum structures are as yet insufficient for capacity building in archaeology in the DR Congo. Rescue archaeology, as part of environmental impact assessments, may present a valuable alternative. It holds great potential given the large scale of infrastructure development in the DR Congo and it may provide the best approach for setting Congolese priorities in archaeological research, for capacity building and for the preservation of the cultural heritage. One of the challenges is to organize training in the DR Congo for this kind of archaeological surveying. The most promising strategy may be found in enlarging the archaeological knowledge of all academics involved in environmental impact assessments and to combine funding and expertise from both foreign universities and museums.

Résumé

Archéologie en République Démocratique du Congo : Stratégies d'antan et d'aujourd'hui pour des questions anciennes

La section de Préhistoire et Archéologie du Musée royal de l'Afrique centrale trouve ses origines dans l'histoire coloniale du pays qui porte aujourd'hui le nom de République Démocratique du Congo. Cet héritage, qui apparaît clairement tant dans les collections et les archives qu'au niveau de l'expertise, explique les efforts continus du musée pour encourager à la fois la recherche archéologique et la collaboration avec des musées congolais. En dépit de ces efforts, d'une politique engagée en RDC et des programmes belges d'aide internationale, les structures des universités et des musées sont aujourd'hui encore insuffisantes pour renforcer les capacités en archéologie en RDC. L'archéologie préventive, liée à l'évaluation de l'impact environnemental, peut représenter une alternative sérieuse. Son potentiel est évident, étant donné le développement d'infrastructures de grande envergure en RDC.

L'archéologie préventive pourrait bien être la meilleureapproche pour établir des priorités congolaises en matière de recherche, pour renforcer les capacités et pour préserver le patrimoine culturel. L'une des difficultés réside dans l'organisation, en RDC, d'une formation pour ce type d'archéologie préventive. La stratégie la plus prometteuse consiste sans doute à étendre les connaissances des universitaires impliqués dans l'évaluation de l'impact environnemental et à combiner le financement et l'expertise des universités et musées étrangers.

Extracto

La Arqueología en la República Democrática del Congo: estrategias antiguas y actuales para asuntos antiguos

El origen de la sección de Prehistoria y Arqueología del Museo Real de África Central en Bélgica se halla en el pasado colonial, en lo que ahora se llama la República Democrática del Congo. Este legado, claramente representado en las colecciones, los archivos y en la experiencia, explica los continuos esfuerzos del museo para estimular tanto la investigación arqueológica como la colaboración con museos en la RD Congo. A pesar de estos esfuerzos, las políticas gubernamentales explícitas en la RD Congo y los programas indirectos belgas de ayuda internacional, las estructuras de las universidades y de los museos son todavía insuficientes para la creación de capacidades en la RD Congo. Arqueología de rescate, como parte de las evaluaciones de impacto medioambiental, podrá ofrecer una alternativa valiosa. Tiene gran potencial visto la gran escala de desarrollo infraestructural en la RD Congo y podrá ofrecer el mejor enfoque para fijar las prioridades en la investigación arqueológica, para la creación de capacidades y para la preservación del patrimonio cultural. La organización de la formación en la RD Congo para este tipo de prospección arqueológica, es uno de los desafíos. La estrategia más favorable se podrá encontrar en la ampliación de los conocimientos arqueológicos de todos los académicos que participan en evaluaciones de impacto medioambiental y en la combinación de subsidios y de experiencia tanto de las universidades como de los museos extranjeros.

ملخص

علم الآثار في جمهورية الكونغو الديمقراطية: إستراتيجيات قديمة وحالية لقضايا قديمة

ألس كورنيليسن

قسم ما قبل التاريخ وعلم الآثار، المتحف الملكي لوسط أفريقيا، بلجيكا

يعود أصل ما قسم ما قبل التاريخ وعلم الآثار في المتحف الملكي لوسط أفريقيا وجمهورية الكونغو فيما يخص الآلام إلى الماضي الاستعماري، في بلجيكا إلى المجموعات، وألرشيفات والخبرة، ويفسر هذا التراث الممثل في المجموعة. الديمقراطية. فقد البحث بتشجيع المتحف لتشجيع البحث المتحف التي بذلها الجهود المستمرة لهذلها التي بذلها المتحف لتشجيع البحث من مؤثري أخرى. من جهة أخرى. واضح، بشكل والتعاون مع المتحف في جمهورية الكونغو والديمقراطية من جهة أخرى. التأسيسات السياسية والسلوك الحكومية والواضحة في جمهورية الكونغو والديمقراطية من هذه الجهود والمتاحف والجماعات على الجانب إن بني المباشرة، غير البلجيكية الدعم البرامج حتى البلاد علم الآثار في جمهورية الكونغو والديمقراطية لا تكفيف لبناء القدرات في علم الآثار الولائي، باعتباره جزءا من تقييمات التأثير الآلان. وقد يشكل علم الآثار الولائي، باعتباره جزءا من تقييمات التأثير لتنمية للحلم نظرا مفيدا تكون قيم. فقد يكون نظرا للحلم الكبير للتنمية على البيئة، بدني قيم. فقد قدم أفضل علم الآثار في جمهورية الكونغو والديمقراطية، كما قد يقدم أفضل البنية التحتية في جمهورية الكونغو وليا والبنانا البنية التحتية بشأننا فيما يتعلق بالبحث الآثاري، إن أحد التحديات هو تنظيم المنهج أو أوضع تاليات الكونغو وليا في البحث الآثاري، إن أحد التحديات هو تنظيم المدربين القدرات والحفاظ على التراث الثقافي. إن القدرات والحفاظ على التراث الثقافي. وقد تكمن القدرات والحفاظ على المسح الآثاري. وقد تكمن في جمهورية الكونغو والديمقراطية لمثل هذا النوع من المسح الآثاري. أكثر إستراتيجية واعدة في تعزيز المعرفة المعرفة زي تعزيز في فرع عاودة إستراتيجية أكثر في جميع الأكاديميين وتمويل المتمولة ووجهة على البيئة وجمع التمويل وليل الخبرة من من الجامعات والمتاحف من جهة أخرى.

Keywords

Democratic Republic of Congo, history of archaeological research, colonial era, capacity building, rescue archaeology, Royal Museum for Central Africa

Introduction

During European colonialism Belgium had one colony, Congo.[1] Today we know it as the Democratic Republic of Congo (*République Démocratique du Congo*, in this article further referred to as the DR Congo). In 1897 King Leopold II organized an exhibition on his royal estate in Tervuren in order to promote Congo, which became the Congo Museum (1898) and later the Museum of the Belgian Congo (*Musée du Congo Belge* or *Museum van Belgisch Congo*) (1908). Nowadays it is known as the Royal Museum for Central Africa.[2] This historical link between the Royal Museum for Central Africa and the Belgian colonial past explains

---

1   After World War I the protectorate of Ruanda-Urundi fell to Belgium, which in 1962 split into the two independent states of Rwanda and Burundi.

2   After Congo's independence in 1960, the Ministry of Colonies in Belgium, which was in charge of the colonial museum, was abolished and the Museum of Belgian Congo was redefined as the Royal Museum for Central Africa and its geographical scope was widened (Cahen 1961, 1973:114; Van Noten 1972; Cornelissen 1998; Plets, Plets and Annaert, this volume).

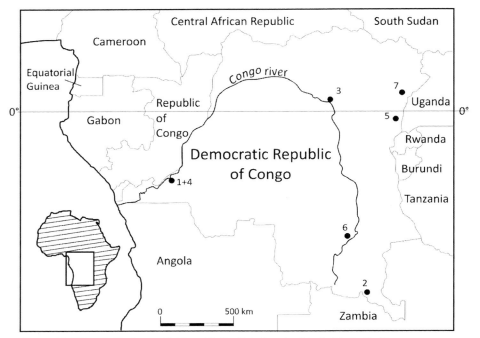

Congo M: Zaire, 1. Kinshasa - C: Léopoldville, 2. Lubumbashi - C: Elisabethville,
3. Kisangani - C: Stanleyville, 4. Gombe - C: Kalina,
5. Ishango, Katanda, Semliki, Virunga National Park - C: National Albert Park
6. Sanga, Upemba basin, Northern Katanga M: Northern Shaba, 7. Matupi

Figure 1. Map of places and archaeological sites mentioned in the text, names currently in use, when applicable former names are indicated, from the colonial era preceded by C and from Mobutu times preceded by M (Illustration: Royal Museum for Central Africa).

its expertise, collections from and archives on archaeological sites as well as its continuous efforts in promoting archaeological research and capacity building in archaeology in the DR Congo. We have been – and still are – in search of the most efficient approach to support archaeological research and capacity building in the DR Congo, considering the various demands and expectations of possible funding agencies through museums within societies facing colonial and post-colonial heritage. Of these strategies, rescue archaeology seems to hold new and promising perspectives for the specific situation of the DR Congo. In this paper, the development of archaeology in the DR Congo and the present situation will be discussed. Three periods are distinguished: the colonial era of Belgian Congo until independence in 1960; the period from 1960 until 1997 and especially the period of the presidency of D. Mobutu Sese Seko (1971-1997) who changed the name of the (Democratic) Republic of Congo into the Republic of Zaire; and the period after 1997, when the Republic of Zaire became the Democratic Republic of Congo under the succeeding regimes of the presidents Laurent D. Kabila and J. Kabila.[3]

---

3   On the various changes of the name of the country, see Ndaywel è Nziem 2009: 39.

The colonial era (1897-1960): a mostly Belgian affair contributing to world prehistory

In his comprehensive paper on the history of archaeology in Central Africa, Pierre de Maret (1990) (see also Plets, Plets and Annaert, this volume) points out that until the eve of independence, archaeology in Congo was essentially focusing on the contributions that Stone Age sites could make to the project of World Prehistory. This was also the case in other colonies on the continent (Robertshaw 1990; see also Sheperd 2002; Stahl 2005: 5-7). Hunter-gatherer communities in the Equatorial rainforest in Central Africa were considered survivors of prehistoric times and a key to understanding prehistoric ways of living. Establishing a chronology and typology for the Stone Age was the main aim and guided as such choices of fieldwork and research design (De Maret 1990: 111-121; Stahl 2005). During this first period, many of those involved in archaeological surveys and collecting were engineers, geologists, religious congregations, colonial administrators and amateurs with an interest in archaeology.

Large-scale excavations were conducted in the capital of Kinshasa (figure 1) and in its vicinity; first by Jean Colette in 1925 at Kalina point (figure 2), and later by Francis Cabu in 1934 and 1935 on the plains. Outside the capital, Jean de Heinzelin excavated in 1950 and in 1959 at Ishango, one of the country's most famous sites. Its exquisite bone industries were the first in the region to be radiocarbon-dated, giving the affiliated microlithic assemblages a Later Pleistocene age of approximately 20,000 years ago. This provoked quite some debate, since the available archaeological record elsewhere, and especially in Europe, called for a Holocene age of microlithic industries (De Heinzelin 1957, 1962). In the south of the country, Jean Hiernaux and Jacques Nenquin excavated in 1957 the site of Sanga, which testified to the existence of a complex socio-political entity from the eighth to the twelfth century AD. These excavations at Sanga were the start of a shift in archaeological interest towards the more recent history and towards the identity of contemporary people (De Maret 1990: 129, 132; Stahl 2005).[4]

The people in charge of the excavations were generally researchers of Belgian nationality. Some were responsible for the unit of Physical Anthropology and Prehistory at the Congo Museum in Tervuren where they were the sole scientists.[5] There were no Congolese scholars trained in archaeology, neither in Belgium nor in the colony. University training in general is a late phenomenon in Belgian Congo, universities did not come into existence until 1954, when the Catholic University of Lovanium in Leopoldville (Kinshasa) opened. Special degrees (*Licence*, after the Belgian academic system) in cultural anthropology were created at the Faculty for Political, Social and Economic Sciences and a degree in African philology was offered at the Faculty of Literature and Philosophy (Mantels 2007: 228). Jan Vansina (1994), the famous historian for Central Africa, taught in the early years

---

4   An exhaustive and comprehensive bibliography for archaeology in the DR Congo is available at http://www.african-archaeology.net/biblio/bibliordc.html.

5   J. Colette from 1934 to 1936, M. Bequaert from 1937 until 1958, J. Nenquin succeeded him until 1967.

Figure 2. J. Colette at the site of Kalina Point in 1925, Leopoldville (Photo: Royal Museum for Central Africa).

at Lovanium, where he promoted the new orientations of the role of oral traditions and of African history.

The artefacts from the excavations – which were mostly stone tools given the research focus – followed their finders. If the researcher had an institutional affiliation, such as a university or an institute in Belgium or in the DR Congo, the material was stored in that institute. The material that was collected by Colette, Cabu and Bequaert was thus registered in the collections of the Museum of Belgian Congo in Tervuren. The material from Ishango ended up in the National Institute for Natural Sciences in Brussels, as it was located in a national park. The finds from the jointly conducted excavations at Sanga went partly to the Museum of Belgian Congo, where Nenquin was responsible for the archaeological collections, and partly to the University of Elisabethville (now called Lubumbashi), where Hiernaux had become rector in 1956. Some collections were in private possession, both in Congo and in Belgium. Several are still privately owned, others were integrated during colonial times in one of the governmental museums. An example is the private collection of Cabu, part of which formed in 1943 the base of the official Congolese Leopold II museum, nowadays called the National Museum of Lubumbashi (De Plaen 1989a, 1989b, 1989c; Muya wa Bitanko Kamwanga 1999).

1960-1997: Archaeology and the authenticity policy

Belgian Congo became an independent state, the Republic of Congo, on 30 June 1960 and a decade later, on 27 October 1971, president Mobutu Sese Seko announced the principle of *le recours à l'authenticité*, the turning (not re-turning) to authenticity and to the roots of the Zairian culture. The country, the river and the currency were named Zaire in order to break with the previous colonial term of Congo.[6] Like elsewhere in post-colonial Africa, archaeology was considered instrumental in constructing this new national identity (Robertshaw 1990; Sheperd 2002: 196; Stahl 2005). Bokonga Ekanga Botombele, who was State Commissioner of Culture and Arts from 2 July 1972 until 7 January 1975 (Mulumba and Mokombo 1986: 61-62), wrote a UNESCO-report on the cultural policy in the Republic of Zaire (Bokonga 1975). In this he refers to the *Manifeste de la N' Sele* of 20 May 1968, which declares that in order to protect and restore past monuments, the Institute of National Museums is created (Bokonga 1975: 87; De Maret 1990: 131).[7] One of the special tasks of the new institute was the protection of archaeological sites. In fact, defining the stratigraphic and chronological framework for the archaeology of Zaire was its most urgent task (Bokonga 1975: 89). Another important task was capacity building, on this Bokonga stated:

> "*Recently we have realized that archaeology in Africa should not be interpreted exclusively in the light of European knowledge. Research should be carried out whenever possible by nationals. Also, we have noticed that training at universities is theoretical and focused on generalities. The institute is therefore to organize practical courses for young researchers so that they obtain practice*" (Bokonga 1975: 89).[8]

Awaiting academically trained Zairians, a specific arrangement between the Zairian and Belgian government was made to place Belgian experts at the position of general director of the institute and of the museums at Kinshasa and Lubumbashi (Konaré and 'O Byrne 1985: 4). From 1971 until 1976 the Institute of the National Museums in Zaire and the Belgian Royal Museum for Central Africa were headed by the same general director, Lucien Cahen.

---

6   On mobutism and authenticity policy see Ndaywel è Nziem 2009: 535-536; Bokonga 1975: 49.

7   On the legislation concerning the Institute see Konaré and O'Byrne 1985: 3-5. In the first years of its existence, the Institute operated directly under the Presidency of the Republic, in 1984 it was integrated in the Department (the later Ministry) of Culture and Arts. Issuing research clearances for excavations became the responsibility of the Ministry of Culture and Arts, but the ministerial permit was still to be prepared and examined by the Institute of National Museums first. This procedure is still in force.

8   Quote translated by the author from Bokonga 1975: 89, "En effet, on s'est rendu compte récemment que l'archéologie de l'Afrique ne doit pas être interprétée exclusivement à la lumière des connaissances européennes. Il importe donc que les recherches soient menées autant que possibles par des nationaux. Par ailleurs, on constate que l'enseignement dispensé par l'université demeure essentiellement théorique et axé sur des généralités. L'institut organise donc des stages pour les jeunes chercheurs, afin qu'ils acquièrent des connaissances pratiques."

Several years after the declaration of authenticity, a special volume on *'L'Archéologie en Afrique Centrale'* was published in the series of *Etudes d'Histoire Africaine*. In his foreword, Ndaywel è Nziem (1978: 6), then president of the Society of Zairian Historians, underlined the importance of archaeology as a historical science, but he also mentioned that the involvement of Zairian scientists in archaeological research was still quite minimal. There was not yet a team of national archaeologists and the National University of Zaire did not yet offer archaeological training. The volume is also important as papers by both young Zairian students in archaeology and researchers from the Royal Museum for Central Africa give an overview of archaeological research in the DR Congo and in Rwanda. Attention is drawn to the post-depositional disturbances at the reference site of Gombe in Kinshasa (figure 3) that put all previous chronostratigraphic subdivisions in the DR Congo at stake. Other topics included a Pleistocene age for the microlithic industries, the Neolithic in lower Congo and new excavations in the Upemba basin (see also Van Noten 1982; De Maret 1990, 2005).

As of the 1970s, researchers from other European countries and from Northern America became involved in the archaeological work in the DR Congo. For example, the River Reconnaissance Project of Manfred Eggert of the University of Hamburg (Germany) covered between 1977 and 1983 4,000 kilometres along the rivers in the interior of the Congo-Zaire basin. In this archaeologically void area, the project acquired new insights into the occupation in the last 3000 years (Eggert 1993, 2005; Wotzka 1995, 2006). Another example is the Semliki River Project, directed by Noel Boaz of the Virginia Museum of Natural History (Boaz 1990). Together with Alison S. Brooks from the Washington DC University, Boaz brought an impressive international interdisciplinary team out in the Western Rift Valley. They excavated the Middle Stone Age sites of Katanda, yielding 70,000 year old bone points, the oldest known in the world (Brooks *et al.* 1995; Yellen 1998). New excavations and dating at Ishango consolidated the Later Pleistocene Age here for the elaborate bone and quartz microlithic industries (Brooks and Smith 1987; Mercader and Brooks 2001).

These international activities lasted until the late 1980s, when the research conditions started to deteriorate due to the general collapse of the regime. In 1990 a total diplomatic rupture between president Mobutu's government and the international community resulted in a suspension of all Belgian funding. As a consequence, all Belgian cooperation agents were called back, including those active in research and education.

The research activities in the period between 1971 and 1995 had highlighted once more the enormous potential of the DR Congo for addressing questions ranging from the origin and characteristics of modern human behaviour to the material traces of Bantu expansions and of historical state formations, but although these research themes might have been of interest to Congolese archaeologists too, they were not set by them. The lack of funding for research activities reflects the general crisis in African archaeology in the years 1980–1990, with African and Africanist archaeology being reduced to 'a cultural puppet on a string for foreign based archaeologists' (Sheperd 2002: 201).

In general, the post-colonial government policy of Zaire was certainly at the outset very encouraging and promising for the development of archaeology. The political concern with identity building and archaeology triggered legislation, fieldwork and education in archaeology; *e.g.* research permits and the export of artefacts were subjected to formal legislation[9] and in this period five Zairian students were trained abroad, four of which obtained a PhD[10] (three of them were employed by the Institute of National Museums). It is mainly due to the withdrawal of funding from international programmes – covering either scientific explorations out in the field or museum aid - and the lack of financial support from the Zairian government that they were not in a position to implement the general policy as outlined by Bokonga (1975) and to conduct their own research programmes.

Figure 3. View on the excavations conducted at the site of Gombe (ex-Kalina) Point in 1973, Kinshasa, by D. Cahen and P. de Maret (Photo: P. de Maret).

---

9   In this period excavated artefacts were in some cases still exported for further analysis and conservation to Belgium, but with a valid licence obtained from the Institute of National Museums. This happened more frequently when the Institute's financial resources and infrastructure diminished due to a decreasing governmental support. The Royal Museum for Central Africa continues to host such archaeological 'guest' collections that are not its property.
10 Bakua Lufu Badibanga 1988; Kanimba Misago 1986; Mulowayi Kayemba 1999; Muya wa Bitanko Kamwanga 1986.

After 1997: new strategies for 'old' issues

When Laurent Désiré Kabila took over power in the DR Congo in 1997, the diplomatic relations between the two countries were slowly restored. In the meantime, the general political scene in Belgium had changed too, as Belgium had become a federal state in 1990. Education, research and culture were gradually becoming regional matters, but the Royal Museum for Central Africa and its scientific institute remained a national federal institute. This implied that it could apply for the so-called *indirect* international development funds. Unlike bilateral cooperation programmes, this indirect cooperation is not negotiated between governments, but it concerns international partnerships between institutions. As this opened up new opportunities for institutional cooperation, the Royal Museum for Central Africa saw in this an excellent opportunity to co-operate with the museums in the DR Congo to assist them with their capacity building task.

In 1998 a general agreement was signed between the Royal Museum for Central Africa and the Belgian General Directorate for Development Cooperation to start the institutional cooperation. D. Muya wa Bitanko Kamwanga, who was in charge of the National Museum of Lubumbashi, had written in 1997 a report on the terrible state his museum was in (Muya wa Bitanko Kamwanga 1999). He made a testimony of the disintegrating buildings and infrastructure, of the lack of research, the lack of motivation of the museum agents and their deficit in training. On the basis of this, the two museums set up a development programme, prioritizing the conservation of the collections, the renewal of the permanent exhibition, the creation of temporary exhibitions and the training for the museum staff. The programme could however not deal with the disintegrated infrastructure or with the poor salaries, since these matters are explicitly not covered by indirect cooperation programmes and have to be taken care of by the partner institution.

The cooperation project also provided individual internships (for a maximum of three months and only one per year) for Congolese museum agents at the Royal Museum for Central Africa. These helped to resolve their academic arrears that had been caused by being cut off from the media and the international scientific community for a long time. Internships could obviously not fill in the gap of the academic education, but they were meant as a 'training the trainers'-programme. The interns could pass on their newly gained knowledge to other Congolese museum agents and to university students.

In addition, foreign specialists visiting the Museum in Lubumbashi gave classes to a selection of students from the University and the Higher Education Institute of Lubumbashi, although this teaching was not part of any formal agreement. As it depended on personal initiatives by the director of the Lubumbashi museum, it was on an irregular base. If – for whatever reason – he was unable to select or to contact students, there were no classes.

This indirect institutional cooperation did not aim to conduct archaeological research, nor to include fieldwork, yet the Royal Museum for Central Africa managed to contribute to that too. Although it had become increasingly difficult for a national institute in Belgium to gain research funding, we initiated 'Crossing

Borders' (2006–2009) – financed by the Belgian Science Policy – (Smith and Van der Veken 2009; Smith and Viseyrias 2010; Smith 2010). Other strategies to support archaeological research in the DR Congo include for instance facilitating initiatives of the University of Brussels in cultural heritage management activities that are part of environmental impact assessments in World Bank financed infrastructure development (De Maret, Lavachery and Gouem Gouem 2008). We also participated in the biodiversity expedition 'Boyekoli Ebale Congo' on the Congo River (2010).[11]

Despite our efforts and the fact that it was a key objective in the case of the biodiversity expedition,[12] the contribution of these projects to capacity building in Congolese archaeology was limited. In 2011, there were still only two professional archaeologists employed by the Institute of the National Museums of Congo; P. Bakua Lufu Badibanga (as Director of Scientific Research in Kinshasa) and D. Muya wa Bitanko Kamwanga (as director of the Museum in Lubumbashi). They both teach archaeology classes at the universities, to anthropology and history students, and in the case of Kinshasa without financial or logistic means to organize fieldwork. Their educational work is surely complicated by the one thousand five hundred kilometres that separate them, by the lack of funding and of access to internet, but the most essential problem for capacity building in archaeology is the absence of an academic degree in archaeology at either of the Congolese universities. This for instance complicates international knowledge exchange. In order to be eligible for an internship at the Royal Museum for Central Africa or for training courses organized in the DR Congo, candidates need to have a university degree in the field that they seek expertise in or an institutional affiliation in that field. Admission to universities abroad is difficult as well; Congolese candidates often do not qualify because they do not correspond to profiles eligible for international funding, for instance due to age constraints or problems of equivalence in academic degrees.

These difficulties not only relate to archaeology, in general the educational sector in the DR Congo encounters severe problems.[13] Schools and universities suffer from a lack of government support and have to operate in totally disintegrating infrastructures and facilities; manuals, books, access to literature and educational tools are rare, and salaries are low. In fact, the entire society is confronted with the problem of daily survival, with competition over limited resources and hence also over the few positions at the universities, which – as a consequence – are often held beyond retirement. It is therefore most likely that there is no room for the creation of new positions in archaeology, that the classes in archaeology will continue to be inserted into other university programmes and that an academic degree in archaeology will not be an option for many years to come.

---

11   Http://www.congobiodiv.org/en/mission.
12   Http://www.congobiodiv.org/en/capacitybuilding.
13   Recent assessments are scarce, but some information can be found in Vwakyanakazi and Anthoine 2003; Lejeune and Gulungana 2009, and Mrsic-Garac 2010.

Rescue archaeology as an alternative to academic archaeology

Whereas the academic and the museum sector in the DR Congo cannot create favourable conditions for research and capacity building in archaeology, cultural heritage management might provide an alternative approach and perhaps a solution. Elsewhere in Central Africa it has been experienced that cultural heritage management, as part of environmental impact assessment studies accompanying infrastructure development, turned structural weaknesses into structural opportunities. Especially in Cameroon and Chad it can been seen how impact assessments during pipeline construction works offered opportunities for conducting archaeological fieldwork – in otherwise remote and inaccessible areas – and has led to spectacular results (Lavachery *et al.* 2010a, 2010b). These experiences also demonstrate that the cultural heritage management sector can provide training and perspectives for employment (De Maret, Lavachery and Gouem Gouem 2008; MacEachern 2010). Perhaps rescue archaeology may come to the rescue of archaeology in DR Congo as well, as large scale construction works, including mining operations, are booming business.

This however is not without caveats (MacEachern 2001, 2010; Arazi 2011). There is a serious incongruity between the cultural heritage management model as applied in Northern America and Europe and the circumstances in Africa (MacEachern 2001, 2010). In Africa there is for instance no structural or governmental infrastructure, nor funding for an academic follow-up of impact studies. Moreover, African archaeologists are not always aware of the specific aims of rescue archaeology, such as limited research goals – fieldwork is restricted to the problem for which funding has been obtained – versus those of impact studies - the recognition and prioritization of finds applies to all periods (MacEachern 2010; Alexander 2011). Also, an analysis of the compliance of safeguard policies regarding physical cultural resources that must be a component of environmental impact assessment and to which the clients of the World Bank need to comply, shows that non-compliance appears to be common with projects in Africa (Arazi 2011).

One of the reasons for such problems is that cultural heritage assessments are left to experts who are totally unfamiliar with cultural resources, as these are mostly done by natural heritage organizations that conduct environmental impact studies (Arazi 2011). It reflects, to some extent, the split in ministerial responsibilities and a lack of communication between organizations that are in charge of cultural heritage and those in charge of natural heritage. In order to enhance mutual understanding amongst all parties and various stakeholders in the DR Congo, the Royal Museum for Central Africa participated in two international conferences for the mining sector[14] and organized a workshop[15] on rescue archaeology. During the second mining conference, the general directors of the Congolese Institute for Nature Conservation and the Institute of the National Museums of Congo were brought together to join efforts (at least in national parks) for an integrated protection of natural and cultural heritage. The most emblematic site in this respect is Ishango, which is situated in the Virunga National Park that is one of the five national parks on the World Heritage in Danger list. We were not very successful; the Institute for Nature Conservation wished to develop a site museum on its own rather than as a joint venture with the Institute of National Museums. Probably this has to do with the fact that natural heritage management does not need to get involved with cultural heritage management; wildlife protection generates tremendous foreign financial support.

Another initiative was much more successful. As training in archaeology and raising awareness of the management of cultural resources is mandatory in environmental impact assessments, the Museum for Central Africa set up a summer school in Kinshasa in 2011 (figure 4). We financed it with support from

Figure 4. Fieldschool in 2011 at the site of the Institute of National Museum of Congo, Mount Ngaliema, Kinshasa (Photo: Royal Museum for Central Africa).

14 'La 'Quête des Ressources' en Afrique Centrale: Evolution and perspectives in the mining sector of the DRC', International conference organized by the University of Lubumbashi (RDC) and the Royal Museum for Central Africa (RMCA), 8-9 December 2008 and 1-3 December 2010; see http://www.africamuseum.be/museum/research/conferences/index_html.

15 The workshop on rescue archaeology was organized on 8.10.2009 by and at the Royal Museum for Central Africa. The programme included contributions from both Congolese and Belgian participants.

the Belgian indirect institutional cooperation and from a scientific grant that was allocated to Prof. Hans-Peter Wotzka of the University of Cologne (Germany), and the Institute of National Museums provided fifteen candidates. This combination of funds brought along the new possibility of accepting candidates with a master degree in anthropology or history that had no job or institutional affiliation. Despite some shortcomings and some logistical and administrative difficulties that were caused by Belgian and Congolese requirements, both organizers and participants considered this experiment highly constructive. It has been recommended to turn this pilot into a more formal, if not institutionalized approach.

Organizing a field school in Kinshasa outside the university but within the setting of the Institute of National Museums offers yet another new perspective. It means that apart from students in anthropology and history who have no prior archaeological training or fieldwork experience, candidates from other disciplines may be invited as well. This may include people working in disciplines relevant to or engaged in environmental impact studies. Including training in issues that relate to rescue archaeology would certainly be an asset to the programme. Moreover, involving candidates from other fields of research would also respond to the growing demand for multidisciplinary research approaches.

Setting agendas for the future

Rescue archaeology offers perhaps the best possibility to foster the archaeological record in the DR Congo. Because of the intrinsic absence of problem-oriented research design and hence the absence of agendas set by either foreign research agencies or by nationalist propaganda aims, it enables African cultural heritage managers to identify the research and conservation priorities. The possibilities and strategies for maintaining archaeological research, and concomitant improvement of the means for capacity building, reside in closer monitoring of environmental impact assessments for cultural heritage. As has been experienced in other Central African countries, this implies however that attention must be given to a correct application of and compliance with World Bank policies, to the promotion of rescue archaeology and to awareness raising for cultural heritage protection among practitioners of environmental impact assessment. Training the latter together with anthropologists and historians in specifically designed programmes within the Congolese Institute of National Museums is in my opinion the most viable option. Given the circumstances in the DR Congo this may suit the present opportunities in the DR Congo best, as insisting on university training is not very useful. Foreign museums, like the Belgian Royal Museum for Central Africa, can play a valuable and pragmatic role by offering their expertise in collection management, in research and analysis and in guiding fieldwork.[16] The museum may also continue to take part in the organization of field courses in rescue archaeology and in cultural

16 An example of such a pragmatic current project of the Royal Museum for Central Africa is the adjusting of archaeological maps of the DR Congo, on the basis of both its own, historically built collections and the Congolese 'guest' collections that are still stored in Belgium.

heritage management. This approach might be perceived as yet another agenda set by 'the outside', however, it will at least provide the concerned authorities in the DR Congo with 'inside' arguments for setting priorities in the protection and promotion of Congolese heritage.

Acknowledgements

I would like to thank the editors for inviting me to write this article, in particular Sjoerd van der Linde for his suggestion to reflect on the topic of capacity building. I also thank him, Monique van den Dries and Corijanne Slappendel for their editorial work. Their comments, as well as those from Gertjan Plets and from anonymous reviewers on an earlier draft, were most helpful and much appreciated. I am indebted to various persons and colleagues who all share a profound and sincere interest in the archaeology of the DR Congo and Central Africa, for answering my sometimes bizarre questions. The final responsibility for all flaws in interpretation and points of view remains, of course, mine alone.

References

Alexander, J. 2011. 'Editorial: Saving the African Heritage is a Global Priority: How Can a New Subdiscipline of Rescue Archaeology Aid It?', *African Archaeological Review* 28: 93-96.

Arazi, N. 2011. 'Safeguarding Archaeological Cultural Resources in Africa - Policies, Methods and Issues of (Non) Compliance', *African Archaeological Review* 28: 27-38.

Bakua Lufu Badibanga, P. 1988. 'Archéologie de la Plaine de la Ruzizi dans son Cadre Géologique', unpublished PhD thesis. Brussels: Vrije Universiteit Brussel.

Boaz, N.T. (ed.). 1990. *Evolution of Environments and Hominidae in the African Western Rift Valley.* Virginia Museum of Natural History Memoir 1. Martinsville: Virginia Museum of Natural History.

Bokonga, E.B. 1975. *La Politique Culturelle en République du Zaïre.* Paris: Les Presses de l'UNESCO.

Brooks, A.S. and C.C Smith. 1987. 'Ishango Revisited: New Age Determinations and Cultural Interpretations', *African Archaeological Review* 5: 65-78.

Brooks, A.S., D. Helgren, J.S. Cramer, A. Franklin, W. Hornyak, J.M. Keating, R.G. Klein, W. J. Rink, H. Schwarcz, J.N.M. Smith, K. Stewart, N.E. Todd, J. Verniers and J.E. Yellen. 1995. 'Dating and Context of Three Middle Stone Age Sites with Bone Points in the Upper Semliki Valley, Zaire', *Science* 268: 548-553.

Cahen, L. 1961. 'Editorial', *Africa-Tervuren* VII(1): 1-2.

Cahen, L. 1973. 'La Collaboration entre le Musée Royal de l'Afrique Centrale et les Musées Nationaux du Zaïre: un Chapitre de la «Politique Scientifique» du Musée de Tervuren', *Africa-Tervuren* 19(4): 111-114.

Cornelissen, E. 1998. 'Onderzoek aan de Afdeling Prehistorie en Archeologie', in D. Thys van den Audenaerde (ed.), *Africa Museum Tervuren 1989-1998*. Tervuren: Koninklijk Museum voor Midden-Afrika, 99-103.

De Heinzelin, J. 1957. *Les Fouilles d'Ishango*. Exploration du Parc National Albert 2. Brussels: Institut des Parcs Nationaux du Congo Belge.

De Heinzelin, J. 1962. 'Ishango', *Scientific American* 26: 105-116.

De Maret, P. 1990. 'Phases and Facies in the Archaeology of Central Africa', in P. Robertshaw (ed.), *A History of African Archaeology*. London: James Currey, 109-34.

De Maret, P. 2005. 'From Pottery Groups to Ethnic Groups in Central Africa', in A.B. Stahl (ed.), *African Archaeology. A Critical Introduction*. Blackwell Studies in Global Archaeology. London: Blackwell Publishing Ltd, 420-440.

De Maret P., P. Lavachery and B. Gouem Gouem. 2008. 'Grands Travaux Publics Grandes Opportunités Archéologiques? Evaluation d'un Siècle d'Expériences en Afrique', in B.O.M. Naffé, R. Lanfranchi and N. Schlanger (eds), *L'Archéologie Préventive en Afrique: Enjeux et Perspectives: Actes du Colloque de Nouakchott, 1er-3 Fevrier 2007*. Saint-Maur-des-Fossés: Editions Sépia, 142-152.

De Plaen, G. 1989a. 'Le Musée de Lubumbashi: un Musée Zaïrois Tout à Fait Particulier', *Museum* 162(XLI, 2): 124-126.

De Plaen, G. 1989b. 'The Lubumbashi Museum: a Museum in Zaire that is Quite Different', *Museum* 162(XLI, 2): 124-126.

De Plaen, G. 1989c. 'El Museo de Lubumbashi: un Museo Singular', *Museum* 162(XLI, 2): 124-126.

Eggert, M.K.H. 1993. 'Central Africa and the Archaeology of the Equatorial Rainforest: Reflections on some Major Topics', in Th. Shaw, P. Sinclair, B. Andah and A. Okpoko (eds), *The Archaeology of Africa: Food, Metals and Towns*. London: Routledge, 289-329.

Eggert, M.K.H. 2005. 'The Bantu Problem and African Archaeology', in A.B. Stahl (ed.), *African Archaeology. A Critical Introduction*. Blackwell Studies in Global Archaeology. London: Blackwell Publishing Ltd, 301-326.

Kanimba Misago, C. 1986. *Aspects Écologiques et Économiques des Migrations des Populations de Langues Bantu*. Europäische Hochschulschriften XXXVIII, Archäologie 8. Frankfurt am Main/New York: P. Lang.

Konaré, A.O. and P. O'Byrne. 1985. *Création du Musée National de Kinshasa*. Développement de l'Institut des Musées Nationaux: Zaire. Paris: UNESCO. Retrieved 16 November 2011 from http://unesdoc.unesco.org/Ulis/cgi-bin/ulis.pl?catno=69601&set=4E9A909A_0_101&gp=0&lin=1&ll=1.

Lavachery, P., S. MacEachern, T. Bouimon and C. Mbida Mindzie. 2010a. *Komé - Kribi: Rescue Archaeology Along the Chad-Cameroon Oil Pipeline, 1999-2004*. Journal of African Archaeology Monograph Series 4. Frankfurt a.M: Africa Magna Verlag.

Lavachery, P., S. MacEachern, T. Bouimon and C. Mbida Mindzie. 2010b. *De Komé à Kribi: Archéologie Préventive le long de l'Oléoduc Tchad-Cameroun, 1999-2004*. Journal of African Archaeology Monograph Series 5. Frankfurt a.M: Africa Magna Verlag.

Lejeune, M. and M. Gulungana. 2009. *Mission d'Identification R.D. du CONGO 27 octobre – 7 novembre 2009, rapport final*. Retrieved 16 November 2011 from http://www.vliruos.be/downloads/Mission_didentification_RDC_Rapport_Final.pdf.

MacEachern, S. 2001. 'Cultural Resource Management and Africanist Archaeology', *Antiquity* 75(290): 866- 871.

MacEachern, S. 2010. 'Seeing Like an Oil company's CHM programme, Exxon and Archaeology on the Chad Export Project', *Journal of Social Archaeology* 10: 347-367.

Mantels, R. 2007. *Geleerd in de Tropen, Leuven, Congo & de Wetenschap, 1885-1960*. Lovaniensia 28. Leuven: Universitaire Pers Leuven.

Mercader, J. and A.S. Brooks. 2001. 'Across Forests and Savannas: Later Stone Age Assemblages from Ituri and Semliki, Democratic Republic of Congo', *Journal of Anthropological Research* 57: 197-217.

Mrsic-Garac, S. 2010. 'Le Modèle Participatif à l'Épreuve du Champ Éducatif Congolais (RDC)', in P. Petit (ed.), *Société Civile et Éducation. Le Partenariat à l'Épreuve du Terrain*. Espace Afrique 8. Louvain-la-Neuve: Bruylant-Academia s.a., 75-102.

Mulowayi Kayemba, G. 1999. 'Le Matériel Lithique des Dépôts Quaternaires de la Vallée de la Mugera (Rift Kivu-Tanganyika/Est-Congo)', unpublished PhD thesis. Brussels: Vrije Universiteit Brussel.

Mulumba, M. and M. Makombo. 1986. *'Les Cadres et Dirigeants au Zaïre Qui Sont-Ils?' Dictionnaire Biographique*. Kinshasa: Editions du Centre de Recherches Pédagogiques.

Muya wa Bitanko Kamwanga, D. 1986. 'Préhistoire du Zaire Oriental. Essai de Synthèse des Âges de la Pierre Taillée', unpublished PhD thesis. Louvain-la-Neuve: Université Catholique de Louvain.

Muya wa Bitanko Kamwanga, D. 1999. 'Ceci n'est pas un Musée', in AFRICOM (ed.), *Actes de l'Assemblée Constituante, Lusaka, Zambie 3–9 Octobre 1999*. Paris: ICOM, 161-164.

Ndaywel è Nziem, I. 1978. 'Avant-propos', in D. Cahen (ed.), *Etudes d'Histoire Africaine, Numéro Spécial: L'Archéologie en Afrique Centrale* IX-X. Lubumbashi: Presses Universitaires du Zaïre, 6-7.

Ndaywel è Nziem, I. 2009. *Nouvelle Histoire du Congo des Origines à la République Démocratique*. Bruxelles: Le Cri/Kinshasa: Afrique Editions.

Robertshaw, R. (ed.). 1990. *A History of African Archaeology*, London: James Currey/ Portsmouth: Heinemann.

Sheperd, N., 2002. 'The Politics of Archaeology in Africa', *Annual Review of Anthropology* 31: 189-209.

Smith, A.L. 2010. 'Pottery Traditions in Katanga (DRC)', *Anthropos* 105: 179-190.

Smith, A.L and A. van der Veken. 2009. 'The «Crossing Borders Project»: Pottery traditions in Katanga (DRC)', *Afrique, Archéologie & Arts* 5: 141-148.

Smith, A.L. and A. Viseyrias. 2010. 'Shaping Kabambian Pottery: Identification and Definition of Technical Features', *The Open Anthropology Journal 3*: 124-141.

Stahl, A.B. 2005. 'Introduction: Changing Perspectives on Africa's Past', in A.B. Stahl (ed.), *African Archaeology. A Critical Introduction.* Blackwell Studies in Global Archaeology. London: Blackwell Publishing Ltd., 1-23.

Van Noten, F. 1972. 'De Afdeling Prehistorie en Archeologie van het Museum te Tervuren', *Africa - Tervuren* XVIII(3-4): 64-66.

Van Noten, F. (ed.). 1982. *The Archaeology of Central Africa.* Grazz: Akademische Druck- und Verlaganstalt.

Vansina, J. 1994. *Living with Africa.* Wisconsin: The University of Wisconsin Press.

Vwakyanakazi, D. and C. Anthoine. 2003. *L'Education à Lubumbashi.* Lubumbashi: Observatoire du Changement Urbain.

Wotzka, H.-P. 1995. *Studien zur Archäologie des Zentral-Afrikanischen Regenwaldes.* Africa Praehistorica 9. Köln: Heinrich Barth Institut.

Wotzka, H.-P. 2006. 'Records of Activity: Radiocarbon and the Structure of Iron Age Settlement in Central Africa', in H.-P. Wotzka (ed.), *Grundlegungen, Beiträge zur Europäischen und Afrikanischen Archäologie für Manfred K.H. Eggert.* Tübingen: Francke, 271-289.

Yellen, J.E. 1998. 'Barbed Stone Points: Tradition and Continuity in Saharan and Sub-Saharan Africa', *African Archaeological Review* 15: 173-198.

2.3 Communicating vessels: a Flemish experience with international collaboration in maritime heritage research

Ine Demerre

Flanders Heritage Agency, Belgium

Abstract

Maritime archaeological heritage does not take territorial borders into account, therefore cross-border collaboration is crucial for the research and management of this heritage. As a scientific but governmental agency, Flanders Heritage is convinced of the importance of international collaboration. It is therefore active in several projects, even though it has limited opportunity because its main task is to serve the Flemish government. For the agency's maritime research unit (established in 2003), this task consists primarily of gathering data to be prepared for the forthcoming legislation and subsequent management. As it is a young research unit, the main motivation for participating in international projects is to gain experience and to build a research network. During its involvement in two European research projects on maritime heritage, 'Managing Cultural Heritage Under water' (MACHU, 2007–2009) and the 'Archaeological Atlas of the 2 Seas' (A2S, 2009–2012), the agency encountered the advantages and disadvantages of working together with other nations. We found that even though partners may have similar visions towards maritime archaeological research, differences in culture, legislation and organization may complicate collaborations. But if an open mind is kept towards the differences, they can be exploited to enrich a project.

Résumé

Vases communicants : une Expérience Flamande avec une Collaboration Internationale en matière de Recherche du Patrimoine Maritime

Le patrimoine archéologique maritime ne tient pas compte des frontières territoriales et donc la collaboration transfrontalière est un élément crucial pour la recherche et la gestion de ce type de patrimoine. En tant qu'agence scientifique mais aussi politique, l'agence du patrimoine flamand, (agentschap Onroerend Erfgoed,

Flanders Heritage Agency), est convaincu de l'importance d'une collaboration internationale. L'agence participe, par conséquent, activement à plusieurs projets, bien que ses possibilités soient limitées puisque sa mission principale est de servir le gouvernement flamand. Pour l'unité des recherches maritimes de l'agence (établie en 2003), la tâche consiste principalement à collecter des données pour être présentées en vue de la prochaine législation et pour la gestion qui en découle. Comme l'unité de recherche est récente, sa principale motivation pour participer aux projets internationaux est d'acquérir de l'expérience et de créer un réseau de recherches. Lors de sa participation à deux projets européens relatifs au patrimoine maritime, 'Gérer le patrimoine culturel sous-marin' ('Managing Cultural Heritage Under water', MACHU, 2007-2009) et 'L'Atlas Archéologique des 2 Mers' ('Archaeological Atlas of the 2 Seas', A2S, 2009-2012), l'agence a eu les avantages et les inconvénients de travailler en coopération avec d'autres pays. On s'est aperçu que, même si les partenaires ont la même vision sur la recherche archéologique maritime, des différences culturelles, de législation et d'organisation peuvent compliquer les collaborations. Cependant, quand ces différences sont abordées avec une ouverture d'esprit, elles peuvent être exploitées pour enrichir un projet.

Extracto

Naves Comunicantes: una Experiencia Belga con Colaboración Internacional en Investigaciones del Patrimonio Marítimo

El patrimonio arqueológico marítimo no cuenta con fronteras territoriales por lo cual la colaboración transfronteriza es determinante para la investigación y gestión de este patrimonio. Como agencia científica y gubernamental, la Agencia del Patrimonio de Flandes está convencida de la importancia de la colaboración internacional. Por eso está implicada en diferentes proyectos, aunque posea de posibilidades limitadas porque su objetivo principal es servir el gobierno de Flandes. Para la sección de investigaciones marítimas de la agencia (establecida en 2003), esta tarea consiste principalmente en la recolección de datos que después serán preparados para la futura legislación y la gestión subsecuente. Como es una sección investigadora joven, la motivación principal para participar en proyectos investigadores europeos es para obtener experiencia y para construir una red investigadora. Durante su implicación en dos proyectos europeos de investigación del patrimonio marítimo, 'Gestionar Patrimonio Cultural Submarino' ('Managing Cultural Heritage Under water', MACHU, 2007-2009) y el 'Atlas Arqueológico de los dos Mares' ('Archaeological Atlas of the 2 Seas', A2S, 2009-2012), la agencia experimentó las ventajas y las desventajas de trabajar junto con otras naciones. Resultó que, aunque los socios tengan semejantes opiniones de la investigación arqueológica marítima, las diferencias en cultura, legislación y organización pueden complicar las colaboraciones. Sin embargo, si uno tiene la mente abierta frente a las diferencias, las puede utilizar para enriquecer un proyecto.

ملخص

التواصل بين السفن، تجربة فلمنكية مع التعاون الدولي في البحث التراثي البحري

إيان ديميري

وكالة التراث الفلمنكية، بلجيكا

لا يأخذ التراث الأثري في البحر البحري ضمن الحدود الإقليمية في عين الاعتبار، ولذلك يعد وكالة علمية لكن وكالة. وإداراته. التراث هذا في البحث سوريا محور عبر الحدود التعاون الدولي. وبالتالي حكومة، اقتنعت وكالة التراث الفلمنكية بأهمية التعاون الدولي. وبالرغم من أن حدودها فرضها من مختلف في مخطط نشاط في تقوم الخاصة الوكالة لوحدة وبالنسبة. الفلمنكية الحكومة خدمة هي الرئيسية اهتمامها بالبحث البحري تأسست في (2003)، تضمنت هذه المهمة أول جمع البيانات المتتالية. وبما هنا وحدة حديثة، فإن بالبحث في مشاركتها بحث. وخلال مشاريع اهتكاها في مشروعي بحث أوربيين خاصين بالتراث الدافع الرئيسي للمشاركة في المشروعات الدولية هو اكتساب الخبرة وبناء البحري، الأ وهما ''إدارة التراث الثقافي بالمغمور بالمياه'' ('Managing Cultural Heritage Under water', MACHU, 2007-2009) و''الأطلس الأثري للبحرين'' ('Archaeological Atlas of the 2 Seas', A2S, 2009-2012)، وقد تبين أنه من مغرم أن الشركاء قد يكون وعبوب التعاون مع الدول الأخرى. وقد تبين أنه من مغرم أن الشركاء قد يكون ونحن مجموعة ممثلة لدهم رؤى ماثلة، إلا أن الأثري البحري، والتشريعية والتنظيمية قد تعدت التعاون. ولكن، إذا تم الحفاظ على وعي منافع هذه الاختلافات، فهم الممكن استغلالها من أجل تعزيز المشروعات.

Keywords

Maritime Archaeology, heritage management, Flanders Heritage Agency, international collaboration, Flanders/Belgium

Introduction

Throughout history, the sea has always been a medium for international contacts across any current boundary. Therefore the maritime heritage is not just the property of one nation, it is also common heritage and therefore common responsibility of humanity (UNESCO 2001). Cross-border collaboration and communication within the maritime heritage research brings benefits and progress to all participating countries (both for partners, scientists, stakeholders and the larger public), regardless of how small they are. It is like in the well-known physical process of the communicating vessels with a homogeneous fluid: regardless of the shape and volume of the containers, if liquid is added to one of them, the liquid will find a new equal level in all the connected vessels (Fontana and Di Capua 2005).

In this paper the international collaboration activities of the maritime heritage unit of the Flanders Heritage Agency[1] will be discussed and personal reflections will be given on these collaborations on the basis of the author's involvement in the 'Managing Cultural Heritage Under water' (MACHU, 2007–2009) and the 'Archaeological Atlas of the 2 Seas' (A2S, 2009–2012) projects. During these projects interesting similarities and differences in the participants' views and approaches were discovered and the reflections are not meant to offend any of our partners, but to provide suggestions for improvement and to enrich future collaboration.

Background on Belgium maritime legislation and heritage management

Although invisible to the eye, the sea is divided into different juridical areas each of which is allocated to different nations and competent authorities, and as such they are subject to different laws. For instance the Belgian federal government is the competent authority of the Belgian Territorial Sea (12 nautical miles) and in a more restricted way of the wider Belgian Continental Shelf, containing the Exclusive Economic Zone (3,454 km²)[2] (Belpaeme, Konings and Vanhooren 2011: 30-33). Concerning the *in situ* maritime heritage, the legislation is more complex as the authority lies with a region of the federal state (Plets, Plets and Annaert, this volume), *i.e.* the region that borders the location of the heritage site. Thus maritime heritage in Belgium is a matter of both the Flemish region and the federal authorities.

To facilitate the communication between the two governments (*e.g.* in relation to exploitation and developments at sea) a collaboration agreement was drafted in 2004.[3] As a result of this agreement and as a first step towards a change in policy concerning the management of the maritime heritage, the region of Flanders developed an interactive database with all maritime heritage in the Belgian North Sea, co-ordinated by the Flemish Heritage Institute (*Vlaams Instituut voor het Onroerend Erfgoed*, VIOE, now Flanders Heritage Agency) in collaboration with the province of West Flanders.[4]

---

1   Flanders Heritage (*Agentschap Onroerend Erfgoed*) is an agency of the Flemish government (under direct authority of the Flemish ministry competent for immobile heritage), responsible for the scientific research, inventorization, protection, management and the outreach of the architectural, archaeological, scenic, heraldic and maritime heritage in Flanders. Since 1 July 2011 the Flemish Heritage Institute (*Vlaams Instituut voor het Onroerend Erfgoed*, VIOE) and the 'heritage' aspect of the 'Flemish Planning Agency for Town and Country Planning and Immovable Heritage' were merged into one agency (https://www.onroerenderfgoed.be/over-ons/). For more information about the development of the Agency since the establishment of the Belgian State Service for Excavations in 1903 see Plets, Plets and Annaert, this volume.

2   See http://www.mumm.ac.be/NL/NorthSea/geography.php.

3   This is an unpublished cooperation agreement '*Samenwerkingsakkoord tussen het Vlaamse Gewest en de federale overheid houdende het maritiem erfgoed*', 5 October 2004 (Pieters *et al.* 2010: 180).

4   See the database '*Maritieme Archeologie*' which was launched in 2007 (http://www.maritime-archaeology.be).

Subsequently, in 2007 the sixteenth century 'Wreck Edict of Charles V' was replaced by a new 'wreck act', to organize the property of wrecks and wreck parts.[5] It laid a modern juridical base for the protection of wrecks within Belgian territorial waters, but unfortunately there is still no implementation order for this new legislation. The Flemish Government did however sign a decree in 2010 that accepts the UNESCO 2001 Convention on the protection of Underwater Cultural Heritage[6] and which is an important step towards a possible federal ratification and thus a better interaction between Belgian and international maritime heritage management (Demerre and Zeebroek 2009).

Flanders Heritage Agency established a unit for maritime heritage research in 2003. It was in fact founded by terrestrial archaeologists who were active in archaeological research of the medieval fishing village of 'Walraversijde' (Raversijde - Ostend) (*e.g.* Tys and Pieters 2009). Its main task was to take an inventory of the maritime heritage on land, under water and still afloat, and to integrate it into an interactive maritime database. In order to gather information on these maritime sites and their condition, since 2006 the unit organizes surveys of archaeological sites in the Belgian part of the North Sea (Demerre, Missiaen and Gevaert 2008). To this day the maritime research unit of Flanders Heritage Agency is still anticipating further developments in legislation, and despite a properly working law and a limited staff capacity, it is mostly thanks to collaborations and international projects that the unit is already a professional and equipollent partner for its foreign colleagues.

Contacts abroad

Situated on the 'crossroads' of Europe, Belgium has a strategic position. International contact is therefore its second nature. Also archaeological heritage is subject to international (and certainly European) collaboration, as archaeological remains are ignorant of territorial borders, especially in the sea. For example, the so far identified wreck sites (over 250 targets) on the Belgian Continental Shelf already represent fifteen nationalities. Moreover, Belgium ratified in 2010 the European 1992 Convention on the Protection of the Archaeological Heritage (Council of Europe 1992), and has plans to ratify the UNESCO Convention on the Protection of the Underwater Cultural Heritage (UNESCO 2001). This all stimulates international collaboration and exchange of information. So, although Flanders Heritage currently does not have a policy of executing or supervising archaeological research abroad (see Plets, Plets and Annaert, this volume),

5   Federale Overheidsdienst Mobiliteit en Vervoer (FMOV). 2007. 'Wet betreffende de Vondst en de Bescherming van Wrakken, 9 April 2007'. *Belgisch Staatsblad*, 21 June 2007, 16-17. Retrieved 17 December 2011 from http://www.ejustice.just.fgov.be/cgi/welcome.pl.

6   Vlaamse Overheid 2010. 'Decreet van 16 juli 2010 houdende Instemming met het Verdrag ter Bescherming van het Cultureel Erfgoed onder Water, aangenomen in Parijs op 2 november 2001'. *Belgisch Staatsblad,* 9 August 2010. Retrieved 17 December 2011 from http://www.ejustice.just.fgov.be/doc/rech_n.htm.

anticipating international developments is part of its mission statement[7] and it is convinced of the importance of international collaborations for networking, for the exchange and gain of knowledge and for its outreach towards the stakeholders in heritage management, *i.e.* the public, the scientific community and the policy officers.

Within this context of international networking the maritime unit co-ordinated for instance the 2006 international colloquium 'to Sea or not to Sea', held in Bruges (Belgium), on maritime and fluvial archaeology (Pieters *et al.* 2006; Zeebroek, Pieters and Gevaert 2007). Flanders Heritage also often participates in international colloquia and conferences with lectures and poster presentations. Thanks to this networking, other activities could be organized that would help to improve our experience in the maritime research field. For example, in collaboration with the British Nautical Archaeology Society, a course was organized to develop the archaeological skills under water of sports divers.[8] To develop its own experience as well, the maritime heritage unit participates since 2009 in sub-aquatic excavation and prospection campaigns in the rivers Canche and Somme (France).[9]

As of 2003, the agency has also been active in several cross-border collaboration projects, *i.e.* in Planarch 2 ('Planning and Archaeology in the North West'), Archaeology in Contemporary Europe, MACHU and A2S. Interestingly, the collaboration with neighbouring countries is often more intensive than the interaction between the neighbouring regions Flanders and Wallonia. As mentioned by Plets, Plets and Annaert, this volume, archaeological research in the federal state of Belgium was split into a Flemish and Walloon region in 1989. This is the reason why within heritage research collaboration is often, unintentionally, forgotten. Moreover, Wallonia does not border the North Sea, so research under water has a different focus, namely mostly on rivers and caves.

Due to the maritime research unit's lasting 'preparatory' status, awaiting further legislative developments since 2003, international collaboration has been a main source of support for its existence and further development. But apart from the financial support through project funding, another major motivation for international collaboration was to acquire academic recognition by the maritime archaeological research community. But its main objective is to gain experience in other research methods other than taking inventories. The more knowledge of the heritage we have, the better the foundation for its future management will be. In the agency's view this has to be achieved through international cooperation and the exchange of research methods and results. It consequently promotes innovation of research and of public outreach, which may help to raise the awareness and appreciation of the Belgian public, the stakeholders and the policy officers regarding our maritime archaeological heritage.

---

7   Https://www.onroerenderfgoed.be/over-ons/agentschap-onroerend-erfgoed/missie-en-visie/.

8   See the website of the *Nautical Archaeology Society at* http://www.nauticalarchaeologysociety.org.

9   These campaigns are organized by the government-funded French Research Centre for Scientific Research (CNRS) and the Sub-aquatic and Submarine Archaeological Research Department of the French Ministry of Culture (DRASSM) (Rieth 2009).

Two case studies

After having participated in the wetland archaeological project 'Planning and Archaeology in the North West' (Planarch 2002–2006),[10] the maritime heritage unit of the Flanders Heritage Agency became a partner in two projects on underwater cultural heritage. The first was the project 'Managing Cultural Heritage Underwater' (MACHU), that ran from 2007 until 2009 as part of the Culture 2000 programme,[11] the second the 'Archaeological Atlas of the 2 Seas' (A2S), that ran from 2009 until 2012 within the Interreg IVA programme.[12]

The MACHU project involved eight partners from seven different European countries, with the Dutch 'National Agency for Cultural Heritage' (RCE) as leading partner.[13] The project was a pilot study on developing, implementing and combining techniques for a better management of the underwater archaeological heritage (for locating, monitoring and protecting sites). It also aimed to make our mutual underwater heritage more accessible to scientists, policy makers and to the general public, to raise the awareness for this kind of heritage.

These goals were to be achieved through models predicting natural and human degradation or sedimentation processes and threats to the heritage, through databases, a Geographic Information System (GIS) for visualizing data, and through a website for public interaction.[14] The project officially ended in September 2009, but it was actually the start of further developments and collaborations within the maritime unit (Manders, Oosting and Brouwers 2008, 2009a, 2009b).

When Flanders Heritage participated in the MACHU project, the maritime heritage research in Flanders was just at its starting point and finding the best way towards a proper management of this heritage was a big issue. It was expected that the project would bring insights into the management situation throughout Europe and that the agency could benefit from the experiences of the other countries. Another motivation for collaboration, especially with our northern neighbour, the

---

10 For information on the project and its results see *e.g.* Dyson, Heppell and Pieters 2006.

11 The Culture 2000 programme aims to develop a common cultural area by promoting cultural dialogue, knowledge of the history, creation and dissemination of culture, the mobility of artists and their works, European cultural heritage, new forms of cultural expression and the socio-economic role of culture. See also website: http://europa.eu/legislation_summaries/culture/l29006_en.htm.

12 The Interreg Community Initiative (Interreg IV A 2007–2013) is a European programme that aims for a dissolution of the borders in Europe. It is funded by the European Union and promotes the cooperation between regional territories in different countries. The organization wants to strengthen the economic cohesion of the EU. The Interreg IVA '2 Mers Seas Zeeën'-programme promotes crossborder cooperation between the coastal regions of four member states: France (Nord-Pas de Calais), England (SW, SE, E), Belgium (Flanders) and The Netherlands (South coastal area). See also the website: http://www.interreg4a-2mers.eu/programme/key-information/en.

13 The other partners were: the Dutch hydrographic service '*Rijkswaterstaat*', the 'Roman Germanic Commission' (RGK) in collaboration with Mecklenburg-Vorpommern (Germany), the 'Polish Maritime Museum' (CMM) of Gdansk, 'English Heritage', the 'National Maritime Museums of Sweden' (SMM), the Portuguese 'Centre for Underwater and Nautical Archaeology' (DANS/CNANS) and the Flemish Heritage Institute in Flanders (VIOE), see the section on partners on the website of the project at http://www.machuproject.eu/partners.htm.

14 See the MACHU GIS section on the website of the MACHU project at http://machuproject.eu/machu_gis.htm.

Netherlands, was that it would be essential for research of the heritage in the border region.

As said, one of the main tasks of the maritime heritage research within Flanders Heritage is to build an interactive database on the national maritime heritage. The GIS system that was planned within the MACHU project, would allow this data (and additional geographic information) to be presented to the public and be better accessible for future management (it shows for example the geographical application range of a certain law, how the areas of aggregate extraction relate to endangered wreck sites, etc.). As the ambition of the project corresponded with the goals of the maritime heritage unit itself, the European co-funding could make further research possible and the registration could be combined with the actual exploration and monitoring of wreck sites in Belgian territorial waters.

During the MACHU project, France started to recruit participants to join in a cross-border collaboration project. This project was to be called 'Archaeological Atlas of the 2 Seas' (A2S). Between mid-2009 and July 2012 Flanders Heritage participated in this European project, together with the British Hampshire and Wight Trust for Maritime Archaeology (HWTMA) and the French *Association pour le Développement de la Recherche en Archéologie Maritime* (Adramar) that managed the project (Bowens *et al.* 2011; Fenwick *et al.* 2012).[15]

Whereas MACHU focused on management and outreach, the A2S project focused on the research and outreach that precedes the management. Apart from sharing and comparing our knowledge and information on the underwater archaeological heritage in our common seas (North Sea, Channel area and Atlantic Ocean), also the skills of the different partners would be brought together to execute archaeological surveys and to analyse and interpret our mutual maritime history. This approach is not only beneficial to the partners, but the knowledge that it generates on excavating and recording the sub-aquatic heritage is also of use for students and recreational divers.

The A2S project would emphasize public outreach as well. All gathered information would be merged into a publicly accessible geo-portal that combines the existing databases of each partner country to create a comprehensive underwater landscape. The maritime heritage research was promised to be brought to the wider public through a website, publications, educational initiatives, an exhibition etc.

As the actual maritime heritage management is preceded by a sites evaluation and assessment, Flanders Heritage needed additional desk-based archival research and on-site recordings in the Belgian territorial waters. The aim was to fill this need through the A2S project as well. Especially for the data gathering and actual fieldwork a close interaction with the other partners was foreseen, in particular with our southern neighbours (France) – with its long history in maritime heritage research (since the 1960s). The result of this research objective is a geo-portal

---

15 See the website of the Archaeological Atlas of the 2 Seas Project at www.atlas2seas.eu / www.atlas2mers.eu / www.atlas2zeeen.eu.

combining the new information and the data from already existing national databases for public use.[16]

Experiences with international collaboration in general

It was noticed during the international collaboration projects that many differences between the partners may be encountered. Often they are due to the cultural dissimilarities between the countries. They can be enriching, but they may also hinder a smooth collaboration. For instance the differences in communication customs can give the impression to some partners that meetings are inefficient if discussions do not yield clear and obvious results. Another example is the approach towards 'deadlines'; these can be quite flexible in certain countries, others respect them more strictly (cf. the more rigid northern attitude versus the southern 'go-with-the-flow' mentality). Also some partners may be more self-confident than others and more talented or skilled in 'selling' their approach. Working together with experienced project partners can be very stimulating to achieve good results and motivating to contribute with fresh ideas, but it also requires a strong project leader who balances the input of both strong and more modest partners.

Using different languages can be a major barrier as well. Most often English is the communication language in science and therefore also for European scientific projects. This sometimes causes difficulties for non-native speakers. Misunderstandings can easily occur during negotiations and in taking decisions. Secondly, the necessary translations (for instance for publications or for preparing educational tools for international schools, such as in A2S) can be very time consuming.

Furthermore, international collaboration projects often involve different types of organizations, like museums, universities, governmental institutes, trusts and other small specialized organizations. These usually have particular aims and priorities, which are reflected in their approaches. Some for instance depend on public relations and are thus experienced in communicating maritime archaeology to the wider public,[17] others are more experienced in communication with policy makers or scientists. It is not only important to exploit their strengths, the partners should also agree on the project goals and be able to contribute to the suggested approaches.

Beside a partner's approach, the organizational framework it has to operate in can be quite different too. For instance, some project partners may be involved in just one project, while others may be embedded in a larger structure and may have to work on multiple assignments. Moreover, some partners may be restricted by decisions or requests from their principals that relate to the policy and/or funding of the organization. An association like Adramar for instance depends on the

---

16   See www.a2s-geoportal.eu.
17   For instance through elaborated educational programmes or exhibitions such as conducted by the National Maritime Museums of Sweden during the MACHU-project (Ekberg 2009) and by the Hampshire and Wight Trust for Maritime Archaeology during the A2S project (Bowens *et al.* 2011: 24-27).

support and decisions of the match funding by the Ministry,[18] and an organization like Flanders Heritage is directed in its policies by the Flemish government. Consequently, unforeseen developments on these organizational levels may have serious consequences for an ongoing project.[19]

Furthermore, some partners may have a large project team in which the different activities can be divided among specialists (*e.g.* finances, IT, communication, project co-ordination, survey, archival research, etc.), while other teams are too small for a specialization. Yet the latter are expected to have more or less the same input as their bigger partners and they usually need to take care of the same amount of administrative work.[20] When applying for a project, it is for that reason important to bear in mind that the tasks of smaller teams should be levelled out and divided among the other partners, or that these teams should get administrative support.

Experiences with collaboration in maritime archaeology

Regarding the content of the international projects, handling maritime heritage, several useful experiences were gained as well. A major lesson is that it is crucial for a good collaboration to know and understand the differences between partners and countries, specifically regarding their approach to maritime heritage research and management. There are for instance crucial differences in legislation. Some countries can base their maritime heritage management on a well-organized legislative structure, while others still have to prepare a stable legislative structure for it. Some countries do not recover any artefacts – even if it concerns stray finds – whereas others do.

Such things not only relate to legislation issues, also to differences in local situations, like preservation circumstances. In the Baltic Sea for instance, small stray finds can be monitored for many years, while in the North Sea these will disappear (washed away, looted or silted up) within a month if they are not recovered (Manders, Oosting and Brouwers 2009b). The local water condition (visibility, sedimentation rate, etc.) therefore defines what survey, excavation and management methods can be applied (*e.g.* Arnshav 2008; Olsson 2011).

Even the definition of maritime archaeological heritage can vary from country to country. It depends on the scope of the heritage that is present in the territorial waters, but it can also be influenced by a country's philosophy on the issue. Some countries or organizations include for example water-linked heritage on land in their maritime research, whereas others focus exclusively on underwater heritage. Some make a distinction between wooden wreck sites and metal World War shipwrecks;

---

18 It is decided on by *Le Département des Recherces Archéologiques Subaquatiques et Sous-Marines* (DRASSM) within the ministry of culture and communication.

19 Examples of such developments are the reorganization of DANS in Portugal (see http://www.machuproject.eu/p-cnans-port.htm), the struggle for survival by the British Hampshire and Wight Trust for Maritime Archaeology, the funding restrictions due to the financial crisis etc. (Manders, Oosting and Brouwers 2009b: 14; Fenwick *et al.* 2012).

20 For instance the partnership of Belgium in A2S mainly involved two people, while the involvement of France and England consisted of five to eight people (Bowens *et al.* 2011: 8-9).

others focus on drowned (prehistoric) landscapes rather than on shipwrecks, and so on (Bailey 2011: 27).

Moreover, the approach towards public accessibility of maritime archaeological data differs strongly as well. Most countries are restricted in publishing wreck sites (*e.g.* Sweden or Germany), or data may even be the property of private companies (cf. in the United Kingdom) (Hootsen and Dijkman 2009: 21; Cornelis *et al.* 2011), but in some countries locations may be publicly known. In Flanders for example, wreck positions are accessible via the hydrographic service.[21]

When creating a mutual 'public' database, like in the MACHU project, such issues may cause serious dilemmas. As many sites are vulnerable to looting or damage, they need to be kept concealed to preserve them effectively (especially protected sites), but it is on the other hand also important to communicate research results (at least in a restricted way) that were acquired with public money, especially since this might help to raise the awareness of the value and vulnerability of these sites. So it sometimes may be difficult to find an acceptable solution for all partners and sites.

Furthermore the maritime heritage management and research approaches may reflect cultural differences which are hard to overcome. The Netherlands for instance are very much focused on applying the principles of the Valletta Convention (Council of Europe 1992). They prefer to look for means to physically protect maritime archaeological sites *in situ*. There are no excavations unless the site is in danger of destruction (Manders 2004). In France, on the other hand, excavations play a much more important role as they are believed to help in maintaining and expanding expertise for the future (Bowens *et al.* 2011: 8). This difference in approaches is clearly illustrated by the fact that the Netherlands did not participate in the A2S project, whereas France was absent in the MACHU project.

A final complicating factor for collaboration may be the lack of a common language. The French can have difficulties understanding English, the Dutch with French. Fortunately, in such cases Belgium/Flanders can act as a 'neutral intermediate'. Due to its shared history – throughout history Belgium was sometimes even used as a 'battlefield' between bigger states (*e.g.* during the Eighty Year's War, in Napoleon's battle of Waterloo, in World Wars I and II) – it is familiar with the (maritime) culture of its different neighbours. Moreover, Belgium has the advantage of being officially trilingual (Dutch, French and German), while most Belgian people understand English well too.

Experiences versus expectations

Despite the differences, the overall methodological and general approaches usually show enough similarities to enable highly successful collaborations. It is in any case important that each partner keeps its own characteristics throughout a mutual project, differences enable enrichment if we understand, accept and even learn

---

21 See the '*Wrakkendatabank*' on the website of the *Agentschap voor Maritieme Dienstverlening en Kust* at http://www.vlaamsehydrografie.be/wrakkendatabank.htm.

Figure 1. Material from a so far unidentified eighteenth century shipwreck on the 'Buiten Ratel' sandbank (Belgian waters) that mainly originates from the Netherlands. Using foreign information sources may help to find information about the ship and its identity (Photo: Flanders Heritage Agency).

from each partners' peculiarities (Fenwick *et al.* 2012). This was the case with both the MACHU and the A2S projects. Both achieved their main goals rather well, although some aspirations were reduced or reoriented.

Thanks to both projects, Flanders Heritage was able to elaborate its data gathering on maritime heritage. It also made its own information accessible for a wider audience. However, the high ambition of the A2S project of exchanging archival information and extensive data collections of most of the sites in the project region, had to be lowered and the exchange was limited to a few test cases. Other big advantages of the cross-border collaborations of both MACHU and A2S are the possibilities of sharing knowledge and information, of having access to archives abroad, of being able to study artefacts that have travelled across borders (figure 1), and of sharing specialized knowledge on maritime heritage (*e.g.* ship constructions, artefacts, etc.) (Demerre 2009: 30-31).

With both the MACHU GIS-database and the A2S geo-portal, a visual medium was created that joins the information of different countries in an easily accessible way and that facilitates comparative studies (Hootsen and Dijkman 2009: 15-30; Bowens *et al.* 2011: 16-19; Fenwick *et al.* 2012: 50-53).[22] Within the GIS database of MACHU, the geographical layers (*e.g.* with the range of the applicability of

22   See also http://machuproject.eu/machu_gis.htm, http://www.atlas2mers.eu/the-project-3/database-2/ and http://a2s-geoportal.eu.

national and international laws) have turned out to be a very good management tool. The A2S portal is especially valuable as it makes the elaborate national databases searchable for quick overviews or for more detailed researches into the data, even across the national borders. All of this is useful for the general public and for scientists, but also stakeholders and policy makers.

Nevertheless, in the realization of the databases several difficulties were encountered. The restrictions of public accessibility of certain data for instance hindered the previously planned public access of the MACHU database.[23] Furthermore the differences in structure of all the national databases of the MACHU partners made it impossible to create a direct link to the mutual GIS tool as planned. Instead, a new database with manually extracted data (from each partner) was developed. This serves its purpose better, but is difficult to maintain. Any update in one of the national databases needs to be manually copied to the MACHU database.

In the A2S project, concerning only three national databases, the data tuning was also time consuming but much easier. In this case the plan was feasible to build an open source geo-portal with a direct link to the local databases, mainly because it contains only little information on individual sites and links to the national database for more information. This implies that the portal requires little maintenance and can easily be kept 'alive' after the project is finished.

All together the actual database development in both projects took more time than planned due to these unforeseen complications. Therefore both databases were only ready in a limited version at the end of the project. Hopefully, in the near future other countries as well as the MACHU GIS can be linked to the geo-portal. It may reduce the number of different maritime databases with comparable content all over Europe (and the world).

Another crucial activity in the projects was the research *in situ*. It was experienced within a large team like in the MACHU project that each partner has its own priorities and is tempted to stick to its own research aims, thus risking to disregard the mutual project goals. The common guideline towards management methods was respected but there were too many partners for a common research.[24] This lack of coherence was fortunately compensated by the exchange of experiences during the frequently held project meetings.

In the A2S project there were fewer partners involved, so national priorities did not influence the mutual goals too much. On the contrary, the partners participated more in most project activities. Especially the mixed teams that conducted the on-site research in each partner country, were a big success. In this way, all partners had the opportunity to participate in various research methods (*e.g.* a *side-scan*

---

23 The GIS tool is only accessible to the scientific community and stakeholders with a password. The wider public has access to a more limited tool, see http://machuproject.eu/machu_gis.htm.

24 Sweden for instance developed a questionnaire for recreational divers and Germany and Poland did research on prehistoric settlements, to prepare for developments at sea (Manders, Oosting and Brouwers 2009b: 80, 88, 93).

Figure 2. Using an underwater planning frame for documenting a wreck site (Photo: A2S-project, Onroerend Erfgoed). Right: The construction of the frame by the A2S project partners during a survey by Flanders Heritage Agency (Photo: A2S, HWTMA).

sonar survey in France, an excavation in England and a detailed wreck registration in Belgium) and to exchange skills and methods (figure 2).

Thanks to the international relations, various (interdisciplinary) research methods could be tested in our waters (*e.g.* electromagnetism and seismic acoustics by Ghent University (Missiaen 2010; Missiaen and Demerre 2012), coring by the University of Utrecht and *multibeam* or *side-scan sonar* imaging by the Flemish Hydrographic Service; under water and above water registration by the project team and by volunteers). In this way a diverse approach of maritime archaeological research was established (Demerre 2009; Fenwick *et al.* 2012).

Public outreach and communication were also an important aspect, because these projects were funded with public money of the European community. From the perspective of Flanders Heritage, raising the awareness on maritime heritage with the public, stakeholders and policy makers is an important step towards the actual management of this heritage. In the MACHU project a lot of attention was therefore given to a website with news items and information about the project, the maritime heritage in the partner countries and in the GIS-database. At the end of the project a conference was organized and a final report was published (Manders, Oosting and Brouwers 2009b).

Although publicity about the MACHU project was generated in each country, it was mostly organized by the lead partner, with little interaction with the other partners. Involvement of the partners would have been better structured if there had been a working group on public outreach from the start. This would have generated a more spontaneous feed of information from all partners, reducing the need for the lead partner to send repeated requests for news feeds and to fill the gaps itself. Fortunately, in the three scheduled project reports more interaction was achieved (Manders, Oosting and Brouwers 2008, 2009a, 2009b).

For the A2S project the plans for outreach were quite ambitious and they did not always suit the limited available time and personnel. Consequently, a few changes had to be made in the original goals and planning. It also made this activity very intense, but challenging. At the start the communication was delayed due to some changes in personnel, but in the end the dedicated communication officer enabled an efficient co-ordination.

Regarding the reporting, some changes were made as well: the planned extensive project reports were reduced to smaller ones (Bowens *et al.* 2011; Fenwick *et al.* 2012) in which – like in the MACHU project – the focus was on the development of the project. This caused a slight misunderstanding with the Flemish partner. We had expected a scientific publication of the research results, intended for an international audience, but the French and English partners used other channels to fill this need. In the final publication this gap was slightly filled by case studies, but in future projects it would be better to consider publishing both a report on the project methodology (for the wider public) and one for the academic audience.

In A2S we furthermore had the chance to implement an innovation: we developed an educational tool for schools. It was co-ordinated by the English team, but all three partners participated equally enthusiastic - as it concerned the research on a Belgian ship, that was chartered by the French government but sunk in British waters (figure 3) – and tested it on a school in their own country

Figure 3. The s/s Londonier (1911), a Belgian wreck on a French mission that sunk in British waters (Photo: MAS, Maritime Collections (AS 1970.045.266)).

(Bowens and Fisher 2012).[25] All in all this activity took more time than intended, but it turned out to be absolutely rewarding, not just for the experience we gained but mostly because it is an ideal tool for awareness building. During both the second steering committee meeting of A2S (December 2011) and the UNESCO colloquium (Cornelis *et al.* 2011) a continuation of this initiative was very much encouraged.

Unfortunately, all these activities bring along a lot of project administration. Especially the time spent on financial matters was heavily underestimated in both projects. In the project proposal, in particular within the Interreg IVA programme, the partners had to predict rather precisely the amount of money that would be needed when and for what activity. Subsequently all costs had to be justified accurately (after each semester) in order to receive the European match-funding. This proved to be extremely time consuming.

The co-ordination of the projects turned out to be a challenge as well. The larger the group, the stronger the need for structural co-ordination. During both projects we had a very good experience with our project leaders. Very useful in the A2S project was an external and independent steering committee which regularly evaluated the results and could adjust the course of the project when necessary (see figure 4).

Figure 4. A steering committee meeting of the A2S project, 7 December 2011 Brussels (Photo: A2S, Flanders Heritage Agency).

---

25   See for the educational tool http://www.atlas2mers.eu/education-3/outreach-a-major-aspect-of-the-a2s-project/.

Regarding the collaboration between the partners, it turned out that working in a large team like in the MACHU project is more difficult than in a small team such as in the A2S project. In the latter there was more interaction within the team, still respecting each partner's own methods and priorities. The number of people involved clearly influences the level of engagement of the partners and the individual participants. The closer the contact is, the stronger the project dynamics are. For instance working together as a team for a full week (*e.g.* during a survey or other fieldwork) is more productive than organizing a meeting twice a year. Dividing the project participants into small teams encourages interaction between the partners as well. Both projects did use working groups during the meetings, but this could also become the general practice during the entire project,[26] as long as the constraints of the smaller partners are taken into account.

Looking back, a major lesson of the A2S project in particular, is that no matter how rewarding the project is, it can sometimes be a little too ambitious. It had high aspirations in many different activities. This meant that even though most objectives were achieved and new initiatives could be developed, some deadlines could only be achieved at the expense of others. We have learned from this that for detailed project proposals, such as for an Interreg programme, more time would have to be spent on the actual preparation of the project. Not all developments in a project can be predicted, but with a well-prepared plan that is accompanied by a realistic time schedule, which allows adaptations to unforeseen circumstances, the project outcome may be more feasible. Finally a good project plan should also contain procedures to safeguard and guarantee the continuity of the project when project partners are pressed by other, non-project assignments or obligations.

Conclusion

During the past decade the maritime heritage research of Flanders Heritage has been in close contact with colleagues from different types of organizations from neighbouring countries bordering the North Sea (the Netherlands, France and Great Britain), and with partners from other European countries. This has not only been very instructive for, but also highly beneficial to, the unit. Maritime archaeology is, as a sub-discipline of the already small world of archaeology, a tiny field of science for which not many financial means are available and participating in projects like MACHU or A2S provides additional funding for research. Moreover, participating in important international collaboration projects also means that maritime researchers can gain a stronger local position.

It is beneficial to the unit's outreach objectives too to work side by side with foreign like-minded but more experienced colleagues. We can compare approaches and learn from their successes and failures. Also working together with young and motivated people stimulates the development of maritime archaeological research. For the research itself, it is important as well. Collaboration projects are in fact

---

26   e.g. The Interreg project 'Heritage and Maritime Memories in the two seas region' (HMS) consists of
      30 partners and is divided into project activity groups, each with a leader (Muyllaert 2009).

the only way to study this mutual heritage (*e.g.* a Dutch wreck in Belgian waters, a Belgian wreck in British waters with a French crew, etc.) and to share sometimes inaccessible sources.

Nonetheless, some challenges were encountered as well. It is for instance difficult in a large group with different cultures present, to agree on mutual approaches and to go beyond the individual views and methodologies. Therefore a project needs a good management and at least in some cases a division into small working groups. Furthermore, European collaboration projects involve heavy administrative procedures. Especially for small project teams these can be quite a workload and may sometimes be conducted at the expense of the actual research and dissemination.

Such difficulties are however of marginal importance if we consider the benefits of international projects. Of major importance is that they help to build new and strong relations across borders, relationships that will last when the projects come to an end and that enable even small countries or organizations to add their input to European maritime archaeology. This input is valuable too. Similar to what happens with the communicating vessels, this input adds to the level of knowledge of all other partners, regardless of their size or experience.

Acknowledgements

I want to thank Rica Annaert, Hein Baes, Guido Demerre, Sofie Debruyne, Marnix Pieters and Inge Zeebroek for providing me with information and for patiently reviewing this paper. And of course a special thanks to the project partners of MACHU and A2S for the many instructive years of working closely together, which were a good inspiration for this paper but of course also for future practice.

References

Arnshav, M. 2008. 'Introduction to the Swedisch Test Areas. The Stockholm Archipelago', in Manders, M., R. Oosting and W. Brouwers (eds), *Machu Report* 1. Amersfoort: Managing Cultural Heritage Underwater, 34-37.

Bailey, G. 2011. 'The Significance of Underwater Cultural Heritage', in C. Cornelis, B. Egger, U. Guérin; S. Khakzad, T. Missiaen, M. Pieters, A. Rey Da Silva and K. Van Balen (eds), *Conference Book: UNESCO Scientific Colloquium on Factors Impacting Underwater Cultural Heritage. Papers from the UNESCO Regional Meeting on the Protection of the Underwater Cultural Heritage, Royal Library of Belgium, Brussels 13-15 December 2011*. Brussels: UNESCO, 27-28.

Belpaeme, K., P. Konings and S. Vanhooren (eds). 2011. *De Kustatlas Vlaanderen/België* 2. Oostende: Coördinatiepunt Duurzaam Kustbeheer, 29-33.

Bowens, A., C. Chatelin, V. Dellino-Musgrave, I. Demerre, C. Georgeault, D. Guyon, A. Hoyau; V. Millership, G. Momber, L. Moran, A. Poudret-Barré and I. Zeebroek (eds). 2011. *Archaeological Atlas of the 2 Seas. Mid-Term Project Report*. Domagné, Brussels and Southampton: Adramar/Flanders Heritage/HWTMA. Retrieved 4 October 2012 from http://www.atlas2mers.eu/wp-content/uploads/reports.pdf.

Bowens, A. and S. Fisher. 2012. 'SS Londonier', in V. Fenwick, A. Poudret-Barré, G. Momber, I. Demerre, I. Zeebroek, A. Bowens and C. Chatelin (eds), *Archaeological Atlas of the 2 Seas. A Cross Border Maritime Archaeology Project. Final report 2009-2012*. Domagné, Brussels and Southampton: Adramar/Flanders Heritage/HWTMA, 60-65.

Cornelis, C., B. Egger, U. Guérin, S. Khakzad, T. Missiaen, M. Pieters, A. Rey Da Silva and K. Van Balen (eds). 2011. *Conference Book: UNESCO Scientific Colloquium on Factors Impacting Underwater Cultural Heritage. Papers from the UNESCO Regional Meeting on the Protection of the Underwater Cultural Heritage, Royal Library of Belgium, Brussels 13-15 December 2011*. Brussels: UNESCO. Retrieved 4 October 2012 from http://www.unesco.org/new/fileadmin/ MULTIMEDIA/HQ/CLT/pdf/UCH_Brussels%20Conference%20BOOK.pdf.

Council of Europe. 1992. *European Convention on the Protection of the Archaeological Heritage (Revised), Valetta, 16 January 1992*. Council of Europe Treaties 143. Retrieved 27 April 2011 from http://conventions.coe.int/Treaty/en/Treaties/Html/143.htm.

Demerre, I. 2009. Cooperation with Non-Archaeological, Scientific Institutes, Organizations and Individuals, in M. Manders, R. Oosting and W. Brouwers (eds), *Machu Report* 2. Amersfoort: Managing Cultural Heritage Underwater, 30-31.

Demerre, I., T. Missiaen and G. Gevaert. 2008. *Maritiem Archeologisch Erfgoedonderzoek in 2006–2007: Twee Jaar Registratie en Verwerking van het Erfgoed in en uit de Noordzee*. Brussels: Vlaams Instituut voor het Onroerend Erfgoed.

Demerre, I. and I. Zeebroek. 2009. Management of the Underwater Cultural Heritage: National Practice in Belgium, in M. Manders, R. Oosting and W. Brouwers (eds), *Machu Final Report* 3. Amersfoort: Managing Cultural Heritage Underwater, 112-115.

Dyson, L., C. Heppell and M. Pieters. 2006. *Archaeological Evaluation of Wetlands in the Planarch Area of North West Europe*. Planarch: Maidstone.

Ekberg, G. 2009. 'Questionnaire on Recreational Diving in Sweden', in M. Manders, R. Oosting and W. Brouwers (eds), *Machu Final Report* 3. Amersfoort: Managing Cultural Heritage Underwater, 88-89.

Fenwick, V., A. Poudret-Barré, G. Momber, I. Demerre, I. Zeebroek, A. Bowens and C. Chatelin (eds). 2012. *Archaeological Atlas of the 2 Seas. A Cross Border Maritime Archaeology Project. Final report 2009-2012*. Domagné, Brussels and Southampton: Adramar/ Flanders Heritage/HWTMA. Retrieved 12 October 2012 from http://www.atlas2mers.eu/wp-content/uploads/ 2011/01/FINAL-REPORT-A2S-Project_EN_LD.pdf.

Fontana, F. and R. Di Capua. 2005. 'Role of Hydrostatic Paradoxes towards the Formation of the Scientific thought of Students at Academic level', *European Journal of Physics* 6: 1017–1030.

Hootsen, H. and W. Dijkman. 2009. 'Building a Geographical Information System in MACHU', in M. Manders, R. Oosting and W. Brouwers (eds), *Machu Final Report* 3. Amersfoort: Managing Cultural Heritage Underwater, 15-30.

Manders, M. 2004. 'Safeguarding a Site: the Master Management Plan. Monitoring, Safeguarding and Visualising North European Shipwreck Sites', *MoSS newsletter* 2004(3). Helsinki: The National Board of Antiquities, 16-17.

Manders, M., R. Oosting and W. Brouwers (eds). 2008. *Machu Report* 1. Amersfoort: Managing Cultural Heritage Underwater. Retrieved 4 October 2012 from http://www.machuproject.eu/ documenten/MACHU_report_1.pdf.

Manders, M., R. Oosting and W. Brouwers (eds). 2009a. *Machu Report* 2. Amersfoort: Managing Cultural Heritage Underwater. Retrieved 4 October 2012 from http://www.machuproject.eu/documenten/MACHU_report_2.pdf.

Manders, M., R. Oosting and W. Brouwers (eds). 2009b. *Machu Final Report* 3. Amersfoort: Managing Cultural Heritage Underwater. Retrieved 4 October 2012 from http://www.machuproject.eu/documenten/MACHU_report_3.pdf.

Missiaen, T. 2010. 'The Potential of Seismic Imaging in Marine Archaeological Site Investigations', *Relicta. Archeologie, Monumenten- en Landschapsonderzoek in Vlaanderen* 6. Brussels: Vlaams Instituut voor het Onroerend Erfgoed, 119-236.

Missiaen, T. and I. Demerre. 2012. 'Integrated Assessment of the Buried Wreck Site of The Dutch East Indiaman 't Vliegent Hart', *Relicta. Archeologie, Monumenten- en Landschapsonderzoek in Vlaanderen* 9. Brussels: Onroerend Erfgoed, 191-208.

Muyllaert, S. 2009. 'Heritage and Maritime Memories in the Two Seas Region (HMS) (presentation)', in *Interreg Iva 2 Cooperation Fair (19-20 November 2009)*. Retrieved 30 November 2011 from http://archive.interreg4a-2mers.eu/cooperationfair/presentation/03_P3-2009_11_19_Workshop%20presentation_P3_HMS.pdf.

Olsson, A. 2011. 'The Valorisation and the Presentation of Underwater Archaeological Heritage: the VASA Museum', in C. Cornelis, B. Egger, U. Guérin, S. Khakzad, T. Missiaen, M. Pieters, A. Rey Da Silva and K. Van Balen (eds). 2011. *Conference Book: UNESCO Scientific Colloquium on Factors Impacting Underwater Cultural Heritage. Papers from the UNESCO Regional Meeting on the Protection of the Underwater Cultural Heritage, Royal Library of Belgium, Brussels 13-15 December 2011*. Brussels: UNESCO, 69.

Pieters M., I. Demerre, T. Lenaerts, I. Zeebroek, M. de Bie, W. de Clercq, B. Dickinson and P. Monsieur. 2010. 'De Noordzee: een Waardevol Archief onder Water. Meer dan 100 jaar Onderzoek van Strandvondsten en Vondsten uit Zee in België: een Overzicht', *Relicta. Archeologie, Monumenten- en Landschapsonderzoek in Vlaanderen* 6. Brussels: Vlaams Instituut voor het Onroerend Erfgoed, 177-218.

Pieters, M., G. Gevaert, J. Mees and J. Seys (eds). 2006. *Colloquium to Sea or not to Sea / Ter Zee of niet Ter Zee. 2nd International Colloquium on Maritime and Fluvial Archaeology in the southern North Sea Area/ 2de Internationaal Colloquium over Maritieme en Fluviale Archeologie in het Zuidelijk Noordzeegebied (Provinciaal Hof Brugge, 21-23 September 2006)*. VLIZ Special Publication 32. Oostende: Vlaams Instituut voor de Zee.

Rieth, E. 2009. *L'Épave Médiévale de la Canche*. Archéologia 463. Dijon: Faton, 40-47.

Tys, D. and M. Pieters. 2009. 'Understanding a Medieval Fishing Settlement along the Southern North Sea: Walraversijde, c. 1200-1630', in L. Sicking and D. Abreu-Ferreira (eds), *Beyond the Catch. Fisheries of the North Atlantic, the North Sea and the Baltic, 900-1850*, 91-121.

UNESCO. 2001. *Convention on the Protection of the Underwater Cultural Heritage, Paris, 2 November 2001*. Retrieved 16 December 2011 from http://portal.unesco.org/en/ ev.php-URL_ID=13520&URL_DO=DO_TOPIC&URL_SECTION=201.html.

Zeebroek, I., M. Pieters and G. Gevaert (eds). 2007. *Verdronken Verleden, Passé Submergé, Drowned Past, Ertrunkene Vergangenheit*. Brussels: Vlaams Instituut voor het Onroerend Erfgoed.

2.4 Constructing from the South: a post-colonial perspective on scientific cooperation in archaeology in Uruguay

Camila Gianotti, David Barreiro**,
Felipe Criado-Boado** and José López Mazz**

* Landscape Archaeology and Heritage Laboratory,
unit associated with the Eastern Regional University Centre
of the University of the Republic of Uruguay, Uruguay

** Institute of Heritage Sciences,
Spanish National Research Council, Spain

Abstract

For the last ten years, the Institute of Heritage Sciences of the Spanish National Research Council (CSIC) and the University of the Republic in Uruguay (*Universidad de la República*, UdelaR) have had co-operative links. These began as research projects, but have now led to the establishment of a joint scientific research and work unit. The recent creation of the Landscape Archaeology and Heritage Laboratory (LAPPU), as a scientific unit of the UdelaR, is the final and most outstanding result of this international cooperation. The LAPPU mainly carries out activities in the field of integrated management of cultural heritage. Its focus is on the consolidation of lines of action aimed at the integration of cultural heritage within public policies, institutional enforcement, knowledge transfer, local development and the socialization and participative construction of heritage through different projects and inter-institutional agreements.

In this paper we will present the epistemological basis and the path towards the cooperation we have maintained, exemplified by one of our main projects, 'The Archaeological Landscape of Lowlands in Uruguay', which took place in the rural areas of Tacuarembó. This archaeological and anthropological project has its foundations in the research project 'Situated in Place' and in the dialogical interaction between local and global, rural and urban, and traditional and modern, as a way of generating practical knowledge and instruments for local community empowerment. The specific act of researching 'other heritages' that represent groups of indigenous peoples and those of African origin who have been marginalized culturally and historically in the construction of the Uruguayan nation-state, has made it possible to create a platform for multi-vocal and post-colonial articulation on different levels (such as academics, politicians, urban public, rural communities and African descendants). It has also led us to deal with new ways of approaching heritage (not only in academic practices but also in social processes), of involving new actors and including inter-generational dialogues. As a result, new participative methodologies emerged. From these experiences, the challenge for the LAPPU will be to de-centralize and create more platforms for the articulation of these multi-vocal approaches to heritage.

Résumé

Construire à partir du Sud : une Perspective Postcoloniale sur la Coopération Scientifique en Archéologie en Uruguay

Au cours des dix dernières années, l'Institut des Sciences du Patrimoine qui fait partie du Conseil supérieure des recherches scientifiques de l'Espagne (CSIC) et l'Université de la République en Uruguay (Universidad de la República, UdelaR) ont eu des relations coopératives. La récente création du Laboratoire de l'archéologie du paysage et du patrimoine (LAPPU), qui fait partie du UdelaR, est le meilleur résultat final de cette coopération internationale. Le LAPPU poursuit principalement des activités dans le cadre de la gestion intégrée du patrimoine culturel. L'accent est placé sur la consolidation de la mise en œuvre de l'intégration du patrimoine culturel dans les politiques publiques, de l'amélioration institutionnelle, du transfert des connaissances, du développement local et de la socialisation par une construction participative du patrimoine culturel, par le biais de différents projets et accords inter-institutionels.

Dans cet article nous voulons présenter le fondement épistémologique et le chemin menant au mode de coopération que nous avons maintenu, illustré par un de nos projets principaux, 'Le paysage archéologique des basses-terres en Uruguay', qui a été effectué dans la région rurale de Tacuarembó. Ce projet archéologique et anthropologique trouve ses origines dans le projet de recherche dénommé 'Situés en lieu' ('Situated in Place') et dans le dialogue interactif entre local et global, rural et urbain et traditionnel et moderne, comme un moyen de générer les connaissances pratiques et les instruments essentiels pour le renforcement des communautés locales. Le fait de rechercher 'd'autres patrimoines', c'est à dire des indigènes et des descendants africains qui ont été marginalisés culturellement et historiquement durant la création de l'État-nation Uruguayen, a permis de créer une plate-forme d'articulation multi-vocale et postcoloniale à différents niveaux (comme des universitaires, des politiciens, le public urbain, des communautés rurales et des descendants africains). Cela nous a également permis d'approcher le partimoine d'une manière différente (pas seulement dans la pratique académique, mais également dans les processus sociaux), d'impliquer de nouveaux acteurs et d'inclure le dialogue intergénérationnel. Par conséquent, de nouvelles méthodologies participatives sont apparues. L'enjeu pour le LAPPU, avec toutes ces expériences, serra de décentraliser et de créer plus de plate-formes pour l'articulation de ces approches multi-vocales du patrimoine.

Extracto

Construyendo Desde el Sur: una Perspectiva Poscolonial de la Cooperación Científica en Arqueología en Uruguay

En la última década el Instituto de Ciencias del Patrimonio y la Universidad de la Republica en Uruguay (UdelaR) han mantenido enlaces cooperativos. La reciente fundación del Laboratorio de Arqueología del Paisaje y Patrimonio (LAPPU) como departamento científico de la UdelaR, es el resultado final y más notable de esta cooperación internacional. El LAPPU en primer lugar emprende actividades en el terreno de la gestión integrada del patrimonio cultural. Enfoca la consolidación de las políticas que se dirigen a la integración del patrimonio cultural en las políticas públicas, la ejecución institucional, la transferencia de conocimientos, el desarrollo local y la socialización y construcción participativa del patrimonio a través de diferentes proyectos y acuerdos interinstitucionales.

En este artículo presentaremos la base epistemológica y el camino hacia la cooperación que hemos realizado, ejemplificado por uno de nuestros proyectos principales, 'El Paisaje Arqueológico de las Tierras Bajas en Uruguay', que se realizó en las zonas rurales de Tacuarembó. Este proyecto arqueológico y antropológico tiene su base en el proyecto investigador 'Situado en el Espacio' y en la interacción dialogante entre la localidad y la globalidad, la ruralidad y la urbanidad y la tradicionalidad y la modernidad, siendo una manera para generar conocimientos prácticos e instrumentos para el empoderamiento de la comunidad local. El acto específico de investigar 'otro patrimonio', que representa a grupos de gente indígena y aquella de origen africano que han sido marginalizados cultural e históricamente en la construcción del estado nación uruguayo, facilitó la creación de una plataforma para la articulación multivocal y poscolonial a diferentes niveles (como los académicos, políticos, el público urbano, las comunidades rurales y los descendientes africanos). Nos ha llevado también al hecho de que planteemos de nuevas maneras el patrimonio (no sólo en las prácticas académicas sino también en los procesos sociales) y de que involucremos a actores nuevos e incluyamos diálogos intergeneracionales. Como efecto han surgido nuevas metodologías participativas. De estas experiencias procede que el desafío del LAPPU será la descentralización y la creación de más plataformas para la articulación de estos planteamientos multivocales del patrimonio.

صخلم

الإنشاء من الجنوب. منظور ما بعد الاستعمار للتعاون العلمي في علم الآثار في أوروغواي

زيبول م. يسوخو**وداوب-وديرك يبلبيف، **ورير بارد ديفاد، *يتونايج الميماك مزا*

*المركز الجامعي للمنطقة الشرقية (CURE)، ومختبر أركيولوجية صور الأرض والتراث (LAPPU-FHCE)، وهي مرتبطة بـ CURE، جامعة الجمهورية، أوروغواي.

** معهد علوم التراث (Incipit)، المجلس الوطني الإسباني للأبحاث (CSIC)، إسبانيا.

منذ السنوات العشر الماضية، هناك علاقات تعاونية بين معهد علوم التراث المجلس الوطني الإسباني للأبحاث جامعة الجمهورية في أوروغواي. ويدعد وحدة علمية لمختبر أركيولوجية صور الأرض والتراث، الإنشاء لخير من التنيجية النهائية والأكثر تفوقا لذل جامعة الجمهورية في أوروغواي، يقوم مختبر أركيولوجية صور الأرض والتراث بشكل رئيسي مركز على تعزيز خط الدولي. ويف التراث الثقافي، تنشط في مجال الإدارة المتكاملة للتراث الثقافي. العمل إلى إثارة التراث الثقافي في أساسيات العامة، وبناء والتنشئة والتنمية المحلية، ونقل المعرفة، والمؤسسات، التشاركية من التراث خلال مشروعات مختلفة وثقافيات بين المؤسسات.

في هذه الورقة سنقدم على أساس عمل يفرط وطريقة للوصول إلى التعاون الذين صور"، الآ وهو الريئيسية، لمشروعنا اتن أحد على مثال لخلال من بهما، فالعاملان في نفذه هذه المشروع تم تنفيذه في أوروغواي"، للأضرار المنخفضة في يضي الأضرار الآثري والأنثروبولوجي. ويقوم هذا المشروع "في الموقع"، ويف همه بحثي اسم على أس مشروع على تنشيط القيمة للتقليدية الثقافة، والريف والحضر، والعالمية، والمحلية أمكن. وقد أمكن للمجتمع المحلي. بالبحث في اتفاقات الأخرى" التي تمثل في فئات من الشعوب الأصلية والدول في اريخيا ثقافيا وتاريخيا في بناء الدولة والشعوب من أصل أفريقية مهمشة ثقافية أصبحت من إنشاء تعبر غير الأصوات المتعددة في ما يخص من الأوروبية، من إنشاء السكان الأوروبيين، والسياسيين، نتعامل على مختلف الاستعمار مثل الأكاديميين الفيريقية وذوي الأصول الأفريقية). كما أدى إلى أننا نتعامل مع التراث بأساليب جديدة (ليس فقط في المراسات الأكاديمية، الحضر أيضا بل أن ندخل فاعلين جدد بحيث نضمن أن تكون هناك كانت في العمليات الاجتماعية وأنا على هذه، وبناء تشاركية جديدة. ونتيجة لذلك، نشأت مناهج تشاركية في كيفك تفكيك المركزي او إنشاء المزيد حوارات بين الآجال. ونتيجة لذلك، الأساس هل؟؟؟؟؟ يمكن التحدث عن هذه غير بعبير ذات جديدة بالأساليب المختلفة للأصوات المختلفة للتعامل مع التراث.

Keywords

cultural heritage, scientific cooperation, post-colonial archaeology, multivocality, public science, Uruguay

From scientific-archaeological research to the public domain: heritage as a collaborative arena

The centrality of heritage for dealing with identities, memoirs and communities in current processes in post-modern societies, means that archaeology is called upon to be a technoscience of heritage (Barreiro-Martínez 2003). The complexity of the incipient knowledge economy has meant that the transfer of technology has been replaced by the transfer of knowledge, which in turn has been replaced by collaborative research and, increasingly, a community science. Multivocality has ceased to be a merely post-modern manifesto. Instead, it is part of the practices of social life, accompanying our complex societies, in which a large number of agents concur and who increasingly call for their own legitimacy and rights.

The experience we present in this paper is situated in this field, at the point at which archaeology, anthropology, heritage, research and the co-construction and co-transfer of knowledge converge. This paper has two central aims. The first is to present the experience of ten years of scientific cooperation between two institutional research groups (belonging to the Spanish National Research Council, CSIC and to the *Universidad de la República* in Uruguay, UdelaR) and to show the process of moving from the study of a specific scientific (archaeological) problem (research on burial mounds in the lowlands of Uruguay) to a trans-disciplinary field such as heritage. The second aim is to elucidate the emergence of heritage as an arena for social and community action, in an attempt to challenge through praxis asymmetrical dualities that are deeply rooted in Uruguay (such as urban versus rural, academic versus social and official rhetoric versus subaltern discourses), and to show how this has been based on a collaborative research concept which not only overcomes European neo-colonialist practices, but also the endo-colonial social structures that still exist in Uruguay. This will allow us to discuss the practice of scientific cooperation and its role in the process of shaping and constructing a Public Science in Latin America, understood as knowledge presented in a public arena and based on the involvement of the public at large.

We have two starting points in different contexts: Uruguay and Spain. In general terms, the Spanish context was marked between 2004 and 2011 by the political priority of international development cooperation, part of which has been focused on scientific cooperation on heritage issues. The case study we are presenting here was supported by the Spanish Agency for International Cooperation for Development (AECID). Therefore, it belongs in a wider sense to a Spanish experience in the field of cooperation for development and archaeological activity in foreign countries. However, we are aware that this is not a normal experience in this country. After 2004, Spain bolstered the politics of international cooperation for development through the AECID. This led to a substantial increase in the Spanish budget dedicated to these purposes. This policy, despite having a number of naive aspects in its development (something we could refer to as para-colonial or paternalist gestures), was deeply and ideologically rooted in the awareness of contributing towards repaying the historical debt with former European colonies. A major part of the cooperation policy for development consisted of different

Figure 1 (above and right). Geographical location of work areas of cooperation projects in Uruguay (South America) (Illustration: LAPPU/Incipit).

budgetary instruments to promote scientific and university cooperation, mainly orientated towards promoting research for development.[1] At one point, the total amount of money devoted to the specific purposes of scientific cooperation for development rose to more than 50 million euro.

On the other hand, the situation of Uruguay was that of a small country covering 176,215 km^2 with a population of 3,241,000, of whom 40 per cent lives in the capital, Montevideo (530 km^2), and the remaining 60 per cent in the rest of the country.[2] Our projects were carried out in rural areas of the region of Tacuarembó and the region of Rocha (see figure 1). Tacuarembó has a population of approximately 90,500, 85 per cent of whom live in urban areas. Rocha has a population of 70,000, with 91 per cent living in urban areas. It is a hyper-

---

1   The different instruments included grants for graduate and postgraduate studies for students from other countries, subsidies to acquire equipment and improve infrastructures, funding for co-operative research projects and specialized courses.

2   The data was retrieved on 12 May 2010 from the National Statistics Institute of Uruguay, http://www.ine.gub.uy.

Tacuarembó

Rocha

centralized country with most of the political and administrative power maintained in the national capital, while the different regions or *departamentos* have very limited decision-making power. It is characterized by an asymmetrical socio-political and economic situation, with major differences between the rural areas and the urban area of Montevideo. These differences have appeared over the last 150 years and still exist at a number of levels. Apart from political centralism, the division between the city and the countryside has become increasingly severe due to dramatic changes in the economic production model over the last fifteen years, *e.g.* the transfer of land into foreign hands, an increase in the number of extensive and more aggressive agricultural and industrial activities (tree reforestations, rice and soya cultivation), and a loss of rural population.

These imbalances had already appeared before the establishment of the nation of Uruguay, during the final stage of the Spanish and Brazilian colonial experiences of the eighteenth and nineteenth centuries. The processes of independence led to a rise in modernity in South America, but in the new independent countries the old colonial relationships continued to exist, leading to new situations of domination by the Creole (*criollo*) elite over 'the others' – the native peoples and/or the Afro-American population. These endo-colonial relationships still dominate the internal social and political structure today, which makes it possible to explore the role of the historical discourse in its reproduction, as was proposed by Gnecco (2008: 23-27). The historical governmental rhetoric, in which history and archaeology played an important role as erudite knowledge, was an important instrument in the reproduction of these practices. The dominant historical discourse emphasized the 'white' and 'western' compounds of Creole people while hiding the presence of indigenous peoples (who were exterminated after independence throughout the nineteenth century) and the descendants of African slaves.

The configuration of the concept of cultural heritage in Uruguay provides a good example to explore the relationship between historic discourse, Creole hegemony and nationalist feeling. The milestone that marked the emergence of heritage as an official and therefore public domain was the creation of the National Commission for Cultural Heritage. It resulted from the passing of the first law in this area in 1971 and it is still the only applicable law in force for heritage issues. Until 2006, Uruguay's cultural heritage (understood as the heritage of the nation) reflected the same governmental discourse from the twentieth century that consecrated national unity and equal rights based on cultural standardization, the inexistence of indigenous groups and the 'European-ness' of the Uruguayans.

In general, this trajectory has been shared with other neighbouring countries, revealing clear signs of fracture in the last ten years due to the return of democracy. Over the last ten years, the social and political context of several South American countries has triggered transformations and debates initiated by social movements, ethnic groups, minority groups and also by social scientists. In countries such as Brazil, Argentina, Bolivia, Colombia, Uruguay and Chile, these collectives have begun to produce alternative discourses and bring new meanings and uses to the hegemonic historical representations that upheld fixed ideas of national identities, allowing for the inclusion of other types of knowledge, or dissident or minority subalternate discourses on the fringes.

This critical review of history was accompanied by constitutional reforms, actions and statutory changes that acknowledge factors such as cultural hybridism, multiculturalism and indigenous and Afro-American roots. However, in Uruguay these transformations have still not taken place, especially at a judicial level and in the sphere of public policies. Towards the end of the dictatorship (c. 1985) and in the early 1990s, a movement appeared in the field of social sciences and humanities that strongly criticized the bases of the national history and its image in terms of identity (Achugar and Caetano 1992; Caetano 1992; Porzecanski 1992; Verdesio 2008, 2009). Its inarguable 'European-ness' was questioned, together with its configuration through the denial or concealment of the presence of indigenous peoples and those of Afro-American descent. Despite the fact that these debates have continued for twenty years, no changes occurred in the public sphere until 2006, when the Uruguayan state ratified the conventions of UNESCO to safeguard intangible heritage and to protect cultural diversity.[3] Subsequently, different laws

---

3   Law 18.035 approved the Convention for the Protection of Immaterial Cultural Heritage and Law
     18.068 integrated the Protection and Promotion of the Diversity of Cultural Expressions.

approved the commemoration of the National Day of Afro-Uruguayan Culture and Racial Equality on 3 December[4], the National Tango Day[5] and the Day of the Charrúa Nation and Indigenous Identity[6]. Some years earlier, the remains of four Charrúa Indians that had been taken to France were repatriated[7], and subsequently a law was passed prohibiting scientific studies on the remains of one of them, who was called *Vaimaca*.[8]

During these events, the radical change was the acknowledgement of the indigenous and Afro-Uruguayan identity and the inclusion into the official discourse of 'other' references with regard to history and identity. Although this trend seems to be gaining strength, it still has not had a tangible effect on the design of a national heritage strategy, nor on any concrete policies with regard to heritage. In fact, the absence of a solid, effective heritage policy is only just being indicated and discussed (Lezama 2004; Gianotti 2005; Carámbula 2006; Criado-Boado, Gianotti and López Mazz 2006). Whilst the awareness of the public, global trends and some partial political support make it possible to construct and manage national heritage, gradually transferring more management competence to the National Commission for Cultural Heritage, the absence of a specific national heritage law clearly illustrates the current political situation.

After 30 years of activity, the main contribution of the National Cultural Heritage Commission has been a brief inventory of colonial and European monuments (*i.e. criollos*), and the restoration and management of some of them. The current law and heritage management system does not provide any tools to deal with the results of the socio-economic changes that have taken place over the last three decades, such as a rise in aggressive models of production (forestation, extensive and intensive monocultivation), industrialization, an increasing number of public works and infrastructures and tourism development. However, other sectors which have been involved in this transformation (territorial planning, environment, etc.) have increasingly called for the integration of cultural heritage and its management. In this context, a series of specific projects have been developed in a non-official manner and by different parties (academia, non-governmental organizations, local organizations, etc.) which, working from the ground up, have helped to fill in some of the gaps (Lezama 2004; Gianotti 2005; Criado-Boado, Gianotti and López-Mazz 2006; Irazábal, Etchegaray and Florines 2006; Capdepont *et al.* 2010; Gianotti *et al.* 2010a; Lezama *et al.* 2010).

Faced with this situation, it seems clear that the recognition by Uruguay of a plural configuration in terms of its society and identity, urgently calls for education and action regarding this 'otherness' and for specific attention for its heritage. The chronological depth of European cultural traditions is not an irreversible *fait accompli*; on the contrary, it is constantly changing, as it is subject to cultural

---

4   Law 18.059, 2006.
5   Law 18.107, 2006.
6   Law 18.589, 2009. This day is commemorated on the 11th of April.
7   This was supported by a specific legislation to repatriate the corpses, Law 17.256 (2000).
8   Law 17.767, 2004.

losses and various types of ethno-genesis. The management of cultural diversity, the study of heritage processes, the dynamism of Latin American identities, and in particular the comparative study of all of these phenomena, offers a budding field of theoretical reflection. Moreover, heritage work may contribute enormously to the project of development; the work of any agent (either because of its sensitive nature, or because of the conflict generated with other agents by the absence of any such sensitivity) gives strength to local voices. The act of taking the floor produces an awareness that empowers alternative channels for dialogue in the face of (and in spite of) the dizzying processes associated with land ownership, the loss of territory and the implantation of new, aggressive economic models.

From co-operative scientific research projects to the strengthening of infrastructures for cultural heritage management

The previous 'evolution', involving a movement from pure research towards the public domain, becomes more meaningful if we examine the trajectory of scientific cooperation between the two research groups involved. This enrichment of our practice of bilateral cooperation took shape in the Laboratory of Landscape Archaeology and Heritage of Uruguay (or LAPPU, the acronym in Spanish for the *Laboratorio de Arqueología del Paisaje y del Patrimonio del Uruguay*), a research unit which was created - after receiving financial support from the AECID – to deal with different aspects (research, education, training, assessment, expert consultancy, etc.) of the integrative management of heritage. Nowadays, the LAPPU forms part of the Faculty of Humanities and Education Sciences (FHCE) of the Eastern Regional University Centre (CURE) in the Department of Rocha. It works together with the Institute of Heritage Sciences (Incipit) of the Spanish National Research Council (CSIC) on joint projects.

With regard to the initiation of LAPPU, we have to look back to the period between 1996 and 2010, in which the bilateral cooperation between Spain and Uruguay developed in four stages. The initial stage (1996-2000) consisted of an exchange of research and researchers on landscape archaeology. This led, as of 2001, to a first joint research project that was funded by the AECID. It aimed to study the origin and development of prehistoric mounds in the rural regions of Tacuarembó and Rocha (Gianotti 2005). The scope of the call under which we received funding was to promote international cooperation in research by combining the interaction between a Spanish team and a team from Latin America. The project, despite being tightly funded, allowed us to consolidate the previously existing relationships.

In the third stage (2004–2009) the aim was to consolidate a genuine programme for the integral management of cultural heritage through a wide-ranging project (Criado-Boado, Gianotti and López Mazz 2006; Gianotti, Criado-Boado and López Mazz 2007; Gianotti *et al.* 2008; Cuesta *et al.* 2009). This project was funded by the Spanish Ministry of Culture, through a specific call that had been running since the 1970s.[9] The main aim of this call was, and still is, to fund field projects in archaeological sites and areas related to relevant research topics. The heritage or social dimensions of the sites were not the primary concern of these projects, although in our case the pure research activity, carried out as part of a project known as 'The Archaeological Landscape of the Lowlands of Uruguay: an integral heritage management model', was gradually integrated into in a much wider social and heritage dimension. Our field research led to us acquiring a more thorough knowledge of pre-Hispanic monumentality in locations such as Caraguatá, Turupí, Los Vázquez, Cerro Pereira and Villa Ansina, in the region of Tacuarembó (see Criado-Boado, Gianotti and López Mazz 2006; Gianotti, Criado-Boado and López Mazz 2007; Gianotti *et al.* 2008; Cuesta *et al.* 2009).

The project itself was based on archaeology, ethnography, anthropology and heritage, applying participatory action research strategies (Wadsworth 1998) and an approach that focused on the local dimension and the anthropological perspective of Place (Escobar 2001). In this sense, the project constituted a trans-disciplinary and even a post-disciplinary experience. It provided an open scenario for research through dialogue and criticism on heritage, material culture and the distant and recent past. It involved scholars from Uruguay and Spain, local agents, the regional government, NGOs, local groups, educators and local inhabitants. The project brought together several of the principles included in the epistemological proposals of 'applied archaeology', as proposed by Barreiro-Martínez 2006, which state that all theoretical considerations with regard to culture, heritage and development, apart from being adapted to the place and its population (Viola 2000), must have a practical value of use for the local people (Barreiro-Martinez 2006).

To do so, we based our work on the concept of the heritage value chain (HVC). The HVC proposes a sequence of procedures that include the identification, characterization, protection, dissemination and socialization of heritage assets. This model for understanding heritage and integrating the work and management associated with it, was initially proposed in Criado-Boado (1996) and has been followed closely in our work. As the transverse axis of the model, we have incorporated the public and participative dimension in all stages, which has been re-conceptualized in our project as the 'participative construction of heritage' (Cuesta *et al.* 2009). The aim was to develop all of the different instances of the HVC in dialogue with the community and to ensure that the heritage values – apart from being scientifically contextualized and evaluated – are socially, culturally and economically relevant.

In practice, this philosophy was shaped through a wide range of activities, publications, technical documents and protocols, dissemination instruments, and documentary films (Criado-Boado, Gianotti and López Mazz 2006; Criado-Boado, Gianotti and Mañana-Borrazás 2006; Cuesta *et al.* 2009; Dabezies and De Souza

---

9   At first the call had a late-colonial name: Archaeological Missions Abroad (*misiones arqueológicas en el exterior*), far removed from the type of name used by other European countries with stronger traditions in colonial research. This name sounded so old-fashioned that the call was recently renamed as Archaeology Abroad.

2009; Gianotti *et al.* 2010a; 2010b).[10] The documentary film *Los Narradores del Caraguatá* (The Narrators of Caraguatá) for instance, presents voices and practices that have been virtually obliterated throughout history in Uruguay. Filmed in small villages in Tacuarembó, local inhabitants and researchers discuss vanished heritage and residual memories (see figure 2). The national identity is reconsidered through sounds and images, shattering the mirror that has been used to reflect it. The journey moves from the empowerment of local heritage – showing children excavating burial mounds together with archaeologists – to the visions of local inhabitants on the landscape and their daily life in these rural areas today. It is as much an artistic expression as it is scientific. It also represents the result of five years of archaeological and anthropological research.[11]

As said, the co-evolution of Incipit and the archaeological teams from the UdelaR finally led to the creation of the LAPPU in the fourth stage of our relationship. This ambitious project was made possible with substantial funding from a call by AECID to support scientific cooperation for development. This inter-university cooperation programme, as it was called, had four main categories. We designed a collaborative project in category four, allocated to promote the transfer of

Figure 2. Moment of ethnographic fieldwork and film documentation in Pueblo de Arriba, Tacuarembó (Photo: LAPPU/Incipit).

10   Most of these papers, and many others connected with these topics, are available through the institutional repository of Digital.CSIC (http://digital.csic.es/simple-search?query=gianotti&boton =[+Buscar). See search results for Gianotti.

11   An English version of the documentary film is available at http://digital.csic.es/handle/10261/28600 (Gianotti et al. 2010b). It was sponsored by the Archaeology in Contemporary Europe project.

knowledge and expertise from Spain to other national contexts calling for specific solutions. Once again, a funding scheme that was mainly uni-directional (from Spain to other countries, from Europe to Latin America, from North to South), was modified by our own design and practice into a completely two-way form of exchange and interactions.

The LAPPU project has four main lines of research. The first is the production of historical knowledge with regard to cultural landscapes. Due to different reasons, and not only because of the imperative that a sustainability strategy must commence in the territory itself, the landscape has been the essential underlying factor of our strategy (as based on Criado-Boado 1993). The multi-vocal dimension of our practical strategy means, for instance, that we not only had to look for an non-existent 'archaeological landscape' but also for the actual landscape embedded in current social practices (such as of local populations, peasants, ranchers or *gauchos*). Therefore, the landscape was the concept and dimension that made it possible to combine archaeology and anthropology with heritage, the academic world with cooperation and heritage, and these with social development. It provided a 'reading' of cultural spaces which, in Uruguay, are conceived as being natural, overlooking the fact that they are a historical product that is not only altered by modernity (Muir 1999). The space in which we work is a cultural landscape, which is fully occupied by heritage and comprised of 'places', rather than just sites, where the communities and individuals who occupy them are those who primarily construct it and give it meaning.

Based on this, the research focused on two types of cultural landscapes, the prehistoric monumental landscape and the contemporary rural landscape of Uruguay. In both cases, the main lines of research included the study of material and immaterial aspects, historical continuities and discontinuities, and the documentation and characterization of the rural landscape in the light of its rapid transformation due to new agricultural practices (see figure 3).[12]

The archaeological surveys carried out made it possible to identify and characterize a remarkable prehistoric and historic cultural record: nearly 2000 sites of different types and from different periods. One of the most significant contributions has been the documentation and research of the monumental spaces of South American hunter-gatherers (see figure 4), making it possible to explore in detail a series of aspects connected with their domestic contexts, social change, the appearance of systems for controlling water resources, technological systems, the use of plants in prehistoric times, and the paleo-environmental evolution of the region (Capdepont, Del Puerto and Inda 2005; Del Puerto and Inda 2005; Gianotti 2005; Gianotti, Criado-Boado and López Mazz 2007; Gianotti *et al.* 2008).

The second line of research of the LAPPU project is integrated heritage management. This dimension of our practice has been one of the central and cross-cutting objectives of all of the actions of the project. The research results have

---

12 The data is being studied and analysed in a series of graduate and postgraduate research projects (Pascual 2008; Dabezies 2009).

Figure 3. Interview with Evenida Duarte in Las Toscas of Caraguatá (Tacuarembó). Evenida is a healer (yuyera) having knowledge of traditional herbal medicine (Photo: LAPPU/Incipit).

been transformed into different management tools, such as in regional inventories and in the first Heritage Information System of Uruguay (SIPAU).[13] Other results worth mentioning are methodologies for heritage management, consultancy on the design of municipal territorial organization regulations, and participation in the debate on Uruguay's new Cultural Heritage Law (López *et al.* 2010).

Third, LAPPU is involved in technological development and professional specialization. The incorporation of new technologies and tools (specifically GPS, GIS, remote detection, etc.) requires specialized training for heritage managers. Thus, next to guidebooks and technical documents, courses have been organized at different levels, ranging from universities (such as post-graduate and specialization courses, research stays and the creation of the Training Site for Archaeological Techniques for university students) to the local level (like training actions for local agents and workshops produced in collaboration with specialists from the National System of Protected Areas of the National Environment Directorate). Moreover, researchers stayed at the centres of the project partners and provided postgraduates students with the required skills (including technological developments, management aspects, conservation strategies, presentation tools and visitor management); distance-learning courses and tutoring sessions were started between the Incipit and LAPPU.

The final line of research concerns heritage and social development. In this context an educational programme on heritage issues was developed for schools in rural areas. It was implemented in fourteen primary and two secondary rural schools, covering a large geographical region in which the population and schools are widely dispersed.[14] Through informal educational activities, based on the daily

13 The SIPAU is currently in the process of validation and testing, through two projects connected with the territorial planning and management of protected areas carried out by the LAPPU.

14 We worked in the rural areas of Caraguatá, Yaguarí, Villa Ansina and Cerro Pereira, with a total of 1131 primary school children, 239 secondary school students, 48 primary teachers and twenty secondary teachers (Cuesta *et al.* 2009).

experiences of the children, their surroundings and their reality, we developed a critical and reflexive approach towards the local heritage, its creation and history, its role in a wide historical context and at a regional level, and its protection and presentation to the public. All of the activities were aimed at contributing towards a (re)configuration and/or (re)interpretation of the space and therefore the landscape. They encouraged to build a new type of relationship with the landscape, bringing previous knowledge, perceptions and attitudes into play that made it possible to put the inhabitants into direct contact with a cultural landscape which is frequently 'naturalized'. For example, the prehistoric mounds (*cerritos de indios*), have re-appeared as local objects of paramount importance, as tangible as they are symbolic, to help guide these experiences and redefine their significance, This can be seen in the documentary produced as part of the project '*Los Narradores del Caraguatá*'. The activities also included the design and production of didactic materials: games ('The River of Time', see figure 5), news bulletins, workshops, guided tours and hands-on experiences for children on excavation sites (figure 6), travelling exhibitions, public lectures in the local communities, workshops with managers and specialists, news items in the press, radio and television, a showing of the film produced by the project followed by a debate, etc. (Cuesta *et al.* 2009).

It would require another article to examine how local communities reinterpreted monuments as part of their life, but one relevant consequence of this multi-vocal practice we would like to mention here is that the *cerritos* (prominent and conspicuous sites within their surroundings) were reintroduced as places and territorial markers in the mental maps of local populations. This was particularly

Figure 4. Prehistoric mounds (cerritos de indios) at the hills of Potrero Grande in Rocha Department (Photo: LAPPU/Incipit).

Figure 5. Scholars playing the game The River of Time about the prehistory and history of Uruguay in a rural school of Caraguatá (Photo: LAPPU/Incipit).

remarkable amongst children, who completely missed any knowledge about the landscape of their own family traditions.

The LAPPU project formalized the joint research group that had been working together for almost ten years (Gianotti *et al.* 2010a). While the project began as a means to transfer research results, techniques, specialized skills and specific tangible products (such as the information system, catalogues, protocols, etc.) from Incipit to UdelaR, it is no longer a one-direction relationship. We jointly constructed a new organizational and theoretical model for scientific practice through a co-operative and collaborative experience. The midterm aim was to develop a new institutional agent that would operate in Uruguay, promoting cooperation and integration in different public policies (Marozzi *et al.* 2009; Capdepont *et al.* 2010), but in the end, ideas, solutions and practices were jointly developed. These took shape in seminal processes that served to produce, transfer and disseminate new knowledge and applications, to exchange mutual experiences, and to raise awareness and debate amongst the agents involved. Cooperation was turned into operating jointly.

Conclusions

In order to draw a conclusion, we first need to recognize that working in the field of heritage gives us the opportunity to discover the multi-dimensional reality of complex modern societies, over which practices from a wide range of agents are constructed, hermeneutics are de-centred, identities are negotiated and rationalities are based. This plurality leads to a wealth of social action, in which dialogue but also incomprehension and conflict may occur, depending on the ability or inability to establish a common horizon of intelligibility. What we call Public Science cannot be excluded from the vicissitudes of comprehension: the scientific construction of objectivity and intersubjectivity develops into a dialogue that interacts with other ways of creating knowledge, an instrument to create intelligibility that overcomes absolute subjectivity, which only leads to isolation or hegemony. Therefore, the necessary transformation of the systems of science and the production of knowledge must serve to make their results congruent and compatible with all of the different voices that are involved; to permit action that helps to transform the existing reality. For this reason, it is necessary to reach agreement on the knowledge production method; it must balance the different intentions and contexts of rationality that are involved. We need a method for dialogue between alternative, frequently opposing models, in order to understand and evaluate them in relation to their positive capacity; this would be a method different from the unilinear positivist model and from the phenomenological-subjective multi-vocal model.

From the practical case of our Spanish-Uruguayan experience we not only learned that a participative and multi-vocal construction of heritage is needed, but also that when one is faced with the absence of institutional directives and a solid public policy on heritage, bottum-up developed projects and initiatives such as our own may lead to the construction of alternative heritage strategies. Our project responded to the needs of different institutions, constructing a communal, multi-vocal space for collaboration, and at the same time, other major gaps were being filled in from a collaborative and community-based space. Research results were jointly constructed by researchers, local agents and inhabitants, but these are not only used to promote locality and cultural identity (through tourism, websites, leaflets, etc.), but also to construct a local heritage practice that consists of creating social heritage maps – providing a greater understanding and improved cultural and historical knowledge – , of undertaking joint projects, and of training local specialists, as the heritage value chain requires.[15] Obviously, such processes are slow and lengthy, but we are optimistic about the fact that at some stage, such circumstances – the absence of a solid public heritage policy and the need for its presence – will stimulate the emergence of a common political strategy and an innovative socio-political strategy. In the midst of these contradictions, a vigour of community science and public archaeology already emerged in Brazil, Bolivia and even in Venezuela (Gnecco 2008; Lopes and Funari 2008).

Based on the experience we have presented in this paper, and especially on its development and the current situation, we would underline the value of both science and heritage as fields of public action. Based on this, we can evaluate our experience as praxis for cooperation. The LAPPU, in materializing all of these aspects, is a powerful figure with post-colonial implications. It goes beyond heritage and reflects a type of interaction that can be useful in other contexts. Scientific cooperation, in particular a joint research unit such as our own, makes it

15 An overall review of this complex and integrative practice is presented in Gianotti and Dabezies 2011.

Figure 6. Children from a rural school of Pago Lindo, excavating an archaeological mound site in Caraguatá river locality (Photo: LAPPU/Incipit).

possible to create structure, to facilitate heritage management and research and to strengthen the capacities of all of those involved (research groups, the community, authorities, etc.). Being optimistic, we predict that our work will contribute towards defining, in the near future, a convergent strategy for the construction of a heritage policy in Uruguay. At the same time, our work has made it possible to generate constant scientific innovation and renewal, to construct common conceptual frameworks, to develop and apply formal methodologies for analysis, diagnosis and intervention, to train local agents in sustainable heritage management, and to think about community-based work to promote participative heritage processes which mirror the cultural diversity of our societies. Finally, this cooperation model means that we help Uruguay as much as Uruguayan experience has changed many Spanish practices. Moreover, the local population has learned as much about its lost knowledge (such as traditions, sites and place names) as we – the archaeologists – have learned about our fields of interest.

Epilogue

In the short period of time between the first version of the paper and its final correction, there has been a significant downturn in the economy in Spain and Europe. This was used as an excuse for the destruction of many of the social policies of the European welfare state, including those of international cooperation. The generous funding that the Spanish government destined from 2004 to 2011 to collaboration through the AECID has been slashed to the point that all of the major scientific cooperation projects for development have been cancelled (grants, cooperation projects, university cooperation, etc.). At the same time, despite the democratic and institutional consolidation of Uruguay (and many other Latin American countries), the Uruguayan national budget has not covered these needs. This means that a lack of funding is compromising the future development of experiences such as the one being reviewed here. But at the same time as we must denounce the new, neo-conservative inspired policy affecting the whole of Europe that has reduced solidarity and replaced European international cooperation with supporting the international interests of the oligarchy of each state,[16] our review allows us to see that the concepts, agents and practices that have contributed to this experience of 'constructing from the South' are quite independent of the respective national policies and the funds that have contributed to these projects. Funding undoubtedly serves as an incentive, but the post-colonial frontier is more a problem of values and ideas than money. It is even possible that without money it could be easier for post-colonial new values to find their way.

Acknowledgements

The cooperation projects would not have been possible without funding from the Spanish Agency for International Development Cooperation (AECID) and the Spanish Ministry of Culture. The different fieldwork and research lines of the LAPPU have been supported by the Faculty of Humanities and Education Sciences, the Sectorial Commission for Scientific Research of the *Universidad de la República* and the Spanish National Research Council (CSIC). We have received collaboration of the Municipal Office of Tacuarembó, the National System of Protected Areas (SNAP-DINAMA), the non-government organization Cardijn, the Local Council of Las Toscas and the Uruguayan Ministry of Education and Culture. We are also particularly grateful to the local communities of Pago Lindo, Las Toscas, Villa Ansina, Turupí and the people who have made possible the work and activities carried out over the last ten years: Walter Mederos, Omar Michoelsson, Ana Laura Martínez and all of the students and colleagues from Uruguay, Brazil, Spain and Argentina that took part in the cooperation projects. We also are due particular acknowledgement to Antoni Nicolau and Alfons Martinell, clear champions of the Spanish policy of cooperation for development during remarkable years.

---

16 The Spanish contribution for cooperation reached in 2008 0.51% of GDP but has decreased in 2012 to 0.12% of GDP, while the budget for foreign actions – support for defending national interests abroad – has increased by 52%.

References

Achugar, H. and G. Caetano (eds). 1992. *Identidad Uruguaya: ¿Mito, Crisis o Afirmación?*. Montevideo: Ediciones Trilce.

Barreiro-Martínez, D. 2003. 'Arqueología y Pragmatismo Crítico', *Claves de Razón Práctica* 133: 36-41.

Barreiro-Martínez, D. 2006. 'Conocimiento y Acción en la Arqueología Aplicada', *Complutum* 17: 205-219.

Caetano, G. 1992. 'Identidad Nacional e Imaginario Colectivo en Uruguay. La Síntesis Perdurable del Centenario', in H. Achugar and G. Caetano (eds), *Identidad Uruguaya: ¿Mito, Crisis o Afirmación?*. Montevideo: Ediciones Trilce, 75-90.

Capdepont, I., L. del Puerto and H. Inda. 2005. 'Análisis de Sedimentos de la Estructura Monticular YALE27 y su Entorno', in C. Gianotti (ed.), *Proyecto de Cooperación Científica: Desarrollo Metodológico y Aplicación de Nuevas Tecnologías para la Gestión del Patrimonio Arqueológico en Uruguay*. TAPA 36. Santiago de Compostela: LAr (IEGPS-CSIC).

Capdepont, I., M. Sotelo, O. Marozzi, E. Villarmarzo and C. Gianotti. 2010. 'Patrimonio Cultural y Políticas Públicas 2010. La Experiencia en Áreas Protegidas en Uruguay', in J.R. Barcena and H. Chiavazza (eds), *Arqueología Argentina en el Bicentenario de la Revolución de Mayo*. Mendoza: Universidad Nacional de Cuyo, CONICET, 491-496.

Carámbula, G. 2006. 'La Diversidad Cultural ante la Otra Violencia. Algunos Casos de la Gestión Cultural Pública de Montevideo', in J.C. Moneta (ed.), *El Jardín de los Senderos que se Encuentran: Políticas Públicas y Diversidad Cultural en el MERCOSUR*. Montevideo: UNESCO, 257-275.

Criado-Boado, F. 1993. 'Límites y Posibilidades de la Arqueología del Paisaje', *SPAL, Revista de Prehistoria y Arqueología* 2: 9-55.

Criado-Boado, F. 1996. 'Hacia un Modelo Integrado de Investigación y Gestión del Patrimonio Histórico: la Cadena Interpretativa como Propuesta', *PH. Boletín Andaluz de Patrimonio Histórico* 16: 73-78.

Criado-Boado, F., C. Gianotti and J.M. López Mazz. 2006. 'Arqueología Aplicada al Patrimonio Cultural: Cooperación Científica entre Galicia y Uruguay', in G. Muñoz Cosme and C. Vidal Lorenzo (eds), *II International Conference on Cultural Heritage and Cooperation Development*. Valencia: UPV, 165-186.

Criado-Boado, F., C. Gianotti and P. Mañana-Borrazás. 2006. 'Before the Barrows: Forms of Monumentality and Forms of Complexity in Iberia and Uruguay', in L. Smejda (ed.), *Archaeology of Burial Mounds*. Czech Republic: Department of Archaeology, Faculty of Philosophy & Arts, University of West Bohemia, 38-52.

Cuesta, A.V., J. Dimuro, C. Gianotti and M. Muttoni. 2009. 'De la Investigación a la Construcción Participativa del Patrimonio. Un Programa de Educación Patrimonial y Divulgación de la Cultura Científica en Uruguay'. *ARKEOS* 4(11). Retrieved 25 September 2012 from http://mileto.pucp.edu.pe/arkeos/content/view/225/26/.

Dabezies, J.M. 2009. *El Discurso Visual en la Elaboración de un Inventario de Patrimonio Inmaterial*, doctoral research paper. Santiago de Compostela: University of Santiago de Compostela.

Dabezies, J.M. and G. de Souza. 2009. 'El Audiovisual y la Gestión del Patrimonio', in S. Romero (ed.), *Anuario de Antropologia Social y Cultural de Uruguay 2009-2010*. Montevideo: Nordan Comunidad, 267-268.

Del Puerto, L., and H. Inda. 2005. 'Paleoetnobotánica de los Constructores de Túmulos del Noreste del Uruguay: Análisis de Silicofitolitos de la Estructura Monticular YALE 27 y su Entorno', in C. Gianotti (ed.), *Proyecto de Cooperación Científica: Desarrollo Metodológico y Aplicación de Nuevas Tecnologías para la Gestión del Patrimonio Arqueológico en Uruguay*. TAPA 36. Santiago de Compostela: LAr (IEGPS-CSIC), 109-120.

Escobar, A. 2001. 'Culture Sits in Places: Reflections on Globalism and Subaltern Strategies of Localization', *Political Geography* 20: 139-174.

Gianotti, C. (ed.) 2005. *Cooperación Científica, Desarrollo Metodológico y Nuevas Tecnologías para la Gestión Integral del Patrimonio Arqueológico en Uruguay.* TAPA Series 36. Santiago de Compostela: LAr (IEGPS-CSIC).

Gianotti, C., F. Criado-Boado, and J.M. López Mazz. 2007. 'Arqueología del Paisaje: la Construcción de Cerritos en Uruguay', in IPCE, Institute of Cultural Heritage of Spain (ed.). *Excavaciones en el Exterior 2007. Informes y Trabajos*. Madrid: Ministerio de Cultura - IPCE, 177-185.

Gianotti, C., F. Criado-Boado, J.M. López-Mazz, C. Parcero-Oubiña. 2010a. 'Paisaje y Territorio como Marcos para la Cooperación en Patrimonio. La experiencia del LAPPU en Uruguay', in *IV International Conference on Heritage and Cooperation Development*. Seville: IAPH, 27-36.

Gianotti, C., F. Criado-Boado, G. Piñeiro, N. Gazzán, I. Capdepont, Y. Seoane and C. Cancela. 2008. 'Dinámica Constructiva y Formación de un Asentamiento Monumental en el Valle de Caraguatá', in IPCE, Institute of Cultural Heritage of Spain (ed.). *Excavaciones en el Exterior (2008). Informes y Trabajos.* Madrid: Ministerio de Cultura - IPCE, 245-254.

Gianotti, C. and J.M. Dabezies (eds). 2011. *Huellas de la Memoria*. ANAINA. Electronic Series of Monographs for Cultural and Didactic Dissemination 1. Santiago de Compostela: Incipit. Retrieved 25 September 2012 from http://hdl.handle.net/10261/41123.

Gianotti, C., J.M. Dabezies, G. de Souza, G. Bendahan and A. Costa. 2010b. 'Los Narradores del Caraguatá' (The Narrators of Caraguatá)'. Retrieved 25 September 2012 from http://digital.csic.es/handle/10261/25625?locale=en.

Gnecco, C. 2008. 'Manifiesto Moralista por una Arqueología Reaccionaria', in D. Jackson, D. Salazar, and A. Troncoso (eds). *Puentes Hacia el Pasado. Reflexiones Teóricas en Arqueología*. Serie Monográfica de la Sociedad Chilena de Arqueología. Santiago de Chile: Editorial LOM, 23-34.

Irazábal H., M. Etchegaray and A. Florines. 2006. *Área Propuesta para ser Integrada al Sistema Nacional de Áreas Protegidas en la categoría Paisaje Protegido*. Technical Paper of Chamangá project, in SNAP. Retrieved 25 September 2012 from http://www.snap.gub.uy/dmdocuments/ manifiestochamanga.pdf.

Lezama, A. 2004. 'El Patrimonio Cultural Frente al Desafío de la Globalización', *Cuadernos del CLAEH* 88: 9-40.

Lezama, A., L. Brum, L. d'Ambrosio, V. Lembo and B. Vienni. 2010. 'Patrimonio Local y Turismo: los deSafíos de la Investigación', in *IV Congreso Internacional de Patrimonio y Cooperación al Desarrollo*. Sevilla: IAPH, 221-228.

Lopes, R. and P.P. Funari 2008. 'Public Archaeology and Management of the Brazilian Archaeological-Cultural Heritage', in H. Silverman and W.H. Isbell (eds.), *Handbook of South American Archaeology*. New York: Springer, 1127-1133.

López J.M, C. Gianotti; F. Criado-Boado; R. Varela, C. Otero and D. Barreiro. 2010. *Comentarios al Borrador de Ley de Patrimonio Cultural de Uruguay. Reunión de Trabajo, Santiago de Compostela 21 de Octubre 2009*. Retrieved 25 September 2012 from http://patrimoniouruguay.blogspot.com/.

Marozzi O., I. Capdepont, F. Carve, E. Villarmarzo, M. Sotelo, J. López Mazz and C. Gianotti. 2009. 'Arqueología Aplicada en el Uruguay. Nuevos Horizontes para la Gestión del Patrimonio Cultural', in *II Jornadas de Investigación en FHCE*. Retrieved 25 September 2012 from http://www.fhuce.edu.uy/jornadas/IIJornadasInvestigacion/PONENCIAS/ponencias.html.

Muir, R. 1999. *Approaches to Landscape*. London: Macmillan Press.

Pascual, C. 2008. *Con las Manos en el Barro. Una Aproximación al Trabajo de Ladrilleros artesanales*. Graduate Thesis in Social and Cultural Anthropology. Facultad de Humanidades. Montevideo: UDELAR.

Porzecanski, T. 1992. 'Uruguay a Fines del s. XX. Mitologías de Ausencia y de Presencia', in H.Achugar and G. Caetano (eds), *Identidad Uruguaya: ¿Mito, Crisis o Afirmación?*. Montevideo: Ediciones Trilce, 51-62.

Verdesio, G. 2008. 'From the Erasure to the Rewriting of Indigenous Pasts: The troubled Life of Archaeology in Uruguay', in H. Silverman and W.H. Isbell (eds), *Handbook of South American Archaeology*. New York: Springer, 1115-1126.

Verdesio, G. 2009. 'Invisible at a Glance. Indigenous Cultures of the Past, Ruins, Archaeological Sites, and Our Regimes of Visibility', in J. Hell and A. Schönle (eds), *Ruins of Modernity. Politics, History, and Culture*. Durham: Duke University Press.

Viola, A. 2000. 'La Crisis del Desarrollo y el Surgimiento de la Antropología del Desarrollo', in A. Viola (ed.), *Antropología del Desarrollo. Teoría y Estudios Etnográficos en América Latina*. Barcelona: Editorial Paidós, 1-30.

Wadsworth, Y. 1998. 'What is Participatory Action Research?', *Action Research International, Paper 2*. Retrieved 25 September 2012 from http://www.aral.com.au/ari/p-ywadsworth98.html.

2.5 BUILDING COUNTRY-RELEVANT PROGRAMMES IN THE CONTEXT OF THE IMPLEMENTATION OF THE UNESCO CONVENTION ON THE PROTECTION OF THE UNDERWATER CULTURAL HERITAGE

Robert Parthesius* and Bill Jeffery**

* Centre for International Heritage Activities, Leiden, The Netherlands
and Leiden University, The Netherlands

** Centre for International Heritage
Activities, Leiden, The Netherlands

Abstract

In this paper three different case studies of international collaboration in developing and implementing maritime and underwater cultural heritage (MUCH) capacity building programmes will be discussed. They were carried out in Sri Lanka, the Federated States of Micronesia (FSM) and in Tanzania, within the context of the implementation of the principles of the *UNESCO Convention on the Protection of the Underwater Cultural Heritage 2001*. The paper describes the various approaches used in this work with the aim of exploring how heritage management policies can be made relevant to local community values.

Résumé

Construire des Programmes Pertinents face aux Pays dans le Cadre de la mise en place de la Convention de l'UNESCO pour la Protection du Patrimoine Culturel Subaquatique

Dans cet article, trois études de cas seront discutées concernant la collaboration internationale pour le développement et la mise en œuvre de programmes de renforcement des capacités relatifs au patrimoine culturel maritime et subaquatique (Maritime and underwater cultural heritage: MUCH). Ces études ont été réalisées au Sri Lanka, aux États fédérés de Micronésie et en Tanzanie, dans le cadre de la mise en œuvre des principes de la Convention de l'UNESCO pour la protection du patrimoine culturel subaquatique de 2001. L'article décrit les différentes approches utilisées dans ces études, visant à explorer la pertinence des politiques de gestion du patrimoine culturel face aux valeurs des communautés locales.

Extracto

La Creación de Programas Relevantes para los Países en el Marco de la Implementación de la Convención de la UNESCO sobre la Protección del Patrimonio Cultural Subacuático

En este artículo se discutirán tres diferentes estudios de caso sobre la colaboración internacional en el desarrollo y la implementación de programas de la creación de capacidad del patrimonio cultural marítimo y subacuático. Se llevaron a cabo los estudios en Sri Lanka, en los Estados Federales de Micronesia (FSM) y en Tanzania, dentro del marco de la implementación de los principios de la *Convención sobre la Protección del Patrimonio Cultural Subacuático 2001* de la UNESCO. El artículo describe los varios planteamientos que se usan en este trabajo con el fin de explorar cómo se pueden hacer relevantes las políticas de gestión del patrimonio para los valores de la comunidad local.

ملخص

إنشاء برامج خاصة بالدول في إطار تطبيق اتفاقية منظمة الأمم المتحدة للتربية والعلوم والثقافة بشأن حماية التراث الثقافي المغمور بالمياه.

روبرت بارثيسيوس* وبيل جيفري**

* مركز الأنشطة الدولية للتراث، ليدن، وجامعة هولندا، ليدن، هولندا

** مركز الأنشطة الدولية للتراث، ليدن، هولندا

في هذه الورقة سنتناول ثلاث دراسات حالة عن التعاون الدولي في إنشاء وتطبيق برامج تنمية القدرات الخاصة بالتراث البحري والثقافي المغمور بالمياه. وقد تم إجراء هذه الدراسات في سري لنكا، وفي تايلاند ميكرونيسيا، داخل إطار تطبيق مبادئ اتفاقية منظمة الأمم المتحدة بالمياه حماية بشأن التراث الثقافي المغمور للتربية والعلوم والثقافة وتصف الورقة المناهج المختلفة التي تم استخدامها في هذا العمل بهدف 2001. استكشاف كيفية جعل سياسات إدارة التراث ذات التراث صلة بقيم المجتمع المحلي.

Keywords

maritime and underwater cultural heritage, shared cultural heritage, Sri Lanka, Chuuk Lagoon, Yap, Federated States of Micronesia, Tanzania, Avondster shipwreck

Introduction

Sri Lanka, the Federated States of Micronesia (islands in the northwest Pacific) and Tanzania have varied and long histories related to seafaring, marine and riverine use. Yet little maritime archaeological or maritime and underwater cultural heritage (MUCH) work has been carried out compared to the terrestrial archaeological investigations that European archaeologists conducted there.[1] The development of diving equipment, allowing archaeologists to effectively work underwater, and the great development in geophysical and deep diving equipment in the recent 20 years, has meant that underwater sites located virtually anywhere can now be systematically studied. It also means however that salvagers wanting to commercially exploit these sites have access too. This has led to governments enacting protective legislation and active underwater cultural heritage programmes. From 2009 an international agreement entitled the UNESCO *Convention on the Protection of the Underwater Cultural Heritage 2001* (UNESCO 2001) came into force to assist in the protection and management of sites located in all waters, including international waters. The development of this framework and approach has stimulated the initiation and implementation of many capacity building programmes in maritime and underwater cultural heritage, all over the world.[2] The authors conducted three of such programmes in very different areas, with particular circumstances and heritage management challenges. This paper describes the various approaches used in Sri Lanka, the Federated States of Micronesia (FSM) and Tanzania and discusses the experiences with this particular form of international collaboration.

The UNESCO convention on the protection of the underwater cultural heritage

The capacity building programmes and the individual projects described in this paper use the approach promoted by the UNESCO 2001 Convention.[3] This convention came into force on 2 January 2009, when twenty countries ratified it. It is considered the standard universal agreement on how to protect and manage

---

1   As of the late nineteenth century in Sri Lanka and the early to mid twentieth century in Tanzania and the FSM.

2   It is not that long ago that the process of capacity building in the field of maritime archaeology commenced. It has been put into practice only from the 1960s and the discipline as we know it today leans heavily on the work that has been done, primarily in the western world. This has included the work of George Bass and the USA Institute of Nautical Archaeology, and major maritime archaeological excavations including the Vasa (1960s), the Dutch East-Indiamen in Western Australia (1970s) and the Mary Rose (1980s) (Bass 1972, 1987; Green 1975; Kvarning 1997; Rule 1982). The path of the development of a maritime archaeological tradition was a long learning curve in which capacity and skills were built over a long time. This process led eventually to the six year debate and adoption of the wording of the Convention in 2001, now considered the universal rule for implementing maritime archaeology and the management of underwater cultural heritage.

3   It was the discovery and exploitation of the Titanic shipwreck, located in international waters, and commercial shipwreck operations such as the work on the Geldermalsen that triggered the need for United Nations guidelines on the best practices of protecting and managing underwater cultural heritage sites in all waters, not just in international waters (O'Keefe 2002: 7-13).

underwater cultural heritage sites, because it uses as its practical base the ICOMOS Charter on the Protection and Management of Underwater Cultural Heritage (1996), which was developed by many eminent maritime archaeologists.[4]

One of the main provisions of this convention is the definition of an underwater cultural heritage site, being: 'all traces of human existence having a cultural, historical or archaeological character which have been partially or totally under water, periodically or continuously, for at least 100 years' (UNESCO 2001). 'Shipwrecks' are not refered to in the UNESCO 2001 Convention under this title, they are integrated with all other types of underwater cultural heritage remains being protected. It appears to have been a particular aim of the authors of the UNESCO 2001 Convention to give maritime archaeology a much broader focus than what has occurred in the past. In places such as Yap and Chuuk in the FSM, this is very relevant given that inhabitants take great pride in, and make underwater cultural heritage a priority in their cultural identity.

Furthermore, the convention contains several general articles on how underwater cultural sites should be managed, complemented with a section on the most appropriate operational procedures (the Rules). It also calls for the establishment of a competent authority in the various countries. It is the responsibility of this authority to implement an active programme in researching, preserving, and interpreting the various underwater cultural heritage sites.

The implementation of the Convention is still in its early days (in April 2012, 41 countries had ratified it) and UNESCO has recently established a scientific and technical advisory body and a working group to assist State Parties in implementing the rules and the development of some operational guidelines. UNESCO is also developing a list of appropriate non-governmental organizations (NGOs) to collaborate with this advisory body.[5]

Sri Lanka: the *Avondster* project

At the request of the Sri Lankan authorities, a joint team of Sri Lankan and international maritime archaeologists, historians and museum curators started in the early 1990s to conduct research in the Bay of Galle and in the extensive archives in Sri Lanka and the Netherlands. This research revealed an impressive number of underwater heritage sites, dating from the thirteenth century up to

---

4   Some of the main objectives and provisions of the Convention are: underwater cultural heritage shall not be commercially exploited, *i.e.* it "shall not be traded, sold, bought or bartered as commercial goods"; countries to co-operate on a number of issues, including site management, training programmes, sharing resources; ratification by a country means all its waters come under the provisions of the Convention, in addition to its nationals (anywhere in the world) needing to comply with the Convention; preservation *in situ* is the first priority but other processes are possible if they are determined as the best practices in preserving the site; ensure proper respect is given to human remains; maintain the sovereign rights of a country – its vessels and aircraft; does not prejudice the jurisdiction and duties under the United Nations Convention on the Law of the Sea 1982 (UNCLOS); encourage public access through public awareness programmes; formation of a scientific and technical advisory body and development of operational guidelines. See http://www.international.icomos.org/charters/underwater_e.pdf.

5   In July 2011, the CIE was accredited as an appropriate NGO.

modern times, and has led to an ambitious capacity building programme that was set up to establish a suitable infrastructure for the management of these sites. Subsequently, in 2001 a Maritime Archaeology Unit (MAU) was formed under the Mutual Heritage Centre, managed by the Sri Lankan government agency, the Central Cultural Fund, in cooperation with international partners from the Netherlands, Australia and Mexico.

The first major project of the MAU was the excavation of the *Avondster* (wrecked in 1659). It is one of five Dutch East-Indiamen that went missing around Galle. The wreck was discovered during the 1993 expedition to Galle Harbour and subsequently identified as the *Avondster* (Green, Devendra and Parthesius 1998). A survey and test excavation in 1998 and 1999 revealed that the site was in an excellent state of preservation; a rich source of finds and historical knowledge was anticipated. The wreck site was situated about 80 metres off the beach in about four metres of water. From a diving perspective it was deemed suitable for training, although visibility was often poor. The site was relatively easy to interpret underwater, enabling the archaeologists to learn about the construction techniques used on a seventeenth century East-Indiaman. The *Avondster* was also historically well documented which allowed the Sri Lankan archaeologists to be introduced to historical-archaeological research (Parthesius 1998).[6]

In addition to the survey, excavation and conservation of the site and the artefacts, one of the primary goals of the *Avondster* project was to involve Sri Lankan archaeologists and conservators in order to develop the local capacity and the associated infrastructure enabling them to continue with a maritime archaeology programme in Sri Lanka. Another important goal was to develop a national maritime museum, based to some extent on the material recovered from the *Avondster* but also incorporating Sri Lanka's broader maritime history, its sites and the people involved.

The *Avondster* site was also selected because it was severely under threat. Due to changes in the dynamics of the seabed, that were caused by the building of a sea wall and the channelling caused by storm-water drains, the *Avondster* had become increasingly exposed throughout the 1990s and serious degradation was observed. For example, the prominent iron anchor found on the site originally had an intact wooden stock but this steadily degraded and by 1997 it had disintegrated completely. The proposal to develop a new small harbour to the east of the *Avondster* was also seen as an additional threat to its preservation. This development could cause changes in the marine environment of the area, such as in the patterns of silting and erosion. Additionally, a new harbour would attract more traffic in the

---

6 The seventeenth century European East-Indiaman Avondster which can be linked to extensive historical documentation and is connected with an important development stage of Galle as an emporium in the Asian shipping network would appear to be an eminent subject of historical and archaeological research. The Avondster took part in a complex VOC/European/Asian trading network that had developed from the late sixteenth century (Parthesius 2010). The vessel served two European East-India companies, participated in various functional roles on all important trading routes and it is therefore an important representative of this complex system.

shallow bay that might impact the *Avondster*. Despite an official ban on diving in Galle Harbour, the site was also vulnerable to looting.

Conducting a professional archaeological excavation on the *Avondster* using the highest possible standards was seen as an appropriate step to take in preserving the ship.[7] It would also demonstrate how archaeological information can be obtained and disseminated to the community. The *Avondster* project consisted of a pre-disturbance survey of the exposed part of the site, an excavation of trenches in the bow, midship and stern areas, and the recovery of about 3,000 artefacts, including an iron cannon and a large iron anchor (figure 1). In addition, the development of a conservation infrastructure and the implementation of conservation techniques were also deemed to be of primary importance (Parthesius, Millar and Jeffery 2005). In cooperation with the conservation department of the Western Australian Maritime Museum, the Amsterdam Historical Museum and The Instituto National de Antropologia e Historia in Mexico, a well-equipped conservation laboratory was built and a small team of conservators was trained in many of the techniques required to conserve maritime archaeological objects.

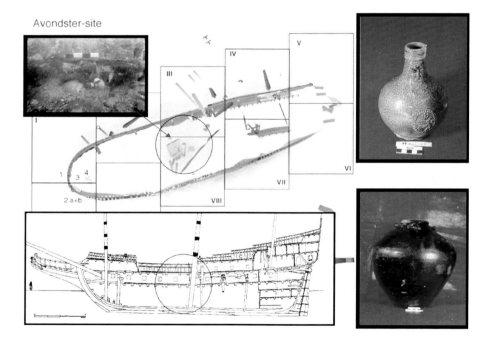

Figure 1. The mid-ship excavation of the Avondster shipwreck site (Photo: Avondster Project).

---

7   Each year a permit was required from the Department of Archaeology to implement the project. The permit conditions were consistent with the UNESCO 2001 even though Sri Lanka had not ratified the Convention.

As *in situ* preservation of underwater cultural heritage sites is an important element of the UNESCO Convention, the team also developed a method for the *in situ* preservation of the *Avondster*. In November 2003, the wreck was covered with a mesh that allowed for sediment to build up over the shipwreck and to inhibit further erosion. While initial work was hindered by the rough sea conditions in Galle Harbour and the mesh was ripped off during the southwest monsoons, a subsequent recovering – with the addition of sandbags – has stood up well even against the tsunami of 2006. Today much of the *Avondster* is covered and in a more stable anerobic environment (Chandraratne 2011).

Since the inception of the *Avondster* project in 1998, the primary aim of the work carried out by the foreign consultants has been to train members of the MAU as conservators and maritime archaeologists so that they would have the skills to function autonomously. This aspect was emphasized during each field season. As part of this training, many foreign consultants with various skills worked with the MAU team. The use of different consultants allowed the MAU team to get acquainted with alternative approaches and different experiences. A very significant outcome of this project was that the Sri Lankan team contributed to the production of a two-volume publication on the *Avondster* (Parthesius 2007).

The devastating 2006 tsunami was a very tragic event in Sri Lanka and for the MAU, with a huge loss of material, equipment and infrastructure. However, with considerable international support the basic MAU facilities and infrastructure could fortunately be rebuilt and it could keep its role as a regional training centre in maritime archaeology for the Asia/Pacific region. In recent years, members of the MAU have participated in training programmes in Australia and Thailand. They have now consolidated their many resources and established an active maritime archaeology programme in Sri Lanka.[8]

It is important to note that The *Avondster* project was financially possible because it was a Dutch VOC vessel that was under threat. As this Dutch shipwreck was considered 'mutual heritage' by the Netherlands, the Netherlands Cultural Fund could be persuaded to invest in a capacity building programme around this heritage site. As of 2001 it provided substantial funding for a three-year project.

This Dutch 'mutual cultural heritage programme' was introduced by Dutch policymakers in the 1990s to label the heritage of the Dutch expansion and colonial period. It is seen as an important period in the Dutch national memory, bringing along mixed feelings of pride and shame. As the overall objective of the Dutch Common Cultural Heritage Policy (Ministry of Education, Culture and Science 2009: 1) is to "collaborate on the sustainable maintenance and management of common cultural heritage, on the basis of reciprocal political and substantive involvement", this provided an excellent framework and funding that could focus on the management of the Dutch East India Company (VOC) and the West India Company (WIC) maritime installations and shipwrecks in Galle Harbour. This is very similar to how the UNESCO 2001 Convention has been designed to operate, through international collaboration.

---

8   Http://www.mausrilanka.lk.

Chuuk Lagoon, Federated States of Micronesia

Quite a different approach to the development and implementation of a maritime and underwater cultural heritage programme was implemented in Chuuk Lagoon. This was done through the recognition and use of a broader perspective, including the multi-vocal values of the underwater heritage sites.

Chuuk Lagoon is a large lagoon with nineteen high volcanic islands. It is the central most populated area of Chuuk State (formerly Truk), which is located in the Western Pacific Ocean, 3,450 km southeast of Manila (Philippines) and is one of the four states of the independent Federated States of Micronesia (FSM). Chuuk has been inhabited for about 2,000 years and the cultural practices, customs and traditions built-up remain inherent in many aspects of daily life (Rainbird 1993).

Chuuk, as with all of Micronesia, had colonial rulers from Spain (1885–1898), Germany (1899–1914), Japan (1914–1945), and the United States of America (1945–1991). Of these, the Japanese and Americans have had the greatest influence on current lifestyles. In the lead up to World War II, the Japanese navy established a base in Chuuk Lagoon, which they considered one of the best anchorages in the world. This was later recognized by the USA, as they called it the "impregnable bastion of the Pacific", the "Japanese Pearl Harbor" and the "Gibraltar of the Pacific" (Denfeld 1981: 4; Peattie 1988: 251). The Imperial Japanese Navy Combined Fleet was based in Chuuk for two years and it was this fleet the USA navy was after in February and May 1944 when it sent a total of 3,450 aircraft bombing flights from an American Carrier Task Force of over 50 ships that killed about 5,000 Japanese and 1,000 Chuukese, sunk more than 60 Japanese ships and destroyed over 300 aircraft.

Led by Jacques Cousteau's 1969 visit to the shipwreck sites, his film ('Lagoon of lost Ships') and the recovery of 'tons of artefacts', the Chuuk Lagoon shipwrecks have built up an international reputation as the world's best shipwrecks to dive and – as a result – to plunder (Bailey 2000: 265-266) (figure 2). They are however also regarded as "a continual source of national sorrow" by many Japanese due to the human remains that are found on the shipwrecks and their disturbance by scuba divers (Bailey 2000: 3).

The Chuukese government greatly values the tourism industry that is based on the shipwrecks and many Chuukese also benefit from the illegal dynamite fishing 'industry' that has been built-up from the shipwrecks. Many munitions can be found on the sites and they are recovered to make dynamite bombs that are used to kill fish on the shipwrecks and elsewhere on the surrounding reefs. This activity is very dangerous and very destructive to the environment, but the Chuukese government seems powerless to stop it.

The maritime archaeological work in Chuuk comprised a comprehensive survey of the submerged World War II sites to gain an understanding of their nature, integrity, condition and value (Jeffery 2007). This work included a range of methods, such as participant observations in Chuuk and the collection of oral histories from the Chuukese which provided broad socio-historical and socio-political views of Chuuk (Jeffery 2007). The underwater surveys combined with an

Figure 2. The 7,000 ton aircraft transport vessel Fujikawa Maru in 2001 (Photo: Greg Adams).

emic approach to research made it possible to interpret information about different societies and their relationships without employing any destructive site analysis.[9] It was revealed that these submerged sites contain both tangible and intangible heritage aspects, but according to a dominant Euro-American perspective their management focuses on the tangible aspects. This is related to the iconic pedestal that the tourism industry has placed on the sites and which is widely promoted through websites and primarily American publications (Bailey 2000). Chuukese do not greatly value the shipwrecks as historic sites; it is the terrestrial World War II sites that have family and suffering connections and that reflect elements of a Chuukese identity (Jeffery 2007).

With regard to the management of the Chuuk Lagoon shipwrecks, the current ineffective approach is indicative of the limitations when using a single dominant western approach to the protection of underwater cultural heritage sites. Local commitment (and one of the most influential and important aspects in site management) is only possible when all site values – the multi-vocal values – are recognized and acted upon by all the stakeholders. This is not to be interpreted as advocating dynamite fishing or tourist diving on sites that still contain many human remains, but rather that all values and conflicts should be placed on the negotiating table and used in developing site management. Dynamite fishing on the submerged war sites is about acquiring food and some financial gain, but it has

---

9   Knowledge about cultures can be gained through an emic approach; a subjective, insider's perspective about what things mean to members of a society, and/or an etic approach which is an objective, analytical interpretation of the same customs.

no traditional ownership impediments as do the natural reefs. An alternative may be to establish another ongoing source of fish and money, through aquaculture, or to consider compensation for the Chuukese, similar to that proposed by the Coalition of Rainforest Nations for rainforest conservation.[10]

Maritime archaeology for communities: Yap fish weirs (*aech*)

Another maritime archaeology project was implemented in Yap. In contrast to the project in Chuuk, the project in Yap was directed by the local Yapese community and focused on traditional sites. While Yap contains colonial and World War II shipwrecks (not to the same extent as in Chuuk), the Yapese were more interested in revealing the value of their traditional sites and revitalizing the associated cultural practices (tangible and intangible). Amongst other things, the project in Yap highlights the role maritime archaeology can play in assisting local communities in preserving and re-using underwater cultural heritage sites.

Yap (Waab is the traditional name) is located 1,950 km southeast of Manila. It comprises three high volcanic islands (Yap Proper) and several outer islands and atolls. Without wanting to overgeneralize, Yap's indigenous and colonial background is similar to Chuuk's. A major effect of the foreign presence was a population decimation from possibly about 40,000 pre-contact to about 2,500 immediately after World War II; today it is about 11,700 (Underwood 1969 cited in Takeda 2001: 118; Useem 1946 cited in Takeda 2001: 118).

Yap has a very unique and enduring culture. Traditions, customs and cultural practices remain at the core of society. The outer islanders are famous for their canoe building, sailing and navigation. In Yap Proper, dances are still performed to honour the spirits and ancestors, and to tell about the suffering during World War II. Yapese society is a very structured society with high and low class families and villages that support each other during good and hard times.

As part of its responsibilities in protecting, preserving and maintaining the many aspects of Yap's heritage, the Yap Historic Preservation Office (HPO) had been interested in their traditional fish weirs (*aech)* for some time and during the last few years funding had been provided to some *aech* owners for restoration work. It was considered that a comprehensive survey of the location, condition and histories of the *aech* was warranted to assist in prioritizing further restoration work. It was known that many of the histories and information on the *aech* construction techniques were being lost with the passing away of older men and there was an urgent need to document this information before more was lost.

An estimated 700 to 800 *aech* are thought to be located on the reef flat, the relatively shallow submerged land between the island coastline and outer reef edge, together with many bamboo weirs.[11] This is supported by early surveys and aerial photographs. While it is not known when exactly the weirs were constructed, all

---

10   A discussion on compensation for not logging in the Indonesian rainforest can be seen at http://www. rainforestcoalition.org/, accessed 7 September 2011.

11   Small bamboo traps are often used in connection with the stone weirs or on their own. Other fishing techniques can include nets, line and spear fishing.

Figure 3. A restored aech (fish weir) in Yap in 2008 (Photo: Bill Jeffery).

are said to be based on seven *aech* built by spirits. Many are reputed to have been built hundreds, if not thousands of years ago. The later *aech* are probably at least 100 years old (figure 3).

In association with the *aech* owners, village chiefs and Yap HPO staff, Bill Jeffery commenced in 2008 – with US National Park Historic Preservation funding[12] – a survey of the *aech*. The project was completed in August 2009 when the location, name, owner's name and history of 432 *aech* were documented. A more detailed survey of 46 *aech* was also implemented to get a good idea of their shape, construction and condition, and information on why that type of *aech* was built in a specific spot (Jeffery and Pitmag 2010). It was found that the *aech* is a unique example of how a society can exploit as well as live in harmony with its natural resources. The *aech* was designed and built to suit the local environment, to take advantage of the way certain fish move along the shoreline as well as further offshore. They were left unused for particular periods, so fish could come-and-go from within the weir and 'feel at home'. The *aech* also provides an insight into Yap's complex social ranking. While it is located in one owner's 'sea-plot', the *aech* could be owned by another person or estate, and it could even be used by a third person or estate. Moreover, many of the coastal villages are high caste villages, but some lower caste villagers could from time to time be given access to sea-plots, sometimes including an *aech*. This would depend for example on whether fish are plentiful and whether there is a famine or another natural disaster. According

---

12   The project was funded through the National Park Service's Historic Preservation Program, which provides funding (on a competitive basis) to Historic Preservation Offices throughout Micronesia.

to Hunter-Anderson this contributed to the development of Yap's social ranking (Hunter-Anderson 1986: 3-4).

On a practical level, maritime archaeology, if implemented in a broad and contemporary manner can help in some important community issues. For example, the Yap Cultural Inventory Group (n.d.) recommended a number of initiatives to reconstitute traditional marine ownership rights and the power to protect this natural resource, amongst which included:

> *"People need to be encouraged to use more ecologically sound fishing methods such as traditional stone weirs and bamboo fish traps. […] The reconstruction of aech could be undertaken as village projects for communal use. Or several could be constructed by owners and used as a type of supermarket, where individuals could select fish from the aech upon paying a small fee or giving a percentage or number of fish to the owner"* (Yap Cultural Inventory Group n.d.: 28).

Yap HPO, the traditional chiefs (through the Council of Pilung) and many Yapese citizens are optimistic that this project can help in reviving traditional knowledge about fishing with an *aech,* and in their construction and maintenance. It could also help to make fishing more sustainable.

There are a number of other issues that need to be considered in this work, such as the impact on the currents through dredging some of the reef flat, sea-level rise, declining fish stocks, unsustainable fishing practices and the establishment of marine protected areas. But this project highlighted how maritime archaeology can be part of a multi-disciplinary investigation and assist contemporary communities with some important daily issues and in helping to revive traditional cultural practices.

The MUCH programme in Tanzania

A third programme was conducted in Tanzania. Since 2009, the Dutch Centre for International Heritage Activities (CIE) has assisted in building the capacity of the citizens in regard to implementing MUCH programmes. This request was also related to the national government intending to ratify the UNESCO Convention on the Protection of Underwater Cultural Heritage. However, when the CIE was approached to implement a capacity building programme in Tanzania that was to be funded by the Dutch government, the focus needed to be much broader than for instance in Sri Lanka, as in Tanzania there is no mutual cultural heritage. Thus the aim of the CIE was to build a Tanzanian programme that would be infused of the ideals and experiences of the work in the Federated States of Micronesia and that would be relevant and beneficial to many Tanzanians through the broad perspective on capacity building and through a multi-vocal and value-based approach.

The overall goal of the MUCH programme was to establish a sustainable infrastructure for MUCH management in Tanzania, in line with the UNESCO Convention on the Protection of Underwater Cultural Heritage, and to work toward the ratification of this convention. A four-phased capacity building programme was started for fourteen staff members of five key Tanzanian

Figure 4: Some members of the Tanzanian team recording the Great Northern shipwreck site in Zanzibar (Photo: Bill Jeffery).

stakeholders: the Department of Antiquities Tanzania, the Marine Parks and Reserves Tanzania, the Department of Archives, Museums and Antiquities Zanzibar, the National Museum of Tanzania,[13] and the Archaeology and History Department of the University of Dar es Salaam.[14] The staff would develop skills to implement non-disturbing site surveys, research and report writing, and the development of a MUCH database (Mahudi 2011) (figure 4). A phased programme that would run over a longer period of time was considered appropriate as it would provide the

---

13   This is a consortium of five Tanzanian museums: the National Museum of Dar es Salaam, the Village Museum in Dar es Salaam, the National History Museum, the Arusha Declaration Museum and the Mwalimu Julius K. Nyerere Memorial Museum.

14   Phase 1: Assessment of, and awareness raising for political, institutional and academic commitment; Phase 2: Building capacity, infrastructure, academic and technical expertise in MUCH protection and management; Phase 3: Development of a Project Design and Management Plan of a site(s) and implementation of a comprehensive site(s) survey; Phase 4: Formulate strategic plans for implementing a sustainable MUCH programme.

necessary time for the team to build its skills and it would give the trainers time to build a programme that is beneficial for the local situation.

Subsequently an action plan (2010–2011) was developed by the Tanzanian stakeholders, which called for more advanced training in conducting a survey of the MUCH sites at Kilwa Kisiwani. This was a pre-eminent Swahili port and city during much of its time (ninth to nineteenth century) but primarily during the twelfth to fifteenth centuries and is a World Heritage Site (Sutton 1998). It was expected that the project would raise the awareness of the value of MUCH sites and would strengthen the need for ratification of the 2001 Convention. In addition, it could help to sustain the MUCH unit as the competent authority. The Kilwa Kisiwani project was also recommended due to the need to assist in the *Integrated Approach to the Protection and Safeguarding of Cultural Heritage of the Ruins of*

Figure 5. *Jiwe la Jahazi (stone dhow) at Kilwa Kisiwani (Photo: Bill Jeffery).*

Figure 6. *The elders of Kisiwani Mafia and some members of the MUCH Team (Photo: Sophie Winton).*

Kilwa Kisiwani and Songo Mnara, Endangered World Heritage sites which had as its major aims to "improve living standards and ensure long-term sustainability of the site" (UNESCO 2008).

The Kilwa project was implemented in November 2010 with the major activities being site investigations, building a relationship with the local community and collecting oral histories. The team also gained experience in the use of a magnetometer to search for ship remains. They located an anchor that possibly belonged to one of the three sixteenth century Portuguese ships that was wrecked in the area.

Of special interest for many of the residents of Kilwa Kisiwani was a site called *Jiwe la Jahazi* (English translation is 'stone dhow'). Local folklore depicts the site as an Arab dhow that turned to stone following prayers offered by the local residents, as they were fearful that the crew of the dhow would come and harm them. The dhow and its crew changed form and were therefore unable to harm the residents of Kilwa Kisiwani. It is now a significant site in the maritime cultural landscape of Kilwa Kisiwani (figure 5).

In a meeting with Kilwa Kisiwani's elders (figure 6), they expressed interest but also some reservations about the MUCH project. They were very keen to obtain some lasting tangible benefits from collaborating with researchers at the site, as from their experience with previous researchers, ongoing benefits were rare. The priorities of the elders were training in new skills, lasting employment and economic benefits.

Lessons to learn

From these very different projects in the three remote regions valuable experiences were gained from which future international collaboration projects could benefit. One of the experiences concerns the financing. No fund was included in the original articles of the UNESCO Convention although an 'account' has now been established to allow for pooling donor donations to support certain projects and programmes. Article 22 of the Convention states: "States Parties shall establish competent authorities or reinforce the existing ones where appropriate, with the aim of providing for the establishment, maintenance and updating of an inventory of underwater cultural heritage, the effective protection, conservation, presentation and management of underwater cultural heritage, as well as research and education". In order to implement these activities, less developed countries with a rich and extensive underwater cultural heritage need access to funding. In the case of sites of 'international interest' (*e.g.* shipwrecks linked with the 'Golden Age of European' expansion) external sources of funding are often available, but in countries where there are no particular interests of foreign countries in the traditional or indigenous sites, often no external source of funding is available.

Heritage does not exist by itself; it is always the product of the interpretation of the past by people. Many factors are influencing this 'heritage making process'. The process becomes extremely interesting when funding opportunities and heritage claims get mixed. The programme in Sri Lanka is a good example of this. Cultural heritage sites from the colonial period take a prominent position in Sri Lanka and through the nature of the European expansion, many of the remains of this period (*e.g.* port cities, harbour installations, fortifications and shipwrecks) can be considered MUCH sites. However, the fact that they are located in prominent places and that the Netherlands consider them 'mutual cultural heritage', does not mean that the partner countries consider it important heritage too and that they link it with their own cultural identity. In fact, this term – which can be translated as 'common cultural heritage' or 'shared cultural heritage' – has been the subject of debate because the remnants of a Dutch presence do not automatically lead to mutual appreciation (Fienieg *et al.* 2008). In Sri Lanka the built heritage of the so-called Dutch Period (1640–1796) is considered heritage of 'dual partnership'. The World Heritage Site at Galle is considered as the highlight of that heritage, but the wreck of the VOC-ship Avondster does not come under that concept. It was in a sense new heritage, because prior to its discovery in 1993 neither the Netherlands nor Sri Lanka was aware of its existence. Placed in the context of Galle, but not as a product of Sri Lankan-Dutch design, the Avondster site is considered 'mutual cultural heritage' instead of 'heritage of dual partnership'. This status made the Avondster very suitable and reciprocal for the development of capacity and heritage management strategies, but it also developed a perspective of MUCH sites in Sri Lanka as very narrow. It focused on a Dutch shipwreck, from predominantly a Dutch perspective, yet Sri Lanka has many shipwrecks of different nationalities that could be investigated to provide a Sri Lankan perspective. It has also many other types of MUCH sites. Fortunately it is now being expanded upon by members of the Sri Lankan MAU. This can be seen in one of their investigations of the British shipwreck *Earl of Shaftsbury* where research about broad Sri Lankan social issues is being implemented. They are using a foreign shipwreck as a means to implement a multi-vocal and value-based approach to MUCH research (Dayananda 2011).

Besides the financial aspects, another limitation of the UNESCO Convention is that it may not always suit the particular local circumstances in the various countries. This could be addressed by developing operational guidelines that can be applied in such a way that they can be adapted to the local situations and needs of the country or region in question. In order to fulfil this, it is necessary to stimulate value-based approaches and discuss new and different perspectives. By listening to local parties, the guidelines can be adapted and new methods developed whereby local communities can take part in and profit from researching and preserving their cultural heritage.

That this is needed was clearly shown by the work in Chuuk Lagoon, where the traditional western management approach is not working. It does not include the many values of all the sites and they continue to be damaged. In a country or region where traditional sites and traditional cultural practices are strongly developed and maintained and contribute to a local cultural identity, there is a need for a MUCH programme to give these sites (and the associated intangible heritage) priority. Moreover, a multi-vocal and value-based approach is required to effectively manage such heritage. And for the sustainability of the created capacity, an awareness of the value of heritage at all levels of society is essential.

Regarding sustainability it was demonstrated by the *Avondster* project, that this can only be achieved when a capacity building programme has been put together in collaboration with all the relevant stakeholders (political, academic, bureaucratic, general community). To obtain this, it is important that an awareness of the different values of underwater cultural heritage is appreciated among all stakeholders. It is indeed stated in the UNESCO Convention (Article 20) that it is necessary to create and implement practicable measures to stimulate public awareness and we believe this can be achieved in part through community engagement programmes which implement underwater cultural heritage projects for the benefit of contemporary communities. In addition to reviving or helping to maintain traditional cultural practices and protect and preserve indigenous sites in less developed countries, one of the benefits could be an economic gain through the re-use of underwater cultural heritage sites and through tourism managed by the local community.

It is our contention that traditional or indigenous sites need equal, if not more attention in the implementation of an underwater cultural heritage programme in many countries. This is what we tried to establish with the work in Tanzania. It has only just begun and it is early days to see whether the Tanzanian MUCH programme can really benefit from the work in Sri Lanka and the Federated States of Micronesia. So more time, surveys, resources and funding is needed to further develop this start, but it is already a great improvement given that the Tanzanian MUCH team now has a permanent staff member within the lead agency, the Department of Antiquites, that co-ordinates the programme. Recently the team undertook the Mafia Island survey, in which three of the five stakeholders were represented. They used the same approach as implemented in the earlier Kilwa Kisiwani survey, being very conscious of the need to build community engagement as a first and ongoing step.

While so far largely successful, the project however also highlighted some major challenges that a MUCH programme will face in developing countries. The first is the already discussed quest for funding, the second are the issues associated with community individuals imparting knowledge where originally traditional laws and custodianship maintained relations. The main challenge, however, will be to make a real difference. Where many communities are poor and in desperate need of basic necessities (water, nutrition, education and housing), a MUCH programme is not particularly relevant, unless it can find ways to benefit these communities.

Acknowledgements

There are many individuals and organizations to thank: the staff of the Historic Preservation Offices in Chuuk and Yap; the National Historic Preservation Office in Pohnpei; the US Historic Preservation Program for Micronesia, particularly Paula Creech the Program Manager; the Tanzanian Ministry of Natural Resources and Environment, Department of Antiquities and the four other agencies from Zanzibar and throughout Tanzania who supported the MUCH programme with staff and funding; the Tanzanian MUCH team members; the Sri Lankan team of the Maritime Archaeological Unit, the Central Cultural Fund, the Departement of Archaeology and the Post Graduate Institute of Archaeological Research; the Embassies of the Kingdom of the Netherlands in Tanzania and Sri Lanka; UNESCO Office in Tanzania; and the office staff of the CIE in Leiden. We would finally like to thank the many community members who we spoke to about the MUCH programme in Sri Lanka, Chuuk, Yap and Tanzania.

References

Bailey, D.E. 2000. *World War II Wrecks of the Truk Lagoon*. Redding: North Valley Diver Publications.

Bass, G. (ed.). 1972. *A History of Seafaring Based on Underwater Archaeology*. London: Thames and Hudson.

Bass, G. 1987. 'Oldest Known ShipWreck Reveals Bronze Age Splendors'. *National Geographic* 172(6): 693-734.

Chandraratne, W.M. 2011. 'In-Situ Preservation in Tropical Seas: Case Study on the Avondster Shipwreck', in *Asia-Pacific Regional Conference on Underwater Cultural Heritage Proceedings*. Retrieved 10 April 2012 from the Museum of Underwater Archaeology Collection at http://www.themua.org/collections/items/show/1250.

Dayananda, A.M.A. 2011. 'Reading of the Contemporary Social Consciousness through the Shipwreck Earl of Shaftsbury', in *Asia-Pacific Regional Conference on Underwater Cultural Heritage Proceedings*. Retrieved 8 October 2012 from the Museum of Underwater Archaeology Collection at http://www.themua.org/collections/items/show/1245.

Denfeld, D.C. 1981. *Field Survey of Truk: World War II Features*. Micronesian Archaeological Survey Report 6. Saipan: Historic Preservation Office, Trust Territory of the Pacific Islands.

Fienieg, A., R. Parthesius, B. Groot, R. Jaffe, S. van der Linde and P. van Roosmalen. 2008. 'Heritage Trails: International Cultural Heritage Policies in a European Perspective', in G. Oostindië (ed.), *Dutch Colonialism, Migration and Cultural Heritage*. Leiden: KITLV Press, 23-62.

Green, J.N. 1975. 'The VOC Ship Batavia, Wrecked in 1629 on the Houtman Abrolhos, Western Australia', *The International Journal of Nautical Archaeology* 4(1): 43-64.

Green, J.N., S. Devendra, and R. Parthesius (eds). 1998. *Report for the Sri Lanka Department of Archaeology Galle Harbour Project 1996–1997 Archaeology, History, Conservation and Training*. Special publication (Australian National Centre of Excellence for Maritime Archaeology) 4. Fremantle: Western Australian Maritime Museum.

Hunter-Anderson, R.L. 1986. 'Yapese Social Stratification and Archaeological Consequences for the Study of Fishing Adaptation', in A. Anderson (ed.), *Traditional Fishing in the Pacific: Ethnographical and Archaeological Papers from the 15th Pacific Science Congress, 1983, Dunedin, N. Z.* Pacific Anthropological Records 37. Honolulu: Department of Anthropology, Bernice Pauahi Bishop Museum.

Jeffery, W.F. 2007. 'War Graves, Munition Dumps and Pleasure Grounds: A Post-Colonial Perspective of Chuuk Lagoon's Submerged World War II Sites', unpublished doctoral dissertation. Townsville: James Cook University. Retrieved 12 April 2012 from http://eprints.jcu.edu.au/2068/.

Jeffery, B. and W. Pitmag. 2010. 'The *Aech* of Yap: a Survey of Sites and their Histories', unpublished report. Colonia, Yap: Yap State Historic Preservation Office.

Kvarning, L.-Å.K. 1997. 'Vasa', in J. Delgado (ed.), *Encyclopedia of Underwater and Maritime Archaeology*. London: British Museum Press, 454-456.

Mahudi, H. 2011. 'Establishing a Maritime and Underwater Cultural Heritage Unit in Tanzania', in *Asia-Pacific Regional Conference on Underwater Cultural Heritage Proceedings*. Retrieved 10 April 2012 from the Museum of Underwater Archaeology Collection at http://www.themua.org/collections/items/show/1252.

Ministry of Education, Culture and Science. 2009. *Common Cultural Heritage Framework 2009-2012 (Bijlage a (engelse versie) van Beleidskader Gemeenschappelijk Cultureel Erfgoed 2009-2012)*. Retrieved 13 September 2012 from http://www.rijksoverheid.nl/documenten-en-publicaties/rapporten/2009/04/07/bijlage-a-engelse-versie-common-cultural-heritage-policy-framework-2009-2012.html.

O'Keefe, P.J. 2002. *Shipwrecked Heritage: A Commentary on the UNESCO Convention on Underwater Cultural Heritage*. Leicester: Institute of Art and Law.

Parthesius, R. 1998. *Archives and Wreckes: Australian-Dutch cooperation*, J. Green, M. Stanbury and F. Gaastra (eds). 1998. *The ANCODS Colloquium. Papers presented at the Australia-Netherlands Colloquium on Maritime Archaeology and Maritime History*. Special Publication - Australian National Centre of Excellence for Maritime Archaeology 3. Fremantle: Western Australian Maritime Museum, 68-74.

Parthesius, R. 2007. *Excavation report of the VOC-ship Avondster, The Anglo-Dutch East-Indiaman that was Wrecked Twice in Ceylon*. Centre of International Heritage Activities special publication 1. Amsterdam: Centre of International Heritage Activities.

Parthesius, R. 2010. *Dutch Ships in Tropical Waters. The Development of the Dutch East India Company (VOC) Shipping Network in Asia 1595-1660*. Amsterdam: Amsterdam University Press.

Parthesius, R., K. Millar, B. Jeffery. 2005. 'Preliminary Report on the Excavation of the 17th-Century Anglo-Dutch East-Indiaman Avondster in Bay of Galle, Sri Lanka', *International Journal of Nautical Archaeology* 34(2): 216-237.

Peattie, M.R. 1988. *Nan'yō: The Rise and Fall of the Japanese in Micronesia, 1885-1945*. Honolulu: University of Hawaii Press.

Rainbird, P. 1993. *Report on the Cultural Resource Management in the Coastal Area of Chuuk Lagoon*. Chuuk: Chuuk Historic Preservation Office.

Rule, M. 1982. *The Mary Rose, the Excavation and Raising of Henry VIII's Flagship*. London: Conway Maritime Press.

Sutton, J.E.G. 1998. *Archaeological Sites of East Africa: Four Studies; Special Volume*. Azania 33. Nairobi: The British Institute in Eastern Africa.

Takeda, J. 2001. 'Fishing-Gleaning Activities on Reef Flats and/or Reef Margins in Coral Ecosystem in Yap, Federated States of Micronesia (FSM)', in T. Aoyama, *The Progress Report of the 1999 Survey of the Research Project "Social Homeostasis of Small Islands in an Island-Zone": Yap Proper, Micronesia and Islands in Southern Japan.* Kagoshima University Research Center for the Pacific Islands, Occasional Papers 34. Kagoshima, Japan: Kagoshima University Research Center for the Pacific Islands, 117-127. Retrieved 13 September 2012 from http://cpi.kagoshima-u.ac. jp/publications/occasionalpapers/occasional/vol-34/34-14.pdf.

Underwood, J.H. 1969. 'Preliminary Investigations of Demographic Features and Ecological Variables of a Micronesian Population', *Micronesia* 5(1): 1-24.

UNESCO. 2001. *Convention on the Protection of Underwater Cultural Heritage, Paris, 2 November 2001.* Retrieved 10 April 2012 from http://www.unesco. org/new/en/culture/themes/underwater-cultural-heritage/

UNESCO. 2008. *Kilwa Draft Comprehensive Project Document.* unpublished manuscript, Dar es Salaam, Tanzania: UNESCO.

Useem, J. 1946. *Economic and Human Resources, Yap and Palau, West Carolines.* Honolulu: United States Commercial Company Economic Survey.

Yap Cultural Inventory Group. n.d., 'Traditional fishing in Yap', unpublished report. Colonia, Yap: Yap Historic Preservation Office.

2.6 The socio-political context of Polish archaeological discoveries in Faras, Sudan

Arkadiusz Klimowicz and Patrycja Klimowicz

Institute of Prehistory, Adam Mickiewicz
University Poznań, Poland

Abstract

The archaeological mission at Faras (Northern Sudan), headed by Professor Kazimierz Michałowski, is one of the most recognized and best-known efforts of Polish archaeology abroad. Despite the fact that the site was explored in the 1960s, the outcome is still considered a great success. Most probably, this is the result of large-scale publicity of the activities developed in Poland as well as in the international arena. Considering the fabulous discoveries, it is impossible to disregard their principal scientific inference, bringing to attention the great cultural and archaeological heritage of Sudan.

This paper presents the circumstances related to the excavation work at Faras by researchers from a communist state in Central-Eastern Europe. In particular, the authors shall look into the political and economic situation in the second half of the twentieth century, when the confrontation between two ideological blocks (communism and capitalism) – also known as 'the Cold War' – played a particular and infamous role. The unique ways of presenting the research achievements will be discussed, which simultaneously resulted in building up the importance of Polish archaeology abroad in the eyes of the citizens of the People's Republic of Poland.[1] Consequently, the paper highlights the effort that was made to popularize the excavation at Faras and its importance to Polish society at the time of communism. Short references to the contemporaneous situation in Sudan and the importance of the discoveries in the local communities will form complementary issues of this paper.

---

1   Eastern European countries governed by communist parties (widely known as 'the Communist States') used the term 'Countries of the People's Democracy'. Accordingly, Poland was called the *People's Republic of Poland* or the *Polish People's Republic*.

Résumé

Le contexte socio-politique des découvertes archéologiques polonaises à Faras, Soudan

La mission archéologique à Faras (au Soudan du Nord), présidée par le professeur Kazimierz Michałowski, est un des efforts les plus connus et les plus renommés de l'archéologie polonaise à l'étranger. Malgré le fait que le site avait été exploré dans les années 1960, le résultat est jusqu'à présent considéré comme une grande réussite. Ceci est sans doute grâce à une grande publicité faite en Pologne ainsi que sur la scène internationale, sur ces activités. Vu les fabuleuses découvertes, il est impossible de faire abstraction de leur inférence scientifique principale, attirant l'attention du grand patrimoine culturel et archéologique du Soudan.

Cet article présente les circonstances dans lesquelles les fouilles ont été effectuées à Faras, par des chercheurs d'un État communiste de l'Europe centrale et orientale. Les auteurs vont se pencher notamment sur la situation économique et politique durant la seconde partie du XXème siècle, quand l'affrontement entre deux blocs idéologiques (le communisme et le capitalisme) – également connu sous le nom de 'guerre froide' - jouait un rôle particulier et bien connu. Les méthodes uniques pour présenter les réalisations en terme de recherche seront discutées, ces méthodes ayant également renforcé l'importance de l'archéologie polonaise à l'étranger dans le regard des citoyens de la République populaire de Pologne.[2] L'article souligne donc l'effort que l'on a fait pour populariser les fouilles à Faras et leur importance pour la société polonaise à l'époque où le communisme régnait. De brèves références à la situation contemporaine au Soudan et à l'importance des découvertes pour les communautés locales, constitueront des questions complémentaires dans cet article.

Extracto

El marco sociopolítico de los descubrimientos arqueológicos polacos en Faras, Sudán

La misión arqueológica en Faras (Sudán del Norte), que es dirigida por el catedrático Kazimierz Michalowski, es uno de los esfuerzos más reconocidos y conocidos de la arqueología polaca en el extranjero. Pese al hecho de que el sitio fuera explorado en los años 60, se lo considera todavía un gran éxito. Esto, muy probablemente es el resultado de la publicidad a gran escala de las actividades que se desarrollan en Polonia tanto como en el campo internacional. Si se tienen en cuenta los maravillosos descubrimientos, es imposible ignorar su interferencia científica. Lleva a la atención el gran patrimonio cultural y arqueológico del Sudán.

---

2   Des pays d'Europe de l'Est, gouvernés pas des partis communistes (connu généralement sous le nom de 'États communistes') utilisaient le terme 'Pays de la démocratie du peuple'. Par conséquent, la Pologne était appelée la République du peuple de Pologne ou la République du Peuple Polonais (connu en français comme 'la République populaire de Pologne').

Este artículo muestra las circunstancias relacionadas al trabajo de excavación en Faras realizado por investigadores de un estado comunista en Europa Central y Oriental. Los autores analizarán en particular la situación política y económica en la segunda mitad del siglo veinte, cuando la confrontación entre los dos bloques ideológicos (el comunismo y el capitalismo) – también conocida como 'La Guerra Fría' – tuvo un papel peculiar e infame. Se discutirán las maneras únicas de presentar los logros de la investigación, que a la vez resultó en la construcción de importancia de la arqueología polaca en el extranjero para los habitantes de la República Popular de Polonia[3]. Por consiguiente el artículo destaca el esfuerzo que se hizo para popularizar la excavación en Faras y su importancia para la sociedad polaca durante la época del comunismo. Referencias breves a la situación contemporánea en Sudán y la importancia de los descubrimientos en las comunidades locales formarán cuestiones complementarias de este artículo.

ملخص

الإطار السياسي الاجتماعي للاكتشافات الأثرية البولندية في فرس، السودان

أركاديوش كليموويتش وبارتريسيا كليموويتش

معهد ما قبل العصور، جامعة آدم ميكيويتش، بوزنان، بولندا

ملخص

تعتبر البعثة الأثرية في فرس (شمال السودان)، التي يرأسها الأساتذة كازيمير ميكالوفسكي، أشهر جهود أثري بولندي أو أكثر مجهود تعترف به في ستينيات القرن العشرين، إلا أن المواقع تم استكشافها في استكشافه أن من من المغرم وبابالرغ. وبالخارج من الأحجار أن هذا كان نتيجة عداعية واسعة كبيرا. ومن الأحجار كبيرا. ومن النتائج التي تدعت تلت ان أن النسبة للمناطق الألنشطة التي تم تطويرها في فيها بولندا على الساحل وعلى الدولية. والسنبة الذي يئيسي العلمي الاها المستحيل إامال استدلاله العلمي الرئيسي إلفت الانتباه للتراث الثقافي والأثري الرائع في السودان.

وتقدم هذه الورقة المعتقلة بعمل حفريات في فرس قام بها هؤلاء من يحثون بشكل خاص، وبشكل خاص، سيتناول المحاضران وضع دولة شيوعية في وسط-شرق أوربا. وبشكل خاص، حيث تعب القرنين العشرين، النصف الثاني للقرن في الاقتصادي والسياسي والتي – (الشيوعية والرأسمالية) الأيديولوجيتين الكتلتين بين بين المواجهة كما سينشقنا. كما المجمعة. دورا خاصا وسيء وبشع ما أسفرت عن بناء أهمية علم لتي التي، للبحث، إنجازات البحث، الفريدة لتقديم الأساسي بالفريد في الأثار البولندي في الخارج في نظر مواطني جمهورية بولندا الشعبية[4] من أجل لتلقي للورقة على ضوء المجهود من المذبول وبالتالي، التقت نفس. عهد في البولندي المجتمع بالنسبة لهميتها وأهميتها في فرس وأهميتها في الحفريات ترويج

---

3   Los países europeos orientales que fueron gobernados por partidos comunistas (ampliamente conocidos como 'los Estados Comunistas'), solían usar la expresión 'los Países de la Democracia Popular'. En consecuencia, Polonia se llamaba la *República Popular de Polonia* o la *República Popular polaca*.

4   دول شرق أوربا التي كانت تحكمها أحزاب شيوعية (والتي هي معروفة على نطاق واسع بولندا سميت فقط لذلك، وفقا ".الشعبية الديمقراطية الدول" مصطلح "الدول الشيوعية") ".البولندية الشعبية الجمهورية" أو ".الشعبية بولندا بجمهورية".

الشيوعية. وستشكك بعض الإشارات القصيرة إلى الوضع الراهن في السودان
وأهمية الاكتشافات في المجتمعات المحلية قضايا إضافية في هذه الرواق.

Keywords

Faras, Polish archaeology abroad, Nubian Salvage Campaign, Kazimierz Michałowski

A historical background

The Polish archaeological mission at Faras was carried out as part of the Nubian Salvage Action. This international campaign under the auspices of the UNESCO was a reaction to the appeal of the government of the United Arab Republic of Egypt and of the government of Sudan, to help save the antiquities of ancient Nubia endangered by the construction of the Aswan great reservoir and the High Dam (El-Sadd Al-Ali) on the Middle Nile Valley at Aswan.[5]

At first sight the involvement of Poland in the project of saving the Nubian monuments fitted perfectly into the foreign policy of the Soviet Union, as well as other states of the Warsaw Pact.[6] Circumstances of the post-war world had been mainly shaped by the USSR and the USA, and concerned also spreading their influence on the African continent (Yahya 1989; Kreutz 1999; Borodziej 2005). The quest for a concession to construct the Aswan High Dam in the early 1960s was of considerable importance. Its outcome was to define the direction of development of post-colonial North Africa and determine the scope of domination of one of the two superpowers in the Middle East. The USA as well as the USSR focused their activities on diplomacy and generously granted assurance of long-term economic, engineering and financial aid, which was to tempt the United Arab Republic. As soon as the American government, displeased with the politics promoted by president Gamal Abdel-Nasser, withdrew their declarations of assistance in the financing of the construction of the gigantic dam, the Soviet Union immediately offered its help.[7]

The situation in the international arena seemingly favoured the prospects of developing Polish excavations on the Nile at that juncture. However, the coincidence of the interests of politicians and archaeologists was not the main factor deciding on the participation of Polish researchers in the Nubian project. One must make

---

5   The vast reservoir (c. 500 km long) created by taming the Nile at Aswan is variously named. The Sudanese call the southern part 'the Nubian Lake', while the greatest part of the water belongs to the territory of Egypt and is widely known as 'the Nasser Lake'.

6   The Warsaw Treaty was a mutual defence treaty, signed in 1955 by the Soviet Union, Poland, Czechoslovakia, Hungary, Bulgaria, Romania, East Germany and Albania. The Treaty of Friendship, Cooperation and Mutual Assistance, was also commonly known as the Warsaw Pact and from a military point of view it was the socialist counterpart of NATO.

7   The extending Soviet influence on the Middle East was demonstrated by the presence of Russian specialists who built the Aswan Dam and a modern air defence system in Egypt (Daigle 2004). In return for this *support*, thousands of Arab students had the opportunity to complete their cost-free university education in the Eastern European countries (Kreutz 1999).

clear at the start that by the middle of the 1950s, the concept of carrying out archaeological activities outside Poland had been treated as a bourgeois reverie, absolutely not worth spending public money on. Indeed the approach to conduct research in the Middle East was evidently against the 'real patriotic attitude' of the working class, whose labour serves the purpose of constructing the socialist republic between the Bug and Oder rivers. Nevertheless, the sixth decade of the twentieth century brought changes in the issue. At that time Professor Kazimierz Michałowski, the unquestioned precursor of the Polish School of Mediterranean Archaeology, decided to take an advantage of conducive conditions in the international arena and to develop scientific research abroad. From his point of view, the change in the wider political context made it possible to continue his activities, which were interrupted in 1939 and then brutally withheld by the communist regime for over ten years (see also Klimowicz and Klimowicz, this volume).

These unpleasant experiences (*i.e.* the World War II and the Stalinist period) almost certainly affected his further approach that is distinguished by a 'neutral' attitude and avoiding any deep political and ideological engagements. Consequently, one of the golden rules transferred by Michałowski, and strictly maintained in the School, was that involvement with policy had a deleterious influence on the discipline. Taking this into consideration, the major aim was to limit relationships with the communist government to a minimum and to exploit the affairs in a unilateral manner. The most noticeable example of the resilient posture towards the authorities had been demonstrated by clever use of the circumstances that occurred in the 1960s, in order to simplify the complex administrative procedures. Consequently, the argument that the excavation work in the Middle East was a matter of international assistance, supported by the UNESCO and officially approved by the Soviet Union, unquestionably made it easier for the members of the expedition to obtain passports, visas and some funding from the budget of the People's Republic of Poland.

Besides officially representing a country belonging to the Soviet Bloc, the researchers did not get involved in international politics. In this sense the activities of the Polish archaeologists abroad have been considered as 'neutral' from the point of view of the East-West confrontation (Szafrański 2007: 55-56). From the very beginning of the missions on the Nile, the work was nothing but academic research, resulting in great scientific achievements. Additionally, their success was strengthened by the fact that the United Arab Republic, Sudan and several newly constituted states in decolonized Africa were searching for their own identity and preferred to host researchers from countries with which they had never had a colonial past (Michałowski 1974a: 30, 47-48; Hassan 1998: 207-209).

The Poles at Faras

The archaeologists led by Professor Kazimierz Michałowski were amongst the first to actively participate in the International Nubian Programme (Michałowski 1959; Hassan 2007: 81; see also Klimowicz and Klimowicz, this volume). Initially, they were only involved in salvage excavations in Egypt. It was at the end of

1960 that the Polish Centre of Mediterranean Archaeology (PCMA) in Cairo was officially invited by the Sudan Antiquities Service to conduct rescue work beyond the second cataract in the Sudanese part of Nubia (Klimowicz and Klimowicz, this volume). Professor Michałowski agreed to expand his archaeological activities to the south in the same campaign, as the Sudanese government offered the very attractive condition that half of the recovered finds would be given to the National Museum in Warsaw. The possibility of obtaining such exquisite exhibits was a decisive argument according to Michałowski, who believed that Polish archaeology could otherwise not afford such excavations for research purposes only. He used to argue that the people of Poland should be able to have direct contact with the real outcome of archaeological work (Michałowski 1974a).

In this context one must realize that Poland has always been at a geographical distance from the great centres of antiquity (Natunewicz 1967: 279-280). Compared with West-European institutions, the financial distance was also noticeable. The difficult economic circumstance of Polish archaeology was caused by a total dependence on public money, gathered and distributed by the 'Polish United Workers' Party'. In this regard, the discipline was still treated as a bourgeois science and it suffered from ongoing under-financing. Therefore, Michałowski realized that the only way to change the general attitude of the officials towards his research abroad was to provide a discovery that would make him an acknowledged authority again.

Having a choice of several sites that were suggested by Jean Vercoutter, the Director of the Sudan Antiquities Service, professor Michałowski chose the concession at Faras, which was a small village destined to become submerged by the rising waters of the Nile. The site was located just on the border with Egypt, north of the second cataract near Wadi Halfa (figure 1). The decision was based on an archaeological inquiry, which had indicated a large soil heap (Great *Kom*), surmounted by ruins of an Arab citadel, and thus a promising site.[8]

A rapid academic and diplomatic effort resulted in the start of the work as early as February 1961 (Michałowski 1974a: 77-78, 1974b: 248). The concession of the Sudanese authorities included an area of 7.5 hectares to be explored by the Polish team (Michałowski 1980; Żurawski 2002: 27). Unfortunately the first season only lasted four weeks, as the PCMA was involved in several projects in Egypt simultaneously and did not have enough funds to continue the research in Sudan. Not only was the financial status of the expedition poor, the team had no car and no local workers were available either. Whoever needed a job had already found employment in American and Scandinavian projects (Michałowski 1974b: 248-250). This was not caused by better social or financial conditions, since the wages for workers was the same in every expedition of the salvage campaign (Jakobielski,

---

8   An archive prospection was supported by an in-depth investigation of available files comprising data about previous excavations at Faras. The latter was based mainly on the results of an Oxford expedition between 1910–1912 and conducted by F.L. Griffith (1921). The result of those excavations brought to light 40 sandstone blocks inscribed with the name of Thotmes III (Żurawski 2002: 27-28). However, due to the presence of the modern village of Faras on the slopes of the Great *Kom*, Griffith's team was unable to excavate the mound.

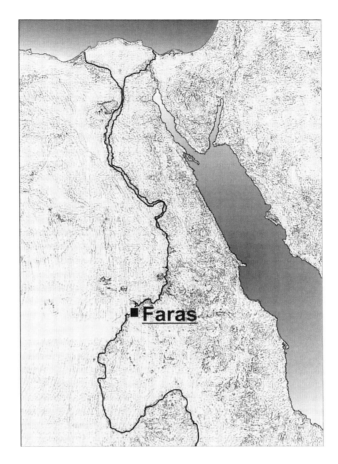

Figure 1. The location of the archaeological site at Faras
(Illustration: A. Klimowicz).

pers. comm.). Most probably it was caused by a delayed start of the work and a general scepticism that there would be interesting archaeological finds under the mound of sand.

Despite these adversities at the beginning of the expedition, the strategy of conducting a 'big dig' soon brought visible results (Żurawski 2002: 28-29). A single large trench, that was meant to reveal the stratigraphy of the site, yielded fragments of a magnificent cathedral that was decorated with frescoes dating back to the Early Christian period (figure 2). Especially two of the discovered mural paintings, Madonna with Child and Archangel Michael in the chapel of Bishop Johannes evoked huge interest, not only among archaeologists but also with the local and international public.

It is important to note that the site of Faras was located in the al-Marīs region, which has been inhabited essentially by Nubians. Most of the workers (*fellaheen*) that were employed during the excavation campaign were *Mahas* (or with a more Arabic sound: *Mahasī*). These inhabitants seem to have occupied the same area,

Figure 2. Model of the Faras Cathedral and a complex of associated buildings (Current collection of the National Museum in Warsaw. Photo: P. Klimowicz).

between the second and third cataract, longer than any other Arab tribe (Hasan 2010a: 143-145). They continued to speak a Nubian dialect, maintaining a large body of genealogical traditions. The present form of the (genealogical) traditions indicates a long term of compilation and a high degree of Arabization (Hasan 2010a: 135-136, 2010b: 47-53). However, the *Mahas* were able to trace their ancestors back to a remote period of time. This illustrates the Nubians extraordinary approach to history. It is characterized by a sensitivity to any evidence of the past. Consequently, the contemporary inhabitants (as well as the *fellaheen* in the 1960s) consider the Christian heritage as part of the long-term Nubian identity.

Most probably this sort of perception results from the general pattern of the Islamization that seems to have been a peaceful process (Hasan 2010b: 209). Hence, Christianity is recognized as a relatively lengthy chapter of Sudanese history, which was gradually superseded by the Islamic faith. Taking this into account, it is no wonder that the *Mahas* expressed awareness and devoted much attention to exposing the cathedral at Faras. It thus seems reasonable to say that there was a deeper motive for their involvement other than the frequent astonishing discoveries.

This led eventually to an increased number of workers at the end of the first excavation season, as local people suddenly wanted to work for the Polish mission (Michałowski 1974b: 249). They were probably encouraged by the newspapers that kept readers posted on the results of the excavation and by the Sudan Post, which issued occasional series of stamps with reproductions of discovered murals while the exploration was still in progress (Jakobielski, pers. comm.). The most remarkable fact was that Christian motives appeared on the stamps, such as the

Figure 3. Mural painting featuring the Nativity of Jesus uncovered in the North Aisle of the Cathedral at Faras. This reproduction was used by the Sudanese National Postal services on its stamps (Current collection of the Sudan National Museum in Khartoum. Photo: A. Chlebowski).

Nativity of Jesus (figure 3). It was interpreted as the ultimate demonstration of approval of the archaeological achievements, given that Islam was the national religion.

Michałowski demonstrated again his unusual organizational skills when he managed to restart the work at the Great *Kom* in the autumn of the same year (Michałowski 1965: 5). This circumstance is particular worth emphasizing, taking into consideration the troublesome restrictions of the Polish financial system. Unfortunately, he was exceptionally modest in his publications and did not reveal the exact arguments he had used in the negotiations with the regime officials. It is even more difficult to determine the conditions that the authorities proposed in return for further co-financing the excavations. He did show that he was self-confident. This is best expressed in his article with the telling title 'Chasing the Lost Time' (1974b), in which he described his undisturbed optimism after the end of the first season: "Unfortunately, we ran out of money and all we had to do was break camp and return to Cairo. But at that point I had no doubts that we hit the jackpot and that there would be no problem finding funds for further exploration" (249-250).

During the following four months of work the sand deposits inside and outside the structure were removed, preparing the church for thorough exploration (Michałowski 1974a: 164-165). It was only during the following two expeditions that the monumental foundations of the basilica were uncovered. The find turned out to be one of the finest specimens of Early Christian architecture and art, dating back to the period between the eighth and twelfth century AD (Michałowski 1964: 325).

In the course of four excavation periods at Faras, over 120 brilliantly coloured religious (Coptic-Byzantine) frescoes were discovered in the church and in associated buildings. They were more magnificent in their design and preservation than any other that had been discovered so far in the Middle Nile Valley and they were published in the most renowned newspapers and magazines in the world. The international press headlined the discoveries as 'The Faras Miracle' (Michałowski 1974b: 250; Żurawski 2002: 27). Of all breathtaking frescoes, presenting bishops as well as scenes from the Bible, the portrait of St. Anna quickly became the most

igure 4. Fragment of fresco featuring Saint Anna (mid eighth century AD), uncovered in the North Aisle of the Cathedral at Faras. The mural painting is known also as 'Mona Lisa from Faras' (Current collection of the National Museum in Warsaw. Photo: P. Klimowicz).

recognizable symbol of the Polish expedition at Faras (figure 4). People from all over the world were enchanted by the charm of this portrait, that was painted on the wall of the basilica in the middle of the eighth century AD. The mural was so admirable that it soon was called the 'Mona Lisa from Faras' (Michałowski 1966: 198).

The results of the work became widely recognized, also by the international scientific community, as the most prominent discovery of Polish Mediterranean Archaeology. The international research authorities that were participating in the Nubian salvage campaign also expressed their admiration for the sensational discoveries near Wadi Halfa. They used to say that "the Poles hit the jackpot in the Nubian lottery" (Michałowski 1983: 63). In addition, the inscriptions in Greek, Old-Nubian and Coptic that were discovered inside the cathedral constituted a tremendous contribution to the history of Nubia (Jakobielski 1986: 90). Especially the so-called 'Bishops' List' was of great importance for determining the historical chronology. It contains the names of the 28 bishops of the old *Pachoras* from the beginning of the capital city until the end of the twelfth century (Jakobielski 1986). The tombs of bishops, a monastery, an Eparchs' palace and a sixth century church that were found beneath the ruins of the cathedral, also helped to extend the chronology of the religious tradition.

Figure 5. Mural painting featuring the Archangel Michael with Three Youths, uncovered in Bishop Johannes's chapel at Faras (Current collection of the Sudan National Museum in Khartoum. Photo: A. Chlebowski).

When people referred to the world famous excavations, no word of praise was too much to honour the interdisciplinary team, which was working under tremendous time pressure, as all the relics had to be properly recorded and removed before the water of the vast artificial Nile reservoir would sweep them away (Emery 1965: 98). The hectic situation is illustrated by the fact that the fourth and last excavation season (1964) was completed only four months before the site was flooded. In this context, the term 'rescue archaeology' seems all too meaningful.

As a result of this institutionalized sharing of monuments by the Sudan Antiquities Service, they retained 37 frescoes, including the two largest (the Nativity and the Archangel Michael with Three Youths, see figure 5). The remaining 62 paintings and various other unique objects (*i.e.* ceramics, bronze artefacts, stone sculptures, decorative architectural elements, and fragments of textiles) became part of the collection of the National Museum in Warsaw (Michałowski 1964: 328, 1966: 198, 1974a: 172; Jeżewska 1966: 110; Żurawski 2002: 30-31).

Public and scientific reverberations of Faras in communist Poland

Although the monuments arrived in Poland in 1964, they were not presented to the public until two years later, as time-consuming conservation work had to be done to save the priceless frescoes. In 1966 a temporary exhibition of the world-famous mural paintings was opened in the National Museum in Warsaw (Michałowski 1966: 198-208). A few years later the Sudanese part of the collection was also displayed in Khartoum.

With regard to post-excavation work, due to a lack of specialists from Sudan, mainly Polish experts were responsible for the conservation, analysis and interpretation of both assemblages. For instance, the restorers worked simultaneously in the two countries. In Khartoum they were supervised by H. Jędrzejewska, whereas J. Gazy managed the renovation in Warsaw. Apart from the restorers, multiple other Polish professionals and students contributed substantially to the multidimensional elaboration of the data (Jakobielski 1972; Kubińska 1974; Godlewski 1979; Karkowski 1981; Martens-Czarnecka 1982; Dzierżykray-Rogalski 1985).

When discussing the question of popularization by the media, one must not overlook the fact that there was no private television in communist Poland, nor was there any private radio station or independent press. Any programme published by the state-owned stations and agencies was carefully planned or rather watchfully censored (Lech 1998).[9] This pertained especially to news from the world at the other side of the 'the Iron Curtain'.

---

9   '*The Central Office for Control the Press, Publications and Public Performances*' operated in Poland until 1989 as an official censorship institution restricting the freedom of speech within the state-owned broadcast stations and press agencies.

The huge interest of the public in the 'miracle of Faras' did not escape the notice of the authorities. They could have treated the apparent sacral nature of the discoveries as inappropriate in terms of communistic ideology. Religion used to be treated in contemporaneous Poland as 'opium for the people', and to the communist regime, the major religious institution in the country (the Roman Catholic Church) was nothing but the enemy, 'influenced and subsidized by imperialist states' (Natunewicz 1967: 280-281).

Nevertheless, it appeared that the international publicity, initiated by Michałowski, could not be easily denied or restricted in Poland, mainly due to the world-wide recognition of Faras and the authority Michałowski had gained. His wisdom, eloquence and persuasive power made the government regard the excavation of an Early Christian Cathedral as the greatest achievement of the Polish researchers and worth subsidizing. In this situation there was nothing left for the cultural policy officials but to formally assume a supporting attitude towards archaeological activities abroad. It was in fact the last chance to turn Michałowski's triumph to their advantage and to demonstrate the political correctness of the communist state, tolerating inimical ideologies (Jakobielski, pers.comm.).

Judging by the number of realized audio-video productions and articles published in the press, the regime authorities most probably believed that the publicity regarding the spectacular results of the Polish archaeologists did not pose any threat to the *socio-cultural order* of the Party. Looking back, one may say that the contemporaneous society witnessed a hitherto unparalleled large-scale and well-organized information action which was to promote the activity of the Polish research in Nubia.

The monographs (Michałowski 1962, 1965), as well as the numerous academic papers on Faras, were probably read only by a small circle of those archaeologists interested in the subject. The most important role in popularizing the Polish achievements during the UNESCO operation of safeguarding the Nubian monuments was played by journalists. One of them was Kazimierz Dziewanowski (1965), who actively participated in the excavations at Faras in 1963 and vividly described the efforts of archaeologists saving the endangered monuments in his book '*Archangels and Jackals. A Report From Before the Flood*'. Another popular-scientific work worth noticing is '*At the Limits of Time*', by Zofia Jeżewska (1966). She was a reporter of the Polish Radio, accredited to archaeological missions during the Nubian Campaign. Based on her voyage to the Middle East she wrote a diary-style book with personal reflections and memories of the time she spent at Faras. Also remarkable was the documentary film made in 1965 by Aleksandra Jaskólska, '*The Frescoes of Faras*'.[10] It presented the history of saving the unique collection of murals from the lost Christian Kingdom of Nubia.

Faras reached its peak of popularity in Poland at the beginning of the 1970s. At that time many actions were taken to present the Nubian treasures to society. For instance, the Polish Post issued in April 1971 a limited series of stamps and postcards featuring the frescoes from Faras (figure 6).

---

10   The original Polish title is '*Freski z Faras*'.

Should be "Figure 6. Limited series of stamps featuring the frescoes discovered at Faras. The collection was issued by the Polish Post in April 1971, to promote Polish archaeological achievements (Photo: Polish Post).

But the most important event for the popularization of Polish archaeology abroad took place in 1972. At that time, the Nubian Art Gallery was officially opened in the National Museum in Warsaw, as an accompanying event of the Second Nubiological Conference. Apart from the opening ceremony, the primarily goal of the meeting was to stregthen mutual scientific relationships, in order to expand the knowledge and discuss issues associated with the results of the archaeological work that was carried out during the salvage campaign of 1960-1967. This led to the establishment of the International Society for Nubian Studies (ISNS), which gathered prominent scholars from all over the world. They soon realized that the scope of interests required a new field within the framework of oriental studies (Jakobielski 1986: 90; Żurawski 2002: 31). In this regard, the advent of Nubiology as a separate discipline can be seen as a result of the need to undertake elaborate research in the art and archaeology of the Meroitic and Christian civilizations that flourished from the third until the fourteenth/fifteenth century AD in the current territory of Northern Sudan and Southern Egypt. Due to a substantial contribution of Polish archaeologists to the subject and to the world's largest permanent exhibition of Nubian art, Warsaw was *the* centre of Nubian studies at that time (Michałowski 1983: 64).

The next stage in publishing the achievements of the Polish archaeologists was Michałowski's book '*From Edfu to Faras*' (1974a), a collection of plainly written memoirs referring to the sites in Egypt and Sudan presenting the subsequent stages of development of the Polish School of Mediterranean Archaeology. Faras occupies a special place in the author's reflections. For him the excavations at Great *Kom* were a great challenge and its sensational results would become the PCMA's showpiece (Michałowski 1974a, 1980). A year later, another noteworthy documentary was made, by Tomasz Pobóg-Malinowski ('*The Frescoes of Faras*'). It was the final chord of the unsurpassed popularization action of the excavation results.

During that period the press, radio and television devoted relatively much time to promote the contribution of the Polish researchers to the rescue of the heritage of Nubia. The contemporaneous Polish society, which was experiencing the ups and down of the centrally planned economy, desperately wanted news from a world that was free of rigorously rationed products and goods. Unfortunately, the prospect of complex passport procedures limited, if not completely eliminated, the possibilities of travelling for the average Polish citizen. This might have been one of the reasons why the general public was so interested in the information from the Middle Valley of the Nile, which transported the reader or viewer to a world full of mysteries, exotics and the Middle Eastern sun. The discoveries not only brought interested recipients closer to an unknown attractive region, they also expanded their cultural and educational horizons. The archaeological activities abroad stimulated a cosmopolitan attitude.

Political circumstances accompanying the excavations at Faras

The relationships between the 'Countries of the People's Democracy' were a complex matter (Milisauskas 1998: 223). For instance the People's Republic of Poland (PRP), as the second state of 'the Eastern Bloc' in regard to size, was totally dependent on the USSR concerning diplomacy and relationships with the outside world. This subordination was demonstrated in the foreign policy of the PRP, which totally corresponded with the Soviet Union's standpoint (Borodziej 2005: 15-17). This reliance counted on taking the same position as Moscow and on conducting negotiations with other nations along with the Soviet approach of extending the sphere of influence. The contacts of the Polish with the Middle Eastern and Near Eastern states were considered as strategic and of utmost importance.[11]

In the light of the political situation of the early 1960s, Michałowski deserves recognition and respect as the organizer of great archaeological missions abroad. He had the unusual skill of coping with adverse situations and to maintain a balance between scientific concerns and political involvement. He took the opportunity to improve the relationship between Middle Eastern and Soviet

---

[11] The amicable relationship of Egypt, under the presidency of Nasser, with the Soviet Union came to an end with the presidency of Anwar al-Sadat (1970-1981). Consequently, in 1972 all Soviet experts and military advisors as well as some diplomats from Eastern Bloc Countries were expelled from Egypt in an insulting way (Saliba 1975; Daigle 2004). In addition, Eastern archaeological institutions and research centres that reported to Ministries of Foreign Affairs (*e.g.* from Czechoslovakia and Hungary) were temporarily closed (Jakobielski 2001). The expulsion of the Soviet personnel emphasized the new Egyptian direction and an inclination towards the United States.

Bloc states in order to continue the research and to develop the Polish School of Mediterranean Archaeology, which was of utmost importance to him. Thanks to his charismatic personality, he could convince the communist authorities to increase the funds for the research at Faras. One must not forget that after World War II, the Polish communist government accomplished a Soviet-like economic regime of nationalization and expropriation of private property (Lech 1998) and of a centralized industry and business in the hands of the ruling party ('the Polish United Workers' Party'). This made the government the one and only depositor of funds and the exclusive funder of archaeological research. A private sector was missing.

Moreover, if researchers were planning to carry out archaeological digs abroad, they had to find a way to organize the so-called 'hard currency'. However, legal access to a reliable and stable currency (*i.e.* US Dollars) required a lot of effort and industriousness in the People's Republic of Poland. The main reason was that the exchange rate regime was entirely controlled by the centrally planned economy in an attempt to limit the internal circulation of foreign currencies. In practice it meant that scientific institutions, like universities, were only allowed to deposit foreign currency in the state-owned bank and the money could only be used during authorized (by the government) travel abroad.

The strict control of the internal circulation of foreign currencies within Poland implied that the budget of all archaeological activities that were carried out abroad, had to be deposited in a special bank account with the Ministry of Finance. This simplified the process of authorized exchange and of receiving money (Jakobielski 2001).

The forceful insertion of the Marxist-Leninist dogma into scientific writings was another academic reality of the communist time in Poland (Lech 1998; Milisauskas 1998). A reinterpretation of history in the spirit of Marxism and *materialism* was more than welcomed. It was also widely known among the authors that references to *class distinction* and *frictions* were sometimes necessary if government subsidies for academic projects were to be received. However, the total amount of ideologically motivated interpretations in archaeology is relatively small. There were very few dedicated Marxists among the Polish scholars in the Humanities, and only a minority (15%) had an official Polish United Workers' Party affiliation (Natunewicz 1967: 280; Milisauskas 1998: 226).

It is noticeable that none of the different types of publications that dealt with the discoveries at Faras promoted communist theory. The fact that the activity of the Polish mission was scientific in nature is owed to professor Michałowski. Thanks to him the entire Nubian salvage programme as well as further activities were not involved with politics, not during the excavations nor in any writings that followed (see also Klimowicz and Klimowicz, this volume).

Conclusion

The aim of this brief historical background is to present the external conditions under which Polish archaeological projects were conducted in the Middle East. The domestic restrictions of the strict communist administration greatly influenced researches outside the country. The general diplomatic policy of the People's Republic of Poland fulfilled a task given by the Soviet Union. In spite of persistent attempts by the communist authorities to convert the Centre of Mediterranean Archaeology into a cultural institution subordinated to the Ministry of Foreign Affairs, the PCMA successfully sustained its academic position (Jakobielski 2001). It could develop its studies without serious turbulences. The seemingly unpleasant conditions constituted incomparable vivid scientific activity in Northern Sudan. Faras became the focal point of the presence of Polish archaeology abroad, both in the eyes of the home country and in the international arena. The autonomous attitude of the PCMA and Polish School of Mediterranean Archaeology also has had remarkable meaning in the context of the permanently altering socio-political configurations during the twentieth century. In particular the East-West confrontation shows how policy could have a deleterious influence on science, especially on research abroad.

In a social sense, the beginning of the Nubian salvage campaign marked an increased popularity of the discipline among the general public. It cannot be measured in figures of course, but the integrated activities using a wide range of opinion-making media clearly affected the fascination with archaeology.

Also remarkable is the exchange of students and experts between Sudan and Poland, that could take place for over 40 years (see also note 4). The main objective was to alter the lack of Sudanese professionals, which had been noticed already during the Nubian salvage campaign. As a consequence, many of the inspectors employed in the Sudan Antiquities Service today still identify themselves with the Polish scholarship (Szafrański 2007: 53). Their presence and full credit studies in Poland surely strengthened the relationship between the countries. In recognition of professor Michałowski's merits in saving the Nubian monuments, the government of Sudan even decided to create favourable conditions for Polish archaeologists, allowing them to continue their work at Old Dongola, the former capital of the ancient united Christian Nubian Kingdoms (Michałowski 1983).

Presently, the scientific community still considers Faras as one of the most significant *milestone*s in the development of Polish archaeology abroad (Szafrański 2007). The unique collection of murals remains a widely recognized symbol of professor Michałowski's legacy (Żurawski 2002: 32). A miniature of the 'Mona Lisa of Faras' became a graphic sign, promoting the National Museum in Warsaw. Her portrait is featured on the tickets allowing entrance to the Nubian Art Gallery where the magnificent original is on permanent display.

Acknowledgements

We would like to express our honest gratitude to dr Stefan Jakobielski for his generous scientific merit as well as for sharing his memories with us. We would also like to thank Arkadiusz Marciniak for his support and Sarunas Milisauskas for the series of conversations about his experiences during communist Poland. We are extremely grateful for the assistance and help in preparing the text for print to Sjoerd van der Linde, Corijanne Slappendel, Monique van den Dries and Nina Schücker, as well as to all scholars who participated in the Archaeology Abroad Project.

References

Borodziej, W. 2005. 'Polityka Zagraniczna Polskiej Rzeczpospolitej Ludowej w Roku 1972 – Szkic do Dyskusji', *Polski Przegląd Dyplomatyczny* 5(1): 15-33.

Daigle, C.A. 2004. 'The Russians are Going: Sadat, Nixon and the Soviet Presence in Egypt', *Middle East Review of International Affairs* 8(1): 1-15.

Dzierżykray-Rogalski, T. 1985. *Faras VIII. The Bishops of Faras. An Anthropological-Medical Study*. Warsaw: PWN.

Dziewanowski, K. 1965. *Archanioły i Szakale. Reportaż Sprzed Potopu*. Warszawa: Iskry.

Emery, W.B. 1965. *Egypt in Nubia*. London: Hutchinson of London.

Godlewski, W. 1979. *Faras VI. Les Baptisteres Nubiens*. Warsaw: PWN.

Griffith, F.L. 1921. 'Oxford Excavations in Nubia', *University of Liverpool Annales of Archaeology and Anthropology* 8.

Hasan, Y.F. 2010a. *The Arabs and the Sudan. From the Seventeenth to the Early Sixteenth Century* (fifth reprint). Khartoum: Sudatek Limited.

Hasan, Y.F. 2010b. *Studies in Sudanese History.* Khartoum: Sudatek Limited.

Hassan, D.T. 1998. 'Memorabilia: Archaeological Materiality and National Identity in Egypt', in L. Meskel (ed.), *Archaeology Under Fire. Nationalism, Politics and Heritage in the Eastern Mediterranean and Middle East*. London: Routledge, 200-216.

Hassan, F.A. 2007. 'The Aswan High Dam and the International Rescue Nubia Campaign', *African Archaeological Review* 24, 73-94.

Jakobielski, S. 1972. *Faras III. A History of the Bishopric of Pachoras*. Warsaw: Éditions Scientifiques de Pologne.

Jakobielski, S. 1986. 'Faras', in Z. Kiss (ed.), *50 Lat Polskich Wykopalisk w Egipcie I na Bliskim Wschodzie*. Warszawa: Uniwersytet Warszawski, 85-90.

Jakobielski, S. 2001. 'Taki był Profesor'. *Podkowiański Magazyn Kulturalny* 4-1(31/32). Retrieved 10 January 2011 from http://free.art.pl/podkowa.magazyn/nr3132/michalowski.htm.

Jeżewska, Z. 1966. *Na Krańcach Czasu. Dziennik Podróży po Egipcie i Sudanie*. Warszawa: Czytelnik.

Karkowski, J. 1981. *Faras V. The Pharaonic Inscriptions from Faras*. Warsaw: PWN.

Kreutz, A. 1999. 'Post-Communist Eastern Europe and the Middle East: the Burden of History and New Political Realities', *Arab Studies Quarterly* 21(2). Retrieved 10 January 2011 from http://findarticles.com/p/articles/mi_m2501/is_2_21/ai_55683884/pg_4/?tag=mantle_skin;content.

Kubińska, J. 1974. *Faras IV. Inscriptions Grecques Chrétiennes*. Warsaw: Éditions scientifiques de Pologne.

Lech, J. 1998. 'Between Captivity and Freedom, Polish Archaeology in the 20th Century', *Archeologia Polona* 35-36: 25-222.

Martens-Czarnecka, M. 1982. *Faras VII. Les Elements Décoratifs sur les Peintures de la Cathédrale de Faras*. Warsaw: PWN.

Michałowski, K. 1959. 'The Polish Archaeological Reconnaissance Trip to Nubia', *Review of the Polish Academy of Sciences* 6(3): 47-85.

Michałowski, K. (ed.). 1962. *Faras – Fouilles Polonaises 1961*. Warszawa: PWN.

Michałowski, K. 1964. 'Archeologia Śródziemnomorska w Ostatnim Dwudziestoleciu w Polsce Ludowej', *Meander* 19: 315-328.

Michałowski, K. (ed.). 1965. *Faras – Fouilles Polonaises 1961-1962*. Warszawa: PWN.

Michałowski, K. 1966. 'The Warsaw National Museum: the New Section of Copto-Byzantine Art', *Museum International* 19(3), 198-208.

Michałowski, K. 1974a. *Od Edfu do Faras. Polskie Odkrycia Archeologii Śródziemnomorskiej*. Warszawa: Wydawnictwa Artystyczne i Filmowe.

Michałowski, K. 1974b. 'Polska Archeologia w Pogoni za Straconym Czasem', in W.H. Boulton, *Wieczność Piramid i Tragedia Pompei*. Warszawa: Wiedza Powszechna, 231-256.

Michałowski, K. 1980. 'Faras, Polish Contribution to the Nubian Campaign', in A. Zajączkowski (ed.), *African Studies in Poland*. Warsaw: Polish Scientific Publishers, 19-28.

Michałowski, K. 1983. 'Polish Mediterranean Archaeology', in W. Tyloch (ed.), *Oriental Studies in the Sixty Years of Independent Poland*. Warsaw: Polish Scientific Publishers, 59-64.

Milisauskas, S. 1998. 'Observations on Polish Archeology 1945-1995', *Archeologia Polona* 35-36: 223-236.

Natunewicz, C.F. 1967. 'The Classics in Post War Poland', *Classical World* 60(7): 271-282.

Saliba, N.E. 1975. 'The Decline of Nasirism in Sadat's Egypt', *World Affairs* 138(1): 51-59.

Szafrański, Z.E. 2007. 'Our Milestones', in E. Laskowska-Kusztal (ed.), *Seventy Years of Polish Archaeology in Egypt*. Warsaw: Wydawnictwa Uniwersytetu Warszawskiego, 41-64.

Yahya, A.M. 1989. *Egypt and the Soviet Union 1955-1972. A Study in the Power of the Small State*. Washington: Harbinger Distributors.

Żurawski, B. 2002. 'Taming the Nile. Polish Archaeology within the Cataracts', *Archaeologia Polona* 40: 23-50.

The Main documentary films mentioned in the paper

Jaskólska, A. 1965. *Freski z Faras*. Łódź: Wytwórnia Filmów Oświatowych.

Pobóg-Malinowski, T. 1975. *Freski z Faras*. Warszawa: Impress-Film.

2.7 ITALIAN ARCHAEOLOGY IN AFRICA: THE ARDUOUS LIBERATION OF A DISCIPLINE FROM COLONIAL IDEOLOGY

Maria Pia Guermandi

Institute for Cultural Heritage,
Region Emilia Romagna, Italy

Abstract

The article highlights the cultural experience of Italian archaeologists in Africa (Libya and Ethiopia) stretching over a century up to the recent political turmoil. During the colonial period (1911–1943), archaeological initiatives went hand in hand with political ones. Italian archaeology in Libya remained substantially focused on classical archaeology until the 1980s. During the fascist period (1922–1943), archaeology became a tool for supporting Mussolini's propaganda based on an alleged continuity of the Augustan Empire. After the Second World War, the missions were no longer a 'cultural' tool serving the colonial ambitions of the Kingdom of Italy and the fascist regime, and they were restored to the realm of a discipline exclusively at the service of scientific research.

A shared trait of archaeological experiences in Libya and Ethiopia is the lack of an explicit, coherent archaeological research policy. The author hopes that Italian archaeology will succeed in transforming the discipline of erudition and aseptic research into a cultural initiative in a wide sense.

Résumé

L'archéologie italienne en Afrique : la pénible libération d'une discipline de l'idéologie coloniale

L'article souligne l'expérience culturelle des archéologues italiens en Afrique (Libye et Éthiopie) depuis plus d'un siècle jusqu'aux récents bouleversements politiques. Pendent la période coloniale (1911-1943) les initiatives archéologiques sont allées de pair avec les initiatives politiques. L'archéologie italienne en Afrique est restée considérablement axées sur l'archéologie classique, jusqu'aux années 1980. Au cours de la période fasciste (1922-1943) l'archéologie est devenue un instrument de soutien de la propagande de Mussolini, fondée sur la continuité présumée de l'Empire d'Auguste. Après la deuxième guerre mondiale, les missions n'étaient plus un instrument 'culturel' au service des ambitions coloniales du royaume d'Italie et du régime fasciste, mais redevenaient la partie d'une discipline exclusivement dédiée à la recherche scientifique.

Le trait commun des expériences archéologiques en Libye et en Éthiopie est le manque d'une politique de recherche cohérente et explicite. L'auteur espère que l'archéologie italienne réussira à transformer la discipline de recherche érudite et aseptisée en une initiative culturelle au sens large du terme.

Extracto

La arqueología italiana en África: la liberación complicada de una disciplina de la ideología colonial

El artículo destaca la experiencia cultural de arqueólogos italianos en África (Libia y Etiopia) que cubre un periodo de más de un siglo hasta la reciente confusión política. Durante la época colonial (1911-1943) las iniciativas arqueológicas iban acompañadas de las políticas. La arqueología italiana en Libia permaneció sustancialmente enfocada en la arqueología clásica hasta los años 80 del siglo pasado. Durante la época fascista (1922- 1943) la arqueología llegó a ser un instrumento para apoyar la propaganda de Mussolini, que se basaba en una supuesta continuidad del Imperio de Augusto. Después de la Segunda Guerra Mundial las misiones dejaron de ser un instrumento 'cultural' que servía las ambiciones coloniales del Reino de Italia y del régimen fascista, y lograron ser restauradas en el ámbito de una disciplina que se dedica exclusivamente a la investigación científica.

Un rasgo común de las experiencias arqueológicas en Libia y Etiopia es la falta de una política arqueológica investigadora coherente y específica. El autor espera que la arqueología italiana logre transformar la disciplina de erudición y de investigación aséptica en una iniciativa cultural en un sentido amplio.

ملخص

علم الآثار الإيطالي في أفريقيا: التحرير الشاق لميدان بحث من أيديولوجية الاستعمار

ماري بيا جرمندي

معهد التراث الثقافي، منطقة إميليا رومانيا، إيطاليا

يلقي هذا المقال الضوء على تجربة إيطاليين ثقافية في أفريقيا (ليبيا واثيوبيا) والتي تمتد عبر فترة تزيد عن قرن حتى الاضطرابات المتبادلة الراهنة (1943-1911)، الاستعمار خلال فترة الاستعمار. السياسة الأخيرة. وقد لظهر علم الآثار الإيطالي في ليبيا تركز على السياسية. وقد لظهر علم الآثار الأحداث الأثرية على حد كبير إلى الكلاسيكي علم الآثار حتى ثمانينيات القرن العشرين. وأثناء الفترة الفاشية (1943-1922)، اصبح علم الآثار وسيلة لدعم دعاية موسوليني على وجه الاستمرارية إمبراطورية أغسطس. وبعد الحرب العالمية الثانية، لم تعد البعثات وسيلة "ثقافية" في خدمة الطموحات الاستعمارية للمملكة

إيطاليا والنظام الفاشي، وتم إعادتها إلى ميدان البحث بشكل لكل حصري في فترة خدمة
البحث العلمي.

ويعتبر عدم وجود سياسة بحث أثري واضحة ومتراطبة من السمات المشتركة
بين التجارب الأثرية في ليبيا وإثيوبيا. ويتمنى الكاتب أن ينجح حجج علم
الآثار الإيطالي في تحويل منهج الاطالع والبحث العقيم إلى مبادرة ثقافية
بالمفهوم الواسع.

Keywords

Libya, Ethiopia, classical archaeology, colonial and cultural policy, Cyrene, Leptis Magna, Sabratha, Axum

Italian archaeology in Libya

In the history of archaeological research in Libya, Italy is acknowledged to have had a leading role. As in other Mediterranean countries, our archaeological missions accompanied the colonial political experience, playing a part that was anything but secondary. This supporting role was destined to diminish considerably, starting from the post-World War II period, though archaeology would once again be at the service of political diplomacy in more recent times, at least episodically. From a scientific standpoint, the numerous missions that took place at many archaeological sites in the country yielded highly significant results. In these brief notes it is not intended, however, to illustrate the scientific results of Italian archaeology in Libya. Specialist publications are available for this.[1] Instead, the characteristics will be highlighted of this cultural experience that stretched over a century, up to the recent uprise events.

Tripoli Bel Suol d'Amore (1910–1945)[2]

As of the colonial period and until the onset of World War II, cultural initiatives, archaeological ones in particular, went hand in hand with political initiatives, often preceding them like a kind of 'cavalry reconnaissance troop' and reproducing their critical elements (see Petricioli 1986, 1990: XIII-XXI, 409-416). Italy's own process of unification (1861), which took place late compared to other European countries, and the structural problems of the unified state had precluded the elaboration of a far-reaching foreign policy. This factor in turn delayed the undertaking of a cultural and archaeological policy abroad. It was not until the start of the twentieth century that archaeological activities began, in Crete, Egypt, Eritrea and Libya (La Rosa 1986; Petricioli 1990).

---

1   See especially *Lybia Antiqua*, the archaeological journal edited since 1964.
2   'Tripoli, fair land of love'. This is the most famous line of a song composed in 1911 to celebrate Italy's conquest of Libya.

It was in 1910, by no coincidence on the eve of a military expedition, that Federico Halbherr, who had already been active in Crete for several years, obtained support from the Italian government for a mission in Cyrenaica,[3] where he would be preceded, albeit only shortly, by an American mission led by Richard Norton and funded by the billionaire Allison V. Armour. The military initiative against the Ottoman Empire, of which Libya was a protectorate, would follow a year later, although the territory was not pacified until many years late (see Del Boca 1986). In that same year Italian archaeologists identified the archaeological areas of interest and managed to get rid of the American mission in Cyrene, with which they had a publicly confrontational relationship. They considered them 'a thorn in the eye' (Di Vita 1986: 88). It was not until the 1920s however, that Italian archaeologists would be able to count on more substantial and continuous sources of funding that enabled them to undertake systematic digging campaigns in Cyrene, Sabratha and Leptis Magna. These three major sites on the Mediterranean coast would remain the most important centres of research for decades, up to the present day.

However, once the Italian occupation had stabilized, the archaeologists found themselves having to battle against the building frenzy of Italian officials who had moved to Libya and were almost always completely indifferent to the needs of scientific research. They did not hesitate to order demolitions and soil removals to make way for buildings to accommodate the new occupiers. Relations with the local population were difficult and Italian archaeologists worked in almost complete isolation from the indigenous social context.

A characterising element of this early phase was that Italian archaeology in Libya was predominantly classical archaeology. Apart from a few notable exceptions, the early twentieth century Italian academy was concerned exclusively with classical archaeology. Hence the Libya of the Italians ideologically coincided with the two provinces of the Roman Empire: Tripolitania and Cyrenaica. For decades and basically up to the second half of the 1980s, the earlier and later cultural periods of Libya's history were substantially ignored. Such an attitude was perfectly in line with the nationalist rhetoric pervading Italian politics at that time, when Italy was seen as heir to Rome, so much so that historians would speak of 'paradigmatic Romanity' (Rainero 1986: 36).

This vision was echoed and emphasized by the propaganda of the succeeding fascist period in Italy. Mussolini's regime would proclaim itself as a direct descendant of the Roman Empire, dominator of the Mediterranean (see Manacorda and Tamassia 1985; Torelli 1986). Classical archaeology, particularly after the 1930s, became a perfect tool for supporting this propaganda and justifying the occupation of the colonies as an inevitable result of historical evolution and the restoration of the link with the past. In this context we may speak of a 'utilitarian vision' of archaeology in those years. Archaeology was called upon to clarify the legitimacy of the colonial conquests, based on this alleged continuity with the Augustan Empire. In a world that – up to World War II – was afflicted by Eurocentrism,

---

3   On the Halbherr mission in Lybia, see Accame 1984, 1986; Di Vita 1986; Petricioli 1990: 91-149.

Romano-centrism became the key feature of Italy's intervention in what again, in an unrealistic parallel, was called *mare nostrum*.

Another result of the nationalist ideology, in Libya as in other territories (from Greece to Turkey), was an attitude of cultural superiority. Archaeological research was interpreted as the 'natural' outcome of cultural primacy. The inevitable consequence of such an attitude was a total indifference towards the indigenous culture and the needs of the local population, an indifference that led to contempt, as is clearly evidenced in the correspondence between the various political and scientific protagonists of that period (see Accame 1984, 1986; Di Vita 1986).

Politically, the provinces of Tripolitania and Cyrenaica were joined together in 1934, in the General Governorate of Libya. But the activity of the two African superintendencies for monuments and excavations that were entrusted with archaeological research, continued to be inspired by a paroxysm of Romanism until the Libyan adventure ended with the start of World War II.

The return (1950–2000)

After the war, and with the arrival of Libya's independence in 1951, Italy naturally went through a period of obscurity. Due to a lack of both training and interest, the new local ruling classes in Libya were however unable to take over management of Libya's archaeological assets. In the previous decades nothing had been done by Italian archaeologists in terms of training and Libyans were employed solely to provide labour. Nobody had even considered the issue of transmitting knowledge to the local populations. It was thus an easy feat for some Italian scholars to recover the ground that had been lost. Thanks above all to the diplomatic initiative of Antonino Di Vita, who was a scientific advisor of the Libyan Department for the Antiquities of Tripolitania[4] from 1962 to 1965, Italy obtained a concession for the previous archaeological missions in the early 1960s (Di Vita 2002). In 1964, again through the initiative of Di Vita, the publication of the periodical *Lybia Antiqua* began. It was intended to accommodate scientific accounts of the archaeological digs in Libya.[5]

The archaeological sites were assigned by Di Vita according to a judicious sharing scheme and saw the involvement of numerous teams from many Italian universities. In the majority of cases they conducted their research through campaigns of a few weeks each, divided between two periods of the year. Compared to contemporary experiences in Italy and Europe, stratigraphic excavation techniques, archaeometric analysis and IT-tools were introduced considerably late (in the 1970s).

The situation changed little after the 1969 revolution that brought Colonel Gaddafi to power. While the old Italian community was expelled from the country, practically all the Italian missions managed to stay. Their isolation from the social context in which they worked continued, however, as did the economic

---

4   The department had been founded in the 1950s.
5   Initially issued on a yearly basis, its publication was first interrupted at the end of the 1970s, then resumed in 1995 and continued until the end of the century. From 2000 to the present day, only one issue has come out, in 2010.

difficulties. Like in the pre-war period, sites were often shut down for years due to a lack of funding. The financial resources were in any case not assigned by research institutions, but by the Italian Ministry of Foreign Affairs, in direct continuity with what had occurred in the first half of the twentieth century (see Ministero degli Affari Esteri 2002). Only the final objective of the cultural initiatives and archaeology changed, from territorial to economic conquest.

Due to the research themes and objects – Roman archaeology – the new Libyan regime and the local population remained indifferent. The subject was linked to the colonial past and was felt to be the heritage of the former colonizers. Archaeological monuments were traces of a history – from ancient to colonial – that the regime wanted to remove as much as possible. They were traces of a culture considered to be alien. Although this attitude enabled the missions to be continued, it prevented archaeological research from being transformed into a fully-fledged cultural project. A problem that for a long time was scarcely perceived by the successive Italian scholars who headed the various missions.

Some missions were even asked to take on commitments involving a great deal of responsibility, not only regarding the scientific aspects, but also with respect to the sites themselves. Examples are the anastylosis of unique monuments in Libya and throughout northern Africa, including the temple of Zeus at Cyrene (figure 1), the four-sided Severan Arch at Leptis (figure 2), and the difficult restoration of the paintings of the sacred funerary area of Sidret el-Balik at Sabratha (see Di Vita 2002).

Starting from the 1980s, the requests of the Libyan Department for Antiquities were extended to the realm of teaching and museology (see Ministero degli Affari Esteri 2002). Courses were organized for local staff of the superintendencies to provide them with training in excavation, classification and restoration methods. In collaboration with the directors of the local superintendencies the new museum of Leptis and the antiquarium at Cyrene were set up to house the sculptures and finds from the excavations. But the projects – overseen by archaeologists and not by museologists – were limited to a re-proposal of the old-fashioned exhibition models that were tied to western traditions. The occasion was not exploited to elaborate an ad hoc communication project, the museum spaces remained little more than orderly storage areas.

The work was conducted, it was repeated, 'in collaboration with the local superintendencies', a formula that did however not succeed in hiding the isolation from the local context in which the Italian archaeologists worked. Only rarely could it be considered collaboration on an equal footing, as is demonstrated by the almost complete absence of Arab scholars from the scientific publications on the results of the mission, from *Lybia Antiqua* (which would continue to be published in Italy) to the various monographs. Moreover, on the occasion of conferences dedicated to analysing the experience of Italian archaeology in the Mediterranean no need was felt, even in more recent times, for an exchange of views with non-Italian scholars. It was almost as if the different missions each operated in a *hortus conclusus* that did not allow for a real cultural interchange.

Figure 1. Cyrene, Temple of Zeus (Wikimedia Commons).

Figure 2. Leptis Magna, four-sided Severan Arch (Photo: Dirk Heldmaier via Wikimedia Commons).

By the end of the 1980s, however, the Libyan political stance changed. Despite the enduring attitude of hostility towards the West, a period of greater openness began, which led to the inauguration of tourist activities that were also open to westerners. These gained in intensity over the years and must-see tourist destinations naturally included the Roman coastal cities of Cyrene, Sabratha and Leptis, which in the meantime (1982) had been included in the UNESCO World Heritage List.[6]

In the 1990s, thanks also to an increase in funding, the archaeological missions enjoyed a major phase of expansion. Moreover, all research was programmatically extended to non-classical periods, from the pre-Roman (Greek and Punic/ Phoenician layers of Leptis and Cyrene) to the Byzantine era. A mission was also undertaken to survey and study the oasis town of Ghadames of the Islamic period and the architecture of Tripoli's Medina, with an eye to a conservative restoration of the buildings (Micara 2002). The prehistoric era also aroused the interest of Italian scholars. After the pioneering research of Fabrizio Mori in the mid-1950s in Acacus, a joint Italian-Libyan mission was undertaken in the 1990s in Tadrart Acacus and Messak (figure 3), in the Libyan Sahara (see Liverani 2002). Another Italian-Libyan mission was started in the Jebel Gharbi (see Barich 2002).

Figure 3. Ancient rock art in Tadrart Acacus (Photo: Roberto D'Angelo via Wikimedia Commons).

---

6   See http://whc.unesco.org/en/list.

As can be seen, the missions started to be referred to as 'Italian-Libyan' and even at traditional sites newly undertaken missions were finally based on a systematic collaboration with local scholars. In the University of Rome's third mission at Leptis (inaugurated in 1995), genuine attention was given to the educational connotations of the project and a bilingual computerized inventory system was created (see Musso 2002).

Today and tomorrow

At the start of the new millennium there were about a dozen Italian missions in Libya (Ministero degli Affari Esteri 2002). Also taking into account partnerships of various types, about twenty Italian universities were involved, next to the Ministry for Cultural Heritage and Activities (MIBAC), the National Research Council (CNR) and other smaller research centres. Before the 2011 spring revolt, Italian missions were active at the sites of Sabratha, Leptis Magna, Cirene, Ghadames, Jebel Gharbi, Tadrart Acacus and Messak (figure 4).[7]

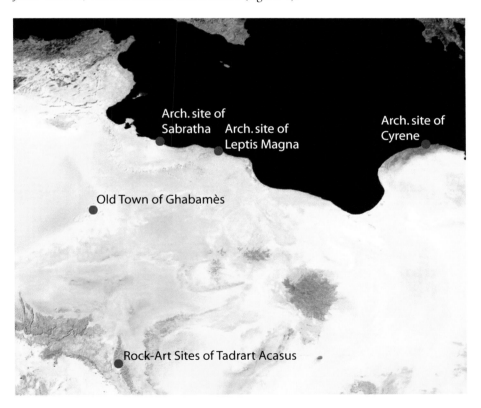

Figure 4. Sites of Italian archaeological missions in Libya, up to recent war events (Illustration: K. Wentink, after an elaboration by Manuela Pereira on UNESCO World Heritage Map file).

---

7   For an updated outline of archaeological initiatives in the Mediterranean see Braemer 2011.

While the Ministry of Foreign Affairs, increasingly the sole funder of Italian archaeological missions, continues to emphasize the role of archaeological research in helping to strengthen political ties, a lot still needs to be done in order to activate the intercultural dialogue that has been identified as a mandatory objective but which is far from being achieved. The training activities for the officials of the Department for Antiquities must evolve into a much broader cultural project and must be extended so as to include not only archaeologists or local scholars, but the whole population.

An extreme example of a utilitarian use of archaeological heritage was the return of the statue of Venus of Cyrene (see Muschella 2008). The headless statue, a marble copy of a Hellenistic original, was found by chance by Italian archaeologists in 1913 and then taken to Italy to be displayed at the National Roman Museum in Palazzo Massimo. In August 2008 it was returned to Colonel Gaddafi by the then Italian Prime Minister Silvio Berlusconi, on the occasion of a state visit to Tripoli. The statue, handed over almost as a personal gift to the Libyan dictator, was however given very little attention. It was seen as the symbol of a foreign culture and the nudity of the statue did not suit the renewed Islamic sensitivity of the colonel's regime.

During the revolt of 2011, the international scientific community and Italian archaeologists in particular had voiced alarm, highlighting the need to safeguard the great coastal cities. It was feared that the sites could be used as a hostage by the opposing factions (see De Giovannangeli 2011; Grande 2011; Rinaldi Tufi 2011). In practice, the sites were simply left to their own fate (see Bongiorni 2011). What happened some months earlier during the mobilization in Egypt and what had led the population to stand guard and to physically defend the sites and museums containing Egyptian antiquities, did not occur in Libya. Yet further proof of how the archaeological heritage of Roman Libya is not considered as an element of the local identity.

At the time of writing, a few weeks after the end of the revolt, a more or less rapid resumption of archaeological activity in Libya can be assumed. The concern about the fate of the archaeological heritage during the months of conflict has in Italy been followed, not coincidentally, by a flurry of seminars and conferences on the future of archaeology in Libya (see Bonino 2011; Garrone 2011; Grande 2011; Moltedo 2011; Sapio 2011). Italian archaeologists will most likely return to Libya sooner or later, but it is by now unthinkable that nothing will change in how missions are managed. In Europe, archaeology has become one of the most effective tools for promoting integration of different cultures.[8] That should become the point of reference for an archaeology that radically rethinks its objectives and, accordingly, its methods. Moreover, it will also be necessary to make sure that the tourism industry – though important for its economic gain – does not degenerate into the exploitation and dissipation of local environmental resources as in other nearby areas (*e.g.* Tunisia). Regarding the fact that Italian scholars promoted the

---

8   A good example is that of Saint Denis in France. See http://www.culture.gouv.fr/fr/arcnat/saint-denis/fr/index.html.

country's immense archaeological wealth to tourists, this is also a task in which Italian archaeologists have a role (Guermandi 2009).

Finally, just as we hope that the overthrow of the Gaddafi regime will serve to launch the country into a process toward full-fledged democracy, on a cultural level it is likewise essential that the country's new rulers acquire a new awareness of the importance of Libya's cultural heritage, which has since the remotest times contributed to the development of a multiple identity. In Libya, as in Italy and everywhere else, multiple roots are present, which cannot be untangled from one another. Recognizing, acknowledging and understanding them is a first indispensable step towards embracing the principles of freedom and democracy.

Italian archaeology in Ethiopia

Faccetta Nera ('Little Black Face')[9] and the country of the Queen of Sheba

On 3 October 1935 Italy attacked the Ethiopian Empire, without declaring war. After the opening of the Suez Canal, the area had taken on new strategic importance, which was a decisive factor in the eyes of the fascist regime. In those years it was desperately striving to play a more aggressive role in terms of foreign policy and in order to broaden the extent of its own colonial empire it was seeking out territories considered easy to conquer. The Italians succeeded in subduing the resistance of the Ethiopians and entered the capital Addis Ababa on 5 May 1936. Ethiopia was thus annexed to Italian East Africa,[10] but the occupation would last only a few years, up until the arrival of the British in 1941. The resistance of the Italian troops ceased altogether in 1943.

As far as archaeological research is concerned, during the years of colonial occupation in East Africa investigations were sporadic and not comparable to the activities then underway in Libya (see Tiné 1986). In Ethiopia, attention was substantially focused on Aksum, where the Deutsche Axum Expedition had been active in the first decade of the twentieth century. Preceded by a topographical study of the area, led by Ugo Monneret de Villard, the first and last Italian archaeological mission began in April 1939. Its aim was to carry out a preliminary survey of the territory and research into prehistoric aspects. The activities were interrupted when the Second World War broke out.[11]

According to a legend, Ethiopia – associated since antiquity with the Land of Punt and mentioned in Homer's works and in religious documents of Pharaonic Egypt – was the native land of the Queen of Sheba, whose son Menelik, fathered

9   These are words from the refrain of a famous Italian song ('Little Black Face') which exalted the fascist regime's conquest of Ethiopia.

10   Italian East Africa was an administrative subdivision of the Italian Empire, proclaimed on 9 May 1936 after Italy's conquest of Ethiopia. Italian East Africa was made up of the Ethiopian Empire and the colonies of Eritrea and Italian Somaliland.

11   The main source for scientific research conducted by Italian scholars in Ethiopia would be the Rassegna di Studi Etiopici ('Review of Ethiopian Studies'), published in Italy from 1941 until today; the journal shortly emerged as one of the most important scientific tools for Ethiopian Studies.

by King Solomon, gave birth to the Ethiopian dynasty. All modern Ethiopian sovereigns linked themselves with this mythical lineage. After a long process of social and economic evolution and thanks to its geographic position of control in the Red Sea, in the first millennium AD, a kingdom of great political importance developed in this region.

The Kingdom of Aksum – named after the site which was its principal city – enjoyed a period of high importance from the fourth to the sixth century AD, when it extended its influence from Sudan to the Arabian Peninsula through the control of several Red Sea ports. It may thus be considered among the greatest empires of its time and a major trading partner of the Roman Empire.[12] Already in the fourth century AD Christianity was introduced into the kingdom and Aksum has remained the most important centre of the Ethiopian Orthodox Church for over 1500 years: Ethiopia's sacred city.[13] Aksum's importance, at least its symbolic importance, also remained after the kingdom's decline, so much so that the last Ethiopian king, Haile Selassié, the 225th direct descendant of Menelik I, went to Aksum to be crowned.

Aksum's importance from a cultural and religious standpoint and its key role in Ethiopian national identity was acknowledged by UNESCO, which included Aksum in the World Heritage List in 1980 (King 2001). From a monumental perspective, one of the distinctive traits of Aksumite civilization – and certainly the best known – are the dozens of finely engraved obelisks in the centre of the sacred city. These are monoliths of varying height (the tallest reaching 34 metres, thus exceeding the height of Egyptian counterparts) whose function, though still not totally clear, is probably connected to funerary rituals, as the presence of tombs and altars in the area suggests (Phillipson 1994, 1997).

The obelisks were erected in the first centuries AD and nearly all are now lying on the ground: one was transported to Italy by the fascist conquerors in 1937. In addition to the Aksum obelisk, countless other objects of Ethiopian culture were removed from the cities, towns and centres of worship to increase the collections of Italian museums. They included a bronze statue of the Lion of Judah, symbol of the Ethiopian dynasty. This practice, common to all colonialist countries, revealed a total indifference toward the local cultures, which were stripped of objects and monuments for the sole purpose of enriching and 'completing' the ethnographic collections displayed in the museums of the occupying countries. Fortunately the Lion was returned in 1970.

Archaeological missions from 1973 to today

The first real archaeological missions conducted by Italian teams date back to 1973, when Lanfranco Ricci undertook a research project in Aksum that would last for two years (Ricci and Fattovich 1987, 1988). From 1975 to the end of 1992,

---

12 For a short sketch of the Aksumite Kingdom, see http://whc.unesco.org/en/list/15.

13 The Saint Mary of Zion church was constructed at Aksum between the fourth and sixth centuries: according to legends the church treasury contains the Ark of Covenant, the box built by Moses to carry the Ten Commandments.

the surveys were largely interrupted because of the turbulent political situation in the region, which exploded into a civil war, and was made even worse by drought and dramatic famines.[14]

Starting from 1993, a team from the Oriental Institute of the University of Naples, headed by Rodolfo Fattovich, in collaboration with Boston University, resumed research in the area, *i.e.* on the site of Ona Enda Aboi Zewgé, a large field of steles associated with artificial stone platforms. The objective was to study the state-building process of the Kingdom of Aksum, which extended across the present-day Eritrea and Northern Ethiopia (Tigray plateau). Thanks to this research, the kingdom's origins, previously dated to the first millennium AD, were traced back to the fourth century BC (Bard *et al.* 1997; Fattovich *et al.* 2000; Fattovich and Bard 2003).

The research continued in a more or less regular manner up to our own times, though the area of investigation shifted to the region of Yeha, near Adua and east of Aksum. For several years, La Sapienza University of Rome has been carrying out a survey aimed at exploring the settlement models and environmental evolution from the Lower Pleistocene to the Holocene in the upper Awash Valley (sites of Melka Kunture and Balchit). As in the case of Libya, research funds are provided by the universities the mission leaders are connected with and above all by the Ministry of Foreign Affairs.[15]

The Aksum obelisk: a symbolic episode

As mentioned earlier, in 1937 the Italian authorities decided to remove one of the obelisks of Aksum. At the time of the Italian conquest, the obelisk, dating from between the first and fourth century, had collapsed and was broken into five parts as a result of an earthquake that had occurred about a thousand years before. The five sections of the obelisk were drawn by hundreds of Italian and Eritrean soldiers to the port of Massaua and transported by ship to Naples. From there they were taken to Rome, where the obelisk was reassembled and set up on 28 October 1937 in Piazza di Porta Capena, in front of the Ministry of the Colonies (today FAO headquarters). This operation, that was extremely complex for the times as the obelisk was a 24 metre high granite monolith weighing 152 tonnes, was entrusted to Ugo Monneret de Villard – a great Italian archaeologist and academic – and coordinated by the minister for Italian Africa.

The erection of the obelisk served to commemorate the fifteenth anniversary of the March on Rome, when the fascists came to power, but it was also inspired by the removals of obelisks by the emperors of ancient Rome. These monuments, largely of Egyptian origin, were transported to the capital of the Roman Empire as of the reign of Augustus, under whose rule Egypt had been conquered after the battle of Actium in 31 BC. With the Aksumite monument, Mussolini meant to

---

14 The war with Eritrea, formally ended in 2000, is still a source of clashes particularly affecting the region at the heart of which Aksum is located. The 1984–1985 famine caused the death of a million people.

15 See http://www.esteri.it/MAE/IT/Politica_Estera/Cultura/ArcheologiaPatrimonioCulturale.htm.

further emphasize the parallel between the fascist regime and the Roman imperial era.

During its removal, travel, reassembly and subsequent stay in Italy, the obelisk suffered a great deal of damage. On 10 September 1943 it came under fire during the battle of Porta San Paolo and in the following decades it was exposed to severe pollution due to its position in an area of heavy traffic. When the war was over, Italy pledged in the peace agreement signed under the auspices of the United Nations on 15 September 1947, that it would return all the war booty taken from Ethiopia after the 1935 occupation. This would be done within eighteen months, but the agreements remained unfulfilled for years, despite the Ethiopian government's numerous requests. Finally, in 1997, in a diplomatic climate that had greatly improved, the commitment was renewed with new vigour (Mariam 2009). However, subsequent political and economic obstacles prevented its immediate fulfilment and in the meantime numerous polemics arose in Italy as to the advisability of the return.[16] Eventually, in 2003 the obelisk was first restored and then disassembled. After lying in barracks for a year and a half because no plane could be found that was capable of transporting it, it finally departed for Ethiopia in 2005. The last of the three fragments it was divided in arrived on 25 April, the date of the liberation from Nazi fascism, and it was welcomed by an enthusiastic Ethiopian crowd.

---

16   See, for example, Conti 2001 and Marco Guidi's article published in the newspaper *Il Messaggero* in November 2003, during the operations to dismantle the obelisk, in which the latter author wrote:

' [...] In the end, it will all cost many millions of euros and the obelisk will return to Aksum to be shown off together with other obelisks (which the various Ethiopian governments have never felt the need to put back into an upright position).

Frankly, after over sixty years, it is hard to understand the reason for the return. So some myths should be debunked: the first is that of the obelisk as a unique, precious document of Aksumite civilization. Something that is not true since, as we have seen, others exist and the one in Rome is not even the largest. Then there are those who demand the return of the monument as reparation for the fascist invasion. Reparation was already made in the 1960s (hospital). But by all means let us admit that Italy still has a further debt to pay back to Ethiopia.

We wonder if it had not been better to allocate the huge sum paid to cover the cost of the operation in aid to one of the poorest countries in the world, maybe in exchange for the symbolic "gift" of the obelisk from the government of Addis Ababa. It might have been better for those populations. But Italy seems to have been seized by a sort of repatriation obsession. A Roman head to Albania, the Venus of Cyrene to Libya, and the Aksum obelisk to Ethiopia. It seems that we are the only country in the world which behaves like that. In Germany, for example, no one thinks about returning the Pergamon Altar to Turkey, though it was carried away by the Germans in a fraudulent manner (unlike the Parthenon marbles, duly purchased by Lord Elgin). Maybe we could have left the obelisk where it had stood for decades and still remains friends of Ethiopia.'

On the other hand, to get an idea of the climate of expectation in Ethiopia, we can read the statements made by the then Ethiopian minister of Culture Wolde-Michael Chemo in an interview published in the newspaper *Corriere della Sera* in July 2001, when the debate in Italy was very heated: 'If the obelisk were to remain in Rome, it would bring shame upon the looter and be an insult to the looted. That presence would continue to be a reminder of the misdeeds committed here by the fascist regime. It would prompt animosity between peoples. It would undermine the notion of forgiveness and desire to forget.'

Figure 5: Obelisk of Aksum (Photo: Ondřej Žváček via Wikimedia Commons).

A decisive stimulus leading to the repatriation of the obelisk was undoubtedly the role Italy had taken on in those years as a major advocate, at an international level, of the policy of returning illicitly removed objects to the countries of origin. The 1990s saw a general rekindling of international debate on cultural heritage, inspired by the UNESCO 1972 Convention concerning the Protection of the World Cultural and Natural Heritage. Italy took a leading role in this debate, pledging to break up, on a juridical, cultural and ethical level, the system of connivances that had favoured theft and clandestine trafficking of archaeological objects on behalf of major international museums and galleries. With a battle conducted above all on 'ethical' grounds, intended to broaden the awareness that the disappearance or degradation of a work of art is a wound inflicted not only on a nation's cultural heritage but also on humanity as a whole, the Italian government reaffirmed the principle that an ancient object belongs to the territory it was found in not because of a desire for property or a merely nationalist spirit, but rather because it can tell its story only in its proper context. Outside of that, its beauty is muted.

The credibility of the cultural battle of Italy, which in those very same years was engaged in negotiations with major institutions like the Getty Trust and the Metropolitan Museum of New York, negotiations that at times involved harsh legal disputes, could not risk being undermined by an issue such as that of the return of the Aksum obelisk, whose removal had always universally been viewed as an illicit act that was against all internationally recognized legal principles.[17]

After its return, the stele remained beneath a shelter in the archaeological park of Aksum, still disassembled. Before it could be reassembled, complex reinforcement operations had to be carried out in the area. The final restoration work and re-erection, that was entirely funded by Italy through UNESCO,[18] ended in 2008 and on 4 September of the same year a large ceremony took place to celebrate the obelisk's return (Figure 5).

In the case of the Venus of Cyrene, as previously discussed, the object was not connected to the local culture and was therefore not felt as a strong identifying symbol: the Hellenistic statue conjured up a past that was deliberately obscured by the dominant political classes because it was similarly perceived as colonial. However, the removal of the Aksum obelisk had always been felt as a wound, not only by the Ethiopian elites, but also by the local populations. The return was thus greeted by the Ethiopian population as a major positive event. Symbolically, in those very same days, a large exhibition – '*Nostoi. I capolavori ritrovati*'[19] – celebrated in Rome the homecoming of a series of illicitly removed archaeological objects returned to Italy under international agreements.

Conclusions

Despite the diversity of the individual situations, the experiences of Italian archaeology in Libya and Ethiopia have some elements in common. After the Second World War, the missions were no longer a 'cultural' tool serving the colonial ambitions of the Kingdom of Italy and the fascist regime, but exclusively serving scientific research again. A shared trait, that clearly distinguished them from other Mediterranean missions undertaken by Italian research teams between the last decades of the nineteenth century and the Second World War, is the lack of any explicit and coherent archaeological research policy. The surveys and digs appear

---

17 Besides the Peace Treaty of 1947, also consider the Hague Convention of 1954 and the UNESCO Convention of 1972. See also Scovazzi 2009.

18 The complex operations of disassembling, reinforcing, moving and reassembling the obelisk, entirely paid for by the Italian government, were entrusted to a team co-ordinated by professor Giorgio Croci, a famous structural engineer who was also placed in charge of other operations such as the restoration of the Tower of Pisa and the basilica of Assisi. See Croci 2009.

19 *Nostoi. Capolavori Ritrovati.* 2007. Roma: Presidenza della Repubblica Italiana, Ministero per i Beni e le Attività Culturali. Retrieved 28 June 2012 from http://www.quirinale. it/qrnw/statico/artecultura/mostre/2007_Nostoi/Nostoihome-a.htm.

to be the fruit of the cultural orientations of individual personalities and at times random in nature. In any case, the objectives and choices proved to be dependent on those guided by foreign policy and were only sporadically autonomous.

Whereas in European countries such as France, Germany and England, archaeological research abroad represented the prevalent area of activity (in terms of quality and resources invested), the opposite was the case with Italy. After a very lively initial period following the unification, from the second decade of the twentieth century onward archaeological policy demonstrated to be increasingly dependent on what has been defined as national *Lumpenimperialismus* and it was limited to a feverish, falsifying exaltation of Romanity (especially in Libya). This cultural backwardness had repercussions on the methodological level as well, considering that stratigraphic excavation techniques were only introduced at the end of the 1970s.[20]

Current archaeological missions, though impacted by the economic difficulties, are aimed exclusively at research. Yet the 'original sin' of Italian archaeological research in these countries has not been completely amended. As was stressed, in both countries the archaeological missions failed to seek full collaboration with the host countries, or did so only episodically. Contact with the local population was limited to organizational and logistic aspects and the teams that worked there, often for many consecutive years, remained enclaves detached from the everyday life of the places they operated or still operate in. Moreover, very few local scholars were involved on a scientific level and publications in the local language were almost non-existent. This confirms that the research groups were separated from the context they worked in, a separation that is difficult to justify as simply the isolation of scientists.

Nevertheless, the publications – in Italian or English – do mention educational activities and attempts to fit the archaeological research within the framework of broader development initiatives which intended to improve the quality of life of the local populations. But the scholars clearly considered such aspects to be secondary, a kind of dues paid to local institutions in exchange for permits and logistic support. These aspects should become the foundation of scientific research and every digging campaign should at all stages seek the widest possible involvement of the population. Only in this way will it be possible to build a full, lasting awareness of the importance of this heritage for the host countries. Only in this way will the populations be able to 'feel' this heritage as a part of their history and identity and, as such, something that is to be protected and brought back to life, not as fossils of a sometimes troublesome past, but as tokens of former civilizations that still exert an influence.

Yet, for the time being, an analogous distant attitude still characterizes the archaeological missions in these areas. A further indication of a substantial detachment of present-day research missions from the contemporary life of the host countries is the indifference that emerges from various scientific reports and

---

20 Concerning the lack of an explicit Italian cultural policy for archaeological research abroad (and at home...), see Torelli 1986.

accounts with respect to the events, at times very grave, which have affected and are still affecting these countries. We are talking about wars, revolts and famine in the case of Ethiopia, and the total absence of democratic guarantees and the very recent civil war in Libya. And yet these events are only mentioned as a source of disruption hindering the normal progress of the missions. It is clear that such an attitude cannot fail to have repercussions on the 'cultural vision' in the full sense of the term: until this separation between archaeology and local society is completely overcome through a collaborative effort that is not opportunistic and superficial, but aimed at setting up a common project, the research initiatives are destined to remain sterile because strictly limited to the academic realm.

The experiences of Italian archaeological missions in Africa, though only very briefly outlined, are clear evidence that – as the ACE project has sought to highlight through its analyses and initiatives – archaeology will have a future only if it succeeds in transforming the discipline of erudition and aseptic research into a cultural initiative whereby research into the past acquires meaning only insofar as it is interpreted in light of the present.

References

Accame, S. 1984. *F. Halbherr e G. De Sanctis. Pionieri delle Missioni Italiane a Creta e in Cirenaica (dal carteggio De Sanctis 1909–1932)*. Roma: Istituto Italiano per la Storia Antica.

Accame, S. 1986. *F. Halbherr e G. De Sanctis (Nuove Lettere dal Carteggio De Sanctis 1892–1932)*. Roma: Istituto Italiano per la Storia Antica.

Bard, K.A., R. Fattovich, A. Manzo and C. Perlingieri. 1997. 'Archaeological Investigations at Bieta Giyorgis (Aksum), Ethiopia: 1993-1995 Field Seasons', *Journal of Field Archaeology* 24: 387-403.

Barich, B.E. 2002. 'Università di Roma "La Sapienza". Missione Archeologica nel Jebel Gharbi', in Ministero degli Affari Esteri (ed.), *Il Dialogo Interculturale nel Mediterraneo: la Collaborazione Italo-Libica in Campo Archeologico*. Roma: Ministero degli Affari Esteri, 49-53.

Bongiorni, R. 2011. 'Leptis Magna Salvata dai Cittadini', *Il Sole 24 Ore,* 9 September 2011. Retrieved 29 March 2012 from http://www.ilsole24ore.com/art/cultura/2011-09-09/leptis-magna-salvata-cittadini-142247.shtml?uuid=Aa5Dns2D&fromSearch.

Bonino, I. 2011. 'Libia, Tunisia, Egitto: Così le Rivoluzioni Cambiano il Lavoro dei nostri Archeologi', *Corriere della Sera – Sette,* 6 October 2011. Retrieved 29 March 2012 from http://host.uniroma3.it/uffici/stampa/ecostampa/pdf/1556/1556FH.PDF.

Braemer, F. 2011. *L'Archéologie en Méditerranée, Situation Internationale, Evolutions*. Rapport de Mission à l'Attention des Directions de l'École Française de Rome et de l'Institut des Sciences Humaines et Sociales du CNRS. Rome: Ecole Française de Rome.

Conti, P. 2001. 'Il Governo Etiope: Ridateci l' Obelisco di Axum', *Corriere della Sera,* 21 July 2001.

Croci, G. 2009. 'From Italy to Ethiopia: the Dismantling, Transportation and Re-erection of the Axum Obelisk', *Museum International* 241-242(61): 61-67.

De Giovannangeli, U. 2011. 'Leptis Magna. Lo Scudo Archeologico del Rais. Razzi nel Gioiello dell'Unesco', *l'Unità,* 15 June 2011. Retrieved 29 March 2012 from http://82.85.28.102/cgi-bin/showfile.pl?file=edizioni/20110615/pdf/NAZ/pages/20110615_28_15NAZ28A.pdf.

Del Boca, A. 1986. *Gli Italiani in Libia. Tripoli bel Suol d'Amore 1860–1922.* Bari: Laterza.

Di Vita, A. 1986. 'Tripolitania e Cirenaica nel Carteggio Halbherr: fra Politica e Archeologia', in V. La Rosa (ed.), *L'Archeologia Italiana nel Mediterraneo fino alla Seconda Guerra Mondiale.* Catania: Centro Studi per l'Archeologia Greca C.N.R., 73-92.

Di Vita, A. 2002. 'Università di Macerata. Missione Archeologica a Leptis Magna e Sabratha', in Ministero degli Affari Esteri (ed.), *Il Dialogo Interculturale nel Mediterraneo: la Collaborazione Italo-Libica in Campo Archeologico.* Roma: Ministero degli Affari Esteri, 26-30.

Fattovich, R. and K.A. Bard. 2003. 'Scavi Archeologici nella Zona di Aksum. K. Bieta Giyorgis', *Rassegna di Studi Etiopici* (New series) II: 23-36.

Fattovich, R., K.A. Bard, L. Petrassi and V. Pisano. 2000. *The Aksum Archaeological Area: a Preliminary Assessment.* Laboratorio di Archeologia, Working Paper 1. Napoli: Istituto Universitario Orientale.

Garrone, L. 2011. 'Il Patrimonio nelle Zone di Guerra', *Corriere della Sera ed. Roma,* 5 November 2011. Retrieved 29 March 2012 from http://archiviostorico.corriere.it/2011/novembre/05/Patrimonio_nelle_zone_guerra_co_10_111105036.shtml.

Grande, C. 2011. 'Archeologia e Guerra. Quali sono i Siti più Minacciati?', *La Stampa,* 15 June 2012. Retrieved 29 March from http://www3.lastampa.it/domande-risposte/articolo/lstp/407203/.

Guermandi, M.P. 2009. 'Neocolonialismi'. *Eddyburg. it, Opinioni e Interventi,* 15 August 2009. Retrieved 31 October 2011 from http://eddyburg.it/article/articleview/3096/1/158.

Guidi, M. 2003. 'La Stele di Axum. Milioni da Spendere Meglio', *Il Messaggero,* 11 November 2003.

King, J. 2001. 'Axum: Toward the Conservation of Ethiopia's Sacred City', in I. Serageldin, E. Shluger and J. Martin-Brown (eds), *Historic Cities and Sacred Sites: Cultural Roots for Urban Futures.* Washington: The World Bank, 358-364.

La Rosa, V. (ed.). 1986. *L'Archeologia Italiana nel Mediterraneo fino alla Seconda Guerra Mondiale.* Catania: Centro Studi per l'Archeologia Greca C.N.R.

Liverani, M. 2002. 'Università di Roma "La Sapienza". Missione Archeologica nel Tadrart Acacus e nel Messak (Sahara Libico) – Centro Interuniversitario di Ricerca sulle Civiltà e l'Ambiente del Sahara Antico e delle Zone Aride', in Ministero degli Affari Esteri (ed.), *Il Dialogo Interculturale nel Mediterraneo: la Collaborazione Italo-Libica in Campo Archeologico*. Roma: Ministero degli Affari Esteri, 54-57.

Manacorda, D. and R. Tamassia. 1985. *Il Piccone del Regime*. Roma: Armando Curcio.

Mariam, H. 2009. 'The Cultural Benefits of the Return of the Axum Obelisk', *Museum International* 241-242(61): 48-51.

Micara, L. 2002. 'Università di Pescara.Missione per lo studio dell'Architettura e della Città di Periodo Islamico in Libia', in Ministero degli Affari Esteri (ed.), *Il Dialogo Interculturale nel Mediterraneo: la Collaborazione Italo-Libica in Campo Archeologico*. Roma: Ministero degli Affari Esteri, 43-48.

Ministero degli Affari Esteri. 2002. *Il Dialogo Interculturale nel Mediterraneo: la Collaborazione Italo-Libica in Campo Archeologico*. Roma: Ministero degli Affari Esteri.

Moltedo, M.L. 2011. 'Leptis Magna Sos, Sito Libico da Salvare', *Terranews,* 19 September 2011. Retrieved 29 March 2012 from http://www.terranews. it/news/2011/09/leptis-magna-sos-sito-libico-da-salvare.

Muschella, E. 2008. 'E la Venere di Cirene Torna in Aereo con Silvio', *Corriere della Sera,* 30 August 2008.

Musso, L. 2002. 'Università Roma Tre - Missione Archeologica a Leptis Magna', in Ministero degli Affari Esteri (ed.), *Il Dialogo Interculturale nel Mediterraneo: la Collaborazione Italo-Libica in Campo Archeologico*. Roma: Ministero degli Affari Esteri, 58–65.

Petricioli, M. 1986. 'Le Missioni Archeologiche Italiane nei paesi del Mediterraneo: uno Strumento di Politica Internazionale', in V. La Rosa (ed.), *L'Archeologia Italiana nel Mediterraneo fino alla Seconda Guerra Mondiale*. Catania: Centro Studi per l'Archeologia Greca C.N.R., 9-31.

Petricioli, M. 1990. *Archeologia e Mare Nostrum. Le Missioni Archeologiche nella Politica Mediterranea dell'Italia 1898/1943*. Roma: Valerio Levi Editore.

Phillipson, D.W. 1994. 'The Significance and Symbolism of Aksumite Stelae', *Cambridge Archaeological Journal* 4(2): 189-210.

Phillipson, D.W. (ed.). 1997. *The Monuments of Aksum*. Addis Ababa: Addis Ababa University Press in collaboration with the British Institute of Eastern Africa.

Rainero, R.H. 1986. 'Reazioni Locali alle Iniziative Culturali Italiane nel Mediterraneo', in V. La Rosa (ed.), *L'Archeologia Italiana nel Mediterraneo fino alla Seconda Guerra Mondiale*. Catania: Centro Studi per l'Archeologia Greca C.N.R., 33-40.

Ricci, L. and R. Fattovich. 1987. 'Scavi Archeologici nella Zona di Aksum. A. Seglamien', *Rassegna di Studi Etiopici* 30: 117-169.

Ricci, L. and R. Fattovich. 1988, 'Scavi Archeologici nella Zona di Aksum. Bieta Giyorgis', *Rassegna di Studi Etiopici* 31: 123-197.

Rinaldi Tufi, S. 2011. 'Scomparsi i Reperti del Tesoro di Bengasi', *Il Messaggero,* 31 August 2011. Retrieved 29 March 2012 from http://www.patrimoniosos.it/rsol. php?op=getarticle&id=88801.

Sapio, S. 2011. 'Sun, Missione di Pace e Cultura per Difendere i Tesori della Libia', *Il Mattino ed. Napoli,* 4 July 2011. Retrieved 29 March 2012 from http://www. patrimoniosos.it/rsol.php?op=getarticle&id=86897.

Scovazzi, T. 2009. 'Legal Aspects of the Axum Obelisk Case', *Museum International* 241-242(61): 52-60.

Tiné, S. 1986. 'L'Archeologia Italiana in Eritrea, Etiopia, Somalia e Fezzan', in V. La Rosa (ed.), *L'Archeologia Italiana nel Mediterraneo fino alla Seconda Guerra Mondiale.* Catania: Centro Studi per l'Archeologia Greca C.N.R., 161-166.

Torelli, M. 1986. 'Archeologia Italiana in Patria e all'Estero. Appunti per una Storia della Politica della Ricerca', in V. La Rosa (ed.), *L'Archeologia Italiana nel Mediterraneo fino alla Seconda Guerra Mondiale.* Catania: Centro Studi per l'Archeologia Greca C.N.R., 189-201.

2.8 THE DELPHI ARCHAEOLOGICAL CONTRACT: LOOKING THROUGH THE EYES OF THE DAILY PRESS OF THE NINETEENTH CENTURY

Eleftheria Theodoroudi and Kostas Kotsakis

Aristotle University of Thessaloniki, Greece

Abstract

The history of the excavations at Delphi was started in the last quarter of the nineteenth century by the French Archaeological School at Athens and the research has continued until today. The initial phase of the project was part of a contract between Greece and France, which took both of them almost ten years (sometimes delicately) to negotiate. The purpose of this paper is to present a brief review of the historical framework of the contract and to highlight the impact this contract had on the general public in Greece, as represented by nineteenth century Greek newspapers. Greek public opinion was vigorous regarding issues such as the protection and management of antiquities, and the feelings toward the work of foreign archaeological institutions in Greece were conflicting. Archaeology has worked as the foundation in the forging of ethnic identity and at the same time as a capital – sometimes literally – to invest in. The Delphi contract is part of that negotiation and the view of the press of that time could shed light onto the little known or even the silent histories that lay underneath one official history.

Résumé

Le contrat archéologique de Delphes : vu par la presse du XIXème siècle

L'histoire des fouilles à Delphes commence au cours du dernier quart du XIXème siècle par l'École Française d'Archéologie d'Athènes, et la recherche continue jusqu'à présent. La phase initiale du projet faisait partie d'un contrat entre la Grèce et la France, dont les négociations (parfois délicates) ont duré près de dix ans. Le présent article vise à montrer brièvement le cadre historique du contrat et de mettre en évidence l'impact que ce contrat a eu sur le grand public en Grèce, comme le démontre les journaux grecs du XIXème siècle. L'opinion publique grecque était vigoureuse concernant les sujets tels que la protection et la gestion des antiquités et les sentiments envers des institutions étrangères travaillant en Grèce étaient contradictoires. L'archéologie a contribué à la fondation et à la construction de l'identité ethnique, tout en étant un investissement, parfois au sens littéral du terme. Le contrat de Delphes fait partie de ces négociations et le point de vue de la presse à cette époque pourrait éclaircir l'histoire peut connue ou inconnue qui sous-tend l'histoire officielle.

Extracto

El contrato arqueológico de Delphi: mirando a través de los ojos de la prensa del siglo diecinueve

La Escuela Arqueológica Francesa en Atenas inició la historia de las excavaciones en Delfi en el último cuarto del siglo diecinueve y la investigación continúa hasta hoy. La fase inicial del proyecto formó parte de un contrato entre Grecia y Francia, que les costó a ambos partidos casi diez años de negociaciones (a veces delicadas). El propósito de este artículo es presentar un breve sinopsis del marco histórico del contrato y para destacar el impacto que este contrato tuvo en el público en general, representado por los periódicos griegos del siglo diecinueve. La opinión publica griega era vigorosa con respecto a cuestiones como la protección y la gestión de antigüedades y los sentimientos hacia el trabajo de instituciones arqueológicas extranjeras en Grecia eran conflictivos. La arqueología ha funcionado como base de la creación de la identidad étnica y al mismo tiempo como capital – a veces literalmente - en el que se puede invertir. El contrato de Delfi es parte de esta negociación y la opinión de la prensa de aquella época puede aclarar las historias poco conocidas, o incluso las calladas, que se hallan debajo de una historia oficial.

ملخص

عقد دلفي الأثري: رؤية من خلال منظور الإعلام اليومي للقرن التاسع عشر

أيفيتيري تيودورودي وكوستاس كوستاكس

جامعة أرطسوط في سالونيك، اليونان

لقد أدب تاريخ الحفريات في دلفي في الربع الأخير من القرن التاسع عشر من خلال المدرسة الأثرية الفرنسية في أثينا ويستمر البحث حتى الآن. وكانت المرحلة البدائية للمشروع جزء من عقد بين اليونان وفرنسا، حيث تخذت الدولتان ما يقرب من عشر سنوات من المفاوضات من أجل (أحيانا إن هذه هدف هو وتقديم مراجعة قصيرة للإطار التاريخي بطريقة دقيقة). وقفا اليونان، للجمهور العام في اليونان وكذا الأرا كان تأثير هذا العقد على الجمهور العام من القرن اليونانية من اليونان دائرة الجريدة في الموجودة المصورة للصور اليونانيي قويا فيما مثل القضايا حماية وإدارة الآثار القديمة، كما كانت وقد كانت المشاعر تجاه عمل المؤسسات الأثرية الأجنبية في اليونان متناقضة. ربتعت أساسا لتكوين الهوية العرقية وفي نفس الوقت كانت تعبر الأركايا أساسا لتكوين الهوية العرقية وفي نفس الوقت كانت تعبر جزءا عقد دلفي -حرفيا. هيه في الاستثمار يجب بشكل حرف أحيانا-الأسمار رأس أو المغمر التاريخ على اضواء كاذنا الإعلام منظور يقلي وقد ضوافتراا هذا من حتى التصامات الذي يمكنه التاريخ الكلاثولكيكي الموحد.

Keywords

Archaeology, Delphi excavation contract, nineteenth century daily press, foreign archaeological schools

Introduction to the context

The present paper is part of a volume exploring practices and policies of European archaeological projects abroad, carried out in 'host countries', outside the national borders of 'home countries'. If we accept this clear dichotomy, Greece would occupy an intermediate place between 'host' and 'home' countries. In some ways, Greece was considered a 'home' country to European archaeology (Kotsakis 1991, 1996), yet also a 'host country' to many foreign archaeological projects. This complex, reciprocal relation echoes the ideological reflections and the historical circumstances of the archaeological practice taking place within the Greek national context of the nineteenth century.

The strong, clear contrast between a 'home' and a 'host' country is mitigated in the specific case of Greece by Herzfeld's concept of 'cryptocolonialism': '[Greece] was compelled to acquire its political independence at the expense of massive economic dependence, this relationship being articulated in the iconic guise of aggressively national culture fashioned to suit foreign models' (Herzfeld 2002: 900-901). There was a deeper dimension in this ideological domination, arguably more complex than a straightforward economic dependence. The special place Greece acquired as the birth place of European identity came with a price: the reliance on western classicism for the signification of their own heritage (Morris 1994: 23).

Modern Greeks, therefore, had to fulfil the expectations of the western Europeans. At the same time, they had to reinvent themselves as the only heirs of their ancient ancestors. This double bind with the past, *i.e.* the self-presentation of the Greek subject and the representation of the Greek self to a non-Greek audience (Herzfeld 1987: 95-122), is central in understanding the core of the formation of Greek identity. There were two dimensions in it, occasionally overlapping or intertwined, often in contrast with each other: an introverted dimension, closely related to the Byzantine Orthodox tradition and the Ottoman rule, appropriate for describing mainly the allegedly negative and mundane characteristics of the modern Greek subject (the *romios*), and an extroverted one, referring mainly to the sublime classical past, used for communicating with non-Greeks (Kotsakis 1998: 54-55). Both dimensions had an equally strong pedagogical effect, which was dragging Greek society relentlessly towards modernity.

The European belief in the cultural ancestry of ancient Greece had also long roots in the eighteenth century philhellenism (Chryssos 1996; Marchand 1996). Therefore, it created a privileged role for archaeology in the process of Greek nation-state building, producing an ideologically charged national narrative (Kotsakis 2003: 57). Within the context of Greek nation-state building, archaeology proved nothing less than a 'national discipline' (Herzfeld 1982: 36) and the newly inaugurated state invested heavily in uncovering and protecting as much material evidence for this descent as possible.[1] Antiquities and ancient heritage were being used to build up the major symbolic capital of modern Greece (Hamilakis and Yialouri 1996). This same capital, however, had strong significance for other cultural descendants, regardless of their national origins. Indeed, while for Greeks the establishment of direct, material links to classical antiquity was a particularly effective means for domestic ideological integration, the call of ancient Greek material culture was equally practised by foreign archaeologists, occasionally in collaboration with the Greeks, often in mutual distrust (Kalpaxis 1990, 1993, 1996; Kotsakis 2003).

Another parameter, highlighting the binary character of archaeological practice as described here, is offered by the absence of direct display of colonial force, in the strict sense of the world. Calotychos (2003: 49) introduces the term self-colonization to describe the ideological role of the westernized local ruling elite that becomes a 'national bourgeoisie' and fashions 'national identities'. Archaeologists of the nineteenth century, as custodians and trustees of the precious symbolic capital of antiquity, constituted an integral part of these elites. Greek archaeologists, as subjects and bearers of Western thoughts and ideals, motivated by their personal agendas and aspirations, created world-views which functioned as coercive structures for the alignment of Greek emerging modernity to the western tropes. Access to the material manifestations of the symbolic capital through archaeological work has always acted as an approving sign from this hegemony.

There are certain aspects, however, that qualify this ideological coercive function. Skopetea (1988: 199-202) has described the tense relationships between Greek and European archaeologists in the nineteenth century, following the details of the conflict of Kyriakos Pitakis with Ludwig Ross. Greek archaeologists at that time often felt alienated by the dominant epistemological paradigm which was mastered by the European scholars and institutions. On the other hand, Greek archaeologists, as representatives of the state, regarded it their duty to defend the value of the official discourse against spontaneous archaeologies produced by the local communities. In a somewhat curious reversal, this defence led on occasion to the rejection of indigenous perceptions when it was felt that their, overtly nationalist, aspirations overshot disciplinary correctness. To set the balance straight, they would normally employ concepts developed and mastered largely by their alienating foreign peers (Alexandri 2002).

Parallel to the mainstream disciplinary discourse, this lower level vivid dialogue is revealed in published articles and notes in newspapers and popular reviews of that time.[2] The fact that the obligations of Greek archaeologists were extended to the ideological integration of local communities, but equally to foreign disciplinary

---

1   Petrakos 1982, aptly describes archaeology as the 'par excellence Greek and national discipline' of the nineteenth century.

2   The reception of archaeology by the local communities and vice versa has been the object of an extensive research project carried out by the Department of Archaeology within the framework of Information Society Operational Programme, under the title 'Digitization and Archiving of Archaeological Publications in the Daily and Periodical Press of the Period 1832–1932' (http://invenio.lib.auth.gr/collection/Archaeological events in Greek press 281832-1932%29?ln=el).

correctness, is an interesting reversal of the image of archaeologists as ideological capacitors in the service of the nation, acting as 'high priests' of nationalism (*e.g.* Hamilakis 1999: 71). Astonishingly, this particular aspect of archaeology of nineteenth century Greece is little studied, let alone understood. The truth is that, as the evidence of the media indicates, the involvement of Greek archaeologists was much more critical of nationalist narratives, a position which, in our opinion, should not be discounted simply as a condescending defence of their monopoly of ideological power. As so often the case, reality does not conform to our analytical stereotypes.

From this point of view, it seems likely that the role of Greece as a host country was determined by two main elements: on the one hand there was a constant concern for national integration, reaching down to the small local communities. On the other, this integration would be attempted by a tenacious adherence to the European archaeological canon, projecting Greek archaeology outside the country to an international audience. While standing at the periphery of theoretical trends, Greek archaeology was thus operating in the core of the European interest for constructing an ancestry stemming from ancient Greek culture. Although for Greece this ancestry had predominantly a national, rather than only cultural, significance, still modern Greece was arguably as much a host as it was a home country for archaeology. Consequently, exporting Greek archaeology abroad, at least during the nineteenth century, was not an objective, not only because of the all too obvious lack of resources.

A drastic change of the historical background occurred in the first quarter of the twentieth century. After the successful Balkan Wars, by which Greece extended its territories to Northern Greece, and as a result of the Treaty of Sèvres in 1920 (Koliopoulos and Veremis 2010: 76), modern Greece acquired for the first time in its history an international geopolitical significance as a key player in southeast Europe. This is precisely the time when the Greek Parliament voted for an act to finance two Greek archaeological schools, one in Rome and one in Istanbul (Pantos 2001: 305).[3] This legislation however never materialized and the Greek state revised the act as late as 1997, giving the Ministers of Culture and Foreign Affairs the right to establish archaeological schools and Greek research institutes abroad (Pantos in press: 17).[4] Significantly, this again was a period of rapid economic growth and convergence to developed European countries, only three years before the Eurozone monetary unification, and ten or so years before the outburst of the debt crisis of 2009.

Despite the since 1920 existing legal framework, up to now no serious and consistent attempt has been made to establish a Greek archaeological school abroad (Pantos in press: 17). During the last decades of the twentieth century, a limited number of excavations and expeditions were carried out in foreign countries, but their research interests have mostly been focused on '*topoi*', traditionally linked

---

3   Law 2447/1920 article 27, §2, *Government Gazette* A' 169, 29 July 1920.
4   Law 2557/1997 article 6, §5, *Government Gazette* A' 271, 24 December 1997.

with the presence of Hellenism.[5] These excavations are often joint projects of institutes and universities and they do not have central planning from the Ministry of Culture or Foreign Affairs, nor a scheduled financing. These efforts are rather personal choices, based on personal connections and networks.

The emphasis on the historical and ideological dimension of Hellenism is articulated officially, in the 3028/2002 Act for the protection of antiquities and national heritage, in which is stated: 'The Greek state should take care, in the framework of International Law, for the protection of the cultural goods *historically associated* to Greece, wherever they are located' (our translation, emphasis added) (Pantos in press).[6] By pointing to the historical associations with Greece as the focus of interest, the act is implicitly aligned with the dominant concept of an internally coherent national narrative devoid of temporal discontinuities. As has been repeatedly pointed out, the notion of continuity is central in national history (Liakos 2001: 28).

There were only few cases, such as those in Albania (1912–1913) or in Western Turkey (1920–1922), where archaeological projects were carried out as a corollary of the national expansion of Greece (Davis 2000; Hamilakis 2007: 40-41).[7] The aim of these short expeditions in regions inhabited by Greek populations and annexed by the Greek army is obvious. Like in many situations of conflict throughout Europe, the programme of nationalism had a profound influence on how the discipline was perceived and practised. The theme has been extensively discussed, especially in the 1990s (*e.g.* Kohl and Fawcett 1995; Atkinson, Banks and O'Sullivan 1996; Díaz-Andreu García and Champion 1996; Meskell 1998). In this paper we can only draw some broad lines on the affinities to our case study. Perhaps it is time to expand the discussion from the organic relationship between the state as a mechanism of homogenization and the archaeological discipline as a means to produce the material evidence, to the different ways and resources with which the shaping of archaeology took place in Greece, as in the rest of Europe.

Without necessarily invoking Foucauldian notions of governmentality (Foucault 2010), it is obvious that the direct domination of the discourse by the state in shaping the perceptions of cultural heritage and national identities, is a broad generalization. For one thing, the assumed uniformity of both the imposed state ideology and 'the people' on which state ideology is imposed, are oversimplified. 'People' especially consist of different groups with different social strategies

---

5   Such as South Italy, the Black Sea (Samoylova 2001, 2004) and Cyprus (Bakirtzis 1976; Bakalakis 1988; Mantzourani 1994, 1996, 2000, 2003, 2009). Archaeological affinities between Cyprus and Greece and the archaeological practice should be examined under the prism of the historical and cultural interaction and national antagonisms, but this is beyond the scope of this article. An exception can be noted for the Greek participation in the Neolithic Catalhoyuk project in Turkey in the years 1996–1998 (http://www.catalhoyuk.com/archive_reports/1996/ar96_04.html; http://www.catalhoyuk.com/archive_reports/1997/ar97_07.html).

6   Law 3028/2002 article 1, §3, *Government Gazette* A' 153, 28 June 2002.

7   Greek irredentism of the nineteenth and early twentieth century should be understood within the context of the 'Great Idea', the dominant ideological narrative which set the territorial limits of Greek nationalism at that time. The Asia Minor Catastrophe (1922) marked the end of Greek expansionist policy (Koliopoulos 1997: 133-197; Koliopoulos and Veremis 2002: 130).

and conflicting interests, which resist the official state discourse and negotiate differently their conditions and possibilities (Kotsakis 2003: 58). This is a complex procedure.

Coming closer to this procedure involves revealing the discourse that the state tries to impose, in this case nationalism, but also the techniques, the strategies and the tactics that construct the apparatus of this imposition. It involves the institutions established, the methodologies endorsed, the visions adopted, but also the resistances experienced and the negations expressed. Such a closer examination sheds more light on the interwoven threads of the discipline and its significance in the formation of national identity. But we should not perceive archaeology as an omnipresent force, imposed on unsuspecting individuals. On the contrary, its discourse has been a battlefield for a number of groups of various ethnic, intellectual and social features, and has served as a means of pressure, and of negotiation. In this battle, archaeologists have not always been the winning team. We will try to illustrate this by describing briefly one example from the Greek-French negotiations for the excavations at Delphi.

The case study of Delphi

In the last quarter of the nineteenth century, Greece as a state only counted 50 years of independent presence. It was a small nation state, formed through the disintegration of the Ottoman Empire and the outbreak of the birth of ethnic entities in the Balkan Peninsula. It became a reality after a series of diplomatic battles and negotiations, but the formation of the Greek nation was an open and tenuous procedure that was addressed both towards the inside and the outside of the country.

Archaeology as a discipline played a vital role in the formation of the ethnic identity of the Greek State. At the same time, foreign institutions rushed to the quest of the past for their own ideological reasons, invested in the pursuit of systematic knowledge. The circumstances were highly appropriate and the antagonism of the great powers, especially of France and Germany, was also felt in the field of archaeological research (Kalpaxis 1996).

The opening of Pandora's box

The first foreign school in Greece was the *École Française d'Athènes* (EFA) in 1846, followed by the *Deutsches Archäologisches Institut, Abteilung Athen* (DAI) in 1874 (Korka 2007). The first priority of the German Institute was to establish a contract for the excavations at Olympia (Kalpaxis 1996: 53-54). The contract, which was signed in December 1874, opened Pandora's box, as term six of the contract gave the excavators the opportunity to obtain 'any double or alike items' unearthed during the excavation, and as the contract provided Germans the exclusive right to take casts of all the antiquities found in Greece (Kalpaxis 1996; Anagnostou 2000). It was fiercely rejected by the Greek Archaeological Society as well as by a major part of the political world.[8] The signing of a contract of that kind, apart from the obvious and rather uncomfortable term of the double antiquities, opened the way to the export of public property (antiquities found in Greece were considered to be public property by law) and to the disregard of the Archaeological Law of 1834, which provided a framework of how foreign institutes would conduct excavations within the Greek state (Petrakos 1982, 1987; Kokkou 2009). Strong objections were raised concerning the precedent that was set by the contract, giving every foreign institute working in Greece the possibility of demanding a similar contract.[9] Concerns were also expressed about the fact that the Greek government would have to pay a considerable amount of money for the excavations, for the expropriation of the land and for the construction of infrastructures (Kalpaxis 1996: 53).[10]

This was the context in which the negotiations between Greece and France for the Delphi excavations began. The negotiations lasted for at least a decade and the whole procedure can be divided into three phases (Delphi 1993): from 1881 to 1883, the phase of preparations and mutual hesitations; from 1886 to 1888, the phase of denial; and the last and fruitful phase from 1889 to 1891, when the contract was finally accepted and voted for by the parliaments of Greece and France.

The contract

At the first phase in 1881, the two sides came to an agreement and presented a plan for the contract which was basically the same as the 1874 one for the Olympia excavations (Amandry 1992: 79). The Prime Minister of Greece, Alexandros Koumoundouros, signed the contract after a series of diplomatic negotiations in February 1882.[11] It was the last thing he did as Prime Minister before going into elections that he lost. Harilaos Trikoupis, his successor, stopped the contract from going to parliament, expressing reservations about the article on the 'double and alike' antiquities. His prime concern, however, was to counterbalance with the archaeological contract an agreement on the French import tax that was imposed

---

8   The impression made on the press was more or less unanimous with regard to the 'disgraceful' terms of the contract. We can see that by a few articles in the daily press, *i.e. Aeon*, 6 May 1874: 1-2; *Paliggenesia*, 4 May 1874: 1-2; *Ethnikon Pneuma*, 24 December 1874: 2-3. About the Archaeological Society see: *Paliggenesia*, 26 November 1974: 3; *Laos*, 29 November 1874: 3; *Nea Hellas*, 14 December 1874: 3; *Efimeris*, 3 December 1874: 5-8. Another interesting feature is that giving up the antiquities which are mentioned as 'national property', Greeks do not differ 'in Hellenism' from the Turks *Aeon*, 2 May 1874: 4. The contrast with the Turks who were seen as a 'barbaric nation' with no interest in the antiquities is a very powerful stereotype produced by the press of that time. But we have to keep in mind that in the Greek press there were voices in support of the German excavation at Olympia in *Nea Hellas*, 28 March 1874: 1; *Nea Hellas* 27 April 1874: 4; *Nea Hellas*, 1 June 1874: 4; *Efimeris*, 31 March 1874: 2. A very illuminative article is that of Koumanoudis in the newspaper *Nea Hellas* against the contract and the answer of the paper in favour of it *Nea Hellas*, 11 May 1874: 4, making clear the very complex and multilayered narratives of archaeological discourses. See also Sofronidou 2002: 380-382.
9   *Aeon*, 2 May 1874: 4.
10   *Paliggenesia*, 4 May 1874: 1-2.
11   21 January/4 February 1882.

on the Greek raisins. This was a commercial contract which was being negotiated since 1878 (Amandry 1992: 89-92; Ntasios 1992: 128-31). The French side refused to relate the two contracts and the whole thing was set aside.

The second phase – after a long period of stasius – started in 1886. Trikoupis was very eager to come to a commercial agreement and insisted on forwarding the two issues as one package (Amandry 1992: 96). The French were still reluctant to accept the commercial contract, but took some courageous steps with regard to the archaeological contract. With some changes favouring the Greek demands, it was signed for the second time (Ntasios 1992: 133). The article on the 'double and alike items' was no longer included in the new contract.

However, another thorny issue came up, concerning the required evacuation of the Kastri village and the reimbursement of the villagers (figure 1). There was a series of negotiations and the Greek part came up with the amount of 60,000 francs, but that was clearly not enough for the relocation of the village. In 1888 the matter reached the French parliament, which voted against the archaeological contract due to the larger sum of money that was demanded for the acquisition of the land (Amandry 1992: 104). The contract was put aside for the second time.

The last phase of the drama introduced a new rival. It was the American School of Classical Studies in Athens (established in 1881), which proposed to the Greek government the idea of undertaking the excavation at Delphi. The American part offered to pay, not only for the excavations but also for the expropriation of the

Figure 1. General view of the Kastri Village (Photo: École Française d'Athènes).

Figure 2. The Athenian Stoa and the Polygonal Wall of the Temple of Apollo (Photo: École Française d'Athènes).

village (Amandry 1992: 108-109).[12] That was something that the French could not ignore. At the same time, the Greek government gave up its expectations of a financially profitable contract, a decision that could open the way for the validation of the archaeological contract (Amandry 1992: 110). That was exactly what happened. The French parliament decided under the American pressure and without the 'raisin issue' to validate the contract and to provide the funds not only for the excavation, but also for the expropriation of the Kastri village. In February 1891, the French parliament finally validated the contract, exactly ten years after the first contract had been signed. In Greece, the contract was validated on 6 March 1891. The excavations (figure 2) did not begin until the spring of 1892.

The impact on the press

The Athenian press was very interested in the contract. Every aspect of the cultural heritage was important for the public, and the French contract on Delphi was warmly accepted by the newspapers. In contrast with the Olympian one, seven years earlier.

In the first phase of the negotiations (1881–1883), the press paid little attention to the incident of the contract and reported only brief notes on it. In 1881, the newspapers covered the demand of the Germans regarding the ownership of the

---

12   The Archaeological Institute of America had published an appeal in the American Journal of Archaeology 1889 5(2) for raising funds for the excavations at Delphi.

double items and the general unwillingness of the Greek statesmen to provide a solution. An interesting series of articles is that of G. Charmes in 1881[13] and an answer to that by E. Kastorchis,[14] the chairman of the Greek Archaeological Society. Charmes pointed to the strict archaeological law of Greece, which did not allow the export of antiquities. The fact that Germany invested so much in the excavation only for theoretical results – a platonic excavation, as Charmes calls it – was common place to the arguments of Western rhetoric (Kalpaxis 1996; Anagnostou 2000). Kastorchis responded with another stereotypical answer namely that Greece is not like Turkey (he had in mind the case of Pergamon), that it has laws that prohibit the looting of antiquities, and he concluded that the Turks cannot appreciate the treasures found in their territory.[15]

At the start of 1882, just before the first contract was signed, there was a short but very insightful clipping presenting the Greek Archaeological Society as being ready to undertake the excavation at Delphi, if the Greek government would be willing to pay for the village of Kastri.[16] A few months later an article by Koummanoudis,[17] then secretary of the Archaeological Society at Athens, expressed the then prevalent academic attitudes of the Greek side towards the contract. In this article, Koummanoudis took a stand against any kind of special contract with foreign archaeological schools. In his opinion, contracts are a burden, generating unnecessary economic obligations for the Greek state, while the existing archaeological law provides an adequate framework for the foreign institutes to excavate. Significantly, he opened his article with stating his belief that 'no civilized nation should stand in the way of scientific progress'.[18]

On the same issue, another important statesman, S. Dragoumis, member of the Archaeological Society and Minister of Foreign Affairs, followed with a reply to S. Reinach[19] who with an article provokingly entitled '*Vandalisme moderne en Oriente*' accused Greece of not willing to co-operate on the advancement of archaeological knowledge.[20] Dragoumis, in a long and detailed response supported Koummanoudis' point of view, rejecting as it were the Delphi contract.

In the following years there was no special mention of the contract. The theme returned to the columns of the press in 1887, when the negotiations were concluded. That year started with a series of articles noticing that the contract, compared to the Olympia one, was altered in favour of the Greek concerns.[21] Now,

---

13   In particular: 'The Excavations at Olympia' (in Greek), *Paliggenesia*, 20 April: 2. See also *Paliggenesia*, 6 April 1881: 2-3; *Paliggenesia*, 20 April 1881: 2; *Paliggenesia*, 22 April 1881: 1-2; *Paliggenesia*, 5 May 1881: 2.

14   'Control of unjust accusations against Greece' (in Greek), *Aeon*, 27 May 1881: 2-3.

15   See also footnote 7.

16   *Nea Efimeris*, 11 November 1882: 1; *Paliggenesia*, 11 January 1882: 2.

17   *Aeon*, 19 April 1882: 2-3.

18   *Aeon*, 19 April 1882: 2-3 (our translation).

19   'Olympia and Delphi' (in Greek), *Aeon*, 25 March 1883: 1-2.

20   Reinach, S. 1883. 'Vandalisme Moderne en Oriente', *Revue des Deux Mondes* 56, 1 March 1883: 132. Retrieved 4 January 2012 from http://gallica.bnf.fr/ark:/12148/bpt6k871070.image.f137. pagination.langEN.

21   *Nea Efimeris*, 15 February 1887: 5; *Paliggenesia*, 13 February 1887: 3.

however, more emphasis was placed on the moving of the Kastri village.[22] Repeated reports in the press made clear that the villagers had very high expectations regarding the compensation and the final relocation of their village, and so the whole project was delayed. The year finished with reports presenting details from the French deliberations regarding the contract[23] and expressing the certainty that the excavations would start soon.[24]

The following year the press presented the actions taken by the Greeks on the issue of the relocation of the Kastri village. The Greek Ministry of Internal Affairs had sent an engineer to report on the claims of the villagers.[25] An interesting report was published on behalf of the villagers of Kastri, who were complaining about the delays of the expropriation of the land and about the compensations.[26] The most interesting article of that year was a reprint from the French press of the minutes of the discussion on the Delphi contract in the French Parliament.[27] The contract was not voted for and the comment of the reporter was that the majority of the political community in France did not consider research expeditions as particularly profitable or useful for diplomatic purposes.

In 1889, entering the last phase of the Delphi contract, two issues emerged in the Greek press. The first one is the lottery of the Archaeological Society and the second the interest of the American school of Classical Studies to take on the excavations at Delphi.[28] The Archaeological Society had gained the right to print a lottery for antiquities by governmental decree (figure 3). The Greek Prime Minister had personally come to an agreement to get a loan from an Austrian bank (Union Bank) and to print bonds in the form of a lottery for antiquities.[29] Unfortunately, the Austrian parliament did not validate the contract and the Union Bank withdrew from the deal.[30] The importance of that deal was shown by a series of articles presenting the Archaeological Society as competent and with enough funds to proceed with the excavations at Delphi.[31] The French objections to the lottery were also described in the press.[32] The year ended with the Archaeological Society getting the right to issue the lottery.[33] Participation was considered a 'national duty for every lover of antiquity'.[34] The income of the lottery was nevertheless rather disappointing, forcing the Archaeological Society to forget the dream of excavating the ancient oracle of Apollo.[35]

---

22   *Nea Efimeris*, 15 February 1887: 5.
23   *Paliggenesia*, 6 March 1887: 2; *Nea Efimeris*, 25 June 1887: 1.
24   *Nea Efimeris*, 15 July 1887: 4.
25   *Paliggenesia*, 17 February 1888: 3; *Acropolis*, 12 March 1888: 2.
26   *Paliggenesia*, 3 June 1888: 1-2.
27   *Efimeris*, 12 December 1888: 4-5.
28   *Efimeris*, 12 February 1889: 2.
29   *Paliggenesia*, 27 January 1889: 1; *Efimeris*, 30 January 1891: 2-3; *Paliggenesia*, 13 February 1889: 1; *Paliggenesia*, 4 February 1889: 3.
30   *Nea Efimeris*, 8 March 1889: 2.
31   *Nea Efimeris*, 7 February 1889: 1; *Efimeris*, 6 February 1889: 2.
32   *Efimeris*, 13 February 1889: 3; *Efimeris*, 1 May 1889: 2.
33   *Efimeris*, 19 March 1889: 2; *Paliggenesia*, 28 June 1889: 2; *Efimeris*, 28 June 1889: 3.
34   *Efimeris*, 30 September 1889: 3.
35   *Efimeris*, 11 March 1889: 2(a).

Figure 3. The lottery of antiquities for 1880 (École Française d'Athènes 1992: 106).

In 1890, the press forgot about the issue of Delphi and only at the end of the year some reprints from the French press appeared, referring to the upcoming budget discussions in the French parliament, which would include the funds for the excavations and the translocation of Kastri village.[36]

In 1891 Waldstein, the director of the American school announced the withdrawal of their interest in Delphi,[37] opening the way for the French to validate the contract. The whole project was presented to the Greek public through long and detailed publications of all the discussions in the French parliament and the subsequent voting.[38] During the year, several articles appeared on the successful culmination of the contract. Simultaneously, the press presented the problems relating to the relocation of the village.[39]

---

36   *Paliggenesia*, 9 October 1890: 3; *Efimeris*, 10 October 1890: 3; *Paliggenesia*, 25 October 1890: 2.
37   *Efimeris*, 14 January 1891: 2; *Nea Efimeris*, 15 January 1891: 4.
38   *Efimeris*, 11 February 1891: 1.
39   *Efimeris*, 27 June 1891: 3.

Conclusions

As stated in the introduction of this paper, archaeologists and archaeological practice are always caught between two parallel discourses; the first one is the official discourse of the state, as represented by statesmen, organic intellectuals and venerable institutions like the Archaeological Society at Athens. The other is an everyday, unofficial one, as expressed by local communities and stakeholders, in our case by the press. Both of these discourses are subject not only to the national significance of classical antiquities, but equally to the necessities of their direct connection with the material remains of the past. The attitude of all parts involved is eventually defined by the realization that both aspects of this relationship are significant. Through the kaleidoscopic view of the press of that time, we can observe how the so-called symbolic capital transformed into a real one.

The Delphi contract was for Prime Minister Harilaos Trikoupis – by definition a representative of the ideology of the state – a lever for something as mundane as the taxes imposed on exported raisins (*Efimeris*, 11 March 1889: 2a), for the villagers of Kastri an opportunity to sell their land for a better price (*Paliggenesia*, 3 June 1888: 1-2). The villagers were urging the French to proceed with the compensations; otherwise they would put pressure on the government to hand over the excavations of the Delphi sanctuary to the Germans. In the same way, the government closed the negotiations with the French using the threat of the Americans (Amandry 1992; Ntasios 1992; Morris 1994: 33).

Two other things are noteworthy here. The first is that the crypto-colonial state (Herzfeld 2002) was in this case using the 'symbolic capital' for the interests of its subjects, to persuade foreigners and to succeed in its purposes. This was recognized by the press, which hinted that the Greek side defended the national interests well (Morris 1994: 33), reinforcing the competition between the European countries to gain access to the Greek antiquities. The second is that the community of Kastri was using its 'symbolic capital' not so much to shape and negotiate a national or even a communal identity, but to gain a more profitable deal for their properties.

The claims of both sides were made, of course, while understanding the enormous significance of the monuments of Delphi. The government was fully aware of the cultural significance that Delphi held for Europe, while the local community realized the national significance of the monuments to the government. Both sides therefore felt safe to exert pressure on the other. However, none of the Greek archaeologists that expressed an opinion in the press seemed to have disregarded, or even belittled, the material concerns involved. In contrast to the articles published in the French press during the time of negotiations, in which the ideological and cultural value of the antiquities overshadowed any other concern, Greek archaeologists – and of course politicians – were aware of the real limitations of an utterly idealistic reading of the past. In this particular case, rather than acting as 'high priests' of nationalism, they acted as firm and efficient tradesmen.

In between the discourses deployed, the 'self-colonized' (Calotychos 2003) archaeologists, therefore, seemed to be the ones producing symbolic capital, but were not always controlling it. The final decisions for its exploitation and transformation rest equally, perhaps even more, with the other parties involved, which archaeology and archaeologists can only influence to a limited extent. Lastly, a word of caution is needed, as we have to keep in mind that the example discussed above is based on information recorded by the press. Reports and articles in newspapers and magazines reflect the attitudes and dispositions of the public of that time, rather than the documented history. Although contemporary archaeological discussions stress the relationship of archaeology with its audiences, this realization limits the arguments presented in this paper.

Acknowledgements

The research on the press was realized through the digital depository of the National Library of Greece (http://www.nlg.gr/digitalnewspapers/ns/main.html), the Library of the Hellenic Parliament (http://catalog.parliament.gr/ipac20/ipac. jsp?session=13256P86L4M83.52320&profile=001&menu=search&submenu=su btab32&ts=1325668703526) and the Aristotle University of Thessaloniki (http:// digital.lib.auth.gr/?ln=el). The database of the AUTh was the result of a project named 'Digitization and Archiving of Archaeological Publications in the Daily and Periodical Press of the Period 1832–1932, and Construction of a Web Site' that was conducted in the framework of the Information Society Operational Program.

References

Alexandri, A. 2002. 'Names and Emblems: Greek Archaeology, Regional Identities and National Narratives at the Turn of the 20th Century', *Antiquity* 76(291): 191.

Amandry, P. 1992. 'Excavations at Delphi and Corinthian Raisins: the History of a Negotiation'(in Greek), in École Française d'Athènes – The Delphi Ephorate of Antiquities (eds), *Delphi. Looking for the lost Shrine* (in Greek). Athens: B. Giannikos and B. Kaldis, 77-126.

Anagnostou, I. 2000. 'Greek and German Archaeology. Parallel Actions and Influences' (in Greek), unpublished PhD Thesis. Thessaloniki: Aristotle University of Thessaloniki.

Atkinson, J.A., I. Banks and J. O'Sullivan. 1996. *Nationalism and Archaeology: Scottish Archaeological Forum*. Glasgow: Cruithne Press.

Bakalakis, G. 1988. *Excavations at Yiorkous Hill: NE of Athiaenou, Cyprus* (in Greek). Athens: Archaeological Society.

Bakirtzis, H. 1976. *Basilica at 'Yiorkous' NE of Athiaenou*. Reports of the Department of Archaeology, Cyprus. Nicosia: Department of Archaeology: 1-24.

Calotychos, V. 2003. *Modern Greece: a Cultural Poetics*. Oxford and New York: Berg.

Chryssos, E. 1996 (ed.). *A New World is Born. The Image of Greek Civilization in German Science in the 19th Century* (in Greek). Athens: Akritas Publishing.

Davis, J.L. 2000. 'Warriors for the Fatherland: National Consciousness and Archaeology in Barbarian Epirus and Verdant Ionia' 1912-22, *Journal of Mediterranean Archaeology* 13(1), 76-98.

Díaz-Andreu García, M. and T.C. Champion. 1996. *Nationalism and Archaeology in Europe*. Boulder, Colo: Westview Press.

École Française d'Athènes – The Delphi Ephorate of Antiquities (eds). 1992. *Delphi. Looking for the lost Shrine* (in Greek). Athens: B. Giannikos and B. Kaldis.

Foucault, M. 2010. *The Government of Self and Others*. New York: Palgrave/Macmillan.

Hamilakis, Y. 1999. 'La Trahison des Archéologues? Archaeological Practice as Intellectual Activity in Post-Modernity', *European Journal of Archaeology* 3(2): 60-79.

Hamilakis, Y. 2007. *The Nation and its Ruins: Antiquity, Archaeology, and National Imagination in Greece*. Oxford and New York: Oxford University Press.

Hamilakis, Y. and E. Yalouri. 1996. 'Antiquities as Symbolic Capital in Modern Greek Society'. *Antiquity* 70(267): 117-129.

Herzfeld, M. 1982. *Ours Once More: Folklore, Ideology, and the Making of Modern Greece*. New York: Pella Publishing.

Herzfeld, M. 1987. *Anthropology through the Looking-glass: Critical Ethnography in the Margins of Europe*. Cambridge and New York: Cambridge University Press.

Herzfeld, M. 2002. 'The Absent Presence: Discourses of Crypto-Colonialism', *The South Atlantic Quarterly* 101(4): 899-926.

Kalpaxis, Th.E. 1990. *Archaeology of Samos 1850-1914* (in Greek). Rethymn: University Press of Crete.

Kalpaxis, Th.E. 1993. *The Excavation of the Temple of Artemis (Corfu 1911)* (in Greek). Rethymn: University Press of Crete.

Kalpaxis, Th.E. 1996. 'The French-German Conflict in the 19th Century in the Image Making of Ancient Greece'. in E. Chryssos (ed.), *A new World is Born. The Image of Greek Civilization in German Science in the 19th Century* (in Greek). Athens: Akritas Publishing, 41-58.

Kohl, P.L. and C.P. Fawcett. 1995. *Nationalism, Politics, and the Practice of Archaeology*. Cambridge and New York: Cambridge University Press.

Kokkou, A. 2009 [1977]. *The Care for Antiquities in Greece and the First Museums* (in Greek). Athens: Kapon.

Koliopoulos, J. 1997. Brigandage and Irredentism in Greece of the 19th Century (in Greek), in T. Veremis (ed.), *National Identity and Nationalism in Modern Greece*. Athens: Morfotiko Idrima tis Ethnikis Trapezis, 133-197.

Koliopoulos, J, Th. and M. Veremis. 2002. *Greece: The Modern Sequel from 1831 to the Present*. London: Hurst.

Koliopoulos, J, Th. and M. Veremis. 2010. *Modern Greece. A History since 1821*. Malaysia: Willey-Blackwell.

Korka, E. (ed.) 2007. *The Foreign Archaeological Schools in Greece from the 19th to 21st Century* (in Greek). Athens: Ministry of Culture.

Kotsakis, K. 1991. 'The Powerful Past: Theoretical Trends in Greek Archaeology', in I. Hodder (ed.), *Archaeological Theory in Europe*. London: Routledge, 65-90.

Kotsakis, K. 1996. 'United we Stand?', *Antiquity* 70: 706-709.

Kotsakis, K. 1998. 'The Past is Ours: images of Greek Macedonia.', in L. Meskell (ed.), *Archaeology under Fire: Nationalism, Politics and Heritage in the Eastern Mediterranean and Middle East*. London: Routledge, 44-67.

Kotsakis, K. 2003. 'Ideological Aspects of Contemporary Archaeology in Greece', in M. Haagsma, P. den Boer and E.M. Moorman (eds.), *The Impact of Classical Greece on European and National Identities. (Proceedings of an International Colloquium, held at the Netherlands Institute at Athens, 2-4 October 2000)*. Amsterdam: J.C. Gieben, 55-70.

Liakos, A. 2001. 'The Construction of National Time: The Making of the Modern Greek Historical Imagination', *Mediterranean Historical Review* 16(1), 27-42.

Mantzourani, E. 1994. *Report of the Excavations' Results at Kantou-Kouphovouno Site* (in Greek). Report of the Department of Antiquities, Cyprus. Nicosia: Department of Antiquities, 1-29.

Mantzourani, E. 1996. *Report of the Excavations' Results at Kantou-Kouphovouno Site at 1994-1995* (in Greek). Report of the Department of Antiquities, Cyprus. Nicosia: Department of Antiquities: 1-28.

Mantzourani, E. 2000. *Kantou-Kouphovouno: Confirmation and Differentiations of the Architecture of 5000 B.C* (in Greek). Minutes of the third Cyprological Conference A' Ancient Part. Nicosia: Society of Cypriotic Studies, 219-235.

Mantzourani, E. 2003. 'Kantou-Kouphovounos. A Late Neolithic Site in the Limassol District', in J. Guilaine and A. le Brun (eds), *Le Néolithique de Chypre, Actes du Colloque International Organisé par le Départment des Antiquités de Chypre et L' École Française d' Athènes*. Nicosie 17-19 Mai 2001. Athens: École Française d'Athènes, 85-98.

Mantzourani, E. 2009. *The Excavation of the Neolithic Site Kantou-Kouphovouno in Cyprus. Part A'. Stratification and Architecture* (in Greek). Nicosia: Department of Antiquities.

Marchand, S.L. 1996. *Down from Olympus: Archaeology and Philhellenism in Germany, 1750-1970*. Princeton, N.J.: Princeton University Press.

Meskell, L. 1998. *Archaeology under Fire: Nationalism, Politics and Heritage in the Eastern Mediterranean and Middle East*. London and New York: Routledge.

Morris, I. 1994. *Classical Greece: Ancient Histories and Modern Archaeologies*. Cambridge and New York: Cambridge University Press.

Ntasios, F. 1992. 'The Adventure of the Negotiation from Greek Point of View (1881-1891)' (in Greek), in École Française d'Athènes – The Delphi Ephorate of Antiquities (eds), *Delphi. Looking for the Lost Shrine* (in Greek). Athens: B. Giannikos and B. Kaldis, 127-142.

Pantos, P. 2001. *Encoding Legislation for Cultural Heritage. A' Greek Legislation* (in Greek). Athens: Ministry of Culture.

Pantos, P. in press. 'The Legal Framework of Excavations in Greece. From 20th to the 21st Century' (in Greek), *Anaskamma* 6: 1-24.

Petrakos, B. 1982. *Proofreading for the Archaeological Legislation* (in Greek). Athens: Fund for Archaeological Resources.

Petrakos, B. 1987. The *Archaeological Society in Athens: 150 Years of History 1837-1987* (in Greek). Athens: Archaeological Society.

Samoylova, T.L. (ed.). 2001. *Ancient Greek Sites on the Northwest Coast of the Black Sea*. Kiev: Hellenic Foundation of Culture, Branch in Odessa.

Samoylova, T.L. (ed.). 2004. *Ancient Greek Sites in the Crimea*. Kiev: Hellenic Foundation of Culture, Branch in Odessa.

Skopetea, E. 1988. '*The Model Kingdom' and 'the Great Idea'* (in Greek). Thessaloniki: Polytropo.

Sofronidou, M.D. 2002. 'Archaeological News in the Newspapers' (in Greek), unpublished PhD. Thesis. Thessaloniki: Aristotle University of Thessaloniki.

Part Three

Critical Reflections

3.1 Colonization and the development of archaeology in Senegal

Ibrahima Thiaw

Archaeology Laboratory,
Fundamental Institute for Black Africa
Cheikh Anta Diop University Dakar, Senegal

Abstract

French archaeology in Senegal and francophone West Africa began in the mid-nineteenth century but it was not until the 1930s, with the creation of the *Institut Français d'Afrique Noire* (IFAN), that it took shape and developed structure. Most French archaeologists operating in Senegal and francophone West Africa were not archaeologically trained and this had profound consequences for methods, goals and paradigms, which were largely articulated in respect of the colonial project. Doing archaeology consisted mainly of collecting artefacts and human remains. With the influence of orientalists and ethnographers, initial interests in stone industries quickly shifted toward the Iron Age period that coincided with the expansion of trans-Saharan commerce that was thought to have brought civilization and progress in the region prior to contact with the Europeans. Archaeology's main interest was in monumental sites, and diffusionism was widely used to explain their presence on African soil. This perspective began to lose ground in the post-colonial period after the 1960s. It was replaced by a normative approach that defined culture areas on the basis of monument types. Also processual archaeology with fine excavations and analysis techniques was introduced in Senegal by the late 1960s. French archaeologists working in Senegal were however reluctant to change and their work remained prevalent until the 1980s. By then, local archaeologists took over but due to a dearth of resources, the scope of their work remained limited. As of the 1990s, the training of local archaeologists outside the traditional French mould has opened up new sources of funding and possibilities of collaboration and brought along exposure to a variety of new paradigms and methodologies. This has begun to reshape Senegalese archaeology.

Résumé

La Colonisation et le Développement de l'Archéologie au Sénégal

L'archéologie française au Sénégal et en Afrique de l'Ouest francophone a commencé au milieu du XIXème siècle mais ce n'est qu'à partir des années 1930, avec la création de l'Institut Français d'Afrique Noire (IFAN), qu'elle a pris forme et qu'elle s'est structurée. La plupart des archéologues français qui ont travaillé au Sénégal et en Afrique de l'Ouest francophone n'ont pas été formés à l'archéologie, ce qui a eu des conséquences profondes sur les méthodes, les objectifs et les paradigmes qui ont été largement articulés dans le cadre du projet colonial. Effectuer une recherche archéologique consiste essentiellement à recueillir des artefacts et des ossements humains. Sous l'influence d'orientalistes et d'ethnographes, l'intérêt initial pour l'industrie lithique s'est rapidement tourné vers l'Age de Fer qui coïncidait avec l'expansion du commerce transsaharien dont on estimait qu'il avait apporté la civilisation et le progrès dans la région avant l'arrivée des Européens. L'intérêt archéologique s'est tourné principalement vers les sites monumentaux, et la notion du diffusionnisme a été largement utilisée afin d'expliquer leur présence sur le sol africain. Ce point de vue a commencé à perdre en importance durant la période postcoloniale après les années 1960. Il fût remplacé par une approche normative qui définissait des zones de culture sur la base du type de monument. A la fin des années 1960 une archéologie processuelle fût également introduite au Sénégal et celle-ci employait des techniques d'excavation et d'analyse détaillée. Cependant, les archéologues français qui travaillaient au Sénégal furent réticents au changement et leur travail a prévalu jusque dans les années 1980. Dès lors, des archéologues locaux ont pris la suite mais leur travail est resté limité en raison du manque de ressources. Depuis les années 1990, la formation des archéologues locaux, en dehors du modèle français traditionnel, a mis à disposition de nouvelles sources de financement et des possibilités de collaboration, et a permis l'introduction d'une variété de paradigmes et de méthodes nouvelles. Ceci a déclenché une refonte de l'archéologie sénégalaise.

Extracto

La Colonización y el Desarrollo de la Arqueología en Senegal

La arqueología francesa en Senegal y en África Occidental francófona empezó a mitad del siglo diecinueve, pero no es hasta los años 30 del siglo pasado, con la fundación del *Institut Français d'Afrique Noire* (IFAN), que se concrete y se desarrolle una estructura. La mayoría de los arqueólogos que trabajan en Senegal y en África Occidental francófona no había recibido instrucción en la arqueología y esto tenía consecuencias profundas para los métodos, fines, y paradigmas que eran ampliamente expresados en relación con el proyecto colonial. Practicar arqueología consistía principalmente en la colección de artefactos y de restos humanos. Bajo la influencia de los orientalistas y los etnólogos, los intereses iniciales en las industrias de la piedra se desplazaron rápidamente hacia la Edad de Hierro que coincidió con la expansión del comercio a través del Sahara, la que se considera responsable de la civilización y el progreso en la región anterior al contacto con los europeos. El interés principal de la arqueología se hallaba en los sitios monumentales y se utilizaba ampliamente el difusionismo para explicar su presencia en tierras africanas. Esta perspectiva empezó a perder valor en la época poscolonial después de los años 60 del siglo pasado. Se la sustituyó por un planteamiento normativo que definía los campos culturales sobre la base de tipos de monumentos. La arqueología procesal con excavaciones y técnicas excelentes de análisis fue introducida en Senegal a fines de los años 60 del siglo pasado. Sin embargo, los arqueólogos franceses que trabajaban en Senegal, rechazaban el cambio y su trabajo quedó prevaleciente hasta los años 80. Para entonces, los arqueólogos locales se hicieron cargo, pero debido a una escasez de recursos el alcance de su trabajo siguió limitado. La formación, a partir de la década de los años 60 del siglo pasado, de arqueólogos locales fuera del modelo francés ha creado posibilidades para nuevas fuentes de fondos y posibilidades de colaboración y llevó consigo la exposición a una variedad de nuevos paradigmas y metodologías. Esto fue el inicio de la remodelación de la arqueología senegalesa.

ملخص

الاستعمار وتنمية علم الآثار في السنغال

ابراهيم ثياو

مختبر علم الآثار، المعهد الأساسي في أفريقيا السوداء – جامعة انتا ديوب، داكار، السنغال

ادب علم الآثار في السنغال وغرب أفريقيا بالمنطقة الفرنسية في فترة ما قبل التاريخ، متخصص جدا ولم يتطور حتى بنية ثلاثينيات القرن التاسع عشر أي ذخذ الشكل ولم تكن أي. ولم نشأ المعهد الأساسي في أفريقيا السودء. معظم الأثريين الفرنسيين العاملين في السنغال وغرب أفريقيا بالمنطقة الفرنسية عند نشأن انشاء المعهد اركيولوجي مما أثر تأثيرا عميقا على الأساليب. والأهداف والمناهج التي تم وضعها احترام المشروع الاستعماري إلى حد كبير. وتحت تأثير وقد تضمن العمل الأثري جمع القطع الأثرية والرفات البشرية. والمستشرقين الفرنسيين، تحولت الاهتمامات الابتدائية بالصناعات الحجرية ونحو مرحلة العصر الحديدي التي تزامنت مع انتشار التجارة عبر الصحراء التي من المعتقد انها تبلبت الحضارة والتقدم إلى المنطقة قبل الاتصال بالأوربيين. إن الأثري الرئيسي كان بالملامح واقع الأثرية، وقد تم استخدام الاستعمار من فترة ما بعد الاستعمار بفقدت موقعه في أدب المنظور هذا ولكن. الأفريقية. في أواخر ستينيات القرن العشرين. وقد استبدل بمنهج معياري يعرف فروع الأثريين الفرنسيين العاملين في السنغال هنا كانوا. غير أن الأثريين العاملين في السنغال في الإجراءي بالحفريات وأساليب التحليل الدقيقة في أضيف إلى ذلك تم إدخال علم الآثار. وبالإضافة إلى ذلك تم إدخال علم الثقافية على أساس نوع أواخر الستينيات.

متددردين في ميما الغتيير الخص واستمر معلمهم على ما كان على حيه حتى ثمانينيات
القرن العشرين. ووقتئذ، تولت الأثريين المحليون الممهمة الا أن نطاق عملهم
ظل محدودا بسبب قلة الموارد. ومنذ تسعينيات القرن العشرين، فتح تدريب
الأثريين المحليين خارج النمط التقليدي الفرنسي الطريق الى موارد تمويل
وامكانيات تعاون جديدة، كما أن ما أدى الى نماذج ومناهج متنوعة جديدة. مما
إعادة تشكيل علم الآثار في السنغال.

Keywords

French, archaeology, colonial, post-colonial, diffusionism, normative, culture areas, processual archaeology, collaboration, Senegal

Introduction

French archaeological research in West Africa and in Senegal in particular, is tightly entangled with the establishment and organization of colonial administration and its supporting research institutions. The French tailored a vast colonial empire in West Africa during the scramble for Africa in the late nineteenth century. Senegal was at the apex of the administrative apparatus of this French colonial empire that was known as *Afrique Occidentale Française* (AOF) or French West Africa. From the initial archaeological finds in Senegal in the mid nineteenth century until the 1970s, Senegal was the hub for French scientific investigations in francophone West Africa. The earliest archaeological activities were primarily conducted by soldiers, colonial administrators, missionaries, ethnographers and explorers. Almost none of them had a background in archaeology and their activities consisted essentially of collecting artefacts and roughly locating sites. Archaeology was a leisure activity carried out by amateurs, who interpreted and disseminated their finds for the French colonial administration and public. Analysis was generally performed with the help of scholars based in France who rarely ventured into the colonies. Therefore they had no control over the methods of collecting and the contextual information on the material they analysed, which was a major flaw in their work.

With the establishment of a French colonial government in the early twentieth century, the need grew for research institutions capable of collecting usable data on the people, the regions and the resources they administered. The first initiative was launched in 1915 with the creation of the *Comité d'Etudes Historiques et Scientifiques de L'Afrique Occidentale Française* (BCEHSAOF). It would later be replaced by the *Institut Français d'Afrique Noire* (IFAN), which existed from 1936 to 1966. From its headquarters in Dakar (Senegal), IFAN pioneered research in archaeology, ethnography, history, geology, botany, zoology, entomology, etc., mostly in the French West-African colonies and sometimes in the neighboring regions that were under other European administration. Like with most other disciplines that emerged at this time, the methodologies and conceptual framework of archaeological enquiry were shaped by the convulsions of colonialism and the ideologies and counter ideologies, such as nationalism, that it inadvertently produced.

As most amateurs were also active collectors, in Senegal as well as in the other colonies, the local communities were expropriated of their culture heritage in order to fill private and public collections in France (*e.g. Musée de l'Homme, Laboratoire de Paléontologie and Musée des Colonies*). As a hub for French research in the West African sub-region, IFAN museums and laboratories were also destinations for material collected throughout the French West-African Empire (Bocoum and Becker 1997). As far as archaeology is concerned, there was little or no public outreach. Publications were in French, a language that the largest majority in Senegal did not speak. Local populations had limited means to counter the way in which they were described or displayed to the rest of the world (Thiaw 2003). However, with the rise of African nationalism in the interwar period, a number of voices began to challenge this view.

This paper explores French archaeology in Senegal, paying particular attention to changes in goals, paradigms and methods. The main focus is on archaeology, but I wink at other disciplines, such as history, ethnography and heritage management, to understand the linkages in paradigms, goals, methods and trajectories. I will also look into the role of the multiple actors involved in archaeological enquiry, to evaluate their strengths and weaknesses in the production of archaeological knowledge.

The first section analyses the period before the existence of IFAN, roughly between 1850 and 1936. Archaeological research during this period was sporadic and unplanned. It generally focused on collecting and describing objects that the French public considered curiosities. The second section examines the role of IFAN during the development of archaeological research under French colonial rule, from 1936 to 1960. The bulk of the archaeological collections from francophone West Africa was constituted in this period. Research was generally oriented toward stone tool typologies, monumental sites and the identification of the capital cities of the western Sudanic medieval kingdoms. However, its scope and outcome were quite limited due to the poor training of the researchers and to a general lack of resources. The first heritage legislation in Senegal dates from this period, but it concerned primarily French colonial architecture, which still dominates Senegal's national heritage list (Thiaw 2003). This legislation has barely changed since then, it was only slightly amended in the early 1970s. The management of archaeological resources was mainly in the form of salvage archaeology, which only occurred occasionally and merely around the major cities. Most of the sites that were discovered in the early twentieth century have been wiped out without any research.

The third section looks at French archaeology in post-colonial Senegal, from 1960 to the 1980s. French archaeologists continued to dominate in the field but the political context following independence in 1960 led to major changes in the organization of research. With the creation of the University of Dakar, archaeology was taught in the History Department and for the first time local students could aspire to a career in archaeology. This was also a time of ideological blossoming, where nation building, pan-Africanism, negritude and the definition of new useable pasts were hotly debated among Senegalese intellectual and political elites.

The last section reflects on the current trends and future of Senegalese archaeology. The post-1980 period is marked by the internationalization of research and a greater presence of Senegalese archaeologists in the field. Thanks to collaboration with nationalities other than French, the new generation of Senegalese archaeologists is exposed to new methods, paradigms, and sources of funding which widens the scope of archaeological inquiry.

French archaeology in Senegal: 1850–1936

Like history and ethnography, archaeology in Senegal and West Africa is an offspring of the colonial experience. The imposition of French colonial rule in the mid-nineteenth century permitted the collection of historical, ethnographic, geographical, geological and archaeological material (Fall 1988; Holl 1995). Archaeology was informed by what Mudimbe aptly called "ethnological reason" that "extracts elements from their context, aestheticizes them, and then uses their supposed differences for classifying types of political, economic, or religious ensembles" (Mudimbe 1994: 52-53).

The colonial project to 'civilize' local populations relied heavily on a diffusionist paradigm in which change was considered inevitable and which would irremediably lead to gradual assimilation and finally to the dissolution of local cultures into the dominant colonial system. To achieve that goal, the past was fashioned by the ethnographer and was anything but a sequential account of events. The rhetoric was either paternalistic, as in the case of Delafosse and his disciples (Grosz-Ngaté 1988; Van Hoven 1990), or racist, like with Henri Hubert (1925). In his discussion of Neolithic industries, Hubert distinguished a northern white race of nomadic pastoralists – who generally worked and used flint according to Capsian, Mousterian and Tardenoisian technological traditions – and southern black agriculturalists, who used a variety of raw material but rarely flint. In both the paternalist and racist approach, French archaeologists and ethnographers not only used their authority to manufacture history, they also gave little credit to African agency in historical processes.

Thus, French colonial archaeology, ethnography and history in Senegal was characterized by two parallel currents of thought: one directed towards the place and role of African societies in world history, the other towards the nature, extent and long-term consequences of external influence on African societies. Both currents were dominant ideologies from the eighteenth to the early twentieth centuries and had major consequences for the production of knowledge.

The first current has its roots in Hegelian universal history, by which sub-Saharan Africa is depicted as stuck in time and outside the realm of history (Fall 1988; Holl 1990, 1995). This assumption was at the foundation of the colonial project that was embellished to become a 'mission' or even a 'burden' to 'civilize' the 'uncivilized' Africans.[1] Some colonial authorities such as Albert Charton (1931) voiced this need to "protect" and "educate" the people they administered. Indeed, education was the key for setting up an efficient administrative apparatus. By the end of the first quarter of the twentieth century, there was an increasing attention for history, ethnology and even for archaeology as they helped to develop knowledge on indigenous people.

Archaeological and ethnographic objects were collected as curiosities, through purchase, theft or by force, disregarding indigenous emotional and symbolic linkages to it. With such collections, General Faidherbe, the founder of the colony of Senegal, set up the first museum in Saint Louis in 1865.[2] The permanent exhibition of this museum displayed material on agriculture, industry, ethnology and natural history (Charpy 1958: 528-532). The aim of the French colonial authorities was to develop knowledge on the available natural and human resources in order to exhibit the potentials of the territories under their administration and to garner support for their policy from France. Thus, archaeology, history, ethnography and cultural heritage were in general cursory to the objectives of these essentially economical endeavours.

Stone material constituted the bulk of archaeological finds. Mostly they were surface finds without a context and as chronologies were missing and some populations continued to recycle and use stone artefacts, these finds were linked to modern populations or their immediate predecessors.[3] Europeans, living in the industrial age, easily interpreted the finds as evidence of African primitiveness and deduced from that their superiority and mission to civilize the Africans.

The second current was born out of the findings of Arab/Islamic texts on Africa and of archaeological discoveries (Fall 1988). Most colonial administrators were trained as orientalists that converted into Africanists historians, ethnographers and amateur archaeologists. Among them was Maurice Delafosse. He played an influential role as he coached and encouraged a number of scholars to investigate iron-using societies, caravan routes and medieval towns that were historically connected to the Arab/Islamic World (Desplagnes 1903, 1951; Bonnel de Mézières 1923a, 1923b; Gaillard 1923; Vidal 1923). Monumental burial architecture such as tumuli and megaliths were also targeted, not only because they fascinated and intrigued Europeans but also because they were seen as a by-product of external influences (Jouenne 1916-17, 1918, 1920, 1930; Bonnel de Mézières 1923a, 1923b, Maes 1924). The initial attribution of these monuments to African populations on the basis of associated human skeletal remains that were identified

---

1   During the colonial era, French scholarship contributed significantly to ethnic stigmatization, which was canonized via transcriptions of oral narratives, census reports, agricultural surveys, ethnographic, religious (Amselle and M'Bokolo 1985) and archaeological cartographies (Thiaw 2003). Although it was later admitted that ethnic construction was not necessarily a by-product of colonization, it may have stimulated it via its multiple modes of classifying people (Chrétien and Prunier 2003).

2   It would be transferred to Dakar in 1869.

3   Even the polished Neolithic stones axes that were collected in the valley of the Falémé in eastern Senegal in the second half of nineteenth and early twentieth centuries were part of such curiosities. They were attributed to a Saharan influence with the assumption that local populations were unable to produce such fine tools (Hamy 1901; Zeltner 1916; Laforgue 1923, 1924, 1925).

as Negro (Hamy 1904; Duchemin 1905, 1906), were rejected in the early second quarter of the twentieth century with diffusionist arguments. As this evidence contradicted the colonial assumption of African backwardness, it threatened the colonial domination, which was grounded on European superiority (Holl 1990: 300; Trigger 1990: 311).

Although racist considerations were largely downplayed by the 1960s, the diffusionist paradigm continued to thrive until recently, even among African intellectual elites. It was a long-lasting legacy of colonial historical studies that continued to passionate debates, particularly among Senegalese Egyptologists, who generally appeal to archaeologists for empirical evidence (C.A. Diop 1974, 1979, 1981, 1987; Lam 1993, 1994, 1997, 2003). While both Europeans and Africans archaeologists are more and more reluctant to engage in such debates, the nature and significance of Arab/Islamic external influences via the trans-Saharan trade network have been largely re-evaluated over the past fifty years, giving greater recognition to African agency in the production of history (McIntosh and McIntosh 1988).

IFAN 1936–1960

The creation of the *Institut Français d'Afrique Noire* (IFAN), in 1936, gave a tremendous impulse to archaeological research in francophone West Africa. From its foundation to the period of local empowerment in the 1960s, IFAN centralized scientific research in the French West-African colonies. Although there was still a strong reliance on stray finds, extrapolation from a handful of artefacts, single site analysis and inadequate chronologies, the work of IFAN played a crucial role in the development of modern academic science in this part of the continent.

One of the main contributors to the expansion of French archaeology in francophone West Africa was Raymond Mauny. As a former law student at the *Ecole Coloniale* (Colonial School), he joined the federal colonial government in Dakar in 1937. At his arrival in Dakar, Mauny met Theodore Monod, the first director of IFAN, who was a naturalist. Monod was engaged in archaeological and historical research and he presumably coached Mauny, who did not have an academic training in archaeology. Mauny (1961: 19) calls Monod his master and the two collaborated in various projects concerning history, prehistory and the historical geography of West Africa.[4]

During World War II Mauny joined the French army and participated in military campaigns in France and Northern Africa. In Northern Africa he devoted his free time to library research in Fès, Rabat, Algiers and Tunis to get acquainted with material that was unavailable in Dakar (Mauny 1961: 13). After the war, he returned to Senegal and in 1947 he was appointed in charge of the archaeology and

---

4   Mauny also read the work of previous colonial administrators, including Maurice Delafosse, Jean Rouch, Charles Monteil, etc., such as their publications in the *Bulletin du Comité d'Etudes Historiques and Scientifiques de l'Afrique Occidentale Française*.

prehistory section of IFAN.[5] He managed to built a large research network through establishing IFAN sections (Centrifan) throughout the French colonial empire in West Africa, and through participating in international conferences worldwide.[6]

Until the late 1950s, Mauny and his colleagues at IFAN reinforced the diffusionist paradigm by "medievalizing" western Africa, which was at that time perceived as a marginal backcountry of the Islamic World (McIntosh 2001). Caravan routes, capital cities, and entrepôts mentioned in Arab chronicles[7] were the primary research focus in the Sahel and Sudanic zones. The main interest was on evidence of Islamic/North African influence, which materialized as luxuries, inscriptions, Islamic architecture, etc. (Monteil 1928, 1942; Mauny 1949a; Desplagnes 1951; Joire 1955). As McIntosh pointed out, there was very little consideration for locally manufactured material remains (McIntosh 2001). Imports were generally used as *fossiles directeurs* for building chronologies while local manufactures (including pottery) were barely considered in the establishing of culture history sequences. Surveys were generally judgmental and written sources and local informants were used to locate old cities.

There was equally little effort to gain an understanding of regional settlement patterns and site variability (McIntosh and McIntosh 1984). Surface collections were unsystematic and there was hardly any interest in local production systems (De Barros 1990). Presumably this approach was as much driven by the limitations of chronological assessments of prehistoric material, as by ideology. Datable imported luxuries were more useful for chronological assessments, but they were only present at sites connected to external trade. Assumptions that only writing, urbanization and monumentality conveyed historicity, subsequently constituted major constraints for an archaeology liberated of the colonial prism. Ultimately, this perspective that negated African agency in the production of culture and history, disqualified the largest majority of African cultures.

In this period there were few archaeological excavations worth mentioning,[8] but as with the support of the French army aerial photos were increasingly employed, lots of sites were discovered, necessitating classifications and typologies (Gard and Mauny 1961; Clos-Arceduc 1962). Towards the end of the military expeditions and explorations and the subsequent consolidation of the territorial administration,

---

5   This section was created in 1944, with Henri Bessac as its first director, but would only become active in 1947 in response to a resolution passed at the Pan-African Archaeological Congress in Nairobi, that deplored the absence of an institutional apparatus for archaeology in francophone West Africa.

6   His work culminated with the publication of his *Tableau Géographique de l'Ouest Africain au Moyen Age* (1961). It is a genuine synthesis of the archaeological work conducted under the auspices of IFAN from 1936 to 1960, as it uses archaeology, oral traditions and written sources. Prior to his return to France, Mauny received the medal of the officer of merit from the government of independent Senegal in 1962. Back in France, he became the chair of Pre-colonial African History at the Sorbonne, president of the *Société des Africanistes* (in 1974) and member of the *Académie des Sciences d'Outre-mer* (Hennion 2000: 35).

7   Such as the Tegdaoust (Robert 1970; Devisse 1983), Kumbi Saleh (Thomassey and Mauny 1951; Berthier 1997), and Niani (Filipowiak 1966, 1968).

8   Joire's excavation in 1955 of the tumuli near Rao (north-west Senegal) yielded the most significant archaeological finds of that time, such as a fabulous golden pectoral.

the majority of the discovered sites were located near major cities.[9] As many of these sites were threatened by urban expansions, archaeological work took more and more the form of salvage interventions, which mainly consisted of collecting artefacts. This is illustrated by the large number of archaeological reports on sites and stray finds that were recovered at the Cap Vert Peninsula around Dakar and other major Senegalese cities.[10]

The salvage operations could however not prevent the destruction and looting of archaeological sites. In an attempt to protect natural monuments and sites of artistic, historical, scientific, legendary or picturesque importance (Descamps 1997: 896), the French colonial authorities had already begun to implement heritage management legislation in the West African territories as of the 1930s, but this legislation was weak and also IFAN was too poorly equipped and staffed to play a significant role in cultural heritage preservation and management. Illustrative is the case of Podor, a town in northern Senegal, where during construction work for an airport in 1958, a chance discovery of jewellery was made. The site was looted and destroyed by the local population well before IFAN's archaeologists could get there (Thilmans 1977) and the archaeologists purchased a large part of the material from the local market. This was the worst way to deal with the situation, as it only encouraged the site being looted further.

French archaeology in post-colonial Senegal (from the 1960s to the 1980s)

With the wave of independancy in the French African colonies in the 1960s, IFAN's archaeological research was increasingly confined to Senegal and nearby countries, including Mauritania and Mali. In 1966, on the eve of the First World Festival of Negro Arts (*Festival Mondial des Arts Nègres*), which marked a turning point in African nationalisms, IFAN was turned into the *Institut Fondamental d'Afrique Noire* (Fundamental Institute for Black Africa) (Touré and Ciss 2008). The acronym remained the same but the institute changed its name to get rid of the French umbrella. It wanted to become more pan-Africanist and to reduce its French personnel.

IFAN's research activities were further restricted to the national boundaries of Senegal and the regional sections (Centrifans) became independent research institutes or museums. The institute nevertheless continued to hire and host a number of African francophone scholars, such as historian Joseph Ki-Zerbo from Burkina-Faso, Hampaté Bâ and Sékéné Modi Cissokho from Mali, Camara Laye from Guinée, etc. IFAN also continued to feed on French government subsidies until the 1970s, a decade after Senegal's independence and after the dissolution of

---

9   A pattern that occured in the other territories of francophone West Africa as well, with archaeological sites and finds mainly being reported near major cities (Bessac 1951; Szumowski 1953, 1955; Cosson 1955).

10 See for instance Laforgue and Mauny 1938; Corbeil 1943, 1951; Joire 1946, 1947; Mauny 1946a, 1946b, 1948, 1949b, 1951; Corbeil, Mauny and Charbonnier 1948; Richard 1951, 1952, 1955, 1956, 1957; Szumowski 1952; Cheneveau 1958.

Figure 1. Collection of human remains in a baobab burial (Photo: IFAN, Archaeology Laboratory).

the French West-African federation. It was only by the 1970s that IFAN's French staff, funding and research activities began to dwindle.

Yet, most archaeological work in Senegal was still carried out by Frenchmen. Prominent French archaeologists working in Senegal included Cyr Descamps, Annie Ravie, Bruno Chavane, Victor Martin and Charles Becker.[11] Guy Thilmans, a Belgian physical anthropologist, who worked closely with his French colleagues of IFAN, may however have been the most dominant figure in Senegalese archaeology from the 1970s to the 1980s. Thilmans had a grand passion for human skeletal remains. He was an unusual grave robber who was primarily interested in human skulls from baobab burials, leaving the rest of the body and possible grave goods on site. With Cyr Descamps he intruded in several burial sites in the hallowed trunks of baobabs, generally in the middle of the night (Thilmans 2006) (figure 1). This was done without any concern for the impact this practice could have on the emotional well-being of the local populations who related to these sites, and without concern for contextual information. Although Thilmans and Cyr Descamps might have thought they were doing this for the benefit of science, this practice is to be condemned because it poses ethical and moral problems. Moreover, the material is largely useless for scientific purposes because it is poorly documented and contextualized.

---

11 Like their predecessors, most of them became archaeologists out of practice with little or no academic training

Already during the political period following World War II, African academics had gained influence. It were these former African students who had new ideas and who challenged colonial ideology. While none or very few of them were trained in archaeology (most were historians), they were well informed and aware of the potentials of archaeology for nation building and identity reconstruction. In the early 1960s, these African historians were able to set the methodological grounds for accepting oral traditions as a reliable source of history too (Fall 1988). This first generation of African historians was also very attentive to archaeology, but it was not until the mid 1970s to early 1980s for the first Senegalese to get a PhD in archaeology (A. Diop 1974; Diagne 1978; Lame 1981).[12]

In response to this African nationalism, interests in Iron Age archaeology grew further. The Iron Age period coincided largely with the development of the trans-Saharan trade and the emergence of most Sudanese medieval kingdoms. For many nascent West-African states, including Senegal, this period was seen as the formative stage for most modern societies prior to the expansion of European influences in the region (Thiaw 1999).

A historian who has contributed considerably to Senegalese archaeology in this period, is Jean Devisse. He was not based at IFAN but at the History Department of the newly-founded University of Dakar and he contributed both via teaching and research. His fieldschool in Tegdaoust (Mauritania), an important trade entrepôt linking the Sahara to the savannah, was the first training ground to archaeology for many of the first generation of historians in francophone West Africa. As a medieval historian, the underlying paradigm in Devisse's work was inspired by the work of aforementioned orientalists and he was primarily interested in evidence of Arab/Islamic influences. However, Devisse would later supervise the groundbreaking doctoral theses of Senegalese archaeologists, including Hamady Bocoum and Mandiomé Thiam. Bocoum's work on iron metallurgy (2000) and Thiam's on pottery (2010) meant a rupture with the past in that they were the first to emphasize local manufactures rather than luxury imports and they devised a way to study them. Devisse also supervised the innovative thesis of Laurence Garenne-Marot (1993), a French archaeologist who worked on the history of copper.

At the University of Dakar, archaeology was taught as part of history and archaeologists were confined to the remote prehistorical or protohistorical past, for which there were few or no documentary or oral records (Thiaw 2003, 2010). Moreover, neither anthropology nor art history or museum studies were taught, even though the field was still dominated by French scholars. The absence of anthropology and ethnography in the curriculum may have to do with their original association with colonialism, but this was not the case with art history and museum studies and it is curious they were not part of the agenda. The immense archaeological and ethnographic collections that IFAN scholars accumulated

---

12 Like his French colleagues in Senegal, the Senegalese physicist Cheikh Anta Diop embraced the diffusionist paradigm identifying Black Egypt as the cradle of Senegalese and African civilizations (C. Diop 1974, 1979, 1981, 1987). His attempts to trace their way back to Egypt were largely ignored by his French colleagues based at IFAN, who neither refuted nor openly accepted his ideas.

should have incited the development of curricula in museum studies and art history. Their absence continues to pose major challenges for conservation and cultural preservation until today.

In an attempt to classify the large amount of recorded finds and sites, the 1960s to the 1980s were also characterized by efforts to identify and delineate regional cultural boundaries on the basis of the geographical distribution of the most visible monumental features. For that purpose the concept of the '*aire culturelle*' (culture area) was introduced (Mauny 1957, 1961).

It distinguised four areas, *i.e.* the Iron Age sites of the middle Senegal valley, the shell mound sites bordering the Atlantic coast, the tumuli in west-central Senegal and, the megaliths also in west-central and central-eastern Senegal (figure 2). It focused on inter-regional variability of sites and monuments, largely ignoring intra-regional variability and the non-monumental sites, and it was based on poor contextual information and small sample sizes.

This normative perspective assumed that within each culture area, only one type of monument was erected and other non-monumental archaeological sites were not worth recording. Excavations and testing were undertaken to define regional patterns of culture (Descamps 1972a; Thilmans and Descamps 1974; Thilmans, Descamps and Khayat 1980; Thilmans and Ravisé 1980; Gallay, Pignat and Curdy 1982; Chavane 1985; Descamps and Thilmans 2001) and oral traditions were gleaned for proof of ethnic affiliation of these archaeological cultural provinces with modern populations (Becker and Martin 1982; Fall 1982; Gravrand 1983, 1990), but variability within the various culture areas was rarely investigated or simply interpreted as chronological change.

The assumption that within each culture area only one type of monument was erected and other non-monumental archaeological sites were not worth recording, was only challenged by the work of American archaeologists working in the Senegambia. The pioneering work of Olga Linares de Sapir (1971) on the shell mounds of Casamance was clearly oriented toward establishing a culture history sequence, triangulating between local production and consumption systems, settlement patterns, and cultural innovations and continuities in time.[13] It did not however influence the French archaeologists working in Senegal.

By the 1970s, the rapid destruction of archaeological sites, particularly near urban areas, required syntheses and new inventories for preservation.[14] Especially Victor Martin and Charles Becker (1970, 1974, 1977), two French priests, undertook an extensive, albeit, unsystematic nationwide survey, recording hundreds, if not, thousands of sites. Although the work was primarily concerned with historical demography and sought to define regional cultural boundaries, as De Barros (1990: 165) rightly pointed out, it remains until now the most exhaustive

---

13   About the same time, the work of another American archaeologist Patrick Munson (1972) on Dar Tichitt Walata in Mauritania, which followed a similar perspective, had a huge impact on archaeologists and historians of West Africa alike, perhaps because it concerned the Empire of Ghana, one of the first historically known polity in the region.

14   Guitat (1970) proposed a first synthesis for Neolithic sites, followed by Ravisé (1975), who took on both Neolithic and Palaeolithic sites.

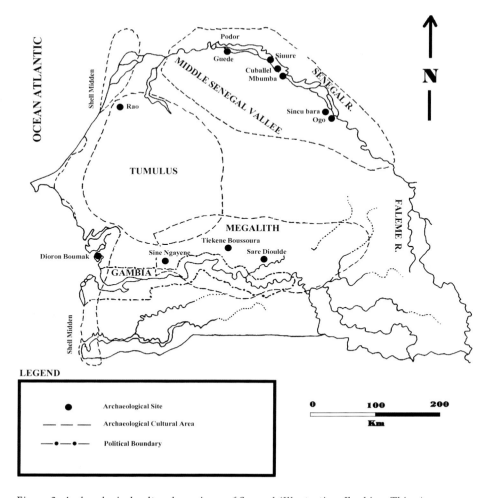

Figure 2. Archaeological cultural provinces of Senegal (Illustration: Ibrahima Thiaw).

inventory of archaeological sites in Senegal. The inventories enlarged the number of known Neolithic and Palaeolithic sites significantly, but a clear unbalance between one region to another persisted, reflecting the traditional concentration of archaeological activity near urban settlements and along the major axis of French penetration routes (roads, rivers, railways).

Moreover, the diffusionist paradigm persisted as well. For instance, for Stone Age sites terms like '*faciès*' were used, but almost always with reference to North African or European-French technical traditions, implicitly suggesting cultural influences. This is reflected in the copying of the terminologies such as Capsian, Iberomaurusian, Mousterian, Aterian, etc. used by the francophone scholars in North Africa (see Descamps 1972b; Descamps and Descamps 2010). Even when local terminologies were employed, it was always assumed that new or different technologies were introduced from the North (see also P. Klimowicz and A. Klimowicz, this volume).

The 1960s to 1970s is also known as a period of political tensions and instability. In many African independent nations, clashes between ethnic and national ideals coincided with a profound economic crisis that jeopardized the hope for a brighter future which the independences had kindled. Senegal was however not affected by political instability resulting from the tensions between ethnic versus national identity. When the Senegalese intellectual and political elites, such as Cheikh Anta Diop, drew on the distant past to foster a national and pan-African identity, most uneducated people showed little interest in prehistoric or protohistoric archaeological sites for which oral memories were very shallow.

Communicating archaeology as prehistory, and associating it with a Stone Age period, was reminiscent of the clichés of primitive and uncivilized that had been applied to local populations during the colonial period. As a result, prehistoric sites are generally unclaimed by populations living nearby. These populations often prefer to attribute such sites to other groups. In contrast, more recent archaeological sites with which populations still have memories and emotional linkages, are intensely negotiated (Thiaw 2003, 2008a). It seems that the subdivision of Senegalese archaeology into culture areas had solely been the concern of the French and Senegalese intelligentsia but not of local uneducated populations.

Current trends and the future of Senegalese archaeology

When by the 1990s the number of French archaeologists working in Senegal diminished and the number of local Senegalese archaeologists grew, important changes started to emerge. Ethnoarchaeology developed rapidly as an inexpensive way of doing archaeology, particularly among colleagues in the history department of the University Cheikh Anta Diop of Dakar who have little time to devote to research due to their heavy teaching load. The popularity of ethnoarchaeology also emanates from the dearth of resources for archaeological research, as it requires less logistics and manpower than archaeology. Most of the students were involved in ethnoarchaeology to conduct ethnographic interviews, generally on modern pottery production. With a few exceptions (Gueye 1998; Sall 2005), these ethnoarchaeological studies were however conceived without a clear research design and therefore they were of little use to archaeological analogical reasoning.

The development of ethnoarchaeology went hand in hand with that of historical archaeology, both at the expense of Paleolithic, Neolithic and Iron Age archaeology, which had been the main interests of the first generation of local Senegalese archaeologists. Ethnoarchaeology was generally associated with Senegalese students trained in Europe. Those trained in North America were more oriented toward historical archaeology and the Iron Age, for which they developed culture history sequences and documented long-term changes for the past two millennia. The reasons for this are unclear, but the interests of these students in ethnoarchaeology and historical archaeology/Iron Age were both motivated by archaeologists' efforts to participate in and contribute to debates on memory and identity, relating to recent historical processes.[15] Unlike prehistory, these issues were the subject of passionate conversations among historians and traditionalists in Senegal (Thiaw 2003).

Another major innovation in Senegalese archaeology was the collaboration with American/English scholars. Apart from some work carried out by French scholars[16] most of the archaeological work in the late 1990s and 2000s was either carried out by Senegalese scholars (Gueye 1998; Thiaw 1999; Deme 2003; Sall 2005; Thiam 2010) or scholars based in American universities (Richard 2007; Croff 2009; Gokee 2012). It was in this period that the perspective on culture sequence that De Sapir had inaugurated in the Senegambia took root in Senegal too. This was due to the work of Susan K. McIntosh and Roderick J. McIntosh. The long-lasting impact of their work, combining regional surveys and large-scale excavations, owes much to the scale of it (McIntosh, McIntosh and Bocoum 1992; McIntosh and McIntosh 1993) but also to their training of four Senegalese students, who would later receive their doctorate degrees in archaeology.

In developing and maintaining ties with archaeologists of different nationalities, Senegalese archaeology opened up to multiple influences. Especially the collaborative fieldschool programmes between American universities and the archaeology laboratory of IFAN have been an important teaching environment for many Senegalese students.[17] In addition to training students in archaeological field techniques and exposing them to an international and multicultural experience, archaeology fieldschools also have the advantage of funding research in regions where resources are scarce.

It is through such collaborative programmes however that the old model (with people in the colonies or post-colonial regions collecting the data and people in the metropolis performing analyses and building theories) started to crumble and fall apart. Illustrative in this respect is the debate on the interpretation of the site of Sincu Bara in the middle Senegal valley as a necropole (Garenne-Marot and Polet 1997). It could not stand up to the mountain of evidence collected through the new way of working, which indicated that it was a settlement site (McIntosh and Bocoum 2000). This debate was a turning point in the history of Senegalese archaeology and marked its definitive emancipation.

Cyr Descamps' recent book on Senegalese prehistory (Descamps and Descamps 2010) has evoked the same kind of reactions among Senegalese archaeologists. It is outmoded by at least thirty years. In some sort of nostalgia of the old days,

---

15 Although historians of the University of Dakar invested early on in the history of the Atlantic World, it is not until the very late 1990s and early 2000s that we see effective archaeological engagement in this recent historical period (Thiaw 1999, 2000, 2008a, 2011; McIntosh and Thiaw 2001; Richard 2007; Croff 2009).

16 Pradines' three days survey in the Siin region in 1996, Garenne-Marot's 1993 thesis on copper and Gelbert's 2000 ethnoarchaeological study on pottery circulation among the Fulbe and Soninke speakers of the middle and upper valley regions. See Pradine, S. 1996. *Les Tumulus Funéraires Sénégambiens (Sénégal)*. Retrieved 8 October 2012 from http://www.senegalaisement.com/senegal/tumulus_funeraires_senegal.php.

17 Collaborations between IFAN and Rice University, IFAN and the University of Michigan, Ann Arbor and between IFAN and the University of Chicago.

Descamps focuses on the golden age of French archaeology in Senegal. As a result, the book displays only broad brushes on the recent development in Senegalese archaeology, largely ignoring work published in English.

The international collaboration generates yet another development, a growing interest in the management of cultural heritage (Bocoum 2008; Thiaw 2008b). Until a decade ago, salvage operations were only carried out here and there in order to collect artefacts from sites that already had been or were in the process of being destroyed, but through collaboration with organizations like SRI inc. and Nexus Heritage, the IFAN archaeology laboratory has begun to develop capacities in systematic heritage management. Although Senegalese legislation remains weak, there is a growing awareness of culture heritage preservation both at the academic and political levels. With a strengthened legislation, heritage management should offer new possibilities and opportunies for archaeology.

For the future, the stake of Senegalese archaeology therefore is to capitalize on past experiences, either French or English, and to develop comprehensive and effective approaches for contemporary archaeology and heritage preservation. To achieve that, grassroot teaching and public outreach on archaeology and heritage management is a must.

Conclusion

In Senegal, the development of archaeology went hand in hand with colonization and the setting up of the French colonial administration. From the mid-nineteenth century until the 1960s, archaeological investigations were primarily the work of colonial administrators and soldiers. The lack of prior and proper academic training in archaeology had a major impact on methods. As colonial agents, French archaeologists working in Senegal systematically used archaeology to legitimate the colonial project. This would result in a sort of fossilizationin paradigms.

Throughout the colonial era and even beyond, the diffusionist paradigm was predominantly used in the interpretation of archaeological finds. The bulk of archaeological work was also too much concentrated on monumental and burial architecture and without research design. In fact, the agenda of archaeological research was primarily guided by the concerns of expatriate French archaeologists who considered architectural monuments as the only feature worthwhile investigating. Monumentality was generally associated with power and authority and therefore offered to the dominant colonial regime a historical lens on past governmentality. It was associated with external groups who allegedly brought civilization and progress in the region and therefore legitimated colonial domination. The focus on monumentality was also based on a conception of the past where only the powerful were considered as the makers of history and the powerless mere subjects to be dominated. Although archaeological research is today an old practice in Senegal, the lack of conversations with local communities and public outreach activities by the colonial pioneers, have resulted in the marginalization of the field, still largely ignored or considered as irrelevant for historical reconstruction (Thiaw 2003).

Even today, archaeology remains largely an academic endeavour, confined to a small circle of individuals at the university.

Until the 1980s, French archaeologists in Senegal had very little academic training and were too often lagging behind the major changes in the field in terms of method, concepts and paradigms. By this time however, even though archaeological research was still predominantly carried out by French expatriates, other European and American nationals were present in Senegal, forcing methodological and conceptual interaction and dialogue. Simultaneously, in response to African nationalisms and the greater demand for history, paradigmatic shifts occured with the development of normative and ethnographic archaeology.

This emergence of ethnoarchaeology and historical archaeology in the late 1990s and early 2000s was an exciting moment in Senegalese archaeology, as it was a means to connect with local concerns. Whereas Senegalese archaeology until the 1980s was characterized by an unclaimed and uncontested prehistorical past, this new era is marked by productive conversations between professional archaeologists, historians and anthropologists on the one hand and the larger public on the other. Recent interests in heritage management are likely to play a significant role in that too, as it is an important venue for conversations with the public on questions that resonate with local concerns. The development of fieldschools and capacity building programmes will result in more professionals who can engage in various and innovative methods of archaeological research and heritage management.

References

Amselle, J-L. and E. M'Bokolo (ed.). 1985. *Au Coeur de l'Ethnie. Ethnie, Tribalisme et Etat en Afrique*. Paris: Editions La Découverte.

Becker, C. and V. Martin. 1982. 'Rites de Sépultures Pré-Islamiques au Sénégal et Vestiges Protohistoriques', *Archives Suisse d'Anthropologie Générale, Genève* 46(2): 261-293.

Berthier, S. 1997. *Recherches Archéologiques sur la Capitale de l'Empire de Ghana. Etude d'un Secteur d'Habitat à Kumbi Saleh, Mauritanie. Campagnes II-III-IV-V (1975-1976)-(1980-1981)*. Britisch Archaeological Reports (International series) 680. Oxford: Archaeopress.

Bessac, H. 1951. 'Matériel Protohistorique de la Region de Nouakchott (Mauritanie)', *Notes Africaines* 50: 315-327.

Bocoum, H. 2000. *L'Âge du Fer au Sénégal: Histoire et Archéologie*. Dakar and Nouakchott: l'Institut Fondamental d' Afrique Noir and Centre Régional Inter-Africain d'Archéologie, Université de Nouakchott.

Bocoum, H. 2008. 'Aménagement du Territoire et Archéologie Préventive au Sénégal: Quels Enjeux pour la Recherche?', in B.O.M. Naffé, R. Lanfranchi and N. Schlanger (eds), *L'Archéologie Préventive en Afrique*. Saint-Maur-des-Fossés: Éditions Sépia, 75-85.

Bocoum, H. and C. Becker. 1997. 'L'Afrique Occidentale Française et la Recherché Archéologique', in C. Becker, S. Mbaye and I. Thioub, *AOF: Réalités et Heritages. Sociétés Ouest-Africaines et Ordre Colonial, 1895-1960, Tome 2*. Dakar: Direction des Archives du Sénégal, 873-889.

Bonnel de Mézières, A. 1923a. 'Recherches sur l'Emplacement de Ghana (Fouilles à Koumbi et à Settah)', *Mémoires Présentés par Divers Savants à l'Académie des Inscriptions et Belles Lettres de l'Institut de France* 13(1): 227-264.

Bonnel de Mézières, A. 1923b. 'Recherches sur l'Emplacement de Tékrour', *Mémoires Présentés par Divers Savants à l'Académie des Inscriptions et Belles Lettres de l'Institut de France* 13(1): 265-273.

Charpy, J. 1958. *La Fondation de Dakar (1845,-1857-1869)*. Paris: Larose.

Charton, A. 1931. *Rapport à Monsieur le Gouverneur General de l'A.O.F. sur un Avant-Projet de Creation d'un Institut d'Etudes Africaines, August 1931*. Dakar: Archives du Gouvernement du Sénégal.

Chavane, B.A. 1985. *Villages de l'Ancien Tékrour. Recherches Archéologiques dans la Moyenne Vallée du Fleuve Sénégal*. Paris: Editions Karthala.

Cheneveau, R. 1958. 'Sur un Anneau de Pierre Polie de l'Île de Ngor', *Notes Africaines* 80: 97-98.

Chrétien, J-P and G. Prunier (ed.). 2003. *Les Ethnies ont une Histoire*. Paris: Editions Karthala.

Clos-Arceduc, A. 1962. 'Les Tumulus de la Région de Mbacké (Sénégal)', *Notes Africaines* 95: 88-91.

Corbeil, R. 1943. 'Etat Actuel de la Question du Paléolithique dans la Region du Cap Vert', *Notes Africaines* 17: 387-390.

Corbeil, R. 1951. 'Les Récentes Découvertes au Cap Vert Concernant le Paléolithique', *Bulletin de l'Institut Fondamental d'Afrique Noire, Série B, Sciences Humaines* 13(2): 384-437.

Corbeil, R., R. Mauny and J. Charbonnier. 1948. 'Préhistoire et Protohistoire de la Presqu'île du Cap Vert et de l'Extrême Ouest Sénégalais', *Bulletin de l'Institut Fondamental d'Afrique Noire, Série B, Sciences Humaines* 10: 378-460.

Cosson, R. 1955. 'Sur Quelques Gisements Préhistoriques des Environs de Bamako (Rive Droite du Niger), *Notes Africaines* 68: 118-119.

Croff, R. 2009. 'Village des Bambara: An Archaeology of Domestic Slavery and Urban Transformation on Goree Island, Senegal, AD 17th-19th Centuries', unpublished doctoral thesis. New Haven: Yale University.

De Barros, P. 1990. 'Changing Paradigms, Goals and Methods in the Archaeology of Francophone West Africa', in P. Robertshaw (ed.), *A History of African Archaeology*. London: James Currey, 155-172.

Deme, A. 2003. 'Archaeological Investigations of Settlement and Long-Term Complexity in the Middle Senegal Valley (Senegal)', unpublished doctoral dissertation. Houston: Rice University.

Descamps, C. 1972a. 'Sites Protohistoriques de la Sénégambie', *Annales de la Faculté des Lettres et Sciences Humaines de Dakar* 9: 303-313.

Descamps, C. 1972b. 'Contribution à la Préhistoire de l'Ouest Sénégalais', unpublished doctoral Thesis. Paris: Paris I Pantheon-Sorbonne.

Descamps, C. 1997. 'Le Patrimoine Archéologique de l'Afrique de l'Ouest Avant, pendant et après l'AOF', in C. Becker, S. Mbaye and I. Thioub, *AOF: Réalités et Heritages. Sociétés Ouest-Africaines et Ordre Colonial, 1895-1960, Tome 2*. Dakar: Direction des Archives du Sénégal, 890-899.

Descamps, C. and F. Descamps. 2010. *La Préhistoire au Sénégal*. Dakar: Les Nouvelles Editions Africaines du Sénégal.

Descamps, C. and G. Thilmans. 2001. 'Fouille de Tumulus à Djouta (Îles du Saloum, Sénégal)', Paper presented at *the XIVème Congrés UISPP, 3-8 September 2001*. Liège: University of Liège.

Desplagnes, L. 1903. 'Etude sur les Tumuli du Killi dans la Region de Goundam', *L'Anthropologie,* 151-172.

Desplagnes, L. 1951 'Fouilles du Tumulus d'El-Oualedji (Soudan)', *Bulletin de l'Institut Fondamental d'Afrique Noire* 13(4): 1159-1173.

Devisse, J. 1983. *Tegdaoust III. Recherches sur Aoudaghoust*. Paris: Editions Recherches sur les Civilisations.

Diagne, I. 1978. 'Le Néolithique dans L'aire Sénégambienne et dans les Régions Adjacentes. Contributions à la Préhistoire de l'Ouest Africain', unpublished doctoral thesis. Nanterre: Paris X.

Diop, A.S. 1974. 'Mégalithisme et Préhistoire Saharo-Soudanienne', unpublished doctoral thesis. Nanterre: Paris X.

Diop, C.A. 1974. *The African Origin of Civilisation: Myth or Reality*. New York: Westport, Lawrence Hill University and Company.

Diop, C.A. 1979. *Nations Nègres et Cultures*. Dakar: Nouvelles Editions Africaines.

Diop, C.A. 1981. *Civilisation ou Barbarie, Anthropologie Sans Complaisance*. Paris: Présence Africaine.

Diop, C.A. 1987. *L'Afrique Noire Précoloniale. Etude Comparée des Systèmes Politiques et Sociaux de l'Europe et de l'Afrique Noire, de l'Antiquité à la Formation des Etats Modernes*. Paris: Présence Africaine.

Duchemin, M. 1905. 'Les Mégalithes de la Gambie', *L'Anthropologie* 16: 633-638.

Duchemin, M. 1906. 'Les Mégalithes de la Gambie', *Bulletin et Mémoires de la Société d'Anthropologie (Paris)* 7: 25-34.

Fall, Y.K. 1982. 'Silla: Problématiques d'un Site de la Vallée du Fleuve', *Archives Suisses d'Anthropologie Générale, Genève* 46: 199-216.

Fall, Y.K. 1988. 'L'Histoire et les Historiens dans l'Afrique Contemporaine', in R. Rémond, *Etre Historien Aujourd'hui: L'Histoire et les Historiens de l'Afrique Contemporaine. Actes du Colloque de Nice*. Paris: UNESCO, 181-218.

Filipowiak, W. 1966. Expédition Archéologique Polono-Guinéenne à Niani (Guinée). *Africana Bulletin* 4: 116-127.

Filipowiak, W. 1968. 'Contributions aux Recherches sur la Capitale du Royaume du Mali à l'Époque de Haut Moyen Age (Afrique Occidentale)', *Archaeologia Polonia* 10: 217-232.

Gaillard, M. 1923. 'Niani, Ancienne Capitale de l'Empire Mandingue'. *Bulletin du Comité d'Etude Historique et Scientifique de l'Afrique Occidentale Française*: 619-637.

Gallay, A., Pignat G. and Curdy, P. 1982. 'Molop Tobé (Santhiou Kohel, Sénégal). Contribution à la Connaissance du Mégalithisme Sénégambien', *Archives Suisses d'Anthropologie Générale, Genève* 46(2): 217-59.

Gard, J. and R. Mauny. 1961. 'Découverte de Tumulus dans la Région de Diourbel (Sénégal)', *Notes Africaines* 89: 10-11.

Garenne-Marot, L. 1993. 'Archéologie d'un Méta: le Cuivre en Sénégambie entre le Xe et le XIVe Siècle', unpublished doctoral thesis. Paris: University of Sorbonne-Paris I.

Garenne Marot, L. and J. Polet. 1997. 'Préjugés et Subjectivités dans l'Approche des Sites Médiévaux Ouest Africains: Tumulus ou Sites d'Habitat? Le cas de Sinthiou Bara, Moyenne Vallée du Sénégal', *Dossiers et Recherches sur l'Afrique* 4: 31-51.

Gelbert, A. 2000. 'Etude Ethnoarchéologique des Phénomènes d'Emprunts Céramiques. Enquêtes dasn les Hautes et Moyenne Vallée du Fleuve Sénégal (Sénégal)', unpubished doctoral thesis. Paris: University of Nanterre-Paris X.

Gokee, C.D. 2012. 'Daily Life in the Land of Bambuk: An Archaeological Study of Political Economy at Diouboye, Senegal', unpublished doctoral thesis. Ann Arbor: The University of Michigan.

Gravrand, H. 1983. *La Civilisation Sereer. Casaan. Les Origines.* Dakar: Nouvelles Editions Africaines.

Gravrand, H. 1990. *La Civilisation Sereer. Pangool. Le Génie Religieux Sereer.* Dakar: Nouvelles Editions Africaines du Sénégal.

Grosz-Ngaté, M. 1988. 'Power and Knowledge. The Representation of the Mande World in the Works of Parks, Caillé, Monteil, and Delafosse', *Cahiers d'Etudes Africaines* 23(3-4): 485-511.

Gueye, N.S. 1998. 'Poteries et Peuplements de la Moyenne Vallée du Fleuve Sénégal du XVIe au XIXe Siècle: Approaches Ethnoarchéologique et Ethnohistoriques', unpublished doctoral thesis. Paris: University of Nanterre Paris X.

Guitat, R. 1970. 'Cartes et Répertoire des Sites Néolithique du Sénégal', *Bulletin de l'Institut Fondamental d'Afrique Noire, Série B, Sciences Humaines* 32(4): 1125-1135.

Hamy, E.T. 1901. 'L'Age de la Pierre de la Falemme', *Bulletin du Musée d'Histoire Naturelle*: 313.

Hamy, E.T. 1904. 'Quelques Observations sur les Tumulus de la Vallée de la Gambie. Présentée à l'Occasion d'une Exploration Récente de M. le Capitaine Duchemin', *Comptes-Rendus des Séances de l'Académie des Inscriptions et Belles-Lettres*: 560-569.

Hennion, S. 2000. *Archéologie et Préhistoire au Sud du Sahara: la Construction d'une Science Colonial-1900-1980.* Mémoire de DEA. Marseille: Université de Aix-Marseille 1, Institut d'Etudes Africaines.

Holl, A. 1990. 'West African Archaeology: Colonialism and Nationalism', in P. Robertshaw, *A History of African Archaeology*. London: James Currey, 296-308.

Holl, A. 1995. 'African History: Past, Present, and Future, The Unending Quest for Alternatives', in P. Schmidt and T.C. Patterson, *Making Alternatives Histories. The Practice of Archaeology and History in Non-Western Settings*. Santa Fe: School of American Research Press, 183-211.

Hubert, H. 1925. 'Description d'Objets Néolithiques de l'A.O.F.', *Bulletin du Comité d'Etude Historique et Scientifique de l'Afrique Occidentale Française* 8(2): 262-297.

Joire, J. 1946. 'Remarques sur l'Industrie Lithique de la Presqu'île du Cap Vert Habituellement désignée sous le nom de Néolithique à Tradition Capsienne et sur la Presence d'Amas de Debris de Cuisine à Proximité du Lac M'Bobeusse', *Notes Africaines* 31: 4-6.

Joire, J. 1947. 'Amas de Coquillage du Littoral Sénégalais dans la Banlieue de Saint Louis', *Bulletin de l'Institut Fondamental d'Afrique Noire* 9: 170-340.

Joire, J. 1955. 'Découvertes Archéologiques dans la Région de Rao (Bas-Sénégal)', *Bulletin de l'Institut Fondamental d'Afrique Noire, Série B, Sciences Humaines* 3-4: 249-333.

Jouenne, P. 1916-17. 'Les Monuments Mégalithiques du Sénégal', *Annuaire et Mémoires du Comité d'Études Historiques et Scientifiques de l'A.O.F.*: 27-36 and 311-327.

Jouenne, P. 1918. 'Les Monument Mégalithiques du Sénégal', *Bulletin du Comité d'Etude Historique et Scientifique de l'Afrique Occidentale Française*: 57-86.

Jouenne, P. 1920. 'Les Roches Gravées du Sénégal', *Bulletin du Comité d'Etude Historique et Scientifique de l'Afrique Occidentale Française*: 1-42.

Jouenne, P. 1930. 'Les Monuments Mégalithiques du Sénégal, les Roches Gravées et leur Interprétation Culturelle', *Bulletin du Comité d'Etude Historique et Scientifique de l'Afrique Occidentale Française* 13(3): 309-399.

Laforgue, P. 1923. 'Essai sur l'Influence de l'Industrie Saharienne en Afrique Occidentale au Cours de la Période Néolithique', *Bulletin de la Société Préhistorique Française* 20: 161-166.

Laforgue, P. 1924. 'L'Outillage Néolithique en Hématite de la Falemme (Sénégal)', *Bulletin de la Société Préhistorique Française* 21: 263-264.

Laforgue, P. 1925. 'Etat Actuel de nos Connaissances sur la Préhistoire en Afrique Occidentale Française', *Bulletin du Comité d'Etude Historique et Scientifique de l'Afrique Occidentale Française* 8(1): 105-171.

Laforgue, P. and R. Mauny. 1938. 'Contribution à la Préhistoire du Cap Vert', *Bulletin du Comité d'Etude Historique et Scientifique de l'Afrique Occidentale Française* 21(2): 325-343.

Lam, A.M. 1993. *De l'Origine Égyptienne des Peuls*. Paris: Présence Africaine/Khepera.

Lam, A.M. 1994. *Le Sahara ou la Vallée du Nil: Aperçu sur la Problématique du Berceau de l'Unité Culturelle de l'Afrique Noire*. Dakar: l'Institut Fondamental d'Afrique Noire/Khepera.

Lam, A.M. 1997. *Les Chemins du Nil: les Relations entre l'Egypte Ancienne et l'Afrique Noire*. Paris: Présence Africaine/Khepera.

Lam, A.M. 2003. *L'Unité Culturelle Égypto-Africaine à Travers les Formes et les Fonctions de l'Appui-Tête*. Dakar: Presses Universitaires de Dakar.

Lame, M.N. 1981. 'Le Néolithique Microlithique Dunaire dans la Presqu'île du Cap-Vert et ses Environs. Essai Typologique', unpublished doctoral thesis. Paris: University of Sorbonne, Paris 1.

Linares de Sapir, O. 1971. 'Shell Middens of the Lower Casamance and Problems of Diola Protohistory', *West African Journal of Archaeology* 1: 23-54.

Maes, E. 1924. 'Notes sur les Pierres Taillées et Gravées, sur les Pierres Alignées et sur une Muraille de Pierre en Ruines Situées prés du Village de Tundidaro (Soudan Français)', *Bulletin du Comité d'Etude Historique et Scientifique de l'Afrique Occidentale Française* 7(1): 31-39.

Martin, V. and C. Becker. 1970. '*Sites et Monument Protohistorique de la Sénégambie. Données Numériques Concernant la Zone des Tumulus et la Zone Mégalithique*'. Kaolack: Ronéotype.

Martin, V. and C. Becker. 1974. '*Répertoire des Sites Protohistorique du Sénégal et de la Gambie*'. Kaolack: Sénégal B.P. 96.

Martin V. and C. Becker. 1977. 'Sites Protohistorique de la Sénégambie', in R. van Chi (ed.), *Atlas National du Sénégal*. Paris: IGN, 48-51.

Mauny, R. 1946a. 'Récentes Découvertes Préhistoriques au Cap Vert (Sénégal)', *Rivista di Scienze Preistoriche* 1, 317-319.

Mauny R. 1946b. 'Du nouveau sur les poteries miniscules du Cap Vert', *Notes Africaines* 32: 16-18.

Mauny, R. 1948. 'Pointe de Fleche d'un Type Inusité Trouvée prés de Dakar', *Bulletin de la Société Préhistorique Française* 45(11-12): 405-406.

Mauny, R. 1949a. 'Perles de Cornaline, Quartz et Verre des Tumulus du Bas-Sénégal', *Notes Africaines* 43: 72-74.

Mauny, R. 1949b. 'Sur la Préhistoire de la Presqu'île du Cap Vert', *Etudes Sénégalaises* 1: 239-251.

Mauny, R. 1951 'Poteries Minuscule du Cap Vert (Sénégal)', *Bulletin de l'Institut Fondamental d'Afrique Noire, Série B, Sciences Humaines* 13(1): 155-167.

Mauny, R. 1957. 'L'Aire des Mégalithes Sénégambiens', *Notes Africaines* 73: 1-3.

Mauny, R. 1961. 'Tableau Géographique de l'Ouest Africain au Moyen Age', *Mémoire de l'Institut Fondamental d'Afrique Noire* 61. Dakar: l'Institut Fondamental d'Afrique Noire.

McIntosh, S.K. 2001. 'Africa, Sudanic Kingdoms', in T. Murray (ed.), *Encyclopedia of Archaeology, History and Discoveries* 1(A-D). Santa Barbara: ABC CLIO, 71-78.

McIntosh S.K. and H. Bocoum. 2000. 'New perspectives on Sincu Bara, a first millennium site in the Senegal Valley', *African Archaeological Review* 17(1): 1-43.

McIntosh, S.K. and R.J. McIntosh. 1984. 'The Early in West Africa: Towards and Understanding', *The African Archaeological Review* 2: 13-98.

McIntosh, S.K. and R.J. McIntosh. 1988. 'From Stone to Metal: New Perspectives on the Later Prehistory of West Africa', *Journal of World Prehistory* 2(1): 89-133.

McIntosh, S.K. and R.J. McIntosh. 1993. 'Field Survey in the Tumulus Zone of Senegal, *The African Archaeological Review* 11: 73-107.

McIntosh, S.K., R.J. McIntosh and H. Bocoum. 1992. 'The Middle Senegal Valley Project: Preliminary Results from the 1990-91 Field Season', *Nyame Akuma* 38: 47-61.

McIntosh S.K. and I. Thiaw. 2001. 'Tools for Understanding Transformation and Continuity in Senegambian Society: 1500-1900', in C.R. Decorse (ed.), *West Africa During the Atlantic Slave Trade: Archaeological Perspectives*. London and New York: Leicester University Press, 14-37.

Monteil, C. 1928. 'Le Site de Goundiourou', *Bulletin du Comité d'Etude Historique et Scientifique de l'Afrique Occidentale Française* 11: 647-653.

Monteil, C. 1942. 'A Propos des Bijoux de Nguiguela', *Notes Africaines* 13: 22-23.

Mudimbe, V.Y. 1994. *The Idea of Africa*. Bloomington: Indiana University Press.

Munson, P.J. 1972. 'The Tichitt Tradition: A Late Prehistoric Occupation of the Southwestern Sahara', unpublished PhD thesis. Urbanna-Champaign: University of Illinois.

Ravisé, A. 1975. 'Recensement des Sites Paléolithiques et Néolithiques du Sénégal', *Bulletin de l'Institut Fondamental d'Afrique Noire, Série B, Sciences Humaines* (37): 234-245.

Richard, F.G. 2007. 'From Cosaan to Colony: Exploring Archaeological Landscapes Formations and Socio-Political Complexity in the Siin (Senegal), AD 500-1900', unpublished doctoral thesis. Syracuse: Syracuse University.

Richard, R. 1951. 'Contribution à l'Étude de Quelques Gisements Néolithiques de Tradition Capsienne de la Presqu'île du Cap Vert', *Bulletin de l'Institut Fondamental d'Afrique Noire, Série B, Sciences Humaines* 13(4): 1181-1202.

Richard, R. 1952. 'Etude d'un Gisement Néolithique d'Aspect Archaique des Environs de Rufisque (Sénégal)', *Notes Africaines* 55: 72-74.

Richard, R. 1955. 'Contribution à l'Étude de la Stratigraphie du Quaternaire de la Presqu'île du Cap Vert (Sénégal)', *Bulletin de la Société Préhistorique Française* 52(1): 80-88.

Richard, R. 1956. 'Contribution à l'Étude des Industries Microlithiques de la Presqu'île du Cap Vert (Sénégal)', *Bulletin de la Société Préhistorique Française* 53(10): 618-636.

Richard, R. 1957. 'Le Toumbien du Cap Manuel Est (Dakar). Hypothèses sur l'Évolution des Industries Toumbiennes en AOF', *Bulletin de la Société Préhistorique Française* 54(9): 555-563.

Robert, D.S. 1970. 'Les Fouilles de Tegdaoust', *Journal of African History* 40(4): 471-493.

Sall, M. 2005. *Traditions Céramiques, Identités et Peuplement en Sénégambie. Ethnographie Comparée et Essai de Reconstitution Historique. Gordon House.* British Archaeological Reports (International Series) 1407. Oxford: Archaeopress.

Szumowski, G. 1952. 'Gisement Paléolithique de Bargny Ouest', *Bulletin de l'Institut Fondamental d'Afrique Noire, Série B, Sciences Humaines* 14(4): 1228-1267.

Szumowski, G. 1953/ Notes sur la Grotte Préhistorique de Bamako, *Notes Africaines*, 58: 35-40.

Szumowski, G. 1955. 'Industrie Préhistorique en Forme de Coup de Poing aux Environs de Bamako', in L. Balout (ed.), *Actes du IIème Congrès Panafricain de Préhistoire d'Alger 1952.* Casablanca: Edita, 478-479.

Thiam, M. 2010. *La Céramique dans l'Espace Sénégambien, un Patrimoine Méconnu.* Paris: L'Harmattan.

Thiaw, I. 1999. 'An Archaeological Investigation of Long-Term Culture Change in the Lower Falemme (Upper Senegal region) A.D. 500-1900', unpublished doctoral thesis. Houston: Rice University.

Thiaw, I. 2000. 'L'Impact de la Traite des Noirs dans le Haut Fleuve du Sénégal: Archéologie des Intéractions Afro-Européennes dans le Gajaaga et le Buundu aux XVIIIe et XIXe siècles', in D. Samb (ed.), *Saint-Louis et l'Esclavage.* Dakar: l'Institut Fondamental d'Afrique Noire - Cheikh Anta Diop, 129-137.

Thiaw, I. 2003. 'Archaeology and the Public in Senegal: Reflections on Doing Fieldwork at Home', *Journal of African Archaeology* 1(2): 27-35.

Thiaw, I. 2008a. 'Every House has a Story: the Archaeology of Gorée Island, Sénégal', in L. Sansone, E. Soumonni and B. Barry (ed.), *Africa, Brazil and the Construction of Trans-Atlantic Black Identities.* Trenton: Africa World Press, 45-62.

Thiaw, I. 2008b. 'Développement Touristique et Mal Gestion des Ressources Culturelles Archéologiques dans le Delta du Saloum', in B.O.M. Naffé, R. Lanfranchi and N. Schlanger (eds), *L'Archéologie Préventive en Afrique: Enjeux et Perspectives: Actes du Colloque de Nouakchott, 1er-3 Fevrier 2007.* Saint-Maur-des-Fossés: Editions Sépia, 86-96.

Thiaw, I. (ed.). 2010. *Espace, Culture Matérielle et Identités en Sénégambie.* Dakar: CODESRIA.

Thiaw, I. 2011. 'Slaves without Shackles: An Archaeology of Everyday Life on Gorée Island', in P. Lane and K. MacDonald (eds.), *Comparative Dimensions of Slavery in Africa: Archaeology and Memory.* Proceedings of the British Academy 168. Oxford: Oxford University Press, 147-165.

Thilmans, G. 1977. 'Sur les Objets de Parure Trouvés à Podor (Sénégal) en 1958', *Bulletin de l'Institut Fondamental d'Afrique Noire, Série B, Sciences Humaines* 39(4): 669-694.

Thilmans, G. 2006. 'Les Baobabs à Griots du Sénégal (1965): Carnet de Fouilles', in C. Descamps and A. Camara, *Senegalia: Etudes sur le Patrimoine Ouest-Africain, Hommage à Guy Thilmans.* Saint-Maur-des-Fossés: Éditions Sépia, 167-182.

Thilmans, G. and C. Descamps. 1974. 'Le Mégalithique de Tiékène-Boussoura (Sénégal). Fouilles de 1973-1974', *Bulletin de l'Institut Fondamental d'Afrique Noire* 36(3): 447-496.

Thilmans, G., C. Descamps and B. Khayat. 1980. *Protohistoire du Sénégal. Recherches Archéologiques 1 (Les Sites Mégalithiques)*. Mémoires de l'Institut Fondamental d'Afrique Noire 91. Dakar: l'Institut Fondamental d'Afrique Noire.

Thilmans, G. and A. Ravisé. 1980. *Protohistoire du Sénégal. Recherches Archéologiques 2 (Sincu Bara et les sites du Fleuve)*. Mémoires de l'Institut Fondamental d'Afrique Noire 91. Dakar: l'Institut Fondamental d'Afrique Noire.

Thomassey, T. and Mauny, R. 1951. 'Campagne de Fouilles à Koumbi Saleh', *Bulletin de L'Institut Fondamental d'Afrique Noire, Série B, Sciences Humaines* 13(2): 438-475.

Touré, A. and I. Ciss. 2008. 'L'Institut Fondamental d'Afrique Noire Cheikh Anta Diop et la Recherche en Afrique', in M.H. Yankori, *La Recherche Scientifique et le Développement en Afrique. Idées Nomades*. Paris: Editions Karthala, 53-86.

Trigger, B.R. 1990. 'The History of African Archaeology in World Perspective', in P. Robertshaw, *A History of African Archaeology*. London: James Currey, 309-319.

Van Hoven, E. 1990. 'Representing Social Hierarchy. Administrators-Ethnographers in the French Sudan: Delafosse, Monteil, and Labouret', *Cahiers d'Etudes Africaines* 118(30-2): 179-98.

Vidal, J. 1923. 'Le Mystère de Ghana', *Bulletin du Comité d'Etude Historique et Scientifique de l'Afrique Occidentale Française*, 512-524.

Zeltner, F. 1916. 'Quelques Gisements Préhistoriques de la Vallée du Sénégal', *Extrait des Bulletins et Mémoires de la Société d'Anthropologie de Paris*: 238-244.

3.2 Preserving knowledge as a basic human need: on the history of European archaeological practices and the future of Somali archaeology

An interview with Sada Mire, SOAS, Department of Art and Archaeology, United Kingdom and Horn Heritage, Somaliland

Sjoerd van der Linde and Monique van den Dries

Faculty of Archaeology, Leiden University, The Netherlands

Abstract

This interview with Sada Mire starts with the history and legacy of European archaeological practices in Somalia, arguing how it has contributed to a situation in which archaeology is viewed by many Somalis as a distant, foreign phenomenon. Touching upon her personal experiences as a Somali-born Swedish archaeologist, living and working in the UK and Somaliland, the interview then delves deeper into the need for preserving knowledge and promoting community engagement and training as a way forward, ultimately arguing how cultural heritage and archaeological knowledge should be regarded as a basic human need. The paper ends with a discussion on the potential of collaborative practices in terms of bringing communities more closely together.

Résumé

Préserver la Connaissance comme un besoin humain fondamental : l'Histoire des Pratiques Archéologiques Européennes et l'Avenir de l'Archéologie Somalienne - Un Interview avec Sada Mire, SOAS, Département d'Art et Archéologie, Royaume-Uni et Patrimoine de la Corne de l'Afrique, Somaliland

Cette interview de Sada Mire commence avec l'histoire et l'héritage des recherches archéologiques européennes en Somalie, en expliquant les raisons pour lesquelles l'archéologie est vue, par beaucoup de Somaliens, comme un phénomène lointain et étranger. En évoquant ses expériences personnelles d'archéologue suédoise, d'origine Somalienne, qui vie et travaille au Royaume-Uni et en Somaliland, Sada Mire aborde plus profondément la nécessitée de préserver la connaissance et de promouvoir l'engagement communautaire et la formation comme une voie de progrès, en faisant valoir, en définitive, que l'héritage culturel et la connaissance archéologique devrait être considérée comme un besoin humain fondamental. L'article se termine par une discussion sur le potentiel des pratiques basées sur la collaboration lorsqu'il s'agit de rapprocher des communautés.

Extracto

La Preservación de Conocimientos como una Necesidad Humana Básica: Sobre la Historia de las Prácticas Arqueológicas Europeas y el Futuro de la Arqueología Somalí - Una entrevista con Sada Mire, SOAS, Departamento de Artes y Arqueología, Patrimonio del Reino Unido y del Cabo de Hornos, País Somalia

Esta entrevista con Sada Mire empieza con la historia y el legado de las prácticas arqueológicas europeas en Somalia y argumenta cómo han contribuido a una situación en que la arqueología es vista por muchos somalíes como un fenómeno lejano y extranjero. Tratando in primera instancia su experiencia personal como una arqueóloga sueca nacida en Somalia, la entrevista luego profundiza en la necesidad de preservar conocimientos y de la promoción de la participación comunitaria y de la formación como un camino hacia adelante. En última instancia argumenta cómo el patrimonio cultural y el conocimiento arqueológico deberían ser considerados una necesidad humana básica. El artículo termina discutiendo el potencial de las prácticas colaborativas en términos de juntar más intensamente las comunidades.

ملخص

الحفاظ على المعرفة كحاجة إنسانية أساسية: عن تاريخ الممارسات الأثرية الأوربية ومستقبل علم الآثار في الصومال

حوار مع سادا ماير، مدرسة الدراسات الشرقية والإفريقية، قسم الفنون وعلم الآثار، المملكة المتحدة وتراث هورن، صومالیلاند

شورد فان در دن لیندە ومونیكە فان دن فاث درین سیر

كلية علم الآثار، جامعة لايدن، هولندا

يبدأ هذا الحوار مع سادا ماير بتاريخ وتراث الممارسات الأثرية الأوربية في يناقش كيف ساهم في إنشاء وضع يرى فيه الكثير من الصوماليين علم الآثار كظاهرة غريبة وبعيدة. وبعد معالجة تجاربها الشخصية كأثرية الصومال، عامله في الصومال مقيمة وعالمة آثار مولودة في السويد وصومالیلاند، يتعمق الحوار في الحاجة إلى الحفاظ على المعرفة وتشجيع مشاركة المجتمع والتدريب كوسيلة للتقدم إلى الأمام، وأخيرا يناقش ضرورة النظر إلى التراث الثقافي والمعرفة الأثرية كحاجة إنسانية أساسية. وتنتهي هذه الورقة بمناقشة إمكانية الممارسات التعاونية من حيث تقريب المجتمعات من بعضها البعض بشكل أوثق

Keywords

Somali archaeology, knowledge, collaboration, development

Background

You have published before on the history of Somali archaeology (Mire 2007; 2011). Could you explain, in short, the history of foreign archaeological practices and influences in Somalia?

During colonial times, Somalia was divided into two regions; southern Somalia, known as Italian Somalia, and northern Somalia, which was the British Protectorate of Somaliland. Focusing first on the British Protectorate of Somaliland, you initially had colonial officers who were not necessarily archaeologists, but who were interested in the remains of the past, and who traveled in vehicles that allowed them access to places where usually people didn't get to.

These officers also visited ruins that were close to villages, but local people traditionally didn't know much about these ruins; they just associated them with past civilizations, past people. The surveys by the colonial officer Alexander T. Curle in 1937 for example, were triggered not because he was there as an archaeologist, but because he was surrounded by ruins in the field, so he started gathering information and doing tests with excavation, and ultimately he wrote an article on his findings.

But during colonial times, these archaeological interests did not lead to systematic studies. Rather, it was more of a sporadic approach whereby people would record the things they found, and whereby they would often bring everything back to for example the UK, or in the case of southern Somalia, to Italy.

Figure 1. Sada Mire (Photo: courtesy by Sada Mire).

Was there a local institutional infrastructure in the field of archaeology or cultural heritage supporting these investigations?

In southern Somalia, there was one important initiative by the Italian colonial administration, when they basically built the first sub-Saharan, African museum in Mogadishu in 1934; the Garesa Museum. They collected a lot of ethnographic material, and they also collected a lot of information from those coastal towns that connect to the Swahili coastal towns in East Africa, such as historical tablets with texts carved on in Arabic. But mostly, the museum's collection was ethnographic; things that were kept in people's homes, things for cooking, for cleaning, for wearing to ceremonies, things from people's households. Such items weren't at all associated with the past for Somalis, but for the Italians, these artifacts adhered to an essentialist image that they had of local people.

Until when would you say this colonial approach to archaeology and heritage continued?

Well, the interesting thing is that in 1960, both British Somaliland and Italian Somalia formed a nation, called Somalia. Mogadishu became the capital, and there was a massive nationalist project to establish educational institutions which lead to the first universities being built in the 1970s, and soon after to what we can call the arrival of the first professional foreign archaeologists.

What happened to the museum in this period?

As I said, I think there was this essentialist element of preserving a past within the Italian museum that didn't fit the post-colonial context at all. This is important, because this was a very critical time when Somalis were fighting for liberation - so they were not interested in foreign people choosing objects that they felt were inferior, and to be put in a museum and immortalized as Somali culture.

Of course, these objects belonged to our culture, but it was something that people wanted to go beyond. They wanted development; they wanted to drive cars themselves, go to universities, learn new languages, build roads, hospitals. Although I can understand the Italians' perspective of trying to preserve artifacts, I actually think they rather displayed their own traditional image of Somali culture – but local people, especially in the cities, felt that these objects stood for backwardness.

What was the result of this clash between foreign and local perspectives?

Well, first of all, we can see how the museum had been left to deteriorate completely, as I understood from interviewing a few former directors of the museum, some of whom stated that they had not interest in preserving such 'backward' collections made by outsiders.

In the 1970's, you had UNESCO come in for the first time to Somalia to advise on the development of the museum that we had inherited from the Italians. When the consultants came, they noted that it had a lot of problems in terms of storage and maintenance, but also in the sense that most of the important collections had already been taken back to Italy; some of the most important objects were not in the museum, and the rest was mainly ethnographic material.

In the framework of subsequent Swedish influences in the region that started important capacity building programs, some additional consultancy reports were written that stated that none of the archaeologists who had come before 1980 had left documentation reports, and this is whether they were working in colonial times or post-colonial times. What this means, is that it is still very difficult to get hold of materials.

Changes

What happened after these recommendations and consultancy reports? Were there any changes?

Well, in the mid-1980's there were some important Swedish initiatives that I mentioned before, that were trying to involve Somalis and that were hoping to train them in archaeology in Sweden, or paying for them to be trained elsewhere. So this new vision towards collaboration was forwarded not so much by British, nor the Italians, but rather by the Swedish in the whole of Eastern Africa, which is interesting. But then the civil war started, so everything collapsed.

Can you explain a little more about what happened during the civil war? What was the impact on archaeology and heritage management?

Well, basically you have this Swedish initiative just taking off but then because of the war, it stops, and then you have a civil war taking place in which archaeology is no longer a concern for anybody. On the contrary - the first things that got looted were the museums, whereby objects were mainly sold to ex-pats, even humanitarian workers. In addition, during the famine in 1992 and 1993, there were a lot of people who had absolutely nothing. When the UN left in 1993, the warlords started to commission illicit excavations of archaeological sites, in order to fund their war. So, the already established connection with selling things to foreigners developed into a full-blown business, which brought in more weapons and gave the warlords more power, but which also meant that extremely poor people started to see the archaeological resource as a source to feed upon.

Apart from these objects being sold to foreigners, do you see a link between these activities and the previous western, colonial approaches to archaeology and heritage management in the region?

Yes. My first impression was, 'why are people looting their own heritage'? But if you look more closely at the past approaches to archaeology and heritage management you can see that in the eye of local people, these sites have never been seen something that was protected, or cared for.

Archaeological heritage has also been something that belonged to the foreigner, as a souvenir – it was not something that belonged to 'us'. In addition, during colonial times, our ruined-towns were accredited to have been built by Arabs. Our forts were said to be built by ancient Egyptians, and our own religion, our own myths already attributed to us being Islamic, coming from Arabia. So, people have never had a link with the archaeological heritage to identify with as a source of pride or as a source of anything – they think 'archaeology is the foreigner's business, it's not us, and it's not even our culture; we come from Arabia'.

You talked about looting and the civil war, and then the issue of the local population not regarding archaeology as something that belongs to them but as a foreign influence. Did this change after the civil war?

Well, I suppose it took until about 2000 before foreign people actually started to feel safe enough to go to Somaliland. From this time onwards, we also see that foreign archaeologists started to return, such as the French expedition out of Djibouti. Still, I believe that many local people saw this return as an opportunity to again sell locally collected artifacts to foreigners; a real awareness about a care for Somali archaeology was not existent yet.

When I came to Somaliland in 2007, to do my first archaeological research after having fled the country during the civil war, a public opinion started to appear on the basis of a publication of an article about me by University College London. The Horn Tribune published the UCL article on its front page two days later. Everybody was basically looking for me when I was doing my research in the field, so when I returned, I was approached by several deans and vice-presidents of university departments, asking me to set up archaeological courses. I found it very strange that there was so much excitement about the fact that there was a Somali person who knew this science called archaeology and who was a PhD student who was coming back.

So as soon as there was a person from Somaliland who was knowledgeable about archaeology, all of a sudden there appeared to be a local interest in a field that was previously regarded as belonging to foreigners?

Yes, I guess so. I mean, the capital Hargeisa is a tiny place in some ways, with a population of about 500,000. Actually, it started with the media. The media got first interested in the French mission. But the French mission couldn't commit to being there all the time, so there was this curiosity - Somaliland was a place where not many foreigners were coming at that time.

So I think that people were somehow waiting for somebody to actually explain to them what archaeology was really about, why foreigners were investigating these things. The interesting thing was that when I did my fieldwork, I saw that there were local people just looting sites who thought that that was fine. They brought their objects to me and thought that I could use them for my research, because that is what they expected. After that I had to take every TV opportunity explaining the problems of illicit digging, how archaeology works and the importance of scientific excavation, stratigraphy and so on.

Challenges and opportunities

This misconception about excavating things seems an important issue for the development of Somali archaeology. What are the other challenges and opportunities facing archaeology and heritage management in Somaliland for instance?

I think there are several major issues. First, you have a lack of infrastructure, which means you can't get to sites. The second problem is financial; there are very little financial resources for archaeology, almost none. Thirdly, you have a lack of effective heritage legislation. This latter issue is something I have tried to address as a government person, but because we've had two governments in the last four years, this means there is a very short institutional memory. So you lose documents, you lose people, and the people who are brought in, you have to start from zero with them. Somaliland is also a country where land rights and land distribution is a massive issue. If you want to mark an area as a national heritage site, regardless of land ownership, there must be legislation facilitating that. But we don't have those policies; there is not even a national heritage law at the moment. Finally, a major problem is a lack of skills and training. We don't have the people that can do the work.

Are you the only Somali archaeologist?

At the moment, yes, but in the last four and a half years, I have trained about 50 people, who are now able to protect sites, who have basic knowledge of archaeology, using basic materials in terms of site protection, tourism management, archaeological survey, archaeological photography, reports writing and IT skills, archiving, things like that. These 50 people are based throughout the country. They are community people who live next to the site. It's not somebody who's been trained in Hargeisa and then been sent to work in a remote place.

The approach is to identify a site, and then identify a person with the help of the community to become a guardian, a custodian of the site, and this person will be getting a salary from the government to do this work. Most of these guardians could not read or write, so they would be on the lowest scale of government work, but still this would be helping their families to have a source of income.

What is the impetus for the government and the local community members to support this archaeological heritage approach?

The interesting thing is that it's not so much about identity – quite often it is because I start talking about the possible economic benefits of archaeology, such as for tourism. But more importantly, there is the element of local knowledge. I work with what I call the knowledge-centered approach, which means that I, as an archaeologist, have certain skills to enable people to understand the site from a scientific perspective, but I also identify a role for the community in the sense that our approaches should be about preserving their knowledge.

Can you explain a little more about this 'knowledge-centered' approach?

When you ask Somalis what their heritage is, they do not talk about objects or monuments – rather, they will talk about the landscape, about the things that they know, about their skills. So if I show a picture of a pot, and I say this pot is 10,000 years old, found in this region, and probably made by people who used to live this way, they will answer me by telling what they know about the pot. They tell me about how their grandmother used to make pots, where she would get the best clay, how she made these pots, and how she taught them how to make them.

By identifying and acknowledging their skills and what they can teach me as an archaeologist, I can subsequently tell them about the archaeological information. This is, so far, how I approached working with communities. This also involves women, because women are always excluded - but traditionally, our women are the ones who create a lot of things, the craft work for the house, who build the huts, nomadic buildings – women actually have a lot of this knowledge, a lot of skills.

It sounds like your approach tries to bridge the divide between archaeological heritage and cultural heritage, by emphasizing the knowledge element and the more socio-economic benefits of archaeological sites and objects. In this respect, how do you relate this to some of your remarks that cultural heritage is a basic human need?

Well let me first say that I didn't start off studying archaeology thinking that cultural heritage was a basic human need. It's something that I gradually realized, mainly by reflecting upon my own experience as a refugee. When I first started studying archaeology in Sweden, it wasn't because I wanted to go back to Somalia at some point to do archaeology. I never thought I would. That was not the point. I was studying archaeology because I was interested in Scandinavia, where I was living, and it helped me to adapt and survive.

I was reading a lot, I loved literature. I was trying to read a lot about what happened in nineteenth century Sweden, because I thought it would help me understand my own experience as a refugee in Sweden, and the experience of poverty. In nineteenth century Sweden, people also had to flee poverty. A lot of people migrated, and had to deal with a new life, where people started living in cities, trying to get jobs. So what was happening in Sweden in the nineteenth century was parallel with my experience of living in Somalia, which made me feel that I somehow fitted into Swedish society.

When you come from a refugee background, and all of a sudden you end up in a new place, everything is like a new planet, a new language, new people. They're all white, they look different, they act different, they speak different, they eat different, they walk different, everything is different. Their buildings are different, their trees are different, their animals are different.

So, there is this intimidating element where you feel a sort of inferiority because you arrived as a refugee. What are my rights, what's the humanity within this context, what do we have in common? In addition, the Swedish people all looked as if they were super humans, and you come from a failed place, a failed people, and you being there is an example of that failure. So for me, by understanding the development that Sweden made in a very short time, from extreme poverty to a welfare state, helped me fit in. Archaeology was something that made sense to me because it made my surroundings make sense to me. It was a way for me to understand things.

Towards a future of Somali archaeology

Can you explain how this influenced your knowledge-centered approach in Somaliland?

Well, when I first started studying Somali archaeology, I first didn't understand why they were not mad about their objects being destroyed, about their museums being looted. But then I realized that their heritage was not in a museum or in a building. It was about their experiences. The things that they knew - the knowledge itself was the heritage. To know how to build that pot, to know what it was used for, to know simple things that actually would help them survive.

I remember when the war broke out in Mogadishu and we had to leave everything in our house - we just had to flee. When I talk about the knowledge-centered approach, it's basically about preserving knowledge, not objects. This is the lesson I've learned. When we were refugees, we were all of a sudden in the middle of the nomadic landscape with nothing. No cups to drink from. And there was no help then, in the beginning.

But what helped us was the knowledge that we had learned from our grandparents. My mother had sent us to our grandparents while we were in school in Mogadishu in the 1980s, although we wanted to be at home and watch TV. We were sent to the nomadic landscape, and at the time it felt useless, but when we were refugees, we were able to build nomadic huts to live in. We could do so many things that we had learned by being in that environment. For me, that element, that experience, of actually using my own knowledge, my own heritage, to survive in the war, to know which trees to use, to know what to eat, to know how to find water - these are the heritage skills worth preserving.

This is an example of what I mean when I say that cultural heritage is a basic need. And the main thing is to sustain those values, and to sustain them very early on. We should deepen the cultural values that hold communities together. For instance, knowing about your past can help people be more open minded and accept the other in a reconciliation context. Currently there is a religious conflict in the Horn of Africa within Islam itself and with other religious groups. By unearthing the multiple heritage that the past represents we can advocate for peace and acceptance. If I accept that my ancestors were perhaps Christians or even 'pagan' a thousand years ago, then I may not have a problem with my neighbor being Christian or something else. For instance, some fundamentalist groups are destroying Sufi shrines and these desecrations of revered ancestral shrines are traumatic for those who venerate these sites. Such heritage is their basic human

Figure 2. Community outreach and capacity building in Somaliland (Photo: courtesy of Sada Mire).

need. We do not need only food and shelter, we are beings who think, with feelings and beliefs. The knowledge-centered approach takes into account these forms of heritage - both intangible and tangible heritage.

How do you see the role of archaeology in deepening this cultural value?

By getting away from thinking about archaeology purely as sites, object, or monuments. Ultimately, it's about knowledge, and archaeological knowledge can really help people in those contexts.

Is it difficult to make international collaborations in archaeology based upon this new kind of heritage approach?

It is. First of all, I should note that the potential for international collaboration has been very limited because I'm a government person, and I'm a government person from a government that's not recognized, and Somalia itself never ratified the World Heritage Convention. So it's been very difficult to gain funding for projects in Somaliland.

Nevertheless, we have had some important international collaborations in the last decade. But some approaches are remnants of the past. Some people still hold an idea of entitlement to places where Europeans once ruled, and this is a very one-sided approach. In my experience, there are certain international approaches that show a self-interest - if you are going to get something, you have to give something in return.

But there are also some funding bodies where you are purely getting this sort of 'humanitarian support'. Without naming names, some of the foundations are really innovative in the sense that they see cultural heritage as a basic human need, and I want to be associated with that. For them, it is about bringing communities closer, and that type of approach tends to attract me more in my search for funding, in my search of collaboration.

Luckily, there are many other archaeologists who have changed their approach to collaboration. And there is a massive potential nowadays because we are dealing with a world where there are so much opportunities. For example, the internet has made communication easier for digital interaction between foreign and local people.

Do you think that social media and digital communication can lead to better collaborations?

Telecommunications is one of the most developed technologies and economies in Somaliland. I know nomads who are using smart phones. So yes, these technologies allow you to easily access the community. You can speak to them, you can have information, you can work with them, and it's not as costly as before. So, it should be much easier to move on towards a situation in which international teams can actually work much closer with local teams, build relationships, and also re-approach the significance of archaeological heritage - because the significance of archaeological heritage has been, from the experience of Somalia, something that is just for the Westerners.

From this perspective, do you think that there still is a place for international collaboration?

Yes, but international groups really have to make a case for their relevance in this, and the way to make it is to share, and to actually tell people about their own experiences. For instance, I use English and Scandinavian sites to explain to people about archaeology. We really have to share why we, as foreigners, find their culture interesting as well. Clearly, we are talking here about world heritage. The world is really small, but full of experiences. We share so much, everything that happens impacts all of us. Environment, piracy, war - but cultural heritage is a core, something that can really help people come closer.

References

Mire, S. 2007. 'Preserving Knowledge, *not* Objects: A Somali Perspective for Heritage Management and Archaeological Research', *African Archaeological Review* 24: 49-71.

Mire, S. 2011. 'The Knowledge-Centered Approach to the Somali Cultural Emergency and Heritage Development Assistance in Somaliland', *African Archaeological Review* 28: 71-91.

3.3 Europe and the people without archaeology

Cristóbal Gnecco

University of Cauca, Colombia

Abstract

A book about European archaeology abroad calls for one of two approaches: either tracing the genealogy of European thought about *the archaeological* in non-European settings or describing the deeds and fates of European archaeologists doing research outside their homelands. Although both approaches can be tackled together, in this paper I have chosen to privilege the former, that is, I will trace the main lines of operation of modern/European archaeology amidst peoples without archaeology in Colombia.

Résumé

l'Europe et le Peuple sans Archéologie

Un livre sur l'archéologie européenne à l'étranger peut faire appel à l'une des ces deux approches : soit suivre la généalogie de la pensée européenne sur l'archéologie dans des contextes non-européens, soit décrire les faits et gestes des archéologues européens qui entreprennent des recherches en dehors de leur propre pays. Bien que ces deux approches peuvent être explorées en même temps, j'ai choisi de me concentrer dans cet article sur la première, ce qui signifie que je vise à tracer les grands axes d'opération de l'archéologie moderne/européenne parmi des peuples sans connaissance en archéologie en Colombie.

Extracto

Europa y los Pueblos sin Arqueología

Un libro sobre la arqueología europea en el extranjero exige uno de dos planteamientos: o bien trazar la genealogía del pensamiento europeo sobre la arqueología en situaciones no europeas o describir los hechos y destinos de los arqueólogos que emprenden investigaciones fuera de sus países de origen. Aunque se podrían tratar ambos planteamientos juntos, en este artículo he optado por concentrarme en el primero, es decir trazaré las líneas operativas principales de la arqueología moderna/europea en medio de pueblos sin arqueología en Colombia.

ملخص

أوروبا والناس بدون علم الآثار

كريستوبال نينكيو

جامعة الكاوكا، كولومبيا

يعد وكتاب عن علم الآثار الأوربي في الخارج إلى تأييد أحد منهجين: إما الاتباع
نسب الفكر الأوربي في علم الآثار في المواقع غير الأوربية أو وصف أفعال
ومصير الأثريين الأوربيين القادمين بالبحث خارج بلدهم. وبالرغم من أن
من الممكن معالجة المنهجين في آن واحد، إلا أنني في هذه الورقة اخترت التركيز
على المنهج الأول، أي أنني سأتبع خطوط العمل الرئيسية لعلم الآثار الحديث/
الأوربي بين الأشخاص بدون علم آثار في كولومبيا.

Keywords

modernity, modern cosmology, archaeology, Europe, Colombia

Introduction

Tracing the influences of an entire continent upon another in terms of ideas and worldviews is quite a task, mostly undertaken by novelists and historians. If Europe and the Americas were at stake, the modern mind had it clear: the former influenced the latter by bestowing upon its societies the gifts of the Enlightenment. However, a wide revisionist literature in the Americas since the beginning of the twentieth century set up to view the matter differently. The elites that designed and controlled national projects in Latin America posited the importance of pre-Columbian legacies for the world at large, not to say for their own countries. Among them figured, prominently, archaeological items of great beauty and craftsmanship, profusely displayed in key global scenarios, such as world fairs and expositions. Those items, mostly of gold and pottery, became the targets of European expeditions that came to American soil to secure them on behalf of the most important museums. Along with those expeditions came archaeologists; in vast numbers to the countries providing richer treasures (Mexico and Peru), and in much more modest numbers to those countries where archaeological goods were meager and not as impressive. Colombia was among the latter. Yet, this paper is not a narrative account of the deeds and fates of European archaeologists in Colombia, very few anyway. It is a story about the general principles of metropolitan storytelling in a peripheral country, which I hold to be much more important and enduring than the mere, physical presence of some individuals.

The arguments I sketch hinge upon the operation of European/modern archaeology by European/modern-minded storytellers (mostly Colombians) which, by virtue of their work amidst peoples without archaeology, established a canon that still pervades the reasoning about *antiquities*. Yet, in the multicultural world that canon has changed, adapting itself to new opportunities and renewed challenges. In such a situation, 'collaboration' nowadays figures prominently in the disciplinary agenda. But is collaboration possible between Europe and the former Third World? If so, what should the terms be on which it can operate? The first part of this paper will argue that collaboration is indeed possible, if not necessary, but only by altering the terms of traditional relationships and by altering the very character of archaeology *qua* modernity.

Archaeology and modernity – Colombia in the European horizon

An idiosyncratic account of the encounter between Europe and the peoples of the Americas posits that it was an anthropophagic act. In the *Cannibal manifesto,* the Brazilian Oswald de Andrade (2002: 173, 179) presented the encounter as cannibalism, an act by which savage Indian America ingested the civilized Europe: 'Only cannibalism unites us. Socially. Economically. Philosophically. The only law of the world... Cannibalism. Absorption of the sacred enemy.' Archaeology was a part of this cannibal act, but upside down and much later, well into the nineteenth century: the history of civilized Europe (that of the *Creole* elites, later reconverted into national bourgeoisies) ingested the history of Indian America and recounted it on its own terms. Archaeology was a way of dealing with temporal heterogeneities, with founding myths and with the creation of communities of historical believers.

A past that the new nations needed, stripped bare of European roots but full of European referent-making strategies (such as objectification, universality and progressive temporality), was provided by well chosen pre-European artefacts and by the romanticized societies that produced them. As such, archaeology was thought to reveal the hidden roots of the national trees. Enlightenment was thus imposed: archaeology, a modern storytelling-machine, was bestowed upon societies that from then on were portrayed as rescued from the tragic impossibility of recounting their own histories. Europe conquered undisciplined temporalities, those of the people without archaeology: the discipline was given to those destitute peoples who did not have it.

Archaeology is 'modern', as it was born out of a desire of (for) modernity. It thus belongs to the wide epistemic tradition of the Enlightenment. In the regions of the world to which the Enlightenment was exported – as if it were just another commodity – modernity was discussed and eventually co-produced *in situ* with vernacular traditions. This was also the case with Colombia. Saying that archaeology practiced outside metropolitan centers is just a reproduction of a global order, is to incur in an analytical blind; saying so implies that the process is just one of mimesis, without much else happening – a form of westernization.

Rather, I suggest that what occurred instead, was a complex, ironical annexation or domestication, by bringing forward the idea that metropolitan discourses were locally 'indigenized'.

The history of archaeology in Colombia began with metropolitan scholars of different academic backgrounds (such as the German Konrad Preuss, the North American Alden Mason and the Spaniard José Pérez de Barradas) at the onset of the twentieth century, but soon after native researchers took over. With a few notable exceptions, foreign archaeologists have avoided doing fieldwork in the country during the last six decades, both because Colombia never witnessed the kind of social and political complexity characteristic of the Central Andes or Mesoamerica (and, thus, was academically unattractive), and because of the dangers inherent in the chronic violence that has swept the country since the 1950s. As a result, archaeology in Colombia has been carried out mostly by Colombians.

Such a particularity, however, needs to be understood and situated in its context. The relative absence of metropolitan archaeologists in Colombia – especially in comparison to several other Latin American countries – is not tantamount to the absence of metropolitan archaeology. *Archaeology* (the broad compositional elements of the discipline) is one thing, but an *archaeologist* (the individual that does archaeology) is quite something different. This apparently disparate difference is important for the arguments I sketch in this paper: although there were very few European archaeologists working in Colombia, 'European' archaeology has been, and still is prominent. But I shall correct myself and proceed to use another adjective instead of appealing to mere quotes: although I could use terms like 'European-like', 'Eurocentric' or 'western archaeology' I will refer to it simply as 'modern', for modernity is as European as the crusade that planted it the world over.

Modern master narratives had at their core a historical operation, in the sense of bringing forward the idea of 'the birth of savages into civilization'. Yet, the implementation of modern temporality into the Americas were characterized by a crucial difference in comparison to the events in the metropolis. Whilst the archaeological discipline in Europe described the 'savages' as *proto-selves* in evolutionary terms (in the sense of primitives that eventually evolved into the civilized westerner), in the Americas and elsewhere the 'savages' were regarded as the 'other', external to modernity. In European countries, the denial of coevalness to their own pre-civilized savages was a function of teleology: they were not part of modernity because they truly belonged to past times. Their rhetorical existence, their presence in archaeological narratives built upon *true* relics, their eventuating into modern selves and their presence in national histories – these were all proofs of the elapsing of progressive time. In the Americas, the 'savages' as 'others' (the paradigmatic Indians) were not part of such a story, as they were believed to not evolve into the 'civilized self'. In Latin America, the call of some Indigenous achievements by national story-tellers – all members of elites that despised the Indians and considered themselves 'white' – was a brutal paradox, as these achievements were carefully selected as to mimic European civilization (such as gold work, domestication of crops, monumental architecture, religious life, centralized governments, even writing-like systems). As such, archaeology became the notary public of the passing of pre-European societies, by legitimizing the disappearance of the Indians as something of the past, and by paving the road to *mestizo* national ideologies.

Similar differences between the colonial metropolis and the colonized areas in terms of storytelling, stood behind the fact that archaeology in Europe was not a part of anthropology. As a result, it didn't partake in the same thematic field of which archaeology in the Americas was a part – that is, the normalization of contemporary savagery. Archaeology and anthropology in the Americas were one and the same; their relationship was a pure brand of the apparently odd complicity between modernity and colonialism. Whilst anthropology set to normalize the 'savages' through indigenism,[1] archaeology normalized them by imposing a new temporality (that of civilization) and by using their chosen civilized traits as national symbols. In short, both were modern disciplines geared to modernize savagery through the production of a national imagination. Yet, although archaeology was also nationalist, it never was indigenist. It never talked about 'the Indian', about the means on how to court him into the national house: it only talked about what past Indians left, which were basically thought to be monuments. Such an emphasis on monumentality, at the expense of 'less civilized' cultural traits, was a part of the rhetoric of civilization, whose origin was located in "civilized" pre-European societies; the contemporary heirs of those "civilized" pre-European societies were banished with the argument that they were just degraded remains of their bright ancestors. In line with the heterodox nationalism of most Latin American countries, discriminatory and anti-modern (no matter how modern its rhetorical outlook may have been), archaeology did not contribute to dissolve the rigid colonial *cosmopolis*; rather, it helped to thicken it.

Here comes archaeology!

Since the mid-nineteenth century Colombian governments enacted, time and again, the same old policy: solving a supposed deficit of modernity. By the first decades of the twentieth century, governing elites had it clear that the modernization of the country was trailing behind its rhetorical promotion. Railroads had been built, connecting roads were replacing the dependence on rivers for communication, there was a standing army, the economy had opened to world markets, and the political life had become relatively democratic. Yet, a large part of the population was still excluded from the welfare promised by the egalitarian ethics of Republican life and from the market economy that was claimed to raise Colombia

---

1 Indigenism was the main anthropological contribution to nationalism: it provided the epistemic means by which indigenous societies would be digested into national society; it was the national anthropological rhetoric *par excellence*.

from underdevelopment. The creation of the 'modern' individual was still fairly incomplete, and so was the 'modern' Colombia. Two issues were prominent in the deficit of modernity: history and alterity. Archaeology acted upon both of them.

History was not firmly addressed in the nineteenth century, leaving an important part of nation-building unattended. In the beginning of the twentieth century the State thus embarked on the full promotion of a national history for the creation of a still non-existent sense of an all-embracing community. The historical narrative was modernized: the first historical text, mandatory for the schools, was adopted in 1910; a National Archaeological Service was created in 1938 and the Gold Museum in 1939; the National Museum was strengthened; and anthropology was established as a professional discipline in 1941. The archaeological discourse, now stripped of amateurism, rushed to help close the gap between modernity as rhetoric and as realization; a unified past came to rescue a clouded future.

As for alterity, although *mestizaje* had replaced the colonial dominance of 'whites' over colored castes and had thus opened the former guarded gates of political and economic participation, native communities and afro-descendents (which together made up more than 30% of the population) were now true outcasts. The Colombian elite, mostly Liberal, foresaw the need for an instrumental knowledge capable of dealing with those peoples placed outside of modernity; 'social sciences' then appeared to discipline discourses about identity – national and otherwise, especially ethnic. Studies from the nineteenth century about 'indigenous antiquities' were also covered by this regulated instrumentality. Archaeology, albeit amateurish, was by the mid-nineteenth century used to provide part of the rhetorical fuel needed to launch the modernist rocket. The Colombian scholar Ezequiel Uricoechea, writing about antiquities during the mid-nineteenth century (about which he considered himself just a *dilettante*), wrote as a Statesman the following:

> '*I am content just to add my wish that this very short and imperfect notice about the antiquities of our homeland may produce some effect among my compatriots. I hope that the taste for homeland archaeology is aroused; I can only see my little text fulfilled if there are archaeological productions in our country, worthy of the object they deal with and of its authors*' (Uricoechea 1984: 108).

Although the professionalization of archaeology would only occur decades later, the discursive consequences of such an amateur enterprise were numerous and far-reaching. Its most important product was central to the weaving of the new social fabric: pre-Hispanic 'otherness' was shown and vindicated as the cornerstone of national identity whilst, simultaneously, contemporary indigenous groups were marginalized and made invisible. One of the basic ingredients in such a separation was evolutionism: the most 'civilized' pre-Hispanic societies were shown as the base of national society, a necessary link in the evolutionary (and unavoidable) path towards plain civilization (modernity), planted by Europeans and tended by their Creole inheritors.

The institutionalization of archaeology in Colombia started with the State-sponsored work of French anthropologist Paul Rivet in 1941 when he founded the National Ethnological Institute, which was devoted to research and academic training. This occurred within an open, liberal environment that led credence to the potential role of social sciences in the construction of a new social fabric. Rivet´s endeavor catalyzed an ongoing and incipient (both in scope and support) archaeological research and established the scientific canon, guiding the nascent discipline through a distant, aseptic relationship with social life. Ethnic otherness was objectified in museums and academic reports; its existence was thus secured and boxed in. A double subduing was set in motion; firstly, an old, vernacular yet strange cultural diversity was domesticated by making it appear as constitutive of national identity; and secondly, social memory was tamed, showing Colombians how the other became part of the self by virtue of its incorporation into the collective project. Archaeology played a prominent role in the promotion of national pride, and monumental sites and their associated paraphernalia became adequate theatres for staging nationalism. In the 1960, archaeologists staged the national pride for its indigenous roots with their imaginative reconstructions of San Agustín, an iconic site in the south-west Andes, and later in Teyuna (also known as the Lost City, in the Sierra Nevada de Santa Marta, in the northern coast), which was converted into a place where contemporary politicians offer the trinkets of ethno-populism.

As such, archaeology entered the scene of national production: it forged a particular temporality (teleological and past-concerned) and contributed to elevate critical symbols – things, places, sequences – to the national imagination, in which the birth to civilization played the major role. Most Latin American archaeologies were carried out by and for *mestizos*, a tool for glorifying and cementing the national unity from where minorities – or majorities, as in Bolivia – were utterly banished. Just as *mestizaje* was a cannibalization of differences (Ribeiro 2003: 48), archaeology was a cannibalization of different times. Archaeology was important to the bourgeoisie *mestiza*: it provided the new temporality that bridged pre-European civilizations with the civilized, modern world implanted by the bourgeois logic while leaping over condemned Colonial times. It also built a homogeneous history which was fracture-less, cumulative, fluid and continuous. Colombian society was thereby portrayed as a hybrid totality whose continuity was provided by temporal depth. The rhetoric of modernity, civilization, and bourgeoisie ripened the times for archaeology, which grew out of the evolutionist impetus that lasted in these countries well beyond its apparent demise in the North Atlantic at the end of the nineteenth century. Evolutionism was not just a matter of ordering for cataloguing; it was the junction of natural and social sciences, the hinge that was missing on split knowledge. Although some archaeologies had a naturalist accent – pre-European societies as a part of the landscape without agency of the unanimated, such as in Argentine – and others a cultural one – those societies as roots of the national tree – it was evolutionism which set the common language. It provided the discourse that confined indigenes to temporal distance, and it gave to national history its origin, its direction and its meaning. Although evolutionist philosophy lost its centrality in the modern globalization at the end of the nineteenth century – due to the dismantling of historical reason by a bourgeoisie threatened by the organization of workers – it never abandoned its chambers in the metaphysical building of Latin American archaeologies, not even where the obsession with space silenced, only apparently, the political value of time.

Archaeology was a eugenic tool for the purification of time, and it reified and fetishicized indigenous 'cultures'. Such a fetishist operation allowed it to cannibalize alien objects which were elevated to national symbols, ignoring the social contexts where they were originally produced, and ignoring contexts of conflict and genocide. The archaeological eulogy of a glorious past was bucolic and aesthetical; it silenced the tragedy of the Conquest and centuries of colonialism. The past was emptied of conflict and of the consequences of power. A double archaeological operation was hereby in place: one pasteurized the past, whilst the other severed indigenous historical continuity. Archaeology constructed the image of an essential and a-temporal unity, that of civilized pre-European societies bringing order and identity to a heterogeneous mess (which were, in fact, the national societies being created). Diffusionism and the comparative gaze thereby imposed similarities where others only saw differences. By mapping unity and by certifying the disappearance of indigenous societies, archaeology supported the bourgeois idea of a cosmic race. The nationalist appropriation of the archaeological heritage severed its connection with contemporary Indians, implying that only the *mestizos* (the national society) were the worthy heirs of the pre-European splendor and the ones in charge of its custody and promotion.

At this point in my story about archaeology, modernity, and nationalism in Colombia, I wish to make a distinction. It is one thing to modernize the archaeological discourse (by enlisting it to serve national needs), but quite another to modernize archaeology itself. The latter only started to occur in Colombia by the late 1980s (which was late considering archaeological modernization had been occurring in the metropolitan world for almost three decades) and ended up contradicting the former. The modernization of the archaeological apparatus meant the replacement of old ideas and techniques (vernacular, unregulated, idiosyncratic) for others that were associated with rationality, universalism, and objectivity. The center-periphery dichotomy arose out of such a desire: the center produces cognitive standards while the periphery strives to adopt them. Science was shown as a natural international goal while vernacular practices were portrayed as anachronistic noises to be exterminated. Modernizing archaeologists, all trained in North Atlantic universities, argued that there was a center producing knowledge (which they saw as the capitalist democracies, notably the US and Great Britain) and a periphery consuming it. The argument was homologous to state that the colonies produce raw materials, whilst the metropolitan centers produce manufactured products adding value. In archaeological terms, this is equivalent to saying that peripheral countries contributed 'the empirical past', and metropolitan countries the archaeological discourse for its interpretation, which is then reproduced in the periphery. Such a tragic situation can then only be solved in the same way that technological *backwardness* can be solved: through knowledge transfer and by establishing an adequate infrastructure. Colombian archaeologists thus learned to write and read in English (such as the fellow writing this paper) and became aware that their entrance into the academic First World demanded publication in international, indexed journals.

The 'modernization' of archaeology had two results. First, it pushed the discipline away from politics, as its nationalism was replaced by a scientific rhetoric which stopped worrying about the annoying events of *reality* and even disdained nationalist primordialism. Secondly, it lead the discipline into a meta-reality to which the use of new techniques and the substantiation of statements were far more important than reflecting in and about the context. The utter paradox is that so much modernizing eagerness – sending students to get doctorates abroad; travelling to international meetings; publishing in widely distributed journals and books, reviewed by equally-converted peers; implementing curricular reforms – occurred just when Colombia was preparing to enter the multicultural world. The archaeologists, busy as they were in their businesses, may have heard about a new Constitution and about terms such as autonomy and recognition but assumed, once more, that the issue was not with them.

Modern archaeology in Colombia today

A couple of decades of multiculturalism have changed the face of traditional (modern, national, European-like) archaeological practice into a distortion: a significant part of practicing archaeologists nowadays strive to please the needs of capitalism, turning themselves into commodities that deal with a primarily legal conception of heritage. Contract, rescue, or urgent archaeologies (many names for the same curse) have abandoned the possibility to intervene in order to indulge in the sad and irresponsible function of complacency. Their tragedy is seen with disdain by academic archaeology that has, in the meanwhile, become marginal, whilst ignoring that its structural functionality in relation to nationalism had ceased to make sense with the arrival of multicultural policies. Indeed, academic archaeologists are rare birds in multicultural contexts: they can be seen as de-contextualized autistics that still court a narrative monopoly lost long ago to empowered local historical actors, mostly ethnic. Some of its practitioners, perhaps the boldest in theoretical terms, have thereby appealed for a curious approach that mixes a bit of old positivism with a bit of new constructivism. This unlikely cocktail is now defining the contours of multicultural archaeology (which is also called 'public archaeology'), which from a distance (this time not aseptic but cynical) has done three things: it has opened its practice to local actors (in research-related activities and in decision-making); it has widened the circulation of its discourses (especially with the promotion of local museums and printed and audiovisual materials); and it has included other historical horizons in its interpretations. However, the first one has only managed to involve local peoples as crew members (the ever-lasting worker, this time using ethnic clothes) or, the most, to train them in the arcane of the discipline (taking them out of their savage practices and bringing them to the course of civilization.)

The second one is (apparently) a good intention that has contributed to the fetishization of the past, as is the case with local museums that have sprouted everywhere, as a plague, without much thinking about their meaning and role. The third one has widened archaeological hermeneutics but has forgotten to build inter-discursive bridges. These characteristics, which seem to militate against epistemic violence, are however deceptive; multicultural archaeology is traditional academic archaeology accommodated to the needs and mandates of multiculturalism. It is a disguise of an old practice that has decided to keep doing what it has been doing for centuries. It has changed everything in order to continue doing the same.

It is not paradoxical – yet it is symptomatic – that many archaeologists refuse to let go of their functionality to the nation by simply ignoring ongoing contextual changes or by accommodating them without much thinking. Archaeology clinches to its modern origin and destiny. It is as if archaeologists have decided to live in the modern/national heaven forever, no matter that it exists no longer, or that it is just phasing out. Such a questionable decision, however, must account for two unavoidable facts. First, ethnic activism will increase its pace of confrontation with the academic establishment in the frame of the multicultural promotion and protection of cultural differences, for which the historical horizon is prominent, albeit conceived way differently. Secondly, colonial political responsibility will eventually fall back upon those disciplines that decided to conserve old privileges and to side with the most reactionary forces of society.

The confrontation of archaeological hegemony by local, mostly indigenous peoples in Colombia was only marginal until a few years ago, but it is growing. The relationship between archaeologists and social movements has changed in the last two decades, in the sense that those groups now have a bearing in the configuration of historical narratives. The relationship is nowadays marked by a struggle for self-determination and decision-making. In short, we might say that the archaeological building has been shaken.

Noting that something happened in the canonical world of archaeology, British archaeologist Michael Rowlands (1994: 130) wrote:

> *'The ideological role of archaeological interpretation was exposed with a second, political, loss of innocence in the furor over the first World Archaeological Congress in Southampton in 1986. That particular event, in fact, demonstrated both the politics of doing academic work as well as the political implications of archaeological representations of alternative pasts. What was striking about this challenge to archaeological naivety was the role of non-European archaeologies in challenging the metanarratives of principally European – and North American – dominated global archaeology. The convenient forgetting of the political construction of European prehistory was challenged more by the experience of writing prehistory in the periphery as resistance to colonial constructions of indigenous pasts than by political events in the archaeological heartlands of Europe and North America'* (Rowlands 1994: 130).

Rowlands was right (a good deal of the strength of postcolonial reasoning in archaeology arises from the geopolitical South), was aware of profound contestations to the discipline, and was outright correct by pointing out to non-metropolitan sources. Yet, he ignored or was not prepared to see that the most important challenge, one with lasting impact, was not coming from inside the discipline – what he calls ' the experience of writing prehistory in the periphery' – but from outsiders, both of archaeology and modernity. The challenge comes from peoples situated in a condition of exteriority, not from a place untouched by modernity (as if it were an ontological outside) but from an externality;

> '…which is, precisely, constituted as difference by the hegemonic discourse. From within the exteriority in which he/she is localized, the Other becomes the original source of the ethical discourse vis a vis a hegemonic totality' (Escobar 2005: 36)

Such a challenge seeks to counteract modernity – and the discourses on which it found support and substance, such as archaeology – with the political and historical legitimacy obtained by talking/acting from within colonial difference and from within a constitutive exteriority.

Europe and the people with archaeology

The positioning of those people who challenge archaeology is not that consensual. Some value archaeological processes and results if they are part of their agendas, considering that material objects and features turned archaeological by academic or community-appropriated discourses can serve to strengthen historical reflection, central in social mobilization and life. Others confront archaeology altogether and reject any possible transaction with it. A perusal of the geographical distribution of these two antithetical positions will show that the former is mostly exercised by native groups in industrialized democracies, while the latter characterizes most indigenous peoples in the old Third World. Such a distribution is not odd; it closely responds to the differential effectiveness of multicultural policies and to how successful they have been in building strong hegemonies – accomplished more completely in those countries where nationalism was more aggressive and triumphant.

Those groups accepting archaeology and making it their own want it as another recourse to enliven the past – a cherished support of social life. Sometimes they even want it to fight other histories (modern/national) in their own terrain, with their own discursive objects. What they do is truly archaeology (a disciplined gaze into time turned material), but this time controlled and designed to serve non-academic needs and expectations. Those who confront archaeology and want to know nothing about it raise their voice from a discursive emergence, from a distance, even from an assumed exteriority. They expose and challenge what the West has done and drag its institutions into the fight, including academia. Confrontation with the West is not new – it is centuries old – but it has gained more coherence and strength since the 1950s, starting with the anti-colonial wars in Africa. It has increased its pace and intensity on the multicultural stage, where actors with opposed agendas concur.

In the interstices of the friction resulting from those two postures, there is yet another approach to the matter, very different than multicultural archaeology; I will call this, in short, archaeology *otherwise*. While the former deals publicly with disciplinary problems (most of them removed from social needs), the latter devotes its efforts to recover the relationship between academia and society from a common agenda of issues to be resolved, the least pressing of which is not colonial domination and epistemic violence. It is not a different disciplinary practice, perhaps complementary to traditional ways of doing; it seeks to build new relations, which can only be found outside disciplinary gates. In such a new political economy of truth there is power and subjects; there is a new house being built: modest, perhaps, but content to receive those who think that academic privileges ought to be questioned, those who side with social projects stressing solidarity and good living.

What can Europe do in this new, multifarious scenario? I don't believe that the issue between European and, say, Colombian archaeologies nowadays should revolve around 'perceived needs and wishes regarding international collaboration' or around 'an 'evolution' in the approach to international collaboration within European practices and policies'; it shouldn't revolve around getting European resources (personnel, funds, new technologies) to non-metropolitan settings, because it would perpetuate the Faustian dream: modernization by bringing the Enlightenment to the savages. Instead, it can revolve around teaming up for a different disciplinary outlook, one that is not based on logo-centrism but pleased in learning from other cosmologies. If this edited volume 'aims at aligning current practices and policies better with the needs and wishes of archaeologists, local communities and other stakeholders in host countries outside contemporary Europe,' (see Schlanger *et al.,* this volume) then the task is broader and more radical than simply establishing networks of modern archaeological practitioners. It is not just a matter of collaborating with European archaeologists (or, for that matter, from the metropolitan elsewhere).

Collaboration has become a scenario nowadays much discussed by archaeologists, who have different concerns and agendas – so many, indeed, that the meanings attributed to the term are multiple and emerge from the various ways in which archaeologists engage local communities and foreign colleagues. For most archaeologists 'collaboration' is more a way of alleviating their guilt (and getting on with their work) than a way of embarking on the path of different practices; more of the 'political correction' that reaches out to marginalized peoples, frequently with an arrogant naiveté built upon selected criteria of authenticity and purity. Many archaeologists are content with offering to local communities cultural crumbs (a local museum, a video, a school booklet) while preserving their control over critical issues (such as research design, curation of findings, production and distribution of archaeological narratives).

In the logic of the anti-imperialist struggle that bloomed worldwide since the 1960s (from European ecological movements to peasant rebellions in Latin America) and that challenged neocolonial geopolitics, the nature of the center-periphery dichotomy has been widely debated in world archaeology. This debate, that has questioned dominant practices and hegemonic disciplinary traditions, has de-centered and de-stabilized discursive enunciations. It is not just a practical demand born out of the establishment of high-level academic training in the countries of the former Third World but an active form of facing subordination, consequently with social practices in contexts of (a) exclusion; (b) social conflict; and (c) political confrontations between hegemonies and subalternities. Modern academic policies are confronted by collaborative investigations between scholars and grass-root organizations that explore new relational forms instead of reproducing the enlightened canon – precisely what public archaeology does. Such a participative/collaborative process is taking place the world over and shows how archaeology changes its practice and discourse. With differences corresponding to the academic and social contexts in which they unfold, such experiences tell about non-academic participation in research, about the need to carry out long-term investigations to comprehend local processes, as well as about dialogue and discussion.

References

Andrade, O. de. 2002. 'Manifiesto Antropófago [1928]', in J. Schwartz (ed.), *Las Vanguardias Latinoamericanas. Textos Programáticos y Críticos*. Mexico: Fondo de Cultura Económica, 171-180.

Escobar, A. 2005. *Más allá del Tercer Mundo. Globalización y Diferencia*. Bogotá: Instituto Colombiano de Antropología e Historia -Universidad del Cauca.

Ribeiro, G. 2003. *Postimperialismo*. Barcelona: Gedisa.

Rowlands, M. 1994. 'The Politics of Identity in Archaeology', in G. Bond and A. Gilliam (eds), *Social Construction of the Past. Representation as Power*. London: Routledge, 129-143.

Uricoechea, E. 1984. *Memoria Sobre las Antigüedades Neo-Granadinas* [1854]. Bogotá: Banco Popular.

3.4 Archaeological fieldwork in the Middle East: academic agendas, labour politics and neo-colonialism

Maria Theresia Starzmann

Institute for Ancient Near Eastern Archaeology,
Free University of Berlin, Germany

Abstract

The discipline of archaeology is embedded in discursive practices shaped by European colonialism and imperialism. The interest of German scholars in the Middle East was long characterized by a colonial obsession, which was not only reflected in scientific expeditions abroad, but has also configured colonial discourses in the metropole. I argue that Middle Eastern archaeology has largely displaced a reflexive critique of these discourses in favour of leaving intact a highly exclusionistic academic agenda and exploitative labour practices, especially during fieldwork, which in the present-day context of global capitalism reveal distinctly neo-colonial features. As this paper shows, based on participant observation and a series of interviews conducted with German archaeologists working in the Middle East, these practices must be understood as both strategic and pervasive in our discipline.

Résumé

Les Travaux Archéologiques sur le Terrain au Moyen Orient : Agendas Académiques, Politique du Travail et le Néo-colonialisme

La discipline de l'archéologie fait partie des pratiques discursives façonnées par le colonialisme et l'impérialisme européens. L'intérêt que les universitaires allemands portaient au Moyen Orient a été pendant longtemps caractérisé par une obsession coloniale qui n'était pas seulement mise en évidence dans les expéditions scientifiques effectuées à l'étranger, mais qui ressortait également dans des discours dans la métropole. J'affirme que l'archéologie du Moyen Orient a largement évité la critique réflective de ces discours, afin de maintenir un agenda académique exclusionniste et des conditions d'exploitation par le travail, notamment sur le terrain, ce qui, dans le contexte actuel de capitalisme mondial, révèle des caractéristiques néocoloniales. Fondé sur l'observation et sur une série d'entretiens avec des archéologues allemands travaillant au Moyen Orient, cet article démontre que ces pratiques doivent être considérées à la fois comme stratégiques et largement rependues dans notre discipline.

Extracto

El Trabajo de Campo Arqueológico en el Medio Oriente: Agendas Académicas, Políticas laborales y Neo Colonialismo.

La disciplina arqueológica está implicada en las prácticas discursivas formadas por el colonialismo e imperialismo. Por mucho tiempo el interés de los escolares alemanes en el medio Oriente se caracterizaba por una obsesión colonial, que no sólo se reflejaba en las expediciones científicas en el extranjero, sino que también configuraba los discursos coloniales en el metrópoli. Argumento que la arqueología del medio Oriente ha sustituido ampliamente a la crítica reflexiva de estos discursos a favor de dejar intactas una agenda de alta exclusión académica y las prácticas laborales de explotación, en particular durante el trabajo de campo que en el marco actual del capitalismo global revela distintivamente rasgos coloniales. Como resulta de este artículo, basándose en la observación de participantes y una serie de entrevistas celebradas con arqueólogos alemanes que trabajaban en el medio oriente, estas prácticas deben ser consideradas como estratégicas y omnipresentes en nuestra disciplina.

ملخص

العمل الميداني في الآثار في الشرق الأوسط: الأجندات الأجنبية، وسياسات العمل والاستعمار الجديد

ماري تيريسيا شتراتمان

معهد علم الآثار في الشرق الأدنى، الجامعة الحرة في برلين، ألمانيا

يمكن نادين بحث علم الآثار في المماراسات الخطابية التي شكلها الاستعمار والإمبريالية الأوروبيين.

فقد تميز اهتمام العلماء الألمان في الشرق الأوسط بهجاس استعماري، لم ينعكس في بعثات علمية في الخارج فقط، بل شكل الحوارات الاستعمارية في البلاد أيضاً. إنني أناقش أن علم الآثار في الشرق الأوسط حاز النقد في إطار جديدة مميزة في الحلول للرأسمالية العالمية. ومثلما تظهر هذه الورقة، عمل اغتيالية، خاصة خلال البحث الميداني، الذي يكشف عن سمات استعمارية المماراسات لصالح الحوارات الحفاظ على أجندة علمية استبعادية ومهيمنة ومنتشرة إستراتيجية كماراسات يجب فهم هذه بحبثنا ميدان عاملين في الشرق الأوسط، بجانب على ملاحظة المشاركين وسلسلة من الحوارات التي تمت مع أثريين ألمان.

Keywords

Neo-colonialism, political economy, archaeological ethnography, discourse analysis

"Archaeological ethics must be politically aware, sensitive to the pain of the other, or they are nothing." (Hamilakis 2003: 108)

The culture of colonialism

Scholars in the social sciences write about colonialism as a project of dominance that focuses on political control and economic exploitation. Anthropologists argue that colonialism is also a cultural process, meaning that the "discoveries and trespasses [of the colonial project] are imagined and energized through signs, metaphors and narratives" (Thomas 1994: 2). Looking at the culture of colonialism, it becomes clear that at the very base of the colonial project lies a variety of asymmetrical relationships that result in the dispossession of certain 'kinds' of people.

In this paper, I examine a set of neo-colonial formations, that is, an ensemble of discursive and material practices characteristic of Middle Eastern Archaeology. My goal is to understand how these formations lock with a neo-colonial culture, which plays out both on the level of political economy and of social and cultural life. I start from the understanding that the colonial project has historically been at the base of knowledge production about the Middle East, especially as it concerns German archaeological expeditions into 'the Orient', which have contributed to the creation of an essentialized image of the 'Oriental Other' (Marchand 1996). While Germany never managed to establish colonies that equalled those of the other European imperial powers, it cultivated colonial fantasies about the Middle East that were comparable to those of France or Britain in Africa and India (Zantrop 1997). In Western Anatolia, for example, Germany once established schools, churches and trading outposts, reflecting how the desired control was cultural just as much as political and economic (Fuhrmann 2006). The fact that Germany's geopolitical strategy in the Middle East was partially successful even without the establishment of de facto colonies is indicative of a neo-colonial praxis of domination.[1]

Because the historically documented colonial obsession of imperial Germany played an important role for early archaeological expeditions abroad, I will investigate how this colonial legacy continues to structure the relationships between foreign archaeologists and local communities. Based on my own experiences of doing archaeological fieldwork in the Middle East[2] and a set of semi-structured, qualitative interviews with German archaeologists, the goal of this paper is to systematically analyse the intersection of our material practices in the field with the discourses that archaeologists produce about their work abroad.[3] However, I am not concerned here with the scientific operations involved in excavation work

---

1   For my use of the term neo-colonialism, see Nkrumah (1965).
2   My previous field experience outside Germany includes work in Austria, Romania, Israel, Yemen, Turkey, Iran, the United States and Indonesia. Universities, public research institutions and cultural resource management companies have undertaken the different projects I have participated in.
3   The interviews were not conducted as part of an archaeological research project in the field, that is, in the context of participant observation, but were carried out 'at home'.

– the uncovering of artefacts, the establishment of stratigraphic sequences, or the documentation of excavation results – and their meaning for the production of academic knowledge (cf. Davidovic 2009; Davidovic-Walther 2011). Rather, my interest lies in understanding how these operations are managed by archaeologists, which includes the organization and administration of labour. Based on my inquiry, I maintain that the labour politics of foreign archaeological teams working in the Middle East aim, in quite strategic ways, at preserving existing power asymmetries between foreign scientists and the locally hired workforce, which are symptomatic of neo-colonial control.

My semi-ethnographic insights into archaeological fieldwork abroad as well as the statements of colleagues with whom I have spoken about their field experiences support my argument that neo-colonial formations continue to structure our relations with local communities in ways that are often oppressive. Yet, how we talk about our practices in the field tends to mask this problematic situation by foregrounding a 'naturalized' cultural difference. Building on this observation, I show how the dialectic that exists between our material and discursive practices points us toward mechanisms of rule that are heavily reliant on the politics of language. As Stoler (2002) has skilfully argued, colonial rule licenses itself through the intimate knowledge of others as different. The language categories used to express this knowledge have variously included notions of the 'exotic' or the 'primitive', though present discourses may favour more tacit expressions. The power of such language categories does not, however, lie in their capacity to tell of hierarchies and differences, but in the fact that they are able "to impose the realities they ostensibly only describe" (Stoler 2002: 8).

Researching back

While language is subject to continual shifts of meaning, the problems discussed here are not confined to terminology, but concern the socio-political conditions that render certain statements possible to begin with (Foucault 1972). These conditions set the parameters for the racialized and otherwise essentializing discourses, which persist in neo-colonial settings, albeit in variable manifestations. For this reason it is important that we not only look at the form of disciplinary discourses, but also critically examine our positionality as researchers. Recently, a number of archaeological projects have adopted a methodology that they refer to as 'archaeological ethnography', which has the goal of decentring, if not overturning, our heuristic privilege (see *e.g.* Meskell 2005; Edgeworth 2006; Castañeda and Matthews 2008; Hamilakis 2011).

For the study presented here, I conducted a total of thirteen interviews with colleagues in Middle Eastern Archaeology who are currently located in Germany.[4] Of my interview partners, six are graduate students holding an MA

4   For the purpose of this article, all interviews have been translated from German into English. Interviews are cited according to the number of the interview I conducted and the date on which I held the interview. In agreement with my interview partners, I am keeping the names of persons and institutions anonymous.

degree, while the other seven are PhDs working either in research institutions or at universities. My interview partners have extended fieldwork experience in a number of countries in the Middle East. Of the persons with PhD degrees, all have carried out or are currently carrying out their own projects as field directors, while most of the graduate students have experience as trench supervisors and some are also employed as acting field directors. I have carried out qualitative rather than quantitative interviews with my colleagues, because I am interested in the experiential aspects of fieldwork situations, the complexities and the messiness of which are most adequately accounted for in face-to-face interview situations that are conversational and do not narrowly prescribe possible answers as is the case with standardized questionnaires. My method is explorative, because the primary goal of my analysis was to understand what kind of problems other practitioners of archaeology have or have not experienced, observed and advocated for/against during fieldwork.

Even though interviews deliver descriptions that are somewhat distanced from the actual practices of fieldwork, they are helpful in learning how archaeologists make sense of their practices by discursively framing them in certain ways. For example, when talking about the fact that local workers are usually paid very low wages by foreign archaeologists, several people explained to me that introducing higher standards of employment would mean 'interfering' with local conditions. This position, which Scheper-Hughes (1995) has called an "artificial moral relativism", defends certain standards as "self-evident at home" while suspending "the ethical in our dealings with the 'other', especially those whose vulnerable bodies and fragile lives are at stake" (Scheper-Hughes 1995: 409). Moreover, it cannot be ruled out that those who insist on a non-involved scholarly practice in the field demand moral high ground regarding the production of academic knowledge at home. Bernbeck (2008: 402) has analysed this as the sort of structural violence of academia, which expects disciplinary obedience from our colleagues abroad who are to adopt, unconditionally, Western-style scholarly thinking and practice. Both attitudes result in exploitative and exclusionary practices with serious consequences for people and their political and economic sovereignty.

Considering this, my paper is a way of "researching back" (Smith 1999: 7) in order to hold ourselves accountable for our praxis in the field. The issue at stake is not, however, the kind of unhinged empiricism that calls for charitable advocacy behind a "humanitarian mask" (Žižek 2008: 22). Rather, the texts of the interviews constitute ethnographic threads that weave through a much more complex set of relationships – specific archaeological practices and discourses that lock with hierarchies structured both by capitalist and neo-colonial relations, in which I am deeply embedded too and in which I have a relative position of power (cf. Said 1994).

Talking behind-the-scenes

In this context, it is very important to recognize that the relationships between foreign archaeologists and local communities are interlaced with other types of hierarchies, including those between professor and student. In fact, academia is perpetually fuelled by the reproduction of hierarchies of various kinds, which usually position one part as more learned than the other.

Such asymmetrical relationships find their expression in unfair labour practices as well, affecting academics who are employed only short-term or part-time (adjunct teachers, for example) and the oft highly-skilled specialists who do freelance work on excavations as surveyors, photographers, graphic designers and so on. The latter are rarely unionized, notoriously underpaid and typically pushed to working more hours than they are contractually obliged to.[5] Among the reasons for doing unpaid overtime work seems to be the conviction of many academics that one's career is to be based on devotion and, at least partly, self-abandonment. In addition, pressure is exerted on part-time employees or freelancers to work more hours when the employer offers prospects for a follow-on contract or a workplace promotion. Finally, a tacit story tells younger generations of archaeologists of strict discipleships. In short, this story goes: students need to perform dedication and self-discipline to such a degree that they abandon concerns for fair labour conditions. According to the logic of such a narrative, unpaid participation on an excavation is considered a 'chance' for the student and is only rarely understood as the exploitation of cheap labour.

Hierarchies between professors and students, or other employees, often get shifted at the moment when boundaries are redrawn. The professor/student relationship, for example, can turn into a tight coalition against the rugged conditions of fieldwork by sharing knowledge about 'the other' – knowledge that is not only stereotyping, but is impermeable to non-Western and non-academic intervention. In addition, in my experience, a rigorous examination of the truth regimes that underlie and give legitimacy to our academic practices is not a routine element of Middle Eastern Archaeology. Of course, this is not to say that most scholars coldly ignore or are altogether unsusceptible to certain problems of archaeological fieldwork. The willingness of my colleagues to have a conversation with me is certainly testimony that they are not indifferent to the communities and individuals they encounter abroad. However, as a colleague of mine put it quite aptly, it is very common in German academia that conversations about the politico-economic conditions of our work take place 'behind-the-scenes', where they tend to quickly slip off into the anecdotal and non-committal. By having more stringent and committed conversations about our practices in the field and our understandings of these practices, I present a methodical analysis of how archaeological fieldwork in the Middle East is entangled with various articulations and circulations of neo-colonialism.

---

5   The issue of unpaid overtime work and short-term contracts in German academia has been criticized by the United Service Union of Germany (VerDi). Retrieved 17 July 2012 from http://biwifo.verdi. de.

The fact that neo-colonial discourses and practices find manifold and particularized expressions might explain why several people whom I have interviewed argue that neo-colonialism is circumstantial to archaeology rather than structural. One interview partner described how the participants in an excavation go through different 'psychological moments', linked to the rhythm of fieldwork. Because foreign archaeological field campaigns in the Middle East usually take place once a year and only last several weeks, the excavators work under extreme time pressure, requiring members of excavation teams to work long hours (12-hour long or longer workdays are typical).[6] After some time of working under these conditions, my interview partner argues, team members begin to voice resentment which would not get voiced, or at least not so blatantly, in other circumstances. As the interviewee put it (Interview 9: 31 May 2012),

> *"one finds everything quite awful then and … uhm … the food and the hygienic conditions are looked at as extremely backwards and also the intelligence of the people. […] But as I have said, I think that this is owed to the general stress and … like … less to [our] demeanour in that country that might perhaps, yes, have colonialist features".*

My colleague's explanation of racist statements as circumstantial is problematic in two ways. First, it deflects from the fact that racialized discourses are pervasive in structuring the relations between colonized populations and colonizers, regardless of when, why or how this type of language is used. Second, it does not acknowledge that the colonial project lives off internal contradictions. Indeed, colonial rule has often been explained to be a matter of both compassion and responsibility, where it was the 'white man's burden' to rule those who supposedly could not rule themselves. Based on this viewpoint and notwithstanding the tense violence of colonial rule, colonization is not merely considered a technique of governmentality, but it is also imagined as a humanitarian act.[7] In this sense, colonialism has always simultaneously been an assimilationist and a segregationist project, where a covert desire for the 'noble savage' went hand in hand with a rejection of the 'primitive'. In the same vein, it is possible to enjoy doing fieldwork in foreign countries while concomitantly dismissing those countries' populations as 'backwards'.

Neo-colonial agendas

The colonial legacy of archaeology has a well-documented political background. Foreign archaeological projects in the Middle East are usually carried out by scholars who come from countries that have at some point or another had colonies or mandates in the Middle East (Luciani 2008: 152). Due to this historical situation, but surely also as a result of unrealized colonial desires of nations such as Germany, certain practices deployed during archaeological fieldwork today have a strong

---

6   For a more detailed discussion of the conditions and constraints (financial as well as administrative) of archaeological fieldwork, see Pollock (2010).

7   Compare also Spivak's (1999: 287) analysis of the notion that white men come to the colony, because they need to save "brown women from brown men".

flavour of a neo-colonial *habitus*. Based on my interviews, the following sections demonstrate how an inherently uneven relationship between foreign archaeologists and local communities is framed discursively, underlining how these discourses license the further dispossession of populations in the Middle East.

Tactics of hiring and firing

Because the management of labour is crucial to fieldwork, in my interviews I discussed the labour conditions of locally hired workers in terms of security of employment. As it turned out (with the exception of excavations conducted in Turkey), local workers are always employed without a written contract. Agreements about the terms of employment, including the wages to be paid, working hours and length of employment, are merely verbal. This kind of practice tends to get justified by saying that local workers do not usually adhere to a regular work schedule, as some may take days off, skip days, or send a replacement (Pollock 2010: 205), rather than understanding this attitude among local workers as a response to the absence of a work contract.

While archaeological projects can offer employment for part of the year, the fact that labour conditions are not contractually regulated results in an extreme lack of employment security. This is intensified through practices of hiring and firing as well as cuts in wages, which serve to discipline the workforce. Several of my interview partners described how field directors cut workers' wages when someone 'misbehaves', while in other cases, field directors threaten workers with layoffs. As one person put it,

> *"they [the workers] also cannot do anything against this, I mean, if you say, you'll only get paid half the day, then they continue to protest and then you say, well, ok, then we'll just take someone else [...]"* (Interview 11: 1 June 2012).

This strategy of threatening to hire someone else is especially effective in locales where rates of unemployment are high and archaeologists can rely on an excess labour supply. As a result, a fired worker has relatively little to no chance of negotiating the employer's decision, thus leaving an individual, whose family may depend on the extra income, in an economically precarious situation. Similarly, there exists the practice of laying off workers before the official end of the excavation, that is, at a time when work in the field is winding down and fewer workers are required for clean-up at the site. This seems to be less common in the context of long-term excavation projects, where foremen often know from the onset that they are employed for more weeks than other workers. However, on those excavations where such layoffs do occur, this moment typically comes as a surprise to the workers, who are rarely properly informed about the exact duration of their employment.

Furthermore, local workers are almost never insured against workplace accidents or cases of illness. All interview partners (with again the exception of those working in Turkey, where social insurance and insurance covering workplace accidents are government requirements) have confirmed this situation. Lack of insurance can be equally detrimental to security of employment. Although most excavation teams readily cover expenses for hospital stays or visits to the doctor, one interviewee told me that re-employment after a work accident is not guaranteed (Interview 8: 31 May 2012).

> *"When they [the workers] have an accident, for example, and they can no longer work, then they're out. So if, for example, they … if someone's hand gets hit by a rock, then they are allowed to go to the hospital, they also get paid the full day, if I'm not mistaken […]. But otherwise they're out. I mean, this is really unfair."*

No difference seems to exist between excavations carried out by German universities or research institutions, or between projects that are privately and those that are publicly funded.

The use of cheap labour

Another severe problem of archaeological fieldwork is constituted by the fact that the local labour hired on excavations is largely unskilled and, as a consequence, inexpensive to maintain. These workers are for the most part deployed for heavy manual tasks such as shovelling soil and moving dirt. Training of workers is only done if it is cheaper than hiring a specialist. As a result, individual workers are occasionally involved in the use of technical instruments, such as total stations, or trained to draw artefacts, but this is certainly not the rule. Usually excavation teams make no effort to explicitly train workers or to systematically share research objectives with them. Even experienced workers are systematically excluded from those aspects of our work that render it 'academic', such as interpretive tasks. It is interesting here to also look at publication processes, because workers are not typically mentioned in published site reports. This is even true for workers who add valuable ethno-archaeological knowledge (regarding construction techniques of local mud brick architecture, for example) to an excavation. If workers are mentioned in an excavation report, this is in the majority of cases done in the aggregate, not by naming individual people, and not in the local language (Pollock 2010: 206).

In the course of the interviews I conducted, it also turned out that the wages paid on excavations are extremely low, occasionally even remaining below the local minimum wage level. With one exception mentioned to me, the wages paid by German archaeological teams do not generally get adjusted to increased costs of living on-site. Indeed, a number of statements by my interview partners make clear that the wages paid to local workers are intentionally kept low. This gets justified by referring to the fact that in many regions of the Middle East it is the antiquity authorities that set local wages. Yet, it is widely known and has been remarked upon by my interview partners that other foreign (notably American and British) archaeological teams often pay their workers more money than suggested by local authorities. One of my interview partners complained about this practice (Interview 5: 30 May 2012), warning that there *"must not be uncontrolled growth [of wages], because there are always a lot of excavations in a relatively small area and if somehow it begins that an excavation … which somehow, well … is rolling in money … then would start distributing this [money] amongst the workers and such, that would then somehow … uhm … cause disagreement and so".*

The same informant compared the role of archaeologists working in foreign countries to being small business owners ('*Kleinunternehmer*'). This means not only that the archaeologist-as-employer engages in a capitalist social relationship, but rather that he or she operates as the consummate boss, extracting as much surplus value as possible. Indeed, even those interview partners who have expressed concern for the implementation of local interests, have told me that fair labour conditions or reasonable wage levels are to be subordinate to the progress of fieldwork. As Pollock (2010: 205) put it, "[t]he archaeologists' interest consists in obtaining the maximum labour for the minimum wage." The distance that such practices create between archaeologists and workers leaves not much of an option for local commitments, such as public outreach or education programmes.

Colonial capitalism

The capitalist nature of the worker-archaeologist relation is also reflected in the fact that most archaeological projects rely on a system of tiered wages, where the highest wages are paid to foremen, lower wages to less experienced workers and the lowest wages (sometimes below minimum wage) to the entirely unskilled or inexperienced workers. In several conversations, my colleagues expressed to me that this system was useful, because it encourages workers to work harder, at times leading some people to do unpaid overtime hours. One informant explained that a system of tiered wages is good, because workers do more work, even

"after their regular work hours they fetch water and … uhm … buy stuff [for us], yes, they can always be reached" (Interview 8: 31 May 2012).

The notion clearly is that archaeologists take for granted services that go beyond excavation-related tasks and that are not necessarily restricted to regular working days or working hours. Most archaeologists are aware that this payment system can lead to sharp competition between workers and frustration among those who get paid less. Yet, it is common in professionalized archaeology to accept as standard rather than to question exploitative work situations (cf. Hamilakis 2012). Indeed, if colonial rule is read as compassion and responsibility, then archaeologists may link the desire to instil a 'capitalist work ethic' in the local labourers not to practices of exploitation, but to ideas of humanitarian uplift instead.

At this point, a note about the payment process is in order. Rarely do workers on excavations get paid in any form other than cash. The procedure is typically such that workers line up at the end of the week to be called before the project director, who will pay the weekly salary in cash against a signature confirming that the worker has received the money. It has been emphasized by several of my interview partners that they think the transparency of this public event is something that the workers desire, as it allows for a certain degree of social control. At the same time, however, these situations also get abused for regimenting workers in front of everyone else. As one person describes (Interview 6: 30 May 2012),

> "They [the workers] were paid in cash and invoiced. And this was for example such a thing where they would be called up and the project director had his [...] money with him ... the banknotes. And this was then counted out, I mean, really in front of ... everyone could overhear who got how much ... uhm ... money. There was also scolding like this: because you didn't do such and such, now you will ... you won't get this."

In addition, the payment process lacks transparency entirely when archaeologists pay some workers extra money on the side – a 'baksheesh' or tip – if someone was, for example, especially hardworking or took on extra tasks. Interestingly, this tip is almost always paid out of sight of the other workers.

As a few of my interview partners have expressed to me, they feel profoundly uncomfortable with the process of paying the workers in public. One person put it like this:

> "So, I mean, we aren't actually used to this, that one makes cash payments, really. I mean, well, except for inferior tasks, when you hire someone illegally or whatever ... I mean, the kind of stuff you, well, wouldn't want to do [at home]" (Interview 1: 22 May 2012).

This statement clearly shows how in the German economy cash payments are usually only done for 'inferior' types of work, including illicit employment and informal labour. In other words, the fact that on excavations even skilled or trained work is compensated in the way that illegal business would be remunerated in Germany accentuates the difference between an employment situation that is merely capitalist and one that is neo-colonial.

Ethics and accountability

As I have indicated throughout this paper, almost all of my interview partners were, to varying degrees, aware of the fact that the relationship between local populations and foreign archaeologists can be problematic. Most of the interviewees recognized that this has to do with unequal access to resources just as much as with neo-colonial attitudes toward cultural difference. At the same time, I acknowledge a decision to talk mainly about the negative issues that characterize some fieldwork situations while leaving out many of the positive examples I was told about as well. Among these are, for example, attempts to implement heritage programmes abroad. I have also heard of sincere and lasting friendships despite the fact that archaeological campaigns are often merely layovers before we move on to other sites.

Yet, I maintain that many archaeologists decline a radical critique of their material and discursive practices, because it is these very practices that ensure smooth functioning of our discipline. In fact, the racist and otherwise essentializing discourses that archaeologists observe or participate in during fieldwork are often considered acceptable as long as they remain relatively tacit or do not involve racial slur. One of my interview partners, having been asked whether neo-colonial or racist attitudes were widespread among archaeologists, replied:

> *"Of course, but mostly this is harmless [...]. If, for example, someone says, "The Arab[8] as such doesn't know how to properly cook eggs." [...] I mean on this level where ... uhm ... cultural differences, for example in regards to cooking eggs ... are being addressed, and then this gets distorted as a chauvinist statement"* (Interview 12: 5 June 2012).

This response to my question proposes that there are worse practices of dispossession than the use of essentializing language. To be sure, it is not my goal to exaggerate the colonial power of archaeological practices, not only because this may make us blind toward localized expressions of resistance. More importantly, a generalized statement at the dinner table – though it can be deeply hurtful – is not the same as the brutal acts that characterize other colonial situations, such as sexual exploitation, settler violence, or forced sterilization. Yet, as I have indicated earlier, "the *quality* and *intensity* of racism vary enormously in different colonial contexts and at different historical moments" (Stoler 1989: 137, emphasis in the original). While we may be rather remote from some colonial or racist projects, we are not unconnected from all of them. It is for this reason that I am unable to let the essentializing discourses and associated practices that I have witnessed in archaeology slide as mere coincidences. The fact that they occur systematically gives reason to be alarmed.

Finally, for those of us working in the Middle East, even a seemingly harmless statement about 'the Arab' as an abstracted figure should be highly disconcerting. What Edward Said (1978) has shown more than 30 years ago in his book 'Orientalism', is even more acute today: the fact that the production of "essentialized collectivities" (Thomas 1994: 24) such as 'the Arab' can quickly blur with other reifications ("the terrorist"). Said's work requires us to reflect upon the processes through which certain ideas and practices acquire such authority and normality that they escape our reflection. With this in mind, my paper is written on the backcloth of the historical formations of European colonialism and imperialism whose normalizing discourses continue to frame our archaeological practice abroad. In their present form, these discourses are essential to a global capitalist system that requires for its own perpetuation exploitative structures in marginalized locales, such as extreme poverty or the lack of educational opportunities. If we can agree that we have ethical and moral obligations toward the communities and individuals who participate in or surround us during our archaeological work abroad, it is

---

8   I have replaced the generic regional designator used in the interview with another generic term commonly used ('the Arab') so as to protect the interviewee's anonymity.

time to develop an academic practice that is able to undermine the generalizing hegemony of neo-colonialism.

Acknowledgements

This article has benefited from insightful comments by several friends and colleagues. Thanks are due to Bilge Fırat and Susan Pietrzyk whose notes allowed me to focus my arguments and engage my methodology more skilfully. Tonia Davidovic and Andrew Epstein have discussed ideas from earlier drafts of this paper with me. I owe them thanks for helping me to rethink in particular the links between capitalism and colonialism, between material and discursive praxis. I would like to express my gratitude to the colleagues who agreed to be interviewed. Thanks for setting aside the time to work through my questions and inquiries, for hearing me out.

References

Bernbeck, R. 2008. 'Structural Violence in Archaeology', *Archaeologies* 4(3): 390-413.

Castañeda, Q.E. and C.N. Matthews (eds). 2008. *Ethnographic Archaeologies: Reflections on Stakeholders and Archaeological Practices*. Lanham: AltaMira Press.

Davidovic, A. 2009. *Praktiken Archäologischer Wissensproduktion: Eine Kulturanthropologische Wissenschaftsforschung*. Altertumskunde des Vorderen Orients 13. Münster: Ugarit-Verlag.

Davidovic-Walther, T. 2011. 'Die Herstellung Archäologischen Wissens: Praxen und Interaktionen', *Zeitschrift für Volkskunde* 107(1): 49-64.

Edgeworth, M. (ed.). 2006. *Ethnographies of Archaeological Practice: Cultural Encounters, Material Transformations*. Lanham: AltaMira Press.

Foucault, M. 1972. *The Archaeology of Knowledge*. New York: Pantheon Books.

Fuhrmann, M. 2006. *Der Traum vom Deutschen Orient: Zwei Deutsche Kolonien im Osmanischen Reich 1851–1918*. Frankfurt: Campus Verlag.

Hamilakis, Y. 2003. 'Iraq, Stewardship and the 'Record': An Ethical Crisis for Archaeology', *Public Archaeology* 3: 104-111.

Hamilakis, Y. 2011. 'Archaeological Ethnography: A Multitemporal Meeting Ground for Archaeology and Anthropology', *Annual Review of Anthropology* 40: 399-414.

Hamilakis, Y. 2012. 'Are we Postcolonial Yet? Tales from the Battlefield', *Archaeologies* 8(1): 67-76.

Luciani, M. 2008. 'Archaeological Field Training for a Variety of Different Types of Sites: From the Near Eastern Tell to the Prehistoric Settlement Camp', in P.J. Ucko, Q. Ling and J. Hubert (eds), *From Concepts of The Past To Practical Strategies: The Teaching of Archaeological Field Techniques*. UCL ICCHA Studies Series. London: Saffron Books, 149-164.

Marchand, S. 1996. 'Orientalismus als Kulturpolitik: German Archaeology and Cultural Imperialism in Asia Minor', in G.W. Stocking, Jr. (ed.), *Volksgeist als Methode und Ethic: Essays on Boasian Ethnography and the German Anthropological Tradition*. Madison: University of Wisconsin Press, 298-336.

Meskell, L. 2005. 'Archaeological Ethnography: Conversations around Kruger National Park', *Archaeologies* 1(1): 81-100.

Nkrumah, K. 1965. *Neo-Colonialism: The Last Stage of Imperialism*. London: Thomas Nelson & Sons, Ltd.

Pollock, S. 2010. 'Decolonizing Archaeology: Political Economy and Archaeological Practice in the Middle East', in R. Boytner, L. Swartz Dodd and B. Parker (eds), *Controlling the Past, Owning the Future: The Political Uses of Archaeology in the Middle East*. Tucson: University of Arizona Press, 196-216.

Said, E. 1978. *Orientalism*. New York: Vintage.

Said, E. 1994. *Representations of the Intellectual*. New York: Pantheon Books.

Scheper-Hughes, N. 1995. 'The Primacy of the Ethical: Propositions for a Militant Anthropology', *Current Anthropology* 36(3): 409-440.

Smith, L.T. 1999. *Decolonizing Methodologies: Research and Indigenous Peoples*. London: Zed Books Ltd.

Spivak, G.C. 1999. *A Critique of Postcolonial Reason: Toward a History of the Vanishing Present*. Harvard: Harvard University Press.

Stoler, A.L. 1989. 'Rethinking Colonial Categories: European Communities and the Boundaries of Rule', *Comparative Studies in Society and History* 31(1): 134-161.

Stoler, A.L. 2002. *Carnal Knowledge and Imperial Power: Race and the Intimate in Colonial Rule*. Berkeley: University of California Press.

Thomas, N. 1994. *Colonialism's Culture: Anthropology, Travel and Government*. Princeton: Princeton University Press.

Zantrop, S. 1997. *Colonial Fantasies: Conquest, Race, and Nation in Pre-Colonial Germany, 1770–1871*. Durham: Duke University Press.

Žižek, S. 2008. *Violence*. New York: Picador.

3.5 Norwegian archaeology and African competence building

An interview with Randi Håland, Department of Archaeology, History, Culture and Religious Studies, University of Bergen, Norway

Sjoerd van der Linde and Monique van den Dries

Faculty of Archaeology, Leiden University, The Netherlands

Abstract

This interview with Randi Håland focuses on the archaeological research and capacity building programmes in Sudan, Tanzania, Kenya, Ethiopia and Zimbabwe that were undertaken with the support from the Norwegian Development Agency (NORAD), through its Programme for Development, Research and Education (NUFU). It touches upon her personal experiences, the motivations of NORAD behind supporting archaeological research as a form of national identity building, the need for mutually intertwined research and capacity building interests, as well as the problems she faced with implementing academic cooperation and educational programmes in Africa. The paper ends with a discussion on the need to include community concerns and heritage management issues in capacity building programmes for archaeological research.

Résumé

L'Archéologie Norvégienne et l'élaboration des Compétences en Afrique - Un Interview avec Randi Håland, Département d'Archéologie, d'Histoire, Culture et Études Religieuses, Université de Bergen, Norvège

Cette interview avec Randi Håland se concentre sur les recherches archéologiques et les programmes de renforcement des capacités au Soudan, en Tanzanie, au Kenya, en Éthiopie et au Zimbabwe, qui ont été entreprises avec le soutien de l'agence norvégienne de développement (NORAD), dans le cadre de son programme pour le développement, la recherche et l'enseignement (NUFU). L'interview parle de ses propres expériences, les objectifs de la NORAD pour soutenir la recherche archéologique sous forme de renforcement de l'identité nationale, la nécessité de mettre en commun les intérêts de la recherche et du développement de capacités, ainsi que les problèmes qu'elle a rencontrés en mettant en œuvre la coopération académique et les programmes d'enseignement en Afrique. L'article se termine par une discussion sur le besoin d'inclure des préoccupations communautaires et les questions de gestion du patrimoine dans les programmes de renforcement des capacités concernant la recherche archéologique.

Extracto

La Arqueología Noruega y el Desarrollo de Competencias Africanas - Una entrevista con Randi Håland, Departamento de Arqueología, Historia, Cultura y Estudios Religiosos, Universidad de Bergen, Noruega

Esta entrevista con Randi Haland enfoca la investigación arqueológica y los programas del desarrollo de Competencias en Sudan, Tanzania, Kenia, Etiopia y Zimbabue que se realizaron con la ayuda de la Agencia Noruega de Desarrollo (NORAD) por medio de su Programa para el Desarrollo, la Investigación y la Educación (NUFU). Habla de sus experiencias personales, de los motivos de NORAD para apoyar la investigación arqueológica como una forma de desarrollo de una identidad nacional, de la necesidad de investigación mutual entrelazada y de intereses por la creación de capacidades, tanto como de los problemas con los cuales se vio confrontada en la implementación de la cooperación académica y de los programas educativos en África. Este artículo acaba con una discusión sobre la necesidad de incluir los intereses de las comunidades y las cuestiones de gestión patrimonial en los programas de creación de capacidades para la investigación arqueológica.

ملخص

علم الآثار النرويجي وبناء القدرات في أفريقيا

حوار مع راندي هالاند، قسم علم الآثار، والتاريخ، والثقافة، والدراسات الدينية، جامعة بيرغن، النرويج

شورد فان دن دندين ومونيك فان دن دريس

كلية علم الآثار، جامعة لايدن، هولندا

يركز هذا الحوار مع راندي هالاند على البحث الأثري وبرامج بناء القدرات في السودان، وتنزانيا، وإثيوبيا، وكينيا، وزيمبابوي التي تم القيام بها بدعم من التنمية النرويجية، من خلال برنامجها للتنمية، والبحث، والتعليم. وتتحدث عن تجارب الحوار الشخصية، ودوافع وكالة التنمية النرويجية لدعم البحث الأثري كنوع من بناء الهوية الوطنية، والحاجة إلى البحث المتشابك وبناء القدرات، إلى جانب المشاكل التي واجهتها هالاند في تنفيذ التعاون الأكاديمي والبرامج التعليمية في أفريقيا. وتنتهي هذه الورقة بمناقشة الحاجة إلى إدخال هموم المجتمع وقضايا إدارة التراث في برامج بناء القدرات من أجل البحث الأثري.

Background

You have worked from 1972 onwards in archaeological projects in Sudan, Tanzania, Kenya, Ethiopia and Zimbabwe, and have since then supervised and trained many African students with support from the Norwegian Development Agency (NORAD), through their Programme for Development, Research and Education (NUFU). In addition, you have also undertaken such projects in Nepal and Palestine. Focusing primarily on Africa, could you explain how these research projects came into being?

We have to begin with Sudan because that is how everything started. My personal involvement with the archaeology of the region started when I undertook my magister thesis on the material that came out of the Norwegian involvement in the Nubian Salvage Project in the 1960s. At that time, all the material was deposited in Norway, nobody was interested in analyzing it. This got me involved in the region.

Shortly after, I was asked to apply for a lectureship at the newly founded Archaeology Department of Khartoum University in 1972, which was a separate department, not a unit under the history department, as is often the case in Africa. I applied because I was very interested in Nile Valley archaeology and in Sudan as a country, and my husband was already working in Khartoum at the Anthropology Department there. It was fantastic when I got the job, and I took it on local salary.

Sudan was a very hot country in terms of people applying for research. Sudan at that time was very liberal, and there were many foreign archaeologists there who had started their research in connection with the rest of the Nile Valley. So you had a lot of foreign researchers from the USA, England, Poland, Italy and France

Figure 1. Randi Håland attending a seminar in Amman in connection with a Palestinian cooperation program (photo: Bert de Vrie).

coming and going. Of course it was the National Museum that was their main contact for excavation permits. But I saw that all these people paid little attention to the Archaeology Department because there was nothing for them to gain. They rarely gave lectures, but went to the museum, got the permit, and went to the field. And only rarely were local students taken on for fieldwork. I felt that they needed to take the Sudanese students into consideration since these students were the future archaeologists of the Sudan.

After I had worked at the University of Khartoum for two years, I wanted to continue with African or Sudanese archaeology. So I applied for a doctorate scholarship at the Norwegian Research Council, and was successful. When I went back to do fieldwork in Khartoum based on this grant, I could involve Sudanese students in my excavations. Many of the students were really good and dedicated, so I thought: is it possible for me to take on these students so they can study in Norway? In 1977, I managed to get NORAD to take on the first students for a doctorate in Norway. They finished their doctorate in 1982 and 1987. When I think of the first class that I had, four of them actually went on for a doctorate – two of them in Norway and two of them ended up in Cambridge.

The projects in Africa were subsequently funded for many decades by NORAD through their NUFU programme, which supports partner-based academic cooperation and capacity building in developing countries. What was their specific interest in terms of funding these scholarships in Sudan?

Norway was interested in the Sudan because of the political situation in the south, and they had started to support projects. Especially Norwegian's involvement in the peace-making process in Sudan, the Addis Ababa Accord, was tremendously important.

Up to then, NORAD had only supported health, water and other practical aid projects. There was one Norad person that had a doctorate in History and who saw the importance of what I was planning to do. I used the argument about the importance of cultural heritage for a country that was trying to build a new national identity.

Does this mean NORAD saw archaeology as a fundamental means for development?

Well yeah, especially in relation to nation building. In Norway, antiquity laws and cultural heritage have always been important. Remember, we were first part of Denmark for 400 years, and then in union with Sweden until 1905. Archaeology and history had been used to build up our national identity and that was the argument that I used also for the importance of archaeology in the Sudan, and later on, in 1986, also in Tanzania and Zimbabwe.

Can you explain how you got involved in Tanzania?

Well, I think NORAD had a good experience with the project in Sudan, and saw that the value of cultural heritage for development might be even more important than it had been in Norway. When I was working in the Sudan, our university director was appointed Norad Country Representative to Tanzania. Lerheim had a keen interest in African countries and development issues. When NORAD was approached by the archaeological unit of the University of Dar es Salaam for support, Lerheim approached me to see if I would like to help by supervising and training students and by giving advice. I agreed, not in the least because I saw there were really interesting research possibilities there on African early Iron Age. In the end, NORAD paid for support to staff recruitment, library and other facilities in the archaeology unit.

Was this the first time that NORAD supported an archaeological capacity project on such a large scale?

Yes, as far as I know it was the first time. I think the reason NORAD put so much money into building up the archaeological unit and support me to take on students and do research, was that Tanzania had always held a special position in Norway. We used to say it was the darling of the Norwegian Labour Party, because they saw it as a peaceful country with a president that was socialist.

So the main argument and vision behind these projects in Sudan and Tanzania were not so much research. It had much more to do with identity building and competence building. What was the impact of this funding framework upon the scope of your projects?

The NORAD support for the two Sudanese students, the first students I had in African archaeology, consisted of scholarships to study in Norway. Money for excavations was not included in the scholarship. In fact, the first fieldwork that I involved them in was actually with my own research money from the Norwegian Research Council. So to get these two students to work with me, I had to take it from my own budget, sometimes even from my *per diem*.

Later on, we got sufficient scholarship funding for the students to participate in excavations, so we didn't have to struggle with money the way I did in the beginning. So in the second phase of my projects in Sudan, from the second half of the 1980s until early 1990s, we didn't have the research council involved at all. It was completely taken over by NORAD.

Would you have been able to do the same kind of projects from research funding?

No, no. The capacity building, in terms of funding the students, would not have been possible with Norwegian Research Council funding.

Did the NORAD funding have an impact on the type of research that you could undertake?

I actually think that I have been able to be quite independent. It was always possible to base the projects around the research interest I had and which was of interest to the students. NORAD did not influence my choice of research topic... Actually, I would probably never have come to Tanzania unless there was something that I was interested in research-wise.

Why so?

I think that the quality of my supervision significantly depends on having a shared research interest with my students. So my research was intertwined with capacity building and I said that quite explicitly to NORAD; the way they could get good African scholars was for me to have a research interest.

So you see research and capacity building as mutually intertwined?

Absolutely. I don't think you could possibly do this kind of projects unless you have that kind of connection between research interest and dedication to the development task.

Challenges and opportunities

If you look at your experience with these projects in Africa, what were the main issues that you encountered? Did it succeed in how you envisioned it?

First of all, being a female made the work sometimes very difficult, an issue that is often deeply rooted in these countries. But also being Norwegian made it difficult, especially in Sudan in the early 1970s. At that time, Sudan was still very much influenced by having been under British dominion. Great Britain, like other colonial powers, had built up a strong archaeological competence both in museums and in University departments. So it was quite understandable that many wondered why I, coming from a country with hardly any tradition of African Archaeology, was hired instead of a British or American archaeologist for the position of a lecturer at the Archaeology Department. English academics in Sudan had a much higher standing than Norwegians. If they could, most of the students would have chosen a university in Britain instead of Norway, if they could have found a scholarship. They wouldn't have picked Norway. The influence of the British was great, and it still is today.

In certain discussions with other European academics, they thought I was a rather marginal archaeologist. I feel that, in a way, they thought that it was odd that Norwegians had the possibility to get funding for African archaeology.

In what way?

In general I think the Sudanese should put more demands on foreign archaeologists when they get permits to excavate. They need to demand a higher percentage of the field budget to be used for museum storerooms, conservation and exhibitions. They should also pay the staff attending fieldwork higher salaries or *per diem*. It is quite low, also compared to other African countries.

So do you mean to say that one of the problems in general in relation to African archaeology, is that many foreign missions...

...I think they pay little back for what they get. But we all get academic reputations from our work in Africa. If I'm frank, I have built my whole academic career on actually being able to do fieldwork in Africa.

Do you think that the 'drying up' of research funds, combined with an increased opportunity for development aid funds, has perhaps improved this situation?

It is coming. It's coming because foreign archaeological missions are changing and it has been much discussed. But in the beginning, capacity building was not part of it. Also, I would say you have people who are much less dedicated to the capacity building element, even if they have found this sort of funds for their research.

Figure 2. Randi Håland in the field, Darfur, studying pottery making (photo: courtesy Randi Håland).

Is this coming due to a change in attitude in European countries or is this coming out of an increasing demand from the African countries?

It's an increasing demand from the African perspective, but I also think that people in Europe are starting to see that they would have to change, that they have to take on training.

Would you go as far as to say that all funding for foreign archaeology should be a combination of research funds and development funds?

That might be to stretch it, but for me, I would say yes. As I said to you, I built my whole academic career on research in African countries. I have built my name on the possibility to work there, and it is up to us to pay something back and I really mean it. But it doesn't mean that I am a do-gooder who does not demand anything back. There should be a true reciprocity in terms of partnerships. If I really work hard for local partners, I expect them to do the same.

Could you delve a little deeper into the problems you were faced with when implementing such capacity building programmes? What were the problems that you encountered at the African end?

The problems related to such aspects as writing reports. It was expected that both donors and recipients would have equal obligations. But quite often we did not receive these reports at the deadline, even if they had received the extra means to handle this. This meant we had to write the reports ourselves. It was very much a dilemma related to the Tanzanian project. There were also frictions as to how funds and facilities such as cars should be used. This often implied that I had to travel to Tanzania to sort out disagreements. This was partly related to the fact that archaeology was a unit under the history department. Archaeology was a field discipline and that meant that they received more money than other disciplines. The frictions were often related to who should have access to these cars. I have experienced the same in other projects as well. Subsequently, to avoid these problems, I rented cars to be used only for fieldtrips.

On the other hand, I think the archaeology department in Tanzania, as well as other departments that I've been involved with, they really managed to sort out the problems through the work of dedicated individuals. At present all staff is currently from Tanzania. It's is running well. So it was worth it.

What interests me if you look at Norwegian archaeology in general, is that apart from the research traditions in the classical world, the main projects seem to have happened in the priority countries of NORAD. You have for instance also worked in Nepal and Palestine. Could you for example explain how the project in Palestine came about?

Nepal and Palestine are also some of the main co-operative countries of NORAD. The Palestine project began with the supervision of two Palestinian students who had got NORAD scholarships to study in Norway. These scholarships were not tied to any kind of research project but I was able to go and work with one of them in the field. So when I came to Palestine in 1996 to supervise, the head of the department of archaeology at the Birzeit university approached me, asking if it was possible to have a cooperation project.

This was 1996, after the Oslo Accord and Norway therefore had a very strong interest in supporting institutional connections including research. This led to a big interdisciplinary project (The Lower Jordan Basin Project led by Leif Manger) including geography, archaeology, history, and anthropology. Unfortunately, none of my Palestinian students actually went back to Palestine to build up archaeology.

Would you say that that is a general problem with capacity building? Have you experienced that often?

No, not at all; the Palestianians were the only two of the 30 students I have trained, who did not return to their home countries. All the other students I trained went back to their countries, as was the intention of the NUFU policies.

If we come back to the challenges you faced with capacity building, are there other examples?

I consider it very important to apply the same quality standards to the degrees we award African students to those we apply to Norwegian students. On a few occasions when I advised that scholarships should be discontinued at our university, I have been met with the argument that this would be an individual tragedy for the person concerned. My counter argument has been that it would be an institutional tragedy to have unqualified people in charge of academic development in their home countries because of their power to stifle the careers of younger bright student they may perceive as threats to their position. Therefore I wanted to make sure that the students that I trained were well qualified and that nobody could say they were second rate.

Do you mean that capacity building programmes have trained students that were very good, but also students who got their doctorate at European universities, who should not have received it?

I see it happen.

Do you have any thoughts on why that happens?

It is many reasons, I think. Perhaps the two things you can say, is that supervisors do it because they think they are helping individual students. The second thing is, of course, that they see it as a strategic advantage to have a person 'on the ground' that is grateful to them and will make sure that they will have permits and straighten things out for them to work in the country. Those two things are there sometimes.

Community archaeology

We have so far talked about capacity building in relation to academic scholarships. What about capacity building in relation to local communities and the management of archaeological sites?

I think I've done much less in this field. But it's one of the things that one of my former Norwegian doctorate students took on for a project in Zimbabwe and Mozambique, involving a community project with a local museum. Another doctorate student has been heavily involved in community work in Sudan. I actually feel a bit guilty about it because I think that I should have included such activities in my projects too. In terms of contribution to nation building I can see the potential of such projects with support to local museums and with involvement of local cultural leaders. However, I have paid less attention to this, because I was very busy with training academics. This is not an excuse, but I felt that this was where I had to focus at the time.

I think such aspects are very important, especially when ethnographic studies are done in parallel with archaeological work, that is an approach more projects should apply. It's also something that NORAD would facilitate without any doubt.

Do you think that in order to develop this type of community archaeology, it also needs to be taught to the students you train? Would you think, from your experience, that the students you trained would adhere to such a view?

Yes, they would – at least, many of them, without a doubt. But I have also encountered much arrogance in local academics that had been trained abroad, a certain way they treat the local communities that I do not like, especially when they insist on being addressed by their superior academic title. But many of them are involved, and it's worth taking this on board in training programmes, absolutely.

Do you see any other challenges, from your experience, in relation to capacity building and community archaeology?

Well, there's something that I think is extremely important in relation to capacity building in African archaeology, and that is south-south relationships between archaeologists.

A south-south relationship?

Yes, I was struck at a certain time when I taught five students from Ethiopia, Sudan, Zimbabwe and Kenya, and they knew very little about the archaeology of each other's region. This is symptomatic in my view, as there is actually too little academic contact between African archaeologists, even at conferences like SAfA (The Society of Africanist Archaeologists). I think it is important that African universities start to use the capacity that the other universities have, and see it as equal, that they do not look only to Europe for prestigious contacts and external examiners. Fortunately, this is finally starting to change.

Thank you very much for this interview. Is there something you wish to add as a final remark?

Let me just say that the moment you actually have an African who gets a permit to work in Norway, we have reached equal footing.